D1469987

Congratulations!

As a student purchasing Parkin, *Economics, Microeconomics,* or *Macroeconomics,* 5e, you are entitled to a prepaid subscription to *The Economics Place™,* Addison Wesley Longman's premier online resource for students and instructors of economics. *The Economics Place* includes activities, study and testing aids, and a wide range of content to help you succeed in your introductory economics course.

To activate your prepaid subscription:

1. Launch your browser and go to www.economicsplace.com
2. Select the graphic for your book.
3. Enter your pre-assigned Activation ID and Password, exactly as they appear below, in the User ID and Password fields:

Activation ID: MAPKST06001384

Password: humpty

4. Select "Login"
5. Complete the online registration form to establish your personal User ID and Password.
6. Once your personal User ID and Password are confirmed, go to www.economicsplace.com/parkin5 to enter the site with your new User ID and Password.

This Activation ID and Password can be used only once to establish a subscription. This subscription to *The Economics Place* is not transferable.

If you did not purchase this product new and in a shrink-wrapped package, this Activation ID and Password may not be valid. However, if your instructor is recommending or requiring use of *The Economics Place,* you can find information on purchasing a subscription at www.economicsplace.com/parkin5.

Fifth Edition

Macroeconomics

MICHAEL PARKIN

The cover depicts dawn at Millennium Island (recently renamed from Caroline Island) in the South Pacific as viewed through the Parkin icon. This is the spot on our planet that many say will see the first dawn of the year 2000. You can look at this cover in many different ways. Here is what I see. ◆ First, this book together with its CD, Web site, and other supplements is the result of an extraordinary publishing effort to guide students into the new millennium and to face the challenges they will encounter armed with a clear and compelling account of the timeless principles of economics illuminated by the issues of our age. ◆ I also see a symbol of what economics (and all scientific endeavor) is about. The Parkin icon is like an economic model. We use models to understand reality. The model is abstract, like the diamond and its hole or aperture. The model distorts our view of the world by omitting some details. But at the same time, it permits us to see the focus of our interest in the brightest and clearest possible light.

Fifth Edition

Macroeconomics

MICHAEL PARKIN
University of Western Ontario

▲ ADDISON-WESLEY

AN IMPRINT OF ADDISON WESLEY LONGMAN, INC.

READING, MASSACHUSETTS • MENLO PARK, CALIFORNIA • NEW YORK • HARLOW, ENGLAND
DON MILLS, ONTARIO • SYDNEY • MEXICO CITY • MADRID • AMSTERDAM

Executive Editor:	Denise J. Clinton
Senior Editor:	Andrea Shaw
Executive Development Manager:	Sylvia Mallory
Supplements Editor:	Deborah Kiernan
Development Assistant:	Judean Patten
Managing Editor:	James Rigney
Senior Production Supervisors:	Mary Sanger, Lou Bruno
Senior Design Supervisor	Gina Hagen
Technical Illustrator:	Richard Parkin
Photo Researcher:	Beth Anderson
Publishing Technology Manager	Sarah McCracken
Electronic Production Administrator:	Sally Simpson
Copyeditor:	Barbara Willette
Proofreaders:	Kathy Smith, Kris Smead
Indexer:	Robin Bade
Senior Manufacturing Manager:	Ralph Mattivello
Manufacturing Supervisor:	Tim McDonald
Marketing Manager:	Amy Cronin
Marketing Coordinator:	Jennifer Thalmann
Printer:	World Color

Library of Congress Cataloging-in-Publication Data

Parkin, Michael, 1939–
    Macroeconomics/Michael Parkin. — 5th ed.
        p.   cm.
    Includes bibliographical references and index.
    ISBN 0-201-47386-0 (softbound)
    1. Macroeconomics.   I. Title.
    HB172.5.P36 1999
    339—dc21   98–55284
                         CIP

1 2 3 4 5 6 7 8 9 – WCT–0302010099

To Robin

About Michael Parkin

Michael Parkin

received his training as an economist at the Universities of Leicester and Essex in England. Currently in the Department of Economics at the University of Western Ontario, Canada, Professor Parkin has held faculty appointments at Brown University, the University of Manchester, the University of Essex, and Bond University. He is a past president of the Canadian Economics Association and has served on the editorial boards of the *American Economic Review* and the *Journal of Monetary Economics* and as managing editor of the *Canadian Journal of Economics*. Professor Parkin's research on macroeconomics, monetary economics, and international economics has resulted in over 160 publications in journals and edited volumes, including the *American Economic Review*, the *Journal of Political Economy*, the *Review of Economic Studies*, the *Journal of Monetary Economics*, and the *Journal of Money, Credit and Banking*. He became most visible to the public with his work on inflation that discredited the use of wage and price controls. Michael Parkin also spearheaded the movement toward European monetary union. Professor Parkin is an experienced and dedicated teacher of introductory economics.

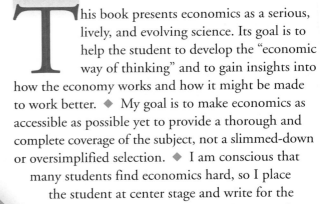

Preface

This book presents economics as a serious, lively, and evolving science. Its goal is to help the student to develop the "economic way of thinking" and to gain insights into how the economy works and how it might be made to work better. ◆ My goal is to make economics as accessible as possible yet to provide a thorough and complete coverage of the subject, not a slimmed-down or oversimplified selection. ◆ I am conscious that many students find economics hard, so I place the student at center stage and write for the student. I use a style and language that don't intimidate and that allow the student to concentrate on the substance. ◆ I open each chapter with a clear statement of learning objectives, a real-world student-friendly vignette to grab attention, and a brief preview. I illustrate principles with examples that are selected to hold the student's interest and to make the subject lively. And I put principles to work by using them to illuminate current real-world problems and issues. ◆ I present some new ideas, such as dynamic comparative advantage, game theory, the modern theory of the firm, public choice theory, rational expectations, new growth theory, and real business cycle theory. But I explain these topics with familiar core ideas and tools. ◆ Today's course springs from today's issues—the information revolution, the East Asian recession, and the expansion of global trade and investment. But the principles that we use to understand these issues remain the core principles of our science. ◆ Governments and international agencies place renewed emphasis on long-term fundamentals as they seek to sustain economic growth. This book reflects this emphasis. ◆ To enable students to access the latest information on the national and global economy, I have developed a companion Web site. And to provide active learning opportunities, I have developed the tutorials and quizzes on the accompanying *Economics in Action* CD.

The Fifth Edition Revision

Economics, FIFTH EDITION, RETAINS ALL THE improvements achieved in its predecessor with its emphasis on core principles, coverage of recent economic developments, brief yet accessible explanations, and strong pedagogy. New to this edition are:

- Revised and updated macro content
- In-text review quizzes
- Parallel end-of-chapter problems
- Part wrap-ups

Revised and Updated Macro Content

The four major revisions in the macro chapters are:

1. Measuring Employment and Unemployment (Chapter 24): A new chapter (based on Chapter 25 of the Fourth Edition) that covers the measurement issues in the labor market.
2. The Economy at Full Employment (Chapter 26): A new chapter that begins to build the story of the aggregate supply side of the economy and that explains how changes in population, capital, and technology change potential GDP, employment, and the real wage rate. This chapter provides the foundation for the theory of aggregate supply and is the jumping-off point for two subsequent chapters on capital accumulation and economic growth.
3. Inflation (Chapter 33): An improved explanation and international illustration of the links between inflation and interest rates.
4. Thorough and extensive updating to reflect the U.S. economy and the global economy of 1998 and 1999, including events such as the evolution of the federal budget from deficit to surplus, the ongoing spectacular performance of the U.S. economy, recession in Asia, and turmoil in global financial markets.

In-Text Review Quizzes

I have replaced the in-text Reviews of the previous editions with Review Quizzes. These brief quizzes invite students to revisit the material they have just studied with a set of questions in mind. I hope that these quizzes will encourage a more critical and thoughtful rereading of any material that proves difficult for the student. The *Instructor's Manual* provides the answers.

Parallel End-of-Chapter Problems

I have reworked the end-of-chapter problems and created pairs of parallel problems. Robin Bade and I have provided the solutions to the odd-numbered problems at the end of the text, and these solutions together with those to the even-numbered problems provided by Melinda Nish appear in the *Instructor's Manual.* This arrangement provides help to students and flexibility to instructors who want to assign problems for credit.

Part Wrap-Ups

A new feature at the *end* of each part:

- Explains how the chapters relate to each other and fit into the larger picture.
- Provides a biographical sketch of the economist who developed the central idea of that part, and places the original contribution in its historical context.
- Presents an interview with a leading contemporary economist.

Features to Enhance Teaching and Learning

HERE I DESCRIBE THE CHAPTER FEATURES that are designed to enhance the learning process. Each chapter contains the following learning aids.

Chapter Opener

A one-page student-friendly, attention-grabbing vignette raises questions that both motivate and focus the chapter.

Chapter Objectives

A list of learning objectives enables students to see exactly where the chapter is going and to set their goals before they begin the chapter. I link these goals directly to the chapter's major headings.

After studying this chapter, you will be able to:

- Explain the fundamental economic problem
- Define the production possibility frontier
- Define and calculate opportunity cost
- Explain the conditions in which resources are used efficiently
- Explain how economic growth expands production possibilities
- Explain how specialization and trade expand production possibilities

---

Chapter 3

The Economic Problem

We live in a style that surprises our grandparents and would have astonished our great-grandparents. Most of us live in more spacious homes than they did. We eat more, grow taller, and are even born larger than they were. Video games, cellular phones, gene splices, and personal computers did not exist even 20 years ago. Economic growth has made us richer than our grandparents. And we are not alone in experiencing an expansion in the goods and services that we consume. Many nations around the world are not only sharing our experience: They are setting the pace. Before the recent Asia crisis, Hong Kong, Taiwan, Singapore, Korea, and China expanded at unheard-of rates. But economic growth does not liberate us from scarcity. Why not? Why, despite our immense wealth, must we still make choices and face costs? Why are there no "free lunches"? ◆ We see an incredible amount of specialization and trade in the world. Each one of us specializes in a particular job—as a lawyer, a car maker, a home maker. We have become so specialized that one farm worker can feed 100 people. Less than one sixth of the U.S. work force is employed in manufacturing. More than half of the work force is employed in wholesale and retail trade, banking and finance, government, and other services. Why do we specialize? How do we benefit from specialization and trade? ◆ Over many centuries, institutions and social arrangements have evolved that we take for granted. One of them is property rights and the political and legal system that protects them. Another is markets. Why have these social arrangements evolved? How do they increase production?

◇ These are the questions that we study in this chapter. We begin with the core economic problem: scarcity and choice and the concept of the production possibility frontier. We then learn about the central idea of economics—efficiency. We also discover how we can expand production by accumulating capital and by specializing and trading. ◆ What you will learn in this chapter is the foundation on which all economics is built. You will receive big dividends from a careful study of this material.

Making the Most of It

After studying this chapter, you will be able to:

- Explain the fundamental economic problem
- Define the production possibility frontier
- Define and calculate opportunity cost
- Explain the conditions in which resources are used efficiently
- Explain how economic growth expands production possibilities
- Explain how specialization and trade expand production possibilities

In-Text Review Quizzes

A review quiz at end of most major sections enables students to determine whether a topic needs further study before moving on.

R E V I E W   Q U I Z

- What is scarcity?
- What is the fundamental economic problem?
- Can you provide a definition of economics?
- What are the resources that can be used to produce goods and services?
- How do we cope with the fact that our wants cannot be satisfied with the available resources?

Key Terms

Highlighted terms within the text simplify the student's task of learning the vocabulary of economics. Each highlighted term appears in an end-of-chapter list with page numbers, an end-of-book glossary, boldfaced in the index, in the *Economics in Action* software, and on the Parkin Web site.

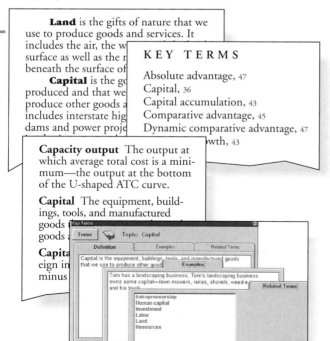

Land is the gifts of nature that we use to produce goods and services. It includes the air, the w... surface as well as the r... beneath the surface of...

Capital is the g... produced and that we... produce other goods a... includes interstate hig... dams and power proje...

KEY TERMS

Absolute advantage, 47
Capital, 36
Capital accumulation, 43
Comparative advantage, 45
Dynamic comparative advantage, 47
...wth, 43

Capacity output The output at which average total cost is a minimum—the output at the bottom of the U-shaped ATC curve.

Capital The equipment, buildings, tools, and manufactured goods... goods...

Capita...
eign in...
minus...

Key Terms
Terms   Topic: Capital
Definition   Examples   Related Terms
Capital is the equipment, buildings, tools, and manufactured goods that we use to produce other goods
Examples
Tom has a landscaping business. Tom's landscaping business owns some capital—lawn mowers, rakes, shovels, weed-e... and his truck
Related Terms
Entrepreneurship
Human capital
Investment
Labor
Land
Resources

Key Figures and Tables

An icon ◆ identifies the most important figures and tables, and the end-of-chapter summary lists them. Instructor's overhead transparencies also contain enlarged and simplified images of most of these key figures.

TABLE 10.3

Efficient Use of Resources ◆

Method		Labor	Capital
a	Robot production	1	1,000
b	Production line	10	10
c	Bench production	100	1
d	Hand tool production	1000	1

FIGURE 3.4

Efficient Use of Resources ◆

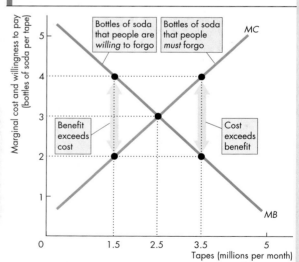

The greater the quantity of tapes produced, the smaller is the marginal benefit (*MB*) from a tape—the fewer bottles of soda people are willing to give up to get an additional tape. But the greater the quantity of tapes produced, the greater is the marginal cost (*MC*) of a tape—the more bottles of soda people must give up to get an additional tape. When marginal benefit equals marginal cost, resources are being used efficiently.

Diagrams That Show the Action

This book has set new standards of clarity in its diagrams. My goal has always been to show "where the economic action is." The diagrams in this book continue to generate an enormously positive response, which confirms my view that graphical analysis is the most important tool available for teaching and learning economics. But many students find graphs hard to work with. For this reason, I have developed the entire art program with the study and review needs of the student in mind. The diagrams feature:

- Shifted curves, equilibrium points, and other important features highlighted in red
- Color-blended arrows to suggest movement
- Graphs paired with data tables
- Diagrams labeled with boxed notes
- Extended captions that make each diagram and its caption a self-contained object for study and review.

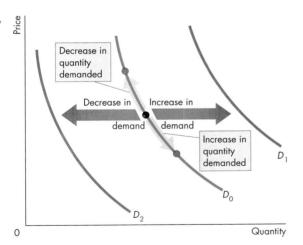

Reading Between the Lines

Each chapter contains an economic analysis of a significant news article from the popular press together with a set of critical thinking questions that relate to the issues raised in the article.

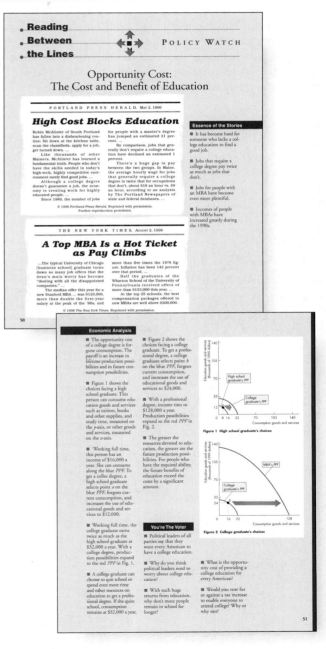

End-of-Chapter Study Material

Each chapter closes with a concise summary organized by major topics; lists of key terms, figures, and tables (all with page references); problems; and critical thinking questions. Items identified by the 🖥 icon link to the *Economics in Action* software CD included with the text. Items identified by the 🌐 icon link to the Parkin Web site at http://www.economicsplace.com. My hope is to encourage students to keep up to date and to become comfortable and efficient in their use of the Internet to access information.

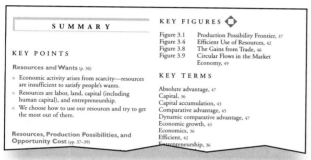

For the Instructor

THIS BOOK ENABLES YOU TO ACHIEVE THREE objectives in your principles course:

- Focus on the core ideas.
- Explain the issues and problems of our time.
- Choose your own course structure.

Focus on the Core Ideas

You know how hard it is to encourage a student to think like an economist. But that is your goal. Consistent with this goal, the text focuses on and repeatedly uses the central ideas: choice; tradeoff; opportunity cost; the margin; incentives; the gains from voluntary exchange; the forces of demand, supply, and equilibrium; the pursuit of economic rent; and the effects of government actions on the economy.

Explain the Issues and Problems of Our Time

Students must *use* the core ideas and tools if they are to begin to understand them. There is no better way to motivate students than by using the tools of economics to explain the issues that confront students in today's world. These issues include the environment, immigration, widening income gaps, the productivity growth slowdown, budget deficits, restraining inflation, watching for the next recession, avoiding protectionism, and the long-term growth of output and incomes.

Choose Your Own Course Structure

You want to teach your own course. I have organized this book to enable you to do so. I demonstrate the book's flexibility in the flexibility chart and alternative sequences table that appear on pp. xxii–xxv. You can use this book to teach a traditional course that blends theory and policy or a current policy issues course. Your micro course can emphasize theory or policy. You can structure your macro course to emphasize long-term growth and supply-side fundamentals. Or you can follow a traditional macro sequence and emphasize short-term fluctuations. The choices are yours.

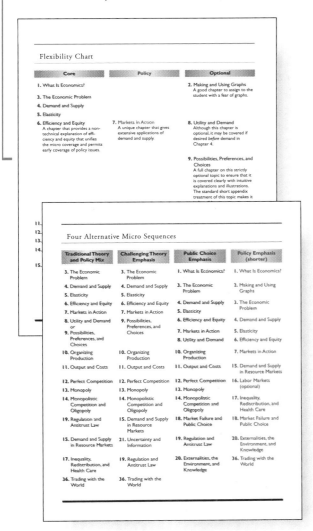

Instructor's Manual

The Instructor's Manual by Melinda Nish of Salt Lake Community College integrates the teaching and learning package and is a guide to all the supplements. An essay by Dennis Hoffman of Arizona State University explains how to use the *Economics in Action* software as a teaching tool.

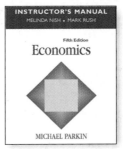

Printed Test Banks

We now have three major test banks. Mark Rush of the University of Florida has thoroughly revised the earlier test banks and has coordinated the development of a new 3,000-question test bank written by fifteen outstanding and dedicated principles instructors. They are Sue Bartlett (University of South Florida), Kevin Carey (American University), Leo Chan (University of Kansas), Carol Dole (University of North Carolina, Charlotte), Donald Dutkowsky (Syracuse University), Andrew Foshee (McNeese State University), Jill H. Boylston Herndon (Hamline University), Veronica Kalich (Baldwin-Wallace College), Melinda Nish (Salt Lake Community College), Terry Olson (Truman State University), Rochelle Ruffer (Youngstown State University), Virginia Shingleton (Valparaiso University), Nora Underwood (University of California, Davis), Peter von Allmen (Moravian College), and Peter Zaleski (Villanova University).

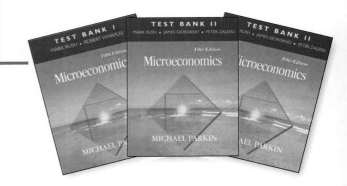

Computerized Test Banks

The test banks are also available in Test Generator Software (TestGen-EQ with QuizMaster-EQ). Version 3.0 of the program, with a wealth of improved features, is now available. This software includes all the questions in the printed test banks. Fully networkable, it is available for Windows and Macintosh. TestGen-EQ's new graphical interface enables instructors easily to view, edit, and add questions; transfer questions to tests; and print different forms of tests. Tests can be formatted by varying fonts and styles, margins, and headers and footers, as in any word-processing document. Search and sort features let the instructor quickly locate questions and arrange them in a preferred order. QuizMaster-EQ, working with your school's computer network, automatically grades the exams, stores the results on disk, and allows the instructor to view or print a variety of reports.

Overhead Transparencies and Overlays

Full-color overhead transparencies (several with overlays) of enlarged and simplified key figures from the text will improve the clarity of your lectures. They are available to qualified adopters of the text (contact your Addison Wesley Longman sales representative).

PowerPoint Lecture Presentations

Charles Pflanz of Scottsdale Community College has developed a full-color Microsoft PowerPoint Lecture Presentation that breaks the chapters into lecture-size bites and includes key figures from the text, animated graphs, and speaking notes. The presentation can be used electronically in the classroom or can be printed to create hard-copy transparency masters. The lecture presentation is available for Macintosh and Windows to qualified adopters of the text (contact your Addison Wesley Longman sales representative).

Economics in Action Software

Instructors can use *Economics in Action* interactive software in the classroom. Its full-screen display option turns its many analytical graphs into "electronic transparencies" for live graph manipulation in lectures. Its real-world data sets and graphing utility bring animated time-series graphs and scatter diagrams to the classroom.

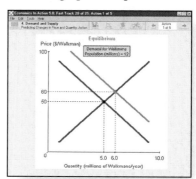

The Parkin Web Site

With the Fifth Edition of the textbook comes the debut of *The Economics Place* at www.economicsplace.com. This Internet-based learning environment contains tools for organizing students' grades from online quizzes, frequent updates of data in the text figures, and news you can use in the classroom. Use the Web site to motivate and organize lectures with electronic *Reading Between the Lines* and *Point-Counterpoint* or to create an online quiz for an in-class review.

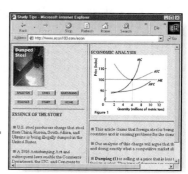

For the Student

Study Guide

The Fifth Edition *Study Guide* by Mark Rush of the University of Florida is carefully coordinated with the main text and the test bank. Each chapter of the Study Guide contains:

- Key concepts
- Helpful hints
- True/false/uncertain questions that ask students to explain their answers
- Multiple-choice questions
- Short-answer questions
- Common questions or misconceptions that the student explains as if he or she were the teacher

Each part allows students to test their cumulative understanding with *Reading Between the Lines* exercises and sample midterm tests.

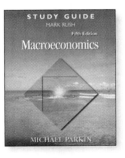

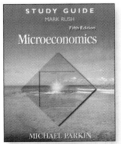

Economics in Action Interactive Software

With *Economics in Action* Release 5.0, which accompanies the Fifth Edition, students will have fun working the tutorials, answering questions that give instant explanations, and testing themselves ahead of their midterm tests. One of my students told me that using *EIA* is like having a private professor in your dorm room!

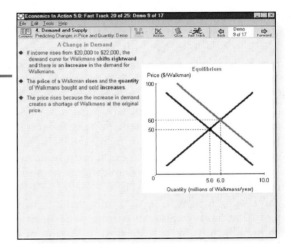

The Parkin Web Site

New for the Fifth Edition, *The Economics Place* Web site provides online quizzes, study tips, office hours, links, electronic *Reading Between the Lines*, a *Point-Counterpoint* feature that encourages students to participate in contemporary policy debates, and much more. You can reach the site at http://www.economicsplace.com.

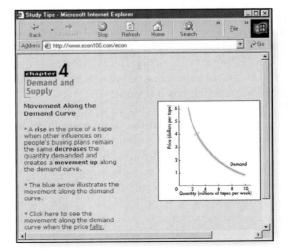

Acknowledgments

I THANK MY CURRENT AND FORMER COLLEAGUES and friends at the University of Western Ontario who have taught me so much. They are Jim Davies, Jeremy Greenwood, Ig Horstmann, Peter Howitt, Greg Huffman, David Laidler, Phil Reny, Chris Robinson, John Whalley, and Ron Wonnacott. I also thank Doug McTaggart and Christopher Findlay, co-authors of the Australian edition, and Melanie Powell and Kent Matthews, co-authors of the European edition. Suggestions arising from their adaptations of earlier editions have been helpful to me in preparing this edition.

I thank the several thousand students whom I have been privileged to teach. The instant response that comes from the look of puzzlement or enlightenment has taught me how to teach economics.

It is an especial joy to thank the many outstanding editors and others at Addison Wesley Longman who have contributed to the concerted publishing effort that has brought this edition to completion. Denise Clinton, Executive Editor for Economics and Finance, has been a constant source of inspiration and encouragement and has provided overall direction. Andrea Shaw, Senior Editor for Economics and my sponsoring editor, has ably coordinated the arrangements for this edition. Sylvia Mallory, Executive Development Manager, has brought her calm, creative, and professional direction to the development effort on this edition. Deborah Kiernan, Senior Supplements Editor, working with the most able team of authors, has managed the creation of a large and complex supplements package. Along with Mark Rush, Sylvia Mallory and Deb Kiernan have pulled together a "dream team" of questions authors and helped to create the best-ever principles of economics test bank. Judean Patten, Editorial Assistant, has cheerfully performed many helpful tasks at a moment's notice. Beth Anderson, Photo Researcher, has diligently persisted in her efforts until the required images were found. Melissa Honig, Senior Project Editor, has directed the development of *Economics in Action* and has been an appreciated and admired source of guidance on many matters relating to the electronic supplements. Amy Cronin, Marketing Manager, has provided inspired marketing direction. Regina Hagen, Senior Designer, has designed the cover, text, and package and surpassed the challenge of ensuring that we meet the highest design standards. Managing Editor James Rigney and Senior Production Supervisors Mary Sanger and Louis Bruno have worked miracles on a tight production schedule and coped calmly with late-changing content. I thank all of these wonderful people. It has been inspiring to work with them and to share in creating what I believe is a truly outstanding educational tool.

I thank the 17 supplements authors whose names appear on pp. xv and xvi. But I especially thank Mark Rush, who has yet again played a crucial role in creating another edition of this text and package. Mark has been a constant source of good advice and good humor. And I thank Art Woolf for his careful accuracy review of near-final pages.

I am most grateful to the thoughtful news clippers who have greatly helped in the task of writing the *Reading Between the Lines* features. They are Richard Fristensky (Bentley College), Susan Glanz (St. John's University), Jim Lee (Fort Hays State University), Kathryn Nantz (Fairfield University), and Paul Storer (Western Washington University).

I thank the people who work directly with me. Jeannie Gillmore has provided outstanding research assistance. Jane McAndrew has provided excellent library help. Richard Parkin has created the electronic art files and offered many ideas that have improved the figures in this book.

As with the previous editions, this one owes an enormous debt to Robin Bade. I dedicate this book to her and again thank her for her work. I could not have written this book without the unselfish help she has given me. My thanks to her are unbounded.

Classroom experience will test the value of this book. I would appreciate hearing from instructors and students about how I can continue to improve it in future editions.

Michael Parkin
London, Ontario, Canada
michael.parkin@ uwo.ca

Reviewers

Tajudeen Adenekan, Bronx Community College
Milton Alderfer, Miami-Dade Community College
William Aldridge, Shelton State Community College
Donald L. Alexander, Western Michigan University
Terence Alexander, Iowa State University
Stuart Allen, University of North Carolina, Greensboro
Sam Allgood, University of Nebraska, Lincoln
Neil Alper, Northeastern University
Alan Anderson, Fordham University
Lisa R. Anderson, College of William and Mary
Jeff Ankrom, Wittenberg University
Fatma Antar, Manchester Community Technical College
Kofi Apraku, University of North Carolina, Asheville
Moshen Bahmani-Oskooee, University of Wisconsin, Milwaukee
Donald Balch, University of South Carolina
Mehmet Balcilar, Wayne State University
A. Paul Ballantyne, University of Colorado
Sue Bartlett, University of South Florida
Valerie R. Bencivenga, University of Texas, Austin
Ben Bernanke, Princeton University
Margot Biery, Tarrant County Community College South
John Bittorowitz, Ball State University
Giacomo Bonanno, University of California, Davis
Sunne Brandmeyer, University of South Florida
Audie Brewton, Northeastern Illinois University
Baird Brock, Central Missouri State University
Byron Brown, Michigan State University
Jeffrey Buser, Columbus State Community College
Alison Butler, Florida International University
Tania Carbiener, Southern Methodist University
Kevin Carey, American University
Kathleen A. Carroll, University of Maryland, Baltimore County
Michael Carter, University of Massachusetts, Lowell
Adhip Chaudhuri, Georgetown University
Gopal Chengalath, Texas Tech University
Daniel Christiansen, Albion College
John J. Clark, Community College of Allegheny County, Allegheny Campus
Meredith Clement, Dartmouth College
Michael B. Cohn, U.S. Merchant Marine Academy
Robert Collinge, University of Texas, San Antonio

Doug Conway, Mesa Community College
Larry Cook, University of Toledo
Bobby Corcoran, Middle Tennessee State University
Kevin Cotter, Wayne State University
James Peery Cover, University of Alabama, Tuscaloosa
Eleanor D. Craig, University of Delaware
Jim Craven, Clark College
Stephen Cullenberg, University of California, Riverside
David Culp, Slippery Rock University
Norman V. Cure, Macomb Community College
Dan Dabney, University of Texas, Austin
Andrew Dane, Angelo State University
Joseph Daniels, Marquette University
David Denslow, University of Florida
Mark Dickie, University of Georgia
James Dietz, California State University, Fullerton
Carol Dole, University of North Carolina, Charlotte
Ronald Dorf, Inver Hills Community College
John Dorsey, University of Maryland, College Park
Amrik Singh Dua, Mt. San Antonio College
Thomas Duchesneau, University of Maine, Orono
Lucia Dunn, Ohio State University
Donald Dutkowsky, Syracuse University
John Edgren, Eastern Michigan University
David J. Eger, Alpena Community College
Harry Ellis, Jr., University of North Texas
Ibrahim Elsaify, State University of New York, Albany
Kenneth G. Elzinga, University of Virginia
M. Fazeli, Hofstra University
Philip Fincher, Louisiana Tech University
F. Firoozi, University of Texas, San Antonio
David Franck, University of North Carolina, Charlotte
Roger Frantz, San Diego State University
Alwyn Fraser, Atlantic Union College
Richard Fristensky, Bentley College
Eugene Gentzel, Pensacola Junior College
Andrew Gill, California State University, Fullerton
Robert Giller, Virginia Polytechnic Institute and State University
Robert Gillette, University of Kentucky
James N. Giordano, Villanova University
Maria Giuili, Diablo College
Susan Glanz, St. John's University
Richard Gosselin, Houston Community College
John Graham, Rutgers University
John Griffen, Worcester Polytechnic Institute
Robert Guell, Indiana State University
Jamie Haag, University of Oregon
Gail Heyne Hafer, Lindenwood University
Rik W. Hafer, Southern Illinois University

Daniel Hagen, Western Washington University
David R. Hakes, University of Northern Iowa
Craig Hakkio, Federal Reserve Bank, Kansas City
Ann Hansen, Westminster College
Jonathan Haughton, Northeastern University
Randall Haydon, Wichita State University
Jolien A. Helsel, Kent State University
Jill H. Boylston Herndon, Hamline University
John Herrmann, Rutgers University
John M. Hill, Delgado Community College
Lewis Hill, Texas Tech University
Steve Hoagland, University of Akron
Tom Hoerger, Vanderbilt University
Calvin Hoerneman, Delta College
George Hoffer, Virginia Commonwealth University
Dennis L. Hoffman, Arizona State University
Paul Hohenberg, Rensselaer Polytechnic Institute
Jim H. Holcomb, University of Texas, El Paso
Harry Holzer, Michigan State University
Djehane Hosni, University of Central Florida
Harold Hotelling, Jr., Lawrence Technical University
Calvin Hoy, County College of Morris
Julie Hunsaker, Wayne State University
Beth Ingram, University of Iowa
Michael Jacobs, Lehman College
Dennis Jansen, Texas A & M University
Frederick Jungman, Northwestern Oklahoma State University
Paul Junk, University of Minnesota, Duluth
Leo Kahane, California State University, Hayward
Veronica Kalich, Baldwin-Wallace College
John Kane, State University of New York, Oswego
E. Kang, St. Cloud State University
Arthur Kartman, San Diego State University
Manfred W. Keil, Claremont McKenna College
Rose Kilburn, Modesto Junior College
Robert Kirk, Indiana University–Purdue University, Indianapolis
Norman Kleinberg, City University of New York, Baruch College
Robert Kleinhenz, California State University, Fullerton
Joseph Kreitzer, University of St. Thomas
David Lages, Southwest Missouri State University
W. J. Lane, University of New Orleans
Leonard Lardaro, University of Rhode Island
Kathryn Larson, Elon College
Luther D. Lawson, University of North Carolina, Wilmington
Elroy M. Leach, Chicago State University
Jim Lee, Fort Hays State University

Jay Levin, Wayne State University
Arik Levinson, University of Wisconsin, Madison
Tony Lima, California State University, Hayward
William Lord, University of Maryland, Baltimore County
Nancy Lutz, Virginia Polytechnic Institute and State University
K.T. Magnusson, Salt Lake City Community College
Mark Maier, Glendale Community College
Beth Maloan, University of Tennessee, Martin
Jean Mangan, California State University, Sacramento
Michael Marlow, California Polytechnic State University
Akbar Marvasti, University of Houston
Wolfgang Mayer, University of Cincinnati
John McArthur, Wofford College
Amy McCormick, College of William and Mary
Russel McCullough, Iowa State University
Gerald McDougall, Wichita State University
Stephen McGary, Ricks College
Richard D. McGrath, College of William and Mary
Richard McIntyre, University of Rhode Island
John McLeod, Georgia Institute of Technology
Charles Meyer, Iowa State University
Peter Mieszkowski, Rice University
John Mijares, University of North Carolina, Asheville
Richard A. Miller, Wesleyan University
Judith W. Mills, Southern Connecticut State University
Glen Mitchell, Nassau Community College
Jeannette C. Mitchell, Rochester Institute of Technology
Khan Mohabbat, Northern Illinois University
W. Douglas Morgan, University of California, Santa Barbara
William Morgan, University of Wyoming
Joanne Moss, San Francisco State University
Edward Murphy, Southwest Texas State University
Kevin J. Murphy, Oakland University
Kathryn Nantz, Fairfield University
William S. Neilson, Texas A & M University
Bart C. Nemmers, University of Nebraska, Lincoln
Melinda Nish, Salt Lake Community College
Anthony O'Brien, Lehigh University
Mary Olson, Washington University
Terry Olson, Truman State University
James B. O'Niell, University of Delaware
Farley Ordovensky, University of the Pacific
Z. Edward O'Relley, North Dakota State University
Jan Palmer, Ohio University
Michael Palumbo, University of Houston

G. Hossein Parandvash, Western Oregon State College
Randall Parker, East Carolina University
Robert Parks, Washington University
David Pate, St. John Fisher College
Donald Pearson, Eastern Michigan University
Mary Anne Pettit, Southern Illinois University, Edwardsville
Kathy Phares, University of Missouri, St. Louis
William A. Phillips, University of Southern Maine
Dennis Placone, Clemson University
Charles Plot, California Institute of Technology, Pasadena
Mannie Poen, Houston Community College
Kathleen Possai, Wayne State University
Ulrika Praski-Stahlgren, University College in Gavle-Sandviken, Sweden
K.A. Quartey, Talladega College
Herman Quirmbach, Iowa State University
Jeffrey R. Racine, University of South Florida
Peter Rangazas, Indiana University–Purdue University, Indianapolis
Vaman Rao, Western Illinois University
Laura Razzolini, University of Mississippi
J. David Reed, Bowling Green State University
Robert H. Renshaw, Northern Illinois University
W. Gregory Rhodus, Bentley College
John Robertson, Paducah Community College
Malcolm Robinson, University of North Carolina, Greensboro
Richard Roehl, University of Michigan, Dearborn
Thomas Romans, State University of New York, Buffalo
David R. Ross, Bryn Mawr College
Thomas Ross, St. Louis University
Robert J. Rossana, Wayne State University
Rochelle Ruffer, Youngstown State University
Mark Rush, University of Florida
Gary Santoni, Ball State University
John Saussy, Harrisburg Area Community College
David Schlow, Pennsylvania State University

Paul Schmitt, St. Clair County Community College
Martin Sefton, Indianapolis University
Rod Shadbegian, University of Massachusetts, Dartmouth
Gerald Shilling, Eastfield College
Dorothy R. Siden, Salem State College
Scott Simkins, North Carolina Agricultural and Technical State University
Chuck Skoro, Boise State University
Phil Smith, DeKalb College
William Doyle Smith, University of Texas, El Paso
Frank Steindl, Oklahoma State University
Jeffrey Stewart, New York University
Allan Stone, Southwest Missouri State University
Courtenay Stone, Ball State University
Paul Storer, Western Washington University
Mark Strazicich, Ohio State University, Newark
Robert Stuart, Rutgers University
Gilbert Suzawa, University of Rhode Island
David Swaine, Andrews University
Kay Unger, University of Montana
Anthony Uremovic, Joliet Junior College
David Vaughn, City University, Washington
Don Waldman, Colgate University
Francis Wambalaba, Portland State University
Rob Wassmer, Wayne State University
Paul A. Weinstein, University of Maryland, College Park
Lee Weissert, St. Vincent College
Robert Whaples, Wake Forest University
Charles H. Whiteman, University of Iowa
Larry Wimmer, Brigham Young University
Mark Witte, Northwestern University
Willard E. Witte, Indiana University
Mark Wohar, University of Nebraska, Omaha
Cheonsik Woo, Clemson University
Douglas Wooley, Radford University
Arthur G. Woolf, University of Vermont
Ann Al Yasiri, University of Wisconsin, Platteville
John T. Young, Riverside Community College
Michael Youngblood, Rock Valley College.

Macroeconomics Flexibility Chart

Core	Policy	Optional

Core

1. What Is Economics?

3. The Economic Problem

4. Demand and Supply

5. A First Look at Macroeconomics

6. Measuring GDP, Economic Growth, and Inflation

7. Measuring Employment and Unemployment

8. Aggregate Supply and Aggregate Demand

This chapter may be delayed and studied after Chapter 11.

9. The Economy at Full Employment

10. Capital, Investment, and Saving
This chapter includes a section on long-run aspects of fiscal policy.

11. Economic Growth
The section on growth theory is optional.

12. Expenditure Multipliers

14. Money

16. Inflation

17. The Business Cycle

Policy

Chapters 9, 10, and 11 may be delayed and studied after any or all of Chapters 12 through 18.

13. Fiscal Policy

15. Monetary Policy

18. Macroeconomic Policy Challenges

Optional

2. Making and Using Graphs
A good chapter to assign to the student with a fear of graphs.

19. Trading with the World

20. International Finance

Four Alternative Macro Sequences

Early Long-Term Growth	Late Long-Term Growth	Keynesian Perspective	Monetarist Perspective
5. A First Look at Macroeconomics	**5.** A First Look at Macroeconomics	**5.** A First Look at Macroeconomics	**5.** A First Look at Macroeconomics
6. Measuring GDP, Economic Growth, and Inflation	**6.** Measuring GDP, Economic Growth, and Inflation	**6.** Measuring GDP, Economic Growth, and Inflation	**6.** Measuring GDP, Economic Growth, and Inflation
7. Measuring Employment and Unemployment	**7.** Measuring Employment and Unemployment	**7.** Measuring Employment and Unemployment	**7.** Measuring Employment and Unemployment
9. The Economy at Full Employment	**8.** Aggregate Demand and Aggregate Supply	**12.** Expenditure Multipliers	**8.** Aggregate Demand and Aggregate Supply
10. Capital, Investment, and Saving	**12.** Expenditure Multipliers	**8.** Aggregate Demand and Aggregate Supply	**14.** Money
11. Economic Growth	**13.** Fiscal Policy	**13.** Fiscal Policy	**15.** Monetary Policy
17. The Business Cycle (Real Business Cycle, pp. 393–397)	**14.** Money	**14.** Money	**16.** Inflation
8. Aggregate Supply and Aggregate Demand	**15.** Monetary Policy	**15.** Monetary Policy	**12.** Expenditure Multipliers
12. Expenditure Multipliers	**16.** Inflation	**16.** Inflation	**13.** Fiscal Policy
13. Fiscal Policy	**17.** The Business Cycle	**17.** The Business Cycle (omit real business cycle)	**17.** The Business Cycle (omit real business cycle)
14. Money	**18.** Macroeconomic Policy Challenges	**18.** Macroeconomic Policy Challenges	**18.** Macroeconomic Policy Challenges
15. Monetary Policy	**9** The Economy at Full Employment (optional)	**9.** The Economy at Full Employment (optional)	**9.** The Economy at Full Employment (optional)
16. Inflation	**10.** Capital, Investment, and Saving (optional)	**10.** Capital, Investment, and Saving (optional)	**10.** Capital, Investment, and Saving (optional)
17. The Business Cycle (rest of chapter)	**11.** Economic Growth	**11.** Economic Growth	**11.** Economic Growth
18. Macroeconomic Policy Challenges	**20.** International Finance	**20.** International Finance	**20.** International Finance

Credits

(continuation from p. IV)

Chapter 1: P. 2 right: PhotoDisc, Inc.; p. 3 top: David Frazier Photolibrary; p. 3 center: George Rose/Gamma Liason; p 3 bottom: Owen Franken/Tony Stone Images; p. 4 top left: MediaFocus International, LLC; p.4 top right: Charles Gupton/The Stock Market; p. 4 bottom left: Chip Henderson/Tony Stone Images; p. 4 bottom right: © Paul Conklin/PhotoEdit Inc.; p. 5 top: David Joel/Tony Stone Images; p. 5 bottom: PhotoDisc Inc.; p. 6 left: PhotoDisc, Inc.; p. 6 right: © David Young-Wolff/PhotoEdit, Inc.; p. 7: PhotoDisc, Inc.;p. 8 left and right: © David Young-Wolff/PhotoEdit Inc.; p. 9 left: courtesy of Intel Corporation; p. 9 right: PhotoDisc, Inc.; p. 10 top left: Karl Cummels/SuperStock; p. 10 bottom left: PhotoDisc, Inc.; p. 10 top right: © David Young-Wolff/Tony Stone Images; p. 10 bottom right: Bob Sacha/Aurora/PNI; p. 11 top left: © Tony Freeman/PhotoEdit Inc.; p. 11 top right: © R. Crandall/The Image Works; p. 11 bottom: Steven Wernberg/Tony Stone Images; p. 12 top and bottom: Scott Foresman/Addison Wesley Longman, Focus on Sports; p. 13 top: PhotoDisc, Inc.; p. 13 bottom: © M. Reinstein/The Image Works; p. 14 top left:

Dick Morton, courtesy of The Weather Channel, Inc. and radar imagery courtesy of WSI Corporation, Inc.; p. 14 bottom left: PhotoDisc, Inc.; p. 14 right: © David Burnett/Contact Press Images/PNI; p. 15 top right: SuperStock; p.15 bottom right: PhotoDisc, Inc.; p. 15 bottom left: PhotoDisc, Inc.; p. 16: AP/Wide World Photos; p. 18: © Jeff Greenberg/PhotoEdit Inc.

Part 1: Adam Smith (p. 56), Corbis-Bettmann. Pin factory (p. 57), Culver Pictures. Silicon wafer (p. 57), Bruce Ando/Tony Stone Images. Douglas North (p. 58), © Bill Stover.

Part 2: Alfred Marshall (p. 88), Stock Montage. Railroad bridge (p.189), National Archives. Airport (p. 89), PhotoDisc, Inc. Paul Milgrom (p. 90), Jenny Thomas.

Chapter 7: The job creation and job destruction data on p. 149 were provided by Steve Davis of the University of Chicago Business School and are used with his permission.

Part 3: John Maynard Keynes (p. 176), Stock Montage. Worker destroying spinning jenny in England (p.177), Corbis/Bettmann. AT&T Networking

Center (p. 177), Hank Morgan. Robert E. Lucas (p. 178), Loren Santow.

Part 4: Joseph Schumpeter (p. 248), Corbis-Bettmann. McCormick's first reaping machine, ca. 1834 (p. 249), North Wind Picture Archives. Fiber optics (p. 249), PhotoDisc, Inc. Paul Romer (p. 250), Christopher Irion.

Part 5: Milton Friedman (p. 378), Marshall Henrichs/Addison-Wesley. German housewife burning Reichmarks in 1923 (p. 379), UPI/Corbis-Bettmann. Brazilians stocking up on food before price increase (p. 379), © Carlos Humberto TDC/Contact Press Images. Bennett T. McCallum (p. 380), David Smith.

Part 6: Irving Fisher (p. 436), Yale University Archives, Manuscripts and Archives, Yale Library. Depositors outside door of closed bank (p. 437), Corbis-Bettmann. Boarded-up shop (p. 437), © Susan van Etten. Frederic S. Mishkin (p. 438), Peter Murphy.

Part 7: David Ricardo (p. 484), Corbis-Bettmann. Clipper ship (p. 485), North Wind Picture Archives. Container ship (p. 485), © M. Timothy O'Keefe/Weststock. Stanley Fisher (p. 486), John Skowronski.

Brief Contents

Contents

Summary (Key Points, Key Figures and Tables, and Key Terms), Problems, and Critical Thinking appear at the end of each chapter.

🖳 Chapters marked with this symbol are
included on the *Economics in Action* CD.

Fifth Edition

Macroeconomics

MICHAEL PARKIN

Chapter 1

What Is Economics?

From the moment you wake up each morning to the moment you fall asleep again each night, your life is filled with *choices*. Your first choice is when to get up. Will you start running the moment the alarm goes off, or will you linger for a few minutes and listen to the radio? What will you wear today? You check the weather forecast and make that decision. Then, what will you have for breakfast? Will you drive to school or take the bus? Which classes will you attend? Which assignments will you complete? What will you do for lunch? Will you play tennis, swim, run, or skate today? How will you spend your evening? Will you study, relax at home with a video, or go to the movies? ◆ You face decisions like these every day. But on some days, you face choices that can change the entire direction of your life.

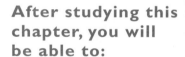

A Day in Your Life

What will you study? Will you major in economics, business, law, or film? ◆ While you are making your own decisions, other people are making theirs. And some of the decisions that other people make will have an impact on your own subsequent decisions. Your school decides its course offerings for next year. Stephen Spielberg decides what his next movie will be. A team of eye doctors decides on a new experiment that will lead them to a cure for nearsightedness. The U.S. Congress decides to reform Social Security. The Federal Reserve Board decides to cut interest rates. ◆ All these choices and decisions by you and everyone else are all examples of economics in your life.

◈ This chapter takes a first look at the subject you are about to study. It defines economics. Then it expands on that definition with five big questions that economists try to answer and eight big ideas that define the economic way of thinking. These questions and ideas are the foundation on which your course is built. The chapter concludes with a description of how economists go about their work, the scientific method they use, and the pitfalls they try to avoid. When you have completed your study of this chapter, you will have a good sense of what economics is about and you'll be ready to start learning economics and using it to gain a new view of the world.

After studying this chapter, you will be able to:

- ■ **Define economics**
- ■ **Explain the five big questions that economists seek to answer**
- ■ **Explain eight ideas that define the economic way of thinking**
- ■ **Describe how economists go about their work**

A Definition of Economics

ALL ECONOMIC QUESTIONS AND PROBLEMS ARISE from **scarcity**—they arise because our wants exceed the resources available to satisfy them.

We want good health and long life, material comfort, security, physical and mental recreation, and knowledge. None of these wants is completely satisfied for everyone, and everyone has some unsatisfied wants. While many people have all the material comfort they want, many others do not. And no one feels entirely satisfied with her or his state of health and expected length of life. No one feels entirely secure, even in the post–Cold War era, and no one has enough time for sport, travel, vacations, movies, theater, reading, and other leisure pursuits.

The poor and the rich alike, face scarcity. A child wants a 75¢ can of soft drink and a 50¢ pack of gum but has only $1.00 in her pocket. She experiences scarcity. A student wants to go to a party on Saturday night but also wants to spend that same night catching up on late assignments. He experiences scarcity. A millionaire wants to spend the weekend playing golf *and* attending a business strategy meeting and cannot do both. She experiences scarcity. Even parrots face scarcity—there just aren't enough crackers to go around!

Faced with scarcity, we must *choose* among the available alternatives.

Economics is the *science of choice*—the science that explains the choices that we make and how those choices change as we cope with scarcity.

Not only do I want a cracker—we all want a cracker!

Drawing by Modell; ©1985 *The New Yorker Magazine,* Inc.

Big Economic Questions

ALL ECONOMIC CHOICES CAN BE SUMMARIZED IN big questions about the goods and services we produce. These questions are: What? How? When? Where? Who?

1: What?

What goods and services are produced and in what quantities? **Goods and services** are all the things that we value and are willing to pay for. We produce a dazzling array of goods and services that range from necessities such as houses to leisure items such as camping vehicles and equipment. We build more than a million new homes every year. And these homes are more spacious and better equipped than they were twenty years ago. We make several million new leisure vehicles, tents, microwaves, refrigerators, telephones, television sets, and VCRs, all of which make outdoor living and vacations more attractive and more comfortable.

What determines whether we build more homes or make more camping gear and develop more campsites? How do these choices change over time? And how are they affected by the ongoing changes in technology that make an ever-wider array of goods and services available to us?

prices. In others, they use a laser scanner. One farmer keeps track of his livestock feeding schedules and inventories by using paper and pencil records, while another uses a personal computer. GM hires workers to weld auto bodies in some of its plants and uses robots to do the job in others.

Why do we use machines in some cases and people in others? Does mechanization and technological change destroy more jobs than it creates? Does it make us better off or worse off?

2: How?

How are goods and services produced? In a vineyard in France, basket-carrying workers pick the annual grape crop by hand. In a vineyard in California, a huge machine and a few workers do the same job that a hundred French grape harvesters do. Look around you and you will see many examples of this phenomenon—the same job being done in different ways. In some supermarkets, checkout clerks key in

3: When?

When are goods and services produced? On a building site, there is a surge of production activity and people must work overtime to keep production flowing fast enough. An auto factory closes for the summer, temporarily lays of its workers, and its production dries up.

Sometimes, economy-wide production slackens off and even shrinks in what is called a *recession*. At other times, economy-wide production expands rapidly. We call these ebbs and flows of production the *business cycle*. When production falls, jobs are lost and unemployment climbs. Once, during the Great Depression of the 1930s, production fell so much that one quarter of the workforce was jobless.

During the past few years, production has decreased in Russia and its Central and Eastern European neighbors as these countries try to change the way they organize their economies.

What makes production rise and fall? When will production fall again in the United States? Can the government prevent production from falling?

4: Where?

Where are goods and services produced? The Kellogg Company, of Battle Creek, Michigan, makes breakfast cereals in 20 countries and sells them in 160 countries. Kellogg's business in Japan is so huge that it has a Japanese language Website to promote its products! Honda, the Japanese auto producer, makes cars and motor cycles on most continents. "Globalization through localization" is its slogan. But it produces some cars in one country and ships them for sale in another.

In today's global economy, people who are separated by thousands of miles cooperate to produce many goods and services. Software engineers in Silicon Valley work via the Internet with programmers in India. American Express card charge slips are processed in Barbados. But there is a lot of local concentration of production as well. Most American carpets are made in Dalton, Georgia. And most of our movies are made in Los Angeles.

What determines where goods and services are produced? And how are changing patterns of production location changing the jobs we do and the wages we earn?

5: Who?

Who consumes the goods and services that are produced? Who consumes the goods and services produced depends on the incomes that people earn. Doctors earn much higher incomes than nurses and medical assistants. So doctors get more of the goods and services produced than nurses and medical assistants.

You probably know about many other persistent differences in incomes. Men, on the average, earn more than women. Whites, on the average, earn more than minorities. College graduates, on the average, earn more than high-school graduates do. Americans, on the average, earn more than Europeans, who in turn earn more on the average than Asians and Africans. But there are some significant exceptions. The people of Japan and Hong Kong now earn a similar amount to that of Americans. And there is a lot of income inequality throughout the world.

What determines the incomes we earn? Why do doctors earn larger incomes than nurses? Why do women and minorities earn less than white males?

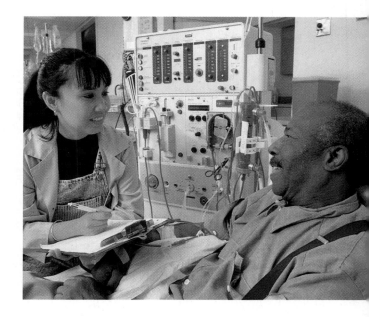

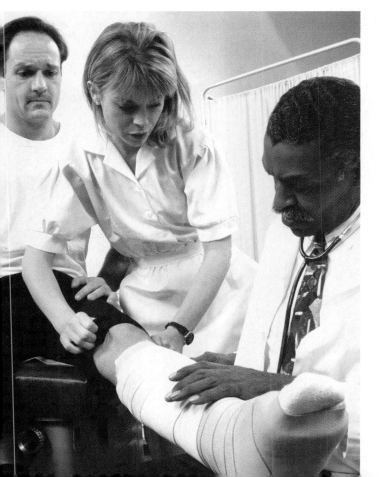

REVIEW QUIZ

- How would you define economics?
- What is scarcity? Give some examples of rich people and poor people facing scarcity.
- Give some examples, different from those in the chapter, of each of the five big economic questions.
- Why do you care about *what* goods and services are produced? Give some examples of goods that you value highly and goods on which you place a low value.
- Why do you care about *how* goods and services are produced? [Hint: Think about cost.]
- Why do you care about *when* or *where* goods and services are produced?
- Why do you care about *who* gets the goods and services that are produced?

These five big economic questions give you a sense of what economics is *about*. They tell you about the *scope of economics*. But they don't tell you what economics *is*. They don't tell you how economists *think* about these questions and seek answers to them. Let's find out how economists approach economic questions by looking at eight big ideas that define the *economic way of thinking*.

Big Ideas of Economics

WE CAN SUMMARIZE THE ECONOMIC WAY OF thinking in eight big ideas. Let's study them.

1: Choice, Tradeoff, and Opportunity Cost

A choice is a tradeoff—we give up something to get something else—and the highest-valued alternative we give up is the opportunity cost of the activity we choose.

Whatever we choose to do, we could have done something else instead. We tradeoff one thing for another. **Tradeoff** means giving up something to get something else. The highest-valued alternative we give up to get something is the **opportunity cost** of the activity chosen. "There's no such thing as a free lunch" is not just a clever throwaway line. It expresses the central idea of economics—that every choice involves a cost.

We use the term *opportunity cost* to emphasize that when we make a choice in the face of scarcity, we give up an opportunity to do something else. The opportunity cost of any action is the highest-valued alternative forgone. The action that you choose not to do—the highest-valued alternative forgone—is the cost of the action that you choose to do.

You can quit school right now or you can remain in school. If you quit and take a job at McDonalds, you might earn enough to buy some CDs, go to the movies, and spend lots of free time with your friends. If you remain in school, you can't afford these things. You will be able to buy these things later, and that is one of the payoffs from being in school. But for now, when you've bought your books, you have nothing left for CDs and movies. And doing assignments means that you've got less time for hanging around with your friends. The opportunity cost of being in school is the alternative things that you would have done if you had quit school.

Opportunity cost is the highest-valued alternative forgone. It is not *all* the possible alternatives forgone. For example, your economics lecture is at 8:30 on a Monday morning. You contemplate two alternatives to the lecture: staying in bed for an hour or jogging for an hour. You can't stay in bed and jog for that same hour. The opportunity cost of attending the lecture is the forgone hour in bed *or* the forgone hour of jogging. If these are the only alternatives you consider, then you have to decide which one you would do if you did not go to the lecture. The opportunity cost of attending a lecture for a jogger is a forgone hour of exercise; the opportunity cost of attending a lecture for a late sleeper is a forgone hour in bed.

2: Margins and Incentives

We make choices in small steps, or at the margin, and choices are influenced by incentives. Everything that we do involves a decision to do a little bit more or a little bit less of an activity. You can allocate the next hour between studying and e-mailing your friends. But the choice is not "all-or-nothing." You must decide how many minutes to allocate to each activity. To make this decision, you compare the benefit of a little bit more study time with its cost—you make your choice at the **margin**.

The mother of a young child must decide how to allocate her time between being with her child and working for an income. Like your decision about study time, this decision too involves comparing the benefit of a little bit more income with the cost of a little bit less time with her child.

The benefit that arises from an increase in an activity is called **marginal benefit**. For example, suppose that a mother is working 2 days a week and is thinking about increasing her work to 3 days. Her marginal benefit is the benefit she will get from the additional day of work. It is *not* the benefit she gets from all 3 days. The reason is that she already has the benefit from 2 days work, so she doesn't count this benefit as resulting from the decision she is now making.

The cost of an increase in an activity is called **marginal cost**. For the mother of the young child, the marginal cost of increasing her work to 3 days a week is the cost of the additional day not spent with her child. It does not include the cost of the 2 days she is already working.

To make her decision, the mother compares the marginal benefit from an extra day of work with its marginal cost. If the marginal benefit exceeds the marginal cost, she works the extra day. If the marginal cost exceeds the marginal benefit, she does not work the extra day.

By evaluating marginal benefits and marginal costs and choosing only those actions that bring greater benefit than cost, we use our scarce resources in the way that makes us as well off as possible.

Our choices respond to incentives. An **incentive** is an inducement to take a particular action. The inducement can be a benefit—a carrot—or a cost—a stick. A change in opportunity cost—in marginal cost—and a change in marginal benefit changes the incentives that we face and leads to changes in our actions.

For example, suppose the daily wage rate rises and nothing else changes. With a higher daily wage rate, the marginal benefit of working increases. For the young mother, the opportunity cost of spending a day with her child has increased. She now has a bigger incentive to work an extra day a week. Whether or not she does so depends on how she evaluates the marginal benefit of the additional income and marginal cost of spending less time with her child.

Similarly, suppose the cost of day care rises and nothing else changes. The higher cost of day care increases the marginal cost of working. For the young mother, the opportunity cost of spending a day with her child has decreased. She now has a smaller incentive to work an extra day a week. Again, whether or not she changes her actions in response to a change in incentives depends on how she evaluates the marginal benefit and marginal cost.

The central idea of economics is that by looking for changes in marginal cost and marginal benefit, we can predict the way choices will change in response to changes in incentives.

3: Voluntary Exchange and Efficient Markets

Voluntary exchange makes both buyers and sellers better off, and markets are an efficient way to organize exchange.

When you shop for food, you give up some money in exchange for a basket of vegetables. But the food is worth the price you have to pay. You are better off having exchanged some of your money for the vegetables. The food store receives a payment that makes its operator happy too. Both you and the food store operator gain from your purchase.

Similarly, when you work at a summer job, you receive a wage that you've decided is sufficient to compensate you for the leisure time you must give up. But the value of your work to the firm that hires you is at least as great as the wage it pays you. So again, both you and your employer gain from a **voluntary exchange**.

You are better off when you buy your food. And you are better off when you sell your labor during the summer vacation. Whether you are a buyer or a seller, you gain from voluntary exchange with others. What is true for you is true for everyone. Everyone gains from voluntary exchange.

In our economy, exchanges take place in **markets** and for money. We sell our labor in exchange for an income in the labor market. And we buy the goods and services we've chosen to consume in a wide variety of markets—markets for vegetables, coffee, movies, videos, muffins, haircuts, and so on. At the other side of these transactions, firms buy our labor and sell us the hundreds of different consumer goods and services we buy.

Markets are **efficient** in the sense that they send resources to the place where they are valued most highly. For example, a frost kills Florida's orange crop and sends the price of orange juice through the roof. This increase in price, with all other prices remaining unchanged, increases the opportunity cost of drinking orange juice. The people who place the highest value on orange juice are the ones who keep drinking it. People who place a lower value on orange juice now have an incentive to substitute other fruit juices.

Markets are not the only way to organize the economy. An alternative is called a command system. In a **command system**, some people give orders (commands) and other people obey those orders. A command system is used in the military and in many firms. And it was used in the former Soviet Union to organize the entire economy. But the market is a superior method of organizing an entire economy.

4: Market Failure

The market does not always work efficiently and sometimes, government action is necessary to make the use of resources efficient.

Market failure is a state in which the market does not use resources efficiently. If you pay attention to the news media, you might get the impression that the market almost never does a good job. It makes credit card interest rates too high. It makes the wages of fast-food workers too low. It causes the price of coffee to go through the ceiling every time Brazil has a serious frost. It increases the world price of oil when political instability threatens the Middle East. These examples are not cases of market failure. They are examples of the market doing its job of helping us to allocate our scarce resources and ensure that they are used in the activities in which they are most highly valued.

Buyers never like it when prices rise. But sellers love it. And sellers never like it when prices fall. But buyers are happy. Rising and falling prices make news because they bring changes in fortunes. Some people win and some lose. Everyone gains from voluntary exchange, as you've just seen, but other things remaining the same, the higher the price, the more the seller gains and the less the buyer gains.

Because a high price brings a bigger gain to the seller, there is an incentive for sellers to try to control a market. When a single producer controls an entire market, the producer can restrict the quantity available and raise the price. This action brings market failure. The quantity of the good available is too small. Some people believe that Intel restricts the quantity of computer chips when it introduces a new design in order to get a high price for it. Eventually, the price falls, but at first, Intel sells its new design for a high price and makes a bigger profit.

Market failure can also arise when producers don't take into account the costs they impose on other people. For example, electric utilities create pollution, such as acid rain, that destroys plants and forests and lowers farm production. If these costs were taken into account, we would produce less electricity.

Market failure can also arise because some goods, such as national defense, must be consumed equally by everyone. None of us has an incentive voluntarily to pay our share of the cost of such a good. Instead, we try to free ride on everyone else. But if everyone tries to free ride, no one gets a ride!

To overcome market failure, governments regulate markets with antitrust laws and environmental protection laws; discourage the production and consumption of some goods and services (tobacco and alcohol for example) by taxing them; encourage the production and consumption of some goods and services (health care and schooling for example) by subsidizing them; and directly provide some goods and services (national defense, for example).

5: Expenditure, Income, and the Value of Production

For the economy as a whole, expenditure *equals* income and *equals* the value of production.

When you buy a coffee milk shake, you spend $2. But what happens to that money? The server gets some of it in wages, the owner of the building gets some of it as rent, and the owner of the milk bar gets some of it as profit. The suppliers of the milk, ice cream, and coffee also get some of your $2. But these suppliers spend part of what they receive on wages and rent. And they keep part of it as profit. Your $2 of **expenditure** creates exactly $2 of **income** for all the people who have contributed to making the milk shake, going all the way back to the farmer in Brazil who grew the coffee beans.

Your expenditure generates incomes of an equal amount. The same is true for everyone else's expenditure. So, for the economy as a whole, total expenditure on goods and services equals total income.

One way to value the things you buy is to use the prices you pay for them. So the value all of the goods and services bought equals total expenditure. Another way to value the items you buy is to use the cost of production. This cost is the total amount paid to the people who produced the items—the total income generated by your expenditure. But we've just seen that total expenditure and total income are equal, so they also equal the **value of production**.

6: Living Standards and Productivity Growth

Living standards improve when production per person increases.

By automating a car production line, one worker can produce a greater output. But if one worker can produce more cars, then more people can enjoy owning a car. The same is true for all goods and services. By increasing output per person, we enjoy a higher standard of living and buy more goods and services.

The dollar value of production can increase for any of three reasons: because prices rise, because production per person—**productivity**—increases, or because the population increases.

But only an increase in productivity brings an improvement in living standards. A rise in prices brings higher incomes, but only in dollars. The extra income is just enough to pay the higher prices, not enough to buy more goods and services. An increase in population brings an increase in *total* production, but not an increase in production per person.

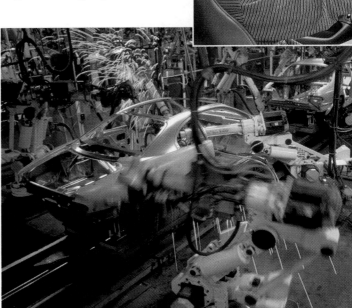

7: Inflation: A Monetary Problem

Prices rise in a process called **inflation** when the quantity of money increases faster than production. This process leads to a situation in which "too much money is chasing too few goods." As people bring more money to market, sellers see that they can raise their prices. But when these sellers go to buy their supplies, they find that the prices they face increase. With too much money around, money starts to lose value.

In some countries, inflation has been rapid. One such country is Poland. Since 1990, prices in Poland have risen more than seven-fold. In the United States, we have moderate inflation of less than 2 percent a year.

Some people say that by increasing the quantity of money, we can create jobs. The idea is that if more money is put into the economy, when it is spent, businesses sell more and so hire more labor to produce more goods and services.

Initially, an increase in money might increase production and create jobs. But eventually, it only increases prices and leaves production and jobs unchanged.

8: Unemployment: Productive and Wasteful

Unemployment can result from market failure and be wasteful. But some unemployment is productive.

Unemployment is ever present. Sometimes its rate is low and sometimes it is high. Also, unemployment fluctuates over the business cycle.

Some unemployment is normal and efficient. We choose to take our time finding a suitable job rather than rushing to accept the first one that comes along. Similarly, businesses take their time in filling vacancies. The unemployment that results from these careful searches for jobs and workers improves productivity because it helps to assign people to their most productive jobs.

Some unemployment results from fluctuations in expenditure and can be wasteful.

R E V I E W   Q U I Z

- Give some examples of *tradeoffs* that you have made and the *opportunity costs* you've incurred today.
- Give some examples of *marginal* cost and *marginal* benefit.
- How do markets enable both buyers and sellers to gain from exchange and why do markets sometimes fail?
- Why for the economy as a whole, does expenditure equal income and the value of production?
- What makes living standards rise?
- What makes prices rise?
- Is unemployment always a problem?

What Economists Do

ECONOMISTS USE THE EIGHT BIG IDEAS THAT YOU have just studied to search for answers to the five big questions that you reviewed at the start of this chapter. But how do they go about their work? What special problems and pitfalls do they encounter? And do they always agree on the answers?

Microeconomics and Macroeconomics

Economists approach their work from either a micro or a macro perspective. These two perspectives define the two major branches of the subject:

- Microeconomics
- Macroeconomics

Microeconomics is the study of the decisions of individual people and businesses and the interaction of those decisions in markets.

Macroeconomics is the study of the national economy and the global economy. It seeks to explain *average* prices and *total* employment, income, and production.

You can take either a micro or a macro view of the spectacular display of national flags in a Korean sports stadium. The micro view is of a single participant and the actions he or she is taking. The macro view is the patterns formed by the joint actions of all the individuals participating in the entire display.

Microeconomics seeks to explain the prices and quantities of individual goods and services. It also

studies the effects of government regulation and taxes on the prices and quantities of individual goods and services. For example, microeconomics studies the forces that determine the prices of cars and the quantities of cars produced and sold. It also studies the effects of regulations and taxes on the prices and quantities of cars.

Macroeconomics studies the effects of taxes, government spending, and the government budget surplus or deficit on total jobs and incomes. It also studies the effects of money and interest rates.

Economic Science

Economics is a social science (along with political science, psychology, and sociology). A major task of economists is to discover how the economic world works. In pursuit of this goal, economists (like all scientists) distinguish between two types of statements:

- What *is*
- What *ought* to be

Statements about what *is* are called *positive* statements. They say what is currently believed about the way the world operates. A positive statement might be right or wrong. And we can test a positive statement by checking it against the facts. When a chemist does an experiment in her laboratory, she is attempting to check a positive statement against the facts.

Statements about what *ought* to be are called *normative* statements. These statements depend on

values and cannot be tested. When Congress debates a motion, it is ultimately trying to decide what ought to be. It is making a normative statement.

To see the distinction between positive and normative statements, consider the controversy over global warming. Some scientists believe that centuries of the burning of coal and oil are increasing the carbon dioxide content of the earth's atmosphere and leading to higher temperatures that eventually will have devastating consequences for life on this planet. "Our planet is warming because of an increased carbon dioxide buildup in the atmosphere" is a positive statement. It can (in principle and with sufficient data) be tested. "We ought to cut back on our use of carbon-based fuels such as coal and oil" is a normative statement. You may agree with or disagree with this statement, but you can't test it. It is based on values. Health-care reform provides an economic example of the distinction. "Universal health care will cut the amount of work time lost to illness" is a positive statement. "Every American should have equal access to health care" is a normative statement.

The task of economic science is to discover and catalog positive statements that are consistent with what we observe in the world and that enable us to understand how the economic world works. This task is a large one that can be broken into three steps:

■ Observation and measurement
■ Model building
■ Testing models

Observation and Measurement First, economists keep track of the amounts and locations of natural and human resources, of wages and work hours, of the prices and quantities of the different goods and services produced, of taxes and government spending, and of the quantities of goods and services bought from and sold to other countries. This list gives a flavor of the array of things that economists can observe and measure.

Model Building The second step toward understanding how the economic world works is to build a model. An **economic model** is a description of some aspect of the economic world that includes only those features of the world that are needed for the purpose at hand. A model is simpler than the reality it describes. What a model includes and what it leaves out result from *assumptions* about what is essential and what are inessential details.

You can see how ignoring details is useful—even essential—to our understanding by thinking about a model that you see every day, the TV weather map. The weather map is a model that helps to predict the temperature, wind speed and direction, and precipitation over a future period. The weather map shows lines called isobars—lines of equal barometric pressure. It doesn't show the interstate highways. The reason is that our theory of the weather tells us that the pattern of air pressure, not the location of the highways, determines the weather.

An economic model is similar to a weather map. It tells us how a number of variables are determined by a number of other variables. For example, an economic model of the 1994 Los Angeles earthquake might tell us the effects of the earthquake and the government's relief efforts on the number of houses and apartments, rents and prices, jobs, and commuting times.

Testing The third step is testing the model. A model's predictions may correspond to or be in conflict with the facts. By comparing the model's predictions with the facts, we are able to test a model and develop an economic theory. An **economic theory** is a generalization that summarizes what we think we understand about the economic choices that people make and the performance of industries and entire economies. It is a bridge between an economic model and the real economy.

A theory is created by a process of building and testing models. For example, meteorologists have a theory that if the isobars form a particular pattern at a particular time of the year (a model), then it will snow (reality). They have developed this theory by repeated observation and by carefully recording the weather that follows specific pressure patterns.

Economics is a young science. It was born in 1776 with the publication of Adam Smith's *The Wealth of Nations* (see pp. 56–57). Over the past 225 years, economics has discovered many useful theories. But in many areas, economists are still looking for answers. The gradual accumulation of economic knowledge gives most economists some faith that their methods will, eventually, provide usable answers to the big economic questions.

But progress in economics comes slowly. Let's look at some of the obstacles to progress in economics.

Obstacles and Pitfalls in Economics

We cannot easily do economic experiments. And most economic behavior has many simultaneous causes. For these two reasons, it is difficult in economics to unscramble cause and effect.

Unscrambling Cause and Effect By changing one factor at a time and holding all the other relevant factors constant, we isolate the factor of interest and are able to investigate its effects in the clearest possible way. This logical device, that all scientists use to identify cause and effect, is called *ceteris paribus*. *Ceteris paribus* is a Latin term that means "other things being equal" or "if all other relevant things remain the same." Ensuring that other things are equal is crucial in many activities, including athletic events, and all successful attempts to make scientific progress use this device.

Economic models (like the models in all other sciences) enable the influence of one factor at a time to be isolated in the imaginary world of the model. When we use a model, we are able to imagine what would happen if only one factor changed. But *ceteris paribus* can be a problem in economics when we try to test a model.

Laboratory scientists, such as chemists and physicists, perform experiments by actually holding all the relevant factors constant except for the one under investigation. In the non-experimental sciences such as economics (and astronomy), we usually observe the outcomes of the *simultaneous* operation of many factors. Consequently, it is hard to sort out the effects of each individual factor and to compare the effects with what a model predicts. To cope with this problem, economists take three complementary approaches.

First, they look for pairs of events in which other things were equal (or similar). An example might be to study the effects of unemployment insurance on the unemployment rate by comparing the United States with Canada on the presumption that the people in the two economies are sufficiently similar. Second, economists use statistical tools—called *econometrics*. And third, when they can, they perform experiments. This relatively new approach puts real subjects (usually students) in a decision-making situation and varies their incentives in some way to discover how they respond to one factor at a time.

Economists try to avoid *fallacies*—errors of reasoning that lead to a wrong conclusion. But two fallacies are common, and you need to be on your guard to avoid them. They are the

- Fallacy of composition
- *Post hoc* fallacy

Fallacy of Composition The fallacy of composition is the (false) statement that what is true of the parts is true of the whole or that what is true of the whole is true of the parts. Think of the true statement, "Speed kills," and its implication, going more slowly saves lives. If an entire freeway moves at a lower speed, everyone on the highway has a safer ride.

But suppose that one driver only slows down and all the other drivers try to maintain their original speed. In this situation, there will probably be more accidents because more cars will change lanes to overtake the slower vehicle. So, in this example, what is true for the whole is not true for a part.

The fallacy of composition arises mainly in macroeconomics, and it stems from the fact that the parts interact with each other to produce an outcome for the whole that might differ from the intent of the parts. For example, a firm lays off some workers to cut costs and improve its profits. If all firms take similar actions, incomes fall and so does spending. The firm sells less, and its profits don't improve.

***Post Hoc* Fallacy** Another Latin phrase—*post hoc ergo propter hoc*—means "after this, therefore because of this." The *post hoc* fallacy is the error of reasoning that a first event *causes* a second event because the first occurred before the second. Suppose you are a visitor from a far off world. You observe lots of people shopping in early December and then you see them opening gifts and partying on Christmas day. Does the shopping cause Christmas, you wonder. After a deeper study, you discover that Christmas causes the shopping. A later event causes an earlier event.

Unraveling cause and effect is difficult in economics. And just looking at the timing of events often doesn't help. For example, the stock market booms, and some months later the economy expands—jobs and incomes grow. Did the stock market boom cause the economy to expand? Possibly, but perhaps businesses started to plan the expansion of production because a new technology that lowered costs had become available. As knowledge of the plans spread, the stock market reacted to *anticipate* the economic expansion. To disentangle cause and effect, economists use economic models and data and, to the extent that they can, perform experiments.

Economics is a challenging science. Does the difficulty of getting answers in economics mean that anything goes and that economists disagree on most questions? Perhaps you've heard the joke: "If you laid all the economists in the world end to end, they still wouldn't reach agreement." Does the joke make a valid point?

Agreement and Disagreement

Economists agree on a remarkably wide range of questions. And surprisingly, the agreed view of economists often disagrees with the popular and sometimes politically correct view. When Fed Chairman Alan Greenspan testifies before the Senate Banking Committee, his words are rarely controversial among economists, even when they generate endless debate in the press and Congress.

Here are twelve propositions[1] with which at least 7 out of every 10 economists broadly agree:

- Tariffs and import restrictions make most people worse off.
- A large federal budget deficit has an adverse effect on the economy.
- Cash payments to welfare recipients make them better off than do transfers-in-kind of equal cash value.
- A minimum wage increases unemployment among young workers and low skilled workers.
- A tax cut can help to lower unemployment when the unemployment rate is high.
- The distribution of income in the United States should be more equal.
- Inflation is primarily caused by a rapid rate of money creation.
- The government should restructure welfare along the lines of a "negative income tax."
- Rent ceilings cut the availability of housing.
- Pollution taxes are more effective than pollution limits.
- The redistribution of income is a legitimate role for the U.S. government.
- The federal budget should be balanced on the average over the business cycle, but not every year.

Which are positive and which are normative? Notice that economists are willing to offer their opinions on normative issues as well as their professional views on positive questions. Be on the lookout for normative propositions dressed up as positive propositions.

---

[1] These are propositions generally supported or supported with provisos by more than 7 out of 10 economists according to a survey by Richard M. Alston, J.R. Kearl, and Michael B. Vaughan, "Is There a Consensus Among Economists," *American Economic Review*, 82 (May 1992), pp. 203–209. I have simplified the language in some cases, and you should check the original for the exact propositions and percentages agreeing.

R E V I E W   Q U I Z

- What is the distinction between microeconomics and macroeconomics? Provide an example (not in the chapter) of a micro issue and a macro issue.
- What is the distinction between a positive statement and a normative statement? Provide an example (different from those in the chapter) of each type of statement.
- What is a model? Can you think of a model that you might use (probably without thinking of it as a model) in your everyday life?
- What is a theory? Why is the statement, "It might work in theory but it doesn't work in practice" a silly statement? [Hint: Think about what a theory is and how it is used.]
- What is the *ceteris paribus* assumption and how is it used?
- Try to think of some everyday examples of fallacies.

You are now ready to start *doing* economics. As you get into the subject, you will see that we rely heavily on graphs. You must be comfortable with this method of reasoning. If you need some help with it, take your time in working carefully through Chapter 2. If you are already comfortable with graphs, then you are ready to jump right into Chapter 3 and begin to study the fundamental economic problem, scarcity.

SUMMARY

KEY POINTS

A Definition of Economics (p. 2)

- Economics is the *science of choice*—the science that explains the choices that we make to cope with scarcity.

Big Economic Questions (pp. 2–5)

- Economists try to answer five big questions about goods and services:
  1. What?
  2. How?
  3. When?
  4. Where?
  5. Who?

  What are the goods and services produced, *how*, *when*, and *where* are they produced, and *who* consumes them?

- These questions interact to determine the standards of living and the distribution of well-being in the United States and around the world.

Big Ideas of Economics (pp. 6–11)

- A choice is a tradeoff and the highest-valued alternative forgone is the opportunity cost of what is chosen.
- Choices are made at the margin and are influenced by incentives.
- Markets enable both buyers and sellers to gain from voluntary exchange.
- Sometimes government actions are needed to overcome market failure.
- For the economy as a whole, expenditure equals income and equals the value of production.
- Living standards rise when production per person increases.
- Prices rise when the quantity of money increases faster than production.
- Unemployment can result from market failure but can also be productive.

What Economists Do (pp. 12–16)

- Microeconomics is the study of individual decisions, and macroeconomics is the study of the economy as a whole.
- Positive statements are about what *is* and normative statements are about what *ought* to be.
- To explain the economic world, economists build and test economic models.
- Economists use the *ceteris paribus* assumption to try to disentangle cause and effect, and they are careful to avoid the fallacy of composition and the *post hoc* fallacy.
- Economists agree on a wide range of questions about how the economy works.

KEY TERMS

Ceteris paribus, 14
Command system, 8
Economics, 2
Economic model, 13
Economic theory, 13
Efficient, 8
Expenditure, 10
Goods and services, 2
Incentive, 7
Income, 10
Inflation, 11
Macroeconomics, 12
Margin, 7
Marginal benefit, 7
Marginal cost, 7
Market, 8
Market failure, 9
Microeconomics, 12
Opportunity cost, 6
Productivity, 10
Scarcity, 2
Tradeoff, 6
Unemployment, 11
Value of production, 10
Voluntary exchange, 8

PROBLEMS

*1. You plan to go to school this summer. If you do, you won't be able to take your usual job that pays $6,000 for the summer and you won't be able to live at home for free. The cost of your tuition will be $2,000, textbooks $200, and living expenses $1,400. What is the opportunity cost of going to summer school?

2. You plan a major adventure trip for the summer. You won't be able to take your usual summer job that pays $6,000 and you won't be able to live at home for free. The cost of your travel on the trip will be $3,000, film and video tape will cost you $200, and your food will cost $1,400. What is the opportunity cost of taking this trip?

*3. The local mall has free parking, but the mall is always very busy and it usually takes 30 minutes to find a parking space. Today when you found a vacant spot, Harry also wanted it. Is parking really free at this mall? If not, what did it cost you to park today? When you parked your car today, did you impose any costs on Harry? Explain your answers.

4. The university has built a new parking garage. There is always an available parking spot but it costs $1 a day. Before the new garage was built, it usually took 15 minutes of cruising to find a parking space. Compare the opportunity cost of parking in the new garage with that in the old parking lot. Which is less costly and by how much?

CRITICAL THINKING

1. Use the link on the Parkin Web site to visit *Resources For Economists on the Internet*. Scroll down the page and click on General Interest. Visit the "general interest" sites and become familiar with the types of information they contain.

2. Use the link on the Parkin Web site to visit *The Dismal Scientist* ®™—the best free lunch on the Web! In the "Economic Profile" box, enter your zip code and click "Get the profile."
    a. What is the number of people employed (nonfarm employment) in your area?

b. Has employment increased or decreased?
c. What is income per person (per capita income) in your area?

3. This man is homeless, and you can see all his possessions in the photograph.

   Use the five big questions and the eight big ideas of economics to organize a short essay about the economic life of the man in the photograph. Does he face scarcity? Does he make choices? Can you interpret his choices as being in his own best interest? Can either his own choices or the choices of others make this man better off? If so, how?

4. Use the link on the Parkin Web site to visit *CNNfn*.
    a. What is the top economic news story today?
    b. With which of the five big questions does it deal? (Hint: It must deal with at least one of them and might deal with more than one.)
    c. Which of the eight big ideas seem to be relevant to understanding this news item?
    d. Write a brief summary of the news item in a few bulleted points, using as much as possible of the economic vocabulary that you have learned in this chapter and that is in the key terms list on p. 17.

---

*Answers to odd-numbered problems appear at the back of the book.

Chapter 2

Making and Using Graphs

British Prime Minister Benjamin Disraeli is reputed to have said that "There are three kinds of lies: lies, damned lies, and statistics." One of the most powerful ways of conveying statistical information is in the form of a graph. And like statistics, graphs can lie. But the right graph does not lie. It reveals a relationship that would otherwise be obscure. ◆ Graphs are a modern invention. They first appeared in the late eighteenth century, long after the discovery of logarithms and calculus. But today, in the age of the personal computer and video display, graphs have become as important as words and numbers. How do economists use graphs? What types of graphs do they use? What do graphs reveal and what can they hide? ◆ The big questions that economics tries to answer—questions that you studied in

Three Kinds of Lies

Chapter 1—are difficult ones. They involve relationships among a large number of variables. Almost nothing in economics has a single cause. Instead, a large number of variables interact with each other. It is often said that in economics, everything depends on everything else. Changes in the quantity of ice cream consumed are caused by changes in the price of ice cream, the temperature, and many other factors. How can we make and interpret graphs of relationships among several variables?

◆ In this chapter, you are going to look at the kinds of graphs that economists use. You are going to learn how to make them and read them. You are also going to learn how to determine the magnitude of the influence of one variable on another by calculating the slope of a line and of a curve. ◆ There are no graphs or techniques used in this book that are more complicated than those described and explained in this chapter. If you are already familiar with graphs, you may want to skip (or skim) this chapter. Whether you study this chapter thoroughly or give it a quick pass, you can use it as a handy reference, returning to it whenever you need extra help in understanding the graphs that you encounter in your study of economics.

After studying this chapter, you will be able to:

■ **Make and interpret a time-series graph, a scatter diagram, and a cross-section graph**

■ **Distinguish between linear and nonlinear relationships and between relationships that have a maximum and a minimum**

■ **Define and calculate the slope of a line**

■ **Graph relationships among more than two variables**

Graphing Data

GRAPHS REPRESENT A QUANTITY AS A DISTANCE on a line. Figure 2.1 gives two examples. A distance on the horizontal line represents temperature, measured in degrees Fahrenheit. A movement from left to right shows an increase in temperature. A movement from right to left shows a decrease in temperature. The point marked 0 represents zero degrees Fahrenheit. To the right of 0, the temperatures are positive. To the left of 0, the temperatures are negative (as indicated by the minus sign in front of the numbers).

A distance on the vertical line represents altitude or height, measured in thousands of feet above sea level. The point marked 0 represents sea level. Points above 0 represent feet above sea level. Points below 0 (indicated by a minus sign) represent feet below sea level.

There are no rigid rules about the scale for a graph. The scale is determined by the range of the variables being graphed.

The main point of a graph is to enable us to visualize the relationship between two variables. And to accomplish this, we set two scales perpendicular to each other, like those in Fig. 2.1.

The two scale lines are called *axes*. The vertical line is called the *y*-axis, and the horizontal line is called the *x*-axis. The letters *x* and *y* appear on the axes of Fig. 2.1. Each axis has a zero point, which is shared by the two axes. This zero point, common to both axes, is called the *origin*.

To show something in a two-variable graph, we need two pieces of information. We need the value of the variable *x* and the value of the variable *y*. For example, off the coast of Alaska on a winter's day, the temperature is 32 degrees, which we will call the value of *x*. A fishing boat is located at 0 feet above sea level, which we'll call the value of *y*. These two bits of information appear as point *a* in Fig. 2.1. A climber at the top of Mount McKinley on a very cold day is 20,320 feet above sea level and the temperature is 0 degrees. These two pieces of information appear as point *b*. The position of the climber on a warmer day might be at the point marked *c*. This point represents the peak of Mt. McKinley when the temperature is 32 degrees.

Two lines, called coordinates, can be drawn from point *c* in the graph. One of these lines runs from *c* to the horizontal axis. This line is called the *y*-coordinate. Its length is the same as the value marked off on

FIGURE 2.1
Making a Graph

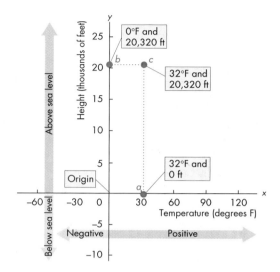

All graphs have axes that measure quantities as distances. Here, the horizontal axis (*x*-axis) measures temperature. A rightward movement shows an increase in temperature. The vertical axis (*y*-axis) measures height. An upward movement shows an increase in height. Point *a* represents a fishing boat at sea level (0 on the *y*-axis) on a day when the temperature is 32° (32° on the *x*-axis). Point *b* represents a climber at the top of Mt. McKinley (20,320 feet above sea level on the *y*-axis) on a day when the temperature on Mt. McKinley is 0° (0° on the *x*-axis). Point *c* represents a climber at the top of Mt. McKinley, 20,320 feet above sea level (on the *y*-axis) on a day when the temperature on Mt. McKinley is 32° (on the *x*-axis).

the *y*-axis. The other of these lines runs from *c* to the vertical axis. This line is called the *x*-coordinate. Its length is the same as the value marked off on the *x*-axis. To describe a point in a graph, we simply use the values of its *x*- and *y*-coordinates.

Graphs like that in Fig. 2.1 can be used to show any type of quantitative data about two variables. Economists use graphs similar to the one in Fig. 2.1 to reveal and describe the relationships among economic variables. To do so, they use three main types of graphs, which we'll now study. They are:

- Scatter diagrams
- Time-series graphs
- Cross-section graphs

Scatter Diagrams

A **scatter diagram** plots the value of one economic variable against the value of another variable. Such a graph is used to reveal whether a relationship exists between two economic variables. It is also used to describe a relationship.

Consumption and Income   Figure 2.2(a) shows a scatter diagram of the relationship between consumption and income. The *x*-axis measures average income, and the *y*-axis measures average consumption. Each point shows consumption per person and income per person (on the average) in the United States in a given year from 1990 to 1997. The points for the eight years are "scattered" within the graph. Each point is labeled with a two-digit number that shows us its year. For example, the point marked 96 shows us that in 1996, income per person was $19,200 and consumption per person was $17,750.

The dots in this graph form a pattern, which reveals that as income increases, consumption also increases.

Phone Calls and Price   Figure 2.2(b) shows a scatter diagram of the relationship between the number of international phone calls made from the United States and the average price per minute.

The dots in this graph reveal that as the price per minute falls, the number of calls increases.

Unemployment and Inflation   Figure 2.2(c) shows a scatter diagram of inflation and unemployment in the United States. The dots in this graph form a pattern that shows us there is no clear relationship between these two variables. By its lack of a distinct pattern, the graph shows us that there is no simple relationship between inflation and unemployment in the United States.

Correlation and Causation   A scatter diagram that shows a clear relationship between two variables, such as Fig. 2.2(a) or Fig. 2.2(b), tells us that the two variables have a high correlation. When a high correlation is present, we can predict the value of one variable from the value of the other variable. But correlation does not imply causation. Sometimes a high correlation is just a coincidence, but sometimes it does

FIGURE 2.2
Scatter Diagrams

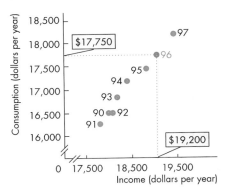

(a) Consumption and income

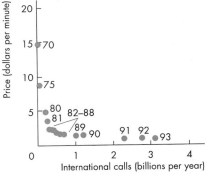

(b) International phone calls and prices

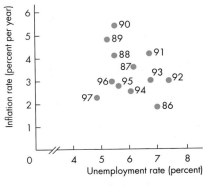

(c) Unemployment and inflation

A scatter diagram reveals the relationship between two variables. Part (a) shows the relationship between consumption and income between 1990 and 1997. Each point shows the values of the two variables in a specific year. For example, in 1996, average income was $19,200 and average consumption was $17,750. The pattern formed by the points shows that as income increases, so does consumption. Part (b) shows the relationship between the price of an international phone call and the number of phone calls made per year between 1970 and 1993. This graph shows that as the price of a phone call has fallen, the number of calls made has increased. Part (c) shows the inflation rate and unemployment rate in the United States between 1986 and 1997. This graph shows that inflation and unemployment are not closely related.

arise from a causal relationship. It is likely, for example, that increasing income causes increasing consumption (Fig. 2.2a) and that falling phone call prices cause more calls to be made (Fig. 2.2b).

Breaks in the Axes   Two of the graphs you've just looked at, Fig. 2.2(a) and Fig. 2.2(c), have breaks in their axes, as shown by the small gaps. The breaks indicate that there are jumps from the origin, 0, to the first values recorded.

In Fig. 2.2(a), the breaks are used because the lowest value of consumption exceeds $15,000 and the lowest value of income exceeds $16,500. With no breaks in the axes of this graph, there would be a lot of empty space, all the points would be crowded into the top right corner, and we would not be able to see whether a relationship exists between these two variables. By breaking the axes, we are able to bring the relationship into view.

Putting a break in the axes is like using a zoom lens to bring the relationship into the center of the graph and magnify it so that it fills the graph.

Misleading Graphs   Breaks can be used to highlight a relationship. But they can also be used to mislead and create a wrong impression—to make a graph that lies. The most common way of making a graph lie is to use axis breaks and to also either stretch or compress a scale. The most effective way to see the power of this kind of lie is to make some graphs that use this technique. For example, redraw Fig. 2.2(a) but make the y-axis that measures consumption run from zero to $45,000 and keep the x-axis the same as the one shown. The graph will now create the impression that despite huge income growth, consumption has barely changed.

To avoid being misled, it is a good idea to get into the habit of always looking closely at the values and the labels on the axes of a graph before you start to interpret it.

Time-Series Graphs

A **time-series graph** measures time (for example, months or years) on the x-axis and the variable or variables in which we are interested on the y-axis. Figure 2.3 shows an example of a time-series graph. In this graph, time (on the x-axis) is measured in years, which run from 1968 to 1998. The variable that we are interested in is the price of coffee, and it is measured on the y-axis.

A time-series graph conveys an enormous amount of information quickly and easily, as this example illustrates. It shows:

1. The *level* of the price of coffee—when it is *high* and *low*. When the line is a long way from the x-axis, the price is high. When the line is close to the x-axis, the price is low.

2. How the price *changes*—whether it *rises* or *falls*. When the line slopes upward, as in 1976, the price is rising. When the line slopes downward, as in 1978, the price is falling.

3. The *speed* with which the price changes—whether it rises or falls *quickly* or *slowly*. If the line is very steep, then the price rises or falls quickly. If the line is not steep, the price rises or falls slowly. For example, the price rose very quickly in 1976 and 1977. The price went up again in 1993 but slowly. Similarly, when the price was falling in 1978, it fell quickly, but during the early 1980s, it fell more slowly.

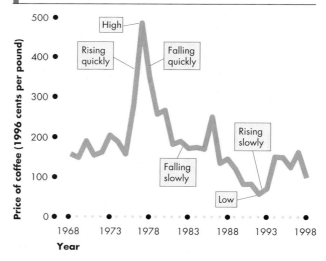

FIGURE 2.3

A Time-Series Graph

A time-series graph plots the level of a variable on the y-axis against time (day, week, month, or year) on the x-axis. This graph shows the price of coffee (in 1996 cents per pound) each year from 1968 to 1998. It shows us when the price of coffee was *high* and when it was *low*, when the price *increased* and when it *decreased*, and when it changed *quickly* and when it changed *slowly*.

A time-series graph also reveals whether there is a trend. A **trend** is a general tendency for a variable to rise or fall. You can see that the price of coffee had a general tendency to fall from the mid-1970s to the early 1990s. That is, although there were ups and downs in the price, there was a general tendency for it to fall.

A time-series graph also lets us compare different periods quickly. Figure 2.3 shows that the 1980s were different from the 1970s. The price of coffee fluctuated more violently in the 1970s than it did in the 1980s. This graph conveys a wealth of information, and it does so in much less space than we have used to describe only some of its features.

Comparing Two Time Series Sometimes we want to use a time-series graph to compare two different variables. For example, suppose you want to know whether the balance of the government's budget fluctuates with the unemployment rate. You can examine the government's budget balance and the unemployment rate by drawing a graph of each of them on the same time scale. But we can measure the government's budget balance either as a surplus or as a deficit. Figure 2.4(a) plots the budget surplus. The scale of the unemployment rate is on the left side of the figure, and the scale of the government's budget surplus is on the right. The orange line shows unemployment, and the blue line shows the budget surplus. This figure shows that the unemployment rate and the government's budget surplus move in opposite directions. For example, when the unemployment rate decreases, the budget surplus increases.

Figure 2.4(b) uses a scale for the government's budget balance measured as a deficit. That is, we flip the right-side scale over. This figure shows that the unemployment rate and the government's budget deficit move in the same direction. The budget deficit and the unemployment rate increase together and decrease together.

Scatter Diagram for Comparing Two Time Series We can compare two time series in a graph like Fig. 2.4 or in a scatter diagram like Fig. 2.2. Which is better? There is no right answer to this question. If the purpose of the graph is to show *both* the way two variables have changed over time and how they are related to each other, then the time-series graph does the better job. But if the purpose of the graph is to check the strength of the relationship between two variables, then a scatter diagram does a better job. A relationship that looks strong in a time-series graph often looks weak in a scatter diagram.

FIGURE 2.4
Time-Series Relationships

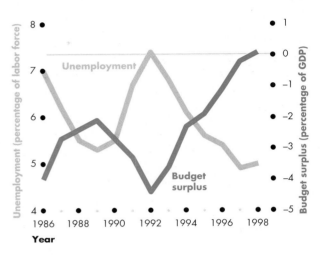

(a) Unemployment and budget surplus

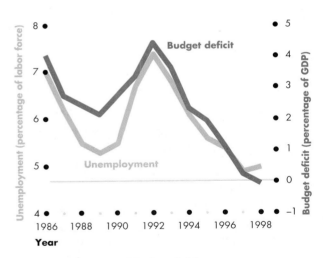

(b) Unemployment and budget deficit

These two graphs show the unemployment rate and the balance of the government's budget. The unemployment line is identical in the two parts. Part (a) shows the budget surplus—*taxes minus spending*—on the right scale. It is hard to see a relationship between the budget surplus and unemployment. Part (b) shows the budget as a deficit—*spending minus taxes*. It inverts the scale of part (a). With the scale for the budget balance inverted, the graph reveals a tendency for unemployment and the budget deficit to move together.

Cross-Section Graphs

A **cross-section graph** shows the values of an economic variable for different groups in a population at a point in time. Figure 2.5 is an example of a cross-section graph. It shows average income per person in the ten largest metropolitan areas in the United States in 1995. This graph uses bars rather than dots and lines, and the length of each bar indicates average income per person. Figure 2.5 enables you to compare the average incomes per person in these ten cities. And you can do so much more quickly and clearly than by looking at a list of numbers.

The cross-section graph in Fig. 2.5 is also an example of a *bar chart*. We often use bars rather than lines in cross-section graphs, but there are no fixed rules about whether to use lines, dots, or bars. It is a matter of taste.

You've now seen how we can use graphs in economics to show economic data and to reveal relationships between variables. Next, we're going to learn how to use graphs in a more abstract way. We'll learn how economists use graphs to construct and display economic models.

FIGURE 2.5
A Cross-Section Graph

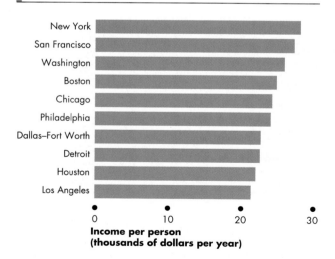

A cross-section graph shows the level of a variable across the members of a population. This graph shows the average income per person in each of the ten largest metropolitan areas in the United States in 1995.

Graphs Used in Economic Models

THE GRAPHS USED IN ECONOMICS ARE NOT always designed to show real-world data. Often they are used to show general relationships among the variables in an economic model.

An **economic model** is a stripped down, simplified description of an economy or of a component of an economy such as a business or a household. It consists of statements about economic behavior that can be expressed as equations or as curves in a graph. Economists use models to explore the effects of different policies or other influences on the economy in ways that are similar to the use of model airplanes in wind tunnels and models of the climate.

You will encounter many different kinds of graphs in economic models, but there are some repeating patterns. Once you've learned to recognize these patterns, you will instantly understand the meaning of a graph. Here, we'll look at the different types of curves that are used in economic models, and we'll see some everyday examples of each type of curve. The patterns to look for in graphs are the four cases in which:

- Variables move in the same direction
- Variables move in opposite directions
- Variables have a maximum or a minimum
- Variables are unrelated

Let's look at these four cases.

Variables That Move in the Same Direction

Figure 2.6 shows graphs of the relationships between two variables that move up and down together. A relationship between two variables that move in the same direction is called a **positive relationship** or a **direct relationship**. Such a relationship is shown by a line that slopes upward.

Figure 2.6 shows three types of relationships, one that has a straight line and two that have curved lines. But all the lines in these three graphs are called curves. Any line on a graph—no matter whether it is straight or curved—is called a *curve*.

A relationship shown by a straight line is called a **linear relationship.** Figure 2.6(a) shows a linear

FIGURE 2.6
Positive (Direct) Relationships

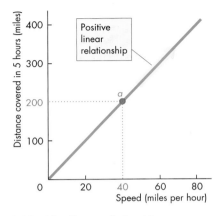

(a) Positive linear relationship

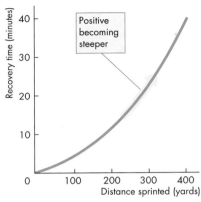

(b) Positive becoming steeper

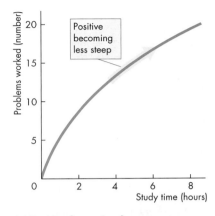

(c) Positive becoming less steep

Each part of this figure shows a positive (direct) relationship between two variables. That is, as the value of the variable measured on the x-axis increases, so does the value of the variable measured on the y-axis. Part (a) shows a linear relationship—as the two variables increase together, we move along a straight line. Part (b) shows a positive relationship such that as the two variables increase together, we move along a curve that becomes steeper. Part (c) shows a positive relationship such that as the two variables increase together, we move along a curve that becomes flatter.

relationship between the number of miles traveled in 5 hours and speed. For example, point *a* shows us that we will travel 200 miles in 5 hours if our speed is 40 miles an hour. If we double our speed to 80 miles an hour, we will travel 400 miles in 5 hours.

Part (b) shows the relationship between distance sprinted and recovery time (the time it takes the heart rate to return to its normal resting rate). This relationship is an upward-sloping one shown by a curved line that starts out fairly flat but then becomes steeper as we move along the curve away from the origin. The reason this curve slopes upward and becomes steeper is because the additional recovery time needed from sprinting an additional 100 yards increases. It takes less than 5 minutes to recover from 100 yards but more than 10 minutes to recover from the third 100 yards.

Part (c) shows the relationship between the number of problems worked by a student and the amount of study time. This relationship is shown by an upward-sloping curved line that starts out fairly steep and becomes flatter as we move away from the origin. Study time becomes less productive as you study for more hours and become more tired.

Variables That Move in Opposite Directions

Figure 2.7 shows relationships between things that move in opposite directions. A relationship between variables that move in opposite directions is called a **negative relationship** or an **inverse relationship**.

Part (a) shows the relationship between the number of hours available for playing squash and the number of hours for playing tennis. One extra hour spent playing tennis means one hour less playing squash and vice versa. This relationship is negative and linear.

Part (b) shows the relationship between the cost per mile traveled and the length of a journey. The longer the journey, the lower is the cost per mile. But as the journey length increases, the cost per mile decreases, and the fall in the cost is smaller, the longer the journey. This feature of the relationship is shown by the fact that the curve slopes downward, starting out steep at a short journey length and then becoming flatter as the journey length increases. This relationship arises because some of the costs are fixed,

FIGURE 2.7
Negative (Inverse) Relationships

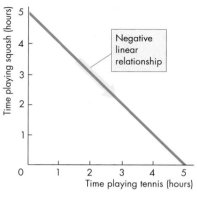

(a) Negative linear relationship

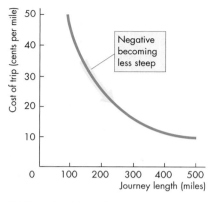

(b) Negative becoming less steep

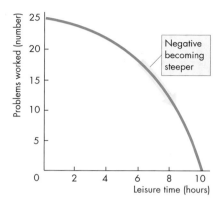

(c) Negative becoming steeper

Each part of this figure shows a negative (inverse) relationship between two variables. Part (a) shows a linear relationship—as one variable increases and the other variable decreases, we move along a straight line. Part (b) shows a negative relationship such that as the journey length increases, the curve becomes less steep. Part (c) shows a negative relationship such that as leisure time increases, the curve becomes steeper.

such as auto insurance, and the fixed costs are spread over a longer journey.

Part (c) shows the relationship between the amount of leisure time and the number of problems worked by a student. Increasing leisure time produces an increasingly large reduction in the number of problems worked. This relationship is a negative one that starts out with a gentle slope at a small number of leisure hours and becomes steeper as the number of leisure hours increases. This relationship is a different view of the idea shown in Fig. 2.6(c).

Variables That Have a Maximum or a Minimum

Many relationships in economic models have a maximum or a minimum. For example, firms try to make the maximum possible profit and to produce at the lowest possible cost. Figure 2.8 shows relationships that have a maximum or a minimum.

Part (a) shows the relationship between rainfall and wheat yield. When there is no rainfall, wheat will

not grow, so the yield is zero. As the rainfall increases up to 10 days a month, the wheat yield also increases. With 10 rainy days each month, the wheat yield reaches its maximum at 40 bushels an acre (point *a*). Rain in excess of 10 days a month starts to lower the yield of wheat. If every day is rainy, the wheat suffers from a lack of sunshine and the yield falls back to zero. This relationship is one that starts out sloping upward, reaches a maximum, and then slopes downward.

Part (b) shows the reverse case—a relationship that begins sloping downward, falls to a minimum, and then slopes upward. An example of such a relationship is the gasoline cost per mile as the speed of travel increases. At low speeds, the car is creeping along in a traffic snarl-up. The number of miles per gallon is low, so the gasoline cost per mile is high. At very high speeds, the car is traveling faster than its most efficient speed, and again the number of miles per gallon is low and the gasoline cost per mile is high. At a speed of 55 miles an hour, the gasoline cost per mile traveled is at its minimum (point *b*). This relationship is one that starts out sloping downward, reaches a minimum, and then slopes upward.

FIGURE 2.8

Maximum and Minimum Points

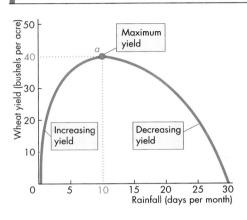

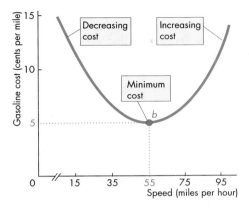

Part (a) shows a relationship that has a maximum point, *a*. The curve slopes upward as it rises to its maximum point, is flat at its maximum, and then slopes downward. Part (b) shows a relationship with a minimum point, *b*. The curve slopes downward as it falls to its minimum, is flat at its minimum, and then slopes upward.

(a) Relationship with a maximum   **(b) Relationship with a minimum**

Variables That Are Unrelated

There are many situations in which no matter what happens to the value of one variable, the other variable remains constant. Sometimes we want to show the independence between two variables in a graph, and Fig. 2.9 shows two ways of achieving this.

In describing the graphs in Fig. 2.6 through 2.9, we have talked about the slopes of curves. Let's look more closely at the concept of slope.

FIGURE 2.9

Variables That Are Unrelated

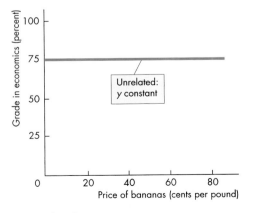

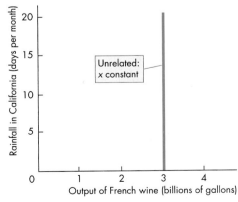

This figure shows how we can graph two variables that are unrelated to each other. In part (a), a student's grade in economics is plotted at 75 percent regardless of the price of bananas on the *x*-axis. The curve is horizontal. In part (b), the output of the vineyards of France does not vary with the rainfall in California. The curve is vertical.

(a) Unrelated: *y* constant   **(b) Unrelated: *x* constant**

The Slope of a Relationship

WE CAN MEASURE THE INFLUENCE OF ONE VARIable on another by the slope of the relationship. The **slope** of a relationship is the change in the value of the variable measured on the y-axis divided by the change in the value of the variable measured on the x-axis. We use the Greek letter Δ (*delta*) to represent "change in." Thus Δy means the change in the value of the variable measured on the y-axis, and Δx means the change in the value of the variable measured on the x-axis. Therefore the slope of the relationship is

$$\Delta y \, / \, \Delta x.$$

If a large change in the variable measured on the y-axis (Δy) is associated with a small change in the variable measured on the x-axis (Δx), the slope is large and the curve is steep. If a small change in the variable measured on the y-axis (Δy) is associated with a large change in the variable measured on the x-axis (Δx), the slope is small and the curve is flat.

We can make the idea of slope sharper by doing some calculations.

The Slope of a Straight Line

The slope of a straight line is the same regardless of where on the line you calculate it. Thus the slope of a straight line is constant. Let's calculate the slopes of the lines in Fig. 2.10. In part (a), when x increases from 2 to 6, y increases from 3 to 6. The change in x is +4—that is, Δx is 4. The change in y is +3—that

---

FIGURE **2.10**

The Slope of a Straight Line

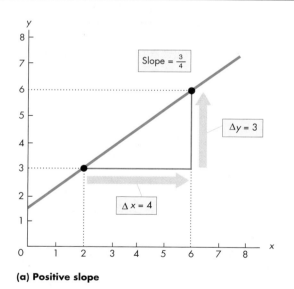

(a) Positive slope

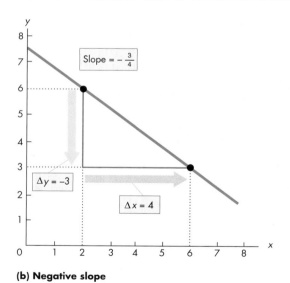

(b) Negative slope

To calculate the slope of a straight line, we divide the change in the value of the variable measured on the y-axis (Δy) by the change in the value of the variable measured on the x-axis (Δx) as we move along the curve. Part (a) shows the calculation of a positive slope. When x increases from 2 to 6, Δx equals 4.

That change in x brings about an increase in y from 3 to 6, so Δy equals 3. The slope ($\Delta y/\Delta x$) equals $3/4$. Part (b) shows the calculation of a negative slope. When x increases from 2 to 6, Δx equals 4. That increase in x brings about a decrease in y from 6 to 3, so Δy equals −3. The slope ($\Delta y/\Delta x$) equals −$3/4$.

is, Δy is 3. The slope of that line is

$$\frac{\Delta y}{\Delta x} = \frac{3}{4}.$$

In part (b), when x increases from 2 to 6, y decreases from 6 to 3. The change in y is *minus* 3—that is, Δy is –3. The change in x is *plus* 4—that is, Δx is 4. The slope of the curve is

$$\frac{\Delta y}{\Delta x} = \frac{-3}{4}.$$

Notice that the two slopes have the same magnitude (3/4), but the slope of the line in part (a) is positive (+3/+4 = 3/4), while that in part (b) is negative (–3/+4 = –3/4). The slope of a positive relationship is positive; the slope of a negative relationship is negative.

The Slope of a Curved Line

The slope of a curved line is trickier. The slope of a curved line is not constant. Its slope depends on where on the line we calculate it. There are two ways to calculate the slope of a curved line: You can calculate the slope at a point, or you can calculate the slope across an arc of the line. Let's look at the two alternatives.

Slope at a Point   To calculate the slope at a point on a curve, you need to construct a straight line that has the same slope as the curve at the point in question. Figure 2.11 shows how this is done. Suppose you want to calculate the slope of the curve at point *a*. Place a ruler on the graph so that it touches point *a* and no other point on the curve, then draw a straight line along the edge of the ruler. The straight red line is this line, and it is the tangent to the curve at point *a*. If the ruler touches the curve only at point *a*, then the slope of the curve at point *a* must be the same as the slope of the edge of the ruler. If the curve and the ruler do not have the same slope, the line along the edge of the ruler will cut the curve instead of just touching it.

Now that you have found a straight line with the same slope as the curve at point *a*, you can calculate the slope of the curve at point *a* by calculating the slope of the straight line. Along the straight line, as x increases from 0 to 4 ($\Delta x = 4$), y increases from 2 to 5

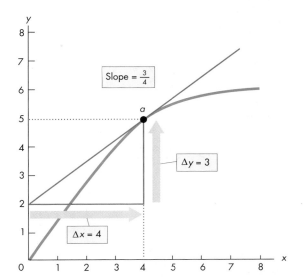

FIGURE 2.11

Slope at a Point

To calculate the slope of the curve at point *a*, draw the red line that just touches the curve at *a*—the tangent. The slope of this straight line is calculated by dividing the change in y by the change in x along the line. When x increases from 0 to 4, Δx equals 4. That change in x is associated with an increase in y from 2 to 5, so Δy equals 3. The slope of the red line is 3/4. So the slope of the curve at point *a* is 3/4.

($\Delta y = 3$). Therefore the slope of the line is

$$\frac{\Delta y}{\Delta x} = \frac{3}{4}.$$

Thus the slope of the curve at point *a* is 3/4.

Slope Across an Arc   An arc of a curve is a piece of a curve. In Fig. 2.12, you are looking at the same curve as in Fig. 2.11. But instead of calculating the slope at point *a*, we are going to calculate the slope across the arc from *b* to *c*. You can see that the slope at *b* is greater than the slope at *c*. When we calculate the slope across an arc, we are calculating the average slope between two points. As we move along the arc from *b* to *c*, x increases from 3 to 5 and y increases from 4 to 5.5. The change in x is 2 ($\Delta x = 2$), and the

FIGURE 2.12
Slope Across an Arc

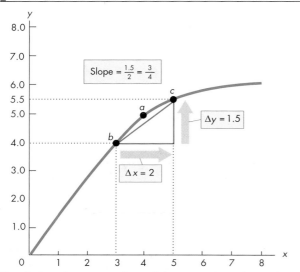

To calculate the average slope of the curve along the arc *bc*, draw a straight line from *b* to *c*. The slope of the line *bc* is calculated by dividing the change in *y* by the change in *x*. In moving from *b* to *c*, Δx equals 2 and Δy equals 1.5. The slope of the line *bc* is 1.5 divided by 2, or $3/4$. So the slope of the curve across the arc *bc* is $3/4$.

change in *y* is 1.5 ($\Delta y = 1.5$). Therefore the slope of the line is

$$\frac{\Delta y}{\Delta x} = \frac{15}{2} = \frac{3}{4}.$$

Thus the slope of the curve across the arc *bc* is $3/4$.

This calculation gives us the slope of the curve between points *b* and *c*. The actual slope calculated is the slope of the straight line from *b* to *c*. This slope approximates the average slope of the curve along the arc *bc*. In this particular example, the slope across the arc *bc* is identical to the slope of the curve at point *a*. But the calculation of the slope of a curve does not always work out so neatly. You might have some fun constructing counterexamples.

You now know how to make and interpret a graph. But so far, we've limited our attention to graphs of two variables. We're now going to learn how to graph more than two variables.

Graphing Relationships Among More Than Two Variables

WE HAVE SEEN THAT WE CAN GRAPH THE RELATION-ship between two variables as a point formed by the *x*- and *y*-coordinates in a two-dimensional graph. You may be thinking that although a two-dimensional graph is informative, most of the things in which you are likely to be interested involve relationships among many variables, not just two. For example, the amount of ice cream consumed depends on the price of ice cream and the temperature. If ice cream is expensive and the temperature is low, people eat much less ice cream than when ice cream is inexpensive and the temperature is high. For any given price of ice cream, the quantity consumed varies with the temperature, and for any given temperature, the quantity of ice cream consumed varies with its price.

Figure 2.13 shows a relationship among three variables. The table shows the number of gallons of ice cream consumed each day at various temperatures and ice cream prices. How can we graph these numbers?

To graph a relationship that involves more than two variables, we use the *ceteris paribus* assumption.

Ceteris Paribus   The Latin phrase **ceteris paribus**, means "other things remaining the same." Every laboratory experiment is an attempt to create *ceteris paribus* and isolate the relationship of interest. We use the same method to make a graph.

Figure 2.13(a) shows an example. There, you can see what happens to the quantity of ice cream consumed when the price of ice cream varies while the temperature is held constant. The line labeled 70°F shows the relationship between ice cream consumption and the price of ice cream if the temperature is 70°F. The numbers used to plot that line are those in the third column of the table in Fig. 2.13. For example, if the temperature is 70°F, 10 gallons are consumed when the price is 60¢ a scoop, and 18 gallons are consumed when the price is 30¢ a scoop. The curve labeled 90°F shows consumption as the price varies if the temperature is 90°F.

We can also show the relationship between ice cream consumption and temperature while the price of ice cream remains constant, as shown in Fig. 2.13(b). The curve labeled 60¢ shows how the consumption

---

FIGURE 2.13
Graphing a Relationship Among Three Variables

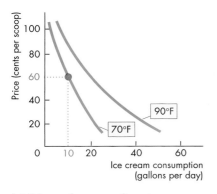

(a) Price and consumption at a given temperature

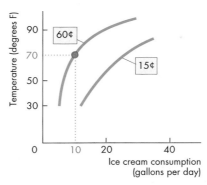

(b) Temperature and consumption at a given price

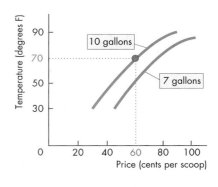

(c) Temperature and price at a given consumption

The quantity of ice cream consumed depends on its price and the temperature. The table gives some hypothetical numbers that tell us how many gallons of ice cream are consumed each day at different prices and different temperatures. For example, if the price is 60¢ a scoop and the temperature is 70°F, 10 gallons of ice cream are consumed. This set of values is highlighted in the table and each part of the figure. To graph a relationship among three variables, the value of one variable is held constant. Part (a) shows the relationship between price and consumption when temperature is held constant. One curve holds temperature at 90°F and the other at 70°F. Part (b) shows the relationship between temperature and consumption when the price is held constant. One curve holds the price at 60¢ a scoop and the other at 15¢ a scoop. Part (c) shows the relationship between temperature and price when consumption is held constant. One curve holds consumption at 10 gallons and the other at 7 gallons.

Price	Ice cream consumption			
(cents per scoop)	(gallons per day)			
	30°F	50°F	70°F	90°F
15	12	18	25	50
30	10	12	18	37
45	7	10	13	27
60	5	7	10	20
75	3	5	7	14
90	2	3	5	10
105	1	2	3	6

---

of ice cream varies with the temperature when ice cream costs 60¢ a scoop, and a second curve shows the relationship when ice cream costs 15¢ a scoop. For example, at 60¢ a scoop, 10 gallons are consumed when the temperature is 70°F and 20 gallons when the temperature is 90°F.

Figure 2.13(c) shows the combinations of temperature and price that result in a constant consumption of ice cream. One curve shows the combination that results in 10 gallons a day being consumed, and the other shows the combination that results

in 7 gallons a day being consumed. A high price and a high temperature lead to the same consumption as a lower price and a lower temperature. For example, 10 gallons of ice cream are consumed at 90°F and 90¢ a scoop, at 70°F and 60¢ a scoop, and at 50°F and 45¢ a scoop.

◆ With what you have learned about graphs, you can move forward with your study of economics. There are no graphs in this book that are more complicated than those that have been explained here.

SUMMARY

KEY POINTS

Graphing Data (pp. 20–24)

- Time-series graphs show trends, cycles, and other fluctuations in economic data.
- Scatter diagrams show the relationship between two variables. They show whether two variables are positively related, negatively related, or unrelated.
- Cross-section graphs show how variables change across the members of a population.

Graphs Used in Economic Models (pp. 24–27)

- Graphs are used to show relationships among variables in economic models.
- Relationships can be positive (an upward-sloping curve), negative (a downward-sloping curve), positive and then negative (have a maximum point), negative and then positive (have a minimum point), or unrelated (a horizontal or vertical curve).

The Slope of a Relationship (pp. 28–30)

- The slope of a relationship is calculated as the change in the value of the variable measured on the y-axis divided by the change in the value of the variable measured on the x-axis—that is, $\Delta y/\Delta x$.
- A straight line has a constant slope.
- A curved line has a varying slope. To calculate the slope of a curved line, we calculate the slope at a point or across an arc.

Graphing Relationships Among More Than Two Variables (pp. 30–31)

- To graph a relationship among more than two variables, we hold constant the values of all the variables except two.
- We then plot the value of one of the variables against the value of another.

KEY FIGURES

KEY TERMS

REVIEW QUIZ

- What are the three types of graphs used to show economic data?
- Give an example of a time-series graph.
- List three things that a time-series graph shows quickly and easily.
- Give three examples, different from those in the chapter, of scatter diagrams that show a positive relationship, a negative relationship, and no relationship.
- Draw some graphs to show the relationships between two variables:
  a. That move in the same direction.
  b. That move in opposite directions.
  c. That have a maximum.
  d. That have a minimum.
- Which of the relationships in the previous question is a positive relationship and which a negative relationship?
- What are the two ways of calculating the slope of a curved line?
- How do we graph a relationship among more than two variables?

PROBLEMS

The spreadsheet provides data on the U.S. economy: Column A is the year, column B is the inflation rate, column C is the interest rate, column D is the growth rate, and column E is the unemployment rate. Use this spreadsheet to answer problems 1, 2, 3, and 4.

	A	B	C	D	E
1	1980	13.5	11.9	–0.1	7.1
2	1981	10.3	14.2	0.8	7.6
3	1982	6.2	13.8	–1.1	9.7
4	1983	3.2	12.0	1.5	9.6
5	1984	4.3	12.7	2.8	7.5
6	1985	3.6	11.4	1.4	7.2
7	1986	1.9	9.0	1.2	7.0
8	1987	3.6	9.4	1.5	6.2
9	1988	4.1	9.7	1.9	5.5
10	1989	4.8	9.3	1.1	5.3
11	1990	5.4	9.3	1.2	5.5
12	1991	4.2	7.9	–0.9	6.7
13	1992	3.0	7.0	2.7	7.4
14	1993	3.0	5.8	2.3	6.8
15	1994	2.6	7.1	3.5	6.1
16	1995	2.8	6.6	2.0	5.6
17	1996	3.0	6.4	2.8	5.4
18	1997	2.3	6.4	3.8	4.9
19	1998	2.0	5.5	2.9	5.0

*1. a. Draw a time-series graph of the inflation rate.
   b. In which year(s) (i) was inflation highest, (ii) was inflation lowest, (iii) did it increase, (iv) did it decrease, (v) did it increase most, and (vi) did it decrease most?
   c. What was the main trend in inflation?

2. a. Draw a time-series graph of the interest rate.
   b. In which year(s) (i) was the interest rate highest, (ii) was it lowest, (iii) did it increase, (iv) did it decrease, (v) did it increase most, and (vi) did it decrease most?
   c. What was the main trend in the interest rate?

*3. Draw a scatter diagram to show the relationship between the inflation rate and the interest rate. Describe the relationship.

4. Draw a scatter diagram to show the relationship between the growth rate and the unemployment rate. Describe the relationship.

*5. Draw a graph to show the relationship between the two variables x and y:

x	0	1	2	3	4	5	6	7	8
y	0	1	4	9	16	25	36	49	64

   a. Is the relationship positive or negative?
   b. Does the slope of the relationship increase or decrease as the value of x increases?
   c. Think of some economic relationships that might be similar to this one.

6. Draw a graph that shows the relationship between two variables x and y:

x	0	1	2	3	4	5
y	50	48	44	32	16	0

   a. Is the relationship positive or negative?
   b. Does the slope of the relationship increase or decrease as the value of x increases?
   c. Think of some economic relationships that might be similar to this one.

*7. In problem 5, calculate the slope of the relationship between x and y when x equals 4.

8. In problem 6, calculate the slope of the relationship between x and y when x equals 3.

*9. In problem 5, calculate the slope of the relationship across the arc when x increases from 3 to 4.

10. In problem 6, calculate the slope of the relationship across the arc when x increases from 4 to 5.

*11. Calculate the slope of the relationship shown at point a in the following figure.

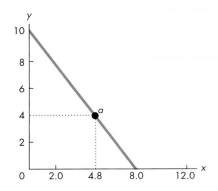

12. Calculate the slope of the relationship shown at point *a* in the following figure.

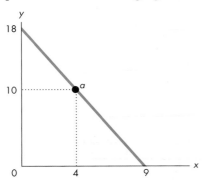

*13. Use the following figure to calculate the slope of the relationship:

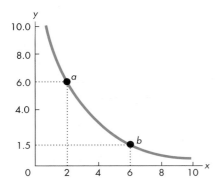

   a. At points *a* and *b*.
   b. Across the arc *ab*.

14. Use the following figure to calculate the slope of the relationship:

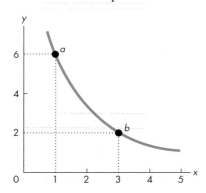

   a. At points *a* and *b*.
   b. Across the arc *ab*.

*15. The table gives the price of a balloon ride, the temperature, and the number of rides a day:

Price (dollars per ride)	Balloon rides (number per day)		
	50°F	70°F	90°F
5.00	32	40	50
10.00	27	32	40
15.00	18	27	32
20.00	10	18	27

Draw graphs to show the relationship between
   a. The price and the number of rides, holding the temperature constant.
   b. The number of rides and temperature, holding the price constant.
   c. The temperature and price, holding the number of rides constant.

16. The table gives the price of an umbrella, rainfall, and the number of umbrellas purchased:

Price (dollars per umbrella)	Umbrellas (number per day)		
	0 mm	2 mm	10 mm
10	7	8	12
20	4	7	8
30	2	4	7
40	1	2	4

Draw graphs to show the relationship between
   a. The price and the number of umbrellas purchased, holding rainfall constant.
   b. The number of umbrellas purchased and rainfall, holding the price constant.
   c. Rainfall and the price, holding the number of umbrellas purchased constant.

17. Use the link on the Parkin Web site and find Consumer Price Index (CPI) for the latest 12 months. Make a graph of the CPI. During the most recent month, is the CPI rising or falling? Is the rate of rise or fall increasing or decreasing?

18. Use the link on the Parkin Web site and find the unemployment rate for the latest 12 months. Graph the unemployment rate. During the most recent month, is it rising or falling? Is the rate of rise or fall increasing or decreasing?

3

The Economic Problem

Making the Most of It

We live in a style that surprises our grandparents and would have astonished our great-grandparents. Most of us live in more spacious homes than they did. We eat more, grow taller, and are even born larger than they were. Video games, cellular phones, gene splices, and personal computers did not exist even 20 years ago. Economic growth has made us richer than our grandparents. And we are not alone in experiencing an expansion in the goods and services that we consume. Many nations around the world are not only sharing our experience: They are setting the pace. Before the recent Asia crisis, Hong Kong, Taiwan, Singapore, Korea, and China expanded at unheard-of rates. But economic growth does not liberate us from scarcity. Why not? Why, despite our immense wealth, must we still make choices and face costs? Why are there no "free lunches"? ◆ We see an incredible amount of specialization and trade in the world. Each one of us specializes in a particular job—as a lawyer, a car maker, a home maker. We have become so specialized that one farm worker can feed 100 people. Less than one sixth of the U.S. work force is employed in manufacturing. More than half of the work force is employed in wholesale and retail trade, banking and finance, government, and other services. Why do we specialize? How do we benefit from specialization and trade? ◆ Over many centuries, institutions and social arrangements have evolved that we take for granted. One of them is property rights and the political and legal system that protects them. Another is markets. Why have these social arrangements evolved? How do they increase production?

◈ These are the questions that we study in this chapter. We begin with the core economic problem: scarcity and choice and the concept of the production possibility frontier. We then learn about the central idea of economics—efficiency. We also discover how we can expand production by accumulating capital and by specializing and trading. ◆ What you will learn in this chapter is the foundation on which all economics is built. You will receive big dividends from a careful study of this material.

After studying this chapter, you will be able to:

- Explain the fundamental economic problem
- Define the production possibility frontier
- Define and calculate opportunity cost
- Explain the conditions in which resources are used efficiently
- Explain how economic growth expands production possibilities
- Explain how specialization and trade expand production possibilities

Resources and Wants

TWO FACTS DOMINATE OUR LIVES:

- We have limited resources.
- We have unlimited wants.

These two facts define **scarcity**, a condition in which the resources available are insufficient to satisfy people's wants.

Scarcity is a universal fact of life. It confronts each one of us individually, and it confronts our families, local communities, and nations.

The fundamental economic problem is to use our limited resources to produce the items that we value most highly. **Economics** is the study of the *choices* people make to cope with *scarcity*. It is the study of how we each individually try to get the most out of our own limited resources and of how in that endeavor, we interact with each other. Let's look a bit more closely at our limited resources and unlimited wants.

Limited Resources

The resources that can be used to produce goods and services are grouped into four categories:

1. Labor
2. Land
3. Capital
4. Entrepreneurship

Labor is the time and effort that we devote to producing goods and services. It includes the physical and mental work of people who make cars and cola, gum and glue, wallpaper and watering cans.

Land is the gifts of nature that we use to produce goods and services. It includes the air, the water, and the land surface as well as the minerals that lie beneath the surface of the earth.

Capital is the goods that we have produced and that we can now use to produce other goods and services. It includes interstate highways, buildings, dams and power projects, airports and jumbo jets, car production lines, shirt factories, and cookie shops.

Capital also includes **human capital**, which is the knowledge and skill that people obtain from education and on-the-job training. You are building human capital right now as you work on your economics course and other subjects. And your human capital will continue to grow when you get a full-time

job and become better at it. Human capital improves the *quality* of labor.

Entrepreneurship is the resource that organizes labor, land, and capital. Entrepreneurs make business decisions, bear the risks that arise from these decisions, and come up with new ideas about what, how, when, and where to produce.

Our limited resources are converted into goods and services by using the technologies available. These technologies are limited by our knowledge—our human capital—and by our other resources.

Unlimited Wants

Our wants are limited only by our imaginations and are effectively unlimited. We want food and drink, clothing, housing, education, and health care. We want some of these things so badly that we call them *necessities*. But we also want many other things. We want cars and airplanes, movie theaters and videos, popcorn and soda, Walkmans and tapes, books and magazines, restaurant meals, vacations at the beach and in the mountains, music and poetry, and instant telecommunication across the globe.

Some of these wants are less pressing than others, but they are all wants. We even want things that are technologically impossible today but about which we fantasize. We want to live longer and healthier lives. Some of us want to hitchhike the galaxy and be beamed around the universe.

Because our wants exceed our resources, we must make choices. We must rank our wants and decide which wants to satisfy and which to leave unsatisfied. We try to get the most out of our resources.

R E V I E W   Q U I Z

- What is scarcity?
- What is the fundamental economic problem?
- Can you provide a definition of economics?
- What are the resources that can be used to produce goods and services?
- How do we cope with the fact that our wants cannot be satisfied with the available resources?

We'll begin our study of the choices people make by looking at the limits to production and at a fundamental implication of choice—opportunity cost.

Resources, Production Possibilities, and Opportunity Cost

EVERY WORKING DAY, IN MINES, FACTORIES, shops, and offices and on farms and construction sites across the United States, 131 million people produce a vast variety of goods and services valued at around $30 billion. The quantities of goods and services that can be produced are limited by our available resources and by technology. That limit is described by the production possibility frontier.

The **production possibility frontier** (*PPF*) is the boundary between those combinations of goods and services that can be produced and those that cannot.

To illustrate the production possibility frontier in a graph, we focus our attention on two goods at a time. In focusing on two goods, we hold the quantities produced of all the other goods and services constant—a device called the *ceteris paribus* assumption. That is, we look at a *model* of the economy in which everything remains the same except for the production of the two goods we are currently considering.

Let's look at the production possibility frontier for two goods that most students buy: bottles of soda and blank audio tapes.

Production Possibility Frontier

The *production possibility frontier* for soda and tapes shows the limits to the production of these two goods, given the total resources available to produce them. Figure 3.1 shows this production possibility frontier. The table lists some combinations of the quantities of tapes and soda that can be produced given the resources available, and the figure graphs these combinations. The quantity of tapes produced is shown on the *x*-axis, and the quantity of soda produced is shown on the *y*-axis. (The numbers are hypothetical.)

Because the *PPF* shows the *limits* to production, we cannot attain the points outside the frontier. They are points that describe wants that cannot be satisfied. We can produce at all the points *inside* the *PPF* and *on* the *PPF*. They are attainable points.

Suppose that in a typical month, 4 million tapes and 5 million bottles of soda are produced. Figure 3.1 shows this combination as point *e* and as possibility *e* in the table. Figure 3.1 also shows other production possibilities. For example, we might stop

FIGURE 3.1
Production Possibility Frontier

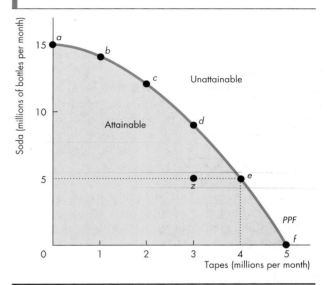

Possibility	Tapes (millions per month)		Soda (millions of bottles per month)
a	0	and	15
b	1	and	14
c	2	and	12
d	3	and	9
e	4	and	5
f	5	and	0

The table lists six points on the production possibility frontier for tapes and soda. Row *a* tells us that if we produce no tapes, the maximum quantity of soda we can produce is 15 million bottles a month. The rows of the table are graphed as points *a, b, c, d, e,* and *f* in the figure. The line passing through these points is the production possibility frontier (*PPF*). It separates the attainable from the unattainable. We can produce at any point inside the orange area or on the frontier. Points outside the frontier are unattainable. Points inside the frontier such as point z are inefficient because it is possible to use the available resources to produce more of either or both goods.

producing tapes and move all the people who produce them into bottling soda. This case is shown as point *a* in the figure and possibility *a* in the table.

The quantity of soda produced increases to 15 million bottles a month, and tape production dries up. Alternatively, we might close down the bottling plants and switch all the resources into producing tapes. In this situation, we produce 5 million tapes a month. This case is shown as point *f* in the figure and possibility *f* in the table.

Production Efficiency

We achieve **production efficiency** if we cannot produce more of one good without producing less of some other good. When production is efficient, we are at a point *on* the *PPF*. If we are at a point *inside* the *PPF*, such as point *z*, production is *inefficient* because we have some *unused* resources or we have some *misallocated* resources or both.

Resources are unused when they are idle but could be working. For example, we might leave some of the bottling plants idle or some workers might be unemployed.

Resources are *misallocated* when they are assigned to tasks for which they are not the best match. For example, we might assign skilled bottling machine operators to work in a tape factory and skilled tape makers to work in a bottling plant. We could get more tapes *and* more bottles of soda from these same workers if we reassigned them to the tasks that more closely match their skills.

If we produce at a point inside the *PPF* such as *z*, we can use our resources more efficiently to produce more tapes, more soda, or more of *both* tapes and soda. But if we produce at a point *on* the *PPF*, we are using our resources efficiently and we can produce more of one good only if we produce less of the other. We face a *tradeoff*.

Tradeoff

On the production possibility frontier, every choice involves a **tradeoff**—we must give up something to get something else. On the *PPF* in Fig. 3.1, we must give up some soda to get more tapes (or give up some tapes to get more soda).

Tradeoffs arise in every imaginable real-world situation. At any given point in time, we have a fixed amount of labor, land, capital, and entrepreneurship. By using our available technologies, we can employ these resources to produce goods and services. But we are limited in what we can produce. This limit defines a boundary between what we can attain and what we

cannot attain. This boundary is the real-world's production possibility frontier, and it defines the tradeoffs that we must make. On our real-world *PPF*, we can produce more of any one good or service only if we produce less of some other goods or services.

When doctors say we must spend more on AIDS and cancer research, they are suggesting a tradeoff: more medical research for less of some other things. When the President says he wants to spend more on education and health care, he is suggesting a tradeoff: more education and health care for less national defense or less private spending (because of higher taxes). When your parents say that you should study more, they are suggesting a tradeoff: more study time for less leisure or less sleep. When an environmental group argues for less logging, it is suggesting a tradeoff: greater conservation of endangered wildlife for less paper.

All tradeoffs involve a cost—an opportunity cost.

Opportunity Cost

The **opportunity cost** of an action is the highest-valued alternative forgone. We can make the concept of opportunity cost more precise by using the production possibility frontier. Along the frontier, there are only two goods, so there is only one alternative forgone—some quantity of the other good. Given our current resources and technology, we can produce more tapes only if we produce fewer bottles of soda. The opportunity cost of producing an additional tape is the number of bottles of soda we must forgo. Similarly, the opportunity cost of producing an additional bottle of soda is the quantity of tapes we must forgo.

For example, at point *c* in Fig. 3.1, we produce fewer tapes and more bottles of soda than we do at point *d*. If we choose point *d* over point *c*, the additional 1 million tapes *cost* 3 million bottles of soda. One tape costs 3 bottles of soda.

We can also work out the opportunity cost of choosing point *c* over point *d* in Fig. 3.1. If we move from point *d* to point *c*, the quantity of soda produced increases by 3 million bottles and the quantity of tapes produced decreases by 1 million. So if we choose point *c* over point *d*, the additional 3 million bottles of soda *cost* 1 million tapes. One bottle of soda costs 1/3 of a tape.

Opportunity Cost Is a Ratio   Opportunity cost is a ratio. It is the decrease in the quantity produced of one good divided by the increase in the quantity produced of another good as we move along the production possibility frontier.

Because opportunity cost is a ratio, the opportunity cost of producing soda is equal to the *inverse* of the opportunity cost of producing tapes. Check this proposition by returning to the calculations we've just worked through. When we move along the *PPF* from *c* to *d*, the opportunity cost of a tape is 3 bottles of soda. The inverse of 3 is 1/3, so if we decrease the production of tapes and increase the production of soda by moving from *d* to *c*, the opportunity cost of a bottle of soda must be 1/3 of a tape. You can check that this number is correct. If we move from *d* to *c*, we produce 3 million more bottles of soda and 1 million fewer tapes. Because 3 million bottles cost 1 million tapes, the opportunity cost of 1 bottle of soda is 1/3 of a tape.

Increasing Opportunity Cost The opportunity cost of a tape increases as the quantity of tapes produced increases. Also, the opportunity cost of soda increases as the quantity of soda produced increases. This phenomenon of increasing opportunity cost is reflected in the *shape* of the *PPF*—it is bowed outward.

When a large quantity of soda and a small quantity of tapes are produced—between points *a* and *b* in Fig. 3.1—the frontier has a gentle slope. A given increase in the quantity of tapes *costs* a small decrease in the quantity of soda, so the opportunity cost of a tape is a small amount of soda.

When a large quantity of tapes and a small quantity of soda are produced—between points *e* and *f* in Fig. 3.1—the frontier is steep. A given increase in the quantity of tapes *costs* a large decrease in the quantity of soda, so the opportunity cost of a tape is a large amount of soda.

The production possibility frontier is bowed outward because resources are not all equally productive in all activities. Production workers with many years of experience working for PepsiCo are very good at producing soda but not very good at making tapes. So if we move these people from PepsiCo to 3M, we get a small increase in the quantity of tapes but a large decrease in the quantity of soda.

Similarly, plastics engineers and production workers who have spent many years working for 3M are good at producing tapes but not so good at bottling soda. So if we move these people from 3M to PepsiCo, we get a small increase in the quantity of soda but a large decrease in the quantity of tapes. The more we try to produce of either good, the less productive are the additional resources we use to produce that good and the larger is the opportunity cost of a unit of that good.

Increasing Opportunity Costs Are Everywhere Just about every activity that you can think of is one with an *increasing* opportunity cost. Two examples are the production of food and the production of health-care services. We allocate the most skillful farmers and the most fertile land to the production of food. And we allocate the best doctors and least fertile land to the production of health-care services. If we shift fertile land and tractors away from farming to hospitals and ambulances and ask farmers to become hospital porters, the production of food drops drastically and the increase in the production of health-care services is small. The opportunity cost of a unit of health-care services rises. Similarly, if we shift our resources away from health care toward farming, we must use more doctors and nurses as farmers and more hospitals as hydroponic tomato factories. The decrease in the production of health-care services is large, but the increase in food production is small. The opportunity cost of a unit of food rises.

This example is extreme and unlikely, but these same considerations apply to any pair of goods that you can imagine: housing and diamonds, wheelchairs and golf carts, pet food and breakfast cereals.

R E V I E W   Q U I Z

- How does the production possibility frontier illustrate scarcity?
- How does the production possibility frontier illustrate production efficiency?
- How does the production possibility frontier show that every choice involves a tradeoff?
- How does the production possibility frontier illustrate opportunity cost?
- Why is opportunity cost a ratio?
- Why does the *PPF* for most goods bow outward so that opportunity cost increases as the quantity produced of a good increases?

We've seen that production possibilities are limited by the production possibility frontier. And we've seen that production on the *PPF* is efficient. But there are many possible quantities we can produce on the *PPF*. How do we choose among them? How do we know which point on the frontier is the best one?

Using Resources Efficiently

HOW DO WE DECIDE WHETHER TO SPEND MORE on AIDS and cancer research? Whether to vote for an education and health-care package or a tax cut? Whether to join an environmental group and press for a greater conservation of endangered wildlife?

These are big questions that have enormous consequences. But the essence of the answer can be seen by thinking about the simpler question: How do we decide how many tapes and how many bottles of soda to produce?

We decide by calculating and comparing two numbers:

■ Marginal cost
■ Marginal benefit

Marginal Cost

Marginal cost is the opportunity cost of producing *one more unit* of a good or service. You've seen how we can calculate opportunity cost as we move along the production possibility frontier. The marginal cost of a tape is the opportunity cost of *one* tape—the quantity of soda that must be given up to get one more tape—as we move along the *PPF*.

Figure 3.2 illustrates the marginal cost of a tape. If all the available resources are used to produce soda, 15 million bottles of soda and no tapes are produced. If we now decide to produce 1 million tapes, how much soda do we have to give up? You can see the answer in Fig. 3.2(a). To produce 1 million more tapes, we move from *a* to *b* and the quantity of soda decreases by 1 million bottles to 14 million a month. So the opportunity cost of the first 1 million tapes is 1 million bottles of soda.

If we decide to increase the production of tapes to 2 million, how much soda must we give up? This time, we move from *b* to *c* and the quantity of soda decreases by 2 million bottles. So the second million tapes cost 2 million bottles of soda.

You can repeat this calculation for an increase in the quantity of tapes produced from 2 million to 3 million, then to 4 million, and finally to 5 million. Figure 3.2(a) shows these opportunity costs as a series of steps. Each additional million tapes costs more bottles of soda than the preceding million did.

We've just calculated the opportunity cost of tapes in blocks of 1 million at a time and generated

FIGURE **3.2**

Opportunity Cost and Marginal Cost

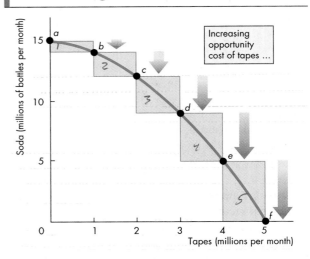

(a) PPF and opportunity cost

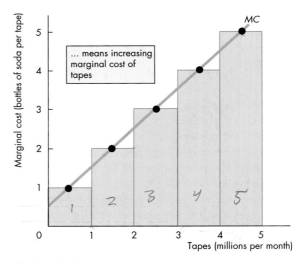

(b) Marginal cost

Opportunity cost is measured along the *PPF* in part (a). If the production of tapes increases from zero to 1 million, the opportunity cost of the first 1 million tapes is 1 million bottles of soda. If the production of tapes increases from 1 million to 2 million, the opportunity cost of the second 1 million tapes is 2 million bottles of soda. The opportunity cost of tapes increases as the production of tapes increases. Marginal cost is the opportunity cost of producing one more unit. Part (b) shows the marginal cost of a tape as the *MC* curve.

the steps in Fig. 3.2(a). If we now calculate the opportunity cost of tapes one at a time, we obtain the *marginal cost* of a tape. In Fig. 3.2(b), the line labeled *MC* shows the marginal cost of a tape. The marginal cost of each additional tape in terms of forgone soda increases, so the marginal cost curve slopes upward.

Marginal Benefit

To use our resources efficiently, we must compare the marginal cost of a tape with its marginal benefit. **Marginal benefit** is the benefit that a person receives from consuming one more unit of a good or service. The marginal benefit from a good or service is measured as the maximum amount that a person is willing to pay for one more unit of it. It is a general principle that the more we have of any good or service, the smaller is our marginal benefit from it—the principle of *decreasing marginal benefit*.

To understand the principle of decreasing marginal benefit, think about your own marginal benefit from tapes. If tapes are very hard to come by and you can buy only one or two a year, you might be willing to pay a high price to get one more tape. But if tapes are readily available and you have as many as you can use, you are willing to pay almost nothing for yet one more tape.

In everyday life, we think of prices as money—as dollars per tape. But you have just been thinking about cost as opportunity cost, which is not a dollar cost but a cost in terms of a forgone alternative. You can also think about prices in the same terms. The price you pay for something is not the number of dollars you give up, but the goods and services that you would have bought with those dollars.

To see this idea more clearly, let's continue with the example we used to study the *PPF* and opportunity cost: tapes and soda. The marginal benefit from a tape can be expressed as the number of bottles of soda that a person is willing to forgo to get a tape. Figure 3.3 illustrates the marginal benefit from tapes. Marginal benefit is the way people feel about different quantities of goods, and we can't derive it from the *PPF*. The numbers in Fig. 3.3 are *assumed*.

In row *a*, 0.5 million tapes a month are available and at that quantity, people are willing to pay 5 bottles of soda for a tape. As the quantity of tapes available increases, the amount that people are willing to pay for a tape falls. When 4.5 million tapes a month are available, people are willing to pay only 1 bottle of soda for a tape.

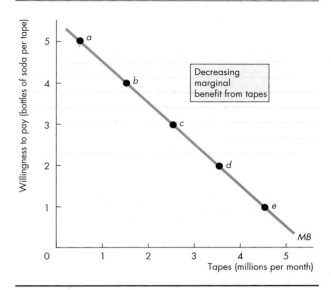

FIGURE 3.3

Marginal Benefit

The fewer the number of tapes available, the more soda people are willing to give up to get an additional tape. If only 0.5 million tapes a month are available, people are willing to pay 5 bottles of soda for a tape. But if 4.5 million tapes a month are available, people will pay only 1 bottle of soda for a tape. Decreasing marginal benefit is a universal feature of people's preferences.

Possibility	Tapes (millions per month)	Willingness to pay (bottles per tape)
a	0.5	5
b	1.5	4
c	2.5	3
d	3.5	2
e	4.5	1

see Notes

The marginal benefit from a tape and the opportunity cost of a tape are both measured in bottles of soda. But they are not the same concept. The *opportunity cost* of a tape is the amount of soda that people *must forgo* to get another tape. The *marginal benefit* from a tape is the amount of soda that people *are willing to forgo* to get another tape.

You now know how to calculate marginal cost and marginal benefit. Let's use these concepts to discover the efficient quantity of tapes to produce.

Efficient Use of Resources

Resource use is **efficient** when we produce the goods and services that we value most highly. That is, when we are using our resources efficiently, we cannot produce more of any good without giving up something that we value even more highly.

We always choose *at the margin*. We compare marginal cost and marginal benefit. If the marginal benefit from a good exceeds the marginal cost of the good, we increase production of that good. If marginal cost exceeds marginal benefit, we decrease production of the good. And if marginal benefit equals marginal cost, we stick with the current production.

This principle is just like the decisions you make when you go shopping. You have $10 to spend and are thinking about buying a CD or a box of floppy disks. You figure that you will get more value from the CD than from the floppy disks, so you spend your $10 on the CD. You have allocated scarce resources to their highest-valued use. The marginal benefit from a CD is greater than (or equal to) its marginal cost, the box of floppy disks. The marginal benefit from a box of floppy disks is less than its marginal cost. No matter what the good or service, if you can afford it and you think it is worth the price, you buy it. If you think it not worth its price, you pass it up.

We can illustrate an efficient use of resources by continuing to use the example of soda and tapes. Figure 3.4 shows the marginal cost and marginal benefit of tapes. Suppose we produce 1.5 million tapes a month. The marginal cost of a tape is 2 bottles of soda. But the marginal benefit from a tape is 4 bottles of soda. Because someone values an additional tape more highly than it costs to produce, we can get more value from our resources by moving some of them out of soda production and into tape production.

Now suppose we produce 3.5 million tapes a month. The marginal cost of a tape is now 4 bottles of soda. But the marginal benefit from a tape is only 2 bottles of soda. Because an additional tape costs more to produce than anyone thinks it is worth, we can get more value from our resources by moving some of them away from tape production and into soda production.

But suppose we produce 2.5 million tapes a month. Marginal cost and marginal benefit are now equal at 3 bottles of soda. This allocation of resources between tapes and soda is efficient. If more tapes are produced, the forgone soda is worth more than the additional tapes. If fewer tapes are produced, the forgone tapes are worth more than the additional soda.

FIGURE 3.4

Efficient Use of Resources

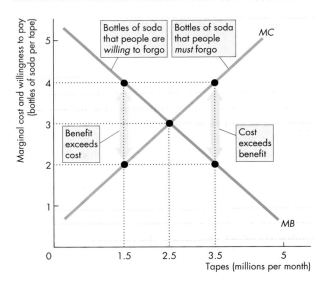

The greater the quantity of tapes produced, the smaller is the marginal benefit (MB) from a tape—the fewer bottles of soda people are willing to give up to get an additional tape. But the greater the quantity of tapes produced, the greater is the marginal cost (MC) of a tape—the more bottles of soda people must give up to get an additional tape. When marginal benefit equals marginal cost, resources are being used efficiently.

REVIEW QUIZ

- What is marginal cost and how is it measured?
- What is the relationship between marginal cost and the production possibility frontier?
- What is marginal benefit and how is it measured?
- How does the marginal benefit from a good change as the quantity of that good increases? Why?
- What conditions must be satisfied if resources are used efficiently? Why?

You now understand the limits to production and the conditions under which resources are used efficiently. Your next task is to study the expansion of production possibilities.

Economic Growth

DURING THE PAST 30 YEARS, PRODUCTION IN THE United States has expanded by 80 percent. Such an expansion of production is called **economic growth**. Can economic growth enable us to overcome scarcity and avoid opportunity cost? You are going to see that economic growth does not overcome scarcity and avoid opportunity cost. You are also going to see that the faster we make production grow, the greater is the opportunity cost of economic growth.

The Cost of Economic Growth

Two key factors influence economic growth: technological change and capital accumulation. **Technological change** is the development of new goods and of better ways of producing goods and services. **Capital accumulation** is the growth of capital resources.

As a consequence of technological change and capital accumulation, we have an enormous quantity of cars that enable us to produce more transportation than when we had only horses and carriages; we have satellites that make global communications possible on a scale that is much larger than that produced by the earlier cable technology. But new technologies and new capital have an opportunity cost. To use resources in research and development and to produce new capital, we must decrease our production of consumption goods and services. Let's look at this opportunity cost.

Instead of studying the *PPF* of tapes and soda, we'll hold the quantity of soda produced constant and examine the *PPF* for tapes and tape-making machines. Figure 3.5 shows this *PPF* as the blue curve *abc*. If we devote no resources to producing tape-making machines, we produce at point *a*. If we produce 3 million tapes a month, we can produce 6 tape-making machines at point *b*. If we produce no tapes, we can produce 10 tape-making machines a month at point *c*.

The amount by which our production possibilities expand depends on the resources we devote to technological change and capital accumulation. If we devote no resources to this activity (point *a*), the frontier remains at *abc*—the blue curve in Fig. 3.5. If we cut the current production of tapes and produce 6 machines a month (point *b*), then in the future, we'll have more capital and our *PPF* rotates outward to the

Eye & Notes (5)

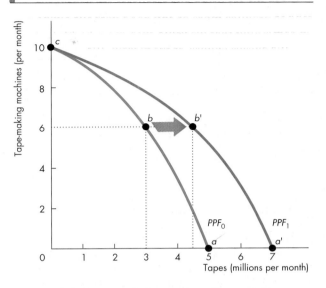

PPF_0 shows the limits to the production of tapes and tape-making equipment, with the production of all other goods and services remaining constant. If we devote no resources to producing tape-making machines and produce 5 million tapes a month, we remain stuck at point *a*. But if we decrease tape production to 3 million a month and produce 6 tape-making machines a month, at point *b*, our production possibilities will expand. After a year, the production possibility frontier shifts outward to PPF_1 and we can produce at point *b'*, a point outside the original *PPF*. We can shift the *PPF* outward, but we cannot avoid opportunity cost. The opportunity cost of producing more tapes in the future is fewer tapes today.

position shown by the red curve. The fewer resources we devote to producing tapes and the more resources we devote to producing machines, the greater is the expansion of our production possibilities.

Economic growth is not free. To make it happen, we devote resources to producing new machines and fewer resources to producing tapes. In Fig. 3.5, we move from *a* to *b*. There is no free lunch. The opportunity cost of more tapes in the future is fewer tapes today. Also, economic growth is no magic formula for abolishing scarcity. On the new production possibility frontier, we continue to face opportunity costs.

The ideas about economic growth that we have explored in the setting of the audio tape industry also apply to nations. Let's look at two examples.

Economic Growth in the United States and Hong Kong

If as a nation we devote all our resources to producing consumer goods and none to research and capital accumulation, our production possibilities in the future will be the same as they are today. To expand our production possibilities in the future, we must devote fewer resources to producing consumption goods and some resources to accumulating capital and developing technologies so we can produce more consumption goods in the future. The decrease in today's consumption is the opportunity cost of an increase in future consumption.

The experiences of the United States and Hong Kong make a striking example of the effects of our choices on the rate of economic growth. In 1960, the production possibilities per person in the United States were more than four times those in Hong Kong (see Fig. 3.6). The United States devoted one fifth of its resources to accumulating capital and the other four fifths to consumption. In 1960, the United States was at point *a* on its *PPF*. Hong Kong devoted one third of its resources to accumulating capital and two thirds to consumption. In 1960, Hong Kong was at point *a* on its *PPF*.

Since 1960, both countries have experienced economic growth, but growth in Hong Kong has been more rapid than in the United States. Because Hong Kong devoted a bigger fraction of its resources to accumulating capital, its production possibilities have expanded more quickly.

In 1998, the *PPF* per person in the United States and Hong Kong were similar. If Hong Kong continues to devote more resources to accumulating capital than we do (at point *b* on its 1998 *PPF*), it will continue to grow more rapidly than the United States and its frontier will move out beyond our own. But if Hong Kong increases consumption and decreases capital accumulation (moving to point *c* on its 1998 *PPF*), then its rate of economic growth will slow.

The United States is typical of the rich industrial countries, which include the United States, Western Europe, and Japan. Hong Kong is typical of the fast-growing Asian economies, which include Taiwan, Thailand, South Korea, and China. Growth in these countries has slowed during the past two years, but before the slowdown, these countries expanded production by between 5 percent and almost 10 percent a year. If these high growth rates are restored, these other countries will eventually

FIGURE 3.6
Economic Growth in the United States and Hong Kong

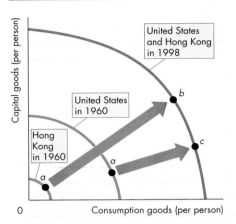

In 1960, the production possibilities per person in the United States were much larger than those in Hong Kong. But Hong Kong devoted more of its resources to accumulating capital than did the United States, so its production possibility frontier has shifted outward more quickly than has that of the United States. In 1998, the two production possibilities per person were similar.

close the gap on the United States as Hong Kong has done.

R E V I E W   Q U I Z

- What are the two key factors that generate economic growth?
- How does economic growth influence the production possibility frontier?
- What is the opportunity cost of economic growth?
- Why has Hong Kong experienced faster economic growth than the United States has?

Next, we're going to study another way we expand our production possibilities—the amazing fact that buyers and sellers gain from specialization and trade.

Gains from Trade

PEOPLE CAN PRODUCE FOR THEMSELVES ALL THE goods that they consume, or they can concentrate on producing one good (or perhaps a few goods) and then trade with others—exchange some of their own goods for those of others. Concentrating on the production of only one good or a few goods is called *specialization*. We are going to discover how people gain by specializing in the production of the good in which they have a *comparative advantage* and trading with each other.

Comparative Advantage

A person has a **comparative advantage** in an activity if that person can perform the activity at a lower opportunity cost than anyone else. Differences in opportunity costs arise from differences in individual abilities and from differences in the characteristics of other resources.

No one excels at everything. One person is an outstanding pitcher but a poor catcher; another person is a brilliant lawyer but a poor teacher. In almost all human endeavors, what one person does easily, someone else finds difficult. The same applies to land and capital. One plot of land is fertile but has no mineral deposits; another plot of land has outstanding views but is infertile. One machine has great precision but is difficult to operate; another machine is fast but often breaks down.

Although no one excels at everything, some people excel and can outperform others in many activities. But such a person does not have a *comparative* advantage in every activity. For example, John Grisham is a better lawyer than most people. But he is an even better writer of fast-paced thrillers. His *comparative* advantage is in writing.

Because people's abilities and the quality of their resources differ, they have different opportunity costs of producing various goods. Such differences give rise to comparative advantage. Let's explore the idea of comparative advantage by looking at two audio cassette factories, one operated by Tom and the other operated by Nancy.

Tom's Factory   To simplify the story quite a lot, suppose that audio cassettes have just two components: a length of tape and a plastic case. Tom has two production lines, one for tape and one for cases.

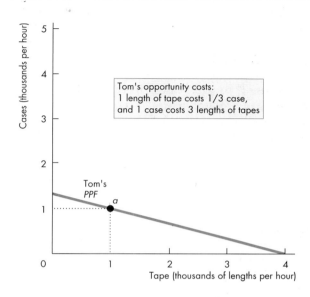

FIGURE 3.7
Production Possibilities
in Tom's Factory

Tom's opportunity costs:
1 length of tape costs 1/3 case,
and 1 case costs 3 lengths of tapes

Tom can produce tape and cassette cases along the production possibility frontier *PPF*. For Tom, the opportunity cost of 1 length of tape is $1/3$ of a case and the opportunity cost of 1 case is 3 lengths of tape. If Tom produces at point *a*, he can produce 1,000 cassette cases and 1,000 lengths of tape an hour.

Figure 3.7 shows Tom's production possibility frontier for tape and cases. It tells us that if Tom uses all his resources to make tape, he can produce 4,000 lengths of tape an hour. The *PPF* in Fig. 3.7 also tells us that if Tom uses all his resources to make cases, he can produce 1,333 cases an hour. But to produce cases, Tom must decrease his production of tape. For each 1 case produced, he must decrease his production of tape by 3 lengths.

See ① on Pg 39

Tom's opportunity cost of producing 1 case is 3 lengths of tape.

Similarly, if Tom wants to increase his production of tape, he must decrease his production of cases. For each 1,000 lengths of tape produced, he must decrease his production of cases by 333. So

Tom's opportunity cost of producing 1 length of tape is 0.333 case.

Nancy's Factory   The other factory, operated by Nancy, can also produce cases and tape. But Nancy's factory has machines that are custom made for case production, so they are more suitable for producing cases than tape. Also, Nancy's work force is more skilled in making cases.

This difference between the two factories means that Nancy's production possibility frontier—shown along with Tom's *PPF* in Fig. 3.8—is different from Tom's. If Nancy uses all her resources to make tape, she can produce 1,333 lengths an hour. If she uses all her resources to make cases, she can produce 4,000 an hour. To produce tape, Nancy must decrease her production of cases. For each 1,000 additional lengths of tape produced, she must decrease her production of cases by 3,000.

Nancy's opportunity cost of producing 1 length of tape is 3 cases.

Similarly, if Nancy wants to increase her production of cases, she must decrease her production of tape. For each 1,000 additional cases produced, she must decrease her production of tape by 333 lengths. So

Nancy's opportunity cost of producing 1 case is 0.333 length of tape.

Suppose that Tom and Nancy produce both tapes and cases and that each produces 1,000 lengths of tape and 1,000 cases—1,000 cassettes—an hour. That is, each produces at point *a* on their production possibility frontiers. Total production is 2,000 cassettes an hour.

In which of the two goods does Nancy have a comparative advantage? Recall that comparative advantage is a situation in which one person's opportunity cost of producing a good is lower than another person's opportunity cost of producing that same good. Nancy has a comparative advantage in producing cases. Nancy's opportunity cost of a case is 0.333 length of tape, whereas Tom's is 3 lengths of tape.

You can see her comparative advantage by looking at the production possibility frontiers for Nancy and Tom in Fig. 3.8. Nancy's production possibility frontier is steeper than Tom's. To produce one more case, Nancy gives up less tape than Tom. Hence Nancy's opportunity cost of a case is less than Tom's. This means that Nancy has a comparative advantage in producing cases.

FIGURE 3.8

The Gains from Trade

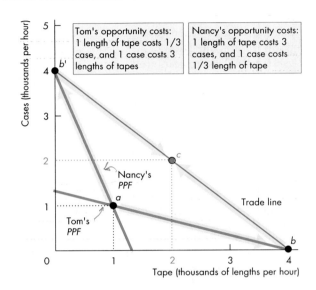

Tom's opportunity costs:
1 length of tape costs 1/3 case, and 1 case costs 3 lengths of tapes

Nancy's opportunity costs:
1 length of tape costs 3 cases, and 1 case costs 1/3 length of tape

Tom and Nancy each produce at point *a* on their respective *PPFs*. Nancy has a comparative advantage in cases, and Tom has a comparative advantage in tape. If Nancy specializes in cases, she produces at point *b'* on her *PPF*. If Tom specializes in tape, he produces at point *b* on his *PPF*. They then exchange cases for tape along the red "Trade line." Nancy buys tape from Tom for less than her opportunity cost of producing it, and Tom buys cases from Nancy for less than his opportunity cost of producing them. Each goes to point *c*—a point outside his or her *PPF*—where each has 2,000 cassettes an hour. Tom and Nancy double their rate of production with no change in resources.

Tom's comparative advantage is in producing tape. His production possibility frontier is less steep than Nancy's. This means that Tom gives up fewer cases to produce one more length of tape than Nancy does. Tom's opportunity cost of producing a length of tape is 0.333 case, which is less than Nancy's 3 cases. So Tom has a comparative advantage in producing tape.

Because Nancy has a comparative advantage in cases and Tom in tape, they can both gain from specialization and exchange.

Achieving the Gains from Trade

If Tom, who has a comparative advantage in tape production, puts all his resources into that activity, he can produce 4,000 lengths of tape an hour—point *b* on his *PPF*. If Nancy, who has a comparative advantage in producing cases, puts all her resources into that activity, she can produce 4,000 cases an hour—point *b* on her *PPF*. By specializing, Tom and Nancy together can produce 4,000 cases and 4,000 lengths of tape an hour, double their total production without specialization. By specialization and exchange, Tom and Nancy can get *outside* their production possibility frontiers.

To achieve the gains from specialization, Tom and Nancy must trade with each other. Suppose they agree to the following deal: Each hour, Nancy produces 4,000 cases, Tom produces 4,000 lengths of tape, and Nancy supplies Tom with 2,000 cases in exchange for 2,000 lengths of tape. With this deal in place, Tom and Nancy move along the red "Trade line" to point *c*. At this point, each produces 2,000 cassettes an hour—double their previous production rate. These are the gains from specialization and trade.

Both parties to the trade share the gains. Nancy, who can produce tape at an opportunity cost of 3 cases per length of tape, can buy tape from Tom for a price of 1 case per length. Tom, who can produce cases at an opportunity cost of 3 lengths of tape per case, can buy cases from Nancy at a price of 1 length per case. Nancy gets her tape more cheaply, and Tom gets his cases more cheaply.

Absolute Advantage

Suppose that Nancy invents and patents a production process that makes her *four* times as productive as she was before in the production of both cases and tape. With her new technology, Nancy can produce 16,000 cases an hour (4 times the original 4,000) if she puts all her resources into that activity. Alternatively, she can produce 5,332 lengths of tape (4 times the original 1,333) if she puts all her resources into that activity. Nancy now has an **absolute advantage** in producing *both* goods—using the same quantity of resources as Tom, she can produce more of both goods than Tom can produce.

But Nancy does not have a *comparative* advantage in both goods. She can produce four times as much of *both* goods as before, but her *opportunity cost* of

1 length of tape is still 3 cases. And this opportunity cost is higher than Tom's. So Nancy can still get tape at a lower cost by exchanging cases for tape with Tom.

A key point to recognize is that it is *not* possible for *anyone* to have a comparative advantage in *everything*. So gains from specialization and trade are always available when opportunity costs diverge.

Dynamic Comparative Advantage

At any given point in time, the available resources and technologies determine the comparative advantages that individuals and nations have. But just by repeatedly producing a particular good or service, people become more productive in that activity, a phenomenon called **learning-by-doing**. Learning-by-doing is the basis of *dynamic* comparative advantage. **Dynamic comparative advantage** is a comparative advantage that a person (or country) possesses as a result of having specialized in a particular activity and, as a result of learning-by-doing, having become the producer with the lowest opportunity cost.

Hong Kong and Singapore are examples of countries that have pursued dynamic comparative advantage vigorously. They have developed industries in which initially they did not have a comparative advantage but, through learning-by-doing, became low opportunity cost producers in those industries. A specific example is the decision to develop a genetic engineering industry in Singapore. Singapore probably did not have a comparative advantage in genetic engineering initially. But it might develop one as its scientists and production workers become more skilled in this activity.

R E V I E W   Q U I Z

- What gives a person a comparative advantage in producing a good?
- Why is not possible for anyone to have a comparative advantage at everything?
- What are the gains from specialization and trade?
- Explain the source of the gains from specialization and trade.
- Distinguish between comparative advantage and absolute advantage.
- What is dynamic comparative advantage and how does it arise?

The Market Economy

INDIVIDUALS AND COUNTRIES GAIN BY SPECIALIZ-
ing in the production of those goods and services in
which they have a comparative advantage and trading
with each other. This source of economic wealth was
identified by Adam Smith in his *Wealth of Nations,*
published in 1776—see pp. 56–57.

To enable billions of people who specialize in
producing millions of different goods and services to
reap these gains, trade must be organized. But trade
need not be *planned* or *managed* by a central authority. In fact, when such an arrangement has been tried,
as it was for 60 years in Russia, the result has been
less than dazzling.

Trade is organized by using social institutions.
The two key ones are:

- Property rights
- Markets

Property Rights

Property rights are social arrangements that govern the ownership, use, and disposal of resources,
goods, and services. *Real property* includes land and
buildings—the things we call property in ordinary
speech—and durable goods such as plant and equipment. *Financial property* includes stocks and bonds
and money in the bank. *Intellectual property* is the
intangible product of creative effort. This type of
property includes books, music, computer programs,
and inventions of all kinds and is protected by copy-
rights and patents.

If property rights are not enforced, the incentive
to specialize and produce the goods in which each
person has a comparative advantage is weakened, and
some of the potential gains from specialization and
trade are lost. If people can easily steal the production
of others, then time, energy, and resources are devoted
not to production, but to protecting possessions.

Establishing property rights is one of the greatest
challenges facing Russia and other Eastern European
nations as they seek to develop market economies.
Even in countries where property rights are well
established, such as the United States, protecting
intellectual property is proving to be a challenge in
the face of modern technologies that make it relatively easy to copy audio and video material, computer programs, and books.

Markets

In ordinary speech, the word *market* means a place
where people buy and sell goods such as fish, meat,
fruits, and vegetables. In economics, a *market* has a
more general meaning. A **market** is any arrangement that enables buyers and sellers to get information and to do business with each other. An example
is the market in which oil is bought and sold—the
world oil market. The world oil market is not a place.
It is the network of oil producers, oil users, whole-
salers, and brokers who buy and sell. In the world oil
market, decision makers do not meet physically. They
make deals throughout the world by telephone, fax,
and direct computer link.

In the example we've just studied, Nancy and
Tom get together and do a deal. They agree to
exchange cassette cases for lengths of tape. But in a
market economy, Nancy sells cassette cases to a dealer
in plastic products and buys lengths of tape from a
dealer in electronic recording media. Similarly, Tom
buys cassette cases and sells lengths of tape in these
same two markets. Tom can use Nancy's cases and
Nancy can use Tom's lengths of tape and yet be
unaware of each other's existence.

Circular Flows in the Market Economy

Figure 3.9 identifies two types of markets: goods
markets and resource markets. *Goods markets* are
those in which goods and services are bought and
sold. *Resource markets* are those in which productive
resources are bought and sold.

Households decide how much of their labor,
land, capital, and entrepreneurship to sell or rent in
resource markets. They receive incomes in the form
of wages, rent, interest, and profit. Households also
decide how to spend their incomes on goods and services produced by firms. Firms decide the quantities
of resources to hire, how to use them to produce
goods and services, what goods and services to
produce, and in what quantities.

Figure 3.9 shows the flows that result from these
decisions by households and firms. The red flows
are the resources that go from households through
resource markets to firms and the goods and services
that go from firms through goods markets to households. The green flows in the opposite direction are
the payments made in exchange for these items.

How do markets coordinate all these decisions?

FIGURE 3.9
Circular Flows in the Market Economy

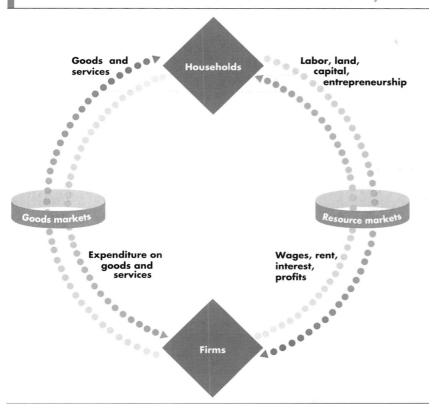

Households and firms make economic choices. Households choose the quantities of labor, land, capital, and entrepreneurship to sell or rent to firms in exchange for wages, rent, interest, and profits. Households also choose how to spend their incomes on the various types of goods and services available. Firms choose the quantities of resources to hire and the quantities of the various goods and services to produce. Goods markets and resource markets coordinate these choices of households and firms. Resources and goods flow clockwise (red), and money payments flow counterclockwise (green).

Coordinating Decisions

Markets coordinate individual decisions through price adjustments. To see how, think about your local market for hamburgers. Suppose that some people who want to buy hamburgers are not able to do so. To make the choices of buyers and sellers compatible, buyers must scale down their appetites or more hamburgers must be offered for sale (or both must happen). A rise in the price of hamburgers produces this outcome. A higher price encourages producers to offer more hamburgers for sale. It also curbs the appetite for hamburgers and changes some lunch plans. Fewer people buy hamburgers, and more buy hot dogs. More hamburgers (and more hot dogs) are offered for sale.

Alternatively, suppose that more hamburgers are available than people want to buy. In this case, to make the choices of buyers and sellers compatible, more hamburgers must be bought or fewer hamburgers must be offered for sale (or both). A fall in the price of hamburgers achieves this outcome. A lower price encour-

ages firms to produce a smaller quantity of hamburgers. It also encourages people to buy more hamburgers.

R E V I E W   Q U I Z

- Why are social arrangements such as markets and property rights necessary?
- What are the main functions of markets?

You have now begun to see how economists approach economic questions. Scarcity, choice, and divergent opportunity cost explain why we specialize and trade and why property rights and markets have developed. You can see the lessons you've learned in this chapter all around you. *Reading Between the Lines* on pp. 50–51 gives an example. It explores the *PPF* of a student like you and the choices that students must make that influence their own economic growth—the growth of their incomes.

Opportunity Cost:
The Cost and Benefit of Education

PORTLAND PRESS HERALD, MAY 2, 1996

High Cost Blocks Education

Robin McAlister of South Portland has fallen into a disheartening routine: Sit down at the kitchen table, scan the classifieds, apply for a job, get turned down. ...

Like thousands of other Mainers, McAlister has learned a fundamental truth: People who don't have the skills needed in today's high-tech, highly competitive environment rarely find good jobs. ...

Although a college degree doesn't guarantee a job, the economy is creating work for highly educated people. ...

Since 1989, the number of jobs for people with a master's degree has jumped an estimated 21 percent. ...

By comparison, jobs that generally don't require a college education have declined an estimated 1 percent.

There's a huge gap in pay between the two groups. In Maine, the average hourly wage for jobs that generally require a college degree is twice that for occupations that don't, about $18 an hour vs. $9 an hour, according to an analysis by The Portland Newspapers of state and federal databases. ...

THE NEW YORK TIMES, AUGUST 2, 1998

A Top MBA Is a Hot Ticket as Pay Climbs

...The typical University of Chicago [business school] graduate turns down so many job offers that the dean's main worry has become "dealing with all the disappointed companies." ...

The median offer this year for a new Stanford MBA ... was $120,000, more than double the first-year salary at the peak of the '80s, and more than five times the 1978 figure. Inflation has been 142 percent over that period. ...

Half the graduates of the Wharton School of the University of Pennsylvania received offers of more than $133,000 this year. ...

At the top 25 schools, the best compensation packages offered to new MBAs are well above $200,000.

Essence of the Stories

- It has become hard for someone who lacks a college education to find a good job.

- Jobs that require a college degree pay twice as much as jobs that don't.

- Jobs for people with an MBA have become even more plentiful.

- Incomes of people with MBAs have increased greatly during the 1990s.

Economic Analysis

■ The opportunity cost of a college degree is forgone consumption. The payoff is an increase in lifetime production possibilities and in future consumption possibilities.

■ Figure 1 shows the choices facing a high school graduate. This person can consume education goods and services such as tuition, books and other supplies, and study time, measured on the *y*-axis, or other goods and services, measured on the *x*-axis.

■ Working full time, this person has an income of $16,000 a year. She can consume along the blue *PPF*. To get a collee degree, a high school graduate selects point *a* on the blue *PPF*, forgoes current consumption, and increases the use of educational goods and services to $12,000.

■ Working full time, the college graduate earns twice as much as the high school graduate at $32,000 a year. With a college degree, production possibilities expand to the red *PPF* in Fig. 1.

■ A college graduate can choose to quit school or spend even more time and other resources on education to get a professional degree. If she quits school, consumption remains at $32,000 a year.

■ Figure 2 shows the choices facing a college graduate. To get a professional degree, a college graduate selects point *b* on the blue *PPF*, forgoes current consumption, and increases the use of educational goods and services to $24,000.

■ With a professional degree, income rises to $128,000 a year. Production possibilities expand to the red *PPF* in Fig. 2.

■ The greater the resources devoted to education, the greater are the future production possibilities. For people who have the required ability, the future benefits of education exceed the costs by a significant amount.

You're The Voter

■ Political leaders of all parties say that they want every American to have a college education.

■ Why do you think political leaders need to worry about college education?

■ With such huge returns from education, why don't more people remain in school for longer?

■ What is the opportunity cost of providing a college education for every American?

■ Would you vote for or against a tax increase to enable everyone to attend college? Why or why not?

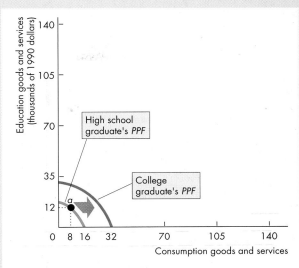

Figure 1 High school graduate's choices

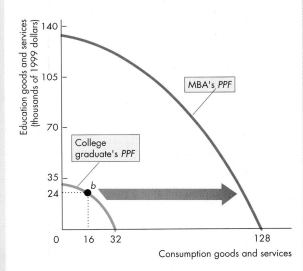

Figure 2 College graduate's choices

SUMMARY

KEY POINTS

Resources and Wants (p. 36)

- Economic activity arises from scarcity—resources are insufficient to satisfy people's wants.
- Resources are labor, land, capital (including human capital), and entrepreneurship.
- We choose how to use our resources and try to get the most out of them.

Resources, Production Possibilities, and Opportunity Cost (pp. 37–39)

- The production possibility frontier, *PPF*, is the boundary between production levels that are attainable and those that are not attainable when all the available resources are used to their limit.
- Production efficiency occurs at points on the *PPF*.
- Along the *PPF*, the opportunity cost of producing more of one good is the amount of the other good that must be given up.
- The opportunity cost of a good increases as the production of the good increases.

Using Resources Efficiently (pp. 40–42)

- The marginal cost of a good is the opportunity cost of producing one more unit.
- The marginal benefit from a good is the maximum amount of another good that a person is willing to forgo to obtain more of the first good.
- The marginal benefit of a good decreases as the amount available increases.
- Resources are used efficiently when the marginal cost of each good is equal to its marginal benefit.

Economic Growth (pp. 43–44)

- Economic growth, which is the expansion of production possibilities, results from capital accumulation and technological change.
- The opportunity cost of economic growth is forgone current consumption.

Gains from Trade (pp. 45–47)

- A person has a comparative advantage in producing a good if that person can produce the good at a lower opportunity cost than everyone else can.
- It is *not* possible for *anyone* to have a comparative advantage at *everything*.
- People gain by specializing in the activity in which they have a comparative advantage and trading with others.

The Market Economy (pp. 48–49)

- Property rights and markets enable people to gain from specialization and trade.
- Markets coordinate decisions and help to allocate resources to *higher*-valued uses.

KEY FIGURES

KEY TERMS

PROBLEMS

*1. Use the figure to calculate Wendell's opportunity cost of an hour of tennis when he increases the time he plays tennis from:
   a. 4 to 6 hours a week.
   b. 6 to 8 hours a week.

O.C. ≈ 5% pts.

O.C. ≈ 10% pts.

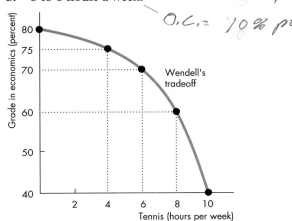

2. Use the figure to calculate Mary's opportunity cost of an hour of skating when she increases her time spent skating from:
   a. 2 to 4 hours a week.
   b. 4 to 6 hours a week.

3) O.C. Ratio
0-4 hrs = 5/4 % pts
4-6 hns = 5/2 % pts
6-8 hns = 10/2 % pts
8-10 hrs = 20/2 % pts
∴ O.C. ↑
As tennis playing ↑

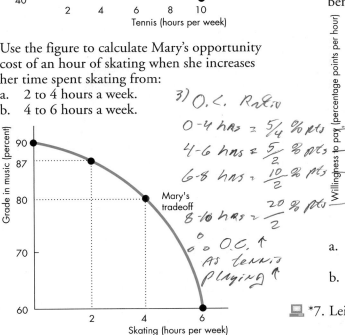

*3. In problem 1, describe the relationship between the time Wendell spends playing tennis and the opportunity cost of an hour of tennis.

4. In problem 2, describe the relationship between the time Mary spends skating and the opportunity cost of an hour of skating.

*5. Wendell, in problem 1, has the following marginal benefit curve:

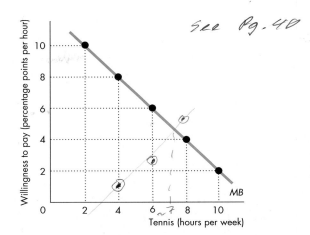

See Pg. 40

   a. If Wendell uses his time efficiently, what grade will he get?
   b. Why would Wendell be worse off getting a higher grade?

6. Mary, in problem 2, has the following marginal benefit curve:

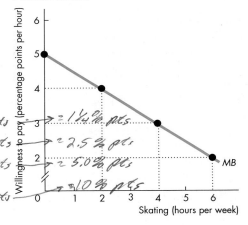

= 1¼% pts.
= 2.5% pts.
= 5.0% pts
= 10% pts

   a. If Mary uses her time efficiently, how much skating will she do?
   b. Why would Mary be worse off spending fewer hours skating?

*7. Leisureland's production possibilities are:

Food (pounds per month)		Sunscreen (gallons per month)
300	and	0
200	and	50
100	and	100
0	and	150

   a. Draw a graph of Leisureland's production possibility frontier.

b. What are Leisureland's opportunity costs of producing food and sunscreen at each output in the table?

8. Jane's Island's production possibilities are:

Corn (pounds per month)		Cloth (yards per month)
3.0	and	0
2.0	and	2
1.0	and	4
0	and	6

a. Draw a graph of the *PPF* on Jane's Island.
b. What are Jane's opportunity costs of producing corn and cloth at each output in the table?

*9. In problem 7, to get a gallon of sunscreen the people of Leisureland are willing to give up 5 pounds of food if they have 25 gallons of sunscreen; 2 pounds of food if they have 75 gallons of sunscreen; and 1 pound of food if they have 125 gallons of sunscreen.
a. Draw a graph of Leisureland's marginal benefit from sunscreen.
b. What is the efficient quantity of sunscreen?

10. In problem 8, to get a yard of cloth Jane is willing to give up 0.75 pound of corn if she has 2 yards of cloth; 0.50 pound of corn if she has 4 yards of cloth; and 0.25 pound of corn if she has 6 yards of cloth.
a. Draw a graph of Jane's marginal benefit from corn.
b. What is Jane's efficient quantity of corn?

*11. Busyland's production possibilities are:

Food (pounds per month)		Sunscreen (gallons per month)
150	and	0
100	and	100
50	and	200
0	and	300

Calculate Busyland's opportunity costs of food and sunscreen at each output in the table.

12. Joe's production possibilities are:

Corn (pounds per month)		Cloth (yards per month)
6	and	0.0
4	and	1.0
2	and	2.0
0	and	3.0

What are Joe's opportunity costs of producing corn and cloth at each output in the table?

*13. In problems 7 and 11, Leisureland and Busyland each produce and consume 100 pounds of food and 100 gallons of sunscreen per month; and they do not trade. Now the countries begin to trade with each other.
a. What good does Leisureland sell to Busyland and what good does it buy from Busyland?
b. If Leisureland and Busyland divide the total output of food and sunscreen equally, what are the gains from trade?

14. In problems 8 and 12, Jane's Island produces and consumes 1 pound of corn and 4 yards of cloth. Joe's Island produces and consumes 4 pounds of corn and 1 yard of cloth. Now the islands begin to trade.
a. What good does Jane sell to Joe and what good does Jane buy from Joe?
b. If Jane and Joe divide the total output of corn and cloth equally, what are the gains from trade?

CRITICAL THINKING

1. After you have studied *Reading Between the Lines* on pp. 50–51, answer the following questions:
a. Why does the *PPF* for education goods and services and consumption goods and services bow outward?
b. At what point on the blue *PPF* in Fig. 1 on p. 51 is the combination of education goods and services and consumption goods and services efficient? Explain your answer.
c. Students face rising tuition. Does higher tuition change the opportunity cost of education?
d. Who receives the benefits from education? Is the marginal cost of education equal to marginal benefit? Is resource use in the market for education efficient?

2. Use the links on the Parkin Web site and obtain data on the tuition and other costs of enrolling in the MBA program of a school that interests you. If an MBA graduate can earn as much as the amounts reported in the news article in *Reading Between the Lines* on pp. 50–51, does the marginal benefit of an MBA exceed its marginal cost? Why doesn't everyone study for an MBA?

Understanding the Scope of Economics

Your Economic Revolution

You are making progress in your study of economics. You've already encountered the big questions and big ideas of economics. And you've learned about the key insight of Adam Smith, the founder of economics: specialization and exchange create economic wealth. ◆ You are studying economics at a time that future historians will call the *Information Revolution*. We reserve the word 'Revolution' for big events that influence all future generations. ◆ During the *Agricultural Revolution*, which occurred 10,000 years ago, people learned to domesticate animals and plant crops. They stopped roaming in search of food and settled in villages and eventually towns and cities, where they developed markets in which to exchange their products. ◆ During the *Industrial Revolution*, which began 240 years ago, people used science to create new technologies. This revolution brought extraordinary wealth for some but created conditions in which others were left behind. It brought social and political tensions that we still face today. ◆ During today's *Information Revolution*, people who have the ability and opportunity to embrace the new technologies are prospering on an unimagined scale. But the incomes and living standards of the less educated are falling behind, and social and political tensions are increasing. Today's revolution has a global dimension. Some of the winners live in previously poor countries in Asia, and some of the losers live here in the United States. ◆ So you are studying economics at an interesting time. Whatever *your* motivation is for studying economics, *my* objective is to help you do well in your course, to enjoy it, and to develop a deeper understanding of the economic world around you. ◆ There are three reasons why I hope that we both succeed: First, a decent understanding of economics will help you to become a full participant in the Information Revolution. Second, an understanding of economics will help you play a more effective role as a citizen and voter and enable you to add your voice to those who are looking for solutions to our social and political problems. Third, you will enjoy the sheer fun of *understanding* the forces at play and how they are shaping our world. ◆ If you are finding economics interesting, think seriously about majoring in the subject. A degree in economics gives the best training available in problem solving, offers lots of opportunities to develop conceptual skills, and opens doors to a wide range of graduate courses, including the MBA, and to a wide range of jobs. You can read more about the benefits of an economics degree in Robert Whaples's essay in your *Study Guide*. ◆ Economics was born during the Industrial Revolution. We'll look at its birth and meet its founder, Adam Smith. Then we'll talk about economic revolutions and other matters with one of today's leading economists, Nobel Laureate, Professor Douglass North of Washington University in St. Louis.

55

The Sources of Economic Wealth

The Father of Economics

Adam Smith *was a giant of a scholar who contributed to ethics and jurisprudence as well as economics. Born in 1723 in Kirkcaldy, a small fishing town near Edinburgh, Scotland, Smith was the only child of the town's customs officer (who died before Adam was born).*

His first academic appointment, at age 28, was as Professor of Logic at the University of Glasgow. He subsequently became tutor to a wealthy Scottish duke, whom he accompanied on a two-year grand European tour, following which he received a pension of £300 a year—ten times the average income at that time.

With the financial security of his pension, Smith devoted ten years to writing An Inquiry into the Nature and Causes of **The Wealth of Nations**, *which was published in 1776. Many people had written on economic issues before Adam Smith, but he made economics a science. Smith's account was so broad and authoritative that no subsequent writer on economics could advance ideas without tracing their connections to those of Adam Smith.*

> "It is not from the benevolence of the butcher, the brewer, or the baker that we expect our dinner, but from their regard to their own interest."
>
> ADAM SMITH
> *The Wealth of Nations*

The Issues

Why are some nations wealthy while others are poor? This question lies at the heart of economics. And it leads directly to a second question: What can poor nations do to become wealthy?

Adam Smith, who is regarded by many scholars as the founder of economics, attempted to answer these questions in his book *The Wealth of Nations*, published in 1776. Smith was pondering these questions at the height of the Industrial Revolution. During these years, new technologies were invented and applied to the manufacture of cotton and wool cloth, iron, transportation, and agriculture.

Smith wanted to understand the sources of economic wealth, and he brought his acute powers of observation and abstraction to bear on the question. His answer:

- The division of labor
- Free markets

The division of labor—breaking tasks down into simple tasks and becoming skilled in those tasks—is the source of "the greatest improvement in the productive powers of labor," said Smith. The division of labor became even more productive when it was applied to creating new technologies. Scientists and engineers, trained in extremely narrow fields, became specialists at inventing. Their powerful skills accelerated the advance of technology, so by the 1820s, machines could make consumer goods faster and more accurately than any craftsman could. And by the 1850s, machines could make other machines that labor alone could never have made.

But, said Smith, the fruits of the division of labor are limited by the extent of the market. To make the market as large as possible, there must be no impediments to free trade both within a country and among countries. Smith argued that when each person makes the best possible economic choice, that choice leads as if by "an invisible hand" to the best outcome for society as a whole. The butcher, the brewer, and the baker each pursue their own interests but, in doing so, also serve the interests of everyone else.

Then

Adam Smith speculated that one person, working hard, using the hand tools available in the 1770s, might possibly make 20 pins a day. Yet, he observed, by using those same hand tools but breaking the process into a number of individually small operations in which people specialize—by the **division of labor**—ten people could make a staggering 48,000 pins a day. One draws out the wire, another straightens it, a third cuts it, a fourth points it, a fifth grinds it. Three specialists make the head, and a fourth attaches it. Finally, the pin is polished and packaged. But a large market is needed to support the division of labor: One factory employing ten workers would need to sell more than 15 million pins a year to stay in business.

Now

If Adam Smith were here today, the computer chip would fascinate him. He would see it as an extraordinary example of the productivity of the division of labor and of the use of machines to make machines that make other machines. From a design of a chip's intricate circuits, cameras transfer an image to glass plates that work like stencils. Workers prepare silicon wafers on which the circuits are printed. Some slice the wafers, others polish them, others bake them, and yet others coat them with a light-sensitive chemical. Machines transfer a copy of the circuit onto the wafer. Chemicals then etch the design onto the wafer. Further processes deposit atom-sized transistors and aluminum connectors. Finally, a laser separates the hundreds of chips on the wafer. Every stage in the process of creating a computer chip uses other computer chips. And like the pin of the 1770s, the computer chip of the 1990s benefits from a large market—a global market—to buy chips in the huge quantities in which they are produced efficiently.

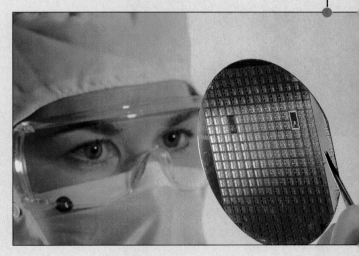

Many economists have worked on the big themes that Adam Smith began. One of these economists is Douglass North, of Washington University, whom you can meet on the following pages.

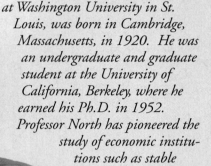

Douglass North

Douglass North, *who*
teaches economics and economic history at Washington University in St. Louis, was born in Cambridge, Massachusetts, in 1920. He was an undergraduate and graduate student at the University of California, Berkeley, where he earned his Ph.D. in 1952. Professor North has pioneered the study of economic institutions such as stable government, the rule of law, and private property rights and the role these institutions play in fostering economic development and sustained income growth. He has used his ideas to explain why the United States and Western Europe have evolved from low-income agricultural societies 200 years ago into high-income complex societies today. In 1993, Professor North was awarded the Nobel Prize for Economic Science for this work. Michael Parkin talked with Professor North about his work and its relevance to today's—and tomorrow's—world.

Professor North, what attracted you to economics?

I grew up during the Great Depression, and when I was a student at the University of California at Berkeley, I became a Marxist. I thought that Marxists had the answers to the economic concerns that were so prevalent during the Depression. If the market economy of capitalism was replaced by the planned economy of socialism, the Depression and other economic ills could, I then believed, be cured.

At Berkeley, I looked for courses that would enable me to understand why some countries were rich and some poor. That is how I was drawn toward economic history.

After I graduated, World War II broke out, and I spent four years in the Merchant Marine. During those years, I read a whole slew of books. I decided that I wanted to save the world—like any good Marxist wanted to—and I decided that the way to save it was to understand what made economies work badly and work well. And I've been pursuing that utopian goal ever since.

How did you abandon your Marxist beginning? Was there a sudden revelation or was it a gradual process?

Converting from Marxism was a very slow process. My first teaching job was at the University of Washington in Seattle in 1950. I used to play chess every day with my colleague, Donald Gordon. He was a good economist, and over three years of playing chess every day and talking economics, I gradually evolved away from Marxism and became a mainstream economist.

What are the key economic principles that guide your work—the principles and perspectives the economist brings to a study of long-term historical processes?

There are two. The first is the importance of transactions costs—the costs that people incur in order to do business with each other.

Economics attempts to understand how societies cope with the problem of scarcity—with the fact that people's wants always outstrip their limited resources. Traditionally, economists have focused on how resources are allocated at a moment of time—what determines today's allocation of spending between high schools and hospitals, computers and cars. Economic history deals with how societies evolve over time and tries to discover why some societies become wealthy while others remain poor. I became convinced that the economic way of reasoning underlying the economic principles is the right way to understand how societies evolve over time. But this conviction led me on a long trail.

Back in the days when I was learning economics, economic theories were based on the *assumption* that people could specialize and exchange their products in markets that function efficiently. They ignored transaction costs—the costs that people incur when they do business with each other and the costs that governments and firms incur to make markets work. So the first problem was to think about how exchange takes place in the face of large transactions costs.

And the second principle?

The second principle is that transactions costs depend crucially on the way that human beings structure the economic order—on their institutions. And this fact gave me my second problem, to think about how institutions evolve to make markets work better over time.

When an economist talks about economic institutions, what exactly is he or she talking about? What are these institutions?

Institutions are rules of the society that structure the interaction among people. Institutions are made up of formal rules, like constitutions and statute law, and common rules and regulations. But they're also more than that. They are the informal ways by which people deal with each other every day, which you could think of as norms of behavior.

Institutions are the framework within which all of human interaction—political, social, and economic—takes place. And so, understanding how those work, why they work well in some circumstances, and why they work badly in others is the key, really, to the wealth of nations. Some examples of economic institutions include antitrust laws, patent laws, and bankruptcy laws.

Can economists explain the radically different institutional evolution of the United States and Russia?

This question is at the very heart of what economic history should be about. The United States inherited a set of institutions—among them common law and property rights—from Great Britain. These institutions had made Britain the world's leading nation by the end of the eighteenth century. The United States modified Britain's institutions and elaborated on them. The result has been two and a half centuries of economic growth. Much of the rest of the world, and Russia in particular, evolved institutions that didn't work very well.

In Britain and the United States, the governments evolved a set of rules that provided a lot of freedom and latitude for people to make contracts and agreements among themselves. These rules produced economic efficiency on an unparalleled scale and led to sustained economic growth.

Russia, as well as some other Eastern European and Third World countries, chose a different economic path based on Communism, which turned out to be an institution that could not sustain economic growth.

The goal of research in economic development and economic history is to understand exactly what led to this very different process of change among countries such as the United States and Russia.

> To have efficient markets, a country needs rules and regulations that provide incentives for people to be creative and become increasingly productive.

How do you explain the economic success of China and economic failure of Russia?

China had political authoritarianism at the top, and those authorities have either deliberately or accidentally loosened control in the provinces. The result has made for a very lucrative combination of local Communist Party officials teaming up with entrepreneurs, who got their capital and sometimes their training from the governments of Hong Kong and Taiwan, being let loose to pursue business ventures. And that's a unique situation. This certainly doesn't appear likely to happen in the former Soviet Union.

I think the biggest economic lessons are from successful Asian economies. Despite recent setbacks, countries such as South Korea and Taiwan show us that a proper dose of government can accelerate the process of creating efficient markets. To have efficient markets, a country needs rules and regulations that provide incentives for people to be creative and to become increasingly productive. We also learn from the Asian crisis and recession of 1998 that the conditions for efficient markets change over time as technologies and market conditions change. This ongoing change requires continual updating of the rules to maintain efficient conditions. It doesn't happen automatically. Asia has shown us that while governments can sometimes hasten the evolution of efficient markets, they can also sometimes thwart the continuation of efficient markets.

How would you characterize the changes that are taking place in today's global and national economy?
I look at economic revolutions as changes in knowledge that fundamentally changed the whole economic social organization of societies. The origin and development of agriculture were the first economic revolution. This economic revolution probably occurred in the eighth millennium

B.C. Agriculture completely altered the pace of economic and all other kinds of human change. Human beings settled down into villages and towns. This eventually led to the growth of exchange and to the whole basis for civilization. Agriculture enormously increased productivity potential and the potential for human progress.

The next real fundamental economic change was the application of science to technology. I would say there's never been a time in human history in which there's been as dramatic a setting of change as we're seeing in the world we live in today. I think it's extraordinary. It's a very exciting world to live in, particularly for an economic historian. I have argued that something happened in the nineteenth century, which I call the Second Economic Revolution: There was a systematic wedding of science to technology that led to the development of the disciplines of physics, chemistry, genetics, and biology. This revolution has completely changed the way in which all of modern economic activity takes place and the way that human beings live and interact.

The personal and social implications of that revolution are enormous. As a result of this revolution, we live packed together in huge cities, many of which are plagued by crime on a scale that frightens us, and we depend for our economic well-being on millions of people we do not know. Many people have benefited from the advances in technology and enjoy unimagined high living standards, while many others have

been left behind and are not sharing in the prosperity that the second economic revolution has created. So, combined with the prosperity of this economic revolution, we've created a set of social, political, and economic problems that we haven't figured out how to solve. And they may overwhelm us down the road.

> I think the most important thing in the world is to have a creative, stimulating, exciting life. . . . Find out what things excite you, and pursue them all your life.

What is your advice to a student who is just setting out to become an economist? How should the student approach his or her work? What are the things to study?
You should find excitement and challenge in the things you do and pursue them. At a university, this means that you ought to bug your professors. You should be continually trying to get a lot out of them. I think most university students don't get out of school what they could. Both in and out of class, you should ask questions and pursue the answers to those questions. I think that's terribly important.

I think the most important thing in the world is to have a creative, stimulating, exciting life. Everybody can do that in their own way, depending on their own curiosities, interests, and talents. Find out what things excite you, and pursue them all your life.

Chapter 4

Demand and Supply

Slide, rocket, and roller coaster—
Disneyland rides? No. Commonly
used descriptions of price changes. ◆ CD
players have taken a price slide from around
$1,100 (in today's money) in 1983 to less than
$100 today. And during these years, the quantity of
CD players bought has increased steadily. What caused
this price slide? Why didn't brisk buying keep the
price high? ◆ The price of health care has rocketed. Yet despite
rocketing prices, people buy more health services every year. Why?
◆ The prices of bananas, coffee, and other agricultural commodities
follow a roller coaster. Why does the price of bananas roller-coaster
even when people's tastes for bananas barely change? ◆ The prices of
many things we buy are remarkably steady. For example, the price of an

Slide, Rocket, and Roller Coaster

audio cassette tape has not changed much.
But despite its steady price, the number of
tapes people buy increases each year. Why do
people buy more tapes even though their
price is no lower than it was a decade ago?
And why do firms sell more tapes even
though they can't get higher prices for them?
◆ Economics is about the choices people
make to cope with scarcity. These choices are guided by costs and benefits and are coordinated through markets. ◆ The tool that explains how
markets work is demand and supply. It is central to the whole of economics. It is used to study issues as diverse as wages and jobs, rents and
housing, pollution, crime, consumer protection, education, welfare,
health care, the value of money, and interest rates.

◆ Your careful study of this topic will bring big rewards both in
your further study of economics and in your everyday life. Once you
understand demand and supply, you will view the world through new
eyes. When you have completed your study of demand and supply,
you will be able to explain how prices are determined and make predictions about price slides, rockets, and roller coasters. But first, we're
going to take a closer look at the idea of price. Just what is a price?

After studying this chapter, you will be able to:

- ■ Distinguish between a money price and a relative price
- ■ Explain the main influences on demand
- ■ Explain the main influences on supply
- ■ Explain how prices and quantities bought and sold are deter-mined by demand and supply
- ■ Explain why some prices fall, some rise, and some fluctuate
- ■ Use demand and supply to make pre-dictions about price changes

Price and Opportunity Cost

ECONOMIC ACTIONS ARISE FROM SCARCITY—WANTS exceed the resources available to satisfy them. Faced with *scarcity*, we must make choices. And to make choices, we compare *costs* and *benefits*. Choices are influenced by opportunity costs. Producers offer items for sale only if the price is high enough to cover their opportunity cost. And consumers respond to changing opportunity cost by seeking cheaper alternatives to expensive items.

We are going to study the way people respond to *prices* and the forces that determine prices. But to pursue these tasks, we need to understand the relationship between a price and an opportunity cost.

In everyday life, the *price* of an object is the number of dollars that must be given up in exchange for it. Economists refer to this price as the *money price*.

The *opportunity cost* of an action is the highest-valued alternative forgone. If, when you buy a cup of coffee, the highest-valued thing you forgo is some gum, then the opportunity cost of buying a coffee is the *quantity* of gum forgone. We can calculate this quantity from the money prices of coffee and gum.

If the money price of coffee is $1 a cup and the money price of gum is 50¢ a pack, then the opportunity cost of one cup of coffee is two packs of gum. To calculate this opportunity cost, we divide the price of a cup of coffee by the price of a pack of gum and find the *ratio* of one price to the other. The ratio of one price to another is called a **relative price**, and a *relative price is an opportunity cost*.

We can express the relative price of coffee in terms of gum or any other good. The normal way of expressing a relative price is in terms of a "basket" of all goods and services. To calculate this relative price, we divide the money price of a good by the money price of a "basket" of all goods (called a *price index*). The resulting relative price is expressed in the buying power of money in a particular year. It tells us the opportunity cost of an item in terms of how much of the "basket" we must give up to buy it.

Figure 4.1 shows the money price and the relative price of wheat. The money price (green) has fluctuated but has tended to rise. The relative price (red) peaked in 1974 and has tended to fall since that year.

The theory of demand and supply that we are about to study determines *relative prices,* and the word "price" means *relative* price. When we predict that a price will fall, we do not mean that its *money*

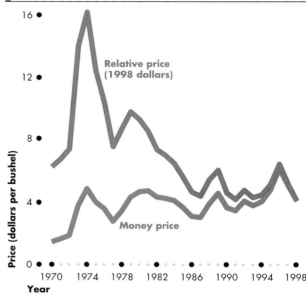

FIGURE 4.1
The Price of Wheat

The money price of wheat—the number of dollars that must be given up for a bushel of wheat—has fluctuated between $1.50 and $6.20. But the *relative* price or *opportunity cost* of wheat, expressed in 1998 dollars, has fluctuated between $4.10 and $16.25 and has tended to fall. The fall in the relative price of wheat is obscured by the behavior of the money price.

Sources: International Financial Statistics, International Monetary Fund, Washington, DC, 1999.

price will fall—although it might. We mean that its *relative* price will fall. That is, its price will fall *relative* to the average price of other goods and services.

R E V I E W   Q U I Z

- Explain the distinction between a money price and a relative price.
- Why is a relative price is an opportunity cost?
- Can you think of an example of a good whose money price and relative price have risen?
- Can you think of an example of a good whose money price and relative price have fallen?

Let's now begin our study of demand and supply, starting with demand.

Demand

IF YOU DEMAND SOMETHING, THEN YOU

1. Want it,
2. Can afford it, and
3. Have made a definite plan to buy it.

Wants are the unlimited desires or wishes that people have for goods and services. How many times have you thought that you would like something "if only you could afford it" or "if it weren't so expensive"? Scarcity guarantees that many—perhaps most—of our wants will never be satisfied. Demand reflects a decision about which wants to satisfy.

The **quantity demanded** of a good or service is the amount that consumers plan to buy during a given time period at a particular price. The quantity demanded is not necessarily the same amount as the quantity actually bought. Sometimes the quantity demanded is greater than the amount of goods available, so the quantity bought is less than the quantity demanded.

The quantity demanded is measured as an amount per unit of time. For example, suppose that you consume one cup of coffee a day. The quantity of coffee that you demand can be expressed as 1 cup a day or 7 cups a week or 365 cups a year. Without a time dimension, we cannot tell whether a particular quantity demanded is large or small.

What Determines Buying Plans?

The amount of any particular good or service that consumers plan to buy depends on many factors. The main ones are:

1. The price of the good
2. The prices of related goods
3. Expected future prices
4. Income
5. Population
6. Preferences

We first look at the relationship between the quantity demanded and the price of a good. To study this relationship, we hold constant all other influences on consumers' planned purchases and ask: How does the quantity demanded of the good vary as its price varies, other things remaining the same?

The Law of Demand

The law of demand states:

Other things remaining the same, the higher the price of a good, the smaller is the quantity demanded.

Why does a higher price reduce the quantity demanded? For two reasons:

1. Substitution effect
2. Income effect

Substitution Effect When the price of a good rises, other things remaining the same, its *relative* price—its opportunity cost—rises. Although each good is unique, it has *substitutes*—other goods that can be used in its place. As the opportunity cost of a good rises, people buy less of that good and more of its substitutes.

Income Effect When a price changes and all other influences on buying plans remain unchanged, the price rises *relative* to people's incomes. So faced with a higher price and an unchanged income, people cannot afford to buy all the things they previously bought. The quantities demanded of at least some goods and services must be decreased. Normally, the good whose price has increased is one of those bought in a smaller quantity.

To see the substitution effect and the income effect at work, think about the effects of changes in the price of blank audio cassette tapes. Many different goods provide a service similar to that provided by a tape. For example, a compact disc, a prerecorded tape, a radio or television broadcast, and a live concert all provide similar services to a tape. Suppose that tapes initially sell for $3 each and then the price doubles to $6. People now substitute compact discs and prerecorded tapes for blank tapes—the substitution effect. And faced with a tighter budget, they buy fewer tapes as well as less of other goods and services—the income effect. The quantity of tapes demanded decreases for these two reasons.

Now suppose the price of a tape falls to $1. People now substitute blank tapes for compact discs and prerecorded tapes—the substitution effect. And with a budget that now has some slack from the lower price of tapes, people buy more tapes as well as more of other goods and services—the income effect. The quantity of tapes demanded increases for these two reasons.

Demand Curve and Demand Schedule

You are now about to study one of the two most used curves in economics, the demand curve. And you are going to encounter one of the most critical distinctions: the distinction between *demand* and *quantity demanded.*

The term **demand** refers to the entire relationship between the quantity demanded and the price of a good, and it is illustrated by the demand curve and the demand schedule. The term *quantity demanded* refers to a point on a demand curve—the quantity demanded at a particular price.

Figure 4.2 shows the demand curve for tapes. A **demand curve** shows the relationship between the quantity demanded of a good and its price when all other influences on consumers' planned purchases remain the same.

The table in Fig. 4.2 is the demand schedule for tapes. A *demand schedule* lists the quantities demanded at each different price when all the other influences on consumers' planned purchases—such as income, population, preferences, and future prices—remain the same. For example, if the price of a tape is $1, the quantity demanded is 9 million tapes a week. If the price of a tape is $5, the quantity demanded is 2 million tapes a week. The other rows of the table show the quantities demanded at prices of $2, $3, and $4.

We graph the demand schedule as a demand curve with the quantity demanded on the horizontal axis and the price on the vertical axis. The points on the demand curve labeled *a* through *e* represent the rows of the demand schedule. For example, point *a* on the graph represents a quantity demanded of 9 million tapes a week at a price of $1 a tape.

Willingness and Ability to Pay Another way of looking at the demand curve is as a willingness-and-ability-to-pay curve. And the willingness-and-ability-to-pay is a measure of *marginal benefit.*

If a small quantity is available, the highest price that someone is willing and able to pay for one more unit is high. But as the quantity available increases, the marginal benefit of each additional unit falls and the highest price that someone is willing and able to pay for it also falls along the demand curve.

In Fig. 4.2, if 2 million tapes are available each week, the highest price that someone is willing to pay for the 2 millionth tape is $5. But if 9 million tapes are available each week, someone is willing to pay only $1 for the last tape bought.

FIGURE 4.2

The Demand Curve

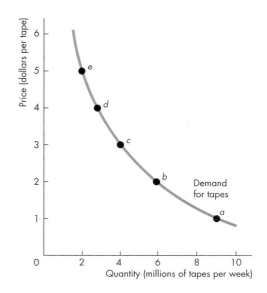

	Price (dollars per tape)	Quantity (millions of tapes per week)
a	1	9
b	2	6
c	3	4
d	4	3
e	5	2

The table shows a demand schedule listing the quantity of tapes demanded at each price if all other influences on buyers' plans remain the same. At a price of $1 a tape, 9 million tapes a week are demanded; at a price of $3 a tape, 4 million tapes a week are demanded. The demand curve shows the relationship between quantity demanded and price, everything else remaining the same.

The demand curve slopes downward: As price decreases, the quantity demanded increases. The demand curve can be read in two ways. For a given price, it tells us the quantity that people plan to buy. For example, at a price of $3 a tape, the quantity demanded is 4 million tapes a week. For a given quantity, the demand curve tells us the maximum price that consumers are willing and able to pay for the last tape available. For example, the maximum price that consumers will pay for the 6 millionth tape is $2.

A Change in Demand

When any factor that influences buying plans other than the price of the good changes, there is a **change in demand**. Figure 4.3 illustrates an increase in demand. When demand increases, the demand curve shifts rightward and the quantity demanded is greater at each and every price. For example, at a price of $5, on the original (blue) demand curve, the quantity demanded is 2 million tapes a week. On the new (red) demand curve, the quantity demanded is 6 million tapes a week. Look closely at the numbers in the table in Fig. 4.3 and check that the quantity demanded is higher at each price.

Let's look at the factors that bring a change in demand. There are five key factors to consider.

1. Prices of Related Goods   The quantity of tapes that consumers plan to buy depends in part on the prices of substitutes for tapes. A **substitute** is a good that can be used in place of another good. For example, a bus ride is a substitute for a train ride; a hamburger is a substitute for a hot dog, and a compact disc is a substitute for a tape. If the price of a substitute for a tape increases, people buy less of the substitute and more tapes. For example, if the price of a CD rises, people buy fewer CDs and more tapes. The demand for tapes increases.

The quantity of tapes that people plan to buy also depends on the prices of complements of tapes. A **complement** is a good that is used in conjunction with another good. Hamburgers and fries are complements. So are spaghetti and meat sauce, and so are tapes and Walkmans. If the price of a Walkman falls, people buy more Walkmans *and more tapes*. It is a fall in the price of a Walkman that increases the demand for tapes in Fig. 4.3.

2. Expected Future Prices   If the price of a good is expected to rise in the future and if the good can be stored, the opportunity cost of obtaining the good for future use is lower now than it will be when the price has increased. So people retime their purchase—they substitute over time. They buy more of the good now before its price is expected to rise (and less after), so the current demand for the good increases.

For example, suppose that Florida is hit by a severe frost that damages the season's orange crop. You expect the price of orange juice to soar. So, anticipating the higher price, you fill your freezer with enough frozen juice to get you through the next six months. Your current demand for frozen orange juice has increased (and your future demand has decreased).

FIGURE **4.3**

An Increase in Demand

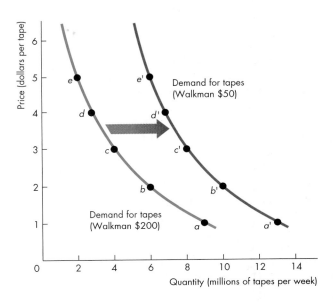

A change in any influence on buyers' plans other than the price of the good itself results in a new demand schedule and a shift of the demand curve. A change in the price of a Walkman changes the demand for tapes. At a price of $3 a tape (row *c* of the table), 4 million tapes a week are demanded when the Walkman costs $200 and 8 million tapes a week are demanded when the Walkman costs only $50. A *fall* in the price of a Walkman *increases* the demand for tapes because the Walkman is a complement of tapes. When demand *increases,* the demand curve shifts *rightward,* as shown by the shift arrow and the resulting red curve.

	Original demand schedule Walkman $200		New demand schedule Walkman $50		
	Price (dollars per tape)	Quantity (millions of tapes per week)		Price (dollars per tape)	Quantity (millions of tapes per week)
a	1	9	a'	1	13
b	2	6	b'	2	10
c	3	4	c'	3	8
d	4	3	d'	4	7
e	5	2	e'	5	6

Similarly, if the price of a good is expected to fall in the future, the opportunity cost of buying the good in the present is high relative to what it is expected to be in the future. So again, people retime their purchases. They buy less of the good now before its price is expected to fall (and more after), so the current demand for the good decreases.

Computer prices are constantly falling, and this fact poses a dilemma. Will you buy a new computer now, in time for the start of the school year, or will you wait until the price has fallen some more? Because people expect computer prices to keep falling, the current demand for computers is less (the future demand is greater) than it otherwise would be.

3. Income   Another influence on demand is consumer income. When income increases, consumers buy more of most goods, and when income decreases, they buy less of most goods. Although an increase in income leads to an increase in the demand for *most* goods, it does not lead to an increase in the demand for *all* goods. A **normal good** is one for which demand increases as income increases. An **inferior good** is one for which demand decreases as income increases. Long-distance transportation has examples of both normal goods and inferior goods. As incomes increase, the demand for air travel (a normal good) increases and the demand for long-distance bus trips (an inferior good) decreases.

4. Population   Demand also depends on the size and the age structure of the population. The larger the population, the greater is the demand for all goods and services. And the smaller the population, the smaller is the demand for all goods and services.

For example, the demand for car parking spaces or movies or tapes or just about anything you can imagine is much greater in New York City (population 7.5 million) than it is in Boise, Idaho (population 150,000).

Also, the larger the proportion of the population in a given age group, the greater is the demand for the types of goods and services used by that age group.

For example, between 1988 and 1998, the number of 20–24 year olds in the United States decreased by 2 million. As a result, the demand for college places decreased during those years. During those same years, the number of Americans aged 85 years and over increased by more than 1 million. As a result, the demand for nursing home services increased.

TABLE 4.1

The Demand for Tapes

The Law of Demand

The quantity of tapes demanded

Decreases if:	*Increases if:*
■ The price of a tape rises	■ The price of a tape falls

Changes in Demand

The demand for tapes

Decreases if:	*Increases if:*
■ The price of a substitute falls	■ The price of a substitute rises
■ The price of a complement rises	■ The price of a complement falls
■ The price of a tape is expected to fall in the future	■ The price of a tape is expected to rise in the future
■ Income falls*	■ Income rises*
■ The population decreases	■ The population increases

*A tape is a normal good.

---

5. Preferences   Demand depends on preferences. *Preferences* are an individual's attitudes toward goods and services. For example, a rock music fanatic has a much greater taste for tapes than does a tone-deaf workaholic. As a consequence, even if they have the same incomes, their demands for tapes will be very different.

Table 4.1 summarizes the influences on demand and the direction of those influences.

A Change in the Quantity Demanded Versus a Change in Demand

Changes in the factors that influence buyers' plans cause either a change in the quantity demanded or a change in demand. Equivalently, they cause either a movement along the demand curve or a shift of the demand curve.

The distinction between a change in the quantity demanded and a change in demand is the same as that between a movement along the demand curve and a shift of the demand curve.

A point on the demand curve shows the quantity demanded at a given price. So a movement along the demand curve shows a **change in the quantity demanded**. The entire demand curve shows demand. So a shift of the demand curve shows a **change in demand**. Figure 4.4 illustrates and summarizes these distinctions.

Movement Along the Demand Curve   If the price of a good changes but everything else remains the same, there is a movement along the demand curve. The negative slope of the demand curve reveals that a decrease in the price of a good or service increases the quantity demanded—the law of demand.

In Fig. 4.4, if the price of a good falls when everything else remains the same, the quantity demanded of that good increases and there is a movement down the demand curve D_0. If the price rises when everything else remains the same, the quantity demanded decreases and there is a movement up the demand curve D_0.

A Shift of the Demand Curve   If the price of a good remains constant but some other influence on buyers' plans changes, there is a change in demand for that good. We illustrate a change in demand as a shift of the demand curve. For example, a fall in the price of the Walkman—a complement of tapes—increases the demand for tapes. We illustrate this increase in the demand for tapes with a new demand schedule and a new demand curve. If the price of the Walkman falls, consumers buy more tapes regardless of whether the price of a tape is high or low. That is what a rightward shift of the demand curve shows—that more tapes are bought at each and every price.

In Fig. 4.4, when any influence on buyers' planned purchases changes, other than the price of the good, the demand curve shifts and there is a *change* (an increase or a decrease) *in demand*. A rise in income (for a normal good), in population, in the price of a substitute, or in the expected future price of the good or a fall in the price of a complement shifts the demand curve rightward (to the red demand curve D_1). This represents an *increase in demand*. A fall in income (for a normal good), in population, in the price of a substitute, or in the expected future price of the good or a rise in the price of a complement shifts the demand curve leftward (to the red demand curve D_2). This represents a *decrease in demand*. (For an inferior good, the effects of changes in income are in the direction opposite to those described above.)

FIGURE 4.4

A Change in the Quantity Demanded Versus a Change in Demand

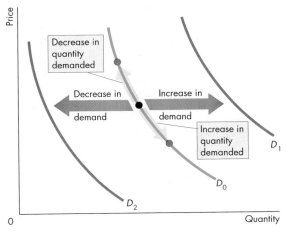

When the price of the good changes, there is a movement along the demand curve and a *change in the quantity demanded*, shown by the blue arrows on demand curve D_0. When any other influence on buying plans changes, there is a shift of the demand curve and a *change in demand*. An increase in demand shifts the demand curve rightward (from D_0 to D_1). A decrease in demand shifts the demand curve leftward (from D_0 to D_2).

REVIEW QUIZ

- Can you define the *quantity demanded* of a good or service?
- What is the *law of demand* and how do we illustrate it?
- If a fixed amount of a good is available, what does the demand curve tell us about the price that consumers are willing to pay for that fixed quantity?
- Can you list all the influences on buying plans that *change demand* and for each influence say whether it increases demand or decreases demand?
- What happens to the quantity of CDs demanded and the demand for CDs if the price of a CD falls and all other influences on buying plans remain the same?

Supply

IF A FIRM SUPPLIES A GOOD OR SERVICE, THE FIRM

1. Has the resources and technology to produce it,
2. Can profit from producing it, and
3. Has made a definite plan to produce it and sell it.

A supply is more that just having the *resources* and the *technology* to produce something. *Resources and technology* are the constraints that limit what is possible.

Many useful things can be produced, but they are not produced unless it is profitable to do so. Supply reflects a decision about which technologically feasible items to produce.

The **quantity supplied** of a good or service is the amount that producers plan to sell during a given time period at a particular price. The quantity supplied is not necessarily the same amount as the quantity actually sold. Sometimes the quantity supplied is greater than the quantity demanded, so the quantity bought is less than the quantity supplied.

Like the quantity demanded, the quantity supplied is measured as an amount per unit of time. For example, suppose that GM produces 1,000 cars a day. The quantity of cars supplied by GM can be expressed as 1,000 a day or 7,000 a week or 365,000 a year. Without the time dimension, we cannot tell whether a particular number is large or small.

What Determines Selling Plans?

The amount of any particular good or service that producers plan to sell depends on many factors. The main ones are:

1. The price of the good
2. The prices of resources used to produce the good
3. The prices of related goods produced
4. Expected future prices
5. The number of suppliers
6. Technology

Let's first look at the relationship between the price of a good and the quantity supplied. To study this relationship, we hold constant all the other influences on the quantity supplied. We ask: How does the quantity supplied of a good vary as its price varies?

The Law of Supply

The law of supply states:

Other things remaining the same, the higher the price of a good, the greater is the quantity supplied.

Why does a higher price increase the quantity supplied? It is because of *increasing marginal cost.* As the quantity produced of any good increases, the marginal cost of producing the good increases. (You can refresh your memory of increasing marginal cost in Chapter 3, p. 40.)

It is never worth producing a good if the price received for it does not at least cover marginal cost. So when the price of a good rises, other things remaining the same, producers are willing to incur the higher marginal cost and increase production. The higher price brings forth an increase in the quantity supplied.

Let's now illustrate the law of supply with a supply curve and a supply schedule.

Supply Curve and Supply Schedule

You are now going to study the second of the two most used curves in economics, the supply curve. And you're going to learn about the critical distinction between *supply* and *quantity supplied*.

The term **supply** refers to the entire relationship between the quantity supplied and the price of a good, and it is illustrated by the supply curve and the supply schedule. The term *quantity supplied* refers to a point on a supply curve—the quantity supplied at a particular price.

Figure 4.5 shows the supply curve of tapes. A **supply curve** shows the relationship between the quantity supplied of a good and its price when all other influences on producers' planned sales remain the same. It is a graph of a supply schedule.

The table in Fig. 4.5 sets out the supply schedule for tapes. A *supply schedule* lists the quantities supplied at each different price when all the other influences on producers' planned sales remain the same. For example, if the price of a tape is $1, the quantity supplied is zero—on row *a* of the table. If the price of a tape is $2, the quantity supplied is 3 million tapes a week—on row *b*. The other rows of the table show the quantities supplied at prices of $3, $4, and $5.

FIGURE 4.5

The Supply Curve

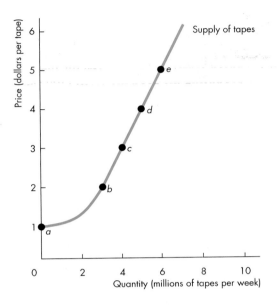

The table shows the supply schedule of tapes. For example, at $2 a tape, 3 million tapes a week are supplied; at $5 a tape, 6 million tapes a week are supplied. The supply curve shows the relationship between the quantity supplied and price, everything else remaining the same. The supply curve usually slopes upward: As the price of a good increases, so does the quantity supplied.

A supply curve can be read in two ways. For a given price, its tells us the quantity that producers plan to sell. And for a given quantity, it tells us the minimum price that producers are willing to accept for that quantity.

	Price (dollars per tape)	Quantity (millions of tapes per week)
a	1	0
b	2	3
c	3	4
d	4	5
e	5	6

To make a supply curve, we graph the quantity supplied on the horizontal axis and the price on the vertical axis, just as in the case of the demand curve. The points on the supply curve labeled *a* through *e* represent the rows of the supply schedule. For example, point *a* on the graph represents a quantity supplied of zero at a price of $1 a tape.

Minimum Supply Price Just as the demand curve has two interpretations, so too does the supply curve. The demand curve can be interpreted as a willingness-and-ability-to-pay curve. The supply curve can be interpreted as a minimum-supply-price curve. It tells us the lowest price at which someone can profitably sell another unit.

If a small quantity is produced, the lowest price at which someone can profitably sell one more unit is low. But if a large quantity is produced, the lowest price at which someone can profitably sell one more unit is high.

In Fig. 4.5, if 6 million tapes are produced each week, the lowest price that a producer is willing to accept for the 6 millionth tape is $5. But if only 4 million tapes are produced each week, the lowest price that a producer is willing to accept for the 4 millionth tape is $3.

A Change in Supply

When any factor that influences selling plans other than the price of the good changes, there is a **change in supply**. Let's look at the five key factors that change supply.

1. Prices of Productive Resources The prices of productive resources influence supply. The easiest way to see this influence is to think about the supply curve as a minimum-supply-price curve. If the prices of productive resources rise, the lowest price a producer is willing to accept rises so supply decreases. For example, during 1996, the price of jet fuel increased and the supply of air transportation decreased. Similarly, a rise in the minimum wage decreased the supply of hamburgers. If the wages of tape producers rise, the supply of tapes decreases.

2. Prices of Related Goods Produced The prices of related goods and services that firms produce influence supply. For example, if the price of prerecorded tapes rises, the supply of blank tapes decreases. Blank tapes and prerecorded tapes are *substitutes in produc-*

tion—goods that can be produced by using the same resources. If the price of beef rises, the supply of cowhide increases. Beef and cowhide are *complements in production*—goods that must be produced together.

3. Expected Future Prices   If the price of a good is expected to rise, the return from selling the good in the future is higher than it is in the present. So the current supply decreases.

4. The Number of Suppliers   Supply also depends on the number of suppliers. The larger the number of firms that produce a good, the greater is the supply of the good. As firms enter an industry, the supply in that industry increases. As firms leave an industry, the supply in that industry decreases. For example, over the past two years, there has been a huge increase in the number of firms that produce and manage World Wide Web sites. As a result, the supply of Internet and World Wide Web services has increased enormously.

5. Technology   New technologies create new products and lower the costs of producing existing products. As a result they change supply. For example, the development of a new technology for tape production by Sony and Minnesota Mining and Manufacturing (3M) has lowered the cost of producing tapes and increased the supply of tapes.

Figure 4.6 illustrates an increase in supply. When supply increases, the supply curve shifts rightward and the quantity supplied is larger at each and every price. For example, at a price of $2, on the original (blue) supply curve, the quantity supplied is 3 million tapes a week. On the new (red) supply curve, the quantity supplied is 6 million tapes a week. Look closely at the numbers in the table in Fig. 4.6 and check that the quantity supplied is larger at each price.

Table 4.2 summarizes the influences on supply and the directions of those influences.

A Change in the Quantity Supplied Versus a Change in Supply

Changes in the factors that influence producers' planned sales cause either a change in the quantity supplied or a change in supply. Equivalently, they cause either a movement along the supply curve or a shift of the supply curve.

A point on the supply curve shows the quantity supplied at a given price. So a movement along the

FIGURE 4.6

An Increase in Supply

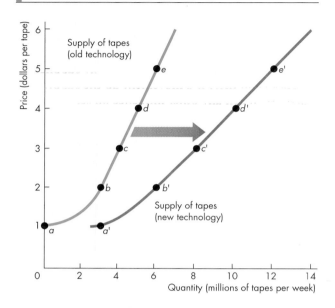

Original supply schedule Old technology			New supply schedule New technology		
	Price (dollars per tape)	Quantity (millions of tapes per week)		Price (dollars per tape)	Quantity (millions of tapes per week)
a	1	0	a'	1	3
b	2	3	b'	2	6
c	3	4	c'	3	8
d	4	5	d'	4	10
e	5	6	e'	5	12

A change in any influence on sellers' plans other than the price of the good itself results in a new supply schedule and a shift of the supply curve. For example, if Sony and 3M invent a new, cost-saving technology for producing tapes, the supply of tapes changes.

At a price of $3 a tape, 4 million tapes a week are supplied when producers use the old technology (row c of the table) and 8 million tapes a week are supplied when producers use the new technology. An advance in technology *increases* the supply of tapes and shifts the supply curve *rightward*, as shown by the shift arrow and the resulting red curve.

supply curve shows a **change in the quantity supplied**. The entire supply curve shows supply. So a shift of the supply curve shows a **change in supply**.

Figure 4.7 illustrates and summarizes these distinctions. If the price of a good falls and everything else remains the same, the quantity supplied of that good decreases and there is a movement down the supply curve S_0. If the price of a good rises and everything else remains the same, the quantity supplied increases and there is a movement up the supply curve S_0. When any other influence on selling plans changes, the supply curve shifts and there is a change in supply. If the supply curve is S_0 and if production costs fall supply increases and the supply curve shifts to the red supply curve S_1. If production costs rise, supply decreases and the supply curve shifts to the red supply curve S_2.

FIGURE 4.7

A Change in the Quantity Supplied Versus a Change in Supply

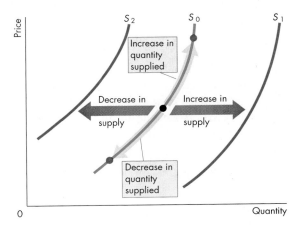

When the price of the good changes, there is a movement along the supply curve and a *change in the quantity supplied,* shown by the blue arrows on supply curve S_0. When any other influence on selling plans changes, there is a shift of the supply curve and a *change in supply.* An increase in supply shifts the supply curve rightward (from S_0 to S_1). A decrease in supply shifts the supply curve shifts leftward (from S_0 to S_2).

TABLE 4.2

The Supply of Tapes

The Law of Supply

The quantity of tapes supplied

Decreases if:	*Increases if:*
■ The price of a tape falls	■ The price of a tape rises

Changes in Supply

The supply of tapes

Decreases if:	*Increases if:*
■ The price of a resource used to produce tapes rises	■ The price of a resource used to produce tapes falls
■ The price of a substitute in production rises	■ The price of a substitute in production falls
■ The price of a complement in production falls	■ The price of a complement in production rises
■ The price of a tape is expected to rise in the future	■ The price of a tape is expected to fall in the future
■ The number of tape producers decreases	■ The number of tape producers increases
	■ More efficient technologies for producing tapes are discovered

---

- Can you define the *quantity supplied* of a good or service?
- What is the *law of supply* and how do we illustrate it?
- If consumers are willing to buy only a given quantity, what does the supply curve tell us about the price at which firms will supply that quantity?
- Can you list all the influences on selling plans that *change supply* and for each influence say whether it increases supply or decreases supply?

Your next task is to use what you've learned about demand and supply and learn how prices and quantities are determined.

Market Equilibrium

WE HAVE SEEN THAT WHEN THE PRICE OF A GOOD
rises, the quantity demanded decreases and the quantity supplied increases. We are now going to see how
prices coordinate the plans of buyers and sellers and
achieve an equilibrium.

An *equilibrium* is a situation in which opposing
forces balance each other. Equilibrium in a market
occurs when the price balances the plans of buyers
and sellers. The **equilibrium price** is the price at
which the quantity demanded equals the quantity
supplied. The **equilibrium quantity** is the quantity bought and sold at the equilibrium price. A
market moves toward its equilibrium because:

- Price regulates buying and selling plans
- Price adjusts when plans don't match

Price as a Regulator

The price of a good regulates the quantities demanded
and supplied. If the price is too high, the quantity
supplied exceeds the quantity demanded. If the price
is too low, the quantity demanded exceeds the quantity supplied. There is one price at which the quantity
demanded equals the quantity supplied. Let's work
out what that price is.

Figure 4.8 shows the market for tapes. The table
shows the demand schedule (from Fig. 4.2) and the
supply schedule (from Fig. 4.5). If the price of a tape
is $1, the quantity demanded is 9 million tapes a
week, but no tapes are supplied. The quantity
demanded exceeds the quantity supplied by 9 million
tapes a week. In other words, at a price of $1 a tape,
there is a shortage of 9 million tapes a week. This
shortage is shown in the final column of the table. At
a price of $2 a tape, there is still a shortage, but only
of 3 million tapes a week. If the price of a tape is $5,
the quantity supplied exceeds the quantity demanded.
The quantity supplied is 6 million tapes a week, but
the quantity demanded is only 2 million. There is a
surplus of 4 million tapes a week. The one price at
which there is neither a shortage nor a surplus is $3 a
tape. At that price, the quantity demanded is equal to
the quantity supplied: 4 million tapes a week. The
equilibrium price is $3 a tape, and the equilibrium
quantity is 4 million tapes a week.

Figure 4.8 shows that the demand curve and supply curve intersect at the equilibrium price of $3 a

FIGURE 4.8
Equilibrium

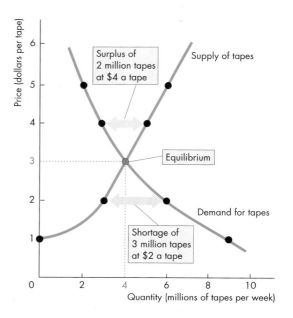

Price (dollars per tape)	Quantity demanded	Quantity supplied	Shortage (−) or surplus (+)
	(millions of tapes per week)		
1	9	0	−9
2	6	3	−3
3	4	4	0
4	3	5	+2
5	2	6	+4

The table lists the quantities demanded and quantities supplied as well as the shortage or surplus of tapes at each price.
If the price is $2 a tape, 6 million tapes a week are demanded
and 3 million are supplied. There is a shortage of 3 million
tapes a week, and the price rises. If the price is $4 a tape, 3
million tapes a week are demanded and 5 million are supplied.
There is a surplus of 2 million tapes a week, and the price falls.
If the price is $3 a tape, 4 million tapes a week are demanded
and 4 million are supplied. There is neither a shortage nor a
surplus. Neither buyers nor sellers have any incentive to
change the price. The price at which the quantity demanded
equals the quantity supplied is the equilibrium price.

tape. At each price *above* $3 a tape, there is a surplus of tapes. For example, at $4 a tape, the surplus is 2 million tapes a week, as shown by the blue arrow. At each price *below* $3 a tape, there is a shortage of tapes. For example, at $2 a tape, the shortage is 3 million tapes a week, as shown by the red arrow.

Price Adjustments

You've seen that if the price is below equilibrium there is a shortage and if the price is above equilibrium there is a surplus. But can we count on the price to change and eliminate a shortage or surplus? We can, because such price changes are mutually beneficial to both buyers and sellers. Let's see why the price changes when there is a shortage or a surplus.

A Shortage Forces the Price Up   Suppose the price of a tape is $2. Consumers plan to buy 6 million tapes a week, and producers plan to sell 3 million tapes a week. Consumers can't force producers to sell more than they plan, so the quantity actually offered for sale is 3 million tapes a week. In this situation, powerful forces operate to increase the price and move it toward the equilibrium price. Some producers, noticing lines of unsatisfied consumers, move their prices up. Some producers increase their output. As producers push their prices up, the price rises toward its equilibrium. The rising price reduces the shortage because it decreases the quantity demanded and increases the quantity supplied. When the price has increased to the point at which there is no longer a shortage, the forces moving the price stop operating and the price comes to rest at its equilibrium.

A Surplus Forces the Price Down   Suppose the price of a tape is $4. Producers plan to sell 5 million tapes a week, and consumers plan to buy 3 million tapes a week. Producers cannot force consumers to buy more than they plan, so the quantity that is actually bought is 3 million tapes a week. In this situation, powerful forces operate to lower the price and move it toward the equilibrium price. Some producers, unable to sell the quantities of tapes they planned to sell, cut their prices. In addition, some producers scale back production. As producers cut prices, the price falls toward its equilibrium. The falling price decreases the surplus because it increases the quantity demanded and decreases the quantity supplied. When the price has fallen to the point at which there is no longer a surplus, the forces moving the price

stop operating, and the price comes to rest at its equilibrium.

The Best Deal Available for Buyers and Sellers
When the price is below equilibrium, it is forced upward toward the equilibrium. Why don't buyers resist the increase and refuse to buy at the higher price? Because they value the good more highly than the current price and they cannot satisfy all their demands at the current price. In some markets— an example is the market for rental accommodation in Atlanta during the 1996 Olympic Games—the buyers might even be the ones who force the price upward by offering higher prices to divert the limited quantities away from other buyers.

When the price is above equilibrium, it is bid downward toward the equilibrium. Why don't sellers resist this decrease and refuse to sell at the lower price? Because their minimum supply price is below the current price and they cannot sell all they would like to at the current price. Normally, it is the sellers who force the price downward by offering lower prices to gain market share from their competitors.

At the price at which the quantity demanded and the quantity supplied are equal, neither buyers nor sellers can do business at a better price. Buyers pay the highest price they are willing to pay for the last unit bought, and sellers receive the lowest price at which they are willing to supply the last unit sold.

When people freely make offers to buy and sell, and when demanders try to buy at the lowest possible price and suppliers try to sell at the highest possible price, the price at which trade takes place is the equilibrium price—the price at which the quantity demanded equals the quantity supplied. The price coordinates the plans of buyers and sellers.

R E V I E W   Q U I Z

- What is the *equilibrium price* of a good or service?
- Over what range of prices does a shortage arise?
- Over what range of prices does a surplus arise?
- What happens to the price when there is a shortage?
- What happens to the price when there is a surplus?
- Why is the price at which the quantity demanded equals the quantity supplied the equilibrium price?
- Why is the equilibrium price the best deal available for both buyers and seller?

Predicting Changes in Price and Quantity

THE DEMAND AND SUPPLY THEORY WE HAVE JUST studied provides us with a powerful way of analyzing influences on prices and the quantities bought and sold. According to the theory, a change in price stems from either a change in demand or a change in supply or a change in both. Let's look first at the effects of a change in demand.

A Change in Demand

What happens to the price and quantity of tapes if the demand for tapes increases? We can answer this question with a specific example. Suppose the price of a Walkman falls from $200 to $50. Because the Walkman and tapes are complements, the demand for tapes increases, as is shown in the table in Fig. 4.9. The original demand schedule and the new one are set out in the first three columns of the table. The table also shows the supply schedule for tapes.

The original equilibrium price is $3 a tape. At that price, 4 million tapes a week are demanded and supplied. When demand increases, the price that makes the quantity demanded equal the quantity supplied is $5 a tape. At this price, 6 million tapes are bought and sold each week. When demand increases, both the price and the quantity increase.

Figure 4.9 shows these changes. The figure shows the original demand for and supply of tapes. The original equilibrium price is $3 a tape, and the quantity is 4 million tapes a week. When demand increases, the demand curve shifts rightward. The equilibrium price rises to $5 a tape, and the quantity supplied increases to 6 million tapes a week, as highlighted in the figure. There is an *increase in the quantity supplied* but *no change in supply*—a movement along, but no shift of, the supply curve.

We can reverse the exercise that we've just conducted. We can work out what happens if we start at a price of $5 a tape with 6 million tapes a week being bought and sold and then demand decreases to its original level. Such a decrease in demand might arise from a fall in the price of CDs or CD players (both substitutes for tapes). The decrease in demand shifts the demand curve leftward. The equilibrium price falls to $3 a tape, and the equilibrium quantity decreases to 4 million tapes a week.

FIGURE 4.9

The Effects of a Change in Demand

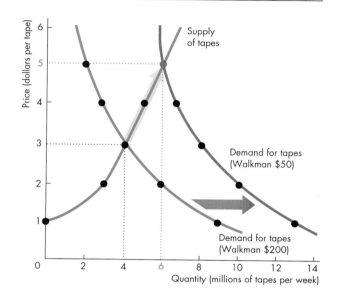

Price	Quantity demanded (millions of tapes per week)		Quantity supplied
(dollars per tape)	Walkman $200	Walkman $50	(millions of tapes per week)
1	9	13	0
2	6	10	3
3	4	8	4
4	3	7	5
5	2	6	6

With the price of a Walkman at $200, the demand for tapes is the blue curve. The equilibrium price is $3 a tape, and the equilibrium quantity is 4 million tapes a week. When the price of a Walkman falls from $200 to $50, the demand for tapes increases and the demand curve shifts rightward to become the red curve.

At $3 a tape, there is now a shortage of 4 million tapes a week. The price of a tape rises to a new equilibrium of $5 a tape. As the price rises to $5, the quantity supplied increases—shown by the blue arrow on the supply curve—to the new equilibrium quantity of 6 million tapes a week. Following an increase in demand, the quantity supplied increases but supply does not change—the supply curve does not shift.

We can now make our first two predictions:

1. When demand increases, both the price and the quantity increase.
2. When demand decreases, both the price and the quantity decrease.

A Change in Supply

Suppose that Sony and 3M introduce a new cost-saving technology in their tape production plants. The new technology increases the supply of tapes. The new supply schedule (the same one that was shown in Fig. 4.6) is presented in the table in Fig. 4.10. What are the new equilibrium price and quantity? The answer is highlighted in the table: The price falls to $2 a tape, and the quantity increases to 6 million a week. You can see why by looking at the quantities demanded and supplied at the old price of $3 a tape. The quantity supplied at that price is 8 million tapes a week, and there is a surplus of tapes. The price falls. Only when the price is $2 a tape does the quantity supplied equal the quantity demanded.

Figure 4.10 illustrates the effect of an increase in supply. It shows the demand curve for tapes and the original and new supply curves. The initial equilibrium price is $3 a tape and the quantity is 4 million tapes a week. When the supply increases, the supply curve shifts rightward. The equilibrium price falls to $2 a tape, and the quantity demanded increases to 6 million tapes a week, highlighted in the figure. There is an *increase in the quantity demanded* but *no change in demand*—a movement along, but no shift of, the demand curve.

The exercise that we've just conducted can be reversed. If we start out at a price of $2 a tape with 6 million tapes a week being bought and sold, we can work out what happens if supply decreases to its original level. Such a decrease in supply might arise from an increase in the cost of labor or raw materials. The decrease in supply shifts the supply curve leftward. The equilibrium price rises to $3 a tape, and the equilibrium quantity decreases to 4 million tapes a week.

We can now make two more predictions:

1. When supply increases, the quantity increases and the price falls.
2. When supply decreases, the quantity decreases and the price rises.

FIGURE 4.10
The Effects of a Change in Supply

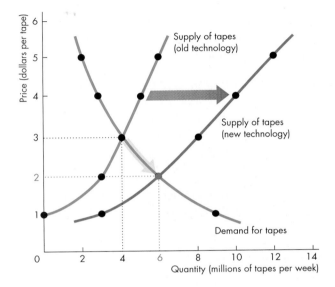

Price (dollars per tape)	Quantity demanded (millions of tapes per week)	Quantity supplied (millions of tapes per week)	
		old technology	new technology
1	9	0	3
2	6	3	6
3	4	4	8
4	3	5	10
5	2	6	12

With the old technology, the supply of tapes is shown by the blue supply curve. The equilibrium price is $3 a tape, and the equilibrium quantity is 4 million tapes a week. When the new technology is adopted, the supply of tapes increases and the supply curve shifts rightward to become the red curve.

At $3 a tape, there is now a surplus of 4 million tapes a week. The price of a tape falls to a new equilibrium of $2 a tape. As the price falls to $2, the quantity demanded increases—shown by the blue arrow on the demand curve—to the new equilibrium quantity of 6 million tapes a week. Following an increase in supply, the quantity demanded increases but demand does not change—the demand curve does not shift.

A Change in Both Demand and Supply

You can now predict the effects of a change in either demand or supply on the price and the quantity. But what happens if *both* demand and supply change together? To answer this question, we look first at the case in which demand and supply move in the same direction—either both increase or both decrease. Then we look at the case in which they move in opposite directions—demand decreases and supply increases or demand increases and supply decreases.

Demand and Supply Change in the Same Direction

We've seen that an increase in the demand for tapes increases the price of tapes and increases the quantity bought and sold. And we've seen that an increase in the supply of tapes lowers the price of tapes and increases the quantity bought and sold. Let's now examine what happens when both of these changes occur together.

The table in Fig. 4.11 brings together the numbers that describe the original quantities demanded and supplied and the new quantities demanded and supplied after the fall in the price of the Walkman and the improved tape production technology. These same numbers are illustrated in the graph. The original (blue) demand and supply curves intersect at a price of $3 a tape and a quantity of 4 million tapes a week. The new (red) supply and demand curves also intersect at a price of $3 a tape but at a quantity of 8 million tapes a week.

An increase in either demand or supply increases the quantity. So when both demand and supply increase, so does quantity.

An increase in demand raises the price, and an increase in supply lowers the price, so we can't say whether the price will rise or fall when demand and supply increase together. In this example, the price does not change. But notice that if demand increases by slightly more than the amount shown in the figure, the price will rise. And if supply increases by slightly more than the amount shown in the figure, the price will fall.

We can now make two more predictions:

1. When *both* demand and supply increase, the quantity increases and the price increases, decreases, or remains constant.
2. When *both* demand and supply decrease, the quantity decreases and the price increases, decreases, or remains constant.

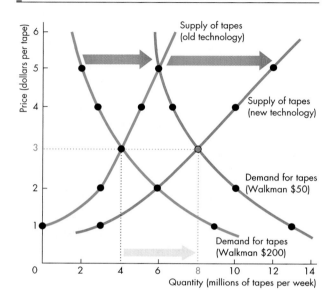

FIGURE 4.11

The Effects of an Increase in Both Demand and Supply

	Original quantities (millions of tapes per week)		New quantities (millions of tapes per week)	
Price (dollars per tape)	**Quantity demanded** Walkman $200	**Quantity supplied** old technology	**Quantity demanded** Walkman $50	**Quantity supplied** new technology
1	9	0	13	3
2	6	3	10	6
3	4	4	8	8
4	3	5	7	10
5	2	6	6	12

When a Walkman costs $200 and the old technology is used to produce tapes, the price of a tape is $3 and the quantity is 4 million tapes a week. A fall in the price of a Walkman increases the demand for tapes, and improved technology increases the supply of tapes. The new supply curve intersects the new demand curve at $3 a tape, the same price as before, but the quantity increases to 8 million tapes a week. These increases in demand and supply increase the quantity but leave the price unchanged.

Demand and Supply Change in Opposite Directions

Let's now see what happens when demand and supply change together but move in *opposite* directions. An improved production technology increases the supply of tapes as before. But now the price of CD players falls. A CD player is a *substitute* for tapes. With less costly CD players, more people buy them and switch from buying tapes to buying discs, and the demand for tapes decreases.

The table in Fig. 4.12 describes the original and new demand and supply schedules. These schedules are shown as the original (blue) and new (red) demand and supply curves in the graph. The original demand and supply curves intersect at a price of $5 a tape and a quantity of 6 million tapes a week. The new supply and demand curves intersect at a price of $2 a tape and at the original quantity of 6 million tapes a week.

A decrease in demand or an increase in supply lowers the price. So when a decrease in demand and an increase in supply occur together, the price falls.

A decrease in demand decreases the quantity, and an increase in supply increases the quantity, so we can't say for sure which way the quantity will change when demand decreases and supply increases at the same time. In this example, the decrease in demand and the increase in supply are such that the increase in quantity brought about by an increase in supply is offset by the decrease in quantity brought about by a decrease in demand—so the quantity does not change. But notice that if demand had decreased by slightly more, the quantity would have decreased. And if supply had increased by slightly more, the quantity would have increased.

We can now make two more predictions:

1. When demand decreases and supply increases, the price falls and the quantity increases, decreases, or remains constant.

2. When demand increases and supply decreases, the price rises and the quantity increases, decreases, or remains constant.

R E V I E W   Q U I Z

- What is the effect on the price of a tape and the quantity of tapes if (a) the price of a CD rises or (b) the price of a Walkman rises or (c) more firms start to produce tapes or (d) tape producers' wages rise or (e) any pair of these events occur at the same time? (Draw the diagrams!)

FIGURE 4.12

The Effects of a Decrease in Demand and an Increase in Supply

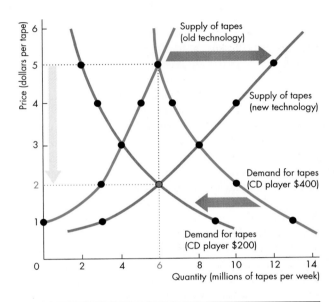

Price (dollars per tape)	Original quantities (millions of tapes per week)		New quantities (millions of tapes per week)	
	Quantity demanded CD player $400	Quantity supplied old technology	Quantity demanded CD player $200	Quantity supplied new technology
1	13	0	9	3
2	10	3	6	6
3	8	4	4	8
4	7	5	3	10
5	6	6	2	12

When a CD player costs $400 and the old technology is used to produce tapes, the price of a tape is $5 and the quantity is 6 million tapes a week. A fall in the price of a CD player decreases the demand for tapes, and improved technology increases the supply of tapes. The new supply curve intersects the new demand curve at $2 a tape, a lower price, but in this case the quantity remains constant at 6 million tapes a week. The decrease in demand and increase in supply lower the price but leave the quantity unchanged.

CD Players, Health Care, and Bananas

Earlier in this chapter, we looked at some facts about prices and quantities of CD players, health care, and bananas. Let's use the theory of demand and supply that we have just studied to explain the movements in the prices and quantities of those goods.

A Price Slide: CD Players   Figure 4.13(a) shows the market for CD players. In 1983, when CD players were first manufactured, very few producers made them and the supply was small. The supply curve was S_0. In 1983, there weren't many titles on CDs and the demand for CD players was small. The demand curve was D_0. The quantities supplied and demanded in 1983 were equal at Q_0, and the price was $1,100 (1994 dollars). As the technology for making CD players improved and as more and more factories began to produce CD players, the supply increased by a large amount and the supply curve shifted rightward from S_0 to S_1. At the same time, increases in incomes, a decrease in the price of CDs, and an increase in the number of titles on CDs increased the demand for CD players. But the increase in demand was much smaller than the increase in supply. The demand curve shifted rightward from D_0 to D_1. With the new demand curve D_1 and the new supply curve S_1, the equilibrium price fell to $170 in 1994 and the quantity increased to Q_1. The large increase in supply combined with a smaller increase in demand resulted in an increase in the quantity of CD players and a dramatic fall in the price. Figure 4.13(a) shows the CD player price slide.

A Price Rocket: Health Care   Figure 4.13(b) shows the market for health-care services. In 1980, the supply curve for health-care services was S_0. Advances in medical technology have greatly increased the range and complexity of conditions that can be treated and have increased the supply of health-care services. But large increases in doctors' compensation and costs have escalated the cost of providing health care and have decreased supply. The net change in supply resulting from these two opposing forces has been an increase. The supply curve has shifted rightward from S_0 to S_1. At the same time that supply increased by a relatively modest amount, the demand for health care increased enormously. Some of the increase resulted from higher incomes, some from an aging population, and some from a demand for newly available treatments. The combination of these influences on demand resulted in the demand curve shifting from D_0 to D_1. The combined effect of a large increase in demand and a small increase in supply was an increase in the quantity from Q_0 to Q_1 and an increase in price from 100 (an index number) in 1980 to 167 in 1998. Figure 4.13(b) shows the health-care price rocket.

A Price Roller Coaster: Bananas   Figure 4.13(c) shows the market for bananas. The demand for bananas—curve D—does not change much over the years. But the supply of bananas, which depends mainly on the weather, fluctuates between S_0 and S_1. With good growing conditions, the supply curve is S_1. With bad growing conditions, supply decreases and the supply curve is S_0. As a consequence of fluctuations in supply, the quantity fluctuates between Q_0 and Q_1. The price of bananas fluctuates between 33 cents per pound (1995 cents), the maximum price, and 20 cents per pound, the minimum price. Figure 4.13(c) shows the banana price roller coaster.

The Invisible Hand   Adam Smith said that each buyer and seller in a market "is led by an invisible hand to promote an end which was no part of his intention." What did he mean? He meant that when each one of us makes decisions to buy or sell to achieve the best outcome for ourselves and when our decisions are coordinated in free markets, we end up achieving the best outcome for everyone.

Although markets are amazing instruments, it turns out that they do not always work quite as perfectly as Adam Smith imagined. If you go on to study *micro*economics, you will discover the conditions under which markets are efficient and why they sometimes fail to achieve the best possible outcome for everyone. If you go on to study *macro*economics, you will discover the reasons why the market economy produces fluctuations in output and employment and sometimes creates persistent unemployment.

◆ You now know the basic theory of demand and supply. By using this theory, you can explain past price and quantity fluctuations and make predictions about future fluctuations. *Reading Between the Lines* on pp. 80–81 shows you the theory in action in the market for oranges. You will see many news articles that you can better understand by using your knowledge of demand and supply. Watch for stories about frosts, droughts, and floods and their effects on the prices of many crops and other items.

FIGURE 4.13

Price Slide, Rocket, and Roller Coaster

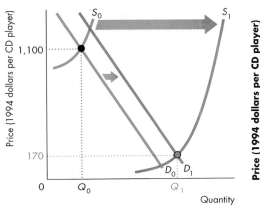

(a) Price slide: CD players

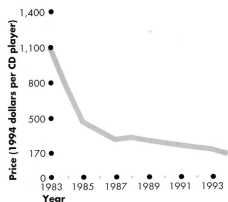

A large increase in the supply of CD players, from S_0 to S_1 combined with a small increase in demand, from D_0 to D_1, resulted in an increase in the quantity of CD players bought and sold from Q_0 to Q_1. The average price of CD players fell from $1,100 in 1983 to $170 in 1994—a price slide.

Source: U.S. Bureau of the Census, Statistical Abstract of the United States: 1994 (114th edition). Washington, D.C., 1994.

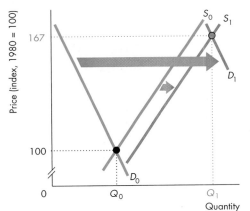

(b) Price rocket: health care

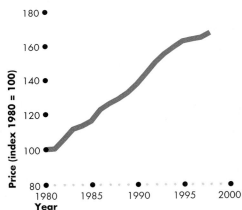

A large increase in demand for health care, from D_0 to D_1, combined with a small increase in the supply, from S_0 to S_1, has resulted in an increase in the quantity of health care, from Q_0 to Q_1 and a rise in the price of health care from 100 in 1980 to 167 in 1998—a price rocket.

Source: Economic Report of the President, 1999.

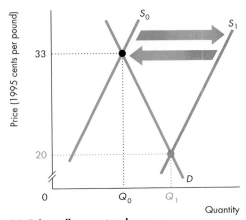

(c) Price roller coaster: bananas

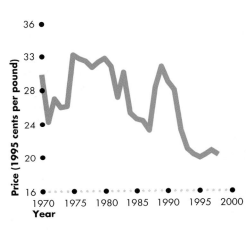

The demand for bananas remains constant at D. But supply fluctuates between S_0 and S_1. As a result, the price of bananas has fluctuated between 20 cents per pound and 33 cents per pound—a price roller coaster.

Source: International Financial Statistics, International Monetary Fund, Washington, D.C., February, 1999.

Demand and Supply: The Price of Oranges

U S A   T O D A Y ,   JANUARY 4, 1999

Orange Prices Start to Rise after Calif. Freeze

LOS ANGELES—Consumers will pay dramatically more for fresh oranges, the result of a killer freeze in California that has already doubled wholesale prices.

The coming price rise is the last in a string of calamities that struck agriculture in 1998.

California navel oranges "will be in very limited quantities," and "what is available will be higher in price," said Paul Bernish, spokesman for Kroger, the nation's largest supermarket chain.

"So far, at least, price increases for citrus products have not been passed along to consumers," Bernish said.

Food Lion, with 1,208 stores mostly in the Southeast, said store prices on fresh oranges will rise 20% to 30% this week, less than the 100% increase it's paying at wholesale. "We're trying to absorb as much of that (the price increase) as we can," spokeswoman Chris Ahearn said.

California supplies about 80% of the nation's eating oranges and lemons. Four days of freezing temperatures in the Central Valley last month caused about $530 million in damage. ...

For fresh oranges, the prices are already rising. A standard 37½-pound box of oranges is selling at wholesale for $20 to $24 depending on size and quality, double the price before the frost, the California Farm Bureau Federation reported. ...

Essence of the Story

- In December 1998, four days of freezing temperatures destroyed a large part of the California crop of navel oranges.

- During early January 1999, the wholesale price of navel oranges doubled.

- At the same time, the store price of navel oranges increased by 20 percent to 30 percent.

■ Orange growers sell their production to major supermarket chains in a **wholesale market**.

■ Supermarket chains sell oranges to consumers in a **retail market**.

■ A serious 4-day freeze in California wiped out a large quantity of navel oranges and led to a rise in their price. The wholesale price increased by more than the retail price.

■ Why did the retail price rise? Why did the wholesale price rise by a larger percentage than the retail price?

■ Figure 1 shows the wholesale market for California navel oranges. The demand curve is D. Before the freeze, the supply curve was S_{98}. The price was $11 a box, and 2 million boxes a week were bought.

■ In December 1998, freezing temperatures destroyed a large quantity of oranges and the supply of oranges decreased. The supply curve shifted leftward to S_{99}.

■ The price increased to $22 a box (a 100 percent increase, as reported in the news article).

■ The increase in price did not change demand. The demand curve did not shift. But the increase in price brought a *decrease in the quantity*

demanded, which is shown by a *movement along the demand curve.*

■ Figure 2 shows the retail market for California navel oranges. The demand curve is D. Before the freeze, the supply curve was S_{98}. The price was 50 cents a pound, and 2 million boxes a week were bought.

■ The decrease in supply shifted the supply curve leftward to S_{99}.

■ The price increased to 65 cents a pound (a 30 percent increase, as reported in the news article).

■ The wholesale price increased by a larger percentage than the retail price, and the profits of supermarkets were squeezed.

■ The percentage rise in the wholesale price exceeded the percentage rise in the retail price because of the way the quantity demanded responds to a price change.

■ A supermarket must stock navel oranges if it is to attract customers who want to buy the oranges even at a higher-than-normal price.

■ A supermarket that does not stock navel oranges loses customers, and its sales of a wide range of items decrease.

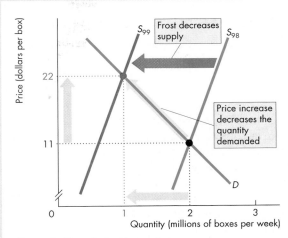

Figure 1 The wholesale market

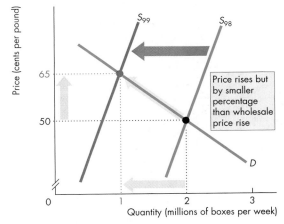

Figure 2 The retail market

■ So a relatively large price rise is needed to allocate the smaller quantity of oranges to the supermarkets.

■ Consumers have many alternatives to navel oranges. When the price of navel oranges rises, some consumers switch to grapefruit and other types of fruit and stop buying oranges. So the quantity of oranges demanded decreases sharply.

■ So a relatively small price rise is sufficient to allocate the smaller quantity of oranges to consumers.

■ In the news article, Chris Ahearn says that Food Lion is trying to absorb the price rise. But the forces of demand and supply prevent supermarkets from raising the retail price by as much as the rise in the wholesale price.

MATHEMATICAL NOTE
Demand, Supply, and Market Equilibrium

Demand Curve

The law of demand says that as the price of a good or service falls, the quantity demanded of it increases. We illustrate the law of demand by setting out a demand schedule, by drawing a graph of the demand curve, or by writing down an equation. When the demand curve is a straight line, a linear equation describes it. The equation that describes a downward-sloping demand curve is

$$P = a - bQ_D,$$

where P is the price and Q_D is the quantity demanded. The a and b are positive constants.

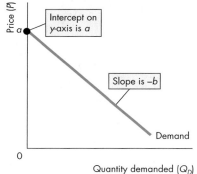

This equation tells us three things:
1. The price at which no one is willing to buy the good (Q_D is zero). That is, if the price is a, then the quantity demanded is zero. You can see the price a on the graph. It is the price at which the demand curve hits the y-axis—what we call the demand curve's "intercept on the y-axis."
2. That as the price falls, the quantity demanded increases. If Q_D is a positive number, then the price P must be less than a. And as Q_D gets larger, the price P becomes smaller. That is, as the quantity increases, the maximum price that buyers are willing to pay for the good falls.
3. The constant b tells us how fast the maximum price that someone is willing to pay for the good falls as the quantity increases. That is, the constant b tells us about the steepness of the demand curve. The equation tells us that the slope of the demand curve is $-b$.

Supply Curve

The law of supply says that as the price of a good or service rises, the quantity supplied of it increases. We illustrate the law of supply by setting out a supply schedule, by drawing a graph of the supply curve, or by writing down an equation. When the supply curve is a straight line, a linear equation describes the supply curve. The equation that describes an upward-sloping supply curve is

$$P = c + dQ_S,$$

where P is the price and Q_S the quantity supplied. The c and d are positive constants.

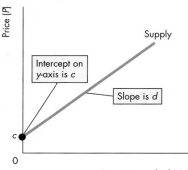

This equation tells us three things:
1. The price at which no one is willing to sell the good (Q_S is zero) That is, if the price is c, then the quantity supplied is zero. You can see the price c on the graph. It is the price at which the supply curve hits the y-axis—what we call the supply curve's "intercept on the y-axis."
2. That as the price rises, the quantity supplied increases. If Q_S is a positive number, then the price P must be greater than c. And as Q_S increases, the price P gets larger. That is, as the quantity increases, the minimum price that sellers are willing to accept rises.
3. The constant d tells us how fast the minimum price at which someone is willing to sell the good rises as the quantity increases. That is, the constant d tells us about the steepness of the supply curve. The equation tells us that the slope of the supply is d.

Market Equilibrium

Demand and supply determine market equilibrium. The figure shows the equilibrium price (P^*) and equilibrium quantity (Q^*) at the intersection of the demand curve and the supply curve.

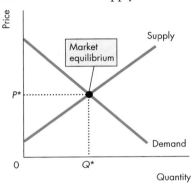

We can use the equations to find the equilibrium price and equilibrium quantity. The price of a good will adjust until the quantity demanded equals the quantity supplied. That is,

$$Q_D = Q_S.$$

So at the equilibrium price (P^*) and equilibrium quantity (Q^*),

$$Q_D = Q_S = Q^*.$$

To find the equilibrium price and equilibrium quantity:

First substitute Q^* for Q_D in the demand equation and Q^* for Q_S in the supply equation. Then the price is the equilibrium price (P^*), which gives

$$P^* = a - bQ^*,$$
$$P^* = c + dQ^*.$$

Notice that,

$$a - bQ^* = c + dQ^*$$

Now, solve for Q^*

$$a - c = bQ^* + dQ^*$$
$$a - c = (b + d)Q^*$$
$$Q^* = \frac{a - c}{b + d}.$$

To find the equilibrium price (P^*), substitute for Q^* in either the demand equation or the supply equation.

Using the demand equation,

$$P^* = a - b\left(\frac{a - c}{b + d}\right)$$
$$P^* = \frac{a(b + d) - b(a - c)}{b + d}$$
$$P^* = \frac{ad + bc}{b + d}.$$

Alternatively, using the supply equation,

$$P^* = c + d\left(\frac{a - c}{b + d}\right)$$
$$P^* = \frac{c(b + d) + d(a - c)}{b + d}$$
$$P^* = \frac{cb + da}{b + d}$$
$$P^* = \frac{ad + bc}{b + d}.$$

An Example

The demand for ice cream cones is
$$P = 800 - 2Q_D.$$
The supply of ice cream cones is
$$P = 200 + 1Q_S.$$
The price of a cone is expressed in cents, and the quantities are expressed in cones per day.

To find the equilibrium price (P^*) and equilibrium quantity (Q^*), substitute Q^* for Q_D and Q_S and P^* for P.

That is,
$$P^* = 800 - 2Q^*$$
$$P^* = 200 + 1Q^*$$
Now solve for Q^*:
$$800 - 2Q^* = 200 + 1Q^*$$
$$600 = 3Q^*$$
$$Q^* = 200$$

And
$$P^* = 800 - 2Q^*$$
$$= 800 - 2(200)$$
$$= 400$$

The equilibrium price is $4 a cone, and the equilibrium quantity is 200 cones per day.

SUMMARY

KEY POINTS

Price and Opportunity Cost (p. 62)

■ Opportunity cost is a relative price. We measure relative price by dividing the price of one good by the price (index) of a basket of all goods.

■ Demand and supply determines relative prices.

Demand (pp. 63–67)

■ Demand is the relationship between the quantity demanded of a good and its price when all other influences on buying plans remain the same.

■ The higher the price of a good, other things remaining the same, the smaller is the quantity demanded.

■ Demand depends on the prices of substitutes and complements, expected future prices, income, population, and preferences.

Supply (pp. 68–71)

■ Supply is the relationship between the quantity supplied of a good and its price when all other influences on selling plans remain the same.

■ The higher the price of a good, other things remaining the same, the greater is the quantity supplied.

■ Supply depends on the prices of resources used to produce a good, the prices of related goods produced, expected future prices, the number of producers, and technology.

Market Equilibrium (pp. 72–73)

■ At the equilibrium price, the quantity demanded equals the quantity supplied.

■ At prices above equilibrium, there is a surplus and the price falls.

■ At prices below equilibrium, there is a shortage and the price rises.

Predicting Changes in Price and Quantity
(pp. 74–79)

■ An increase in demand brings a rise in price and an increase in the quantity supplied. (A decrease in demand brings a fall in price and a decrease in the quantity supplied.)

■ An increase in supply brings a fall in price and an increase in the quantity demanded. (A decrease in supply brings a rise in price and a decrease in the quantity demanded.)

■ An increase in demand and an increase in supply bring an increased quantity but an ambiguous price change. An increase in demand and a decrease in supply raise the price and bring an ambiguous quantity change.

KEY FIGURES ◆

KEY TERMS

PROBLEMS

*1. What is the effect on the price of a tape and the quantity of tapes sold if:
   a. The price of a CD rises?
   b. The price of a Walkman rises?
   c. The supply of CD players increases?
   d. Consumers' incomes increase?
   e. Workers who make tapes get a pay raise?
   f. The price of a Walkman rises at the same time as the workers who make tapes get a pay raise?

2. What is the effect on the price of hotdogs and the quantity of hotdogs sold if:
   a. The price of a hamburger rises?
   b. The price of a hotdog bun rises?
   c. The supply of hotdog sausages increases?
   d. Consumers' incomes decrease?
   e. The wage rate of a hotdog seller increases?
   f. If the wage rate of the hotdog seller rises and at the same time prices of ketchup, mustard, and relish fall?

*3. Suppose that one of the following events occurs:
   a. The price of crude oil rises.
   b. The price of a car rises.
   c. All speed limits on highways are abolished.
   d. Robot technology cuts car production costs.
   Which of the above events increases or decreases (state which):
      (i) The demand for gasoline.
      (ii) The supply of gasoline.
      (iii) The quantity of gasoline demanded.
      (iv) The quantity of gasoline supplied.

4. Suppose that one of the following events occurs:
   a. The price of wool rises.
   b. The price of sweaters falls.
   c. A close substitute for wool is invented.
   d. A new high-speed loom is invented.
   Which of the above events increases or decreases (state which):
      (i) The demand for wool.
      (ii) The supply of wool.
      (iii) The quantity of wool demanded.
      (iv) The quantity of wool supplied.

*5. The figure illustrates the market for pizza.
   a. Label the curves in the figure.
   b. What are the equilibrium price of a pizza and the equilibrium quantity of pizza?

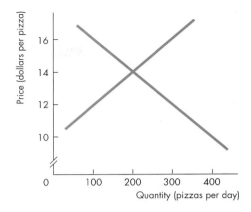

6. The figure illustrates market for bread.
   a. Label the curves in the figure.
   b. What are the equilibrium price of bread and the equilibrium quantity of bread?

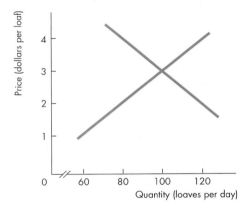

*7. The demand and supply schedules for gum are:

Price (cents per pack)	Quantity demanded	Quantity supplied
	(millions of packs a week)	
20	180	60
30	160	80
40	140	100
50	120	120
60	100	140
70	80	160
80	60	180

   a. What are the equilibrium price and equilibrium quantity of gum?
   b. If gum was 70 cents a pack, describe the situation in the gum market and explain what would happen to the price of gum.

8. The demand and supply schedules for potato chips are:

Price (cents per bag)	Quantity demanded	Quantity supplied
	(millions of bags per week)	
40	170	90
50	160	100
60	150	110
70	140	120
80	130	130
90	120	140
100	110	150
110	100	160

a. What are the equilibrium price and equilibrium quantity of potato chips?

b. If chips were 60 cents a bag, describe the situation in the market for potato chips and explain what would happen to the price of a bag of chips.

*9. In problem 7, suppose that a fire destroys some gum-producing factories and the supply of gum decreases by 40 million packs a week.

a. Has there been a shift in or a movement along the supply curve of gum?

b. Has there been a shift in or a movement along the demand curve for gum?

c. What is the new equilibrium price and quantity of gum?

10. In problem 8, suppose a new snack food comes onto the market and as a result the demand for potato chips decreases by 40 million bags per week.

a. Has there been a shift in or a movement along the supply curve of chips?

b. Has there been a shift in or a movement along the demand curve for chips?

c. What is the new equilibrium price and quantity of chips?

*11. In problem 9, suppose an increase in the teenage population increases the demand for gum by 40 million packs per week at the same time as the fire occurs. What is the new equilibrium price and quantity of gum?

12. In problem 10, suppose that a flood destroys several potato farms and as a result supply decreases by 20 million bags a week at the same time as the new snack food comes onto the market. What is the new equilibrium price and quantity of gum?

CRITICAL THINKING

1. After you have studied *Reading Between the Lines* on pp. 80–81, answer the following questions:

a. Why does the supply of oranges decrease but the demand for oranges not change? How can the demand not change when the quantity available decreases?

b. Explain to Chris Ahearn and Paul Bernish (the spokespeople for Food Lion and Kroger) why the retail price of oranges is out of their control. How would you explain the forces that determine the prices in both the wholesale market and the retail market?

c. Gray Davis, the governor of California, wants your advice on what to do about the effects of the freeze on the orange market. In particular, he wants to know what can be done to keep the price of oranges down and the incomes of the orange growers up. Write a brief report to Mr. Davis outlining his options, if he has any, or explaining why there is nothing he can do, if that is your opinion.

c. Use the links on the Parkin Web site and obtain the latest data on the quantities of oranges produced in the United States.

2. Use the links on the Parkin Web site and obtain data on the prices and quantities of wheat.

a. Make a figure similar to Fig. 1 on page 81 to illustrate the market for wheat in 1998.

b. Show the changes in demand and supply and the changes in the quantity demanded and the quantity supplied that are consistent with the price and quantity data.

3. Use the link on the Parkin Web site and read the story about the prices of millennium cruises.

a. Describe how the millennium changes the price of a cruise.

b. Use the demand and supply model to explain what happens to the price when there is an increase in demand and no change in supply.

c. What do you predict would happen to the price of a cruise if air fares to Australia and the South Pacific decreased?

d. What do you predict would happen to the price of a cruise if the price of oil increased?

Understanding How Markets Work

The Amazing Market

The chapter that you've just studied explain how markets work. The market is an amazing instrument. It enables people who have never met and who know nothing about each other to interact and do business. It also enables us to allocate our scarce resources to the uses that we value most highly. Markets can be very simple or highly organized. ◆ A simple market is one that the American historian Daniel J. Boorstin describes in *The Discoverers* (p. 161). In the late fourteenth century,

> The Muslim caravans that went southward from Morocco across the Atlas Mountains arrived after twenty days at the shores of the Senegal River. There the Moroccan traders laid out separate piles of salt, of beads from Ceutan coral, and cheap manufactured goods. Then they retreated out of sight. The local tribesmen, who lived in the strip mines where they dug their gold, came to the shore and put a heap of gold beside each pile of Moroccan goods. Then they, in turn, went out of view, leaving the Moroccan traders either to take the gold offered for a particular pile or to reduce the pile of their merchandise to suit the offered price in gold. Once again the Moroccan traders withdrew, and the process went on. By this system of commercial etiquette, the Moroccans collected their gold.

An organized market is the New York Stock Exchange, which trades many millions of stocks each day. Another is an auction at which the U.S. government sells rights to broadcasters and cellular telephone companies for the use of the airwaves. ◆ All of these markets determine the prices at which exchanges take place and enable both buyers and sellers to benefit. ◆ Everything and anything that can be exchanged is traded in markets. There are markets for goods and services; for resources such as labor, capital, and raw materials; for dollars, pounds, and yen; for goods to be delivered now and for goods to be delivered in the future. Only the imagination places limits on what can be traded in markets. ◆ The chapter that you've just studied begins by explaining the crucial distinction between a money price and a relative price. This distinction runs right through the macroeconomics that you will meet in the rest of this book. The chapter then explains the laws of demand and supply. You have discovered that these forces make prices adjust to coordinate buying plans and selling plans. You have also learned how the forces of demand and supply make some prices rise, some fall, and some rise and fall in a price roller coaster ride. What you have learned about demand and supply is fundamental to your entire study of economics. It will help you to understand price movements in the world around you. And it will help you in your study of *macroeconomics*. ◆ The laws of demand and supply were discovered during the nineteenth century by some remarkable economists. We conclude our study of demand and supply and markets by looking at the lives and times of some of these economists and by talking one of today's most influential economists who studies and creates sophisticated auction markets.

Discovering the Laws of Demand and Supply

Alfred Marshall

(1842–1924) grew up in an England that was being transformed by the railroad and by the expansion of manufacturing. Mary Paley was one of Marshall's students at Cambridge, and when Alfred and Mary married, in 1877, celibacy rules barred Alfred from continuing to teach at Cambridge. By 1884, with more liberal rules, the Marshalls returned to Cambridge, where Alfred became Professor of Political Economy.

Many others had a hand in refining the theory of demand and supply, but the first thorough and complete statement of the theory as we know it today was set out by Alfred Marshall, with the acknowledged help of Mary Paley Marshall. Published in 1890, this monumental treatise, The Principles of Economics, *became the textbook on economics on both sides of the Atlantic for almost half a century. Marshall was an outstanding mathematician, but he kept mathematics and even diagrams in the background. His supply and demand diagram appears only in a footnote.*

"The forces to be dealt with are . . . so numerous, that it is best to take a few at a time. . . . Thus we begin by isolating the primary relations of supply, demand, and price"

ALFRED MARSHALL
The Principles of Economics

The Issues

The laws of demand and supply that you studied in Chapter 4 were discovered during the 1830s by Antoine-Augustin Cournot (1801–1877), a professor of mathematics at the University of Lyon, France. Although Cournot was the first to use demand and supply, it was the development

and expansion of the railroads during the 1850s that gave the newly emerging theory its first practical applications. Railroads then were at the cutting edge of technology just as airlines are today. And as in the airline industry today, competition among the railroads was fierce.

Dionysius Lardner (1793–1859), an Irish professor of philosophy at the University of London, used demand and supply to show railroad companies how they could increase their profits by cutting rates on long-distance business on which competition was fiercest and by raising rates on short-haul business on which they had less to fear from other transportation suppliers. Today, economists use the principles that Lardner worked out during the 1850s to calculate the freight rates and passenger fares that will give airlines the largest possible profit. And the rates calculated have a lot in common with the railroad rates of the nineteenth century. On local routes on which there is little competition, fares per mile are highest, and on long-distance routes on which the airlines compete fiercely, fares per mile are lowest.

Known satirically among scientists of the day as "Dionysius Diddler," Lardner worked on an amazing range of problems from astronomy to railway engineering to economics. A colorful character, he would have been a regular guest of David Letterman if late-night talk shows had been around in the 1850s. Lardner visited the École des Ponts et Chaussées (School of Bridges and Roads) in Paris and must have learned a great deal from Jules Dupuit.

In France, Jules Dupuit (1804–1866), a French engineer/economist, used demand to calculate the benefits from building a bridge and, once the bridge was built, for calculating the toll to charge for its use. His work was the forerunner of what is today called *cost-benefit analysis.* Working with the principles invented by Dupuit, economists today calculate the costs and benefits of highways and airports, dams, and power stations.

Then

Dupuit used the law of demand to determine whether a bridge or canal would be valued enough by its users to justify the cost of building it. Lardner first worked out the relationship between the cost of production and supply and used demand and supply theory to explain the costs, prices, and profits of railroad operations. He also used the theory to discover ways of increasing revenue by raising rates on short-haul business and lowering them on long-distance freight.

Now

Today, using the same principles that Dupuit devised, economists calculate whether the benefits of expanding airports and air-traffic control facilities are sufficient to cover their costs. Airline companies use the principles developed by Lardner to set their prices and to decide when to offer "seat sales." Like the railroads before them, the airlines charge a high price per mile on short flights, for which they face little competition, and a low price per mile on long flights, for which competition is fierce.

Markets do an amazing job. And the laws of demand and supply help us to understand how markets work. But in some situations, a market must be designed and institutions must be created to enable the market to operate. In recent years, economists have begun to use their tools to design and create markets. And one of the chief architects of new style markets is Paul Milgrom, whom you can meet on the following pages.

Paul R. Milgrom

is Professor of Economics at Stanford University and an Associate Editor of the American Economic Review, *the leading journal that publishes economic research. He is founder and president of Market Design, Inc., a young company that designs new auction and market rules for businesses and governments. Born in Detroit, Michigan, in 1948, Professor Milgrom was an undergraduate at the University of Michigan and a graduate student at Stanford University (Ph.D. 1979). He taught at Northwestern University and Yale University before returning to Stanford in 1987.*

Professor Milgrom is an economic theorist, which means that he uses mathematical techniques to study economic behavior. His work on auctions has been especially influential and has found practical applications in auctioning items ranging from radio spectrum (used in paging and cellular telephones) to mining rights.

Michael Parkin talked with Professor Milgrom about his work and how it connects with the theory of demand and supply developed by Cournot and Marshall.

Paul R. Milgrom

Professor Milgrom, how did you become an economist?

I came into the house of economics through an unmarked side door, not knowing where I was until I was well inside. The main entrance is through a graduate degree in economics, but I have no university degree in economics at any level. My undergraduate studies were in mathematics and statistics, and my graduate studies were in business. It was in graduate school that I stumbled across a brilliant study of auction theory by William Vickrey—work for which he was awarded the Nobel Prize 21 years later, in 1996. Vickrey's work surprised me and convinced me that mathematical analysis could help me to understand auctions and could even point the way to new, improved types of auctions.

Auctions, like all market arrangements, bring buyers and sellers together. Doesn't the supply and demand model explain how auctions work?

The supply and demand model is the economist's workhorse for day-to-day market analysis. It provides a wonderful way to summarize some of the main factors affecting prices and quantities and to explain how prices guide important choices.

But the model is silent about how the rules that govern trade are set or how they affect economic outcomes. Also, it is not very helpful for thinking about technology decisions that can have a huge impact on economic outcomes. For example, the way standards are set for cellular telephone systems determines whether the same phone will work on different systems in different parts of the nation and the world. In Europe, a single standard allows a consumer to go from country to country and still have a working telephone. In the United States, where no single standard exists, a consumer may find that her telephone fails to operate even with the system in the next town.

Obviously, that failure depresses the sales of cellular phone service, although it has nothing to do with the consumer preferences for communications or with the cost or availability of the cellular telephone technology.

So institutions influence prices and quantities and the kinds of plans that people make. And sometimes, institutions such as standards-setting bodies can solve problems that a market guided only by prices can't deal with effectively.

Let's return to auctions. What is auction theory? How does it relate to supply and demand?

Auctions are institutions that determine the prices and other terms at which buyers and sellers will trade. Auction theory explains how the rules of an auction affect its outcome.

Sellers want auctions that generate the highest price. Buyers want auctions that generate the lowest price. Auction houses want auctions that balance the interests of buyers and sellers and ensure a continuing flow of customers for future auctions.

In the U.S. auctions of radio spectrum, the government's main objective was to assign spectrum efficiently.

The supply and demand model does not include a place for auction rules. It supposes that buyers and sellers know all the relevant prices

when they make their decisions. In reality, that is not always true.

Often in an auction, bidders must make a choice without knowing all the relevant prices.

What are the main types of auctions and why are there so many different types? Why isn't one type best?

An auction may be either sealed or open. In a sealed auction, the bids are written and the best bids win. In open auctions, there is usually a sequence of bids with each bidder getting an opportunity to respond to the bids of others. Within these two auction types, there is great variety.

The sealed bid has two advantages over the open auction. First, the bidders don't have to be gathered together physically at one time to conduct the auction. In bidding at a used car warehouse, for example, the bidders (usually used car dealers) examine the cars at times that are convenient for themselves and leave behind a sealed envelope with their bids. There is a deadline for bids. When the deadline passes, the bids are opened and the bidders are notified of the results.

Second, it is harder for bidders to collude and depress the price received by the seller. With sealed bids, a member of a ring of buyers who agree to keep prices low might be tempted to submit a slightly higher bid and take advantage of the low bids by other ring members. The temptation to cheat in an open auction is much less, because the other ring members can punish the cheater by driving up the price when the member violates the agreement.

Open auctions have advantages, too. When a single item is being sold and price is the key factor, an open auction eliminates the guesswork of sealed bids. The bidder with the highest value can outbid the competitors. Also, when a large number of items are to be sold and the bidders are present for an open auction, the items can be sold quickly in sequence.

What advances have we made in auction theory?

Since Vickrey initiated auction theory some 35 years ago, we have improved our ability to predict how different types of auctions perform. And we've learned how to design auctions with particular objectives in mind. We even have developed mathematical descriptions of "optimal auctions," which are theoretically the best auction designs for achieving particular objectives.

We still haven't implemented an optimal auction in a real situation, but a small group of economists have used auction theory to design significant new auctions. Recently, I was among a group that proposed a brand-new auction design called a "simultaneous ascending auction." This type of auction is an open auction of many different items, all of which can be bid for simultaneously.

The U.S. Federal Communications Commission used such an auction to sell licenses to use radio spectrum for telecommunications services. The auction was the largest in history and generated gross revenues of $24 billion.

More important to me, the new auction design performed as predicted and led to much more efficient license assignments than other kinds of auctions could have achieved.

The radio spectrum auctions have shaped competition in wireless communications and have determined which firms will operate businesses in which parts of the country.

Why did selling the frequency spectrum need a simultaneous ascending bid auction? And how does such an auction work?
Bidders want to acquire licenses to provide a wireless communications service covering certain geographic areas. A bidder might want to use one of two available bands of spectrum to provide services in, say, Los Angeles County. If either spectrum band will do and the bidder needs just one, then the licenses to use these bands are economic substitutes.

But a bidder might also be willing to pay more to acquire a license covering southern California if he or she could also acquire a license covering northern California. These licenses are complements. One reason why licenses might be complements is that the two areas can share some facilities and lower costs. Another reason is that an owner of both licenses might be able to provide a more valuable service to consumers and so charge a higher price for it.

The simultaneous ascending bid auction handles both situations well. In such an auction, the bid-

ding for the northern and southern California licenses, and in fact *all* the licenses, goes on at the same time, and bidding remains open on all the individual licenses until bidding for all licenses is complete. In an auction like this, a bidder who is interested in the California licenses can bid for both and can cease bidding when the combination price gets too high. This is a far from perfect solution, but it is much better than any of the traditional alternatives and seems to have performed well in the sale of spectrum licenses in the United States.

What differences are today's information technologies making to the problems of auction design?
Without modern information technology, the simultaneous ascending auction of radio spectrum licenses couldn't have been conducted. In a large version of the auction, both the auctioneer and the bidders need to keep track of bids on hundreds or even thousands of licenses simultaneously. Software programs have been created to facilitate submitting bids and tracking the auction results.

> The best economists are technically able, curious about the world, concerned about human welfare, flexible in their perspectives, and dedicated to clear, analytical thinking.

How do you advise today's undergraduate to prepare for a career in economics? What besides economics should he or she study?
The best economists are technically able, curious about the world, concerned about human welfare, flexible in their perspectives, and dedicated to clear, analytical thinking. Courses can help with some of these things. Students can certainly learn mathematical and statistical concepts as undergraduates.

To enjoy a career as an economist, you have to go beyond the academic abstractions and incorporate elements that excite you. Many students study economics because of their specific social concerns, for example, wanting to understand the sources of poverty in their home countries and to discern the paths out of poverty. For those students, I recommend reading widely and studying other social sciences to learn about the culture and politics of poverty and the kinds of barriers they create to good economic policies. There are so many ways to incorporate one's pleasures in an economics career! I have friends and colleagues who've studied the economics of sports, of wine prices, of the performing arts, and of the Internet. By weaving their personal and professional interests together, they eliminate the sharp divide between their career and their leisure. These are the folks I hold up as role models.

Chapter 5

A First Look at Macroeconomics

During the past 100 years, the quantity of goods and services produced in the nation's farms, factories, shops, and offices has expanded more than twentyfold. As a result, we have a much higher living standard than our grandparents had. Will production always expand? Will your world be more prosperous than today's? ◆ For most of us, a high standard of living means finding a good job. What kind of job will you find when you graduate? Will you have lots of choice, or will you face a labor market with a high unemployment rate in which jobs are hard to find? ◆ A high standard of living means being able to afford to buy life's necessities and some fun. If prices rise too quickly, some people get left behind and must trim what they buy. Prices have increased slowly over the past few years. But can we count on them rising

What Will Your World Be Like?

slowly in the future? What will the dollar buy next year? What will it buy in 10 years when you are paying off your student loan? And what will it buy in 50 years when you are spending your life's savings in retirement? ◆ Every year from 1970 to 1997, the government has spent more than it has raised in taxes. And most years, we have imported more goods and services from the rest of the world than we have exported to it. We have experienced large and persistent government and international deficits. How will these deficits affect your future? ◆ To keep production expanding and prevent an economic slowdown, the federal government and the Federal Reserve Board—the nation's financial managers—take policy actions. What kinds of actions do they take? How do their actions influence production, jobs, prices, and the ability of Americans to compete in the global marketplace?

◆ These are the questions of macroeconomics. The macroeconomic events through which we are now living are tumultuous and exciting. With what you learn in these chapters, you will be able to understand these events, the policy challenges they bring, and the political debate they stir. You will be able to prepare yourself better for your world, the economic world that you will enter when you graduate and in which you will earn your living.

After studying this chapter, you will be able to:

■ **Describe the origins of macroeconomics and the problems it deals with**

■ **Describe the long-term trends and short-term fluctuations in economic growth, unemployment, inflation, and government and international deficits**

■ **Explain why economic growth, unemployment, inflation, and deficits matter**

■ **Identify the macroeconomic policy challenges and describe the tools available for meeting them**

Origins and Issues of Macroeconomics

ECONOMISTS BEGAN TO STUDY LONG-TERM economic growth, inflation, and international payments as long ago as the 1750s, and this work was the origin of macroeconomics. But modern macroeconomics did not emerge until the **Great Depression**, a decade (1929–1939) of high unemployment and stagnant production throughout the world economy. In the Depression's worst year, 1933, the production of U.S. farms, factories, shops, and offices was only 70 percent of its 1929 level and 25 percent of the labor force was unemployed. These were years of human misery on a scale that is hard to imagine today. They were also years of extreme pessimism about the ability of the market economy to work properly. Many people believed that private ownership, free markets, and democratic political institutions could not survive.

The science of economics had no solutions to the Great Depression. The major alternative system of central planning and socialism seemed increasingly attractive. It was in this climate of economic depression and political and intellectual turmoil that modern macroeconomics emerged with the publication in 1936 of John Maynard Keynes' *The General Theory of Employment, Interest, and Money* (see p. 466).

Short-Term Versus Long-Term Goals

Keynes' theory was that depression and high unemployment result from insufficient private spending and that to cure these problems, the government must increase its spending. Keynes' focused primarily on the *short term*. He wanted to cure an immediate problem almost regardless of the *long-term* consequences of the cure. "In the long run," said Keynes, "we're all dead."

But Keynes believed that after his cure for depression had restored the economy to a normal condition, the long-term problems of inflation and slow economic growth would return. And he suspected that his cure for depression, increased government spending, might trigger inflation and might lower the long-term growth rate of production. With a lower long-term growth rate, the economy would create fewer jobs. If this outcome did occur, a policy aimed at lowering unemployment in the short run might end up increasing it in the long run.

By the late 1960s and through the 1970s, Keynes' predictions became a reality. Inflation increased, economic growth slowed down, and in some countries, unemployment became persistently high. The causes of these developments are complex. But they point to an inescapable conclusion: The long-term problems of inflation, slow growth, and persistent unemployment and the short-term problems of depression and economic fluctuations intertwine and are most usefully studied together. So although macroeconomics was reborn during the Great Depression, it has now returned to its older tradition. Today, macroeconomics studies long-term economic growth and inflation as well as short-term business fluctuations and unemployment.

The Road Ahead

There is no unique way to study macroeconomics. Because its rebirth was a product of depression, the common practice for many years was to pay most attention to short-term output fluctuations and unemployment but to never completely lose sight of the long-term issues. When a rapid inflation emerged during the 1970s, this topic returned to prominence. During the 1980s, when long-term growth slowed in the United States and other rich industrial countries but exploded in East Asia, economists redirected their energy toward economic growth. During the 1990s, as information technologies continue to shrink the globe, the international dimension of macroeconomics has become more prominent. The result of these developments is that modern macroeconomics is a broad subject that studies all the issues we've just identified: long-term economic growth, unemployment, and inflation. It also studies two new problems: the government budget and international deficits.

Over the past 40 years, economists have developed a clearer understanding of the forces that determine macroeconomic performance and have devised policies that they hope will improve this performance. Your main goal is to become familiar with the theories of macroeconomics and the policies they make possible. To set you on your path toward this goal, we're going to take a first look at economic growth, unemployment, inflation, and surpluses and deficits and learn why these macroeconomic phenomena merit our attention.

Economic Growth

YOUR PARENTS ARE RICHER THAN YOUR GRAND-parents were when they were young. But are you going to be richer than your parents? And are your children going to be richer than you? The answers depend on the rate of economic growth.

Economic growth is the expansion of the economy's production possibilities. It can be pictured as an outward shift of the production possibility frontier (*PPF*)—see Chapter 3, pp. 43–44.

We measure economic growth by the increase in real gross domestic product. **Real gross domestic product** (also called **real GDP**) is the value of the total production of all the nation's farms, factories, shops, and offices linked back to the prices of a single year. Real GDP in the United States is currently linked back to the prices of 1992 (called 1992 dollars). We link back to the dollar prices of a single year to eliminate the influence of *inflation*—the increase in prices—and determine how much production has grown from one year to another. (Real GDP is explained more fully in Chapter 6 on pp. 118–121.)

Real GDP is not a perfect measure of total production because it does not include everything that is produced. It excludes the things we produce for ourselves at home (preparing meals, doing laundry, house painting, gardening, and so on). It also excludes production that people hide to avoid taxes or because it is illegal—the underground economy. But despite its shortcomings, real GDP is the best measure of total production available. Let's see what it tells us about economic growth in the United States.

Economic Growth in the United States

Figure 5.1 shows real GDP in the United States since 1960 and highlights two features of economic growth:

■ The growth of potential GDP
■ Fluctuations of real GDP around potential GDP

The Growth of Potential GDP   When all the economy's resources are fully employed, the value of production is called **potential GDP**. Real GDP fluctuates around potential GDP, and the rate of long-term economic growth is measured by the growth rate of potential GDP. It is shown by the steepness of the potential GDP line (the black line) in Fig. 5.1.

During the 1960s, real GDP grew at an unusually rapid rate of 4.4 percent a year. But the growth rate of output per person slowed during the 1970s, a phenomenon called the **productivity growth slowdown**. Real GDP began to grow more rapidly during the late 1980s and through the 1990s. But the high growth rate of the 1960s did not return.

Why did the productivity growth slowdown occur? This question is controversial. One possible cause is a sharp rise in the relative price of energy. How this factor might have slowed productivity growth is explored in Chapter 11 on pp. 234. Whatever its cause, the productivity growth slowdown means that we all have smaller incomes today than we would have had if the economy had continued to grow at its 1960s rate.

Let's now look at GDP fluctuations.

FIGURE 5.1

Economic Growth in the United States

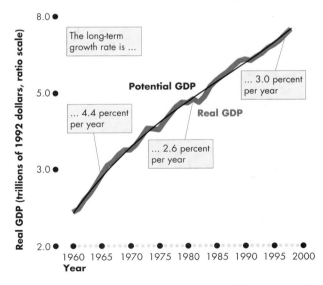

The long-term economic growth rate, measured by the growth of potential GDP, was 4.4 percent a year during the 1960s but slowed to 2.6 percent a year during the 1970s. Growth speeded up again during the 1980s and 1990s but did not return to its 1960s rate. Real GDP fluctuates around potential GDP.

Source: U.S. Department of Commerce, *National Income and Product Accounts of the United States.*

Fluctuations Around Potential GDP   Real GDP fluctuates around potential GDP in a business cycle. A **business cycle** is the periodic but irregular up-and-down movement in production. It is measured by fluctuations in real GDP around potential GDP. When real GDP is less than potential GDP, some resources are underused. For example, some labor is unemployed and capital is underutilized. When real GDP is greater than potential GDP, resources are being *over*used. Many people work longer hours than they are willing to put up with in the long run, capital is worked so intensively that it is not maintained in prime working order, delivery times lengthen, bottlenecks occur, and backorders increase.

Business cycles are not regular, predictable, or repeating cycles like the phases of the moon. Their timing changes unpredictably. But cycles do have some things in common. Every business cycle has two phases:

1. A recession
2. An expansion

and two turning points:

1. A peak
2. A trough

Figure 5.2 shows the most recent business cycle in the United States. A **recession** is a period during which real GDP decreases—the growth rate of real GDP is negative—for at least two successive quarters. The most recent recession began in the third quarter of 1990 and ended in the first quarter of 1991. An **expansion** is a period during which real GDP increases. The most recent expansion began in the second quarter of 1991 and was still in progress during 1999. If this expansion continues through January 2000, it will become the longest expansion on record. An earlier expansion ended with the onset of recession in the second quarter of 1990.

When a business cycle expansion ends and a recession begins, the turning point is called a *peak*. The most recent peak occurred in the second quarter of 1990. When a business cycle recession ends and a recovery begins, the turning point is called a *trough*. The most recent trough occurred in the first quarter of 1991.

FIGURE 5.2

The Most Recent U.S. Business Cycle

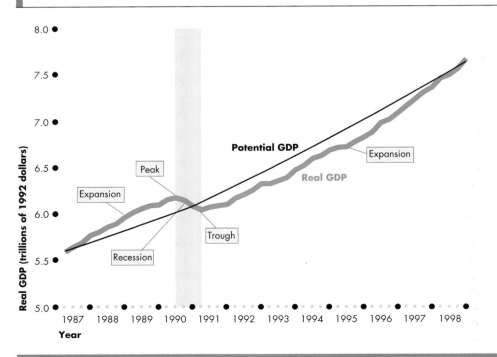

A business cycle has two phases: recession and expansion. The most recent recession (highlighted) ran from the third quarter of 1990 through the first quarter of 1991. Then a new expansion began in the second quarter of 1991. A business cycle has two turning points, a peak and a trough. In the most recent business cycle, the peak occurred in the second quarter of 1990 and the trough occurred in the first quarter of 1991.

The Recent Recession in Historical Perspective

The recession of 1990–1991 seemed severe while we were passing through it, but compared with earlier recessions, it was mild. You can see how mild it was by looking at Fig. 5.3, which shows a longer history of U.S. economic growth. The biggest decrease in real GDP occurred during the Great Depression of the 1930s. A large decrease also occurred in 1946 and 1947, immediately after World War II. In more recent times, severe recessions occurred during the mid-1970s, following oil price hikes by the Organization of Petroleum Exporting Countries (OPEC), and during the early 1980s.

Each of these economic downturns was more severe than that in 1990–1991. But you can see that the Great Depression was much more severe than anything that followed it. This episode was so extreme that we don't call it a recession. We call it a *depression*.

This last truly great depression occurred before governments started taking policy actions to stabilize the economy. It also occurred before the birth of modern macroeconomics. Is the absence of another great depression a sign that macroeconomics has contributed to economic stability? Some people believe it

is. Others doubt it. We'll evaluate these opinions on a number of occasions in this book.

We've looked at real GDP growth and fluctuations in the United States. But is the U.S. experience typical? Do other countries share our experience? Let's see whether they do.

Economic Growth Around the World

A country might have a rapid growth rate of real GDP, but it might also have a rapid population growth rate. To compare growth rates over time and across countries, we use the growth rate of real GDP *per person*. Real GDP per person is real GDP divided by the population. For example, U.S. real GDP in 1998 was $7,550 billion, and the population of the United States was 271.8 million. So U.S. real GDP per person was $7,550 billion divided by 271.8 million, which equals $27,778.

Figure 5.4 shows real GDP per person between 1962 and 1998 for the world's three largest economies: the United States, Japan, and Germany.

FIGURE 5.3

Long-Term Economic Growth in the United States

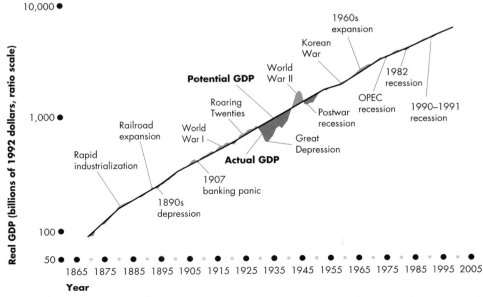

The thin black line shows potential GDP. Along this line, real GDP grew at an average rate of 3.3 percent a year between 1870 and 1994. The blue areas show when real GDP was above potential GDP, and the red areas show when it was below potential GDP. During some periods, such as World War II, real GDP expanded quickly. During other periods, such as the Great Depression and more recently in 1975 (following the OPEC oil price hike), 1982, and 1990–1991, real GDP declined.

Sources: 1869–1928, Christina D. Romer, "The Prewar Business Cycle Reconsidered: New Estimates of Gross National Product, 1869–1908," *Journal of Political Economy* 97, (1989) 1–37. 1929–1996, U.S. Department of Commerce, *National Income and Product Accounts of the United States.*

In these countries, four features of the paths of real GDP per person stand out:

- Similar 1970s growth slowdowns
- Similar business cycles before 1990
- Different business cycles in 1990s
- Different long-term growth trends

Similar 1970s Growth Slowdowns   U. S. real GDP per person grew at a rate of 2.9 percent a year from 1960 through 1973, but slowed to 1.3 percent a year between 1974 and 1988. For the same periods, Germany's growth slowed from 3.5 percent a year to 2 percent a year and Japan's growth slowed from 8.5 percent a year to 3.1 percent a year.

Similar Business Cycles Before 1990   Each of the three big economies had an expansion running from the early or mid-1960s through 1973, a recession from 1973 to 1975, an expansion through 1979, another recession in the early 1980s, and a long expansion through the rest of the 1980s.

Different Business Cycles in 1990s   The 1990s saw the United States in a long and strong business cycle expansion. But the decade brought severe recession in Japan and only moderate expansion in Germany. This divergence of business cycle experience is relatively uncommon and creates a concern that recession in Japan and the rest of Asia might spread.

Different Long-Term Growth Trends   Perhaps the most striking feature of Fig. 5.4 is the variation in the long-term growth rates of the three big economies. In 1960, real GDP per person in the United States was 50 percent greater than that in Germany and more than three times that of Japan.

During the 1960s, Japan's production streaked upward like a rocket departing Cape Canaveral. When U.S. long-term growth of real GDP per person was 2.9 percent a year, Germany's was 3.5 percent a year, and Japan's was an astonishing 8.5 percent a year. The differences in long-term growth trends survived the productivity growth slowdown of the 1970s. But Japan's economic growth disappeared in the 1990s.

FIGURE 5.4
Economic Growth in the Three Largest Economies

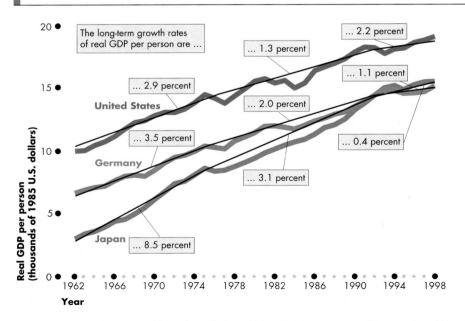

Economic growth in three large economies, the United States, Germany, and Japan, has followed a similar pattern. The growth rate in all three countries slowed during the 1970s, and each country has had similar business cycles. But Japan has grown fastest, and Germany too has grown faster than the United States.

Sources: The data for 1960 through 1992 are from "The Penn World Table," *Quarterly Journal of Economics,* May 1991, pp. 327–368. New computer disk supplement (Mark 5.6a). The data use comparable international relative prices converted to 1985 U.S. dollars. The data for 1993–1998 are from International Monetary Fund, *World Economic Outlook,* Washington, D.C., October 1998, p. 145.

Because it achieved such a high growth rate before 1990, Japan narrowed the gap between its own real GDP per person and that of the United States and it overtook Germany. But Japan's slow growth of the 1990s reversed these changes. During the 1990s, its real GDP per person fell below Germany's and fell further behind that of the United States.

Figure 5.5 compares the growth of the U.S. economy with that of several other countries and regions since 1980. Among the advanced economies (the red bars), the European Union has grown the slowest and the other advanced economies have grown fastest. Among the developing economies (the green bars) the most rapid growth has occurred in Asia, where the average growth rate has exceeded 7 percent a year. The slowest growing developing countries are in Africa and the Western Hemisphere (Central and South America). The transition economies (purple bars) have grown slowest. These are countries such as Russia and the other countries of Central Europe that are making a transition from a state managed economy to a market economy. Production has been shrinking severely in these countries.

World average growth (the blue bar) has been just over 3 percent a year. The U.S. growth rate is slightly below the world average and much below the growth rates that the developing economies of Asia have achieved.

Benefits and Costs of Economic Growth

What are the benefits and costs of economic growth? Does it matter whether the long-term growth rate slows as it did during the 1970s?

The main benefit of long-term economic growth is expanded consumption possibilities, including more health care for the poor and elderly, more cancer and AIDS research, more space research and exploration, better roads, and more and better housing. We can even have cleaner lakes, more trees, and cleaner air by devoting more resources to environmental problems.

When the long-term growth rate slows, some of these benefits are lost, and the loss can be large. For example, if long-term growth had not slowed in the United States during the 1970s, real GDP in 1996 would have been $8,650 billion, or $32,600 per person. Instead, it was $6,903 billion, or $26,000 per person. So if the long-term trend of the 1960s

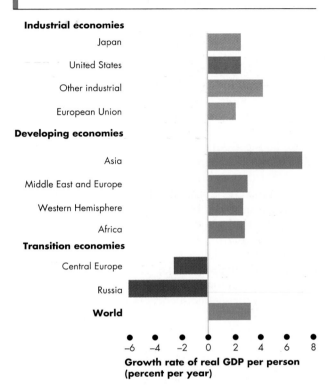

FIGURE 5.5

Growth Rates Around the World

Since 1980, the growth rate of real GDP has been lower in the United States than in some other advanced economies. The developing economies of Asia have had the most rapid growth rates and those of Central Europe and Russia have had the slowest growth.

Source: International Monetary Fund, *World Economic Outlook*, Washington, D.C., October 1998, p. 145.

had persisted, as a nation we would have had $1,750 billion more to spend. Each person (on the average) would have had $6,600 more. If the government had taken one third of this extra income, it could have provided more health care, education, day-care services, highways, space shuttle launches and space stations with no decrease in its provision of other goods and services, and its budget would be in a huge surplus. At the same time, you might have had another $4,400 a year to spend on whatever pleased you.

The main cost of economic growth is forgone consumption. To sustain a high growth rate, resources must be devoted to advancing technology and accumulating capital rather than to producing goods and services for current consumption. But this cost brings the benefit of greater consumption in the future.

Two other possible costs of faster growth are a more rapid depletion of exhaustible natural resources such as oil and natural gas and increased pollution of the air, rivers, and oceans. But neither of these two costs is inevitable. The technological advances that bring economic growth help us to economize on natural resources and to clean up the environment. For example, more efficient auto engines cut gasoline use and tailpipe emissions.

A fourth possible cost of faster growth is more frequent job changes and more frequent moves from one region of the country to another. For example, during the 1990s, the South expanded and people migrated there from the Northeast and Midwest.

The pace of economic growth is determined by the choices that people make to balance the benefits and costs of economic growth. You'll study these choices and their consequences in Chapters 10 and 11.

R E V I E W   Q U I Z

- What is economic growth and how is the long-term economic growth rate measured?
- What is the distinction between real GDP and *potential* GDP?
- What is a business cycle and what are its phases?
- What is a *recession*?
- In what phase of the business cycle was the U.S. economy during 1998?
- What happened to U.S. productivity growth during the 1970s?
- What are the similarities and differences in growth among the major economies?
- What are the benefits and the costs of long-term economic growth?

We've seen that real GDP grows and that it fluctuates over the business cycle. The business cycle brings fluctuations in jobs and unemployment. Let's now examine these macroeconomic problems.

Jobs and Unemployment

WHAT KIND OF LABOR MARKET WILL YOU ENTER when you graduate? Will there be plenty of good jobs to choose from, or will there be so much unemployment that you will be forced to take a low-paying job that doesn't use your education? The answer depends, to a large degree, on the total number of jobs available and on the unemployment rate.

Jobs

The U.S. economy is an incredible job-creating machine. In 1999, 133 million people had jobs. That number is 16 million more than in 1989 and 35 million more than in 1979. Every year, on the average, the U.S. economy creates an *additional* 1.8 million jobs.

During the past four years, the economy has created 7.8 million jobs. Most of these jobs are in the service industries. Jobs in manufacturing shrink each year as we become more efficient and as we buy more of our consumer goods from cheaper foreign sources of supply.

The pace of job creation and destruction is not constant. It fluctuates over the business cycle. More jobs are destroyed than created during a recession, so the number of jobs decreases. But more jobs are created than destroyed during an expansion, so the number of jobs increases. For example, during the recession of 1990–1991, the number of jobs fell by more than 1 million, but through the expansion that followed, 2 million jobs were created each year. During the expansion of the 1980s, jobs were created at an even faster pace of 2.5 million jobs each year.

Unemployment

Not everyone who wants a job can find one. On any one day in a normal or average year, 7 million people are unemployed, and during a recession or depression, unemployment rises above this level. For example, in the recession of 1991, almost 9 million people were looking for jobs. In the booming economic conditions of 1999, the number of job seekers fell to 6 million.

These unemployment numbers are large. The number of people unemployed during a recession is equivalent to the population of Los Angeles. And in a boom, the number is equivalent to the population of Chicago!

In order to place the number of unemployed people in perspective we use a measure called the **unemployment rate**, <u>which is the number of unemployed people expressed as a percentage of all the people who have a job or are looking for one.</u> (The concept of the unemployment rate along with some other labor market measures is explained more fully in Chapter 7 on pp. 139–140.)

The unemployment rate is not a perfect measure of the underutilization of labor for two main reasons. First, it excludes people who are so discouraged that they've given up the effort to find work. Second, the unemployment rate measures unemployed people rather than unemployed labor hours. So it doesn't tell us about the numbers of part-time workers who want full-time jobs. Despite these two limitations, the unemployment rate is the best available measure of underused labor resources. Let's look at some facts about the unemployment rate.

Unemployment in the United States

Figure 5.6 shows the unemployment rate in the United States from 1929 through 1998. Three features stand out. First, during the Great Depression of the 1930s, the unemployment rate climbed to an all-time high of 25 percent in 1933 and remained high throughout the 1930s. After 1934, the official rate probably overstates unemployment because it counts as unemployed the people who had make-work jobs created by governments.

Second, although in recent years we have not experienced anything as devastating as the Great Depression, we have seen some high unemployment rates during recessions. Figure 5.6 highlights three of them: the OPEC recession of the mid-1970s, the 1982 recession, and the 1990–1991 recession.

Third, unemployment never falls to zero. In the period since the Great Depression, the average unemployment rate has been close to 6 percent.

How does U.S. unemployment compare with unemployment in other countries?

FIGURE 5.6

Unemployment in the United States

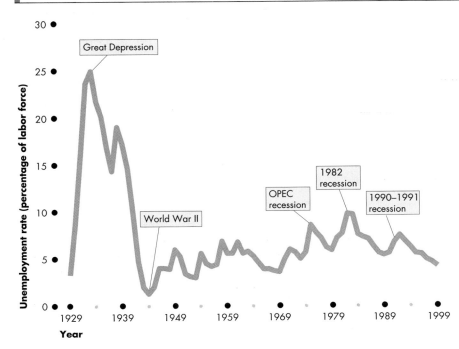

Unemployment is a persistent feature of economic life, but its rate varies. At its worst—during the Great Depression—25 percent of the labor force was unemployed. Even in recent recessions, the unemployment rate climbed toward 10 percent. Between the late 1960s and 1982, there was a general tendency for the unemployment rate to increase. The unemployment rate has remained below its peak during the 1982 recession and has fallen during the 1990s.

Source: Economic Report of the President, 1999.

Unemployment Around the World

Figure 5.7 shows the unemployment rate in Canada, Western Europe, and Japan and compares those unemployment rates with that of the United States. Over the period shown in this figure, U.S. unemployment averaged 6.5 percent, much higher than Japanese unemployment, which averaged 2.7 percent, but lower than Canadian unemployment, which averaged 9.5 percent, and European unemployment, which averaged 9.3 percent.

U.S. unemployment fluctuates over the business cycle. It increases during a recession and decreases during an expansion. Like U.S. unemployment, Canadian and European unemployment increase during recessions and decrease during expansions. The cycles in Canadian unemployment are similar to those in U.S. unemployment, but the European cycle is out of phase with the U.S. cycle. Also, European unemployment was on a rising trend through the 1980s. In contrast with the other countries, Japanese unemployment has remained remarkably stable.

We've looked at some facts about unemployment in the United States and in other countries. Let's now look at some of the consequences of unemployment that make it the serious problem that it is.

Why Unemployment Is a Problem

Unemployment is a serious economic, social, and personal problem for two main reasons:

■ Lost production and incomes
■ Lost human capital

Lost Production and Incomes The loss of a job brings an immediate loss of income and production. These losses are devastating for the people who bear them and make unemployment a frightening prospect for everyone. Unemployment insurance creates a safety net, but it does not provide the same living standard as having a job provides.

Lost Human Capital Prolonged unemployment can permanently damage a person's job prospects. For example, a manager loses his job when his employer downsizes. Short of income, he becomes a taxi driver. After a year in this work, he discovers that he can't compete with new MBA graduates. He eventually gets hired as a manager but in a small firm and at a low wage. He has lost some of his human capital.

FIGURE 5.7

Unemployment in Industrial Economies

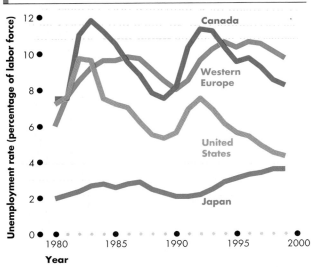

The unemployment rate in the United States has been lower than that in Canada and Western Europe but higher than that in Japan. The cycles in Canadian unemployment are similar to those in the United States. Western European unemployment has a cycle that is out of phase with the U.S. unemployment cycle. Unemployment in Japan has drifted upward in recent years.

Source: World Economic Outlook, October 1998. International Monetary Fund, Washington, D.C, p. 149.

The costs of unemployment are spread unequally, which makes unemployment a political as well as a serious economic problem.

R E V I E W   Q U I Z

■ What is unemployment?
■ What have been the main trends and cycles in the unemployment rate in the United States since 1929?
■ How does unemployment in the United States compare with unemployment in Canada, Europe, and Japan?
■ What are the main costs of unemployment that make it a serious problem?

Let's turn to the third major problem: inflation.

Inflation

COMPUTER PRICES FALL STEADILY. TICKET PRICES for ball games rise steadily. In microeconomics, we try to explain these individual price changes. But in macroeconomics, we are interested in prices *on the average* that we call the **price level**. And we measure the price level by using an index number called the *Consumer Price Index* (CPI). The CPI tells us how the average price of all the goods and services bought by a typical urban household changes from month to month. (The CPI and another measure of the price level are explained in Chapter 6, p. 123).

The price level might be rising, falling, or stable. If the price level is rising, we have inflation. **Inflation** is a process of rising prices. We measure the *inflation rate* as the percentage change in the price level.

In December 1998, the CPI was 163, and in December 1997, it was 160.5, so the change in the price level during 1998 was 2.5. Expressing this change as a percentage of the CPI in December 1997 gives the inflation rate during 1998 as 1.6 percent.

Inflation in the United States

Figure 5.8 shows the U.S. inflation rate from 1962 through 1996. You can see from this figure that during the early 1960s, the inflation rate was between 1 and 2 percent a year. Inflation began to increase in the late 1960s at the time of the Vietnam War. But the largest increases occurred in 1974 and 1980, years in which the actions of the Organization of Petroleum Exporting Countries (OPEC) resulted in exceptionally large increases in the price of oil. Inflation was brought under control in the early 1980s when Federal Reserve chairman Paul Volcker pushed interest rates up and people cut back on their spending. Since 1983, inflation has been relatively mild, and during the 1990s, its rate fell yet further.

The inflation rate rises and falls over the years, but it rarely becomes negative. If the inflation rate is negative, the price *level* is falling and we have **deflation**. Since the 1930s, the price level has generally risen—the inflation rate has been positive. Thus even when the inflation rate is low, as it was in 1961 and 1986, the price level is rising.

FIGURE 5.8

Inflation in the United States

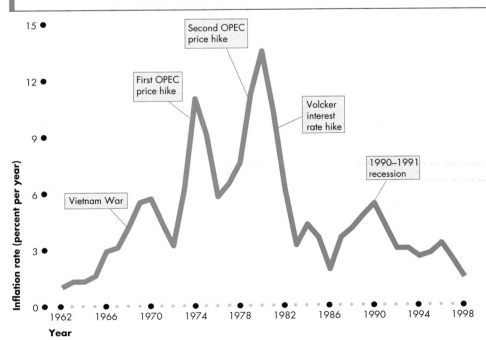

Inflation is a persistent feature of economic life in the United States. The inflation rate was low in the first half of the 1960s, but it increased during the Vietnam War years. It increased further with the OPEC oil price hikes but eventually declined in the early 1980s because of policy actions taken by the Federal Reserve. Since 1983, inflation has been mild, and during the 1990s, it has fallen further.

Source: Economic Report of the President, 1999.

Inflation Around the World

Figure 5.9 shows inflation around the world since 1978. It also shows the U.S. inflation rate in a broader perspective. Part (a) shows that the U.S. inflation rate has been similar to that of other industrial countries. You can also see that all the industrial countries shared the burst of double-digit inflation during the 1970s and the fall in inflation during the 1980s. Part (b) shows that the average inflation rate of industrial countries has been very low compared with that of the developing counties. Among the developing countries, the most extreme inflation in recent times has occurred in the former Yugoslavia, where its rate has exceeded 6,000 percent per year.

Is Inflation a Problem?

If inflation were predictable, it would not be much of a problem. But inflation is not predictable. Unpredictable inflation makes the economy behave a bit like a casino in which some people gain and some lose and no one can predict where the gains and losses will fall. Gains and losses occur because of unpredictable changes in the value of money. Money is used as a measuring rod of value in the transactions that we undertake. Borrowers and lenders, workers and employers, all make contracts in terms of money. If the value of money varies unpredictably over time, then the amounts *really* paid and received—the quantity of goods that the money will buy—also fluctuate unpredictably. Measuring value with a measuring rod whose units vary is a bit like trying to measure a piece of cloth with an elastic ruler. The size of the cloth depends on how much the ruler is stretched.

In a period of rapid, unpredictable inflation, resources get diverted from productive activities to forecasting inflation. It becomes more profitable to forecast the inflation rate correctly than to invent a new product. Doctors, lawyers, accountants, farmers—just about everyone—can make themselves better off, not by specializing in the profession for which they have been trained but by spending more of their time dabbling as amateur economists and inflation forecasters and managing their investment portfolios.

From a social perspective, this diversion of talent resulting from inflation is like throwing scarce resources onto the garbage heap. This waste of resources is a cost of inflation.

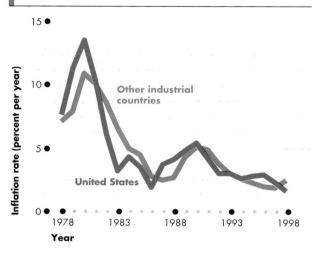

FIGURE 5.9

Inflation Around the World

(a) The United States and other industrial countries

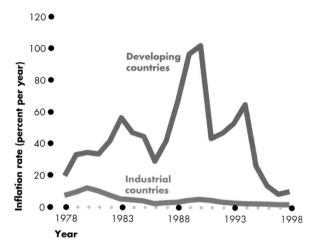

(b) Industrial countries and developing countries

Inflation in the United States is similar to that in the other industrial countries. Compared with the developing countries, inflation in the industrial countries is low.

Sources: International Monetary Fund, *International Financial Statistics Yearbook 1997*, Washington, D.C., 1997 and *World Economic Outlook*, International Monetary Fund, Washington, D.C, October 1998, p. 156.

The most serious type of inflation is called *hyperinflation*—an inflation rate that exceeds 50 percent a month. At the height of a hyperinflation, workers are often paid twice a day because money loses its value so quickly. As soon as workers are paid, they rush out to spend their wages before they lose too much value.

Hyperinflation is rare but there have been some spectacular examples of it. Several European countries experienced hyperinflation during the 1920s after World War I and again during the 1940s after World War II. But hyperinflation is more than just a historical curiosity. It occurs in today's world. In 1994, the African nation of Zaire had a hyperinflation that peaked at a *monthly* inflation rate of 76 percent. Also in 1994, Brazil almost reached the hyperinflation stratosphere with a monthly inflation rate of 40 percent. A cup of coffee that cost 15 cruzeiros in 1980 cost 22 *billion* cruzeiros in 1994.

Inflation imposes costs, but getting rid of inflation is also costly. Policies that lower the inflation rate increase the unemployment rate. Most economists think the increase in the unemployment rate that accompanies a fall in the inflation rate is temporary. But some economists say that higher unemployment is a permanent cost of low inflation. The cost of lowering inflation must be evaluated when an anti-inflation policy is pursued. You will learn more about inflation and the costs of curing it in Chapter 16.

R E V I E W   Q U I Z

- What is inflation and how does it influence the value of money?
- How is inflation measured?
- What has been the U.S. inflation record since 1962?
- How does inflation in the United States compare with inflation in other industrial countries and in developing countries?
- What are some of the costs of inflation that make it a serious economic problem?

Now that we've studied economic growth and fluctuations, unemployment, and inflation, let's turn to the fourth macroeconomic problem: deficits. What happens when a government spends more than it collects in taxes? And what happens when a nation buys more from other countries that it sells to them? Do governments and nations face the problem that you and I would face if we spent more than we earned? Do they run out of funds? Let's look at these questions.

Surpluses and Deficits

IN 1998, FOR THE FIRST TIME IN ALMOST 30 YEARS, the U.S. federal government had a budget surplus. At the same time, the United States had a large international deficit. What are the government budget surplus and the nation's international deficit?

Government Budget Surplus and Deficit

If a government collects more in taxes than it spends, it has a surplus—a **government budget surplus**. If a government spends more than it collects in taxes, it has a deficit—a **government budget deficit**. The U.S. federal government had a surplus in 1998.

Figure 5.10(a) shows the federal government budget surplus and deficit measured as a percentage of GDP since 1962. (The concept of GDP, which is explained more fully in Chapter 6, pp. 114–117, equals total income in the economy.)

We measure the budget surplus or deficit as a percentage of GDP so that we can compare the surplus or deficit in one year with that in another year. You can think of this measure as the number of cents of surplus or deficit per dollar of income earned by an average person.

The government had a budget surplus in 1969 and again in 1998. In every year from 1970 through 1997, the government had a deficit that fluctuated and swelled during recessions. From 1980 through 1995, the deficit was never less than 2 percent of GDP.

Since 1992, the government deficit has been shrinking and a surplus emerged in 1998. In 1998, the government budget surplus was almost 1 percent of GDP and in 1999 and beyond, it is projected to become larger.

International Deficit

When we import goods and services from the rest of the world, we make payments to foreigners. When we export goods and services to the rest of the world, we receive payments from foreigners. If our imports exceed our exports, we have an international deficit.

Figure 5.10(b) shows the history of the international deficit of the United States since 1962. The figure shows the balance on the **current account**, which includes our exports minus our imports but

FIGURE 5.10

Government Budget and International Deficits

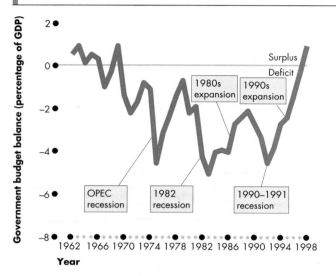

(a) U.S. government budget deficit

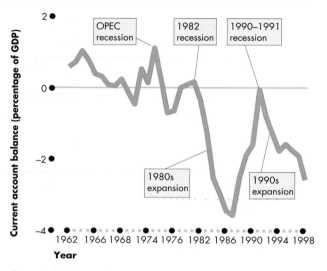

(b) U.S. international deficit

In part (a), the federal government deficit increased as a percentage of GDP before 1982 and shrank after 1982. A surplus emerged in 1998. In part (b), the U.S. current account shows the balance of our exports minus our imports. Until the early 1980s, our current account was generally in surplus. During the expansion of the 1980s, a large international deficit emerged. The deficit almost disappeared during the 1990–1991 recession, but it reappeared during the 1990s expansion.

Sources: The government budget balance is the U.S. federal government's budget deficit, *Economic Report of the President*, 1999. The international balance is the current account balance, U.S. Department of Commerce, *Survey of Current Business*, March 1999.

---

also takes interest payments paid to and received from the rest of the world into account. To compare one year with another, the figure shows the current account as a percentage of GDP. The U.S. current account deficit has fluctuated, and since 1980, it has ranged from close to zero to almost 4 percent of GDP. Our imports have usually exceeded our exports.

Do Deficits Matter?

Why do deficits cause anxiety? What happens when a government cannot cover its spending with taxes or when a country buys more from other countries than it sells to them?

If you spend more than you earn, you have a deficit. And to cover your deficit, you have to borrow. But when you borrow, you must pay interest on your debt. Just like you, if a government or a nation

has a deficit, it must borrow. And like you, the government and the nation must pay interest on their debts.

Whether borrowing and paying out huge amounts of interest are a good idea depends on what the borrowed funds are used for. If you borrow to finance a vacation, you must eventually tighten your belt, cut spending, and repay your debt as well as pay interest on the debt. But if you borrow to invest in a business that earns a large profit, you might be able to repay your debt and pay the interest on it while continuing to increase your spending. It is the same with a government and a nation. A government or a nation that borrows to increase its consumption might be heading for trouble later. But a government or a nation that borrows to buy assets that earn a profit might be making a sound investment.

You will learn more about government budget deficits in Chapter 13 and about the international current account deficit in Chapter 20.

REVIEW QUIZ

- What determines a government's budget deficit?
- How has the U.S. federal government deficit evolved since the 1960s?
- What is a country's international deficit?
- How has the U.S. international deficit changed since the 1960s?

Macroeconomic Policy Challenges and Tools

FROM THE TIME OF ADAM SMITH'S *THE WEALTH of Nations* in 1776 until the publication of Keynes' *General Theory of Employment, Interest, and Money* in 1936, it was widely believed that the only economic role for government was to enforce property rights. The economy behaves best, it was believed, if the government leaves people free to pursue their own best interests. The macroeconomics of Keynes challenged this view. Keynes' central point was that the economy will not fix itself and that government actions are needed to achieve and maintain full employment. The U.S. government declared full employment as a policy goal soon after World War II ended.

Policy Challenges and Tools

Today, the five widely agreed challenges for macroeconomic policy are to:

1. Boost economic growth
2. Stabilize the business cycle
3. Reduce unemployment
4. Keep inflation low
5. Reduce the government and international deficits

But how can we do all these things? What are the tools available to pursue the macroeconomic policy challenges? Macroeconomic policy tools are divided into two broad categories:

- Fiscal policy
- Monetary policy

Fiscal Policy   Making changes in taxes and government spending is called **fiscal policy**. This range of policy actions is under the control of the federal government. Fiscal policy can be used to try to boost long-term growth by creating incentives that encourage saving, investment, and technological change. Fiscal policy can also be used to try to smooth out the business cycle. When the economy is in a recession, the government might cut taxes or increase its spending. Conversely, when the economy is in a rapid expansion, the government might increase taxes or cut its spending in an attempt to slow real GDP growth and prevent inflation from increasing. Fiscal policy is discussed in Chapter 13.

Monetary Policy   Changing interest rates and the amount of money in the economy is called **monetary policy**. These actions are under the control of the Federal Reserve (the Fed). The principal aim of monetary policy is to keep inflation in check. To achieve this objective, the Fed prevents the quantity of money from expanding too rapidly. Monetary policy can also be used to smooth the business cycle. When the economy is in recession, the Fed might lower interest rates and inject money into the economy. And when the economy is in a rapid expansion, the Fed might increase interest rates in an attempt to slow real GDP growth and prevent the inflation from increasing. Monetary policy is discussed in Chapters 14 and 15.

REVIEW QUIZ

- What are the main challenges of macroeconomic policy?
- What are the main tools of macroeconomic policy?
- Can you distinguish between fiscal policy and monetary policy?

In your study of macroeconomics, you will learn what is currently known about the causes of economic growth, business cycles, unemployment, inflation, and government and international deficits and about the policy choices and challenges that the government and the Fed face. *Reading Between the Lines* on pp. 108–109 looks at the state of the U.S. macroeconomy in 1998 and examines the long expansion, falling unemployment, and low inflation of the 1990s.

Economy Watching

C N N f n , MARCH 31, 1999

GDP grew 6% in 4Q 1998

NEW YORK (CNNfn)—In case there was need for another reminder, 1998 ended on a high note for the U.S. economy, as the government confirmed Wednesday that its broadest measure of goods and services rose to record levels during the fourth quarter last year.

In its second and final revision, the Commerce Department said Wednesday that fourth-quarter GDP rose 6 percent. That's down incrementally from February's 6.1 percent revision and up from the 5.6 percent expansion originally reported.

Wednesday's number, the highest since the second quarter of 1996, confirmed the buoyancy of a domestic economy that grew last year with little inflation and despite overseas slowdowns.

"We know the economy's been strong," said Robert Brusca, chief economist at Nikko Securities. For the full year 1998, GDP grew 3.9 percent, matching 1997's growth for the strongest annual performance since 1984, when the economy expanded 7 percent.

The GDP price deflator, a closely watched inflation gauge, was revised back up to 0.8 percent from 0.7 percent. It was the smallest quarterly gain in prices in nearly four decades, since a 0.6 percent rise in the third quarter of 1959.

...

Despite vigorous economic growth, corporate profits after taxes contracted for a second straight quarter by 1 percent in last year's fourth quarter. Profits for all of 1998 fell 2.2 percent to $477.7 billion—the first year company profits declined since 1989, when they fell 4.8 percent.

Looking ahead, analysts generally forecast 1999's economy growing at a slower pace of about 3.5 percent. Brusca said 1999 GDP will hinge upon the stock market's performance and the prospects for rising inflation, which thus far remains tame.

Essence of the Story

■ The Commerce Department originally, in January 1999, estimated that GDP had grown by 5.6 percent (annual rate) in the fourth quarter of 1998. In February, it revised the estimate upward to 6.1 percent, and in March, it provided the final (and last) revision and estimated a growth rate of 6 percent.

■ This growth rate is the highest since the second quarter of 1996.

■ Inflation during the fourth quarter of 1998 was estimated to be 0.8 percent a year, its lowest level since 1959.

■ Company profits after taxes decreased by 1 percent during the fourth quarter of 1998 and decreased by 2.2 percent for the whole of 1998, the first year of falling company profits since 1989.

Economic Analysis

■ Figure 1 shows the expansions in real GDP since 1921. The longest expansion lasted for almost 10 years during the 1960s. The 1990s expansion is now the second longest. If it persists through March 2000, it will exceed the length of the 1960s expansion.

■ Figure 2 shows the 1990s expansion. Real GDP started out below potential GDP in the recession of 1990–1991. Real GDP expanded, and by 1996, it was close to potential GDP. Both real GDP and potential GDP have grown at a similar rate since 1996.

■ Figure 3 shows the unemployment rate during the 1990s expansion. Unemployment peaked in 1992, fell quickly through 1994, and continued to fall through 1998.

■ Figure 4 shows the inflation rate during the 1990s expansion. Beginning at almost 5 percent a year, the inflation rate has fallen to around 1 percent a year, its lowest level since the 1960s.

■ Expansions that last as long as the 1990s expansion are rare, and the current expansion will at some time come to an end. But we cannot predict when.

■ The news article says that company profits decreased in 1998 and that the last time they decreased was 1989. The last recession began in June 1990.

■ The next recession will begin when some *currently unforeseeable* event brings a fall in spending and a surge in layoffs. In the past, such events have occurred on the average every four years but with a range that runs from one year to ten years.

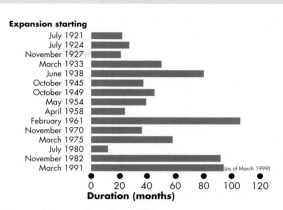

Figure 1 Expansion since 1921

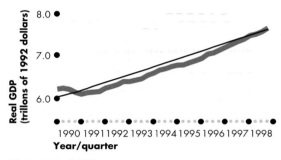

Figure 2 Real GDP

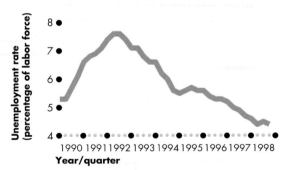

Figure 3 Unemployment

Figure 4 Inflation

109

SUMMARY

KEY POINTS

Origins and Issues of Macroeconomics (p. 94)

■ Macroeconomics studies economic growth and fluctuations, unemployment, inflation, and surpluses and deficits.

Economic Growth (pp. 95–100)

■ Economic growth is the expansion of potential GDP. Real GDP fluctuates around potential GDP in a business cycle.

■ Countries have similar productivity growth slowdowns and business cycles but different long-term trends in potential GDP.

■ The main benefit of long-term economic growth is higher future consumption, and the main cost is lower current consumption.

Jobs and Unemployment (pp. 100–102)

■ The U.S. economy creates 1.8 million jobs a year, but unemployment persists.

■ Unemployment increases during a recession and decreases during an expansion. The U.S. unemployment rate is lower than that in Canada and Western Europe but higher than that in Japan.

■ Unemployment can permanently damage a person's job prospects.

Inflation (pp. 103–105)

■ Inflation, a process of rising prices, is measured by the percentage change in the CPI.

■ Inflation is a problem because it lowers the value of money and makes money less useful as a measuring rod of value.

Surpluses and Deficits (pp. 105–107)

■ When its tax receipts exceed spending, a government has a budget surplus. When its spending exceeds tax receipts, a government has a budget deficit.

■ When imports exceed exports, a nation has an international deficit.

■ Deficits are financed by borrowing.

Macroeconomic Policy Challenges and Tools (p. 107)

■ The macroeconomic policy challenge is to use fiscal policy and monetary policy to boost long-term growth, stabilize the business cycle, lower unemployment, tame inflation, and prevent large deficits.

KEY FIGURES ◆

KEY TERMS

PROBLEMS

*1. Use Variable Graphing in Chapter 5 of *Economics in Action* to answer the following questions. In which country in 1992 was
   a. The growth rate of real GDP highest: the United States, France, Japan, or Canada?
   b. The unemployment rate highest: the United States, Japan, the United Kingdom, or Canada?
   c. The inflation rate lowest: the United States, Germany, the United Kingdom, or Canada?
   d. The government budget deficit (as a percentage of GDP) largest: the United States, Japan, the United Kingdom, or Canada?

2. Use Variable Graphing in Chapter 5 in the *Economics in Action* to answer the following questions. In which country in 1996 was
   a. The growth rate of real GDP highest: The United States, France, Japan, or Canada?
   b. The unemployment rate lowest: the United States, Japan, the United Kingdom, or Canada?
   c. The inflation rate lowest: the United States, Finland, Ireland, or Canada?
   d. The government budget deficit (as a percentage of GDP) smallest: the United States, Australia, Ireland, or Canada?
   e. Is it possible to say in which country consumption possibilities are growing faster? Why or why not?

*3. The figure shows real GDP growth rate in India and Pakistan from 1989 to 1996.

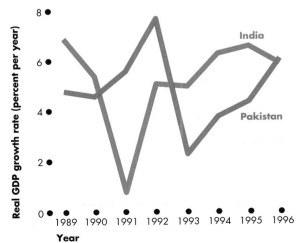

In which years did economic growth in
   a. India increase? And in which year was growth fastest?
   b. Pakistan decrease? And in which year was growth slowest?
   c. Compare the paths of economic growth in India and Pakistan during this period.

4. The figure shows real GDP per person in Australia and Japan from 1989 to 1996.

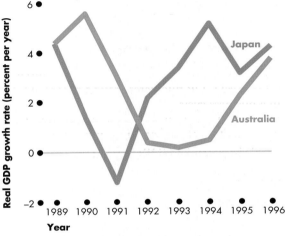

In which years did economic growth in
   a. Australia increase? And in which year was growth fastest?
   b. Japan decrease? And in which year was growth slowest?
   c. Compare the paths of economic growth in Australia and Japan during this period.

*5. The figure shows real GDP in Germany from the first quarter of 1991 to the second quarter of 1994.

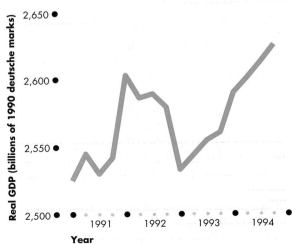

a. How many recessions did Germany experience during this period?

b. In which quarters, if any, did Germany experience a business cycle peak?

c. In which quarters, if any, did Germany experience a business cycle trough?

d. In which quarters, if any, did Germany experience an expansion?

6. Use the links on the Parkin Web site to obtain data on quarterly real GDP for the United States since the fourth quarter of 1998 and update Fig. 5.2. Use what you have discovered to answer the following questions:

a. Is the U.S. economy now in a recession or an expansion?

b. If the economy is still in an expansion, how long has the expansion lasted? If the economy is now in recession, how long the economy been in recession?

c. During the last year, has the growth rate sped up or slowed?

*7. Use Variable Graphing in Chapter 5 in the *Economics in Action* to answer the following questions. Which country, in 1988, had

a. The largest budget deficit: the United States, Japan, the United Kingdom, or Canada?

b. A current account surplus: the United States, Japan, Germany, or Canada?

8. Use Variable Graphing in Chapter 5 in the *Economics in Action* to answer the following questions. Which country, in 1988, had

a. The largest budget surplus: the United States, Japan, the United Kingdom, or Canada?

b. The largest current account deficit: the United States, Japan, Germany, or Canada?

*9. Use Variable Graphing in Chapter 5 in the *Economics in Action* to make a scatter diagram of inflation and unemployment in the United States.

a. Describe the relationship.

b. Do you think that low unemployment brings an increase in the inflation rate?

10. Use Variable Graphing in Chapter 5 in the *Economics in Action* to make a scatter diagram of the government budget deficit as a percentage of GDP and the unemployment rate.

a. Describe the relationship.

b. Do you think that low unemployment brings a decrease in the budget deficit?

CRITICAL THINKING

1. Study *Reading Between the Lines* on pp. 108–109 and then answer the following questions:

a. When did the most recent expansion begin?

b. How long has the most recent expansion lasted? Is it an unusually long expansion? Compare the length of the most recent expansion with those of other expansions since World War II and before World War II?

c. Can you think of convincing reasons why the 1990s expansion has been a long one?

2. Use the links on the Parkin Web site to obtain the latest data on real GDP, unemployment, and inflation.

a. Update the figures on pages 476, 481, and 483.

b. What dangers does the U.S. economy face today?

c. What actions, if any, do you think might be needed to keep the economy strong?

3. Use the links on the Parkin Web site to obtain data on unemployment in your home state.

a. Compare unemployment in your home state with that in the United States as a whole.

b. Why do you think your state might have a higher or a lower unemployment rate than the U.S. average?

4. Use the links on the Parkin Web site to obtain data on the Consumer Price Index for the large city that you live closest to.

a. Compare the inflation rate in your chosen city with that in the United States as a whole.

b. Compare the inflation rate in your chosen city with that in other large cities.

5. Use the links on the Parkin Web site to obtain data on each of the following variables for the United States for the most recent period. Describe how the variables have changed over the last year.

a. The unemployment rate

b. The inflation rate

c. The government budget deficit

d. The international deficit?

6

Measuring GDP, Economic Growth, and Inflation

When Motorola contemplates spending $1 billion developing a cellular telephone system in China, it pays close attention to forecasts of China's real GDP. When AT&T plans to expand its fiber-optic network, it uses forecasts of long-term growth in the U.S. economy. The outcomes of many business decisions turn on the quality of forecasts of economic conditions. ◆ A key input for making economic forecasts is Gross Domestic Product, or GDP, which is like a barometer of a nation's economy. Economists pore over the numbers, looking at past trends and seeking patterns that might give a glimpse of the future. How do economic statisticians add up all the production of the country to arrive at the number called GDP? What exactly *is* GDP? ◆ Most of the time, our economy grows, but sometimes it shrinks. To reveal the rate of growth (or shrinkage), we must remove the effects of inflation on GDP and assess how *real* GDP is changing. How do we remove the inflation component of GDP to reveal real GDP? ◆ Some countries are rich while others are poor and only now are in the process of developing their industries and reaching their productive potential. How do we compare incomes in one country with incomes in another? How can we make international comparisons of GDP? ◆ From economists to homemakers, all types of people pay close attention to another economic barometer, the Consumer Price Index, or CPI. The Department of Labor publishes new figures each month, and analysts in newspapers and on TV quickly leap to conclusions about the causes of recent changes in prices and the prospects for future changes. How does the government determine the CPI? How well does it measure a consumer's living costs and the inflation rate?

Economic Barometers

◆ In this chapter, you will find out how economic statisticians measure GDP, the price level, and real GDP. You will also learn how they measure the economic growth rate and the inflation rate and about the limitations of these measures.

After studying this chapter, you will be able to:

■ Explain why aggregate income, expenditure, and product are equal

■ Explain how we measure GDP

■ Explain how we measure the price level using the Consumer Price Index (CPI)

■ Explain how we measure *real* GDP and the GDP deflator

■ Explain how we use real GDP to measure economic growth and describe the limitations of our measure

■ Explain how we use the CPI and the GDP deflator to measure inflation and describe the limitations of our measures

Gross Domestic Product

WHAT EXACTLY IS GDP, HOW IS IT CALCULATED, what does it mean, and why do we care about it? You are going to discover the answers to these questions in this chapter. First, what *is* GDP? **GDP**, or **gross domestic product**, is the value of the *aggregate* production of goods and services in a country during a given time period—usually a year. The GDP of the United States, which measures the value of aggregate production in the United States during a year, was $8,511 billion in 1998.

How is GDP calculated? In a nutshell, GDP is calculated by valuing everything that is produced and adding all the values together. But precisely *what* is valued and *how* it is valued? To answer these questions, you need to understand two fundamental principles of economic accounting:

■ The distinction between flows and stocks
■ The equality of income, expenditure, and the value of production

Flows and Stocks

To keep track of our personal economic transactions and the economic transactions of a country, we distinguish between flows and stocks. A **flow** is a quantity per unit of time. The water that is running from an open faucet into a bathtub is a flow. So are the number of CDs that you buy during a month and the amount of income that you earn during a month. GDP is a flow. It is the value of the goods and services produced in a country *during a given time period*.

A **stock** is a quantity that exists at a point in time. The water in a bathtub is a stock. So are the number of CDs that you own and the amount of money in your savings account.

Capital and Investment The key macroeconomic stock is capital. **Capital** is the plant, equipment, buildings, and inventories of raw materials and semifinished goods that are used to produce other goods and services. The amount of capital in the economy exerts a big influence on GDP. Two flows change the stock of capital: investment and depreciation. Investment is the purchase of new capital. It increases the stock of capital. (Investment includes additions to inventories.) **Depreciation** is the decrease in the stock of capital that results from wear and tear and obsolescence. Another

name for depreciation is *capital consumption*. The total amount spent on adding to the stock of capital and on replacing depreciated capital is called **gross investment**. The amount spent on adding to the stock of capital is called **net investment**. Net investment equals gross investment minus depreciation.

Figure 6.1 illustrates these concepts. On January 1, 2000, Tom's Tapes, Inc. had 3 machines. This quantity was its initial capital. During 2000, Tom's scrapped an older machine. This quantity is its depreciation. After depreciation, Tom's stock of capital was down to 2 machines. But also during 2000, Tom's bought 2 new machines. This amount is its gross investment. By December 31, 2000, Tom's Tapes had 4 machines, so its capital had increased by 1 machine. This amount is Tom's net investment. Tom's net investment equals its gross investment (the pur-

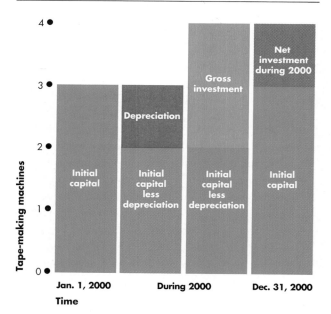

FIGURE 6.1
Capital and Investment

Tom's Tapes has a capital stock at the end of 2000 that equals its capital stock at the beginning of the year plus its net investment. Net investment is equal to gross investment less depreciation. Tom's gross investment is the 2 new machines bought during the year, and its depreciation is the 1 machine that Tom's scrapped during the year.

chase of 2 new machines) minus its depreciation (1 machine scrapped).

The example of Tom's Tapes factory can be applied to the economy as a whole. The nation's capital stock decreases because capital depreciates and increases because of gross investment. The change in the nation's capital stock from one year to the next equals its net investment.

Wealth and Saving   Another macroeconomic stock is **wealth**, which is the value of all the things that people own. What people *own*, a stock, is related to what they *earn*, a flow. People *earn* an *income*, which is the amount they receive during a given time period from supplying the services of resources. Income that is left after paying taxes is either consumed or saved. **Consumption expenditure** is the amount spent on consumption goods and services. **Saving** is the amount of income remaining after meeting consumption expenditures. Saving adds to wealth, and dissaving (negative saving) decreases wealth.

For example, suppose that at the end of the school year, you have $250 in a savings account and some textbooks that are worth $300. That's all you own. Your wealth is $550. Suppose that you take a summer job and earn an income of $5,000. You are extremely careful and spend only $1,000 through the summer on consumption goods and services. At the end of the summer, when school starts again, you have $4,250 in your savings account. Your wealth is now $4,550. Your wealth has increased by $4,000, which equals your saving of $4,000. Your saving of $4,000 equals your income of $5,000 minus your consumption expenditure of $1,000.

National wealth and national saving work just like this personal example. The wealth of a nation at the start of a year equals its wealth at the start of the previous year plus its saving during the year. Its saving equals its income minus its consumption expenditure.

We'll make the idea of the nation's income and consumption expenditure more precise a bit later in this chapter. Before doing so, let's see what the stocks and flows that we've just learned about imply for the recurring theme of macroeconomics: short-term fluctuations in actual real GDP and long-term growth in potential GDP.

The Short Term Meets the Long Term   You saw in Chapter 5 that potential GDP grows incessantly, year after year. You also saw that actual real GDP grows and fluctuates around potential GDP. The stocks and

flows that you've just studied influence *both* the long-term growth in potential GDP and the short-term fluctuations in actual GDP. One of the reasons why potential GDP grows is that the capital stock grows. One of the reasons that real GDP fluctuates is that investment fluctuates. So capital and investment as well as wealth and saving are part of the key to understanding the growth of potential GDP and the fluctuations of real GDP.

The flows of investment and saving together with the flows of income and consumption expenditure interact in a circular flow of income and expenditure. In this circular flow, income equals expenditure, which also equals the value of production. This amazing equality is the foundation on which a nation's economic accounts are built and from which its GDP is measured.

Income, Expenditure, and the Value of Production

To see that for the economy as a whole, income equals expenditure and also equals the value of production, we study the circular flow of income and expenditure.

Figure 6.2 illustrates the circular flow of income and expenditure. In the figure, the economy consists of four sectors: households, firms, governments, and the rest of the world (the purple diamonds). It has three types of markets: resource markets, goods (and services) markets, and financial markets. Focus first on households and firms.

Households and Firms   Households sell and firms buy the services of labor, capital, land, and entrepreneurship in resource markets. For these resource services, firms pay income to households: wages for labor services, interest for the use of capital, rent for the use of land, and profits for entrepreneurship. Firms' retained earnings—profits that are not distributed to households—are also part of the household sector's income. You can think of retained earnings as being income that households save and lend back to firms. Figure 6.2 shows the *aggregate income* received by all households in payment for the services of resources by the blue dots labeled *Y*.

Firms sell and households buy consumer goods and services—such as popcorn and soda, movies and chocolate bars, microwave ovens and inline skates, dental and dry cleaning services—in the markets for goods and services. The total payment that households make for these goods and services is *consumption*

FIGURE 6.2

The Circular Flow of Income and Expenditure

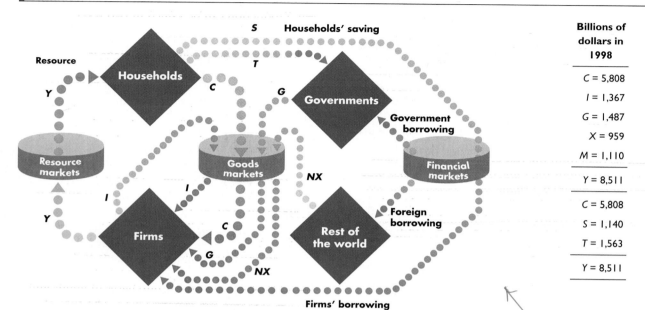

Billions of dollars in 1998
C = 5,808
I = 1,367
G = 1,487
X = 959
M = 1,110
Y = 8,511
C = 5,808
S = 1,140
T = 1,563
Y = 8,511

In the circular flow of income and expenditure, households receive incomes (Y) from firms (blue flow) and make consumption expenditures (C); firms make investment expenditures (I); governments purchase goods and services (G); the rest of the world purchases net exports (NX)—(red flows). Aggregate income (blue flow) equals aggregate expenditure (red flows). Households' saving (S) and net taxes (T) leak from the circular flow. Firms borrow to finance their investment expenditures, and governments and the rest of the world borrow to finance their deficits or lend their surpluses (green flows). The values shown are for 1998.

Source: U.S. Department of Commerce, *Survey of Current Business* (April 1999).

expenditure. Figure 6.2 shows consumption expenditure by the red dots labeled *C*.

Firms buy and sell new capital equipment in the goods market. For example, IBM sells 1,000 PCs to General Motors, or Boeing sells an airplane to United Airlines. Some of what firms produce might not be sold at all and is added to inventory. For example, if GM produces 1,000 cars and sells 950 of them, the other 50 cars remain unsold and GM's inventory of cars increases by 50. When a firm adds unsold output to inventory, we can think of the firm as buying goods from itself. The purchase of new plant, equipment, and buildings and the additions to inventories are **investment**.

Figure 6.2 shows investment by the red dots labeled *I*. Notice that in the figure, investment flows from firms through the goods markets and back to firms. Some firms produce capital goods, and other

firms buy them (and firms "buy" inventories from themselves).

Firms finance their investment by borrowing from households in financial markets. Households' saving flows into financial markets, and firms' borrowing flows out of financial markets. Figure 6.2 shows these flows by the green dots labeled "Households' saving" or *S* and "Firms' borrowing." These flows are neither income nor expenditure. Income is a payment for the services of a resource, and expenditure is a payment for goods or services.

Governments   Governments buy goods and services, called **government purchases**, from firms. In Fig. 6.2 these government purchases are shown as the red flow *G*. Governments use taxes to pay for their purchases. Figure 6.2 shows taxes as net taxes by the green dots labeled *T*. **Net taxes** are equal to taxes paid to governments minus transfer payments received from governments and minus interest payments from the government on its debt. *Transfer payments* are cash transfers from governments to households and firms such as social security benefits, unemployment compensation, and subsidies.

When government purchases (*G*) exceed net taxes (*T*), the government has a budget deficit, which it finances by borrowing in financial markets (shown by the green dots labeled "Government borrowing.")

Rest of World Sector Firms export goods and services to the rest of the world and import goods and services from the rest of the world. The value of exports minus the value of imports is called **net exports**. Figure 6.2 shows net exports by the red flow *NX*. If the value of exports exceeds the value of imports, net exports are positive and dollars flow from the rest of the world to firms. But if the value of exports is less than the value of imports, net exports are negative and dollars flow from firms to the rest of the world.

If net exports are positive, the rest of the world is in deficit and we are in surplus. To finance its deficit, the rest of the world borrows from the U.S. economy or sells U.S. assets that it owns. For example, Korean Airlines can borrow in New York to finance the purchase of new airplanes from Boeing. These transactions take place in financial markets, and they are shown by the green flow labeled "Foreign borrowing."

If net exports are negative, we are in deficit and the rest of the world is in surplus. To finance our deficit, we borrow from the rest of the world or we sell foreign assets that we own. For example, a California winemaker might borrow in Frankfurt, Germany, to finance the purchase of a German-made grape-picking machine. Again, these transactions take place in financial markets. To illustrate this case in Fig. 6.2, we would reverse the directions of the flows of net exports and foreign borrowing.

To help you keep track of the different types of flows that make up the circular flow of income and expenditure, the flows are color-coded in Fig. 6.2. The red flows are expenditures on goods and services, the blue flow is income, and the green flows are financial transfers. The expenditure flows (red flows) are consumption expenditure, investment, government purchases, and net exports. The income flow (blue flow) is aggregate income. The financial transfers (green flows) are saving, net taxes,

government borrowing, foreign borrowing, and firms' borrowing.

Gross Domestic Product Gross domestic product is the value of *aggregate production* in a country during a year. Production can be valued in two ways:

1. By what buyers pay for it
2. By what it costs producers to make it

From the viewpoint of buyers, goods are worth the prices paid for them. From the viewpoint of producers, goods are worth what it costs to make them. Fortunately, the value of production is the same regardless of which viewpoint we take. Let's see why.

Expenditure Equals Income The total amount that buyers pay for the goods and services produced is *aggregate expenditure*. Let's focus on aggregate expenditure in Fig. 6.2. The expenditures on goods and services are shown by the red flows. Firms' revenues from the sale of goods and services equal consumption expenditure (*C*) plus investment (*I*) plus government purchases of goods and services (*G*) plus net exports (*NX*). The sum of these four flows is equal to aggregate expenditure on goods and services.

The total amount it costs producers to make goods and services is equal to the incomes paid for resource services. This amount is shown by the blue flow in Fig. 6.2.

The sum of the red flows equals the blue flow. The reason is that everything a firm receives from the sale of its output is paid out as incomes to the owners of the resources that it employs. That is,

$$Y = C + I + G + NX,$$

or aggregate income (*Y*) equals aggregate expenditure (*C* + *I* + *G* + *NX*).

The buyers of aggregate production pay an amount equal to aggregate expenditure, and the sellers of aggregate production pay an amount equal to aggregate income. Because aggregate expenditure equals aggregate income, these two methods of valuing aggregate production give the same answer. So

Aggregate production, or GDP, equals aggregate expenditure and equals aggregate income.

The circular flow of income and expenditure is the foundation on which the national economic accounts are built. It is used to provide the two approaches to measuring GDP. And it is used to create other accounts that help us to keep track of the flows of saving and investment, the government's budget, and the balance of our exports and imports.

Let's look next at how the circular flows you've just studied enable us to keep track of how investment is financed.

How Investment Is Financed

Investment, which adds to the stock of capital, is one of the determinants of the rate at which production grows. Investment is financed by:

- National saving
- Borrowing from the rest of the world

National Saving   The amount of saving by households and businesses plus government saving is called **national saving**. Saving by households and businesses, S, equals income minus taxes minus consumption expenditure. Government saving equals net taxes minus government purchases of goods and services, $(T - G)$. If the government has a budget surplus, $(T - G)$ is positive and this surplus is a source of finance for investment. But if the government has a budget deficit, $(T - G)$ is negative and part of saving is used to finance the government deficit. So

$$\text{National saving} = S + (T - G).$$

Borrowing from the Rest of the World   If we spend more on foreign goods and services than the rest of the world spends on ours, we must borrow from the rest of the world to pay the difference. That is, if the value of our imports (M) exceeds the value of our exports (X), we must borrow from the rest of the world an amount equal to $(M - X)$. In this case, part of the rest of the world's saving finances our negative net exports and frees up an equal amount of national saving to finance investment in the United States. Conversely, if foreigners spend more on U.S.-made goods and services than we spend on theirs, foreigners must borrow from us to pay the difference. That is, part of U.S. national saving flows to the rest of the world and is not available to finance U.S. investment.

In 1998, U.S. investment was $1,367 billion. This investment was financed by $1,216 billion of national saving and $151 billion of funds borrowed from the rest of the world.

Let's now see how the Department of Commerce uses the circular flows to measure GDP.

Measuring U.S. GDP

To measure GDP, the Department of Commerce uses two approaches:

- Expenditure approach
- Income approach

The Expenditure Approach

The *expenditure approach* measures GDP by using data on consumption expenditure, investment, government purchases, and net exports. Table 6.1 shows this approach. The first column gives the terms used in the *National Income and Product Accounts of the United States* (published by the Department of Commerce). The next column gives the symbol we've used in our GDP equations. GDP using the expenditure approach is the sum of personal consumption expenditures (C), gross private domestic investment (I), government purchases of goods and services (G), and net exports of goods and services (NX).

Personal consumption expenditures are the expenditures by households on goods and services produced in the United States and in the rest of the world. They include goods such as CDs and books and services such as banking and legal advice. They do *not* include the purchase of new homes, which is counted as part of investment.

TABLE 6.1

GDP: The Expenditure Approach

Item	Symbol	Amount in 1998 (billions of dollars)	Percentage of GDP
Personal consumption expenditures	C	5,808	68.2
Gross private domestic investment	I	1,367	16.1
Government purchases of goods and services	G	1,487	17.5
Net exports of goods and services	NX	−151	−1.8
Gross domestic product	Y	8,511	100.0

The expenditure approach measures GDP by adding together personal consumption expenditures (C), gross private domestic investment (I), government purchases of goods and services (G), and net exports (NX). In 1998, GDP measured by the expenditure approach was $8,509 billion. Two thirds of aggregate expenditure is on personal consumption goods and services.

Source: U.S. Department of Commerce, *Survey of Current Business* (April 1999).

Gross private domestic investment is expenditure on capital equipment and buildings by firms and expenditure on new homes by households. It also includes the change in business inventories.

Government purchases of goods and services are the purchases of goods and services by all levels of government. This item includes expenditures on national defense and garbage collection. But it does *not* include *transfer payments*. These payments, such as medical aid and social security benefits, are not purchases of goods and services. They are transfers of funds from government to households.

Net exports of goods and services are the value of exports minus the value of imports. This item includes computers that IBM sells to Volkswagen, the German car producer (a U.S. export), and Japanese VCRs that Circuit City buys from Japan (a U.S. import).

Table 6.1 shows the relative importance of the four items of aggregate expenditure. The largest component is personal consumption expenditures, and the smallest is net exports (negative in 1998).

Expenditures Not in GDP Aggregate expenditure, which equals GDP, does not include all the things that people and businesses buy. To distinguish total expenditure on GDP from other items of spending, we call the expenditure included in GDP *final expenditure.* Spending that is not part of final expenditure and not part of GDP includes the purchase of:

- Intermediate goods and services
- Used goods
- Financial assets

Intermediate goods and services are the goods and services that firms buy from each other and use as inputs in the goods and services that they eventually sell to final users. When Dell Corp. buys computer chips from Intel Corp., it buys an intermediate good. A Dell computer is a final good, but an Intel chip is an intermediate good. To count the expenditure on intermediate goods and services as well as the expenditure on the final good involves counting the same thing twice—called *double counting.*

A good can sometimes be an intermediate good and sometimes a final good. For example, the ice cream that you buy on a hot summer day is a final good, but the ice cream that a diner buys and uses to make sundaes is an intermediate good. Whether a good is intermediate or final depends on what it is used for, not on what it is.

Expenditure on *used goods* is not part of GDP because these goods were counted as part of GDP in the period in which they were produced and in which they were new goods. For example, a 1990 automobile was part of GDP in 1990. If the car is traded on the used car market in 1998, the amount paid for the car is not part of GDP in 1998.

Firms often sell *financial assets* such as bonds and stocks to finance purchases of newly produced capital goods. The expenditure on newly produced capital goods is part of GDP, but the expenditure on financial securities is not. GDP includes the amount spent on new capital, not the amount spent on pieces of paper.

Let's look at the second way of measuring GDP, the income approach.

The Income Approach

The *income approach* measures GDP by summing the incomes that firms pay households for the resources they hire: wages for labor, interest for capital, rent for land, and profits for entrepreneurship. Let's see how the income approach works.

The *National Income and Product Accounts* divide incomes into five categories:

1. Compensation of employees
2. Net interest
3. Rental income
4. Corporate profits
5. Proprietors' income

Compensation of employees is the payment for labor services. It includes net wages and salaries (called "take-home pay") that workers receive plus taxes withheld on earnings plus fringe benefits such as social security and pension fund contributions.

Net interest is the interest households receive on loans they make minus the interest households pay on their own borrowing.

Rental income is the payment for the use of land and other rented inputs. It includes payments for rented housing and imputed rent for owner-occupied housing. (Imputed rent is an estimate of what homeowners would pay to rent the housing they own and use themselves. By including this item in the national income accounts, we measure the total value of housing services, whether they are owned or rented.)

Corporate profits are the profits of corporations. Some of these profits are paid to households in the form of dividends, and some are retained by corporations as undistributed profits. They are all income.

Proprietors' income is a mixture of the previous four items. It is difficult to split the income earned by the owner-operator of a business into compensation for labor, payment for the use of capital, and profit, so the national income accounts lump all these items into a single category.

Table 6.2 shows these five incomes and their relative magnitudes. Compensation of employees is the largest income category.

The sum of these five categories of incomes is called *net domestic income at factor cost*. The term *factor cost* is used because *factor of production* is another name for a productive resource. But *net domestic income at factor cost* is not GDP. We must make two further adjustments to get to GDP, one from *factor cost* to *market prices* and another from *net* product to *gross* product.

Factor Cost to Market Prices   When we add up all the final expenditures on goods and services, we arrive at a total called domestic product at *market prices*. These expenditures are valued at the market prices that people pay for the various goods and services. Another way of valuing goods and services is at factor cost. *Factor cost* is the value of a good or service measured by adding together the costs of all the resources used to produce it. If the only economic transaction were between households and firms—if there were no government taxes or subsidies—the market price and factor cost values would be the same. But the presence of indirect taxes and subsidies makes these two methods of valuation differ.

An *indirect tax* is a tax paid by consumers when they buy goods and services. (In contrast, a *direct tax* is a tax on income.) State sales taxes and taxes on alcohol, gasoline, and tobacco products are indirect

TABLE 6.2
GDP: The Income Approach

Item	Amount in 1998 (billions of dollars)	Percentage of GDP
Compensation of employees	4,981	58.5
Net interest	449	5.3
Rental income	163	1.9
Corporate profits	825	9.7
Proprietors' income	577	6.8
Indirect taxes *less* Subsidies	608	7.1
Capital consumption (depreciation)	908	10.7
Gross domestic product	8,511	100.0

The sum of all incomes plus indirect taxes less subsidies equals net domestic income. GDP equals net domestic income plus capital consumption (depreciation). In 1998, GDP measured by the income approach was $8,511 billion.

Source: U.S. Department of Commerce, Survey of Current Business (April 1999).

taxes. Because of indirect taxes, consumers pay more for some goods and services than producers receive. Market price exceeds factor cost. For example, if the sales tax is 7 percent, when you buy a $1 chocolate bar you pay $1.07. The factor cost of the chocolate bar including profit is $1. The market price is $1.07.

A *subsidy* is a payment by the government to a producer. Payments made to grain growers and dairy farmers are subsidies. Because of subsidies, consumers pay less for some goods and services than producers receive. Factor cost exceeds market price.

To get from factor cost to market price, we add indirect taxes and subtract subsidies. Making this adjustment brings us one step closer to GDP, but it does not quite get us there. We must make one further adjustment.

Net Domestic Product to Gross Domestic Product

What do the words *gross* and *net* mean? *Gross* means *before* subtracting *depreciation*—the decrease in the value of the capital stock that results from wear and tear and obsolescence. *Net* means *after* subtracting depreciation.

Gross investment is a component of aggregate expenditure. So total expenditure includes depreciation and is a gross measure. The *net profit* of businesses—profit *after* subtracting depreciation—is a component of aggregate incomes. So total income excludes depreciation and is a net measure.

To get *gross* domestic product from the income approach, we must add depreciation to aggregate income.

Table 6.2 summarizes these calculations and shows how the income approach leads to the same estimate of GDP as the expenditure approach after the adjustments that we've just described have been made.

Valuing the Output of Industries

The methods used to measure GDP can also be used to measure the contribution that an industry makes to GDP. But to measure the value of production of an individual industry, we count only the value added by that industry. **Value added** is the value of a firm's production minus the value of the *intermediate goods* that the firm buys from other firms. Equivalently, it is the sum of the incomes (including profits) paid to the resources used by the firm.

Figure 6.3 illustrates value added by looking at the brief life of a loaf of bread. It starts with the

farmer, who grows the wheat. The farmer hires labor, capital, and land and pays wages, interest, and rent for these resources. The farmer also earns a profit. The entire value of the wheat produced is the farmer's value added. The miller buys wheat from the farmer and turns it into flour. The miller hires labor and capital, pays wages and interest, and earns a profit. The miller has now added value to the wheat bought from the farmer. The baker buys flour from the miller. The price of the flour includes the value added by both the farmer and the miller. The baker adds more value by turning the flour into bread. The grocer buys the bread from the baker. The price paid by the grocer includes the value added by the farmer, the miller, and the baker. At this stage, the value of the loaf is its *wholesale* value. The grocer adds further value by

FIGURE 6.3
Value Added and Final Expenditure

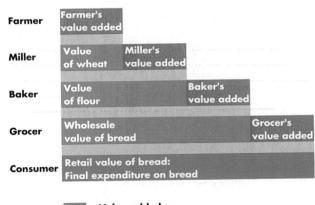

A consumer's expenditure on bread (the green bar) is equal to the sum of the value added at each stage in its production (the red bars). The blue bars illustrate intermediate expenditure. Intermediate expenditure, for example the amount paid by the baker for the purchase of flour from the miller, equals the value added by the farmer and the miller. So to include intermediate expenditure and final expenditure double counts some value added.

making the loaf available at a convenient place and time. The consumer buys the bread for a price—its *market price*—that includes the value added by the farmer, the miller, the baker, and the grocer.

Final Goods and Intermediate Goods   To value output, we count only *value added* because the sum of the value added at each stage of production equals expenditure on the *final good*. By using value added, we avoid double counting. In the above example, the only thing that has been produced and consumed is a loaf of bread—shown by the green bar in Fig. 6.3. The value added at each stage is shown by the red bars, and the sum of the red bars equals the green bar. The transactions involving intermediate goods, shown by the blue bars, are not part of value added and are not counted as part of the value of output or of GDP.

Aggregate Expenditure, Income, and GDP   You've seen that aggregate expenditure equals aggregate income. And you've seen that the Department of Commerce uses both aggregate expenditure and aggregate income to measure GDP. Why does it use two approaches when they are supposed to be the same? The answer is that although the two concepts of the value of aggregate production are identical, the actual measurements, which are based on samples of information, give slightly different answers. The expenditure approach uses data from surveys of retail stores, house building, and business investment; the accounts of the federal, state, and local government; customs records; and many other sources. The income approach uses data supplied by the Internal Revenue Service. None of these sources gives a complete coverage of all the items that make up aggregate expenditure and aggregate income. So by using the two approaches, the Department of Commerce can check one aggregate against the other. The small discrepancy between the approaches is used to adjust both approaches to make them equal.

Figure 6.4 shows this equality between the approaches to measuring GDP and summarizes the expenditure, income, and product concepts.

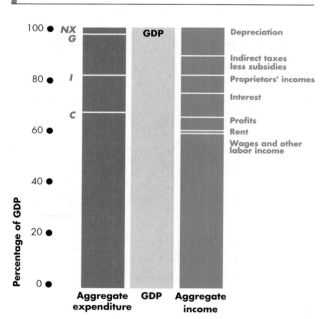

FIGURE 6.4

Aggregate Expenditure, Output, and Income

The red bar illustrates the components of aggregate expenditure as well as their relative magnitudes. Net exports, the smallest component, is shown here as a positive quantity, but in some years it is negative. The green bar illustrates the components of aggregate income and their relative magnitudes. The figure illustrates the equality between aggregate expenditure, aggregate income, and GDP (the yellow bar).

R E V I E W   Q U I Z

- What is the expenditure approach to measuring GDP?
- What is the income approach to measuring GDP?
- What is the distinction between expenditure on final goods and expenditure on intermediate goods?
- What is value added? How is it calculated?

So far, in our study of GDP and its measurement, we've been concerned with the dollar value of GDP and its components. But the dollar value of GDP can change either because prices change or because there is a change in the volume of goods and services produced—a change in *real* GDP. Let's now see how we measure the price level and distinguish between the dollar value and the real value of GDP.

The Price Level and Real GDP

THE PRICE LEVEL IS THE AVERAGE LEVEL OF PRICES measured by a *price index*. The best known price index in the United States is the Consumer Price Index. Let's see how this price index is calculated.

The Consumer Price Index

The **Consumer Price Index (CPI)** measures the average level of prices of the goods and services that a typical urban family buys. The Bureau of Labor Statistics (BLS) calculates the CPI every month.

To construct the CPI, the BLS first selects a base period (currently the three-year period 1993–1995) and surveys consumer spending patterns to determine the "basket" of goods and services that people bought in the base period. That basket contains around 400 different goods and services. Then, every month, the BLS sends observers to more than 50 urban centers to record the prices of the 400 items. The CPI is calculated by valuing the basket at the current month's prices and expressing its value as a percentage of the value of the same basket in the base period.

Table 6.3 shows a simplified example of the CPI calculation. Here, the basket contains only three

goods and services: oranges, haircuts, and bus rides. The table shows the quantities in the base period and the prices in the base period and the current period. In the base period, a typical consumer buys 100 bus rides at $1.40 each and spends $140 on bus rides. Expenditure on oranges and haircuts is worked out in the same way. Total expenditure is the sum of expenditures on the three goods, which is $210.

To calculate the CPI for the current period, we need only discover the prices of the goods in the current period. Suppose that the prices are those shown in Table 6.3 under "Current period." We can now calculate the current period's value of the basket. For example, the current price of oranges is $1.20 per pound, so the current period's value of the oranges in the basket (5 pounds) is 5 multiplied by $1.20, which is $6. The quantities of haircuts and bus rides are valued at the current period's prices in a similar way. The total value of the base-period basket in the current period is $231.

The CPI is the ratio of the current period's value of the base period's basket to the base period's value, multiplied by 100. In Table 6.3, the CPI is 110 in the current period. The current period's price of the basket is 10 percent higher than it was in the base period.

The CPI is just one of two types of price index. An alternative price index uses the *current-period basket* of goods and services and values them at both the base period's prices and the current period's prices.

TABLE 6.3

The Consumer Price Index: A Simplified Calculation

Base-period basket	Base period Price	Base period Expenditure	Current period Price	Current period Value of basket
5 pounds of oranges	$ 0.80/pound	$ 4	$ 1.20/pound	$ 6
6 haircuts	$ 11.00 each	$ 66	$ 12.50 each	$ 75
100 bus rides	$ 1.40 each	$ 140	$ 1.50 each	$ 150
Total expenditure		$210		$231
CPI	$\dfrac{\$210.00}{\$210.00} \times 100 = 100$		$\dfrac{\$231.00}{\$210.00} \times 100 = 110$	

A fixed base-period basket of goods—5 pounds of oranges, 6 haircuts, and 100 bus rides—is valued in the base period at $210. Prices change, and that same basket is valued at $231 in the current period. The CPI is equal to the current-period value of the basket divided by the base-period value of the basket, multiplied by 100. In the base period, the CPI is 100, and in the current period, the CPI is 110.

A Current-Period Basket Price Index

Table 6.4 shows how to calculate price index that uses a current-period basket. In the *current* period, a typical consumer buys 136 bus rides at $1.50 each and spends $204 on bus rides. Expenditure on oranges and haircuts is worked out in the same way. Total expenditure in the current period is $270.10.

We can calculate the base period's value of the current-period basket by valuing it at the base period's prices. For example, the base period's price of oranges is 80¢ per pound, so the base period's value of the oranges in the basket (3 pounds) is 3 multiplied by 80¢, which is $2.40. The current-period quantities of haircuts and bus rides are valued at the base period's prices in a similar way. The total value of the current-period basket in the base period is $247.80.

The current-period basket price index is the ratio of the current period's expenditure to the base period's value of the basket, multiplied by 100. In Table 6.4, the price index is 109 in the current period. The current period's price of the current-period basket is 9 percent higher than it was in the base period.

The price index that uses current-period quantities increases by less than the CPI, which uses base-period quantities. The reason is that consumers make substitutions when prices change. Here, consumers buy fewer oranges and haircuts and more bus rides.

Real GDP

Real gross domestic product (real GDP) is GDP valued in the prices of a base year. Currently, 1992 is the base year for real GDP calculations in the United States. To calculate real GDP, we begin with GDP in the base year and then use a **chain-weighted output index**, to calculate the growth of real GDP from one year to the next. Real GDP each year is linked to the preceding year's real GDP, all the way back to the base year.

An *output* index is a *quantity* index. It compares the quantities in two periods using the prices of one of the periods. (A *price* index, in contrast, compares the prices in two periods using the quantities of one of the periods.) To learn how to calculate an *output* index, let's use the same simplified situation that Tables 6.3 and 6.4 describe.

In Table 6.3, the value of the base period's quantities at the base-period prices is $210. In Table 6.4, the value of the current period's quantities at the base-period prices is $247.80. In these two value calculations, the prices are the same but the quantities are different. To calculate an output index (a quantity index), express the current period's quantities valued at base-period prices as a percentage of the base period's quantities valued at the base-period prices. The quantity index number is $247.80 ÷ $210 × 100 = 118. Using the base-period prices, the quantity

---

TABLE 6.4

A Current-Period Basket Price Index

Current-period basket	Base period		Current period	
	Price	Value of basket	Price	Expenditure
3 pounds of oranges	$ 0.80/pound	$2.40	$ 1.20/pound	$3.60
5 haircuts	$ 11.00 each	$55.00	$ 12.50 each	$62.50
136 bus rides	$ 1.40 each	$190.40	$ 1.50 each	$204.00
Total expenditure		$247.80		$270.10
Price Index	$\frac{\$247.80}{\$247.80} \times 100 = 100$		$\frac{\$270.10}{\$247.80} \times 100 = 109$	

A fixed current-period basket of goods—3 pounds of oranges, 5 haircuts, and 136 bus rides—is valued in the current period at $270.10. In the base period, that same basket is valued at $247.80. A price index that uses the current-period basket is equal to the current-period value of the basket divided by the base-period value of the basket, multiplied by 100. In the base period, the price index is 100, and in the current period, the price index is 109.

of goods and services is 18 percent higher in the current period than in the base period.

Just as we can calculate two price indexes, we can also calculate two quantity indexes. The second quantity index uses the current-period prices. In Table 6.3, the value of the base period's quantities at current-period prices is $231. In Table 6.4, the value of the current period's quantities at current-period prices is $270.10. In these two value calculations, the prices are the same but the quantities are different. To calculate an output index (a quantity index), express the current period's quantities valued at current-period prices as a percentage of the base period's quantities valued at the current-period prices. The quantity index number is $270.10 ÷ $231 × 100 = 116.9. So using the current-period prices, the quantity of goods and services increased 16.9 percent between the base period and the current period.

The Department of Commerce uses an average of *both* of these quantity indexes to calculate real GDP. The average is a special one called a *geometric mean*, which is the square root of the product of the two indexes. In this simplified example, the average index number is 117.5. If we multiply last period's real GDP by this number (and divide by 100), we get this period's real GDP.

The GDP Deflator

The CPI is a popular index, but it includes only consumer prices. In macroeconomics, we use a broader index called the **GDP deflator**, which measures the average level of prices of all the goods and services that are included in GDP. To calculate the GDP deflator, we use the formula

$$\text{GDP deflator} = \frac{\text{GDP}}{\text{Real GDP}} \times 100.$$

GDP, also called **nominal GDP** for emphasis, is the value of the current period's production in current-period prices. Real GDP is the value of the current period's production in base-period prices. So the GDP deflator is a current-period basket price index. Unlike the CPI, the weights for the GDP deflator are constantly changing.

You can think of GDP as a balloon that is blown up by growing production and rising prices. In Fig. 6.5, the GDP deflator lets the inflation air out of the nominal GDP balloon—the contribution of rising

FIGURE 6.5

The U.S. GDP Balloon

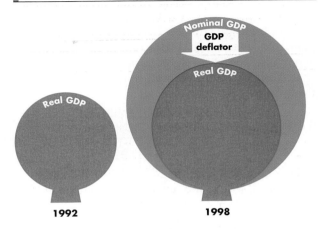

Part of the rise in GDP comes from inflation and part from increased production—an increase in real GDP. The GDP deflator lets some air out of the GDP balloon so that we can see the extent to which production has grown.

prices—so that we can see what has happened to *real* GDP. The red balloon for 1992 shows real GDP in that year. The green balloon shows *nominal* GDP in 1998. The red balloon for 1998 shows real GDP for that year. To see real GDP in 1998, we *deflate* nominal GDP using the GDP deflator.

R E V I E W Q U I Z

- What is the CPI and how is it calculated?
- What is a current-period basket price index?
- How are real GDP and the GDP deflator calculated?
- How does the CPI differ from the GDP deflator?

You now know how to calculate real GDP and the price level. Your next task is to learn how to use these measures to calculate economic growth and inflation. We also look at some limitations of real GDP as a measure of economic growth. And we look at some potential biases in the CPI as a measure of inflation.

Measuring Economic Growth

WE USE ESTIMATES OF REAL GDP TO CALCULATE the economic growth rate. The **economic growth rate** is the percentage change in the quantity of goods and services produced from one year to the next. To calculate the economic growth rate, we use the formula

$$\text{Economic growth rate} = \frac{\text{Real GDP this year} - \text{Real GDP last year}}{\text{Real GDP last year}} \times 100.$$

For example, real GDP was $7,552 in 1998 and $7,270 in 1997. So the economic growth rate (percent per year) during 1998 was

$$\text{Economic growth rate} = \frac{(\$7,552 - \$7,270)}{\$7,270} \times 100$$

$$= 3.7 \text{ percent per year.}$$

We want to measure the economic growth rate so that we may make:

- Economic welfare comparisons
- International comparisons
- Business cycle forecasts

Although the real GDP growth rate is used for these three purposes, it is not a perfect measure for any of them. But nor is it a totally misleading measure. We'll evaluate the limitations of real GDP and its growth rate in each of the three cases.

Economic Welfare Comparisons

Economic welfare is a comprehensive measure of the general state of economic well-being. Economic welfare improves when the production of *all* the goods and services grows. The goods and services that make up real GDP growth are only a part of all the items that influence economic welfare.

Today, because of real GDP growth, real GDP per person in the United States of $28,000 is twice what it was in 1963. But are we twice as well off? Does this growth of real GDP provide a full and accurate measure of the change in economic welfare?

It does not. The reason is that economic welfare depends on many other factors that are not measured by real GDP or that are not measured accurately by real GDP. Some of these factors are:

- Over adjustment for inflation
- Household production
- Underground economic activity
- Health and life expectancy
- Leisure time
- Environment quality
- Political freedom and social justice

Over Adjustment for Inflation   The price indexes used to measure inflation give an upward-biased estimate of true inflation. (We learn about the sources of this bias on pp. 130-131.) If we overestimate the rise in prices, we underestimate of the growth of real GDP. When car prices rise because cars have gotten better (safer, more fuel efficient, more comfortable), the CPI and the GDP deflator count the price increase as inflation. So what is really an increase in production is counted as an increase in price rather than an increase in real GDP. It is deflated away by the wrongly measured higher price level. The magnitude of this bias is probably less than 1 percentage point a year, but its exact magnitude is not known.

Household Production   An enormous amount of production takes place every day in our homes. Preparing meals, cleaning the kitchen, changing a light bulb, cutting the grass, washing the car, and helping a high school student with homework are all examples of productive activities that do not involve market transactions and are not counted as part of GDP.

If these activities grew at the same rate as real GDP, not measuring them would not be a problem. But it is likely that market production, which is part of GDP, is increasingly replacing household production, which is not part of GDP. Two trends point in this direction. One is the number of people who have jobs, which has increased from 57 percent in 1970 to 64 percent in 1998. The other is the trend in the purchase of traditionally home-produced goods and services in the market. For example, more and more families now eat in fast-food restaurants— one of the fastest-growing industries in the United States—and use day-care services. This trend means that an increasing proportion of food preparation and child care that were part of household production are now measured as part of GDP. So real GDP grows more rapidly than does real GDP plus home production.

Underground Economic Activity   The *underground economy* is the part of the economy that is purposely hidden from the view of the government in order to avoid taxes and regulations or because the goods and services being produced are illegal. Because underground economic activity is unreported, it is omitted from GDP.

The underground economy is easy to describe, even if it is hard to measure. It includes the production and distribution of illegal drugs, production that uses illegal labor that is paid less than the minimum wage, and jobs done for cash to avoid paying income taxes. This last category might be quite large and includes tips earned by cab drivers, hairdressers, and hotel and restaurant workers.

Estimates of the scale of the underground economy range between 9 and 30 percent of GDP ($770 billion to $2,550 billion) in the United States and much more in some countries. It is particularly large in some Eastern European countries that are making a transition from communist economic planning to a market economy.

Provided that the underground economy is a reasonably stable proportion of the total economy, the growth rate of real GDP still gives a useful estimate of changes in economic welfare. But sometimes, production shifts from the underground economy to the rest of the economy, and sometimes it shifts the other way. The underground economy expands relative to the rest of the economy if taxes become especially high or if regulations become especially restrictive. And the underground economy shrinks relative to the rest of the economy if the burdens of taxes and regulations are eased. During the 1980s, when tax rates were cut, there was an increase in the reporting of previously hidden income and tax revenues increased. So some part (but probably a very small part) of the expansion of real GDP during the 1980s represented a shift from the underground economy rather than an increase in production.

Health and Life Expectancy   Good health and a long life—the hopes of everyone—do not show up in real GDP, at least not directly. A higher real GDP does enable us to spend more on medical research, health care, a good diet, and exercise equipment. And as real GDP has increased, our life expectancy has lengthened—from 70 years at the end of World War II to approaching 80 years today. Infant deaths and death in childbirth, two fearful scourges of the nineteenth century, have almost been eliminated.

But we face new health and life expectancy problems every year. AIDS and drug abuse are taking young lives at a rate that causes serious concern. When we take these negative influences into account, we see that real GDP growth overstates the improvements in economic welfare.

Leisure Time   Leisure time is an economic good that adds to our economic welfare. Other things being equal, the more leisure we have, the better off we are. Our working time is valued as part of GDP, but our leisure time is not. Yet from the point of view of economic welfare, that leisure time must be at least as valuable to us as the wage that we earn on the last hour worked. If it was not, we would work instead of taking the leisure. Over the years, leisure time has steadily increased. The workweek has become shorter, more people take early retirement, and the number of vacation days has increased. These improvements in economic well-being are not reflected in real GDP.

Environment Quality   Economic activity directly influences the quality of the environment. The burning of hydrocarbon fuels is the most visible activity that damages our environment. But it is not the only example. The depletion of exhaustible resources, the mass clearing of forests, and the pollution of lakes and rivers are other major environmental consequences of industrial production.

Resources that are used to protect the environment are valued as part of GDP. For example, the value of catalytic converters that help to protect the atmosphere from automobile emissions is part of GDP. But if we did not use such pieces of equipment and instead polluted the atmosphere, we would not count the deteriorating air that we were breathing as a negative part of GDP.

An industrial society possibly produces more atmospheric pollution than an agricultural society does. But such pollution does not always increase as we become wealthier. One of the things that wealthy people value is a clean environment, and they devote resources to protecting it. Compare the pollution that was discovered in East Germany in the late 1980s with pollution in the United States. East Germany, a relatively poor country, polluted its rivers, lakes, and atmosphere in a way that is unimaginable in the United States or in wealthy West Germany.

Political Freedom and Social Justice   Most people value political freedoms such as those provided by the U.S. Constitution. And they value social justice or fairness—equality of opportunity and of access to social security safety nets that protect people from the extremes of misfortune.

A country might have a very large real GDP per person but have limited political freedom and equity. For example, a small elite might enjoy political liberty and extreme wealth while the vast majority are effectively enslaved and live in abject poverty. Such an economy would generally be regarded as having less economic welfare than one that had the same amount of real GDP but in which political freedoms were enjoyed by everyone. Today, China has rapid real GDP growth but limited political freedoms, while Russia has a decreasing real GDP and an emerging democratic political system. Economists have no easy way to determine which of these countries is better off.

The Bottom Line   Do we get the wrong message about the growth in economic welfare by looking at the growth of real GDP? The influences omitted from real GDP are probably important and could be large. Developing countries have a larger underground economy and a larger amount of household production than do developed countries. So as an economy develops and grows, part of the apparent growth might reflect a switch from underground to regular production and from home production to market production. This measurement error overstates the rate of economic growth and the improvement in economic welfare.

Other influences on living standards include the amount of leisure time available, the quality of the environment, the security of jobs and homes, the safety of city streets, and so on. It is possible to construct broader measures that combine the many influences that contribute to human happiness. Real GDP will be one element in those broader measures, but it will by no means be the whole of them.

International Comparisons

All the problems we've just reviewed affect economic welfare of every country, so to make international comparisons of economic welfare, factors additional to real GDP must be used. But real GDP comparisons are major components of international welfare comparisons and two special problems arise in making these comparisons. First, the real GDP of one country must be converted into the same currency units as the real GDP of the other country. Second,

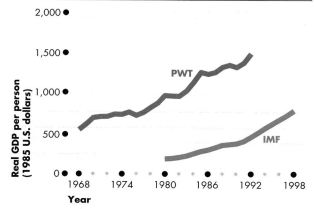

FIGURE 6.6
Two Views of Real GDP in China

According to the official statistics of the International Monetary Fund (IMF) and the World Bank, China is a poor developing country. But according to an alternative view, Penn World Table (PWT), which is based on purchasing power prices, China has a real GDP more than 3.3 times the official view and has the world's third largest total production.

Sources: IMF, *International Financial Statistics Yearbook*, 1998, Washington, D.C., World Bank, *World Development Report, 1998*, Washington, D.C.; "The Penn World Table (Mark 5.5): An Expanded Set of International Comparisons, 1950–1988," *Quarterly Journal of Economics*, May 1991, pp. 327–368; new computer diskette, Mark 5.6a, 1995; and the author's calculations.

the same prices must be used to value the goods and services in the countries being compared. Let's look at these two problems by using a striking example, a comparison of the United States and China.

In 1992 (the most recent year for which we can make this comparison), GDP per person in the United States was $24,451. The official Chinese statistics published by the International Monetary Fund (IMF) say that GDP per person in China in 1992 was 2,402 yuan. (The yuan is the currency of China.) On the average, during 1992, $1 U.S. was worth 5.762 yuan. If we use this exchange rate to convert Chinese yuan into U.S. dollars, we get a value of $417.

The official comparison of China and the United States makes China look extremely poor. In 1992, GDP per person in the United States was 59 times that in China.

Figure 6.6 shows the official story of real GDP in China between 1980 and 1998. But Fig. 6.6 also shows another story. It shows an estimate of real GDP per person in China that is much larger than the official measure. Let's see how this alternative measurement is made.

GDP in the United States is measured by using prices that prevail in the United States. China's GDP is measured by using prices that prevail in China. But the relative prices in the two countries are very different. Some goods that are expensive in the United States cost very little in China. These items get a small weight in China's real GDP. If, instead of using China's prices, all the goods and services produced in China are valued at the prices prevailing in the United States, then a more valid comparison can be made of GDP in the two countries. Such a comparison uses prices called *purchasing power parity prices.*

Robert Summers and Alan Heston, economists in the Center for International Comparisons at the University of Pennsylvania, have used purchasing power parity prices to construct real GDP data for more than one hundred countries. These data, which are published in the Penn World Table (PWT), tell a remarkable story about China. The PWT data use 1985 as the base year, so they are measured in 1985 dollars. According to the Penn World Table, in 1992, real GDP per person in the United States was 12 times that of China, not the 59 times shown in the official data.

Figure 6.6 shows the PWT view of China and compares it with the official view. The difference in the two views arises from the prices used. The official statistics use Chinese prices, while the PWT data use purchasing power parity prices.

Despite large differences in estimates of the *level* of China's real GDP, there is much less doubt about its growth rate. The economy of China is expanding at an extraordinary rate, and it is for this reason that most businesses are paying a great deal of attention to the prospects of expanding their activities in China and the other Asian economies.

U.S. real GDP is measured quite reliably. But China's is not. The alternative measures of China's real GDP are somewhat unreliable, and the truth about GDP in China is not known.

Business Cycle Forecasts

When the Fed decides to raise interest rates to slow an expansion that it believes is too strong, it looks at the latest estimates of real GDP and inflation. But

suppose that for the reasons that we've just discussed, real GDP is mismeasured. Does this mismeasurement hamper our ability to identify the phases of the business cycle? It does not. The reason is that although the omissions from real GDP do change over time, they probably do not change in a systematic way with the business cycle. So inaccurate measurement of real GDP does not necessarily cause a wrong assessment of the phase of the business cycle.

The fluctuations in economic activity measured by real GDP tell a reasonably accurate story about the phase of the business cycle that the economy is in. When real GDP grows, the economy is in a business cycle expansion; when real GDP shrinks (for two quarters), the economy is in a recession. Also, as real GDP fluctuates, so do employment and unemployment.

But real GDP fluctuations probably exaggerate or overstate the fluctuations in total production and economic welfare. The reason is that when business activity slows in a recession, household production increases, and so does leisure time. When business activity speeds up in an expansion, household production and leisure time decrease. Because household production and leisure time increase in a recession and decrease in an expansion, real GDP fluctuations tend to overstate the fluctuations in total production and in economic welfare. But the directions of change of real GDP, total production, and economic welfare are probably the same.

REVIEW QUIZ

- Does real GDP measure economic welfare? If not, why not?
- Does real GDP measure total production of goods and services? If not, what are the main omissions?
- How can we make valid international comparisons of real GDP?
- Does the growth of real GDP measure the long-term growth rate accurately?
- Do the fluctuations in real GDP measure the business cycle accurately?

Let's now see how we use the CPI data to measure inflation and learn about the limitations of our measurement of this important feature of our economy.

Measuring Inflation

A MAJOR PURPOSE OF THE CPI IS TO MEASURE inflation, and the measure is put to practical use. For example, it is used to determine cost of living adjustments to Social Security payments and changes in tax brackets—the income ranges over which different income tax rates apply. The data generated by the CPI survey are also used, along with other information, in the calculations of real GDP, nominal GDP, and the GDP deflator.

The **inflation rate** is the percentage change in the price level from one year to the next. To calculate the inflation rate, we use the formula

$$\text{Inflation rate} = \frac{(\text{CPI this year} - \text{CPI last year})}{\text{CPI last year}} \times 100.$$

For example, the CPI was 164 in December 1998 and 161.3 in December 1997. So the inflation rate during 1998 was

$$\text{Inflation rate} = \frac{(164 - 161.3)}{161.3} \times 100.$$

$$= 1.67 \text{ percent per year.}$$

An alternative measure of inflation replaces the CPI with the GDP deflator in the formula above.

How different are the two measures of inflation based on the CPI and the GDP deflator? And how good a measure of inflation do these index numbers provide?

Figure 6.7 answers the first question. The average inflation rate over the period shown is 4.9 percent a year for the CPI and 4.8 percent a year for the GDP deflator. So on the average, the two measures are similar. But the CPI fluctuates more than the GDP deflator. Worse, *both* measures of inflation probably overstate the inflation rate, and especially the CPI.

The Biased CPI

The main sources of bias in the CPI are:

- New goods bias
- Quality change bias
- Commodity substitution bias
- Outlet substitution bias

FIGURE 6.7
Two Measures of Inflation

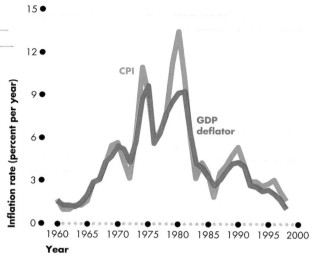

The CPI and the GDP deflator have similar averages over the period shown here—4.9 percent a year for the CPI and 4.8 percent a year for the GDP deflator—but the CPI fluctuates more than the GDP deflator, and both measures probably overstate the inflation rate.

Source: Economic Report of the President, 1999.

New Goods Bias   New goods keep replacing old goods. For example, PCs have replaced typewriters. If you want to compare the price level in 1998 with that in 1978, you must somehow compare the price of a computer today with that of a typewriter in 1978. Because PCs are more expensive than typewriters, the arrival of these new goods puts an upward bias into the CPI and its inflation rate.

Quality Change Bias   Cars, CD players, and many other items get better every year. Part of the rise in the prices of these items is a payment for improved quality and is not inflation. But the CPI counts the price rise as inflation and so overstates inflation.

Commodity Substitution Bias   Changes in relative prices lead consumers to change the items they buy. For example, if the price of beef rises and the price of chicken remains unchanged, people buy more chicken and less beef. Suppose they switch from beef to chicken on a scale that provides the same amount of protein and the same enjoyment as before and costs the same as before. Because the CPI ignores the substitution, it says the price of protein has increased when in fact it is constant.

Outlet Substitution Bias When confronted with higher prices, people use discount stores more frequently and convenience stores less frequently. This phenomenon is called *outlet substitution*. The CPI surveys do not monitor outlet substitutions.

The Magnitude of the Bias

You've reviewed the sources of bias in the CPI. But how big is the bias? This question was tackled in 1996 by a Congressional Advisory Commission on the Consumer Price Index, chaired by Michael Boskin, an economics professor at Stanford University. This commission said that the CPI overstates inflation by 1.1 percentage points a year. That is, if the CPI reports that inflation is 3.1 percent a year, most likely inflation is actually 2 percent a year.

Reducing the Bias To reduce the bias in the CPI, the Bureau of Labor Statistics has decided to undertake consumer spending surveys at more frequent intervals and to revise the basket used for calculating the CPI every 2 years.

Some Consequences of the Bias

The bias in the CPI has three main consequences. It

- Distorts private contracts
- Increases government outlays
- Biased estimates of real earnings

Many private agreements, such as wage contracts, are linked to the CPI. For example, a firm and its workers might agree to a 3-year wage deal that increases the wage rate by 2 percent a year *plus* the percentage increase in the CPI. Such a deal ends up giving the workers more real income than the firm intended.

Close to a third of federal government outlays are linked directly to the CPI. And while a bias of 1 percent a year seems small, accumulated over a decade, it adds up to almost a trillion dollars of additional expenditures.

According to official government statistics, since 1973, real hourly earnings in manufacturing industry have *fallen* by 13 percent. If the CPI is adjusted for the bias estimated by the Boskin Commission, this picture is transformed into one in which real earnings have *increased* by 13 percent!

Is the GDP Deflator Biased?

The GDP deflator is calculated from nominal GDP and the chain-linked estimate of real GDP growth. In principle, real GDP includes new goods and quality improvements. It is also based on people's actual expenditures and so reflects substitutions of both commodities and retail outlets. So in principle, the GDP deflator is not subject to the biases of the CPI. But in practice, the GDP deflator suffers from some of the CPI's problems. To arrive at its estimate of real GDP, the Commerce Department does not directly measure the physical quantities produced. Instead, it estimates quantities by dividing expenditures by price indexes. And one of these price indexes is the CPI. So the biased CPI injects a bias into the GDP deflator.

R E V I E W   Q U I Z

- What are the four main ways in which the CPI is an upward-biased measure of the price level?
- By how much is the CPI estimated to overstate the inflation rate? Is the amount the same in all countries?
- Why might the GDP deflator be a biased measure of the price level?
- What are the main problems that arise from a bias in the measurement of the price level?

◆ You've now studied the methods used to measure GDP, economic growth, and inflation. And you've learned about some of the limitations of these measures. Your next task, in Chapter 7, is to study the methods used to measure employment and unemployment and other indicators of economic health in labor markets.

Before you embark on this next topic, spend a few minutes with *Reading Between the Lines* on pp. 132–133, which explores the consequences of the bias in the CPI for the measurement of real GDP and real hourly earnings. You'll be surprised by the numbers.

Correcting the CPI Bias

THE NEW YORK TIMES, DECEMBER 1, 1996

Essence of the Story

Sorry, Wrong Numbers So Maybe It Wasn't the Economy

BY FLOYD NORRIS

Economic statistics are thrust into the news every day, with a portentous exactitude that can send Wall Street soaring or reeling, influence Government policy, even sway elections. Did consumer prices rise one-tenth of a percent more than was expected? Was economic growth a half percentage point less than people had been hoping?

But what if the statistics are wrong? And what if they are consistently wrong in the same direction? Over time, that can produce a very distorted picture of the economy, with unfortunate effects brought about not by the economy but by our perceptions of it and with those perceptions having effects of their own. ...

This week a commission headed by Michael Boskin, the Stanford economist and former adviser to President Bush, will report to the Senate Finance Committee that inflation, as measured by the Consumer Price Index, has been rising at a far slower pace than we had thought. Economists who have studied the issue now generally agree that inflation has been overstated, although some argue that the error is relatively

small and may not make a significant difference.

The commission was appointed last year because of serious doubts about how changes in benefits and tax brackets, which have a major effect on the deficit, are calculated. A conclusion that the Consumer Price Index [CPI] has been overstated could lead to efforts to reduce the automatic increases in certain benefits, notably Social Security. That's sure to provoke a fight.

But perhaps even more important are changes that may be necessary in our view of the economy for the last two decades. For much of that time, even as America came roaring back into a preeminent position in technological leadership and the stock market zoomed, economists have been looking at statistics that showed a weak economy. And politicians have been trying to address public angst over economic decline. ...

Leonard Nakamura, an economist with the Federal Reserve Bank of Philadelphia, is known for his work on inflation. ... His estimates of the overstatement are among the largest ... at about 1.25 percent annually in the mid-1970s, rising to about 2.75 percent now. ...

- Economic statistics can influence stock markets and government policy, and, if inaccurate, economic statistics can produce a distorted picture of the economy.

- In December 1996, a commission headed by Michael Boskin reported to the Senate Finance Committee that the CPI overstates the inflation rate.

- Economists generally agree that the CPI overstates the inflation rate but are uncertain about the magnitude of the overstatement.

- For the last 20 years, technology has advanced and the stock prices have increased, but economic statistics have shown slow economic growth.

- Leonard Nakamura, an economist at the Federal Reserve Bank of Philadelphia, says the economic statistics are wrong and that inflation has been overstated—by 1.25 percent a year during the mid-1970s to 2.75 percent a year in 1996.

■ Leonard Nakamura, a research economist at the Federal Reserve Bank of Philadelphia, believes that inflation has been overstated for at least 20 years. He says that the overstatement was approximately 1.25 percent annually during the mid-1970s, rising to approximately 2.75 percent annually by the mid-1990s.

■ Figure 1 shows Mr. Nakamura's estimate of the Consumer Price Index. His index equals 100 in 1975. According to Mr. Nakamura, the price level doubled between 1975 and 1996, not tripled as has been reported in the official data.

■ If we accept Mr. Nakamura's revised price level, we must change other economic indicators that are expressed in constant dollars.

■ Figure 2 shows the implications of Mr. Nakamura's assumptions for real GDP. According to his new inflation figures, real GDP has increased by twice as much as reported in the official data.

■ Figure 3 shows the impact of the new view of prices on real hourly earnings. The official

view is that since 1975, real hourly earnings have *decreased* by 9 percent. The new view is that real hourly earnings have *increased* by 35 percent!

■ Mr. Nakamura's views are toward the upper end of the range of what economists believe, but they are not outrageous. He could be correct. If he is correct, the U.S. economy is in even better shape than Alan Greenspan, President Clinton, and many other leading public commentators dared to believe.

You're The Voter

■ As a taxpayer and voter, do you care whether the government's economic statistics are accurate?

■ Try to think of reasons why is matters *to you* that the official statistics are accurate.

■ Would you be willing to see government funds diverted from some existing use and spent on data gathering and processing to get better measures of prices, real GDP, and real earnings?

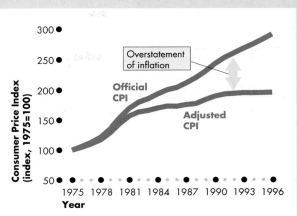

Figure 1 Consumer Price Index

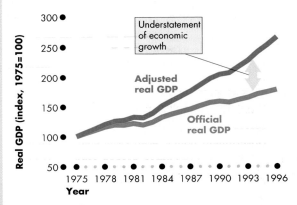

Figure 2 Real GDP

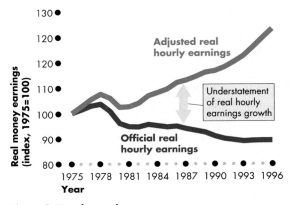

Figure 3 Hourly earnings

SUMMARY

KEY POINTS

Gross Domestic Product (pp. 114–118)

- Gross domestic product (GDP), which is the value of total production in a country during a given period, is calculated by using the circular flow of income and expenditure.
- Aggregate expenditure on goods and services equals aggregate income and GDP.

Measuring U.S. GDP (pp. 118–122)

- Because aggregate expenditure, aggregate income, and the value of aggregate production are equal, we can measure GDP by using the expenditure approach or the income approach.
- The expenditure approach sums consumption expenditure, investment, government purchases of goods and services, and net exports.
- The income approach sums wages, interest, rent, and profit (and indirect taxes and depreciation).

The Price Level and Real GDP (pp. 123–125)

- The Consumer Price Index (CPI) is an index number that measures average price of goods and services typically consumed by American families.
- Real GDP is measured by a chain-weighted output index that compares the value of production each year with its value at the previous year's prices.
- The GDP deflator measures the price level based on the prices of the items that make up GDP.

Measuring Economic Growth (pp. 126–129)

- We measure the economic growth rate as the percentage change in real GDP.
- Real GDP growth is not a perfect measure of economic growth because it excludes quality improvements, household production, the underground economy, environmental damage, health and life expectancy, leisure time, political freedom, and social justice.
- The growth rate of real GDP gives a good indication of the phases of the business cycle.

Measuring Inflation (pp. 130–131)

- We measure the inflation rate as the percentage change in the CPI (or GDP deflator).
- The CPI is biased upward because it does not take proper account of the effects of changes in spending patterns.
- Attempts are being made to reduce the CPI bias.

KEY FIGURES AND TABLES

KEY TERMS

PROBLEMS

*1. Martha owns a copy shop that has 5 copiers. One copier wears out each year and is replaced. In addition, this year Martha will expand her business to 7 copiers. Calculate Martha's initial capital stock, depreciation, gross investment, net investment, and final capital stock.

2. Wendy operates a weaving shop with 10 looms. One loom wears out each year and is replaced. But this year, Wendy will expand her business to 12 looms. Calculate Wendy's initial capital stock, depreciation, gross investment, net investment, and final capital stock.

*3. The figure shows the flows of income and expenditure on Lotus Island. During 1997, A was $10 million, B was $30 million, C was $12 million, D was $15 million, and E was $3 million. Calculate:

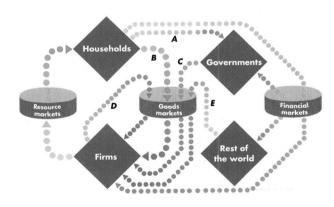

a. Aggregate expenditure.
b. Aggregate income.
c. GDP.
d. Government budget deficit.
e. Household saving.
f. Government saving.
g. Foreign borrowing.
h. National saving.

4. In problem 3, during 1998, A was $10 million, B was $50 million, C was $15 million, D was $15 million, and E was –$5 million. Calculate the quantities in problem 3 during 1998.

*5. The transactions in Ecoland last year were:

Item	Dollars
Wages paid to labor	800,000
Consumption expenditure	600,000
Taxes	250,000
Transfer payments	50,000
Profits	200,000
Investment	250,000
Government purchases	200,000
Exports	300,000
Saving	300,000
Imports	250,000

a. Calculate Ecoland's GDP.
b. Did you use the expenditure approach or the incomes approach to make this calculation?
c. How is investment financed?

6. The transactions in Highland last year were:

Item	Dollars
Wages paid to labor	800,000
Consumption expenditure	650,000
Net taxes	200,000
Profits	250,000
Investment	300,000
Government purchases	250,000
Exports	250,000
Saving	200,000
Imports	300,000

a. Calculate Highland's GDP.
b. What extra information do you need to calculate net domestic product?
c. Where does Highland get the funds to finance its investment?

*7. A typical family on Sandy Island consumes only juice and cloth. Last year, which was the base year, the family spent $40 on juice and $25 on cloth. In the base year, juice was $4 a bottle and cloth was $5 a length. In the current year, juice is $4 a bottle and cloth is $6 a length. Calculate:
a. The basket used in the CPI.
b. The CPI in the current year.
c. The inflation rate in the current year.

8. A typical family on Lizard Island consumes only mangoes and nuts. Last year, which was the base year, the family spent $60 on nuts and $10 on mangoes. In the base year, mangoes were $1 each and nuts were $3 a bag. In the

current year, mangoes are $1.50 each and nuts are $4 a bag. Calculate:
a. The basket used in the CPI.
b. The CPI in the current year.
c. The inflation rate in the current year.

*9. Bananaland produces only bananas and sunscreen. The base year is 1997, and the tables give the quantities produced and the prices.

| Good | Quantity | |
	1997	1998
Bananas	1,000 bunches	1,100 bunches
Sunscreen	500 bottles	525 bottles

| Good | Price | |
	1997	1998
Bananas	$2 a bunch	$3 a bunch
Sunscreen	$10 a bottle	$8 a bottle

Calculate Bananaland's:
a. GDP and real GDP in 1997 and 1998.
b. Growth rate of real GDP in 1998.
c. GDP deflator in 1998.

10. Sea Island produces only lobsters and crabs. The base year is 1997, and the tables give the quantities produced and the prices.

| Good | Quantity | |
	1997	1998
Lobsters	1,000	1,100
Crabs	500	525

| Good | Price | |
	1997	1998
Lobsters	$20 each	$25 each
Crabs	$10 each	$12 each

Calculate Sea Island's:
a. GDP and real GDP in 1997 and 1998.
b. Growth rate of real GDP in 1998.
c. GDP deflator in 1998.

CRITICAL THINKING

1. Study *Reading Between the Lines* on pp. 132–133 and then answer the following questions:
    a. How large does Mr. Nakamura believe the bias in the CPI to be?
    b. How does Mr. Nakamura's estimate of the CPI bias compare with that of the Boskin commission?
    c. Write a brief description of the U.S. economy since 1975 based on the view of the official statistics and based on the view of Mr. Nakamura.
    d. If Mr. Nakamura's view of the economy is correct, how different does economic growth look during the terms of Presidents Carter, Reagan, Bush, and Clinton compared with each other and compared with the official data?
    e. Should Social Security benefits be linked to the measured CPI or to an estimate of the true CPI? Why or why not?
    f. What difference, if any, do you think there would be in the distribution of income between workers and business owners if the bias in the CPI had been discovered 10 years ago? Explain your answer.

2. Use the link on the Parkin Web site to visit the Federal Reserve Economic Data (FRED) Web site at the Federal Reserve Bank of St. Louis. There you can obtain the latest data on real GDP, nominal GDP, and the GDP deflator as well as the data for the previous year.
    a. What was the GDP deflator in the most recent year?
    b. What was the GDP deflator in the previous year?
    c. What is the inflation rate as measured by the GDP deflator between these two years?
    d. What was real GDP in the most recent year?
    e. What was real GDP in the previous year?
    f. What is the real GDP growth rate between these two years?
    g. Check that, for the data you have obtained, nominal GDP divided by real GDP equals the GDP deflator.

Chapter 7

Measuring Employment and Unemployment

Vital Signs

Each month, we chart the course of the unemployment rate as a measure of U.S. economic health. How do we measure unemployment? What does it tell us? Is it a reliable vital sign for the economy? ◆ June 1992 was a month in which unemployment peaked at almost 10 million. How can such a large number of people be unemployed? How do people become unemployed? Do most of them get fired, or do most quit their jobs to look for better ones? How long do spells of unemployment last for most people—a week, two weeks, or several months? And how does the length of unemployment spells vary over the business cycle? ◆ You probably know that unemployment is more common among young people than among older people. It is also more common among minorities than among whites. Why are some groups more frequently unemployed than others? ◆ We also chart every month the number of people working. This number fluctuates as the unemployment rate fluctuates, but it also trends upward. At the start of 1999, more than 130 million people in the United States had jobs. What does this vital sign tell us about the health of the U.S. economy? Does the number of jobs grow quickly enough to keep pace with increases in the population? ◆ Yet other signs of economic health are the hours people work and the wages they receive. Are work hours growing as quickly as the number of people with jobs? Are most of the new jobs full time or part time? Also, are most new jobs high-wage or low-wage jobs?

◆ These are the questions we study in this chapter. You will discover that a lot of ideas that people have about the U.S. labor market are just plain wrong. The economy has created millions of jobs, including good jobs that pay high wages and provide good benefits. But most people have seen a slowdown in their rate of wage increase, and many have seen their wages fall. We begin by looking at the key labor market indicators and the way they are measured.

After studying this chapter, you will be able to:

■ Define the unemployment rate, the labor force participation rate, the employment-to-population ratio, and aggregate hours

■ Describe the trends and fluctuations in the indicators of labor market performance

■ Describe the sources of unemployment, its duration, and the groups that are most affected by it

■ Describe the relationship between employment, unemployment, and real GDP

Employment and Wages

FOR MOST OF US, THE LABOR MARKET IS THE source of almost all our income. We become concerned when jobs are hard to find. And we become more relaxed when jobs are plentiful. We also care about the kinds of jobs that are available. We want good jobs, which means we want well-paid and interesting jobs. In this chapter, we study the way that economists track the health of the labor market.

Population Survey

Every month, the U.S. Census Bureau surveys 60,000 households and asks a series of questions about the age and job market status of its members. This survey is called the Current Population Survey. The Census Bureau uses the answers to describe the anatomy of the labor force.

Figure 7.1 shows the population categories used by the Census Bureau and the relationships among the categories. It divides the population into two groups: the working-age population and others who are too young to work or who live in institutions and are unable to work. The **working-age population** is the total number of people aged 16 years and over who are not in jail, hospital, or some other form of institutional care. The Census Bureau divides the working-age population into two groups: those in the labor force and those not in the labor force. It also divides the labor force into two groups: the employed and the unemployed. So the **labor force** is the sum of the employed and the unemployed.

To be counted as employed in the Current Population Survey, a person must have either a full-time job or a part-time job. To be counted as *un*employed, a person must be available for work and must be in one of three categories:

1. Without work but has made specific efforts to find a job within the previous four weeks
2. Waiting to be called back to a job from which he or she has been laid off
3. Waiting to start a new job within 30 days

Anyone surveyed who satisfies one of these three criteria is counted as unemployed. People in the working-age population who are neither employed nor unemployed are classified as not in the labor force.

FIGURE 7.1
Population Labor Force Categories

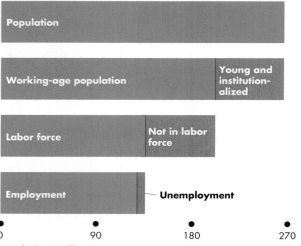

Population (millions)

The population is divided into the working-age population and the young and institutionalized. The working-age population is divided into the labor force and those not in the labor force. The labor force is divided into the employed and the unemployed.

Source: Economic Report of the President, 1999.

In 1998, the population of the United States was 270.2 million. There were 65 million people under 16 years of age or living in institutions. The working-age population was 205.2 million. Of this number, 67.5 million were not in the labor force. Most of these people were in school full time or had retired from work. The remaining 137.7 million people made up the U.S. labor force. Of these, 131.5 million were employed and 6.2 million were unemployed.

Three Labor Market Indicators

The Census Bureau calculates three indicators of the state of the labor market, which are shown in Fig. 7.2. They are:

- The unemployment rate
- The labor force participation rate
- The employment-to-population ratio

The Unemployment Rate   The amount of unemployment is an indicator of the extent to which people who want jobs can't find them. The **unemployment rate** is the percentage of the people in the labor force who are unemployed. That is,

$$\text{Unemployment rate} = \frac{\text{Number of people unemployed}}{\text{Labor force}} \times 100,$$

and

$$\text{Labor force} = \text{Number of people employed} + \text{Number of people unemployed}.$$

In 1998, the number of people employed was 131.5 million and the number unemployed was 6.2 million. By using the above equations, you can verify that the labor force was 137.7 million (131.5 million plus 6.2 million) and the unemployment rate was 4.5 percent (6.2 million divided by 137.7 million, multiplied by 100).

Figure 7.2 shows the unemployment rate (orange line) and two other labor market indicators between 1960 and 1998. The average unemployment rate has been 6 percent, and it reached peak values during the OPEC recession and the recessions of 1982 and 1990—1991.

The Labor Force Participation Rate   The number of people who join the labor force is an indicator of the willingness of people of working age to take jobs. The **labor force participation rate** is the percentage of the working-age population who are members of the labor force. That is,

$$\frac{\text{Labor force}}{\text{participation rate}} = \frac{\text{Labor force}}{\text{Working-age population}} \times 100.$$

In 1998, the labor force was 137.7 million and the working-age population was 205.2 million. By using the above equation, you can calculate the labor force participation rate. It was 67.1 percent (137.7 million divided by 205.2 million, multiplied by 100).

The labor force participation rate (graphed in red and plotted on the left scale) has followed an upward trend and has increased from 59 percent during the early 1960s to 67 percent during the 1990s. It has also had some mild fluctuations. They result from unsuccessful job seekers becoming discouraged

FIGURE 7.2

Employment, Unemployment, and the Labor Force: 1960–1998

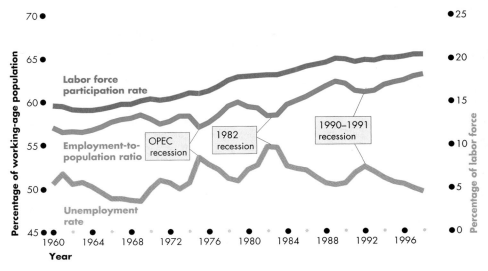

The unemployment rate increases in recessions and decreases in expansions. The labor force participation rate and the employment-to-population ratio have upward trends and fluctuate with the business cycle. The employment-to-population ratio fluctuates more than the labor force participation rate and reflects cyclical fluctuations in the unemployment rate. Fluctuations in the labor force participation rate arise mainly because of discouraged workers.

Source: Economic Report of the President, 1999.

workers. **Discouraged workers** are people who are available and willing to work but have not made specific efforts to find a job within the previous four weeks. These workers often temporarily leave the labor force during a recession and reenter during an expansion and become active job seekers.

The Employment-to-Population Ratio   The number of people of working age who have jobs is an indicator of both the availability of jobs and the degree of match between people's skills and jobs. The **employment-to-population ratio** is the percentage of people of working age who have jobs. That is,

$$\text{Employment-to-population ratio} = \frac{\text{Number of people employed}}{\text{Working-age population}} \times 100.$$

In 1998, employment was 131.5 million and the working-age population was 205.2 million. By using the above equation, you can calculate the employment-to-population ratio. It was 64.1 percent (131.5 million divided by 205.2 million, multiplied by 100).

The employment-to-population ratio (graphed in blue and plotted against the left scale) has increased from 55 percent during the early 1960s to 64 percent in 1998. The increase in the employment-to-population ratio means that the U.S. economy has created jobs at a faster rate than the working-age population has grown. This labor market indicator also fluctuates, and its fluctuations coincide with but are opposite to those in the unemployment rate. It falls during a recession and increases during an expansion.

Why have the labor force participation rate and the employment-to-population ratio increased? The main reason is an increase in the number of women in the labor force. Figure 7.3 shows this increase. Between 1960 and 1998, the female labor force participation rate increased from 38 percent to 60 percent. Shorter work hours, higher productivity, and an increased emphasis on white-collar jobs have expanded the job opportunities and wages available to women. At the same time, technological advances have increased productivity in the home and freed up women's time to take jobs outside the home.

Figure 7.3 also shows another remarkable trend in the U.S. labor force: The labor force participation rate and the employment-to-population ratio for men have *decreased*. Between 1960 and 1998, the male labor force participation rate decreased from

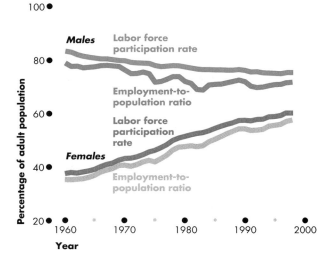

FIGURE 7.3

The Changing Face of the Labor Market

The upward trends in the labor force participation rate and the employment-to-population ratio are accounted for mainly by the increasing participation of women in the labor market. The male labor force participation rate and employment-to-population ratio have decreased.

Source: Economic Report of the President, 1999.

83 percent to 75 percent. It has decreased because increasing numbers of men are remaining in school longer and because some are retiring earlier.

Aggregate Hours

The three labor market indicators that we've just examined are useful signs of the health of the economy and directly measure what matters to most people: jobs. But they don't tell us the quantity of labor used to produce GDP, and we cannot use them to calculate the productivity of labor. The productivity of labor is significant because it influences the wages people earn.

The reason why the number of people employed does not measure the quantity of labor employed is that jobs are not all the same. People in part-time jobs might work just a few hours a week. People in full-time jobs work around 35 to 40 hours a week.

And some people regularly work overtime. For example, a 7-11 convenience store might hire six students who work three hours a day each. Another 7-11 store might hire two full-time workers who work nine hours a day each. The number of people employed in these two stores is eight, but the total hours worked by six of the eight is the same as the hours worked by the other two. To determine the total amount of labor used to produce GDP, we measure labor in hours rather than in jobs. **Aggregate hours** are the total number of hours worked by all the people employed, both full time and part time, during a year.

Figure 7.4(a) shows aggregate hours in the U.S. economy from 1960 to 1998. Like the employment-to-population ratio, aggregate hours have an upward trend. But aggregate hours have not grown as quickly as have the number of people employed. Between 1960 and 1998 the number of people employed in the U.S. economy increased by 100 percent. During that same period, aggregate hours increased by only 80 percent. Why the difference? Because average hours per worker decreased.

Figure 7.4(b) shows average hours per worker. After hovering at almost 39 hours a week during the early 1960s, average hours per worker decreased to about 34 hours a week during the 1990s. This shortening of the average workweek has arisen partly because of a decrease in the average hours worked by full-time workers but mainly because the number of part-time jobs has increased faster than the number of full-time jobs.

Fluctuations in aggregate hours and average hours per worker line up with the business cycle. Figure 7.4 highlights the past three recessions, during which aggregate hours decreased and average hours per worker decreased more quickly than trend.

Wage Rates

The **real wage rate** is the quantity of goods and services that an hour's work can buy. It is equal to the money wage rate (dollars per hour) divided by the price level. If we use the GDP deflator to measure the price level, the real wage rate is expressed in 1992 dollars because the GDP deflator is 100 in 1992. The real wage is a significant economic variable because it measures the reward for labor.

What has happened to the real wage rate in the United States? Figure 7.5 answers this question. It shows four measures of the average hourly real wage rate in the U.S. economy between 1960 and 1998.

FIGURE 7.4

Aggregate Hours: 1960–1998

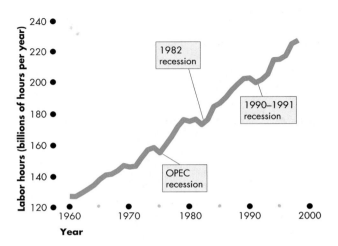

(a) Aggregate hours

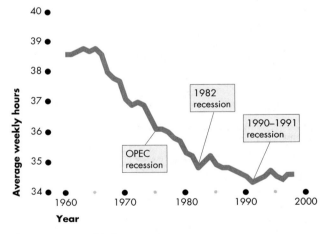

(b) Average weekly hours per person

Aggregate hours (part a) measure the total labor used to produce real GDP more accurately than does the number of people employed because an increasing proportion of jobs are part time. Between 1960 and 1998, aggregate hours increased by an average of 1.5 percent a year. Fluctuations in aggregate hours coincide with business cycle fluctuations. Aggregate hours have increased at a slower rate than the number of jobs because the average workweek has shortened (part b).

Source: Economic Report of the President, 1999, and the author's calculations.

FIGURE 7.5
Real Wage Rates: 1960–1998

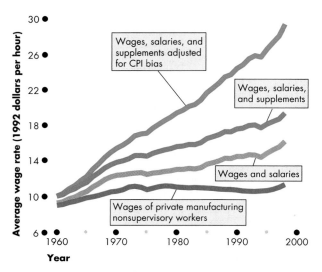

The average hourly real wage rate of private manufacturing nonsupervisory workers peaked in 1978, fell through 1993, then increased again to exceed the 1978 level. Broader measures of the average hourly real wage rate increased. All the official measures show a productivity growth slowdown during the 1970s. An unofficial view is that inflation has been overestimated by 1.1 percent a year and the real wage rate has increased at roughly a constant rate.

Source: Economic Report of the President, 1999, and the author's calculations and assumptions.

The first measure of the real wage rate is the Department of Labor's calculation of the average hourly earnings of private manufacturing nonsupervisory workers. This measure increased to a maximum of $11.16 in 1978 (in 1992 dollars) and then followed a fifteen-year downward trend.

The second measure of the real wage rate is calculated by dividing total wages and salaries in the national income accounts by aggregate hours. This measure is broader than the first and includes the incomes of all types of labor, whether their rate of pay is calculated by the hour or not. This broader measure did not follow a downward trend, but its growth rate slowed during the mid-1970s and remained low through the early 1980s. It then speeded up during the late 1980s and 1990s.

An increasing proportion of labor compensation takes the form of fringe benefits such as pension contributions and the payment by employers of health insurance premiums. Figure 7.5 shows a third measure of the hourly real wage rate that reflects this trend. It is *total labor compensation*—wages, salaries, and supplements—divided by aggregate hours. This measure is the most comprehensive one available, and it shows that the real wage rate has increased. But it also shows that no matter how we measure the wage rate, the productivity growth slowdown also slowed real wage rate growth.

The decline in the average wage rate of manufacturing nonsupervisory workers and the slowdown in the growth rate of the broader measures of the average wage rate coincide with the *productivity growth slowdown* that you saw in Chapter 5. This productivity growth slowdown is the main reason for this behavior of average real wage rates. But whether this slowdown actually occurred depends on what actually happened to the price level. The three measures of real wages that we've just described are based on the official measure of inflation. If inflation has been overestimated by the 1.1 percent that the Boskin Commission (see Chapter 6, p. 131) estimates it has, then real wages have grown at a constant rate, as shown by the fourth line in Fig. 7.5.

R E V I E W   Q U I Z

- What are the trends in the labor force participation rate, the employment-to-population ratio, and the unemployment rate?
- How do the labor force participation rate, the employment-to-population ratio, and the unemployment rate fluctuate over the business cycle?
- Has the female labor force participation rate been similar to or different from the male labor force participation rate?
- How have aggregate hours changed?
- How have average hourly real wage rates changed since 1970?

You've now seen how we measure employment, unemployment, and wage rates. Your next task is to study the anatomy of unemployment and see why it never disappears, even at full employment.

Unemployment and Full Employment

HOW DO PEOPLE BECOME UNEMPLOYED, HOW long do they remain unemployed, and who is at greatest risk to become unemployed? Let's answer these questions by looking at the anatomy of unemployment.

The Anatomy of Unemployment

People become unemployed if they:

1. Lose their jobs and search for another job
2. Leave their jobs and search for another job
3. Enter or reenter the labor force to search for a job

People end a spell of unemployment if they:

1. Are hired or recalled
2. Withdraw from the labor force

People who are laid off, either permanently or temporarily, from their jobs are called **job losers**. Some job losers become unemployed, but some immediately withdraw from the labor force. People who voluntarily quit their jobs are called **job leavers**. Like job losers, some job leavers become unemployed and search for a better job, while others withdraw from the labor force temporarily or permanently retire from work. People who enter or reenter the labor force are called **entrants** and **reentrants**. Entrants are mainly people who have just left school. Some entrants get a job right away and are never unemployed, but many spend time searching for their first job, and during this period, they are unemployed. Reentrants are people who have previously withdrawn from the labor force. Most of these people are formerly discouraged workers. Figure 7.6 shows these labor market flows.

Let's see how much unemployment arises from the three different ways in which people can become unemployed.

The Sources of Unemployment   Figure 7.7 shows unemployment by reason for becoming unemployed. Job losers are the biggest source of unemployment. Also, their number fluctuates a great deal. In the recession of 1990–1991, on any given day, more than

FIGURE 7.6

Labor Market Flows

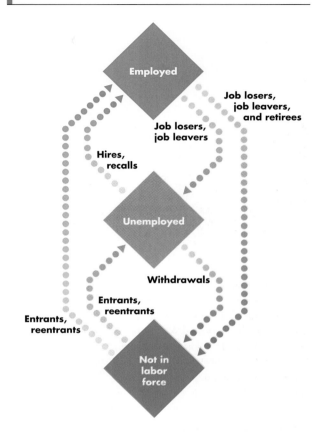

Unemployment results from employed people losing or leaving their jobs (job losers and job leavers) and from people entering the labor force (entrants and reentrants). Unemployment ends because people get hired or recalled or because they withdraw from the labor force.

5 million of the 9.4 million people who were unemployed were job losers. In contrast, in 1998, only 2.8 million of the 6.2 million people who were unemployed were job losers.

Entrants and reentrants also are a large component of the unemployed, and their number fluctuates mildly. On any given day, between 2.5 million and 3 million unemployed people are entrants and reentrants.

Job leavers are the smallest and most stable source of unemployment. On any given day, fewer than 1 million people are unemployed because they

FIGURE 7.7

Unemployment by Reasons

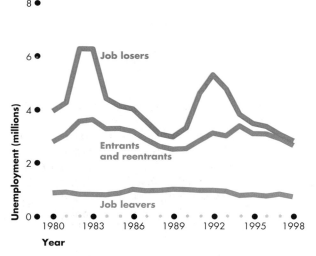

Everyone who is unemployed is either a job loser, a job leaver, or an entrant or reentrant into the labor force. Most of the unemployment that exists results from job loss. The number of job losers fluctuates more closely with the business cycle than do the numbers of job leavers and entrants and reentrants. Entrants and reentrants are the second most commonly unemployed people. Their number fluctuates with the business cycle because of discouraged workers. Job leavers are the least common unemployed people.

Source: Economic Report of the President, 1999.

FIGURE 7.8

Unemployment by Duration

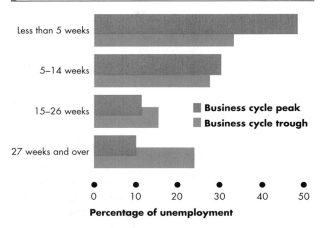

In the business cycle peak of 1989, when the unemployment rate was 5.3 percent, 49 percent of unemployment lasted for less than 5 weeks and 30 percent lasted for 5 to 14 weeks. So 79 percent of unemployment lasted for less than 15 weeks, and 21 percent lasted for 15 weeks or more. In the business cycle trough of 1983, when the unemployment rate was 9.7 percent, 33 percent of unemployment lasted for less than 5 weeks and 27 percent lasted for 5 to 14 weeks. So 60 percent of unemployment lasted for less than 15 weeks, and 40 percent lasted for 15 weeks or more.

Source: Economic Report of the President, 1999.

are job leavers. The number of job leavers is remarkably constant, although to the extent that it fluctuates, it does so in line with the business cycle: A slightly larger number of people leave their jobs in good times than in bad times.

The Duration of Unemployment   Some people are unemployed for a week or two, and others are unemployed for periods of a year or more. The longer the spell of unemployment, the greater the personal cost to the unemployed. The average duration of unemployment varies over the business cycle. Figure 7.8 compares the duration of unemployment in a business cycle peak in 1989, when the unemployment rate was low, with that at the business cycle trough of 1983, when the unemployment rate was high. In 1989, when unemployment hit a low of 5.3 percent, almost 50 percent of the unemployed were in that state for less

than 5 weeks and only 21 percent of the unemployed were jobless for longer than 15 weeks. In 1983, when unemployment reached a high of 9.7 percent, only 33 percent of the unemployed found a new job in less than 5 weeks and 40 percent were unemployed for more than 15 weeks. At both low and high unemployment rates, about 30 percent of the unemployed take between 5 weeks and 14 weeks to find a job.

The Demographics of Unemployment   Figure 7.9 shows unemployment for different demographic groups. The figure shows that high unemployment rates occur among young workers and also among blacks. In the business cycle trough in 1992, the unemployment rate of black teenagers was almost 40 percent. Even in 1998, when the unemployment rate was 4.5 percent, the black teenage rate was 30 percent. The unemployment rates for white teenagers are less than half those of black teenagers. The racial

FIGURE 7.9

Unemployment by Demographic Group

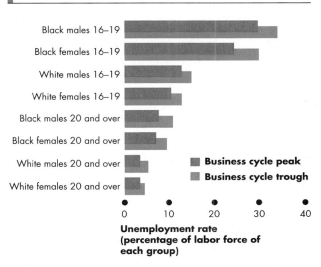

Black teenagers experience unemployment rates that average three times those of white teenagers, and the unemployment rates of teenagers are much higher than those of people aged 20 years and over. Even in a business cycle trough, when unemployment is at its highest rate, only 6 percent of whites aged 20 years and over are unemployed.

Source: Economic Report of the President, 1999.

differences also exist for workers aged 20 years and over. The highest unemployment rates that whites 20 years and over experience are less than the lowest rates experienced by the other groups.

Why are unemployment rates of teenagers so high? There are three reasons. First, young people are still in the process of discovering what they are good at and trying different lines of work. So they leave their jobs more frequently than older workers do. Second, firms sometimes hire teenagers on a short-term or trial basis. So the rate of job loss is higher for teenagers than for other people. Third, most teenagers are not in the labor force but are in school. This fact means that the percentage of the teenage population that is unemployed is much lower than the percentage of the teenage labor force that is unemployed. In 1998, for example, 1.2 million teenagers were unemployed and 7.5 million were employed. So the teenage unemployment rate (all races) was 14 percent. But 11.6 million teenagers were in school.

Teenage unemployment as a percentage of the teenage labor force plus the school population was 6 percent. That is, 14 percent of the teenage labor force or 6 percent of the teenage population is unemployed.

Types of Unemployment

Unemployment is classified into three types that are based on its causes. They are:

■ Frictional
■ Structural
■ Cyclical

Frictional Unemployment   **Frictional unemployment** is the unemployment that arises from normal labor turnover—from people entering and leaving the labor force and from the ongoing creation and destruction of jobs. Frictional unemployment is a permanent and healthy phenomenon in a dynamic, growing economy.

The unending flow of people into and out of the labor force and the processes of job creation and job destruction create the need for people to search for jobs and for businesses to search for workers. Always there are businesses with unfilled jobs and people seeking jobs. Look in your local newspaper, and you will see that there are always some jobs being advertised. Businesses don't usually hire the first person who applies for a job, and unemployed people don't usually take the first job that comes their way. Instead, both firms and workers spend time searching out what they believe will be the best match available. By this process of search, people can match their own skills and interests with the available jobs and find a satisfying job and income. While these unemployed people are searching, they are frictionally unemployed.

The amount of frictional unemployment depends on the rate at which people enter and reenter the labor force and on the rate at which jobs are created and destroyed. During the 1970s, the amount of frictional unemployment increased as a consequence of the postwar baby boom that began during the late 1940s. By the late 1970s, the baby boom had created a bulge in the number of people leaving school. As these people entered the labor force, the amount of frictional unemployment increased.

The amount of frictional unemployment is influenced by unemployment benefits. The greater the number of unemployed people covered by unemployment insurance and the more generous the unemployment insurance and the more generous the unemployment benefit they receive, the longer is the average time taken in job search and the greater is the amount of frictional unemployment. In the United States in 1998, 36 percent of the unemployed received unemployment benefit. And the average benefit check was $167 a week. Canada and Western Europe have more generous benefits than those in the United States and have higher unemployment rates.

Structural Unemployment **Structural unemployment** is the unemployment that arises when changes in technology or international competition change the skills needed to perform jobs or change the locations of jobs. Structural unemployment usually lasts longer than frictional unemployment because workers must usually retrain and possibly relocate to find a job. For example, when a steel plant in Gary, Indiana, is automated, some jobs in that city are destroyed. Meanwhile, new jobs for security guards, life-insurance salespeople, and retail clerks are created in Chicago, Indianapolis, and other cities. The unemployed former steelworkers remain unemployed for several months until they move, retrain, and get one of these jobs. Structural unemployment is painful, especially for older workers for whom the best available option might be to retire early but with a lower income than they had expected.

At some times the amount of structural unemployment is modest. At other times it is large, and at such times, structural unemployment can become a serious long-term problem. It was especially large during the late 1970s and early 1980s. During those years, oil price hikes and an increasingly competitive international environment destroyed jobs in traditional U.S. industries, such as auto and steel, and created jobs in new industries, such as electronics and bioengineering, as well as in banking and insurance. Structural unemployment was also present during the early 1990s as many businesses and governments "downsized."

Cyclical Unemployment **Cyclical unemployment** is the fluctuating unemployment over the business cycle. Cyclical unemployment increases during a recession and decreases during an expansion. An autoworker who is laid off because the economy is in a recession and who gets rehired some months later when the expansion begins has experienced cyclical unemployment.

Full Employment

There is always *some* unemployment—someone looking for a job or laid off and waiting to be recalled. So what do we mean by *full employment?* **Full employment** occurs when there is no cyclical unemployment or, equivalently, when all the unemployment is frictional and structural. The divergence of the unemployment rate from full employment is cyclical unemployment. The unemployment rate at full employment is called the **natural rate of unemployment**.

There can be a lot of unemployment at full employment, and the term "full employment" is an example of a technical economic term that does not correspond with everyday language. The term "natural rate of unemployment" is another example of a technical economic term that does not correspond with everyday language. For most people—especially for unemployed workers—there is nothing *natural* about unemployment.

So, why are do economists call a situation with a lot of unemployment one of full employment? And why is the unemployment at full employment called "natural"?

The reason is that the complex mechanism that we call the U.S. economy undergoes constant changes in its players, structure, and direction. This process of change creates frictions and dislocations that are unavoidable. And they create unemployment.

In 1998, the U.S. economy employed 131 million people. More than 2.5 million retired during that year and more than 3 million new workers entered the labor force. All these people worked in some 20 million businesses, some of which downsized or failed and others of which expanded. All these people and businesses produced goods and services valued at more than $8 trillion.

Figure 7.10 illustrates full employment and cyclical unemployment in the United States between 1980 and 1998. Part (a) shows the fluctuations of real GDP around potential GDP. Part (b) shows fluctuations in the unemployment rate around the natural rate. Notice that cyclical unemployment is positive at a business cycle trough but is *negative* at a business cycle peak. At the cycle peak, total unemployment is less than the sum of frictional and structural unemployment.

In Fig. 7.10 the unemployment rate fluctuates around the natural rate of unemployment (part b) as real GDP fluctuates around potential GDP (part a).

FIGURE 7.10

Unemployment and Real GDP

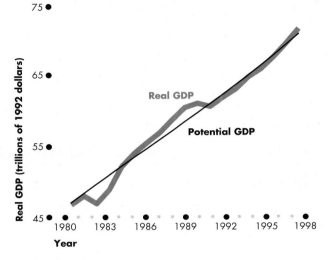

(a) Real GDP

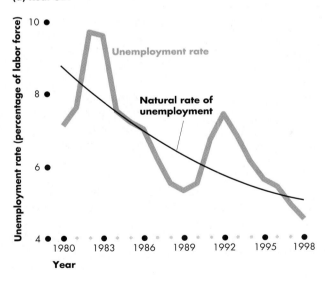

(b) [Unemployment rate / Natural rate of unemployment]

As real GDP fluctuates around potential GDP (part a), the unemployment rate fluctuates around the natural rate of unemployment (part b). In the deep recession of 1982, unemployment reached almost 10 percent. In the milder recession of 1990–1991, the unemployment rate peaked at less than 8 percent. The natural rate of unemployment decreased during the 1980s and 1990s.

Source: Economic Report of the President, 1999, and the author's assumptions.

When there is full employment and the rate equals the natural rate of unemployment, real GDP equals potential GDP. When the unemployment rate is less than the natural rate of unemployment, real GDP is greater than potential GDP. And when the unemployment rate is greater than the natural rate of unemployment, real GDP is less than potential GDP.

There is not much controversy about the existence of a natural rate of unemployment. Nor is there much controversy that it changes. The natural rate of unemployment arises from the existence of frictional and structural unemployment, and it fluctuates because the frictions and the amount of structural change fluctuate. But economists don't agree about the size of the natural rate of unemployment and the extent to which it fluctuates. Some economists believe that the natural rate of unemployment fluctuates frequently and that at times of rapid demographic and technological change, its rate can be high. Others think that it changes slowly.

In Fig. 7.10(b), the natural rate of unemployment is 8.5 percent in 1980 and it falls steadily through the 1980s and 1990s to less than 5 percent by 1999. This estimate of the natural rate of unemployment in the United States is one that many, but not all economists would accept.

REVIEW QUIZ

- What are the categories of people who become unemployed?
- Can you define *frictional* unemployment, *structural* unemployment, and *cyclical* unemployment and provide an example of each type of unemployment?
- What is the *natural rate of unemployment*?

You now know how we measure the key macroeconomic variables—real GDP, the price level, employment, and unemployment. And you understand the link between employment and real GDP. *Reading Between the Lines* on pp. 148–149, looks at the U.S. labor market today.

Your next task is to study the forces that determine real GDP and the price level (and employment and unemployment). You'll begin this task by learning about the *aggregate supply–aggregate demand model*. This aggregate model serves as a backdrop against which to place your further study of the forces that determine economic growth, unemployment, and inflation.

Technological Change and Jobs

T H E   W A S H I N G T O N   P O S T ,   December 5, 1998

Jobless Rate Falls Despite Layoff Plans

John M. Berry

The nation's unemployment rate fell to 4.4 percent last month, as stronger-than-expected hiring by builders, retailers, restaurants and other service providers more than offset layoffs by manufacturers, the government reported yesterday.

The gain of 267,000 payroll jobs in November, which was much greater than many analysts had anticipated, showed that the nation's labor markets remained strong despite the recent flurry of corporate layoff announcements. ...

"The U.S. growth story remains a tale of two economies, with the manufacturing sector shedding 47,000 jobs in November, purchasing agents reporting the weakest factory conditions since February 1996 and (new factory) orders dropping in October," said Bill Dudley, chief economist at Goldman Sachs & Co. in New York.

More than compensating for those job losses were a jump of 55,000 jobs at firms providing business services, including temporary help, and of 47,000 in construction.

Unusually strong holiday hiring boosted retail trade employment by 65,000 jobs, the Labor Department said. ...

Bill Parks, a special assistant to the commissioner of labor statistics, ... (says) ... that each month's labor market report is "a snapshot of the net effects of the movements of millions of people into and out of" employment, unemployment and the labor force itself. ...

For example, the department's figures for 1997 show that about 13.5 million people make such movements in a typical month. That's almost one of every 10 people in the labor force—which consists of those who are working or seeking a job.

Last month's "snapshot" showed that the civilian labor force increased by 277,000, to 138.3 million. Compared with October, when the unemployment rate was 4.6 percent, an additional 477,000 people got jobs last month, while 6.1 million were unemployed, a drop of 200,000. But those were the "net" changes resulting from those millions of decisions.

Essence of the Story

■ In November 1998, the civilian labor force increased by 277,000 to 138.3 million.

■ An additional 477,000 people got jobs, but employment increased by only 267,000. (210,000 people who had jobs became unemployed.)

■ Unemployment decreased by 200,000 to 6.1 million, an unemployment rate of 4.4 percent.

■ The Department of Labor estimates that one of every 10 people in the labor force changes their labor market status in a typical month.

■ In November 1998, the number of jobs in manufacturing decreased by 47,000, but the number of jobs in business services increased by 55,000, in construction by 47,000, and in retail trade by 65,000.

■ The labor market is in a constant state of churning. Millions of decisions each month result in small *net* changes in the labor force, employment, and unemployment.

■ Figure 1 shows the rate of job destruction in U.S. manufacturing industries between 1980 and 1993. These data are compiled infrequently and are not yet available beyond 1993. But the available data tell us a lot.

■ The rate of job destruction fluctuates with the business cycle. But on the average, about 1 percent of jobs get destroyed each month.

■ Much of the job destruction arises because technological advances enable companies to produce more output with fewer workers. This process has been going on almost uninterrupted since the Industrial Revolution began around 1760.

■ At the normal rate of job destruction, more than a million people lose their jobs each month.

■ When a large employer cuts jobs, the news media pays attention. But when a small employer cuts jobs or creates jobs, the media does not usually notice.

■ Because most of the newly created jobs are in small businesses, they go unreported. Consequently, the media often creates the impression that jobs are only being destroyed. This news article does not give this wrong impression. It puts job losses and gains in their proper perspective.

■ Job cuts are serious for the people whom they affect. But they would be even more serious if jobs were not being created in even larger numbers.

■ Figure 1 also shows the rate of job creation and the net change in the number of jobs in manufacturing. In most years, more jobs have been destroyed than created in the manufacturing industries. But (not shown in the figure) more jobs have been created in other sectors such as business services, construction, and retail trade, than the number lost in manufacturing.

■ Technological change creates more jobs than it destroys. It increases the productivity of labor and leads to an increase in the demand for labor.

■ Figure 2 shows the total amount of job creation and job destruction in manufacturing and the relationship between this number and the

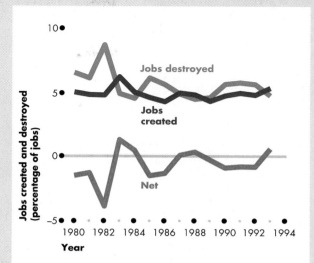

Figure 1 Job creation and destruction rates

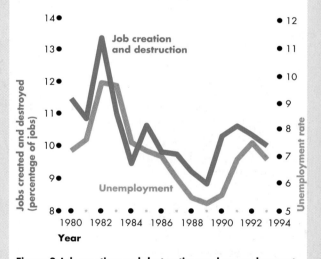

Figure 2 Job creation and destruction and unemployment

Source: Steven J. Davis, John Haltiwanger, and Scott Schuh, *Job Creation and Job Destruction*, Cambridge: MIT Press 1996. Professor Davis kindly updated to 1993.

unemployment rate. It shows that the total amount of job creation and job destruction fluctuates in line with fluctuations in the unemployment rate.

■ What policy actions, if any, can the government take to protect people from job losses?

■ List all the policy actions you can think of and attach to each policy its pros and cons.

149

SUMMARY

KEY POINTS

Employment and Wages (pp. 138–142)

- The labor force participation rate and the employment-to-population ratio have an upward trend and fluctuate with the business cycle.

- The labor force participation rate has increased for females and decreased for males.

- Aggregate hours have an upward trend, and they fluctuate with the business cycle.

- Based on the CPI, real hourly wage rates in manufacturing fell after 1973. Broader real wage measures did not fall, but their growth rates slowed.

Unemployment and Full Employment (pp. 143–147)

- People are constantly entering and leaving the state of unemployment.

- The duration of unemployment fluctuates over the business cycle. But the demographic patterns of unemployment are constant.

- Unemployment can be frictional, structural, and cyclical.

- When all the unemployment is frictional and structural, unemployment is at its natural rate and there is *full employment*. The natural rate of unemployment fluctuates because of fluctuations in frictional and structural unemployment.

KEY FIGURES

KEY TERMS

PROBLEMS

*1. The Bureau of Labor Statistics reported the following data for December 1997:
Labor force: 137,169,000
Employment: 130,777,000
Working-age population: 204,020,000
Calculate for that month the
a. Unemployment rate
b. Labor force participation rate
c. Employment-to-population ratio

2. The Bureau of Labor Statistics reported the following data for December 1998:
Labor force: 138,547,000
Employment: 132,526,000
Working-age population: 206,270,000
Calculate for that month the
a. Unemployment rate
b. Labor force participation rate
c. Employment-to-population ratio

*3. During 1997, the working-age population increased by 2,287,000, employment increased by 2,878,000, and the labor force increased by 2,109,000. Use these numbers and the data in problem 1 to calculate the change in unemployment and the change in the number of discouraged workers during 1997.

4. During 1998, the working-age population increased by 2,172,000 employment increased by 1,888,000, and the labor force increased by 1,461,000. Use these numbers and the data in problem 2 to calculate the change in unemployment and the change in the number of discouraged workers during 1998.

*5. In August 1994, the unemployment rate was 10.1 percent. In August 1995, the unemployment rate was 9.6 percent. Use this information to predict what happened between August 1994 and August 1995 to the numbers of
a. Job losers and job leavers
b. Labor force entrants and re-entrants

6. In January 1998, the unemployment rate was 4.6 percent. In January 1999, the unemployment rate was 4.3 percent. Use these numbers to predict what happened in 1998 to the numbers of
a. Job losers and job leavers
b. Labor force entrants and re-entrants

*7. The figure shows the numbers of working-age people who were employed, unemployed, and not in the labor force in Labecon in July 1997 and the labor market flows during August 1997.

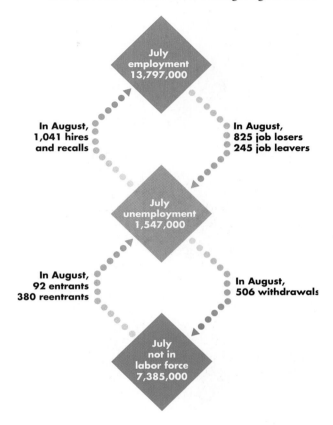

Calculate for July 1997:
a. The labor force
b. The unemployment rate
c. The working-age population
d. The employment-to-population ratio
Calculate for the end of August 1997:
e. The number of people unemployed
f. The number of people employed
g. The labor force
h. The unemployment rate
i. The employment-to-population ratio if the labor force participation rate is 65.5 percent

8. The figure shows the numbers of working-age people who were employed, unemployed, and not in the labor force in Ecolab in July 1998 and the labor market flows during August 1998.

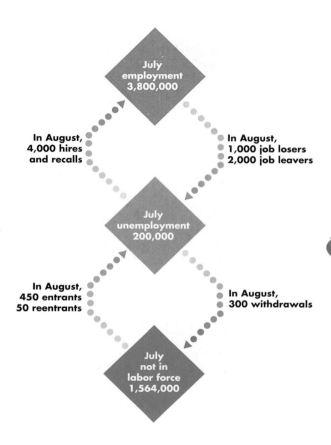

Calculate for July 1998:
a.   The labor force
b.   The unemployment rate
c.   The working-age population
d.   The employment-to-population ratio

Calculate for the end of August 1998:
e.   The number of people unemployed
f.   The number of people employed
g.   The labor force
h.   The unemployment rate
i.   The employment-to-population ratio if the labor force participation rate is 60 percent

*9. Describe the main features of the labor market at the peak of business cycle.

10. Describe the main features of the labor market at the trough of business cycle.

CRITICAL THINKING

1. Study *Reading Between the Lines* on pp. 148–149 and then answer the following questions:
   a.   What types of jobs have been destroyed and created in the United States in the past 15 years?
   b.   What types of businesses create jobs and what types of business destroy jobs?
   c.   Do all the jobs created get reported in the newspapers? Explain why or why not.
   d.   Do all the jobs destroyed get reported in the newspapers? Explain why or why not.
   e.   What information would you need to determine whether the job losses reported will create frictional, structural, or cyclical unemployment?
   f.   Which fluctuates more: the rate of job creation or the rate of job destruction?

2. Use the link on the Parkin Web site to visit the Bureau of Labor Statistics and find labor market data for your own state.
   a.   What have been the trends in employment, unemployment, and labor force participation in your own state during the past two years?
   b.   On the basis of what you know about your own region, how would you set about explaining these trends?
   c.   Try to identify the industries that have expanded most and those that have shrunk.
   d.   What are the problems in your state labor market that you think need state government action to resolve?
   e.   What actions do you think your state government must take to resolve them? Use the demand and supply model of the labor market to answer this question and to make predictions about the effects of the actions you prescribe.
   f.   Compare the labor market performance of your own state with that of the nation as a whole.
   g.   If your state is performing better than the national average, to what do you attribute the success? If your state is performing worse than the national average, to what do you attribute its problems? What federal actions are needed in your state labor market?

Chapter 8

Aggregate Supply and Aggregate Demand

What Makes Our Garden Grow?

During the past 30 years, U.S. real GDP has more than doubled. In fact, a doubling of real GDP every 30 years has been routine. What forces drive our economy to grow? ◆ At the same time that real GDP has grown, we've experienced first a rise and then a fall in inflation. In 1967, U.S. prices were rising at a rate of 3 percent a year. In 1981, the peak inflation year, prices increased by 10 percent. Today, the inflation rate stands at less than 2 percent a year. The result of all this inflation is that you need $400 today to buy what $100 bought in 1967. What causes inflation? And why did its rate explode during the 1970s? ◆ Our economy does not expand at a constant pace. Instead, it ebbs and flows over the business cycle. For example, we had a recession during 1990 and early 1991. For half a year, real GDP decreased. Then began a long period of expansion that was still in progress in 1999. What makes real GDP grow at an uneven pace? Why does growth sometimes speed up, and why does real GDP sometimes shrink? ◆ When economic growth speeds up in Asia and Europe, we benefit because we sell more goods and services abroad. And when economic growth slows in the rest of the world, we suffer because the demand for our goods and services decreases. But some influences on our economy are home made and stem from the actions of the government and the Federal Reserve Board (the Fed) in Washington. How do events in the rest of the world and the policy actions of the government and the Fed affect production and prices?

◆ To answer these questions, we need a *model* of real GDP and the price level. Our main task in this chapter is to study such a model: the *aggregate supply—aggregate demand model*. Our second task is to use the aggregate supply—aggregate demand (or *AS-AD*) model to answer the questions we've just posed. You'll discover that this model enables us to understand the forces that make our economy expand, that bring inflation, and that cause business cycle fluctuations. You will also find that this model is a useful tool with which to organize your entire study of macroeconomics.

After studying this chapter, you will be able to:

- Explain what determines aggregate supply

- Explain what determines aggregate demand

- Explain macroeconomic equilibrium

- Explain the effects of changes in aggregate supply and aggregate demand on economic growth, inflation, and business cycles

- Explain U.S. economic growth, inflation, and business cycles by using the AS-AD model.

Aggregate Supply

THE AGGREGATE SUPPLY-AGGREGATE DEMAND model enables us to understand three features of macroeconomic performance:

- Growth of potential GDP
- Inflation
- Business cycle fluctuations

The model uses the concepts of *aggregate* supply and *aggregate* demand to determine *real GDP* and the *price level* (the *GDP deflator*). We begin by looking at the limits to production that influence aggregate supply.

Aggregate Supply Fundamentals

The *quantity of real GDP supplied* (Y) depends on:

- The quantity of labor (N)
- The quantity of capital (K)
- The state of technology (T)

The influence of these three factors on the quantity of real GDP supplied are described by the **aggregate production function**, which is written as the equation:

$$Y = F(N, K, T).$$

In words, the quantity of real GDP supplied is determined by (is a function F of) the quantities of labor and capital and of the state of technology. The larger are N, K, or T, the greater is Y.

At any given time, the quantity of capital and the state of technology are fixed. They depend on decisions that were made in the past. The population is also fixed. But the quantity of labor is not fixed. It depends on decisions made by people and firms about the supply of and demand for labor.

The labor market can be in any one of three states: at full employment, above full employment, or below full employment.

Even at full employment, there are always some people looking for jobs and some firms looking for people to hire. The reason is that there is a constant churning of the labor market. Every day, some jobs are destroyed as businesses reorganize or fail. Some jobs are created as new businesses start up or existing ones expand. Some workers decide, for any of a thousand personal reasons, to quit their jobs. And other people decide to start looking for a job. This constant churning in the labor market prevents unemployment from ever disappearing. The unemployment rate at full employment is called the **natural rate of unemployment**.

Another way to think about full employment is as a state of the labor market in which the quantity of labor demanded equals the quantity supplied. Firms demand labor only if it is profitable to do so. And the lower the wage rate, which is the cost of labor, the greater is the quantity of labor demanded. People supply labor only if doing so is the most valuable use of their time. And the higher the wage rate, which is the return to labor, the greater is the quantity of labor supplied. The wage rate that makes the quantity of labor demanded equal to the quantity of labor supplied is the equilibrium wage rate. At this wage rate there is full employment. (You can study the labor market at full employment further in Chapter 9 on pp. 190-192).

The quantity of real GDP supplied at full employment is **potential GDP**, which depends on the full-employment quantity of labor, the quantity of capital, and the state of technology. Over the business cycle, employment fluctuates around full employment and real GDP fluctuates around potential GDP.

To study aggregate supply in different states of the labor market, we distinguish two time frames:

- Long-run aggregate supply
- Short-run aggregate supply

Long-Run Aggregate Supply

The economy is constantly bombarded by events that move real GDP away from potential GDP and, equivalently, that move the unemployment rate away from full employment. Following such an event, forces operate to take real GDP back toward potential GDP and restore full employment. The **macroeconomic long run** is a time frame that is sufficiently long for these forces to have done their work so that real GDP equals potential GDP and full employment prevails.

The **long-run aggregate supply curve** is the relationship between the quantity of real GDP supplied and the price level in the long run when real GDP equals potential GDP. Figure 8.1 shows this relationship as vertical line labeled *LAS*. Along the long-run aggregate supply curve, as the price level changes, real GDP remains at potential GDP, which in Fig. 8.1 is $7 trillion. The long-run aggregate

FIGURE 8.1
Long-Run
Aggregate Supply

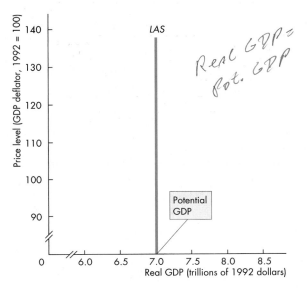

The long-run aggregate supply (LAS) curve shows the relationship between potential GDP and the price level. Potential GDP is independent of the price level, so the LAS curve is vertical at potential GDP.

supply curve is always vertical and is located at potential GDP.

The long-run aggregate supply curve is vertical because potential GDP is independent of the price level. The reason for this independence is that a movement along the LAS curve is accompanied by a change in *two* sets of prices: the prices of goods and services—the price level—and the prices of productive resources. A 10 percent increase in the prices of goods and services is matched by a 10 percent increase in wage rates and other resource prices. That is, the price level, wage rate, and other resource prices all change by the same percentage, and *relative prices* and the *real wage rate* remain constant. When the price level changes but relative prices and the real wage rate remain constant, real GDP also remains constant.

Production at a Pepsi Plant You can see why real GDP remains constant when all prices change by the same percentage by thinking about production

decisions at a Pepsi bottling plant. The plant is producing the quantity of Pepsi that maximizes profit. The plant can increase production, but only by incurring a higher *marginal cost* (see Chapter 3, pp. 40–41). So the firm has no incentive to change production.

Short-Run Aggregate Supply

The **macroeconomic short run** is a period during which real GDP has fallen below or risen above potential GDP. At the same time, the unemployment rate has risen above or fallen below the natural rate.

The **short-run aggregate supply curve** is the relationship between the quantity of real GDP supplied and the price level in the short run when the money wage rate, other resource prices, and potential GDP remain constant. Figure 8.2 shows a short-run aggregate supply curve as the upward-sloping curve labeled *SAS*. This curve is based on the short-run aggregate supply schedule, and each point on the aggregate supply curve corresponds to a row of the aggregate supply schedule. For example, point *a* on the short-run aggregate supply curve and row *a* of the schedule tell us that if the price level is 100, the quantity of real GDP supplied is $6 trillion.

At point *c*, the price level is 110 and the quantity of real GDP supplied is $7 trillion, which equals potential GDP. If the price level is higher than 110, real GDP exceeds potential GDP; if the price level is below 110, real GDP is less than potential GDP.

Back at the Pepsi Plant You can see why the short-run aggregate supply curve slopes upward by returning to the Pepsi bottling plant. The plant produces the quantity that maximizes profit. If the price of Pepsi rises and wage rates and other costs don't change, the *relative price* of Pepsi rises and the firm has an incentive to increase its production. The higher relative price of Pepsi covers the higher marginal cost of producing more Pepsi, so the firm increases production.

Similarly, if the price of Pepsi falls and wage rates and other costs don't change, the lower relative price is not sufficient to cover the marginal cost of Pepsi, so the firm decreases production.

Again, what's true for Pepsi bottlers is true for the producers of all goods and services. So when the price level rises and the money wage rate and other resource prices remain constant, the quantity of real GDP supplied increases.

FIGURE 8.2

Short-Run Aggregate Supply

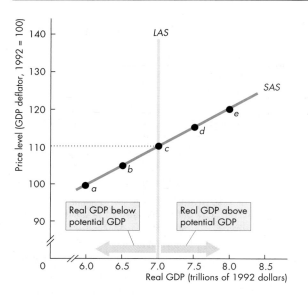

	Price Level (GDP deflator)	Real GDP (trillions of 1992 dollars)
a	100	6.0
b	105	6.5
c	110	7.0
d	115	7.5
e	120	8.0

The short-run aggregate supply (SAS) curve shows the relationship between the quantity of real GDP supplied and the price level when the money wage rate, other resource prices, and potential GDP are constant. The short-run aggregate supply curve SAS is based on the schedule in the table. The short-run aggregate supply curve is upward-sloping because firms' costs increase as the rate of output increases, so a higher price is needed, relative to the prices of productive resources, and bring forth an increase in the quantity produced. On the SAS curve, when the price level is 110, real GDP equals potential GDP. If the price level is greater than 110, real GDP exceeds potential GDP; if the price level is below 110, real GDP is less than potential GDP.

Movements Along the *LAS* and *SAS* Curves

Figure 8.3 summarizes what you've just learned about the *LAS* and *SAS* curves. When the price level, the money wage rate, and other resource prices rise by the same percentage, relative prices remain constant and real GDP remains at potential GDP. There is a *movement along* the *LAS* curve. *(pg 85)*

When the price level rises but the money wage rate and other resource prices remain constant, the quantity of real GDP supplied increases and there is a *movement along* the *SAS* curve.

Let's next study the influences that bring changes in aggregate supply.

FIGURE 8.3

Movements Along the Aggregate Supply Curves

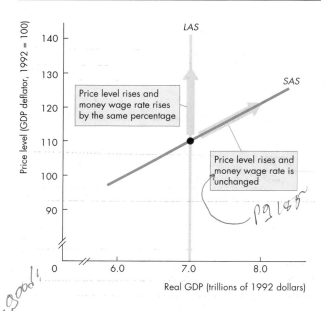

A rise in the price level with no change in the money wage rate and other resource prices brings an increase in the quantity of real GDP supplied and a movement along the short-run aggregate supply curve. A rise in the price level with equal percentage rises in the money wage rate and other resource prices keeps the quantity of real GDP supplied constant and brings a movement along the long-run aggregate supply curve.

Changes in Aggregate Supply

You've just seen that a change in the price level brings a movement along the aggregate supply curves but it does not change aggregate supply. Aggregate supply changes when influences on production plans other than the price level change. Let's begin by looking at factors that change potential GDP.

Changes in Potential GDP   When potential GDP changes, both long-run aggregate supply and short-run aggregate supply change. Potential GDP changes for three reasons:

1. Change in the full-employment quantity of labor
2. Change in the quantity of capital
3. Advance in technology

An increase in the full-employment quantity of labor, an increase in the quantity of capital, or an advance in technology increases potential GDP. And an increase in potential GDP changes both long-run aggregate supply and short-run aggregate supply.

Figure 8.4 shows these effects of a change in potential GDP. Initially, the long-run aggregate supply curve is LAS_0 and the short-run aggregate supply curve is SAS_0. If an increase in the quantity of capital or a technological advance increases potential GDP to $8 trillion, long-run aggregate supply increases and the long-run aggregate supply curve shifts rightward to LAS_1. Short-run aggregate supply also increases, and the short-run aggregate supply curve shifts rightward to SAS_1.

Let's look more closely at the influences on potential GDP and the aggregate supply curves.

A Change in the Full-Employment Quantity of Labor   A Pepsi bottling plant that employs 100 workers bottles more Pepsi than an otherwise identical plant that employs 10 workers. The same is true for the economy as a whole. The larger the quantity of labor employed, the greater is real GDP.

Over time, potential GDP increases because the labor force increases. But (with constant capital and technology) *potential* GDP increases only if the full-employment quantity of labor increases. Fluctuations in employment over the business cycle bring fluctuations in real GDP. But these changes in real GDP are fluctuations around potential GDP. They are not changes in potential GDP and long-run aggregate supply.

FIGURE 8.4
A Change in Potential GDP

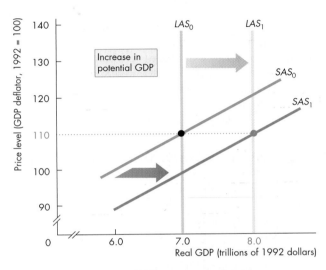

An increase in potential GDP increases both long-run aggregate supply and short-run aggregate supply and shifts both aggregate supply curves rightward from LAS_0 to LAS_1 and from SAS_0 to SAS_1.

A Change in the Quantity of Capital   A Pepsi plant with two production lines bottles more Pepsi than an otherwise identical plant that has only one production line. For the economy, the larger the quantity of capital, the more productive is the labor force and the greater is its potential GDP. Potential GDP per person in the capital-rich United States is vastly greater than that in capital-poor China or Russia.

Capital includes *human capital*. One Pepsi plant is managed by an economics major with an MBA and has a labor force with an average of 10 years experience. This plant produces a much larger output than an otherwise identical plant that is managed by someone with no business training or experience and has a young labor force that is new to bottling. The first plant has a greater amount of human capital than the second. For the economy as a whole, the larger the quantity of *human capital*—the skills that people have acquired in school and through on-the-job training—the greater is potential GDP.

An Advance in Technology A Pepsi plant that has pre–computer age machines produces less than one that uses the latest robot technology. Technological change enables firms to produce more from any given amount of inputs. So even with fixed quantities of labor and capital, improvements in technology increase potential GDP.

Technological advances are by far the most important source of increased production over the past two centuries. Because of technological advances, one farmer in the United States today can feed 100 people, and one auto worker can produce almost 14 cars and trucks in a year.

Let's now look at the effects of changes of money wages.

Changes in Money Wages and Other Resource Prices

When the money wage rate or the money prices of other resources such as the price of oil changes, short-run aggregate supply changes but long-run aggregate supply does not change.

Figure 8.5 shows the effect on aggregate supply of an increase in the money wage rate. Initially, the short-run aggregate supply curve is SAS_0. A rise in the money wage rate *decreases* short-run aggregate supply and shifts the short-run aggregate supply curve leftward to SAS_2.

Money wages (and resource prices) affect short-run aggregate supply because they change firms' costs. The higher the money wage rate, the higher are firms' costs and the smaller is the quantity that firms are willing to supply at each price level. So an increase in the money wage rate decreases short-run aggregate supply.

Changes in the money wage rate do not change long-run aggregate supply because on the *LAS* curve, a change in the money wage rate is accompanied by an equal percentage change in the price level. With no change in *relative* prices, firms have no incentive to change production and real GDP remains constant at potential GDP.

In Fig. 8.5, the vertical distance between the original *SAS* curve and the new *SAS* curve is determined by the percentage change in the money wage rate. That is, the percentage increase in the price level between point *a* and point *b* equals the percentage increase in the money wage rate.

Because potential GDP does not change when the money wage rate changes, long-run aggregate supply does not change. The long-run aggregate supply curve remains at *LAS*.

FIGURE 8.5
A Change in the Money Wage Rate

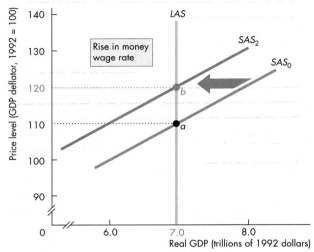

A rise in the money wage rate decreases short-run aggregate supply and shifts the short-run aggregate supply curve leftward from SAS_0 to SAS_2. A rise in the money wage rate does not change potential GDP, so the long-run aggregate supply curve does not shift.

R E V I E W   Q U I Z

- If the price level rises and if the money wage rate also rises by the same percentage, what happens to the quantity of real GDP supplied? Along which aggregate supply curve does the economy move?

- If the price level rises and the money wage rate remains constant, what happens to the quantity of real GDP supplied? Along which aggregate supply curve does the economy move?

- If potential GDP increases, what happens to aggregate supply? Is there a shift of or a movement along the *LAS* curve and the *SAS* curve?

- If the money wage rate rises and potential GDP remains the same, what happens to aggregate supply? Is there a shift of or a movement along the *LAS* curve and the *SAS* curve?

Aggregate Demand

THE QUANTITY OF REAL GDP DEMANDED IS THE sum of the real consumption expenditure (C), investment (I), government purchases (G), and exports (X) minus imports (M). That is,

$$Y = C + I + G + X - M.$$

The *quantity of real GDP demanded* is the total amount of final goods and services produced in the United States that people, businesses, governments, and foreigners plan to buy. What determines these buying plans?

Buying plans depend on many factors. Some of the main ones are:

■ The price level
■ Expectations
■ Fiscal policy and monetary policy
■ The world economy

We first focus on the relationship between the quantity of real GDP demanded and the price level. To study this relationship, we hold constant all other influences on buying plans. We then ask: How does the quantity of real GDP demanded vary as the price level varies?

The Aggregate Demand Curve

Other things remaining the same, the higher the price level, the smaller is the quantity of real GDP demanded. This relationship between the quantity of real GDP demanded and the price level is called **aggregate demand**. Aggregate demand is described by an *aggregate demand schedule* and an *aggregate demand curve*.

Figure 8.6 shows an aggregate demand curve (*AD*) and an aggregate demand schedule. Each point on the *AD* curve corresponds to a row of the schedule. For example, point c' on the *AD* curve and row c' of the schedule tell us that if the price level is 110, the quantity of real GDP demanded is $7 trillion.

The aggregate demand curve slopes downward for two reasons:

■ Wealth effect
■ Substitution effects

FIGURE 8.6

Aggregate Demand

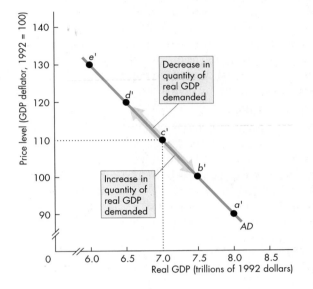

	Price Level (GDP deflator)	Real GDP (trillions of 1992 dollars)
a'	90	8.0
b'	100	7.5
c'	110	7.0
d'	120	6.5
e'	130	6.0

The aggregate demand curve (*AD*) shows the relationship between the quantity of real GDP demanded and the price level. The aggregate demand curve is based on the schedule in the table. Each point a' through e' on the curve corresponds to the row in the table identified by the same letter. Thus when the price level is 110, the quantity of real GDP demanded is $7.0 trillion, shown by point c' in the figure.

Wealth Effect When the price level rises but other things remain the same, *real* wealth decreases. Real wealth is the amount of money in the bank, bonds, stocks, and other assets that people own, measured not in dollars but in terms of the goods and services that this money, bonds, and stock will buy.

People save and hold money, bonds, and stocks for many reasons. One reason is to build up funds for college expenses. Another reason is to build up enough funds to meet possible medical or other big bills. But the biggest reason is to build up enough funds to provide a retirement income.

If the price level rises, real wealth decreases. People then try to restore their wealth. To do so, they must increase saving and, equivalently, decrease consumption. Such a decrease in consumption is a decrease in aggregate demand.

Maria's Wealth Effect   You can see how the wealth effect works by thinking about Maria's buying plans. Maria lives in Moscow, Russia. She has worked hard all summer and saved 20,000 rubles (the ruble is the currency of Russia), which she plans to spend attending graduate school when she's finished her economics degree. So Maria's wealth is 20,000 rubles. Maria has a part-time job, and her income from this job pays her current expenses. The price level in Russia rises by 100 percent, and now Maria needs 40,000 rubles to buy what 20,000 once bought. To try to make up some of the fall in value of her savings, Maria saves even more and cuts her current spending to the bare minimum.

Substitution Effects   When the price level rises and other things remain the same, interest rates rise. But the basic reason for the rise in the interest rate is easy to see. A rise in the price level decreases the real value of the money in people's pockets and bank accounts. With a smaller amount of real money around, banks and other lenders can get a higher interest rate on loans. But faced with higher interest rates, people and businesses delay plans to buy new capital and consumer durable goods and cut back on spending.

This substitution effect involves substituting goods in the future for goods in the present and is called an *intertemporal* substitution effect—a substitution across time. Saving increases to increase future consumption.

To see this intertemporal substitution effect more clearly, think about your own plan to buy a new computer. At an interest rate of 5 percent a year, you might borrow $2,000 and buy the new machine you've been researching. But at an interest rate of 10 percent a year, you might decide the payments would be too high. You don't abandon your plan to buy the computer, but you decide to delay your purchase.

A second substitution effect works through international prices. When the U.S. price level rises and other things remain the same, some of those other things are the prices in other countries. So a rise in the U.S. price level makes U.S.-made goods and services more expensive relative to foreign-made goods and services. This change in relative prices encourages people to spend less on U.S.-made items and more on foreign-made items. For example, if the U.S. price level rises relative to the Canadian price level, Canadians buy fewer U.S.-made cars (U.S. exports decrease) and Americans buy more Canadian-made cars (U.S. imports increase). U.S. real GDP decreases.

Maria's Substitution Effects   In Moscow, Russia, Maria makes some substitutions. She was planning on trading in her old motor scooter and getting a new one. But with a higher price level, and faced with higher interest rates, she decides to make her old scooter last one more year. Also, with the prices of Russian goods sharply increasing, Maria substitutes a low cost dress made in Malaysia for the Russian-made dress she had originally planned to buy.

Changes in the Quantity of Real GDP Demanded
When the price level changes and other things remain the same, the quantity of real GDP demanded changes. Such a change is shown by a movement along the aggregate demand curve. The arrows in Fig. 8.6 illustrate changes in the quantity of real GDP demanded.

We've now seen how the quantity of real GDP demanded changes when the price level changes. How do other influences on buying plans affect aggregate demand?

Changes in Aggregate Demand

A change in any factor that influences buying plans other than the price level brings a change in aggregate demand. The main factors are:

- Expectations
- Fiscal policy and monetary policy
- The world economy

Expectations   Expectations about future incomes, inflation, and profits influence buying plans today. An increase in expected future income increases the amount of consumption goods (especially big-ticket items such as cars) that people plan to buy today and increases aggregate demand.

An increase in the expected future inflation rate increases aggregate demand because people decide to buy more goods and services at today's relatively lower prices. An increase in expected future profit increases the investment that firms plan to undertake today and increases aggregate demand.

Fiscal Policy and Monetary Policy   The government's attempt to influence the economy by setting and changing taxes, transfer payments, and government purchases is called **fiscal policy**. A decrease in taxes or an increase in transfer payments—unemployment benefits, social security benefits, and welfare payments—with no change in government purchases increases aggregate demand. Both of these influences operate by increasing households' *disposable* income. **Disposable income** is aggregate income minus taxes plus transfer payments. The greater the disposable income, the greater is the quantity of consumption goods and services that households plan to buy and the greater is aggregate demand.

Government purchases of goods and services are one component of aggregate demand. So if taxes and transfer payments don't change but the government plans to buy more spy satellites and highways, aggregate demand increases.

Monetary policy consists of changes in interest rates and in the quantity of money in the economy. The quantity of money is determined by the Fed and by the banks (in a process described in Chapters 14 and 15). An increase in the quantity of money in the economy increases aggregate demand. To see why money affects aggregate demand, imagine that the Fed borrows the army's helicopters, loads them with millions of new $10 bills, and sprinkles them like confetti across the nation. People gather the newly available money and plan to spend some of it. So the quantity of goods and services demanded increases. But people don't plan to spend all the new money. They plan to save some of it and lend it to others through the banks. Interest rates fall, and with lower interest rates, people plan to buy more consumer durables and firms plan to increase their investment.

The World Economy   Two main world economy influences on aggregate demand are the foreign exchange rate and foreign income. The *foreign exchange rate* is the amount of a foreign currency that you can buy with a U.S. dollar. Other things remaining the same, a rise in the foreign exchange

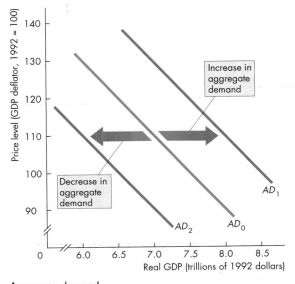

FIGURE 8.7

Changes in Aggregate Demand

Aggregate demand

Decreases if	*Increases if*
■ Expected future incomes, inflation, or profits decrease	■ Expected future incomes, inflation, or profits increase
■ Fiscal policy decreases government purchases, increases taxes, or decreases transfer payments	■ Fiscal policy increases government purchases, decreases taxes, or increases transfer payments
■ Monetary policy decreases the quantity of money and increases interest rates	■ Monetary policy increases the quantity of money and decreases interest rates
■ The exchange rate increases or foreign income decreases	■ The exchange rate decreases or foreign income increases

rate decreases aggregate demand. To see how the foreign exchange rate influences aggregate demand, suppose that $1 exchanges for 100 Japanese yen. A Fujitsu phone (made in Japan) costs 12,500 yen, and an equivalent Motorola phone (made in the

United States) costs $110. In U.S. dollars, the Fujitsu phone costs $125, so people around the world buy the cheaper U.S. phone. Now suppose the exchange rate rises to 125 yen. At 125 yen per dollar, the Fujitsu phone costs $100 and is now cheaper than the Motorola phone. People will switch from the U.S. phone to the Japanese phone. U.S. exports will decrease and U.S. imports will increase, so U.S. aggregate demand will decrease.

An increase in foreign income increases U.S. exports and increases U.S. aggregate demand. For example, an increase in income in Japan and Germany increases the purchases of U.S.-made goods and services that Japanese and German consumers and producers plan to make.

Shifts of the Aggregate Demand Curve   When aggregate demand changes, the aggregate demand curve shifts. Figure 8.7 shows two changes in aggregate demand and summarizes the factors bringing about such changes.

The aggregate demand curve shifts rightward, from AD_0 to AD_1, when expected future incomes, inflation, or profits increase, government purchases on goods and services increase, taxes are cut, transfer payments increase, the quantity of money increases and interest rates fall, the foreign exchange rate falls, or foreign income increases. The aggregate demand curve shifts leftward, from AD_0 to AD_2, when expected future incomes, inflation, or profits decrease, government purchases of goods and services decrease, taxes increase, transfer payments decrease, the quantity of money decreases and interest rates rise, the foreign exchange rate rises, or foreign income decreases.

R E V I E W   Q U I Z

- What does the aggregate demand curve show and what factors change and what factors remain the same when there is a movement along the aggregate demand curve?
- Why does the aggregate demand curve slope downward?
- How do changes in expectations, fiscal policy and monetary policy, and the world economy change aggregate demand and shift the aggregate demand curve?

Macroeconomic Equilibrium

THE PURPOSE OF THE AGGREGATE SUPPLY—aggregate demand model is to explain changes in real GDP and the price level. To achieve this purpose, we combine aggregate supply and aggregate demand and determine macroeconomic equilibrium. There is a macroeconomic equilibrium for each of the time frames for aggregate supply: a long-run equilibrium and a short-run equilibrium. Long-run equilibrium is the state toward which the economy is heading. Short-run equilibrium is the normal state of the economy as it fluctuates around potential GDP.

We'll begin our study of macroeconomic equilibrium by looking first at the short run.

Short-Run Macroeconomic Equilibrium

The aggregate demand curve tells us the quantity of real GDP demanded at each price level, and the short-run aggregate supply curve tells us the quantity of real GDP supplied at each price level. **Short-run macroeconomic equilibrium** occurs when the quantity of real GDP demanded equals the quantity of real GDP supplied. That is, short-run equilibrium occurs at the point of intersection of the *AD* curve and the *SAS* curve. Figure 8.8 shows such an equilibrium at a price level of 110 and real GDP of $7 trillion (points *c* and *c'*).

To see why this position is the equilibrium, think about what happens if the price level is something other than 110. Suppose, for example, that the price level is 120 and that real GDP is $8 trillion (at point *e*) on the *SAS* curve. The quantity of real GDP demanded is less than $8 trillion, so firms are unable to sell all their output. Unwanted inventories pile up, and firms cut both production and prices. Production and prices are cut until firms can sell all their output. This situation occurs only when real GDP is $7 trillion and the price level is 110.

Now suppose the price level is 100 and real GDP is $6 trillion (at point *a*) on the *SAS* curve. The quantity of real GDP demanded exceeds $6 trillion, so firms are unable to meet the demand for their output. Inventories decrease, and customers clamor for goods and services. So firms increase production and raise prices. Production and prices increase until firms can

FIGURE **8.8**
Short-Run Equilibrium

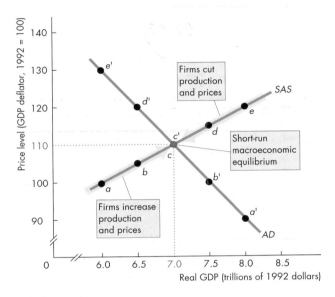

Short-run macroeconomic equilibrium occurs when real GDP demanded equals real GDP supplied— at the intersection of the aggregate demand curve (*AD*) and the short-run aggregate supply curve (*SAS*). Here, such an equilibrium occurs at points *c* and *c'*, where the price level is 110 and real GDP is $7 trillion. If the price level is 120 and real GDP is $8 trillion (point *e*), firms will not be able to sell all their output. They will decrease production and cut prices. If the price level is 100 and real GDP is $6 trillion (point *a*), people will not be able to buy all the goods and services they demand. Firms will increase production and raise their prices. Only when the price level is 110 and real GDP is $7 trillion can firms sell all that they produce and people buy all that they demand. This is the short-run macroeconomic equilibrium.

meet demand. This situation occurs only when real GDP is $7 trillion and the price level is 110.

In short-run equilibrium, the money wage rate is fixed. It does not adjust to bring full employment. So in the short run, real GDP can be greater than or less than potential GDP. But in the long run, the money wage rate does adjust and real GDP moves toward potential GDP. We are going to study this adjustment process. But first, let's look at the economy in long-run equilibrium.

Long-Run Macroeconomic Equilibrium

Long-run macroeconomic equilibrium occurs when real GDP equals potential GDP—equivalently, when the economy is on its *long-run* aggregate supply curve. Figure 8.9 shows long-run equilibrium, which occurs at the intersection of the aggregate demand curve and the long-run aggregate supply curve (the blue curves). Long-run equilibrium comes about because the money wage rate adjusts. Potential GDP and aggregate demand determine the price level, and the price level influences the money wage rate. In long-run equilibrium, the money wage rate has adjusted to put the (green) short-run aggregate supply through the long-run equilibrium point.

We'll look at this adjustment process later in this chapter. But first, let's use the *AS-AD* model to study economic growth and inflation.

FIGURE **8.9**
Long-Run Equilibrium

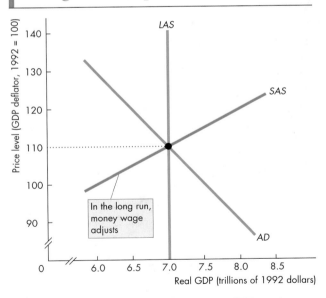

In long-run macroeconomic equilibrium, real GDP equals potential GDP. So long-run equilibrium occurs where the aggregate demand curve intersects the long-run aggregate demand curve. In the long run, aggregate demand determines the price level and has no effect on real GDP. The money wage rate adjusts in the long run, so the *SAS* curve intersects the *LAS* curve at the long-run equilibrium price level.

Economic Growth and Inflation

Economic growth occurs because, over time, the quantity of labor grows, capital is accumulated, and technology advances. These changes increase potential GDP and shift the long-run aggregate supply curve rightward. Figure 8.10 shows such a shift. The growth rate of potential GDP is determined by the pace at which labor grows, capital is accumulated, and technology advances.

Inflation occurs when, over time, aggregate demand increases by more than long-run aggregate supply. That is, inflation occurs if the aggregate demand curve shifts rightward by more than the rightward shift in the long-run aggregate supply curve. Figure 8.10 shows such shifts.

If aggregate demand increased at the same pace as long-run aggregate supply, we would experience real GDP growth with no inflation.

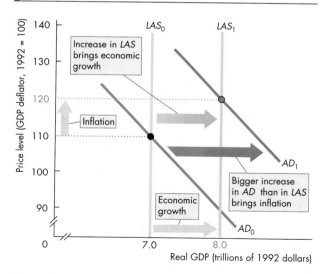

FIGURE 8.10
Economic Growth and Inflation

Economic growth is the persistent increase in potential GDP. Economic growth is shown as an ongoing rightward movement in the *LAS* curve. Inflation is the persistent rise in the price level. Inflation occurs when aggregate demand increases by more than the increase in long-run aggregate supply.

In the long run, the main influence on aggregate demand is the growth rate of the quantity of money. At times when the quantity of money increases rapidly, aggregate demand increases quickly and the inflation rate is high. When the growth rate of the quantity of money slows, other things remaining the same, the inflation rate eventually decreases.

Our economy experiences growth and inflation, like that shown in Fig. 8.10. But it does not experience *steady* growth and *steady* inflation. Real GDP fluctuates around potential GDP in a business cycle, and inflation also fluctuates. When we study the business cycle, we ignore economic growth. By doing so, we can see the business cycle more clearly.

Business Cycles

The business cycle occurs because aggregate demand and short-run aggregate supply fluctuate but the money wage rate does not adjust quickly enough to keep real GDP at potential GDP. Figure 8.11 shows three types of short-run equilibrium.

Figure 8.11(a) shows a below full-employment equilibrium. A **below full-employment equilibrium** is a macroeconomic equilibrium in which potential GDP exceeds real GDP. The amount by which potential GDP exceeds real GDP is called a **recessionary gap**. This name reminds us that a gap has opened up between potential GDP and real GDP either because the economy has experienced a recession or because real GDP, while growing, has grown more slowly than potential GDP.

The below full-employment equilibrium shown in Fig. 8.11(a) occurs where the aggregate demand curve AD_0 intersects short-run aggregate supply curve SAS_0 at a real GDP of $6.8 trillion and a price level of 110. The recessionary gap is $0.2 trillion. The U.S. economy was in a situation similar to that shown in Fig. 8.11(a) in the early 1980s and again in the early 1990s. In those years, real GDP was less than potential GDP.

Figure 8.11(b) is an example of *long-run equilibrium* in which real GDP equals potential GDP. In this example, the equilibrium occurs where the aggregate demand curve AD_1 intersects the short-run aggregate supply curve SAS_1 at an actual and potential GDP of $7 trillion. The U.S. economy was in a situation such as that shown in Fig. 8.11(b) in 1999.

Figure 8.11(c) shows an above full-employment equilibrium. An **above full-employment equilibrium** is a macroeconomic equilibrium in which real

GDP exceeds potential GDP. The amount by which real GDP exceeds potential GDP is called an **inflationary gap**. This name reminds us that a gap has opened up between real GDP and potential GDP and that this gap creates inflationary pressure.

The above full-employment equilibrium shown in Fig. 8.11(c) occurs where the aggregate demand curve AD_2 intersects the short-run aggregate supply curve SAS_2 at a real GDP of $7.2 trillion and a price level of 110. There is an inflationary gap of $0.2

trillion. The U.S. economy was in a situation similar to that depicted in Fig. 8.11(c) in 1988–1990.

The economy moves from one type of equilibrium to another as a result of fluctuations in aggregate demand and in short-run aggregate supply. These fluctuations produce fluctuations in real GDP and the price level. Figure 8.11(d) shows how real GDP fluctuates around potential GDP.

Let's now look at some of the sources of these fluctuations around potential GDP.

FIGURE 8.11

The Business Cycle

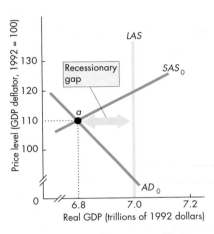

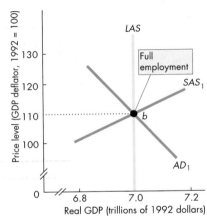

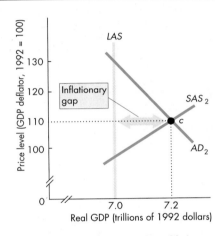

(a) Below full-employment equilibrium

(b) Long-run equilibrium

(c) Above full-employment equilibrium

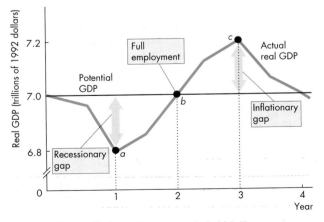

(d) Fluctuations in real GDP

Part (a) shows a below full-employment equilibrium in year 1; part (b) shows a long-run equilibrium in year 2; part (c) shows an above full-employment equilibrium in year 3. Part (d) shows how real GDP fluctuates around potential GDP in a business cycle. In year 1, there is a recessionary gap and the economy is at point *a* (in parts a and d). In year 2, there is long-run equilibrium and the economy is at point *b* (in parts b and d). In year 3, there is an inflationary gap and the economy is at point *c* (in parts c and d).

Fluctuations in Aggregate Demand

One reason real GDP fluctuates around potential GDP is that aggregate demand fluctuates. Let's see what happens when aggregate demand increases.

Figure 8.12(a) shows an economy in long-run equilibrium. The aggregate demand curve is AD_0, the short-run aggregate supply curve is SAS_0, and the long-run aggregate supply curve is LAS. Real GDP equals potential GDP at $7 trillion, and the price level is 110.

Now suppose that the world economy expands and that the demand for U.S.-made goods increases in Japan and Europe. The increase in U.S. exports increases aggregate demand, and the aggregate demand curve shifts rightward from AD_0 to AD_1 in Fig. 8.12(a).

Faced with an increase in demand, firms increase production and raise prices. Real GDP increases to $7.5 trillion, and the price level rises to 115. The economy is now in an above full-employment equilibrium. Real GDP exceeds potential GDP, there is an inflationary gap.

The increase in aggregate demand has increased the prices of all goods and services. Faced with higher prices, firms have increased their output rates. At this stage, prices of goods and services have increased but wage rates have not changed. (Recall that as we move along a short-run aggregate supply curve, wage rates are constant.)

The economy cannot produce in excess of potential GDP forever. Why not? What are the forces at work that bring real GDP back to potential GDP?

Because the price level has increased and wage rates are unchanged, workers have experienced a fall in the buying power of their wages and firms' profits have increased. In these circumstances, workers demand higher wages and firms, anxious to maintain their employment and output levels, meet those demands. If firms do not raise wage rates, they will either lose workers or have to hire less productive ones.

As wage rates rise, the short-run aggregate supply curve begins to shift leftward. In Fig. 8.12(b), the short-run aggregate supply curve moves from SAS_0

FIGURE 8.12

An Increase in Aggregate Demand

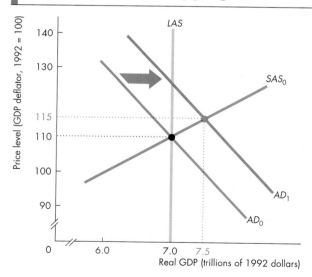

(a) Short-run effect

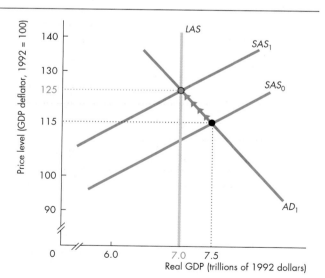

(b) Long-run effect

An increase in aggregate demand shifts the aggregate demand curve from AD_0 to AD_1. In the short-run equilibrium, real GDP is $7.5 trillion and the price level rises to 115 in part (a). In this situation, there is an inflationary gap. The money wage rate rises, and the short-run aggregate supply curve shifts

leftward from SAS_0 to SAS_1 in part (b). As it shifts, it intersects the aggregate demand curve AD_1 at higher price levels and lower real GDP levels. Eventually, the price level rises to 125 and real GDP decreases to $7.0 trillion—potential GDP.

toward SAS_1. The rise in wages and the shift in the *SAS* curve produce a sequence of new equilibrium positions. Along the adjustment path, real GDP falls and the price level rises. The economy moves up along its aggregate demand curve as shown by the arrowheads in the figure.

Eventually, wage rates rise by the same percentage as the price level. At this time, the aggregate demand curve AD_1 intersects SAS_1 at a new long-run equilibrium. The price level has risen to 125, and real GDP is back where it started, at potential GDP.

A decrease in aggregate demand has similar but opposite effects to those of an increase in aggregate demand. That is, a decrease in aggregate demand shifts the aggregate demand curve leftward. Real GDP decreases to less than potential GDP, and a recessionary gap emerges. Firms cut prices. The lower price level increases the purchasing power of wages and increases firms' costs relative to their output prices because wages remain unchanged. Eventually, the slack economy leads to falling wage rates and the short-run aggregate supply curve shifts rightward. But wage rates change slowly, so real GDP slowly returns to potential GDP and the price level falls slowly.

Let's now work out how real GDP and the price level change when aggregate supply changes.

Fluctuations in Aggregate Supply

Fluctuations in short-run aggregate supply can bring fluctuations in real GDP around potential GDP. Suppose that initially real GDP equals potential GDP. Then there is a large but temporary rise in the price of oil. What happens to real GDP and the price level?

Figure 8.13 answers this question. The aggregate demand curve is AD_0, the short-run aggregate supply curve is SAS_0, and the long-run aggregate supply curve is *LAS*. Equilibrium real GDP is $7 trillion, which equals potential GDP, and the price level is 110. Then the price of oil rises. Faced with higher energy and transportation costs, firms decrease production. Short-run aggregate supply decreases, and the short-run aggregate supply curve shifts leftward to SAS_1. The price level rises to 120, and real GDP decreases to $6.5 trillion. Because real GDP decreases, the economy experiences recession. Because the price level increases, the economy experiences inflation. A combination of recession and inflation, called *stagflation*, actually occurred in the United States in the mid-1970s and early 1980s. But events like this are not common.

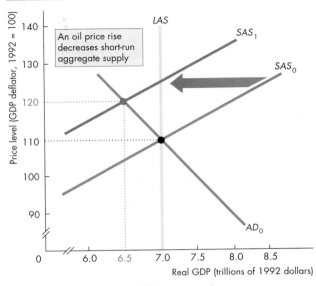

FIGURE 8.13

A Decrease in Aggregate Supply

An oil price rise decreases short-run aggregate supply

An increase in the price of oil decreases short-run aggregate supply and shifts the short-run aggregate supply curve from SAS_0 to SAS_1. Real GDP decreases from $7.0 trillion to $6.5 trillion, and the price level rises from 110 to 120. The economy experiences both recession and inflation—stagflation.

R E V I E W   Q U I Z

- Does economic growth result from increases in aggregate demand, short-run aggregate supply, or long-run aggregate supply?
- Does inflation result from increases in aggregate demand, short-run aggregate supply, or long-run aggregate supply?
- Can you describe three types of short-run macroeconomic equilibrium?
- How do fluctuations in aggregate demand and short-run aggregate supply bring fluctuations in real GDP around potential GDP?

Let's put our new knowledge of aggregate supply and aggregate demand to work and see how we can explain recent U.S. macroeconomic performance.

U.S. Economic Growth, Inflation, and Cycles

THE ECONOMY IS CONTINUALLY CHANGING. IF you imagine the economy as a video, then an aggregate supply–aggregate demand figure such as Fig. 8.13 is a freeze-frame. We're going to run the video—an instant replay—but keep our finger on the freeze-frame button and look at some important parts of the previous action. Let's run the video from 1960.

Figure 8.14 shows the state of the economy in 1960 at the point of intersection of its aggregate demand curve AD_{60} and short-run aggregate supply curve SAS_{60}. Real GDP was $2.3 trillion, and the GDP deflator was 23 (about a fifth of its 1998 level). In 1960, real GDP equaled potential GDP—the economy was on its long-run aggregate supply curve, LAS_{60}.

By 1998, the economy had reached the point marked by the intersection of aggregate demand curve AD_{98} and short-run aggregate supply curve

SAS_{98}. Real GDP was $7.6 trillion, and the GDP deflator was 113. The LAS curve assumes that potential GDP in 1998 was $7.6 trillion. The path traced by the blue and red dots shows three key features:

- Economic growth
- Inflation
- Business cycles

Economic Growth

Over the years, real GDP grows—shown in Fig. 8.14 by the rightward movement of the points. The faster real GDP grows, the larger is the horizontal distance between successive dots in the figure. The forces that generate economic growth are those that increase potential GDP. Potential GDP grows because the quantity of labor grows, we accumulate physical capital and human capital, and our technologies advance.

These forces that bring economic growth were stronger during the early 1970s and mid-1980s than at other times. During the late 1970s, growth was slow.

FIGURE 8.14

Aggregate Supply and Aggregate Demand: 1960–1998

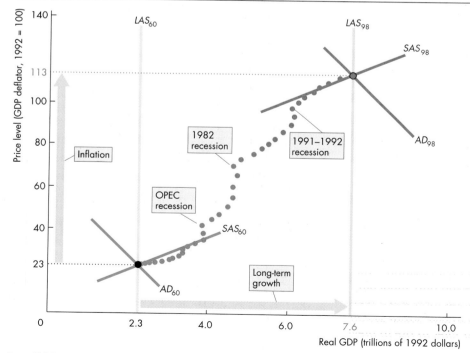

Each point shows the GDP deflator and real GDP in a given year. In 1960, these variables were determined by the aggregate demand curve AD_{60} and the short-run aggregate supply curve SAS_{60}. Each point is generated by the gradual shifting of the AD and SAS curves. By 1998, the curves were AD_{98} and SAS_{98}. Real GDP grew, and the price level increased. Real GDP grew quickly and inflation was moderate during the 1960s; real GDP growth sagged in 1974–1975 and again in 1982. Inflation was rapid during the 1970s but slowed after the 1982 recession. The period from 1982 to 1989 was one of strong, persistent expansion. A recession began in 1991, and a further strong and sustained expansion then followed.

Source: U.S. Department of Commerce, *Survey of Current Business*, (March 1999) and the author's assumptions.

Inflation

The price level rises over the years—shown in Fig. 8.14 by the upward movement of the points. The larger the rise in the price level, the larger is the vertical distance between successive dots in the figure. The main force generating the persistent increase in the price level is a tendency for aggregate demand to increase at a faster pace than the increase in long-run aggregate supply. All of the factors that increase aggregate demand and shift the aggregate demand curve influence the pace of inflation. But one factor—the growth of the quantity of money—is the main source of *persistent* increases in aggregate demand and persistent inflation.

Business Cycles

Over the years, the economy grows and shrinks in cycles—shown in Fig. 8.14 by the wavelike pattern made by the points, with the recessions highlighted. The cycles arise because both the expansion of short-run aggregate supply and the growth of aggregate demand do not proceed at a fixed, steady pace. Although the economy has cycles, recessions do not usually follow quickly on the heels of their predecessors; "double-dip" recessions like the one in the cartoon are rare.

The Evolving Economy: 1960–1998

During the 1960s, real GDP growth was rapid and inflation was low. This was a period of rapid increases in aggregate supply and of moderate increases in aggregate demand.

The mid-1970s were years of rapid inflation and recession—of stagflation. The major source of these developments was a series of massive oil price increases that shifted the short-run aggregate supply curve leftward and rapid increases in the quantity of money that shifted the aggregate demand curve rightward. Recession occurred because the short-run aggregate supply curve shifted leftward at a faster pace than the aggregate demand curve shifted rightward.

The rest of the 1970s saw high inflation—the price level increased quickly—and only moderate growth in real GDP. By 1980, inflation was a major problem and the Fed decided to take strong action against it. It permitted interest rates to rise to previously unknown levels. Consequently, aggregate demand decreased. By 1982, the decrease in aggregate demand put the economy in a deep recession.

"Please stand by for a series of tones. The first indicates the official end of the recession, the second indicates prosperity, and the third the return of the recession."

Drawing by Mankoff; © 1991 *The New Yorker Magazine, Inc.*

During the years 1982 to 1990, capital accumulation and steady technological advance resulted in a sustained rightward shift of the long-run aggregate supply curve. Wage growth was moderate, and the short-run aggregate supply curve also shifted rightward. Aggregate demand growth kept pace with the growth of aggregate supply. Sustained but steady growth in aggregate supply and aggregate demand kept real GDP growing and inflation steady. The economy moved from a recession with real GDP less than potential GDP in 1982 to above full-employment in 1990. It was in this condition when a decrease in aggregate demand led to the 1991 recession. The economy again embarked on a path of expansion through 1998. The expansion took real GDP to a level that probably exceeded potential GDP and took employment to above-full employment.

◆ The aggregate supply–aggregate demand model explains economic growth, inflation, and the business cycle. The model is a useful one because it enables us to keep our eye on the big picture. But it lacks detail. It does not tell us as much as we need to know about the deeper forces that lie behind aggregate supply and aggregate demand. The chapters that follow begin to fill in the details. We begin with the supply side and study the forces that make our economy grow. But before you embark on this next stage, take a look at *Reading Between the Lines* on pages 170–171, which gives you a look at the U.S. economy in 1999.

Aggregate Supply and Aggregate Demand in Action

CNNfn, MARCH 30, 1999

Economy Full-Steam Ahead

By staff writer Steven Radwell

NEW YORK—The American economy, the big engine that could, has made the rest of the world green with envy for most of this decade and 1999 is shaping up as no exception.

Most forecasters expect growth of 3 percent or better this year with little inflation—a mix that has Federal Reserve Chairman Alan Greenspan and many other forecasters scratching their heads. Traditional economic theory says growth of 3 to 4 percent—seen in four of the last five years—should have pushed wages and prices sharply higher by now, but inflation is all but absent after eight years of growth, the longest peace time expansion in the history of the United States. ...

Is there an end in sight? Most forecasters say not yet, though many see growth slowing in 2000. Some others say there is about a one-in-three chance of a recession next year.

"As long as Alan Greenspan's not frowning, I'm not too worried," said David Blitzer, chief economist at Standard & Poor's, who sees strong corporate and consumer spending, the solid job market and low inflation adding up to GDP growth of about 3.6 percent this year, up from his earlier forecast of 3.1 percent.

... Productivity, an important measure of output per worker, grew at a 4.6 percent rate in the fourth quarter, the fastest rise in six years and something Fed Chairman Greenspan considers crucial if economic growth is going to continue with low inflation. ...

"I don't believe the business cycle has been conquered. There'll (eventually) be another recession," (said Blitzer) ..., noting it will be more like the 1990–1991 downturn than the 1981–1982 recession, when unemployment rose to 10.7 percent, the highest since the Great Depression, and interest rates touched 20 percent, levels unseen in the United States since the Civil War. ...

Essence of the Story

■ At the beginning of 1999, most economic forecasters expected real GDP to grow by 3 percent or more during 1999 and to slow during 2000. A few forecasters predicted a recession for 2000.

■ Traditional economic theory predicts that growth of 3 to 4 percent maintained for several years will push wages and prices sharply higher. But inflation has remained low after eight years of growth.

■ Productivity growth is the key to expansion with low inflation.

■ There will eventually be another recession, but it will be more like the mild 1990–1991 recession rather than the severe 1981–1982 recession.

Economic Analysis

■ In 1998, U.S. real GDP grew by 4.2 percent to $7.6 trillion and the price level (which equaled 100 in 1992) increased by only 1 percent to 113.

■ No one can forecast next year's real GDP and price level. And no one knows for sure the current level of potential GDP. But at the beginning of 1999, most forecasters believed that real GDP would continue to grow with low inflation during 1999. A minority believed that a recession would occur in 1999.

■ Figure 1 shows the majority view. Real GDP ($7.6 trillion) and the price level (113) are determined at the intersection of the aggregate demand curve, AD_{98} and the short-run aggregate supply curve SAS_{98}. Potential GDP in 1998 was $7.6 trillion so the long-run aggregate supply curve was LAS_{98}.

■ During 1999, potential GDP was expected to grow by 3 percent to $7.8 trillion so the long-run aggregate supply curve shifts rightward to LAS_{99}. Aggregate demand was expected to increase to AD_{99} and short-run aggregate supply to SAS_{99}. Real GDP was expected to grow by 3 percent and the price level to rise by less than 1 percent.

■ Figure 2 shows a minority view of the U.S. economy in 1999. Potential GDP is $7.5 trillion on long-run aggregate supply curve LAS in 1999. This LAS curve assumes that the growth rate of potential GDP has been around its historical average rate.

■ Aggregate demand was expected to remain at level AD through 1999. At the beginning of 1999, real GDP is $7.6 trillion and there was an inflationary gap.

■ With an inflationary gap, wage rates were expected to rise more rapidly and the SAS curve was expected to shift leftward to SAS_{99}.

■ Real GDP was expected to shrink to $7.5 trillion and the inflation rate will increase.

■ Real GDP was expected to decrease for at least two quarters, so a recession was forecasted. But the recession was expected to be mild, and the pickup in the inflation rate modest

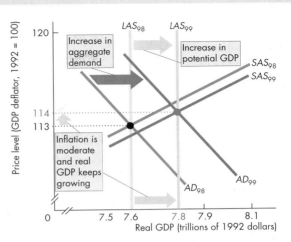

Figure 1 Expansion continues

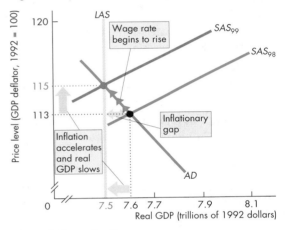

Figure 2 Recession ?

You're The Voter

■ Do you think the Fed should increase interest rates to keep inflation in check? Or do you think the Fed should cut interest rates to prevent a recession? Explain your answer.

■ Do you think the federal government should cut taxes to prevent a recession? Explain your answer.

171

SUMMARY

KEY POINTS

Aggregate Supply (pp. 154–158)

- In the long run, the quantity of real GDP supplied is potential GDP, which is independent of the price level. The long-run aggregate supply curve is vertical.

- In the short run, the money wage rate is constant, so a rise in the price level increases the quantity of real GDP supplied. The short-run aggregate supply curve is upward sloping.

- A change in potential GDP changes both long-run and short-run aggregate supply. A change in the money wage rate or resource prices changes only short-run aggregate supply.

Aggregate Demand (pp. 159–162)

- A rise in the price level decreases the quantity of real GDP demanded, other things remaining the same.

- The reason is that the higher price level decreases the quantity of *real* wealth, raises the interest rate, and raises the cost of domestic goods compared with foreign goods.

- Changes in expected future incomes, profits, and inflation, changes in fiscal policy and monetary policy, and changes in world real GDP and the foreign exchange rate change aggregate demand.

Macroeconomic Equilibrium (pp. 162–167)

- In the short run, real GDP and the price level are determined by aggregate demand and short-run aggregate supply.

- In the long run, real GDP equals potential GDP and aggregate demand determines the price level and the money wage rate.

- Economic growth occurs because potential GDP increases.

- Inflation occurs because aggregate demand grows more quickly than potential GDP.

- Business cycles occur because aggregate demand and aggregate supply fluctuate.

U.S. Economic Growth, Inflation, and Cycles (pp. 168–169)

- U.S. potential GDP grew fastest during the 1960s and mid-1980s and slowest during the 1970s.

- U.S. inflation persists because aggregate demand grows faster than potential GDP.

- U.S. business cycles occur because aggregate supply and aggregate demand change at an uneven pace.

KEY FIGURES

KEY TERMS

PROBLEMS

🖳 *1. The following events occur that influence the economy of Toughtimes:
- A deep recession hits the world economy.
- Oil prices rise sharply.
- Businesses expect huge losses in the near future.

a. Explain the separate effects of each of these events on real GDP and the price level in Toughtimes, starting from a position of long-run equilibrium.

b. Explain the combined effects of these events on real GDP and the price level in Toughtimes, starting from a position of long-run equilibrium.

c. Explain what the Toughtimes government and central bank can do to overcome the problems faced by the economy.

2. The following events occur that influence the economy of Coolland:
- A strong expansion in the world economy.
- Businesses expect huge profits in the near future.
- The Coolland government cuts its expenditure.

a. Explain the separate effects of each of these events on real GDP and the price level in Coolland, starting from a position of long-run equilibrium.

b. Explain the combined effects of these events on real GDP and the price level in Coolland, starting from a position of long-run equilibrium.

c. Explain why the Coolland government or central bank might want to take action to influence the Coolland economy.

🖳 *3. The economy of Mainland has the following aggregate demand and supply schedules:

Price level	Real GDP demanded	Real GDP supplied in the short run
	(billions of 1992 dollars)	
90	450	350
100	400	400
110	350	450
120	300	500
130	250	550
140	200	600

a. In a figure, plot the aggregate demand curve and the short-run aggregate supply curve.

b. What are the values of real GDP and the price level in Mainland in a short-run macroeconomic equilibrium?

c. Mainland's potential GDP is $500 billion. Plot the long-run aggregate supply curve in the same figure in which you answered part (a).

4. The economy of Miniland has the following aggregate demand and supply schedules:

Price level	Real GDP demanded	Real GDP supplied in the short run
	(billions of 1992 dollars)	
90	600	150
100	500	200
110	400	250
120	300	300
130	200	350
140	100	400

a. In a figure, plot the aggregate demand curve and the short-run aggregate supply curve.

b. What are the values of real GDP and the price level in Miniland in a short-run macroeconomic equilibrium?

c. Miniland's potential GDP is $250 billion. Plot the long-run aggregate supply curve in the same figure in which you answered part (a).

🖳 *5. In problem 3, aggregate demand is increased by $100 billion. How do real GDP and the price level change in the short run?

6. In problem 4, aggregate demand is decreased by $150 billion. How do real GDP and the price level change in the short run?

🖳 *7. In problem 3, aggregate supply decreases by $100 billion. What now is the short-run macroeconomic equilibrium?

8. In problem 4, aggregate supply increases by $150 billion. What now is the short-run macroeconomic equilibrium?

*9. In the economy shown in the figure, initially the short-run aggregate supply is SAS_0 and aggregate demand is AD_0. Then some events change aggregate demand, and the aggregate demand curve shifts rightward to AD_1. Later, some other events change aggregate supply and shifts the short-run aggregate supply curve leftward to SAS_1.

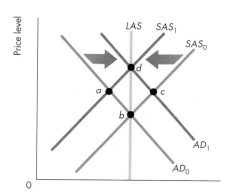

a. What is the equilibrium point after the change in aggregate demand?
b. What is the equilibrium point after the change in aggregate supply?
c. What events could have changed aggregate demand from AD_0 to AD_1?
d. What events could have changed aggregate supply from SAS_0. SAS_1?

10. In the economy shown in the figure, initially long-run aggregate supply is LAS_0, short-run aggregate supply is SAS_0, and aggregate demand is AD_0. Then some events change aggregate supply, and the aggregate supply curves shifts rightward to LAS_1 and SAS_1.

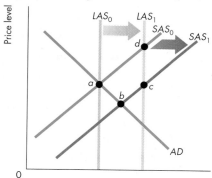

a. What is the equilibrium point after the change in aggregate supply?
b. What events could have changed long-run aggregate supply from LAS_0 to LAS_1?
c. What events could have changed short-run aggregate supply from SAS_0 to SAS_1?
d. After the increase in aggregate demand but before the increase in aggregate supply, is real GDP greater than or less than potential GDP?
e. What change in aggregate demand will make real GDP equal to potential GDP?

CRITICAL THINKING

1. After you have studied the forecasts for the U.S. economy during 1999 in *Reading Between the Lines* on pp. 170–171, answer the following questions:
   a. What were most economists predicting for the U.S. economy during 1999? Why?
   b. Why might some economists have thought that an inflationary gap existed at the beginning of 1999?
   c. Use the *AS-AD* model to show the economy in 1999 if the Fed cuts interest rates.
   d. Use the *AS-AD* model to show the economy in 1999 if the Fed raises interest rates.

2. Use the links on the Parkin Web site to obtain the latest data on real GDP and the price level. Then:
   a. Create a figure similar to those on p. 171 to interpret the latest numbers.
   b. In light of the events that occurred during 1999, which of the two figures on p. 171 is the more likely description of the U.S. economy at the end of 1999? Explain.

3. You are the President's economic advisor and have the following forecasts of aggregate demand and aggregate supply for next year:

Price level	Real GDP demanded	Real GDP supplied	Potential GDP
	(trillions of 1992 dollars)		
100	8.3	5.3	7
105	7.8	6.3	7
110	7.3	7.3	7
115	6.8	8.3	7

This year, real GDP is $6.8 trillion, potential GDP is also $6.8 trillion, and the price level is 107. The President wants answers to the following questions:
   a. What is your forecast of next year's real GDP?
   b. What is your forecast of next year's price level?
   c. What is your forecast of the inflation rate?
   d. What is your forecast of the growth rate of real GDP?
   e. What is your forecast of the growth rate of potential GDP?
   f. Will there be a recessionary gap or an inflationary gap? By how much?

Understanding the Themes of Macroeconomics

The Big Picture

Macroeconomics is a large and controversial subject that is interlaced with political ideological disputes. And it is a field in which charlatans as well as serious thinkers have much to say. This page is a map that looks back at the road you've just traveled and forward at the path you will take from here. ◆ You began your study of macroeconomics with the core questions of the subject. What are the causes of:

- Economic growth?
- Business cycles?
- Unemployment?
- Inflation?

In Chapter 5, you took your first look at each of these questions. You learned some facts about economic growth, business cycles, unemployment, and inflation in the United States and around the world. ◆ In Chapter 6, you learned how we measure the economy's output and the price level. These measures are used to calculate the rate of economic growth, business cycle fluctuations, and inflation. You discovered that making these measurements is not straightforward and that small measurement errors can have a big effect of our perceptions about how we are doing. ◆ In Chapter 7, you learned how we measure the state of the labor market—the levels of employment and unemployment and wages. And in Chapter 8, you studied the macroeconomic version of supply and demand—*aggregate supply* and *aggregate demand*. You saw that the aggregate supply–aggregate demand model is the big picture model. It explains both the long-term trends in economic growth and inflation and the short-term business cycle fluctuations in production, jobs, and inflation. ◆ The chapters that lie ahead of you look behind aggregate supply and aggregate demand. First, in Chapters 9 through 11, you study aggregate supply and economic growth. This material is so central to the oldest question in macroeconomics that Adam Smith tried to answer. You'll begin in Chapter 9 by looking at the economy at full employment and study the forces that determine potential GDP and make it change. In Chapter 10, you will study the role played by saving and investment in increasing the amount of capital and creating economic growth. Then, in Chapter 11, you will study the growth process and the roles of capital accumulation and technological change in bringing economic growth about. ◆ Second, in Chapters 12 through 18, you will study aggregate demand, inflation, and deflation. This material is central to the macroeconomics that Keynes developed as a response to the Great Depression. Here you will learn about economic fluctuations and the policies that might limit their severity. ◆ Before continuing your study of macroeconomics, spend a few minutes with John Maynard Keynes and Jean Baptiste Say, the leading scholars who developed this subject. And spend a few minutes with today's leading macroeconomist, Robert E. Lucas, Jr. of the University of Chicago.

The Economist

John Maynard Keynes,

born in England in 1883, was one of the outstanding minds of the twentieth century. He wrote on probability as well as economics, represented Britain at the Versailles peace conference at the end of World War I, was a master speculator on international financial markets (an activity he conducted from bed every morning and which made and lost him several fortunes), and played a prominent role in creating the International Monetary Fund. He was a member of the Bloomsbury Group, a circle of outstanding artists and writers that included E. M. Forster, Bertrand Russell, and Virginia Woolf. Keynes was a controversial and quick-witted figure. A critic once complained that Keynes had changed his opinion on some matter, to which Keynes retorted: "When I discover I am wrong, I change my mind. What do you do?"

"The ideas of economists and political philosophers, both when they are right and when they are wrong, are more powerful than is commonly understood. Indeed the world is ruled by little else."

JOHN MAYNARD KEYNES
The General Theory of Employment, Interest, and Money

The Issues

During the Industrial Revolution, as technological change created new jobs and destroyed old ones, people began to wonder whether the economy could create enough jobs and sufficient demand to buy all the things that the new industrial economy could produce.

Jean-Baptiste Say argued that production creates incomes that are sufficient to buy everything that is produced—supply creates its own demand—an idea that came to be called *Say's Law.*

Say and Keynes would have had a lot to disagree about. Jean-Baptiste Say, born in Lyon, France, in 1767 (he was 9 years old when Adam Smith's *Wealth of Nations* was published), suffered the wrath of Napoleon for his views on government and the economy. In today's world, Say would be leading a radical conservative charge for a smaller and leaner government. Say was the most famous economist of his era on both sides of the Atlantic. His book, *Traité d'économie politique (A Treatise in Political Economy),* published in 1803, became a best-selling university economics textbook in both Europe and North America.

As the Great Depression of the 1930s became more severe and more prolonged, Say's Law looked less and less relevant. John Maynard Keynes revolutionized macroeconomic thinking by turning Say's Law on its head, arguing that production does not depend on supply. Instead, it depends on what people are willing to buy—on demand. Or as Keynes put it, production depends on *effective demand.* It is possible, argued Keynes, for people to refuse to spend all of their incomes. If businesses fail to spend on new capital the amount that people plan to save, demand might be less than supply. In this situation, resources might go unemployed and remain unemployed indefinitely.

The influence of Keynes persists even today, more than 60 years after the publication of his main work. But during the past 20 years, Nobel Laureate Robert E. Lucas, Jr., with significant contributions from a list of outstanding macroeconomists too long to name, has further revolutionized macroeconomics. Today, we know a lot about economic growth, unemployment, inflation, and business cycles. And we know how to use fiscal policy and monetary policy to improve macroeconomic performance. But we don't yet have all the answers. Macroeconomics remains a field of lively controversy and exciting research.

Then

In 1776, James Hargreaves, an English weaver and carpenter, developed a simple hand-operated machine called a spinning jenny (pictured here). Using this machine, a person could spin 80 threads at once. Thousands of handwheel spinners, operators of machines that could spin only one thread, lost their jobs. They protested by wrecking spinning jennies. In the long run, the displaced handwheel spinners found work, often in factories that manufactured the machines that had destroyed their previous jobs. From the earliest days of the Industrial Revolution to the present day, people have lost their jobs as new technologies have automated what human effort had previously been needed to accomplish.

Now

Advances in computer technology have made it possible for us to dial our own telephone calls to any part of the world and get connected in a flash. A task that was once performed by telephone operators, who made connections along copper wires, is now performed faster and more reliably by computers along fiber-optic cables. Just as the Industrial Revolution transformed the textile industry, so today's Information Revolution is transforming the telecommunications industry. In the process, the mix of jobs is changing. There are fewer jobs for telephone operators but more jobs for telephone systems designers, builders, managers, and marketers. In the long run, as people spend the income they earn in their changing jobs, supply creates its own demand, just as Say predicted. But does supply create its own demand in the short run, when displaced workers are unemployed?

Keynes and Robert E. Lucas, Jr, would have had plenty of disagreements too. Lucas, of the University of Chicago, has led a revolution in macroeconomics that has enabled economists to build model (artificial) economies that display properties similar to those of the actual economy and to use these models to study the effects of alternative policies on macroeconomic performance. A cornerstone of the new macroeconomics is the idea of "rational expectations"— people use all the available information to make economic forecasts. This information includes theories about how the economy works. Lucas, like Say, believes that it is easier for government intervention to do harm than good. Said Lucas, "I don't want to manage the U.S. economy. And I don't think anybody else should take the job either." You can meet Professor Lucas on the following pages.

Robert E. Lucas, Jr.,

is a professor of economics at the University of Chicago, a position he has held since 1975. Professor Lucas was born in Yakima, Washington, in 1937. He earned his B.A. and his Ph.D. from the University of Chicago in 1959 and 1963, respectively.

In 1995, Professor Lucas received the Nobel Prize for Economic Science for his work on developing the theory of rational expectations. Challenging the Keynesian theories of economic fluctuations, this new macroeconomic theory is based on the hypothesis that people and businesses make rational decisions based on rational expectations and markets reconcile individual decisions by balancing supply and demand, even in a recession.

Michael Parkin spoke with Professor Lucas about rational expectations macroeconomics, his views of economic policy, and the legacy of Keynes.

Robert E. Lucas, Jr.

Why are you an economist?
I grew up in a family where everyone talked about politics and economics every night at dinner. So I've been concerned with social questions as long as I can remember. My experience as an undergraduate history major confirmed my belief in the importance of economic forces.

You applied the idea of rational expectations to macroeconomics and to expectations about inflation. How has that hypothesis changed the way we think about things?
It ties down a loose end that shouldn't have been there. Any important economic decision depends on what you think about the future. Rational expectations is a way of dealing with that.

What do you see as the chief criticism of the rational expectations hypothesis?
Here's the genuine difficulty people have with the idea. You would never discover the idea of rational expectations by introspection. Rational expectations describes something that has to be true of the outcome of a much more complicated underlying process. But it doesn't describe the actual thought process people use in trying to figure out the future. Our behavior is adaptive. We try some mode of behavior. If it's successful, we do it again. If not, we try something else. Rational expectations describes the situation when you've got it right.

Can you give an example?
In economics, we're mostly concerned about repetitive events and decisions of some consequence. Our capitalist economy has been operating under pretty much the same laws for 200 years now. People aren't reacting to every monetary contraction as if it's the first time it ever happened: That is just inconceivable. I think people have developed certain ways of living with regular events as best they can.

One of the most significant developments in macroeconomics in recent years has been real business cycle

theory. How do you evaluate this approach?

Real business cycle theory asks what the time path of the economy's GDP or employment would be under the best possible macroeconomic policy. The early authors of this approach asked themselves what fraction of the actual variation in GDP you could account for if you restricted yourself to the fluctuations in the rate of technological change. Their initial answer was: All of it, that there is nothing left over for traditional macroeconomic theory to account for. I don't think that can be right.

For example, you can't account for something like the events of 1929 to 1933, when real output fell by a quarter in four years, as if it resulted from the changes in the rate at which technology was decaying. The Depression didn't occur because production techniques got worse. But real business cycle theory has shown us that real forces are much more important than we had thought and that the questions addressed by traditional macroeconomics are not as important as we once thought. That's the important message.

How can we introduce monetary forces into a macroeconomic model that at the same time pays serious attention to real forces, one that shows fluctuations in price as well as in output?

This question is the subject of my Nobel Lecture, "Monetary Neutrality." I think it is the central question of macroeconomics, but it remains unresolved today, as it did when David Hume first addressed it in the eighteenth century.

Your early work focused primarily on short-term macroeconomic problems. For the past 10 years, you've increasingly devoted your life to thinking about long-term growth. Why has your work changed in that direction?

When I began taking economics courses in the early 1960s, the Great Depression of the 1930s was a key topic of discussion for all my professors. The study of macroeconomics was, at that time, the study of how to prevent depressions and how to get out of them. The United States has not had a serious depression since the 1930s, and we should not be surprised that macroeconomic study has switched from a depression focus to a growth focus. If you ask what determines our income today relative to what it was in the 1960s, 99 percent of the answer is economic growth.

What can we bring to the study of growth today that Smith couldn't bring to it when he tried to figure out what caused the wealth of nations?

When Adam Smith wrote about the wealth of nations, he was thinking about a world in which no country had ever experienced sustained growth in living standards. Some countries had higher *levels* of income than others, and Smith was interested in understanding why those differences existed. But Smith never observed or imagined a country where production could grow at 3 percent per year for a century and more. Smith also lacked good data, by modern standards. We now have tremendous data sets on income and the growth of income for the richest and poorest countries. During the past 10 years, growth theory has evolved from being the study of the United States, the United Kingdom, and a few other very wealthy economies to being the comparative study of rich and poor economies. The hope is that the same general theoretical principles will apply to both.

There's about a 25 to 1 difference between the United States and India in per capita production. How do you explain that difference?

Only a small fraction can be explained by the differences in physical capital. U.S. workers have better equipment than Indian workers, and that's certainly a factor in making them more productive, but a much more important factor is human capital. The level of education and training of the U.S. worker is much higher than the typical Indian worker. Once human capital is introduced—and placed at the center of growth theory—a lot of things start falling into place and it becomes much easier to understand the enormous differences in incomes.

How do you explain the astonishing growth rates of per capita incomes in East Asia compared with the 1 to 2 percent growth rates of North America?

The countries of East Asia are catching up with those of Europe and North America. The Industrial Revolution has opened them up to trade with the more advanced countries of the world. East Asia is experiencing annual growth rates of 6 to 8 percent. Nothing like that ever occurred in the United States or the United Kingdom, the countries that were leaders from the start of the Industrial Revolution. East Asian countries are rapidly learning technology that took decades to produce.

You were a student of Milton Friedman, the architect of the movement called monetarism. How do you distinguish this approach from the kind of macroeconomics that you are responsible for creating?

I'm not that big on the distinction. I think of myself as a monetarist. But the term does refer to several different things. One aspect of what people call monetarism is just an emphasis on the quantity of some money as a determinant of prices and of economic activity. In some ways, I think that revolution has been so successful that it doesn't seem like a revolution any more. In this day and age, no one talks about the price level, exchange rates, or interest rates without talking about the quantity of money. In that sense, we're all monetarists. The second aspect of monetarism

> Economics is a great major. ... economics is a good pre–almost anything major.

is a hostility toward the government's continual management of the economy. The role of government, in a monetarist perspective, is to make its own behavior on fiscal or monetary policy simple and predictable and then just to let the system operate without fine tuning. That view, I think, is absolutely right.

In recent years, we've experienced the biggest peacetime government budget deficit ever. How have you viewed the deficit over the years?

I was a deficit alarmist in the early years of the Reagan administration because I thought the deficits would be inflationary. Well, that just hasn't happened. I've become more sympathetic to people like Larry Kotlikoff, who argued that the deficit just doesn't measure anything we care about, since things like future social security liabilities are arbitrarily excluded.

What for you is the legacy of Keynes?

Keynes' influence was almost entirely political. He wrote *The General Theory* in the 1930s at a time when many of the major countries were in the process of moving away from liberal democracy and capitalism toward fascism in Germany and Italy and toward Communism in Russia. These countries appeared to deal better with the depression of the 1930s than countries like ours that stayed with liberal institutions. Keynes' message in *The General Theory* is that we can deal with depressions within the framework of a basically capitalistic economy and liberal democratic institutions. This is an important message to get across.

The intellectual forefathers of modern macroeconomics are, for me, the classical economists, Smith and Ricardo, the neoclassical work of Marshall, and the generation of our teachers, Arrow, Friedman, and Samuelson.

Would you advise undergraduates to major in economics?

Economics is a great major. I feel economics is a good pre–almost anything major. Most of the economics majors at the University of Chicago will go to law school, professional school, or work for a while. Our students have a lot of electives to choose from; they have a broad, liberal arts education.

Chapter 9

The Economy at Full Employment

In 1943, at the height of World War II, total production in the United States was a staggering 83 percent higher than it had been just four years earlier. How could production increase by such a large amount in such a short time? ◆ Over longer periods, we gradually become more productive and our incomes grow. On the average, each hour that we worked in 1998 earned us 70 percent more than it did in 1960. Despite setbacks during the past few years, the economies of Japan and China have expanded more rapidly than ours has and incomes in these countries have grown more quickly than ours. What makes production and incomes grow over the years? ◆ What are the forces that determine employment, wage rates, and real GDP when our economy is at full employment? ◆ Our population grows every year. Some of this population growth comes from immigration. What effect does population size have on employment, wage rates, and potential GDP? ◆ We also hear a lot about the importance of increasing our national saving to invest in new capital, about the importance of education, and about the need to support science and technology. How do capital accumulation, education, and advances in technology influence employment, wage rates, and potential GDP? ◆ When we talk about full employment, we don't mean that there is *no* unemployment. What determines the amount of unemployment when the economy is at full employment?

Production and Jobs

◆ In this chapter, we study the economy at full employment. We'll study the relationship between production and employment and learn about the forces that determine the quantity of employment. We'll also discover how changes in population, capital, and technology influence employment and incomes. And we'll learn about the forces that create unemployment when the economy is at full employment.

After studying this chapter, you will be able to:

■ Describe the relationship between the quantity of labor employed and real GDP

■ Explain what determines the demand for labor and the supply of labor

■ Explain what determines employment, the real wage rate, and potential GDP

■ Explain the influences on employment, the real wage rate, and potential GDP of an increase in the population, an increase in capital, and an advance in technology

■ Explain what determines unemployment when the economy is at full employment

Real GDP and Employment

TO PRODUCE MORE OUTPUT, WE MUST USE MORE inputs. We can increase real GDP by employing more labor, increasing the quantity of capital, or developing technologies that are more productive. In the short term, the quantity of capital and the state of technology are fixed. So to increase real GDP in the short term, we must increase the quantity of labor employed. Let's look at the relationship between real GDP and the quantity of labor employed.

Production Possibilities

When you studied the limits to production in Chapter 3 (see pp. 37–38), you learned about the **production possibility frontier**, which is the boundary between those combinations of goods and services that can be produced and those that cannot. We can think about the production possibility frontier for any pair of goods or services when we hold the quantities of all other goods and services constant. Let's think about the production possibility frontier between two special items—real GDP and the quantity of leisure time.

Real GDP is a measure of the final goods and services produced in the economy in a given time period (see Chapter 6, pp. 114–117). We measure real GDP as a number of 1992 dollars, but the measure is a *real* one. Real GDP is not a pile of dollars. It is a pile of goods and services. Think of it as a number of big shopping carts filled with goods and services. Each cart contains some of each of the different goods and services produced, and one cartload of items costs $1 billion. To say that real GDP is $7,000 billion means that real GDP is 7,000 big shopping carts of goods and services.

The quantity of leisure time is the number of hours we spend not working. It is the time we spend playing sports, seeing movies, and hanging out with friends. Leisure time is a special type of good or service.

Each hour that we spent pursuing fun could have been an hour that we spent at work. So when the quantity of leisure time increases by one hour, the quantity of labor employed decreases by one hour. If we spent all our time having fun rather than working, we would not produce anything. Real GDP would be zero. The more leisure time we forgo to work, the greater is the quantity of labor employed and the greater is real GDP.

The relationship between leisure time and real GDP is a *production possibility frontier*. Figure 9.1(a) shows an example of this frontier. Here, an economy has 450 billion hours of leisure time available. If people use all these hours to pursue leisure, no labor is employed and real GDP is zero. As people forgo leisure and work more, real GDP increases. If people spent 200 billion hours working and took 250 billion hours in leisure, real GDP would be $7 trillion at point *a*. If people spent all the available hours working, real GDP would be $10 trillion.

The bowed-out *PPF* displays increasing opportunity cost. In this case, the opportunity cost of a given amount of real GDP is the amount of leisure time forgone to produce the real GDP. The additional hours of leisure forgone to produce a given additional amount of real GDP increases as real GDP increases. The reason is that we use the most productive labor first, and as we use more labor, we use increasingly less productive labor.

The Production Function

The **production function** is the relationship between real GDP and the quantity of labor employed when all other influences on production remain the same. The production function shows how real GDP varies as the quantity of labor employed varies, other things remaining the same.

Because one more hour of labor employed means one less hour of leisure, the production function is like a mirror image of the leisure time-real GDP *PPF*. Figure 9.1(b) shows the production function for the economy whose *PPF* is shown in Fig. 9.1(a). You can see that when the quantity of labor employed is zero, real GDP is also zero. And as the quantity of labor employed increases, so does real GDP. When 200 billion labor hours are employed, real GDP is $7 trillion (at point *a*).

A decrease in leisure hours and the corresponding increases in the quantity of labor employed and real GDP bring a movement along the production possibility frontier and along the production function. The arrows along the *PPF* and production function in Fig. 9.1 show these movements. Such movements occurred when employment and real GDP surged during the first four years of World War II.

But the increase in real GDP during World War II changed for an additional reason. Labor became more productive. Let's study the influences on the productivity of labor.

Changes in Productivity

When we talk about *productivity*, we usually mean the labor productivity. **Labor productivity** is real GDP per hour of labor. Three factors influence labor productivity:

- Physical capital
- Human capital
- Technology

Physical Capital A farm worker equipped with only a stick and primitive tools can cultivate almost no land and grow barely enough food to feed a single family. One equipped with a steel plow pulled by an animal can cultivate more land and produce enough food to feed a small village. One equipped with a modern tractor, plow, and harvester can cultivate thousands of acres and produce enough food to feed hundreds of people.

By using physical capital on our farms and in our factories, shops, and offices, we enormously increase labor productivity. And the more physical capital we use, the greater is our labor productivity, other things remaining the same.

Human Capital An economy's **human capital** is the knowledge and skill that people have obtained from education and on-the-job training.

The average college graduate has a greater amount of human capital than the average high school graduate possesses. Consequently, the college graduate is able to perform some tasks that are beyond the ability of the high school graduate. The college graduate is more productive. For the nation as a whole, the greater the amount of schooling completed by its citizens, the greater is its real GDP, other things remaining the same.

Regardless of how much schooling a person has completed, not much production is accomplished on the first day at work. Learning about the new work environment consumes the newly hired worker's time. But as time passes and experience accumulates, the worker becomes more productive. We call this activity of on-the-job education **learning-by-doing**.

Learning-by-doing can bring incredible increases in labor productivity. The more experienced the work force, the greater is its labor productivity, and, other things remaining the same, the greater is real GDP.

World War II provides a carefully documented example of the importance of this source of increase

---

FIGURE 9.1

Production Possibilities and the Production Function

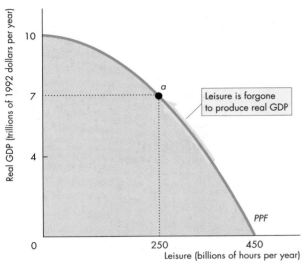

(a) Production possibility frontier

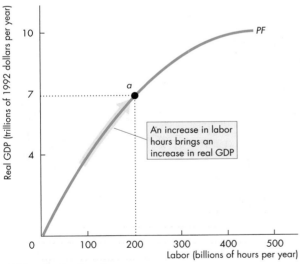

(b) Production function

On the production possibility frontier in part (a) if we enjoy 450 billion hours of leisure, we produce no real GDP. If we forgo 200 billion hours of leisure time and spend 250 billion hours on leisure, we produce a real GDP of $7 trillion, at point *a*.

The production function in part (b) is like a mirror image of the *PPF*. At point *a* on the production function, we use 200 billion hours of labor to produce $7 trillion of real GDP.

in labor productivity. In the shipyards that produced transport vessels called *Liberty ships*, labor productivity increased by an astonishing 30 percent purely as a result of learning-by-doing.

Technology   A student equipped with a pen can complete a readable page of writing in perhaps 10 minutes. This same task takes 5 minutes with a typewriter and 2 minutes with a computer. Traveling on foot from New York to Los Angeles takes a person (a fit person!) more than 100 days. In a car, the trip takes a comfortable 5 days. And in an airplane, the trip takes 5 hours. These are examples of the enormous impact of technology on productivity. Imagine the profound effect of these advances in technology on the productivity of a movie director who works in New York and Los Angeles!

Shift in the Production Function

Any influence on production that increases labor productivity shifts the production function upward. Real GDP increases at each level of labor hours. In Fig. 9.2(a), the production function is initially PF_0. Then an increase in physical capital and human capital and an advance in technology occur. The production function shifts upward to PF_1.

At each quantity of labor employed, real GDP is greater on the new production function than it was on the original one. For example, at 200 billion hours in Fig. 9.2(a), real GDP increases from $7 trillion (point *a*) to $9 trillion (point *b*).

Figure 9.2(b) shows how the production function in the United States has shifted upward between 1980 and 1998. Along the production function PF_{98}, labor productivity is 38 percent greater than on PF_{80}. Labor productivity in the United States increases by almost 2 percent a year.

R E V I E W   Q U I Z

- What is the relationship between the leisure hours–real GDP *PPF* and the production function?
- What does the bowed-out shape of the leisure hours–real GDP *PPF* imply about the opportunity cost of real GDP and why is the *PPF* bowed out?
- Why does the production function shift upward when capital increases and technology advances?

FIGURE 9.2

An Increase in Labor Productivity

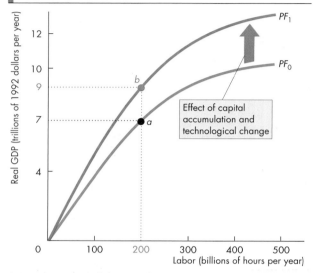

(a) An increase in labor productivity

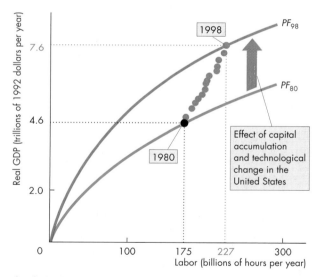

(b) The U.S. production function

The production function is initially PF_0 and 200 billion labor hours produces a real GDP of $7 trillion (point *a*). An increase in capital or an advance in technology that increases labor productivity shifts the production function upward to PF_1 and 200 billion labor hours produces a real GDP of $9 trillion (point *b*). U.S. real GDP has increased (part b) because labor has become more productive and the quantity of labor has increased.

The Labor Market and Aggregate Supply

YOU'VE SEEN THAT IN A GIVEN YEAR, WITH A given amount of physical and human capital and given technology, real GDP depends on the quantity of labor hours employed. To produce more real GDP, we must employ more labor hours. The labor market determines the quantity of labor hours employed and the quantity of real GDP supplied. We'll learn how by studying:

- The demand for labor
- The supply of labor
- Labor market equilibrium
- Aggregate supply

The Demand for Labor

The **quantity of labor demanded** is the labor hours hired by all the firms in the economy. The **demand for labor** is the relationship between the quantity of labor demanded and the real wage rate when all other influences on firms' hiring plans remain the same. The **real wage rate** is the quantity of goods and services that an hour of labor earns. In contrast, the **money wage rate** is the number of dollars that an hour of labor earns. A real wage rate is equal to a money wage rate divided by the price of a good. For the economy as a whole, the average real wage rate equals the average money wage rate divided by the price level multiplied by 100. So we express the real wage rate in constant dollars. (Today, we express this real wage rate in 1992 dollars.)

The *real* wage rate influences the quantity of labor demanded because what matters to firms is not the number of dollars they pay (the money wage rate) but how much output they must sell to earn those dollars.

We can represent the demand for labor as either a demand schedule or a demand curve. The table in Fig. 9.3 shows part of a demand for labor schedule. It tells us the quantity of labor demanded at three different real wage rates. For example, if the real wage rate falls from $30 an hour to $25 an hour, the quantity of labor demanded increases from 150 billion hours a year to 200 billion hours a year. (You can find these numbers in rows *a* and *b* of the table.)

The demand for labor curve is *LD*. Points *a*, *b*, and *c* on the curve correspond to rows *a*, *b*, and *c* of the demand schedule.

FIGURE 9.3

The Demand for Labor

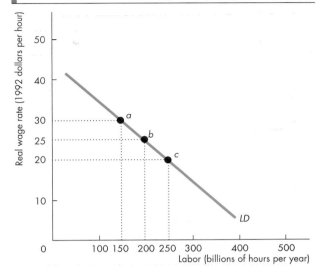

	Real wage rate (1992 dollars per hour)	Quantity of labor demanded (billions of hours per year)
a	30	150
b	25	200
c	20	250

The table shows part of a demand for labor schedule. Points *a*, *b*, and *c* on the demand for labor curve correspond to the rows of the table. The lower the real wage rate, the greater is the quantity of labor demanded.

Why does the quantity of labor demanded *increase* as the real wage rate *decreases*? That is, why does the demand for labor curve slope downward? To answer these questions, we must first return to the production function and learn about the marginal product of labor.

The Marginal Product of Labor The **marginal product of labor** is the additional real GDP produced by an additional hour of labor when all other influences on production remain the same. We calculate the marginal product of labor as the change in real GDP divided by the change in the quantity of labor employed. Figure 9.4(a) shows some marginal product calculations and Fig. 9.4(b) shows the marginal product curve.

In Fig. 9.4(a), when the quantity of labor employed increases from 100 billion hours to 200 billion hours, an increase of 100 billion hours, real GDP increases from $4 trillion to $7 trillion, an increase of $3 trillion. The marginal product of labor equals the increase in real GDP ($3 trillion) divided by the increase in the quantity of labor employed (100 billion hours), which is $30 an hour.

When the quantity of labor employed increases from 200 billion hours to 300 billion hours, an increase of 100 billion hours, real GDP increases from $7 trillion to $9 trillion, an increase of $2 trillion. The marginal product of labor equals the increase in real GDP ($2 trillion) divided by the increase in the quantity of labor employed (100 billion hours), which is $20 an hour.

In Fig. 9.4(b), as the quantity of labor employed increases, the marginal product of labor diminishes. Between 100 billion and 200 billion (at 150 billion), marginal product is $30 an hour. And between 200 billion and 300 billion (at 250 billion), marginal product is $20 an hour.

Diminishing Marginal Product The marginal product of labor diminishes as the quantity of labor employed increases because all the labor, both the old and the new, work with the same fixed amount of physical capital and given technology. As more labor hours are hired, the physical capital is worked more intensively, and more breakdowns and bottlenecks arise. Eventually, as more labor hours are hired, workers get in each other's way and output increases barely at all.

The diminishing marginal product of labor limits the demand for labor.

Diminishing Marginal Product and the Demand for Labor Firms are in business to maximize profits. Each hour of labor that a firm hires increases output and adds to costs. Initially, an extra hour of labor produces more output than the real wage that the labor costs. Marginal product exceeds the real wage rate. But each additional hour of labor produces less additional output than the previous hour—the marginal product of labor diminishes.

As a firm hires more labor, eventually the extra output from an extra hour of labor is exactly what that hour of labor costs. At this point, marginal product equals the real wage rate. Hire one less hour and marginal product exceeds the real wage rate. Hire one more hour and the real wage rate exceeds the marginal product. In either case, profit is less.

FIGURE 9.4

Marginal Product and the Demand for Labor

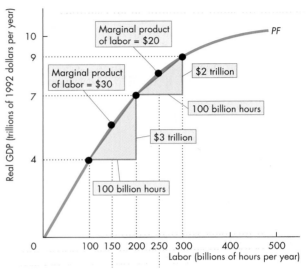

(a) Calculating marginal product

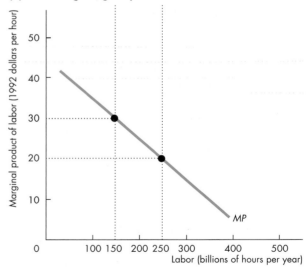

(b) The marginal product curve

An increase in labor from 100 billion to 200 billion hours increases real GDP by $3 trillion. The marginal product of labor is $30 an hour. An increase from 200 billion to 300 billion hours increases real GDP by $2 trillion. Marginal product is $20 an hour. At point *a* on the *MP* curve, marginal product is $30 an hour at 150 billion hours (midpoint between 100 billion and 200 billion). The *MP* curve is the demand for labor curve.

Because marginal product diminishes as the quantity of labor employed increases, the lower the real wage rate, the greater is the quantity of labor that a firm can profitably hire. The marginal product curve is the same as the demand for labor curve.

You might gain a clearer understand of the demand for labor by looking at an example.

The Demand for Labor in a Soda Factory Suppose that when a soda factory employs one additional hour of labor, output increases by 11 bottles. Marginal product is 11 bottles an hour. If the money wage rate is $5.50 an hour and soda sells for 50¢ a bottle, the real wage rate is 11 bottles an hour. (We calculate the real wage rate as the money wage rate of $5.50 an hour divided by a price of 50¢ a bottle, which equals a real wage rate of 11 bottles an hour.) Because marginal product diminishes, we know that if the firm did not hire this hour of labor, marginal product would exceed 11 bottles. Because the firm can hire the hour of labor for a real wage rate of 11 bottles, it just pays the firm to do so.

If the price of soda remains at 50¢ a bottle and the money wage rate falls to $5.00 an hour, the real wage rate falls to 10 bottles an hour and the firm increases the quantity of labor demanded.

Similarly, if the money wage rate remains at $5.50 an hour and the price of soda rises to 55¢ a bottle, the real wage rate falls to 10 bottles an hour and the firm increases the quantity of labor demanded.

When the firm pays a real wage rate equal to the marginal product of labor, it is maximizing profit.

Changes in the Demand for Labor When the marginal product of labor changes, the demand for labor changes and the demand curve for labor shifts. You've seen that an increase in capital (both physical and human) and an advance in technology that increase productivity shift the production function upward. These same forces increase the demand for labor and shift the demand for labor curve rightward.

The Supply of Labor

The **quantity of labor supplied** is the number of labor hours that all the households in the economy plan to work. The **supply of labor** is the relationship between the quantity of labor supplied and the real wage rate when all other influences on work plans remain the same.

The table in Fig. 9.5 shows a supply of labor schedule. It tells us the quantity of labor supplied at three different real wage rates. For example, if the real wage rate rises from $11 an hour (row *a*) to $25 an hour (row *b*), the quantity of labor supplied increases from 150 billion hours a year to 200 billion hours a year. The curve *LS* is a supply of labor curve. Points *a*, *b*, and *c* on the curve correspond to rows *a*, *b*, and *c* of the supply schedule.

The *real* wage rate influences the quantity of labor supplied because what matters to people is not the number of dollars they earn (the money wage rate) but what those dollars will buy.

The quantity of labor supplied increases as the real wage rate increases for two reasons:

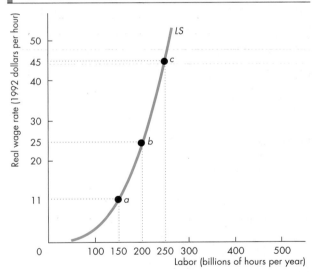

FIGURE 9.5

The Supply of Labor

	Real wage rate (1992 dollars per hour)	Quantity of labor supplied (billions of hours per year)
a	11	150
b	25	200
c	45	250

The table shows part of a supply of labor schedule. Points *a*, *b*, and *c* on the supply of labor curve correspond to the rows of the table. The higher the real wage rate, the greater is the quantity of labor supplied.

- Hours per person increase
- Labor force participation increases

Hours Per Person   In choosing how many hours to work, a household considers the opportunity cost of not working. This opportunity cost is the real wage rate. The higher the real wage rate, the greater is the opportunity cost of taking leisure and not working. And as the opportunity cost of taking leisure rises, other things remaining the same, the more the household chooses to work.

But other things don't remain the same. The higher the real wage rate, the greater is the household's income. And the higher the household's income, the more it wants to consume. One item that it wants to consume more of is leisure.

So a rise in the real wage rate has two opposing effects. By increasing the opportunity cost of leisure, it makes the household want to consume less leisure and to work more. And by increasing the household's income, it makes the household want to consume more leisure and to work fewer hours. For most households, the opportunity cost effect is stronger than the income effect. So the higher the real wage rate, the greater is the amount of work that the household chooses to do.

Labor Force Participation   Some people have productive opportunities outside the labor force. These people choose to work only if the real wage rate exceeds the value of these other productive activities. For example, a parent might spend time caring for her or his child. The alternative is day care. The parent will choose to work only if he or she can earn enough per hour to pay the cost of child care and have enough left to make the work effort worthwhile. The higher the real wage rate, the more likely it is that a parent will choose to work and so the greater is the labor force participation rate.

Labor Supply Response   The quantity of labor supplied increases as the real wage rate rises. But the quantity of labor supplied is not highly responsive to the real wage rate. A large percentage change in the real wage rate brings a small percentage change in the quantity of labor supplied.

Let's now see how the labor market determines employment, the real wage rate, and potential GDP.

Labor Market Equilibrium

The forces of supply and demand operate in labor markets just as they do in the markets for goods and services. The price of labor is the real wage rate. A rise in the real wage rate eliminates a shortage of labor by decreasing the quantity demanded and increasing the quantity supplied. A fall in the real wage rate eliminates a surplus of labor by increasing the quantity demanded and decreasing the quantity supplied. If there is neither a shortage nor a surplus, the labor market is in equilibrium.

In macroeconomics, we study the economy-wide labor market to determine the total quantity of labor employed and the average real wage rate.

Labor Market Equilibrium   Figure 9.6(a) shows a labor market in equilibrium. The demand curve *LD* and the supply curve *LS* are the same as those in Fig. 9.3 and Fig. 9.5.

If the real wage rate exceeds $25 an hour, the quantity of labor supplied exceeds the quantity demanded and there is a surplus of labor. In this situation, the real wage rate falls.

If the real wage rate is less than $25 an hour, the quantity of labor demanded exceeds the quantity supplied and there is a shortage of labor. In this situation, the real wage rate rises.

If the real wage rate is $25 an hour, the quantity of labor demanded equals the quantity supplied and there is neither a shortage nor a surplus of labor. In this situation, the labor market is in equilibrium and the real wage rate remains constant. The equilibrium level of employment is 200 billion hours a year. This equilibrium is *full-employment equilibrium*.

Potential GDP   You've seen that the quantity of real GDP depends on the quantity of labor employed. The production function tells us how much real GDP a given amount of employment can produce. At the equilibrium level of employment, there is full employment. And the level of real GDP at full employment is **potential GDP**. So the equilibrium level of employment produces potential GDP.

Figure 9.6(b) shows potential GDP. The equilibrium level of employment in Fig. 9.6(a) is 200 billion hours. The production function in Fig. 9.6(b) tells us that 200 billion hours of labor can produce a real GDP of $7 trillion. This amount is potential GDP.

FIGURE 9.6

The Labor Market and Potential GDP

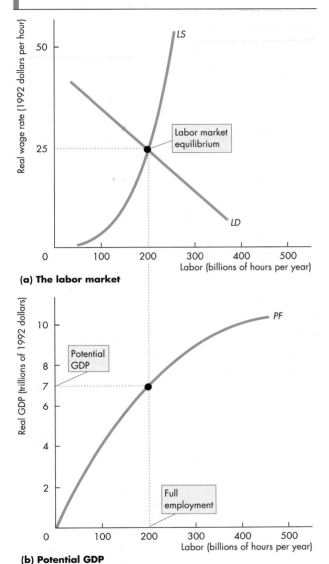

(a) The labor market

(b) Potential GDP

Full employment occurs (part a) when the quantity of labor demanded equals the quantity of labor supplied. The equilibrium real wage rate is $25 an hour, and employment is 200 billion hours a year.

Part (b) shows how potential GDP is determined. It is the quantity of real GDP determined by the production function and the full-employment quantity of labor.

Aggregate Supply

The **long-run aggregate supply curve** is the relationship between the quantity of real GDP supplied and the price level when real GDP equals potential GDP. Figure 9.7 shows this relationship as the vertical *LAS* curve. Along the long-run aggregate supply curve, as the price level changes, the money wage rate also changes to keep the real wage rate at the full-employment equilibrium level in Fig. 9.6(a). With no change in the real wage rate and no change in employment, real GDP remains at potential GDP.

The **short-run aggregate supply curve** is the relationship between the quantity of real GDP supplied and the price level when the money wage rate and potential GDP remain constant. Figure 9.7

FIGURE 9.7

The Aggregate Supply Curves

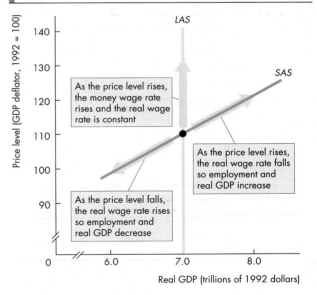

A rise in the price level with a rise in the money wage rate that keeps the real wage rate at its full-employment equilibrium level keeps the quantity of real GDP supplied at potential GDP—a movement along the long-run aggregate supply curve. A rise in the price level with no change in the money wage rate lowers the real wage rate and brings an increase in employment and in the quantity of real GDP supplied—a movement along the short-run aggregate supply curve.

shows a short-run aggregate supply curve as the upward-sloping *SAS* curve. Along the short-run aggregate supply curve, as the price level rises, the money wage rate remains fixed, so the real wage rate *falls*. In Fig. 9.6, when the real wage rate falls, the quantity of labor demanded increases and real GDP increases.

When the economy is at a point on its short-run aggregate supply curve above potential GDP, the real wage rate is below the full-employment equilibrium level. And when the economy is at a point on the short-run aggregate supply curve below potential GDP, the real wage rate is above the full-employment equilibrium level. In both cases, the quantity of labor that firms employ departs from the quantity that households would like to supply.

Production is efficient in the sense that the economy operates on its production possibility frontier. But production is inefficient in the sense that the economy operates at the wrong point on the frontier. When the real wage rate is below the full-employment equilibrium, people do too much work and produce too much real GDP. When the real wage rate is above the full-employment equilibrium, people do too little work and produce too little real GDP.

When the real wage rate departs from its full-employment equilibrium level, the resulting shortage or surplus of labor brings market forces into play that move the real wage rate and quantity of labor employed back toward their full-employment levels.

R E V I E W   Q U I Z

- Why does a rise in the real wage rate bring a decrease in the quantity of labor demanded, other things remaining the same?
- Why does a rise in the real wage rate bring an increase in the quantity of labor supplied, other things remaining the same?
- What happens in the labor market if the real wage rate is above or below the full-employment level?
- How is potential GDP determined?
- What is the relationship between the labor market and long-run aggregate supply?
- What is the relationship between the labor market and short-run aggregate supply?

You studied the forces that determine full-employment real wages, employment, and potential GDP. Let's now look at *changes* in full-employment equilibrium.

Changes in Potential GDP

REAL GDP WILL INCREASE IF:

1. The economy recovers from recession
2. Potential GDP increases

Recovery from recession means the economy moves along the real GDP–leisure *PPF* from a point at which real GDP and employment are too low to the full-employment equilibrium point. Equivalently, the economy moves along the short-run aggregate supply curve. Economists have a lot to say about such a move. And you can learn about this type of short-run change in real GDP in Chapters 12–18.

Increasing potential GDP means expanding production possibilities. We're going to study such an expansion in the rest of this chapter and in Chapters 10 and 11. We begin this process here by examining two influences on potential GDP:

- An increase in population
- An increase in labor productivity

An Increase in Population

As the population increases and the additional people reach working age, the supply of labor increases. With more labor available, the economy's production possibilities expand.

But does the expansion of production possibilities mean that potential GDP increases? And does it mean that potential GDP *per person* increases?

The answers to these questions have intrigued economists for many years. And they cause heated political debate today. In China, for example, families are under enormous pressure to limit the number of children they have. In some other countries, France is an example, the government encourages large families. We can study the effects of an increase in population by using the model of the full-employment economy in Fig. 9.8.

In Fig. 9.8(a), the demand for labor is *LD* and initially the supply of labor is LS_0. At full employment, the real wage rate is $25 an hour and the level of employment is 200 billion hours a year. In Fig. 9.8(b), the production function (*PF*) shows that with 200 billion hours of labor employed, potential GDP is $7 trillion. We're now going to work out what happens when the population increases.

FIGURE 9.8

An Increase in Population

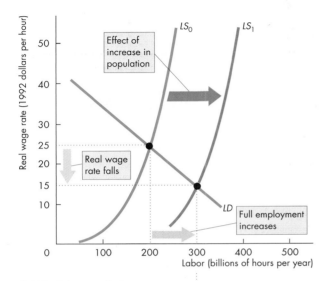

(a) The labor market

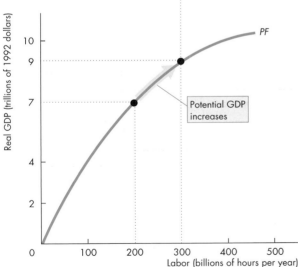

(b) Potential GDP

An increase in population increases the supply of labor and shifts the supply curve rightward (in part a). The real wage rate falls, and the quantity of labor employed at full employment increases. In part (b), the increase in full-employment equilibrium employment increases potential GDP. Because the marginal product of labor diminishes, the increased population produces a greater potential GDP but a smaller potential GDP per hour of work.

An increase in the population increases the number of people of working age and the supply of labor increases. The labor supply curve shifts rightward to LS_1. At a real wage rate of $25 an hour, there is now a surplus of labor. So the real wage rate falls. In this example, it falls until it reaches $15 an hour. At $15 an hour, the quantity of labor demanded equals the quantity of labor supplied. Equilibrium employment increases to 300 billion hours a year.

Figure 9.8(b) shows the effect of the increase in equilibrium employment on real GDP. As the full-employment quantity of labor increases from 200 billion hours to 300 billion hours, potential GDP increases from $7 trillion to $9 trillion.

So at full employment, an increase in population increases employment, increases potential GDP, and lowers the real wage rate.

An increase in population also decreases potential GDP per hour of work. You can see this decrease by dividing potential GDP by total labor hours. Initially, with potential GDP at $7 trillion and labor hours at 200 billion, potential GDP per hour of work was $35. With the increase in population, potential GDP is $9 trillion and labor hours are 300 billion. Potential GDP per hour of work is $30. Diminishing returns is the source of the decrease in potential GDP per hour of work.

You've seen that an increase in population increases potential GDP and decreases potential GDP per work hour. Some economists challenge this conclusion and argue that people are the ultimate economic resource. They claim that a larger population brings forth a greater amount of scientific discovery and technological advance. Consequently, these economists argue, an increase in population never takes place in isolation. It is always accompanied by an increase in labor productivity. Let's now look at the effects of this influence on potential GDP.

An Increase in Labor Productivity

We've seen that three factors increase labor productivity:

- An increase in physical capital
- An increase in human capital
- An advance in technology

The quantity of physical capital increases over time because of saving and investment. We study the factors that influence saving and investment decisions in Chapter 10. Human capital increases because of education and on-the-job training and experience. And technology advances because of research and development efforts. We study the way all these forces interact to determine the growth rate of potential GDP in Chapter 11.

Here, we study the *effects* of an increase in physical capital, an increase in human capital, or an advance in technology on the labor market and potential GDP. We'll see how potential GDP, employment, and the real wage rate change when any of these three influences on labor productivity changes.

An Increase in Physical Capital   If the quantity of physical capital increases, labor productivity increases. With labor being more productive, the economy's production possibilities expand. How does such an expansion of production possibilities change the equilibrium real wage rate, employment, and potential GDP?

The additional capital increases the real GDP that each quantity of labor can produce. It also increases the marginal product of labor and so increases the demand for labor. Some physical capital replaces some types of labor. So the demand for those types of labor decreases when capital increases. But an increase in physical capital creates a demand for the types of labor that build, sell, and maintain the additional capital. The increases in demand for labor are always larger than the decreases in demand and the economy-wide demand for labor increases.

With an increase in the economy-wide demand for labor, the real wage rate rises and the quantity of labor supplied increases. Equilibrium employment increases.

Potential GDP now increases for two reasons. First, a given level of employment produces more real GDP. Second, equilibrium employment increases.

An Increase in Human Capital   If the quantity of human capital increases, labor productivity increases. Again, with labor being more productive, the economy's production possibilities expand. And this expansion of production possibilities changes the equilibrium real wage rate, employment, and potential GDP in a similar manner to the effects of a change in physical capital.

An Advance in Technology   As technology advances, labor productivity increases. And exactly as in the case of an increase in capital, the economy's production possibilities expand. Again, just as in the case of an increase in capital, the new technology increases

the real GDP that each quantity of labor can produce and increases the marginal product of labor and the demand for labor.

With an increase in the demand for labor, the real wage rate rises, the quantity of labor supplied increases, and equilibrium employment increases. And again, potential GDP increases because a given level of employment produces more real GDP and because equilibrium employment increases.

Illustrating the Effects of an Increase in Labor Productivity   Figure 9.9 shows the effects of an increase in labor productivity that results from an increase in capital or an advance in technology. In part (a), the demand for labor initially is LD_0 and the supply of labor is LS. The real wage rate is $25 an hour, and full employment is 200 billion hours a year.

In part (b), the production function initially is PF_0. With 200 billion hours of labor employed, potential GDP is $7 trillion.

Now an increase in capital or an advance in technology increases the productivity of labor. In Fig. 9.9(a), the demand for labor increases and the demand curve shifts rightward to LD_1. In Fig. 9.9(b), the productivity of labor increases and the production function shifts upward to PF_1.

In Fig. 9.9(a), at the original real wage rate of $25 an hour, there is now a shortage of labor. So the real wage rate rises. In this example, it keeps rising until it reaches $35 an hour. At $35 an hour, the quantity of labor demanded equals the quantity of labor supplied and full employment increases to 220 billion hours a year.

Figure 9.9(b) shows the effects of the increase in full employment combined with the new production function on potential GDP. As employment increases from 200 billion hours to 220 billion hours, potential increases from $7 trillion to $10 trillion.

Potential GDP per hour of work also increases. You can see this increase by dividing potential GDP by total labor hours. Initially, with potential GDP at $7 trillion and labor hours at 200 billion, potential GDP per hour of work was $35. With the increase in labor productivity, potential GDP is $10 trillion and labor hours are 220 billion, so potential GDP per hour of work is $45.45.

We've just studied the effects of a change in population and an increase in labor productivity separately. In reality, these changes occur together. We can see the combined effects by examining an episode in the life of the U.S. economy.

FIGURE 9.9

An Increase in Labor Productivity

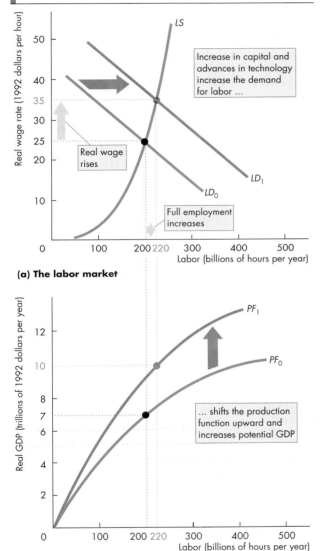

(a) The labor market

(b) Potential GDP

An increase in labor productivity shifts the demand for labor curve rightward from LD_0 to LD_1 (part a) and the production function upward from PF_0 to PF_1 (part b). The real wage rate rises from $25 to $35 an hour, and full employment increases from 200 billion to 220 billion hours. Potential GDP increases from $7 trillion to $10 trillion. Potential GDP increases because labor becomes more productive and full employment increases.

Population and Productivity in the United States

The U.S. economy was close to full employment in 1998. It was also close to full employment 14 years earlier, in 1984. We're going to compare these two years and look at the forces that moved the economy from one full-employment equilibrium to another.

In 1984, real GDP in the United States was $5.1 trillion, employment was 185 billion hours, and the real wage rate was $16 an hour. (We are using 1992 dollars.)

By 1998, real GDP had increased to $7.6 trillion, labor hours had increased to 227 billion, and the real wage rate had risen to $19 an hour. (Again, we are using 1992 dollars.)

The factors that you've just studied—an increase in population, an increase in physical and human capital, and advances in technology—brought these changes.

Population Increase In 1984, the working-age population of the United States was 176 million. By 1998, this number had increased to 205 million. The 1998 working-age population was 16 percent greater than the 1984 population. Recall that labor hours were 185 billion in 1984. A 16 percent increase would take labor hours in 1998 to 215 billion. But labor hours actually increased to 227 billion. Why? The answer is that an increase in capital and advances in technology increased labor productivity, which increased the labor force participation rate.

Capital Increase In 1984, the capital stock in the United States was estimated to be $16 trillion (1992 dollars). By 1998, the capital stock had increased to $22 trillion. This increase in capital increased labor productivity. But the increase in capital was not the only influence on labor productivity. Technological advances also occurred.

Technological Advances In 1984, we were just getting into the information revolution. Personal computers were around, but they were slow, had little memory, and had no hard drive. The Internet existed as a tool used by academic researchers for e-mail and file transfers, but no one had imagined the World Wide Web. Telephones couldn't remember numbers and record messages. Communication was slower and more costly than it was to become by 1998.

Production processes were beginning to be computerized but on a limited scale. Banks equipped

FIGURE 9.10

Full Employment in the United States: 1984 and 1998

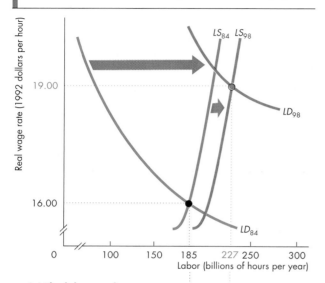

(a) The labor market

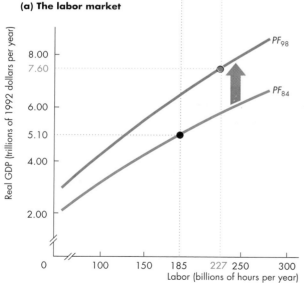

(b) The U.S. production function in 1984 and 1998

In 1984, the real wage rate was $16 an hour and the quantity of labor employed was 185 billion hours at the intersection of LD_{84} and LS_{84} (part a). Potential GDP was $5.1 trillion on PF_{84} (part b). By 1998, the real wage rate had increased to $19 an hour and the quantity of labor employed had increased to 227 billion hours at the intersection of LD_{98} and LS_{98} (part a). Potential GDP had increased to $7.6 trillion on PF_{98} (part b).

with ATMs were in the future. Supermarkets with laser scanners were only a dream. Robots in car factories and coal mines were still unknown. The biotechnology sector had still to be developed. The combined effects of capital accumulation and technological advance have made our farms and factories, shops, and offices more productive.

Figure 9.10 shows their effects along with the effects of the increase in population that occurred. In 1984, the demand for labor curve was LD_{84}, the supply of labor curve was LS_{84}, the full-employment real wage rate of $16 an hour and 185 billion hours of labor were employed. The production function in 1984 was PF_{84}. With 185 billion hours of labor employed, real GDP (and potential GDP) was $5.1 trillion.

By 1998, the increase in population had increased the working-age population by 16 percent. This increase in population increased the supply of labor and shifted the labor supply curve rightward to LS_{98}.

The accumulation of capital and advances in technology increased labor productivity. The demand for labor increased, and the demand for labor curve shifted rightward to LD_{98}. And the production function shifted upward to PF_{98}.

The real wage rate increased to $19 an hour, and employment increased to 227 billion hours. At this quantity of labor, real GDP (and potential GDP) increased to $7.6 trillion.

So in the United States, the effects of an increase in capital and advances in technology have been larger than the effects of increases in population. The forces that increase labor productivity have been sufficiently strong to overcome the effects of an increasing population.

REVIEW QUIZ

- When the population increases but nothing else changes, why does real GDP per hour of work decrease?
- How does an increase in capital change the real wage rate, full employment, and potential GDP?
- How do advances in technology change the real wage rate, full employment, and potential GDP?
- If, as some people suggest, capital accumulation and technological change always accompany an increase in population, is it possible for potential GDP per hour of work to decrease?

Unemployment at Full Employment

So far, we've focused on the forces that determine the real wage rate, the quantity of labor employed, and potential GDP. And we've studied the effects of changes in population, capital, and technology on these variables. We're now going to bring unemployment into the picture.

In Chapter 7 (pp. 138–140), we learned how unemployment is measured. We *described* how people become unemployed—they lose jobs, leave jobs, and enter or reenter the labor force—and we *classified* unemployment—it can be frictional, structural, and cyclical. We also learned that we call the unemployment rate at full employment the **natural rate of unemployment**.

But measuring, describing, and classifying unemployment do not *explain* it. Why is there always some unemployment? Why does its rate fluctuate? Why was the unemployment rate lower during the 1960s and the late 1990s than during the 1980s and early 1990s?

The forces that make the unemployment rate fluctuate around the natural rate take some time to explain, and we study these forces in Chapters 12–18. Here, we look at the churning economy and the reasons why we have unemployment at full employment.

Unemployment is ever present for two broad reasons:

- Job search
- Job rationing

Job Search

Job search is the activity of looking for an acceptable vacant job. There are always some people who have not yet found a suitable job and who are actively searching for one. The reason is that the labor market is in a constant state of change. The failure of existing businesses destroys jobs. The expansion of existing businesses and the startup of new businesses that use new technologies and develop new markets create jobs. As people pass through different stages of life, some enter or reenter the labor market. Still others leave their jobs to look for better ones, and others retire. This constant churning in the labor market

means that there are always some people looking for jobs. These people are the unemployed.

The amount of job search depends on a number of factors, one of which is the real wage rate. In Figure 9.11, when the real wage rate is $25 an hour, the economy is at a full-employment equilibrium. The amount of job search that takes place at this wage rate generates unemployment at the natural rate. If the real wage rate is above the full-employment equilibrium, for example at $35 an hour, there is a surplus of labor. At this higher real wage rate, more job search takes place and the unemployment rate rises above the natural rate. If the real wage rate is below the full-employment equilibrium, for example at $15 an hour, there is a shortage of labor. At this real wage rate, less job search takes place and the unemployment rate falls below the natural rate.

The market forces of supply and demand move the real wage rate toward the full-employment equilibrium. These same forces move the amount of job search toward the level that creates unemployment at the natural rate.

But other influences on the amount of job search bring changes, over time, in the natural rate of unemployment. The main sources of these changes are:

- Demographic change
- Unemployment compensation
- Structural change

Demographic Change   An increase in the proportion of the population that is of working age brings an increase in the entry rate into the labor force and an increase in the unemployment rate. This factor has been important in the U.S. labor market in recent years. The bulge in the birth rate that occurred in the late 1940s and the 1950s increased the proportion of new entrants into the labor force during the 1970s and brought an increase in the unemployment rate.

As the birth rate declined, the bulge moved into higher age groups and the proportion of new entrants declined during the 1980s. During this period, the natural rate of unemployment decreased.

Another demographic trend is an increase in the number of households with two paid workers. When unemployment comes to one of these workers, it is possible, with income still flowing in, to take longer to find a new job. This factor might have increased frictional unemployment.

FIGURE 9.11

Job Search Unemployment

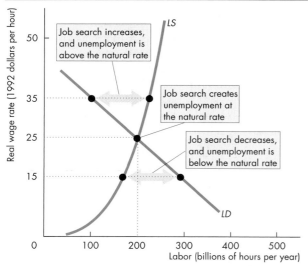

When the real wage rate is at its full-employment level—$25 an hour in this example—job search puts unemployment at the natural rate. If the real wage rate is above the full-employment level, there is a surplus of labor. Job search increases, and unemployment rises above the natural rate. If the real wage rate is below the full-employment level, there is a shortage of labor. Job search decreases, and unemployment falls below the natural rate.

Unemployment Compensation   The length of time that an unemployed person spends searching for a job depends, in part, on the opportunity cost of job search. An unemployed person who receives no unemployment insurance benefits faces a high opportunity cost of job search. In this situation, search is likely to be short and the person is likely to accept a less attractive job rather than continue a costly search process. An unemployed person who receives generous unemployment insurance benefits faces a low opportunity cost of job search. In this situation, search is likely to be prolonged. The unemployed worker will continue to search for an ideal job.

The extension of unemployment benefits to larger groups of workers during the late 1960s and 1970s lowered the opportunity cost of job search. Consequently, the amount of job search and the natural rate of unemployment increased during those years.

Structural Change   Labor market flows and unemployment are influenced by the pace and direction of technological change. Sometimes, technological change brings a *structural slump,* a condition in which some industries die and some regions suffer while other industries are born and other regions flourish. When these events occur, labor turnover is high—the flows between employment and unemployment increase and the number of people unemployed increases. The decline of industries in the "Rust Belt" and the rapid expansion of industries in the "Sun Belt" illustrate the effects of technological change and were a source of the increase in unemployment during the 1970s and early 1980s. While these changes were taking place, the natural rate of unemployment increased.

Job Rationing

You've learned that markets *allocate* scarce resources by adjusting the market price to make buying plans and selling plans agree. Another word that has a meaning similar to that of "allocate" is "ration." Markets *ration* scarce resources by adjusting prices. In the labor market, the real wage rate rations employment and therefore rations jobs. Changes in the real wage rate keep the number of people seeking work and the number of jobs available in balance.

But the real wage rate is not the only possible instrument for rationing jobs. And in some industries, the real wage rate is set above the market equilibrium level. **Job rationing** is the practice of paying a real wage rate above the equilibrium level and then rationing jobs by some method.

Two reasons why the real wage rate might be set above the equilibrium level are:

- Efficiency wage
- Minimum wage

Efficiency Wage   It is costly for a firm to pay its workers more than the market wage rate. But to do so also brings benefits. An **efficiency wage** is a real wage rate that is set above the full-employment equilibrium wage rate and that balances the costs and benefits of this higher wage rate to maximize the firm's profit.

The cost of paying a higher wage rate is direct. It is the addition to the firm's wage bill. The benefits of paying a higher wage rate are indirect.

First, a firm that pays a high wage rate can attract the most productive workers. Second, the firm can get greater productivity from its work force if it threatens to fire those who do not perform at the desired standard. The threat of losing a well-paid job stimulates greater work effort. Third, workers are less likely to quit their jobs, so the firm faces a lower rate of labor turnover and lower training costs. Fourth, the firm's recruiting costs are lower. The firm always faces a steady stream of available new workers.

Faced with benefits and costs, a firm offers a wage rate that balances productivity gains from the higher wage rate against its additional cost. This wage rate maximizes the firm's profit and is the efficiency wage.

The Minimum Wage A **minimum wage** is the lowest wage rate at which a firm may legally hire labor. If the minimum wage is set *below* the equilibrium wage, the minimum wage has no effect. The minimum wage and market forces are not in conflict. But if a minimum wage is set *above* the equilibrium wage, the minimum wage is in conflict with the market forces and does have some effects on the labor market.

The minimum wage in the United States is set by the federal government's Fair Labor Standards Act. Some state governments have passed state minimum wage laws that exceed the federal minimum. In 1999, the minimum wage is $5.15 an hour. The minimum wage increases from time to time and has fluctuated between 35 percent and more than 50 percent of the average wage of production workers.

Job Rationing and Unemployment

Regardless of the reason, if the real wage rate is set above the equilibrium level, the natural rate of unemployment increases. The above-equilibrium real wage rate decreases the quantity of labor demanded and increases the quantity of labor supplied. So even at full employment, the quantity of labor supplied exceeds the quantity of labor demanded.

The surplus of labor is an addition to the amount of unemployment. The unemployment that results from a nonmarket wage rate and job rationing increases the natural rate of unemployment because it is added to the job search that takes place at full-employment equilibrium.

Economists broadly agree that efficiency wages can create persistent unemployment. Most economists believe that the minimum wage contributes to unemployment, especially among low-skilled young workers. But David Card of the University of California at Berkeley and Alan Krueger of Princeton University have challenged this view. And the challenge has been rebutted.

Card and Krueger say that an increase in the minimum wage works like an efficiency wage. It makes workers more productive and less likely to quit. Most economists remain skeptical about this suggestion. If higher wage rates make workers more productive and reduce labor turnover, why don't firms freely pay the wage rates that encourage the correct work habits? Daniel Hamermesh of the University of Texas at Austin says that firms anticipate increases in the minimum wage and cut employment *before* they occur. Looking for the effects of an increase in the minimum wage *after* it has occurred misses its effects. Finis Welch of Texas A&M University and Kevin Murphy of the University of Chicago say that regional differences in economic growth, not changes in the minimum wage, explain the facts that Card and Krueger found.

R E V I E W   Q U I Z

- Why does the economy experience unemployment at full employment?
- Why does the natural rate of unemployment fluctuate?
- What is job rationing and why does it occur?
- How does an efficiency wage influence the real wage rate, employment, and unemployment?
- How does the minimum wage create unemployment?

◈ In this chapter, you've seen how the economy operates at full employment. *Reading Between the Lines* on pp. 198–199 looks at recent productivity gains in the United States. In the next two chapters, we study the rate of growth of the full-employment economy. In Chapter 10, we study decisions by firms to increase the amount of capital they employ and the decisions by households about the amount to save to finance capital accumulation. Then in Chapter 11, we study the interactions of capital accumulation, technological change, and population growth in the process of economic growth.

Productivity and Real Wages in the United States

T H E   W A S H I N G T O N   P O S T ,   FEBRUARY 10, 1999

Productivity Gains Give Wages a Boost

JOHN M. BERRY

Strong economic growth last year gave a healthy boost to labor productivity, allowing firms to give their workers solid pay increases while raising the prices of what they produced only slightly, the Labor Department reported yesterday.

Gains in productivity—the amount of goods and services produced for each hour worked—are a key ingredient in raising the nation's living standards. Consider this arithmetic:

Last year businesses other than farms increased their workers' compensation 4.2 percent while raising the prices they charged only 0.7 percent. The companies could do that without clobbering their profits because productivity gains offset 2.2 percentage points of that difference. And other cost-saving actions reduced non-labor costs by 1.4 percent on each unit of output.

The overall result was a combination that's hard to beat. The firms eked out a small increase in profit on each unit sold, workers' real pay went up 2.6 percent faster than consumer prices, and inflation went down. (The Labor Department

uses the consumer price index, which rose 1.6 percent last year, to adjust compensation for inflation.)

However, many analysts and policymakers are questioning whether such good news is likely to continue for long.

Many economists believe that better education and on-the-job training, major investments in computers and other information processing technology and improved management may have increased the long-term trend in productivity growth in the United States. But even the optimists generally believe that trend is still much closer to the 1.3 percent annual productivity gain of the past two decades than last year's 2.2 percent increase. Over the past five years, for example, the average has been 1.4 percent.

Usually, productivity spurts along with economic growth, with the gain slowing markedly when growth slows. That's exactly what many forecasters expect to happen this year as growth tapers to a 2 percent to 3 percent pace from last year's 4 percent. One consequence could be higher inflation and smaller inflation-adjusted pay gains. ...

Essence of the Story

■ Labor productivity in businesses other than farms increased in 1998 by 2.2 percent. Wages increased by 4.2 percent while prices increased by only 0.7 percent. Non-labor costs per unit of output fell by 1.4 percent, and profits increased.

■ For the economy as a whole, profits increased slightly, real wages rose by 2.6 percent, and inflation fell to 1.6 percent.

■ Many economists think that better education and on-the-job training, investment in information technologies, and improved management may have increased the long-term trend in productivity growth.

■ But most believe that the trend growth rate is closer to the 1.3 percent annual productivity gain of the past two decades than to the 2.2 percent gain of 1998.

■ Figure 1 shows what happened in the labor market during 1998 in the United States.

■ In 1997, the demand for labor curve was LD_{97} and the supply of labor curve was LS_{97}.

■ The labor market was in equilibrium with 224 billion hours of labor employed at an average real wage rate of $18.74 (measured in 1992 dollars).

■ During 1998, technological change and capital accumulation increased the marginal product of labor. The demand for labor increased, and the demand curve shifted rightward to LD_{98}.

■ Because the working-age population increased by 1 percent, the supply of labor increased by this percentage. The supply of labor curve shifted rightward to LS_{98}.

■ The increase in the demand for labor was large compared to the increase in the supply of labor. Employment increased to 227 billion hours, and the real wage rate increased to $19.43.

■ Figure 2 shows the effect of the increase in labor productivity on the production function.

■ In 1997, the production function was PF_{97}. With employment at 224 billion hours, real GDP was $7.3 trillion. Real GDP per hour of work was $32.77 (in 1992 dollars).

■ The same technological change and capital accumulation that increased the demand for labor shifted the production function upward to PF_{98} in 1998. With employment at 227 billion hours, real GDP was $7.6 trillion. Real GDP per hour of work was $33.21.

■ The increase in real GDP per hour of work is the broadest and best measure of labor productivity. On this measure, labor productivity increased by 1.3 percent in 1998—equal to the annual productivity increase of the past two decades.

■ Real GDP grew by 2.8 percent in 1998 because employment increased by 1.5 percent.

■ The growth rate of labor productivity in the business sector reported in the news article is greater than the rate for the economy as a whole.

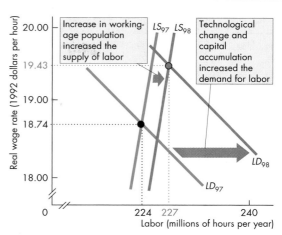

Figure 1 The labor market in 1998

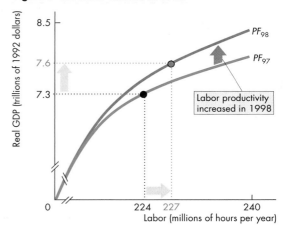

Figure 2 The production function in 1998

SUMMARY

KEY POINTS

Real GDP and Employment (pp. 182–184)

- To produce real GDP, we must forgo leisure time.
- As the quantity of labor increases, real GDP increases.
- Labor productivity increases if physical capital or human capital increases or if technology advances.

The Labor Market and Aggregate Supply (pp. 185–190)

- The quantity of labor demanded increases as the real wage rate falls, other things remaining the same.
- The diminishing marginal product of labor is the reason the quantity of labor demanded increases as the real wage rate falls.
- The quantity of labor supplied increases as the real wage rate rises, other things remaining the same.
- At full-employment equilibrium, the quantity of labor demanded equals the quantity of labor supplied.
- Potential GDP is real GDP produced by the full-employment quantity of labor.
- Along the long-run aggregate supply curve, the real wage rate is constant at its full-employment level. Along the short-run aggregate supply curve, the real wage rate, employment, and real GDP change.

Changes in Potential GDP (pp. 190–194)

- An increase in population increases the supply of labor, lowers the real wage rate, increases the quantity of labor employed, and increases potential GDP. It decreases potential GDP per hour of work.
- An increase in capital or an advance in technology increases labor productivity. It shifts the production function upward and the demand for labor curve rightward. The real wage rate rises, the quantity of labor employed increases, and potential GDP increases.

Unemployment at Full Employment (pp. 195–197)

- The unemployment rate at full employment is the natural rate of unemployment.
- Unemployment is ever present because of job search and job rationing.
- Job-search unemployment is influenced by demographic change, unemployment compensation, and structural change.
- Job-rationing unemployment arises from efficiency wages and the minimum wage.

KEY FIGURES

KEY TERMS

PROBLEMS

*1. Robinson Crusoe lives on a desert island on the equator. He has 12 hours of daylight every day to allocate between leisure and work. The table shows seven alternative combinations of leisure and real GDP in the economy of Crusoe:

Possibility	Leisure (hours per day)	Real GDP ($ per day)
a	12	0
b	10	10
c	8	18
d	6	24
e	4	28
f	2	30
g	0	30

a. Make a graph of Crusoe's *PPF* for leisure and real GDP.
b. Make a table and a graph of Crusoe's production function.
c. Find the marginal product of labor for Crusoe at different quantities of labor.

2. The people of Nautica have 100 hours every day to allocate between leisure and work. The table shows the opportunity cost of real GDP in terms of leisure time forgone in the economy of Nautica:

Possibility	Leisure (hours per day)	Opportunity cost of leisure ($ of real GDP per hour)
a	0	0
b	20	5
c	40	10
d	60	15
e	80	20
f	100	25

a. Make a table and a graph of Nautica's *PPF* for leisure and real GDP.
b. Make a table and a graph of Nautica's production function.
c. Find the marginal product of labor for Nautica at different quantities of labor.

*3. Use the information provided in problem 1 about the economy of Crusoe. Also, use the information that Crusoe must earn $4.50 an hour. If he earns less than this amount, he does not have enough food on which to live. He has no interest in earning more than $4.50 an hour. At a real wage rate of $4.50 an hour, he is willing to work any number of hours between zero and the total available to him.

a. Make a table that shows Crusoe's demand for labor schedule and draw Crusoe's demand for labor curve.
b. Make a table that shows Crusoe's supply of labor schedule and draw Crusoe's supply of labor curve.
c. What is the full-employment equilibrium real wage rate and quantity of labor in Crusoe's economy?
d. Find Crusoe's potential GDP.

4. Use the information provided in problem 2 about the economy of Nautica. Also, use the information that the people of Nautica are willing to work 20 hours a day for a real wage rate of $10 an hour. And for each 50¢ an hour *increase* in the real wage, they are willing to work an *additional* hour a day.

a. Make a table that shows Nautica's demand for labor schedule and draw Nautica's demand for labor curve.
b. Make a table that shows Nautica's supply of labor schedule and draw Nautica's supply of labor curve.
c. Find the full-employment equilibrium real wage rate and quantity of labor in Nautica's economy.
d. Find Nautica's potential GDP.

*5. Crusoe, whose economy is described in problems 1 and 3, gets a bright idea. He diverts a stream and increases his food production by 50 percent. That is, each hour that he works produces 50 percent more real GDP than before.

a. Make a table that shows Crusoe's new production function and new demand for labor schedule.
b. Find the new full-employment equilibrium real wage rate and quantity of labor in Crusoe's economy.
c. Find Crusoe's new potential GDP.
d. Explain and interpret the results you obtained in parts (a), (b), and (c).

6. Nautica's economy, described in problems 2 and 4, experiences a surge in its population. The supply of labor increases, and 50 percent more hours are supplied at each real wage rate.

a. Make a table that shows Nautica's new supply of labor schedule.
b. Find the new full-employment equilibrium real wage rate and quantity of labor in Nautica's economy.
c. Find Nautica's new potential GDP.
d. Explain and interpret the results you obtained in parts (a), (b), and (c).

*7. The figure describes the labor market on Cocoa Island. In addition (not shown in the figure), a survey tell us that when Cocoa Island is at full employment, people spend 1,000 hours a day in job search.

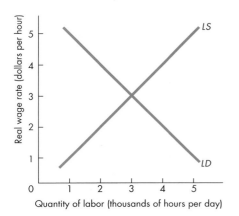

Quantity of labor (thousands of hours per day)

a. Find the full-employment equilibrium real wage rate and quantity of labor employed.
b. Find potential GDP in Cocoa Island. (Hint: The demand for labor curve tells you the *marginal* product of labor. How do we calculate the marginal product of labor?)
c. Calculate the natural rate of unemployment in Cocoa Island.

8. On Cocoa Island described in the figure and in problem 7, the government introduces a minimum wage of $4 an hour.
a. Find the new equilibrium real wage rate and quantity of labor employed.
b. What now is potential GDP in Cocoa Island?
c. Calculate the new natural rate of unemployment in Cocoa Island.
d. How much of the unemployment results from the minimum wage?

CRITICAL THINKING

1. Study the news article about productivity growth in the United States in *Reading Between the Lines* on pp. 198–199 and then answer the following questions:
a. By how much did labor productivity grow in the business sector in 1998?
b. By how much did real wages increase?
c. What, according to the news article, caused the increase in labor productivity?
d. Was the growth rate of labor productivity for the economy as a whole greater or smaller than that for the business sector? What do you think accounts for the difference?
e. Why does employment increase by a relatively small amount while the real wage rate increases by a relatively large amount?

2. Visit the Parkin Web site and use the links provided to obtain information about the economy of Russia during the 1990s. Try to figure out what has happened to the production possibility frontier and production function and to the demand for labor and supply of labor in Russia during the 1990s. Describe the Russian economy during these years, using only the concepts and tools that you have learned about in this chapter.

3. Visit the Parkin Web site and use the links provided to obtain information about the economy of China during the 1990s. Try to figure out what has happened to the production possibility frontier and production function and to the demand for labor and supply of labor in China during the 1990s. Describe the Chinese economy during these years, using only the concepts and tools that you have learned about in this chapter.

4. You are working for the President's Council of Economic Advisors and must write a memo for the President that provides a checklist of policy initiatives that will increase potential GDP. Be as imaginative as possible, but justify each of your suggestions with reference to the concepts and tools that you have learned about in this chapter.

10

Capital, Investment, and Saving

The 1996 Olympic Games in Atlanta were watched, as they happened, by more than two billion people (two fifths of the world's population). This media event was made possible by an enormous investment in a global video network. An even larger investment in a vast network of computers, telecommunications equipment, and databases enables a grade school student in Alice Springs, Australia, to click her mouse button and surf the Internet or send an e-mail message to her "pen-friend" in Akron, Ohio. How do businesses make the investment decisions that create the amazing tools that are building a global village? ◆ Each one of us decides how much income to save and how much to spend on consumption goods and services. Some of us spend everything we earn and can't wait for the next payday to come around. Others of us save large amounts of income. How do people make their saving decisions? ◆ Investment and saving decisions combine to determine interest rates and the long-term growth of potential GDP. Fluctuations in investment create cycles in real GDP. How do investment and saving decisions influence the interest rate you pay on your credit card balance and the interest rate you'll pay when you take a mortgage to buy a home? How do they influence the size of your pension when you retire?

Building the Global Village

◆ In this chapter, we study the decisions that determine the amount of capital in the economy and the return—the interest rate—that capital earns. When you have completed your study of this topic, you will be ready to learn about the forces that make potential GDP grow, which are explained in Chapter 11. ◆ We begin by looking at some facts about investment, capital, and interest rates in the United States and around the world.

After studying this chapter, you will be able to:

■ Describe the growth and fluctuations of investment and the capital stock

■ Describe the fluctuations in the real interest rate

■ Explain how investment decisions are made

■ Explain how household saving decisions are made

■ Explain how investment and saving determine the real interest rate

■ Explain how government influences the real interest rate, saving, and investment

■ Explain how international borrowing and lending are determined

Capital and Interest

POTENTIAL GDP DEPENDS ON THE QUANTITIES of our productive resources. One of these resources is the economy's **capital stock**, which is the total quantity of plant, equipment, buildings, and inventories. The capital stock includes business capital such as auto assembly lines and supermarkets together with the inventories that businesses carry. It includes houses and apartments. And it includes government-owned *social infrastructure capital* such as the courts and the justice system that establish and enforce property rights, highways, dams and canals, schools and state universities, and national defense systems. All of these types of capital contribute to our production possibilities and potential GDP.

The size of the capital stock is a consequence of our *investment decisions.* The purchase of new capital, called **gross investment**, increases the capital stock. The wearing out and scrapping of capital, called **depreciation**, decreases the capital stock. The capital stock changes by the amount of **net investment**, which equals gross investment minus depreciation (see Chapter 6, p. 114). Investment, like the capital stock, includes private and government components. Private investment is business investment plus purchases of new homes and additions to inventories. Government investment is the part of government purchases that creates social infrastructure capital.

People decide how much investment to undertake, and these decisions help to determine the rate at which potential GDP grows. This chapter explains these decisions. We begin by looking at the facts about investment and the capital stock.

Investment and Capital

Figure 10.1(a) shows gross investment and depreciation. In recession years such as 1975, 1982, and 1991, gross investment decreases, and in the expansion years, it grows quickly. Depreciation also grows and fluctuates but it does not line up neatly with the business cycle. In Fig. 10.1(a), the vertical distance between the two lines shows net investment (gross investment minus depreciation). Net investment fluctuates like gross investment.

Figure 10.1(b) provides a more direct view of net investment, which fluctuates with the business cycle, and the capital stock, which grows steadily every year.

FIGURE 10.1

Investment and the Capital Stock: 1970–1998

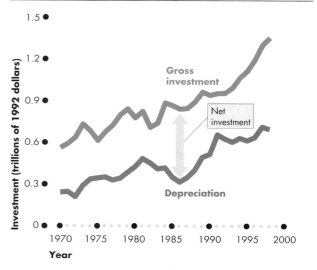

(a) Investment

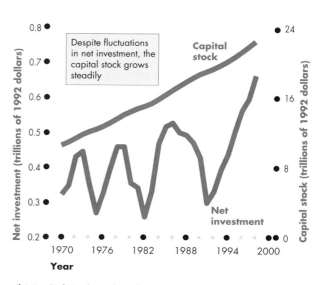

(b) Capital stock and net investment

Net investment fluctuates between $0.25 trillion a year in a recession and $0.65 trillion a year in an expansion. The capital stock grew steadily to $22 trillion in 1998.

Source: U.S. Department of Commerce, *National Income and Product Accounts of the United States* and *The Capital Stock of the United States*, and author's assumptions and calculations.

The capital stock increased from $10 trillion in 1970 to $22 trillion in 1998. The growth *rate* of the capital stock slows during the recessions, but the growth rate has always been positive because net investment has always been positive. When net investment increases during an expansion, the capital stock grows at about 3 percent a year, but on the average, the capital stock grows at around 2.5 percent per year.

Investment Around the World

Figure 10.2 compares investment in the United States with that in other parts of the world. Here, investment includes both business investment and government investment. And so that we can make comparisons, we measure investment as a percentage of GDP—called the investment rate.

Figure 10.2 shows that the investment rate in the United States has fluctuated and, throughout

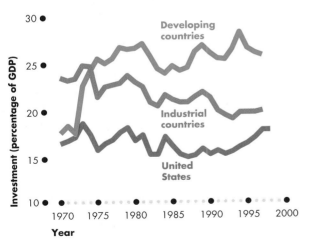

FIGURE 10.2

Investment in the United States and World: 1970–1998

Investment in the United States fluctuates between 15 percent and 19 percent of GDP. The United States has invested a smaller percentage of GDP than many other countries have. Since 1975, the developing countries have invested a larger percentage of GDP than have the industrial countries.

Sources: U.S. Department of Commerce, *National Income and Product Accounts of the United States* and *International Financial Statistics, Yearbook*, 1998.

the period shown in the figure, has been less than the investment rate in the other industrial countries and the developing countries. The industrial countries are Canada, Japan, Australia, New Zealand, and 18 rich countries in Western Europe. The developing countries comprise the rest of the world.

Investment in the industrial countries has fluctuated and has been on a downward trend. Investment in the developing countries has fluctuated and has followed two distinct trends: a strong upward trend from 1970 through 1976 and a moderate upward trend through the 1980s and 1990s. Since 1975, the investment rate in the developing countries has exceeded that in the industrial countries.

Within the developing economies, those in Asia (such as China, Korea, Taiwan, and Malaysia) have the highest investment rates and those in Africa and Central and South America have the lowest investment rates. But most of these countries have higher investment rates than that of the United States.

Interest Rates

When we studied labor in Chapter 7, we discovered that both the quantity of labor and the real wage rate per hour of labor have increased over the years. We've seen that the capital stock has grown steadily over time. But what has happened to the return on capital? Has it grown also? To find out, we must first define the return on capital.

The return on capital is the **real interest rate**, which is equal to the *nominal* interest rate adjusted for inflation. The nominal interest rate is the interest rate expressed in terms of money.

The real interest rate is approximately equal to the nominal interest rate minus the inflation rate. The exact calculation allows for the change in the purchasing power of the interest as well as the amount of the loan.[1]

Here, we'll work with the approximate formula. Suppose the nominal interest rate is 6 percent a year and there is no inflation. The real interest rate is also 6 percent a year.

Now suppose the inflation rate is 4 percent a year. In this situation, prices are rising and money is

---

[1] To calculate the *exact* real interest rate, use the formula: *real interest rate = nominal interest rate − inflation rate* divided by $(1 + $ *inflation rate*$/100)$. If the nominal interest rate is 10 percent and the inflation rate is 4 percent, the real interest rate is $(10 − 4) \div (1 + 0.04) = 5.77$ percent. The lower the inflation rate, the better is the approximation.

losing value at a rate of 4 percent a year. If the real interest rate remains at 6 percent a year, the nominal interest rate must rise to 10 percent a year.

To see why the nominal interest rate is 10 percent when inflation is 4 percent and the real interest rate is 6 percent, think about the following example. You borrow $1,000 for one year. If the real interest rate is 6 percent a year, the people who loaned you the money must be able to buy goods and services valued in today's prices at $1,060 when you repay them. But after a year in which prices rise by 4 percent, they need $1,100 to buy the goods and services that today cost $1,060. So if you pay them $1,100, you are only paying them $1,060 in today's prices and the *real* interest paid is $60—6 percent a year.

In the world economy, there are thousands of different interest rates. The real interest rate at which homebuyers and risky businesses can borrow is higher than the rate at which large corporations can borrow. And large corporations pay a higher interest rate than the U.S. government pays. But all real interest rates tend to move up and down together.

One real interest rate that fluctuates with many others is the real interest rate at which big U.S. corporations borrow. This rate is higher than that at which the U.S government can borrow but lower than the rate that you must pay on a bank loan or credit card balance. But it moves up and down in the same way as all these other interest rates.

Figure 10.3 shows the real interest rate paid by big U.S. corporations from 1970 through 1998. The average real interest rate during these years is 4 percent a year. The real interest rate does not rise steadily like the real wage rate rises. It fluctuates around a constant level.

Four subperiods are striking:

1. The 1970s—low (and negative in 1975)
2. Between 1980 and 1985—increased to exceed 8 percent a year
3. Between 1985 and 1989—decreased to about 5 percent a year
4. The 1990s—steady between 4 percent and 6 percent a year

The 1970s were years of economic turmoil that resulted from huge oil price hikes. The 1980s began with a deep recession but then went into a long expansion. The 1990s also began in recession and then had a long expansion. We'll learn in this chapter *why* these events influenced the real interest rate.

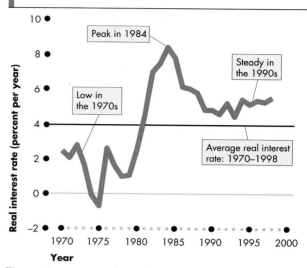

FIGURE 10.3

The Real Interest Rate

The real interest rate (here, the rate at which big U.S. corporations can borrow) was low during the 1970s and negative in 1975. It increased strongly between 1980 and 1984 and then decreased through 1989. It remained relatively steady at between 4 percent and 6 percent a year during the 1990s.

Source: Economic Report of the President, 1999, and the author's calculations.

REVIEW QUIZ

- What are the relationships among gross investment, net investment, depreciation, and the capital stock?
- Provide some examples of private capital and of government social infrastructure capital.
- Which item fluctuates most and which fluctuates least: net investment, depreciation, or the capital stock?
- How does the U. S. investment rate (percentage of GDP invested) compare with the investment rates in other industrial countries and in the developing countries?
- What is the return on capital and how has it changed over the past 30 years? Is the return ever negative?

We are now going to study businesses investment decisions and learn what determines the demand for new capital.

Investment Decisions

INVESTMENT CONSISTS OF PRIVATE INVESTMENT and government investment. We'll look at the role of government later in this chapter and first focus on private investment decisions.

How does Chrysler decide how much to spend on a new car assembly plant? How does AT&T decide how much to spend on fiber-optic cables? Business investment decisions are influenced by:

■ The expected profit rate
■ The real interest rate

To decide whether to invest in a new assembly line, Chrysler compares the expected profit rate with the real interest rate. The real interest rate is the opportunity cost of an investment. Let's look more closely at the expected profit rate and the real interest rate.

The Expected Profit Rate

Other things remaining the same, the greater the expected profit rate from new capital, the greater is the amount of investment.

Imagine that Chrysler is trying to decide whether to build a new $100 million automobile assembly line that will produce cars for one year and then be scrapped. Chrysler expects a net revenue of $120 million from operating the plant. Net revenue is equal to total revenue from sales minus the cost of labor and materials. The firm's expected profit from this assembly line is $20 million, which equals $120 million (net revenue) minus $100 million (cost of the plant). The expected *profit rate* is 20 percent a year—($20 million ÷ $100 million) × 100.

Of the many influences on the expected profit rate, the three that stand out are:

1. The phase of the business cycle
2. Advances in technology
3. Taxes

The phase of the business cycle influences the expected profit rate because sales fluctuate over the business cycle. In an expansion, an increase in sales brings a higher profit rate. In a recession, a decrease in sales brings a lower profit rate.

As technologies advance, profit expectations change. When a new technology first becomes available, firms expect to be on a learning curve and so expect a modest profit rate from the new technology. But as firms gain experience with a new technology, they expect costs to fall and the profit rate to increase.

It is the *after-tax* profit rate that a firm receives, so changes in tax rates influence the firm's after-tax profit rate. Firms go to extreme lengths to avoid taxes, and for multinational firms, the decision about *where* to invest often turns on the effect of taxes on profit.

The Real Interest Rate

Other things remaining the same, the lower the real interest rate, the greater is the amount of investment.

The funds used to finance investment might be borrowed, or they might be the financial resources of the firm's owners (the firm's retained earnings). But regardless of the source of the funds, the opportunity cost of the funds is the real interest rate. The real interest paid on borrowed funds is an obvious cost. The real interest rate is also the cost of using retained earnings because these funds could be loaned to another firm. The real interest income forgone is the opportunity cost of using retained earnings to finance an investment project.

In the Chrysler example, the expected profit rate is 20 percent a year. So it is profitable for Chrysler to invest as long as the real interest rate is less than 20 percent a year. That is, at real interest rates below 20 percent a year, Chrysler will build this assembly line, and at real interest rates in excess of 20 percent a year, it will not. Some projects are profitable at higher real interest rates, but other projects are profitable only at low real interest rates. Consequently, the higher the real interest rate, the smaller is the number of projects that are worth undertaking and the smaller is the amount of investment.

We summarize the influences on investment decisions in an investment demand curve.

Investment Demand

If the real interest rate rises, other things remaining the same, investment decreases. The table in Fig. 10.4 shows an example of this relationship. It lists the levels of investment that occur at three real interest rates and with three expected profit rates. The relationship between investment and the real interest rate, other things remaining the same, is called **investment demand**.

Figure 10.4(a) shows an investment demand curve when the expected profit rate is average. Each point (*a* through *c*) corresponds to a row in the table. If the real interest rate is 6 percent a year, investment is $1 trillion. A change in the real interest rate brings a movement along the investment demand curve. If the real interest rate rises to 8 percent a year, investment decreases to $0.8 trillion; there is a movement up the investment demand curve. If the real interest rate falls to 4 percent a year, investment increases to $1.2 trillion; there is a movement down the investment demand curve.

Figure 10.4(b) shows how investment demand depends on the expected rate of profit. When firms expect an average profit rate, the investment demand curve is ID_0, the same as in part (a). But when the expected profit rate increases, investment demand increases and the investment demand curve shifts rightward to ID_1. When the expected profit rate decreases, investment demand decreases and the investment demand curve shifts leftward to ID_2. Fluctuations in the expected profit rate are the main source of fluctuations in investment demand.

Let's now see how the investment demand curve helps us to understand the changes in investment in the United States.

FIGURE 10.4

Investment Demand

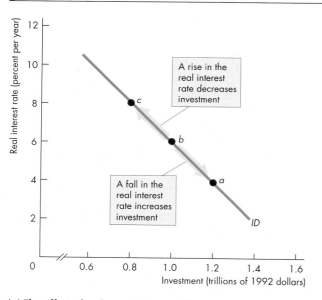

(a) The effect of a change in the real interest rate

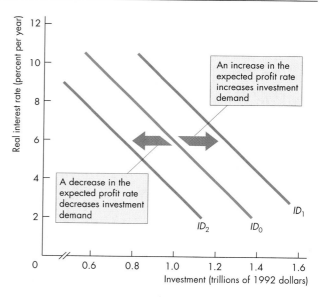

(b) The effect of a change in the expected profit rate

	Real interest rate (percent per year)	Investment (trillions of 1992 dollars)		
		Expected profit rate		
		Low	**Average**	**High**
a	4	1.0	1.2	1.4
b	6	0.8	1.0	1.2
c	8	0.6	0.8	1.0

The table shows the level of investment for three different expected profit rates—low, average, and high—and three different interest rates. When the real interest rate is 6 percent a year and the expected profit rate is average, investment is $1.0 trillion. Part (a) shows the investment demand curve, *ID*, for an average expected profit rate. A change in the interest rate brings a movement along the investment demand curve. In part (b), a high expected profit rate shifts the curve rightward to ID_1 and a low expected profit rate shifts it leftward to ID_2.

Investment Demand in the United States

Fluctuations in the real interest rate and in the expected profit rate bring fluctuations in investment. Figure 10.5 shows the relative importance of these two factors in the United States. The blue dots show net investment and the real interest rate each year

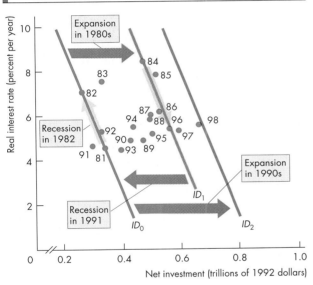

FIGURE 10.5

Investment Demand in the United States

The blue dots show net investment and the real interest rate in the United States for each year between 1981 and 1998. When the expected profit rate was low in the recession of the early 1980s, the investment demand curve was ID_0. Then, as the real interest rate increased in 1982, investment decreased. During the 1980s, the expected profit rate increased and the investment demand curve shifted rightward. By 1984, it had shifted to ID_1. Then, as the real interest rate fell during 1985 and 1986, investment increased. When the expected profit rate decreased in the late 1980s and the recession of 1991, the investment demand curve shifted leftward to ID_0. Then as the expected profit rate increased again through 1998, the investment demand curve shifted rightward through ID_1 to ID_2. Both swings in profit expectations and changes in interest rates bring fluctuations in net investment.

Source: Figures 10.1, 10.3, and the author's assumptions.

from 1981 to 1998. The curves labeled ID_0, ID_1, and ID_2 are three U.S. investment demand curves.

During the early 1980s, the investment demand curve was ID_0. A rise in the interest rate in 1982 brought a decrease in investment and a movement along the investment demand curve. The expected profit rate increased during the expansion of 1983 and 1984, and investment demand increased. The investment demand curve shifted rightward to ID_1. Between 1984 and 1986, the real interest rate fell and there was a movement downward along the investment demand curve ID_1.

During the late 1980s, profit expectations decreased and investment demand decreased. By 1991, the investment demand curve had shifted leftward back to ID_0. The expected profit rate increased again during the expansion of the 1990s and investment demand increased. By 1996, the investment demand curve had shifted rightward to ID_1 and by 1998, to ID_2.

You can see in Fig. 10.5 that investment fluctuates for two reasons: The real interest rate changes, which brings movements along an investment demand curve, and the expected profit rate changes, which shifts the investment demand curve.

REVIEW QUIZ

- If the real interest rate falls and other things remain the same, what happens to investment? If the real interest rate rises and other things remain the same, what happens to investment? How would you use an investment demand curve to illustrate these events?
- If the expected profit rate increases and other things remain the same, what happens to investment? If the expected profit rate decreases and other things remain the same, what happens to investment? How would you illustrate these events using an investment demand curve?
- In which years have changes in the real interest rate changed U.S. investment and in which years have changes in other factors had the larger influence on U.S. investment?

Next, we study the decisions that create the funds that finance investment: saving and consumption decisions.

Saving Decisions

PRIVATE INVESTMENT IS FINANCED BY NATIONAL saving and by borrowing from the rest of the world (see Chapter 6, p. 118). **National saving** is the sum of private saving and government saving. We first study private saving. Later in the chapter, we'll see how government actions influence the saving decisions.

Households must decide how to allocate their *disposable income* between saving and consumption. Of the many factors that influence a household's saving decision, the more important ones are:

- The real interest rate
- Disposable income
- Purchasing power of net assets
- Expected future income

The Real Interest Rate

Other things remaining the same, the lower the real interest rate, the smaller is the amount of saving and the greater is the amount of consumption. The real interest rate is the opportunity cost of consumption. A dollar consumed is a dollar not saved, so the interest that could have been earned on that saving is forgone. This opportunity cost arises regardless of whether a person is a lender or a borrower. For a lender, saving less this year means receiving less interest next year. For a borrower, saving less this year means paying less off a loan this year and paying more interest next year.

You can see why the real interest rate influences saving by thinking about student loans. If the real interest rate on student loans jumped to 20 percent a year, students would save more (buying cheaper food and finding lower-rent accommodations) to pay off their loans as quickly as possible. If the real interest rate on student loans fell to 1 percent a year, students would save less and take larger loans.

Disposable Income

The greater a household's disposable income, other things remaining the same, the greater is its saving. For example, a student works during the summer and earns a disposable income of $10,000. She spends the entire $10,000 on consumption during the year and saves nothing. When she graduates as an economics

major, her disposable income jumps to $20,000 a year. She now saves $4,000 and spends $16,000 on consumption. The increase in disposable income of $10,000 has increased saving by $4,000.

Purchasing Power of Net Assets

A household's assets are what it *owns,* and its debts are what it *owes.* A household's *net assets* are its assets minus its debts. The purchasing power of a household's net assets is the *real* value of its net assets. It is the quantity of goods and services that its net assets can buy. The greater the purchasing power of a household's net assets, other things remaining the same, the less is its saving.

Patty is a department store executive who earns a disposable income of $30,000 a year. She has been saving and now has $15,000 in the bank and no debts. Patty's colleague, Tony, also earns a disposable income of $30,000, but he has no money in the bank. Patty decides that this year, she will take a vacation and save only $1,000. But Tony decides to skip a vacation and save $5,000.

Expected Future Income

The lower a household's expected future income, other things remaining the same, the greater is its saving. That is, if two households have the same disposable income in the current year, the household with the larger expected future income will spend a larger portion of current disposable income on consumption goods and services.

Look at Patty and Tony again. Patty has just been promoted and will receive a $10,000 pay raise next year. Tony has just been told that he will be laid off at the end of the year. On receiving this news, Patty buys a new car—increases her consumption expenditure—and Tony sells his car and takes the bus—decreases his consumption expenditure.

Every young household expects to have a higher future income for some years and then to have a lower income during retirement. Because of this pattern of income over the life cycle, young people save a small amount, middle-aged people save a lot, and retired people gradually spend their accumulated savings.

We've studied households' saving decisions so that we can see how their saving decisions interact with firms' investment decisions to determine the real interest rate, investment, and saving. The next step is to learn about the saving supply curve.

Saving Supply

If the real interest rate rises, other things remaining the same, saving increases. The relationship between saving and the real interest rate, other things remaining the same, is called **saving supply**.

Figure 10.6 illustrates saving supply. The table shows a saving supply schedule, and the graph shows the saving supply curve. The points *a* through *c* on the saving supply curve *SS* in Fig. 10.6(a) correspond to the rows of the table. For example, point *b* indicates that when the real interest rate is 6 percent a year, saving is $1.0 trillion. If the real interest rate

rises from 6 percent a year to 8 percent a year, saving increases from $1 trillion to $1.1 trillion and there is a movement along the saving supply curve from *b* to *c*. If the real interest rate falls from 6 percent a year to 4 percent a year, saving decreases from $1 trillion to $0.9 trillion and there is a movement along the saving supply curve from *b* to *a*.

Along the saving supply curve, all other influences on saving remain the same. A change in any influence on saving other than the real interest rate changes saving supply and shifts the saving supply curve. An increase in disposable income, a decrease in the purchasing power of net assets, or a decrease

---

FIGURE 10.6

Saving Supply

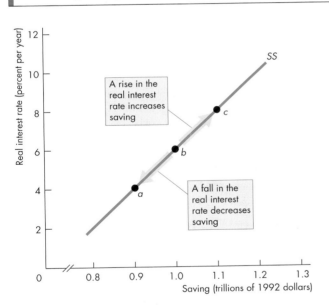

(a) The effect of a change in the real interest rate

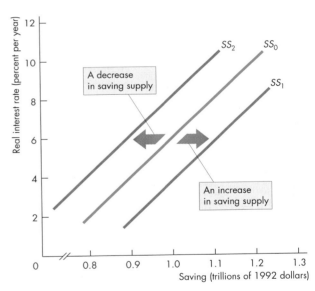

(b) The effects of other influences on saving

The table shows saving at three real interest rates. Part (a) shows the saving supply curve. Along the saving supply curve, the real interest rate changes but all other influences on saving remain the same. In part (b) an increase in disposable income (or a decrease in the purchasing power of net assets or a decrease in expected future income) increases saving and shifts the saving supply curve rightward from SS_0 to SS_1. A decrease in disposable income (or an increase in the purchasing power of net assets or an increase in expected future income) decreases saving and shifts the saving supply curve leftward from SS_0 to SS_2.

	Real interest rate (percent per year)	Saving (trillions of 1992 dollars)
a	4	0.9
b	6	1.0
c	8	1.1

in expected future income increases saving supply and shifts the saving supply curve rightward from SS_0 to SS_1. Changes in these factors in the opposite direction decrease saving and shift the saving supply curve leftward from SS_0 to SS_2.

Let's now see how the saving supply curve helps us to understand changes in saving in the United States.

Saving Supply in the United States

Fluctuations in the real interest rate, disposable income, the purchasing power of net assets, and expected future income change saving. Figure 10.7 shows the relative importance of these factors in the United States. The blue dots show net private saving and the real interest rate each year from 1980 to 1998. The curves labeled SS_0, and SS_1 are two U.S. saving supply curves.

The saving supply curve shows that when the real interest rate rises, saving increases. For example, between 1980 and 1983, the real interest rate rose and saving increased. But a large change in the real interest rate brings only a small change in saving.

The saving supply curve shifts rightward over time and by 1995, it was SS_1. Increasing disposable income is the main factor that increases saving and shifts the saving supply curve rightward.

Increases in the purchasing power of net assets and expected future income decrease saving. During the 1980s, with a booming stock market and increasing personal wealth, the purchasing power of net assets and expected future incomes both increased. Expectations of continued rapid economic expansion, which increased expected future incomes, reinforced the effect of increasing personal wealth. The result was an increase in consumption expenditure that almost equaled the increase in disposable income and the increase in saving was small.

In some years, such as 1998, a rising stock market and rising expected future income were so strong that saving decreased. In these years, the saving supply curve shifts leftward.

But on the average, rising disposable income has increased saving supply and the rightward shifts in the saving supply curve have been greater than the leftward shifts.

We've now studied the decisions that determine investment and saving and seen that both sets of decisions depend on the real interest rate. Next, we're going to see how the real interest rate, investment, and saving are simultaneously determined.

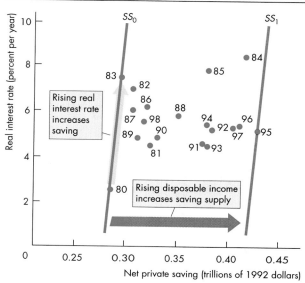

FIGURE 10.7

Saving Supply in the United States: 1980–1998

Each blue dot shows net private saving and the real interest rate for a particular year from 1980 through 1998. The blue curve SS_0 is an estimate of the saving supply curve for 1980. As disposable income increased, saving supply increased and the saving supply curve shifted rightward through SS_1 to SS_2. But in some years, the supply of saving decreases because a rising stock market and rising expected future income encourage consumption and discourage saving.

Source: U.S. Department of Commerce, *National Income and Product Accounts of the United States,* Figure 10.3, and the author's assumptions.

REVIEW QUIZ

- How do the real interest rate, disposable income, the purchasing power of net assets, and expectations of future income influence saving?
- If the real interest rate falls and other things remain the same, what happens to saving? If the real interest rate rises and other things remain the same, what happens to saving? How would you illustrate these events using a saving supply curve?
- How has the U.S. saving supply curve shifted in recent years and what have been the main reasons for the shifts?

Equilibrium in the World Economy

WE ARE NOW GOING TO SEE HOW INVESTMENT decisions and saving decisions determine the real interest rate. To do so, we study the economy of the entire world. The reason is that there is a single world capital market. Capital is free to roam the globe and seek the highest possible real rate of return. In 1998, for example, loans from the rest of the world to the developing countries and countries in transition were $2.1 trillion. So the saving of one country is not always used to finance the investment of that country.

Real interest rates are not the same in every country because some countries are riskier than others. The riskier countries have higher real interest rates. But interest rates move up and down together. If two countries with equal risk had different interest rates, people would want to borrow in the country with a low interest rate and lend in the country with a high interest rate. But no one would want to lend in the country with a low interest rate, so its interest rate would rise. And no one would want to borrow in the country with a high interest rate, so its interest rate would fall. Interest rates would quickly become equal in the two countries. The real interest rate in the world economy is determined by global investment and global saving.

Determining the Real Interest Rate

In Fig. 10.8, the world investment demand curve is *ID* and the world saving supply curve is *SS*. The higher the real interest rate, the greater is the amount of saving and the smaller is the amount of investment.

In the figure, when the real interest rate exceeds 6 percent a year, saving exceeds investment. Borrowers have an easy time finding the loans they want, but lenders are unable to lend all the funds they have available. The real interest rate falls, and as it does so, investment increases and saving decreases. The interest rate continues to fall until saving equals investment.

Alternatively, when the interest rate is less than 6 percent a year, saving is less than investment. Borrowers can't find the loans they want, but lenders are able to lend all the funds they have available. So the real interest rate rises. As the real interest rate rises, investment decreases and saving increases. The interest rate continues to rise as long as saving exceeds investment.

FIGURE 10.8

Equilibrium in the World Capital Market

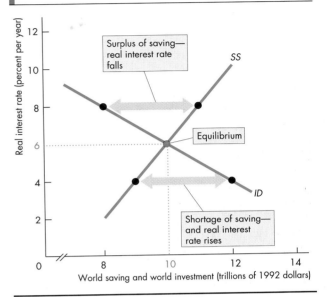

Real interest rate (percent per year)	Investment	Saving
	(trillions of 1992 dollars)	
a	4	12	9
b	6	10	10
c	8	8	11

The table shows world investment and saving at three interest rates, and the figure shows the world investment demand curve, *ID*, and world saving supply curve, *SS*. If the real interest rate is 4 percent a year, investment exceeds saving. There is a shortage of saving, and the real interest rate rises. If the real interest rate is 8 percent a year, investment is less than saving. There is a surplus of saving, and the real interest rate falls. When the real interest rate is 6 percent a year, investment equals saving. There is neither a shortage nor a surplus of saving, and the real interest rate is at its equilibrium level.

The real interest rate changes and is pulled toward an equilibrium level. In Fig. 10.8, this equilibrium is 6 percent a year. At this interest rate, there is neither a surplus nor a shortage of saving. Investors can get the funds they demand, and savers can lend all the funds they have available. The plans of savers and investors are consistent with each other.

Let's use the global saving supply and investment demand curves to explain changes in the real interest rate in the world economy.

Explaining Changes in the Real Interest Rate

In 1998, the real interest rate paid on long-term loans by the biggest and safest U.S. corporations was about 6 percent a year. It was more than 6 percent a year for homebuyers and risky businesses. Fourteen years earlier in 1984, the real interest rate reached a peak level for big companies of 8 percent a year. In contrast, 23 years earlier in 1975, the real interest rate was *negative*. Big companies could borrow at about 9 percent

a year, and the inflation rate was about 10 percent a year. So the real interest rate was close to *minus* 1 percent a year.

Figure 10.9 explains why these changes in the real interest rate occurred. In 1973 (in part a), the saving supply curve was SS_{73} and the investment demand curve was ID_{73}. The real interest rate was 2 percent a year, and the amount of saving and investment in the world economy was $4 trillion.

Between 1973 and 1975, world saving supply increased and the world saving supply curve shifted rightward to SS_{75}. The main reason for this increase was a huge rise in the price of oil, which increased the incomes and saving of oil producers and exporters.

At the same time, world investment demand collapsed and the world investment demand curve

---

FIGURE 10.9

Explaining Changes in the Real Interest Rate

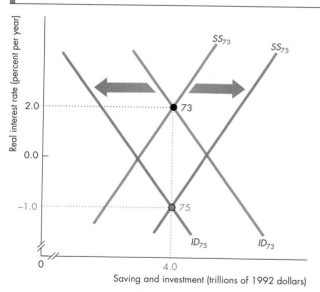

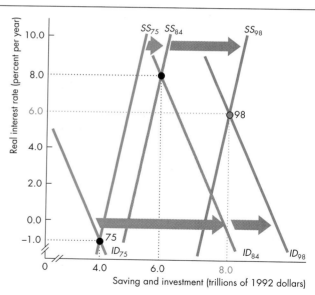

(a) Onset of growth slowdown

In 1973 (part a), world saving supply was SS_{73}, world investment demand was ID_{73}, and the real interest rate was 2 percent a year. A large increase in the world price of oil increased world saving supply and decreased world investment demand. By 1975, saving supply was SS_{75}, investment demand was ID_{75}, and the real interest rate was negative. By 1984 (part b), a

(b) 1975–1998

strong expansion increased investment demand to ID_{84}, but saving supply increased to only SS_{84}. The real interest rate increased to 8 percent a year. After 1984, saving supply increased by more than investment demand, and by 1998, the saving supply was SS_{98}, the investment demand was ID_{98}, and the real interest rate was 6 percent a year.

Sources: International Monetary Fund, *World Economic Outlook,* (Washington D.C., October 1998); International Monetary Fund, *International Financial Statistics, Yearbook,* (Washington D.C., 1998); *Economic Report of the President,* 1999; and the author's assumptions, calculations, and approximations.

shifted leftward to ID_{75}. The reason was that same oil price shock that increased saving supply. On the demand side of the capital market, oil users and importers faced steep cost increases and a collapse of profits, which decreased investment demand.

So by 1975, world saving supply had increased and world investment demand had decreased. The real interest rate fell to −1 percent a year.

Figure 10.9(b) takes up the story at this point. Gradually, investment demand recovered and, except for severe recession in 1982, increased each year. By 1984, the investment demand curve had shifted rightward to ID_{84}. Through these same years, saving supply increased slowly. The reasons for slow saving growth are complex. But one factor at work, which we examine later in this chapter, was the emergence of large government deficits, which must be subtracted from private saving to determine total saving. The combination of a large increase in investment demand and a small increase in saving supply increased the real interest rate to 8 percent a year in 1984, and world investment and world saving increased to $6 trillion.

The rest of the 1980s and the 1990s saw a growth in the supply of saving relative to the increase in investment demand. By 1998, the investment demand curve had shifted rightward to ID_{98} and the saving supply curve had shifted to SS_{98}. Because of these changes, the real interest rate fell to 6 percent a year.

R E V I E W   Q U I Z

- How is the real interest rate is determined? Why is it determined in the *world* capital market?
- What event simultaneously increased saving supply and decreased investment demand in 1973–1974. What was the effect on the real interest rate?
- What were the trends in world investment demand, world saving supply, and the real interest rate during the 1980s? Can you explain the trends?
- What were the trends in world investment demand, world saving supply, and the real interest rate during the late 1980s and 1990s? Can you explain the trends?

So far in our study of investment, saving, and the real interest rate, we've ignored government saving. Let's now bring government saving into the picture.

The Role of Government

PART OF THE CAPITAL STOCK ARISES FROM government investment. And investment is financed by total saving, which is made up of private saving plus government saving. So government actions influence investment demand, saving supply, and the real interest rate. In order to complete our study of the forces that determine the quantity of capital and the real interest rate, we must investigate the role played by governments.

But because the real interest rate is determined in the *world* capital market, it is the *aggregate* investment and *aggregate* saving of all governments that matters, not the investment and saving of one government.

Most governments are tiny and many U.S. corporations have a bigger impact on the world capital market than do some governments. Even the biggest governments have a relatively small impact on the world capital market. For example, the saving of the U. S. government is less than 1 percent of world saving.

But governments in total are large. The saving of world total government is close to 10 percent of world total saving. And the direction of that saving is negative. World total government saving is *negative!*

Let's see why government saving is negative and how government investment and saving influence total investment demand, saving supply, and the real interest rate.

Government Budgets

You learned in Chapter 6, (pp. 118–119) that GDP equals the sum of consumption expenditure, C, investment, I, government purchases, G, and net exports. We'll ignore net exports for the moment and consider only a closed economy (such as the world economy). So, in a closed economy,

$$GDP = C + I + G.$$

GDP also equals the sum of consumption expenditure, saving, S, and net taxes, T. That is,

$$GDP = C + S + T.$$

By combining these two ways of looking at GDP, you can see that:

$$I = S + T - G.$$

■ If net taxes, *T*, exceed government purchases, *G*, the government has a budget surplus and government saving is positive.

■ If government purchases exceed net taxes, the government has a budget deficit and government saving is negative.

When the government has a budget surplus, it contributes toward financing investment. Its saving must be added to private saving. But when the government has a budget deficit, it competes with businesses for private saving. In this situation, government saving must be subtracted from private saving.

Government saving can influence the world capital market in two ways, one direct and one indirect. We'll begin with the direct effect.

Direct Effect of Government Saving

Figure 10.10 shows the direct effect of government saving for the case in which government saving is negative—governments have a deficit. The world investment demand curve, *ID*, is the same as that in Fig. 10.8. The *private* saving supply curve, *PS*, shows the relationship between private saving and the real interest rate. The world saving supply curve *SS* shows the sum of private saving and government saving.

The horizontal distance between the private saving curve and the world saving supply curve is government saving. In this example, government saving is a negative $2 trillion. That is, the governments of all the nations have a total budget deficit of $2 trillion. (This number is larger than the actual total government deficit in the world economy in 1998.)

The effect of government negative saving, which is also called *dissaving*, is to decrease world saving and increase the real interest rate. Investment decreases. In this example, with a government deficit of $2 trillion, the world saving supply curve shifts leftward, and the real interest rate rises from 6 percent a year to 7 percent a year. Investment decreases from $10 trillion to $9 trillion.

Investment does not decrease by the full amount of the government deficit because the higher real interest rate induces an increase in private saving. In this example, private saving increases by $1 trillion to $11 trillion. In reality, the increase in private saving might be quite small, at least in the short term.

The tendency for a government budget deficit to decrease investment is called a **crowding-out effect**. By raising the real interest rate, the government

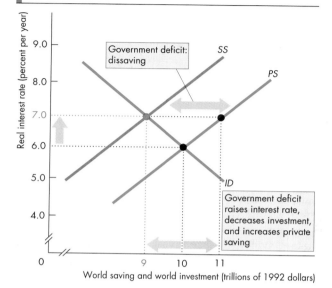

FIGURE 10.10

A Crowding-Out Effect

The world investment demand curve is *ID*, and the world private saving supply curve is *PS*. With balanced government budgets, the real interest rate is 6 percent a year and investment equals saving at $10 trillion a year. A government budget deficit is negative government saving (dissaving). We subtract the government deficit from private saving to determine the world saving supply curve *SS*. The real interest rate rises, investment decreases (is crowded out), and private saving increases.

deficit crowds out private investment and slows the rate of economic growth.

A government surplus has the opposite effect: It increases world saving supply, lowers the real interest rate, and stimulates investment and economic growth.

We've just studied the direct effect of government saving on the world capital market. But there is an indirect effect that we must also take into account.

Indirect Effect of Government Saving

Government saving has an indirect effect on the world capital market because it influences private saving. In the crowding-out story we've just told, the *quantity of private saving* changes because the real interest rate changes. There is a movement along the *PS* curve. But private saving supply does not change. That is, the *PS* curve does not shift. The indirect effect arises from the possibility that a change in government saving changes private saving supply and shifts the *PS* curve. In an extreme version of this effect, private saving changes to offset the government deficit and the deficit has no effect on the real interest rate or investment. Let's look at this extreme case.

The Barro-Ricardo Effect So named because it was first suggested by the English economist David Ricardo in the eighteenth century and refined by Robert J. Barro of Harvard University during the 1980s, the Barro-Ricardo effect holds that a government budget deficit has no effect on the real interest rate or investment. Another way of stating this view is that financing government purchases by taxes or by borrowing is equivalent.

The reasoning behind the Barro-Ricardo effect is the following. A government that runs a deficit must sell bonds to pay for the goods and services that are not paid for by taxes. And the government must pay interest on those bonds. It must also collect more taxes *in the future* to pay the interest on the larger quantity of bonds that are outstanding. Taxpayers are rational and have good foresight. They can see that their taxes will be higher in the future, so their disposable income will be smaller. With a smaller expected future disposable income, saving increases. And if taxpayers want to neutralize the effects of the government deficit on their own consumption plans, they increase their saving by the same amount that the government is dissaving through its deficit.

Figure 10.11 shows this outcome. Initially, the government has a balanced budget—neither a deficit nor a surplus—so the world saving supply curve *SS* is the private saving supply curve PS_0. With world investment demand *ID*, the equilibrium real interest rate is 6 percent a year and investment and saving are $10 trillion.

Governments now run deficits that total $2 trillion. But these deficits induce an increase in private saving. In Fig. 10.11, the increase in private saving equals the government deficit. So the private saving supply curve shifts rightward to PS_1. But the world saving supply curve *SS* remains unchanged, and the real interest rate remains at 6 percent a year. Investment also remains at $10 trillion a year. Private saving increases by $2 trillion to $12 trillion.

The outcome shown in Fig. 10.11 is extreme and probably does not actually occur. Taxpayers probably respond in the *direction* suggested by Ricardo and Barro but not in the *amount* they suggest. So the effect of government deficits probably lies between

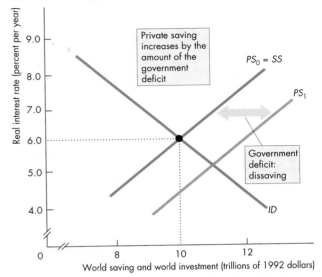

FIGURE 10.11

A Barro-Ricardo Effect

The world investment demand curve is *ID*, and initially, the world saving supply curve *SS* is the same as the private saving supply curve, PS_0. With balanced government budgets, the real interest rate is 5 percent a year and investment equals saving at $10 trillion a year. A government budget deficit induces an increase in private saving to PS_1, but the world saving supply curve remains at *SS*. The real interest rate, investment, and *total* saving remain constant.

the two cases shown in Figs. 10.10 and 10.11. That is, a government deficit increases the real interest rate and partly crowds out investment, but it also induces a partial increase in private saving in anticipation of lean times later when the tax bill rises to pay the interest on a rising debt.

Government Deficits Today

Government deficits have been large in recent years and have probably been responsible for the high real interest rates of the 1990s. Figure 10.12 shows the deficits of the United States, the other advanced countries, and the developing and transitional countries from 1990 through 1998 and the projected deficits for 1999. During the early 1990s, deficits in the United States and the other advanced countries increased to more than 4 percent of GDP. But after

FIGURE 10.12
Government Surpluses and Deficits

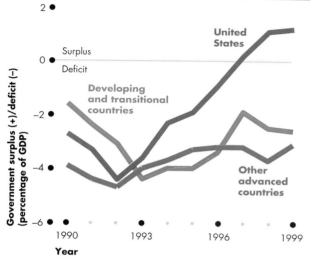

A U.S. government surplus emerged in the late 1990s after a long run of deficits. Government budget deficits in the other advanced countries and the developing and transition countries have shrunk slightly since the early 1990s but deficits persist.

Source: International Monetary Fund, *World Economic Outlook*, (Washington D.C., October 1998).

1993, government deficits in the advanced countries decreased, and spectacularly so in the United States, where by the late 1990s a surplus emerged.

Government deficits in the developing countries and transitional countries (the countries of central and eastern Europe that are introducing market economies and private enterprise) have also persisted but have fallen somewhat through the 1990s. These countries have decreased their deficits because doing so has been a condition for receiving loans, most notably from the International Monetary Fund. (To learn about the International Monetary Fund, see Talking with Stanley Fischer on pp. 486–490.)

During the 1990s, real interest rates were higher than average. The reason is that world investment demand was high relative to world saving supply. During the 1990s, investment opportunities were large and saving rates were low compared with average times. Figure 10.3 shows that real interest rates averaged 4 percent between 1970 and 1995. But even this number is above the long-term average, which

over the past 100 years is 2 percent a year. If government deficits continue to decrease, real interest rates will also decrease (other things remaining the same).

Saving and Investment in the National Economy

SAVING SUPPLY AND INVESTMENT DEMAND IN the world economy determine the world real interest rate. At the equilibrium real interest rate, world saving equals world investment.

Although saving equals investment in the world economy, it does not necessarily do so in a national economy. In a nation, investment is financed by *national* saving plus borrowing from the rest of the world (see Chapter 6, p. 118). Nations in which investment exceeds national saving borrow from the rest of the world, and nations in which national saving exceeds investment lend to the rest of the world. For the world as a whole, international borrowing equals international lending.

But as you also learned in Chapter 6, a nation's international lending equals its net exports. So a nation that has a net export surplus is also one that lends to the rest of the world. A nation whose imports exceed its exports has negative net exports and borrows from the rest of the world. Whether a nation has a surplus or deficit in its international trade depends on whether its national saving exceeds or falls short of its investment.

Let's take a closer look at the role played by national saving and investment decisions and see how they determine international borrowing. There are two channels of influence to consider.

First, each nation contributes to world saving and investment and so influences the world real interest rate. The larger the country, the greater is that influence. For example, investment and saving decisions in the United States, the European Union, and Japan have a big impact on world investment demand and world saving supply. So they have a big influence on the world real interest rate. The investment and saving of other nations individually have a small impact on world investment demand and world saving supply. So they have a negligible influence on the world real interest rate.

Second, a nation's saving and investment decisions, along with the world real interest rate, determine the amount the nation borrows from or lends to the rest of the world. They also, equivalently, determine a nation's net exports.

Figure 10.13 shows the determination of a nation's international borrowing and net exports. The nation's investment demand curve is *ID*, and its saving supply curve (including any government saving) is *SS*. The world real interest rate is 6 percent a year. At this real interest rate, investment is $1.5 trillion and saving is $1.0 trillion. International borrowing fills the gap between investment and saving. In the example in Fig. 10.13, investment exceeds saving, so the nation borrows from the rest of the world. If, at the world real interest rate, saving exceeds investment, the nation lends to the rest of the world.

Government Saving and International Borrowing

The greater the amount of government saving, other things remaining the same, the greater is national saving. And the greater the national saving, the smaller is international borrowing (or the larger is international lending). An increase in the government deficit decreases national saving and increases international borrowing.

You can now see why U.S. net exports have been negative for the past 20 years. It is because U.S. national saving has been less than investment. Government dissaving (a government budget deficit) has contributed to the shortfall. A low private saving rate has also contributed.

You can also see that one popular view about the U.S. budget deficit is incorrect. Because the capital market is a global market and the U.S. government is a small player, the U.S. government deficit cannot cause much damage to growth by crowding out investment. But it does damage the growth of U.S disposable incomes because it increases international borrowing and increases the interest payments that we must make to the rest of the world.

FIGURE 10.13

Saving, Investment, and International Borrowing

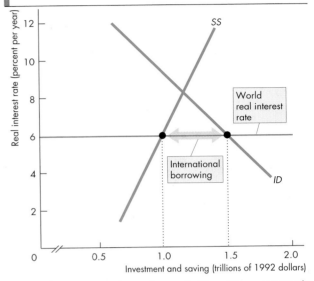

A nation's investment demand curve is *ID*, and its saving supply curve (including government saving) is *SS*. The world real interest rate is 6 percent a year. At this interest rate, investment, which is $1.5 trillion, exceeds saving, which is $1.0 trillion. The nation borrows $0.5 trillion from the rest of the world.

R E V I E W Q U I Z

- If, in a country, investment exceeds saving at the world real interest rate, does that country have positive or negative net exports? Does it lend to or borrow from the rest of the world?
- Does an increase in a government's deficit crowd out investment? Explain why or why not.

◆ In this chapter, we've seen that the quantity of capital depends on investment and saving, and we've seen how the real interest rate is determined in the world capital market. Your next task is to see how technological change brings capital accumulation and economic growth.

Before embarking on this task, take a look at *Reading Between the Lines* on pp. 220–221, which examines the private saving performance of the United States in recent years.

Saving in the United States

THE WALL STREET JOURNAL, FEBRUARY 4, 1999

The Economy Is Safe From a 'Savings Crisis'

BY MICKEY D. LEVY

A specter is haunting our economic boom—the specter of low personal savings. As measured by the Department of Commerce, the rate of personal savings, which averaged 7.7% in the 1960s and 1970s and 7% in the 1980s, fell steadily toward zero in the 1990s, and even turned negative during parts of 1998.

But these concerns are largely misplaced, for they rely on an incomplete picture of the economy. The rate of personal savings is a very limited measure, and although it has fallen, the stock of household wealth has soared, while gross national savings have actually risen as a share of gross domestic product. The relatively modest rise in the current-account deficit (the amount by which national investment exceeds national savings) as a share of the economy is attribut-able to continued strong gross investment with high expected rates of return, and has been consistent with a firm dollar. And while the recent strong growth in consumption seems unsustainable, the fundamentals do not point toward collapse.

A comprehensive measure of savings would capture all changes in the stock of wealth. But the rate of personal savings, measured for national income purposes, is calculated as the ratio of disposable personal income (income minus taxes) minus consumption to disposable personal income. As such, it excludes key sources of savings: business savings and the appreciation of stock values, rising housing values and even the appreciation of individual retirement accounts. Nor does it include personal claims on private pensions and other forms of deferred compensation.

Essence of the Story

■ The rate of *personal* saving measured in the national income accounts fell toward zero during the 1990s.

■ The personal saving rate excludes business saving and the increase in stock values, house values, and individual retirement accounts.

■ A full measure of saving equals the change in the stock of wealth.

■ The falling saving rate is not a problem because the measured saving rate ignores the fact that the stock of household wealth has increased.

■ The current account deficit, which is the amount by which national investment exceeds national saving, has increased because a high expected rate of return has increased investment.

■ Figure 1 shows the falling saving rate in the United States. Two measures, the gross saving rate and the personal saving rate, show a similar downward trend after 1980. But after 1993, while the personal rate continued to decrease, the national saving rate began to increase. The news article notes this fact.

■ The personal saving rate depends on the real interest rate, the purchasing power of net assets, and expected future income.

■ The higher the real interest rate, the greater is the saving rate, other things remaining the same. The real interest rate was higher during the 1980s and 1990s than during the 1970s. So this influence has lessened the decrease in the saving rate.

■ The greater the purchasing power of net assets, other things remaining the same, the smaller is the saving rate. As the news article notes, a full measure of saving includes the change in the value of net assets.

■ So when the value of net assets increases, saving properly measured has increased, and house-holds feel comfortable increasing the percentage of disposable income consumed. The measured saving rate decreases.

■ A large increase in stock market values has increased the value of net assets and decreased the saving rate.

■ The higher is expected future income, other things remaining the same, the smaller is the saving rate. This factor, too, has probably decreased the saving rate as people have come to expect more rapid economic growth during the 1990s.

■ One consequence of the decreased saving rate is a decrease in world saving and a higher real interest rate.

■ Other consequences are a larger amount of U.S. borrowing from the rest of the world and imports that exceed exports.

■ Figure 2 shows how an increasing amount of U.S. investment has been financed by foreign borrowing.

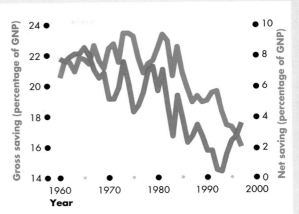

Figure 1 Saving rates in the United States

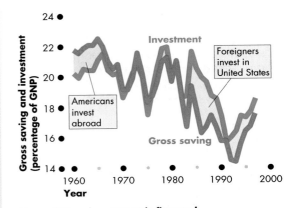

Figure 2 How investment is financed in the United States

■ What do you think the federal government should do about the low U.S. saving rate?

■ Can you think of any tax reforms that might increase saving?

■ How do you think Social Security and Medicare might influence personal saving?

■ Would you vote for tax incentives, a cut in Social Security, neither, or both, and why?

SUMMARY

KEY POINTS

Capital and Interest (pp. 204–206)

- The capital stock grows steadily because net investment is usually positive.
- The return on capital is the real interest rate—the nominal interest rate adjusted for inflation.

Investment Decisions (pp. 207–209)

- Other things remaining the same, the lower the real interest rate or the higher the expected profit rate, the greater is the amount of investment.
- Investment demand is the relationship between investment and the real interest rate, other things remaining the same. Investment demand changes when the expected profit rate changes.

Saving Decisions (pp. 210–212)

- Other things remaining the same, the higher the real interest rates, the greater is saving.
- Saving supply is the relationship between saving and the real interest rate, other things remaining the same.
- Saving supply changes when disposable income, the purchasing power of net assets, or expected future income changes.

Equilibrium in the World Economy (pp. 213–215)

- Because capital is free to move internationally to seek the highest possible real rate of return, the real interest rate is determined in a global market.
- The equilibrium real interest rate makes world saving equal to world investment.

The Role of Government (pp. 215–218)

- National saving equals private saving plus government saving.
- Government saving equals net taxes minus government purchases.
- A government budget deficit might increase the real interest rate and crowd out private investment.

- A government budget deficit might also increase private saving supply because it decreases expected future disposable income.

Saving and Investment in the National Economy (pp. 218–219)

- In the national economy, foreign borrowing fills the gap between national saving and investment.
- An increase in the government budget deficit of a country decreases national saving and increases foreign borrowing, but it does not decrease investment.

KEY FIGURES

Figure 10.4   Investment Demand, 208
Figure 10.6   Saving Supply, 211
Figure 10.8   Equilibrium in the World Capital Market, 213
Figure 10.10   A Crowding-Out Effect, 216
Figure 10.11   A Barro-Ricardo Effect, 217
Figure 10.13   Saving, Investment, and International Borrowing, 219

KEY TERMS

Capital stock, 204
Crowding-out effect, 216
Depreciation, 204
Gross investment, 204
Investment demand, 207
National saving, 210
Net investment, 204
Real interest rate, 205
Saving supply, 211

PROBLEMS

*1. A cellular phone assembly plant costs $10 million and has a life of one year. The firm will have to hire labor at a cost of $3 million and buy parts and fuel at a cost of a further $3 million. If the firm builds the plant, it will be able to produce cellular telephones that will sell for a total revenue of $17 million. Does it pay the firm to invest in this new production line at the following real interest rates:

   a.   5 percent a year?
   b.   10 percent a year?
   c.   15 percent a year?

2. A natural gas deposit contains gas that can be pumped out in one year and sold for a total revenue of $40 million. It will take a $36 million investment in equipment and pipelines to access the gas and deliver it to the buyers. Does it pay to undertake this investment at the following real interest rates:

   a.   5 percent a year?
   b.   10 percent a year?
   c.   15 percent a year?

*3. In 1999, the Batman family (Batman and Robin) had a disposable income of $50,000, net assets of $100,000, and an expected future income of $50,000 a year. At an interest rate of 4 percent a year, the Batmans would save $10,000. At an interest rate of 6 percent a year, they would save $12,500. And at an interest rate of 8 percent a year, they would save $15,000.

   a.   Draw a graph of the Batman family's saving supply curve for 1999.
   b.   In 2000, everything remained the same as the year before except that the Batmans expected their future income to rise to $60,000 a year. Show the influence of this change on the Batman family's saving supply curve.
   c.   In 2001, everything remained the same as the year before except that the Batmans' disposable income increased to the $60,000 a year they expected it would the year before. The Batmans now expect their income to remain at $60,000 a year. Show the influence of this change on the Batman family's saving supply curve.

4. It is now 2002, and the Batman family has net assets of $120,000. Its disposable income is

$60,000, and its expected future income is also $60,000 a year. The Batmans will save $15,000 at an interest rate of 6 percent a year. If the interest rate falls to 4 percent a year, they will cut their saving to $10,000. And if the interest rate rises to 8 percent a year, they will increase their saving to $20,000.

   a.   Draw a graph of the Batman family's saving supply curve for 2002.
   b.   In 2002, the stock market boomed and the Batmans' net assets increased by 50 percent. Indicate the direction of influence of this change on the Batman family's saving supply curve.
   c.   In 2003, the stock market crashed and the Batmans' net assets were wiped out. Indicate the direction of influence of this change on the Batman family's saving supply curve.

*5. The year is 3053. The economy of Planet Earth, still isolated from all other planets, has the following saving supply and investment demand:

Real interest rate (percent per year)	Saving	Investment (trillions of 3050 dollars)
4	2	7
5	6	6
6	10	5
7	14	4
8	18	3

Planet Earth's government budget is balanced.
   a.   What is the equilibrium real interest rate?
   b.   What is equilibrium investment?
   c.   What is equilibrium saving?

6. The year is 3053. The economy of Alpha Centura, still isolated from all other planets, has the following saving supply and investment demand:

Real interest rate (percent per year)	Saving	Investment (trillions of 3050 zips)
4	1	16
5	3	13
6	5	10
7	7	7
8	9	4

Alpha Centura's government budget is balanced.

a. What is the equilibrium real interest rate?

b. What is equilibrium investment?

c. What is equilibrium saving?

*7. The government of Planet Earth spends big on a space program and incurs a deficit of 5 trillion dollars. But the citizens of Planet Earth have a long memory and remember the Ricardo-Barro principle, which they apply to their saving and spending decisions.

a. What is the new equilibrium real interest rate?

b. What are the new equilibrium investment and saving?

8. The government of Alpha Centura spends big on a space program and incurs a deficit of 5 trillion zips. The citizens of Alpha Centura have never heard of David Ricardo and Robert Barro, so they keep spending as if there were no government deficit.

a. What is the new equilibrium real interest rate?

b. What are the new equilibrium investment and saving?

*9. The space programs of Alpha Centura and Planet Earth pay off. The Alpha Centurans and Earth people discover each other and begin to pursue intergalactic economic trade, borrowing, and lending. They establish a common currency: 1 zip equals one dollar. They terminate their government deficits and return to the levels of saving and investment described in problems 5 and 6.

a. What is the real interest rate in the galactic economy?

b. What is the level of galactic investment?

c. What is the level of galactic saving?

d. Do investment and saving on Alpha Centura increase or decrease?

10. In the galactic economy consisting of Alpha Centura and Planet Earth described in problem 9,

a. Do investment and saving on Planet Earth increase or decrease?

b. Do investment and saving on Alpha Centura increase or decrease?

c. Which planet borrows from the other and how much?

CRITICAL THINKING

1. Study *Reading Between the Lines* on pp. 220–221 and then answer the following questions:

a. What has happened to the personal saving rate in the United States during the past 30 years?

b. What has happened to the national saving rate in the United States during the past 30 years?

c. What are the main reasons you can think of that might account for the patterns that you describe in your answers to parts (a) and (b)?

d. What are the likely effects of a decrease in U.S. saving supply? Explain the effects on national saving, investment, the world real interest rate, and U.S. international borrowing and lending.

e. If the U.S. saving rate increases during the 2000s, how will that change influence the quantity of U.S. and world capital by 2010?

2. Suppose that the U.S. government cuts the tax rate on business profits.

a. How do you think this tax cut will influence firms' investment plans?

b. How will the tax cut influence personal saving decisions?

c. How will the tax cut influence the real interest rate?

d. How will the tax cut influence U.S. international borrowing?

For each part, draw a figure to illustrate the effects. Then think about and answer the following questions:

e. Who would benefit from such a tax cut?

f. Who would pay for such a tax cut?

g. On balance, do you favor or oppose such a tax cut? Why?

3. Use the link on the Parkin Web site to obtain data on government budget deficits from the latest *World Economic Outlook* published by the International Monetary Fund.

a. What are the trends in these deficits? Are they the same as or different from those in Fig. 10.12 on p. 218?

b. What influence do you expect these deficits to have on the real interest rate and investment next year?

Chapter 11

Economic Growth

Real GDP *per person* in the United States more than doubled between 1960 and 1998. If you live in a dorm, chances are it was built during the 1960s and equipped with two electricity outlets, one for a desk lamp and one for a bedside lamp. Today, with the help of a power bar (or two), your room bulges with a television and VCR, CD player, microwave, refrigerator, coffee maker, toaster, computer—and the list goes on. What has brought about this growth in production and incomes? What can be done to speed up economic growth? ◆ We see greater extremes of economic growth if we look at modern Asia. On the banks of the Li River in Southern China, Songman Yang breeds cormorants, amazing birds

Transforming People's Lives

that he trains to fish and to deliver their catch to a basket on his simple bamboo raft. Songman's work, the capital equipment and technology he uses, and the income he earns are similar to those of his ancestors going back some 2,000 years. Yet all around Songman, in China's bustling villages, towns, and cities, people are participating in an economic miracle. They are creating businesses, investing in new technologies, developing local and global markets, and experiencing income growth of more than 6 percent a year. Despite a slowdown in 1998, similar rapid economic growth has taken place in Hong Kong, South Korea, and Taiwan. In these countries, real GDP doubled *three times*—an eightfold increase—between 1960 and 1998. Why have incomes in these Asian economies grown so rapidly? What makes an economic miracle?

◆ In this chapter, we study the forces that make real GDP grow, that make some countries grow faster than others, and that make our own growth rate sometimes slow down and sometimes speed up. We'll also look at policies for achieving faster economic growth.

After studying this chapter, you will be able to:

- Describe the long-term growth trends in the United States and other countries and regions
- Identify the main sources of long-term or real GDP growth
- Explain the productivity growth slow-down in the United States during the 1970s
- Explain the rapid economic growth rates being achieved in East Asia
- Explain the theories of economic growth
- Describe the policies that might be used to speed up economic growth

Long-Term Growth Trends

THE LONG-TERM GROWTH TRENDS THAT WE study in this chapter are the trends in *potential GDP*. We are interested in long-term growth primarily because it brings rising incomes *per person*. So we begin by looking at some facts about the level and growth rate of real GDP per person in the United States and around the world. Let's look first at real GDP per person in the United States over the past hundred years.

Growth in the U.S. Economy

Figure 11.1 shows real GDP per person in the United States for the hundred years from 1898 to 1998. The average growth rate over this period is 2 percent a year. But the long-term growth rate has varied from a low of 1.1 percent a year between 1973 and 1984 to a high of 3 percent a year during the 1920s and the 1960s.

Figure 11.1 shows you the recent productivity growth slowdown in a longer perspective. It also shows that productivity growth slowdowns have occurred before. The early years of the 1900s and the mid-1950s had even slower growth than we have today. The rapid growth of the 1960s was not unusual either. The decade of the 1920s was a period of similarly rapid growth.

In the middle of the graph are two extraordinary events: the Great Depression of the 1930s and World War II of the 1940s. The fall in real GDP during the Depression and the bulge during the war obscure any changes in the long-term growth trend that might have occurred within these years. But between 1930 and 1950, averaging out the Depression and the war, the long-term growth rate was 2.2 percent a year.

A major goal of this chapter is to explain why our economy grows and why the long-term growth rate varies. A related goal is to explain variations in the economic growth rate across countries. Let's look at some facts about these variations.

FIGURE 11.1

A Hundred Years of Economic Growth in the United States

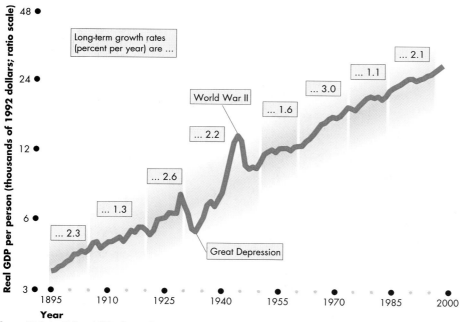

During the 100 years from 1898–1998, real GDP per person in the United States grew by 2 percent a year, on the average. The growth rate was above average during the 1920s, 1960s, and 1983–1998 and it was below average in 1903–1920, the 1950s, and 1973–1983.

Source: Christina D. Romer "The Prewar Business Cycle Reconsidered: New Estimates of Gross National Product, 1869–1908," *Journal of Political Economy* Vol. 97 (1989); *National Income and Product Accounts of the United States; Historical Statistics of the United States Colonial Times to 1957* (U.S. Department of Commerce, 1960); and *Economic Report of the President,* 1999.

Real GDP Growth in the World Economy

Figure 11.2 shows real GDP per person in the United States and in other countries between 1960 and 1998. (The data shown in this figure are in 1985 dollars.) Part (a) looks at the richest countries. The United States has the highest real GDP per person.

In 1998, Canada had the second highest real GDP per person and Japan the third highest. Before the 1990s, both of these countries grew faster than the United States and were catching up. Japan also grew faster than the Europe Big 4 (France, Germany, Italy, and the United Kingdom) and overtook them in the mid-1980s. The Europe Big 4 also grew faster than United States but only by a small margin.

Not all countries are growing faster than, and catching up with, the United States. Figure 11.2(b) looks at some of these. Western Europe (other than the Big 4) grew faster than the United States before 1975, slowed to the U.S. growth rate during the 1980s, and fell behind during the 1990s. After a brief period of catch-up, the former Communist countries of Central Europe fell increasingly behind the United States and by 1998, they were as far behind as they had been 30 years earlier.

Africa and Central and South America have persistently grown more slowly than the United States. Real GDP per person in Central and South America slipped from a comparative high of 30 percent of the U.S. level of real GDP per person in 1980 to 23 percent in 1998. Africa slipped from 8 percent of the U.S. level of real GDP per person in 1960 to 6 percent in 1998.

FIGURE 11.2

Economic Growth Around the World: Catch-Up or Not?

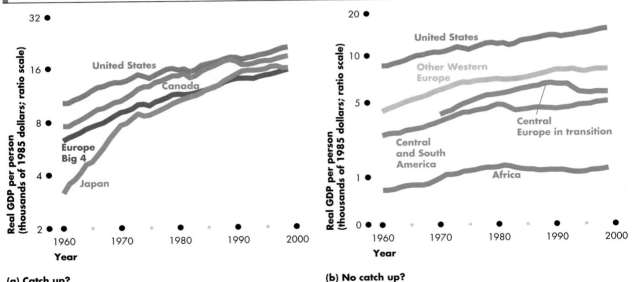

(a) Catch up?

(b) No catch up?

Real GDP per person has grown throughout the world economy. Among the rich industrial countries (part a), real GDP growth has been faster in Canada, the Europe Big 4 (France, Germany, Italy, and the United Kingdom), and Japan than in the United States and they are catching up. The most spectacular growth was in Japan during the 1960s. Real GDP per person in

Canada has also become closest to the U.S. real GDP per person. Among a wider range of countries (part b), there is little sign of catch-up. The gaps between the levels of real GDP per person in the United States, other Western European countries, Central Europe, Central and South America, and Africa have remained remarkably constant.

Sources: 1960–1992, Robert Summers and Alan Heston, New Computer Diskette (Mark 5.6a), January 15, 1995, distributed by the National Bureau of Economic Research to update "The Penn World Table: An Expanded Set of International Comparisons, 1950–1988," *Quarterly Journal of Economics*, May 1991, 327–368; 1993–1998, International Monetary Fund, *World Economic Outlook*, (Washington D.C., October 1998).

Taking both parts of Fig. 11.2 together, we can see that the catch-up in real GDP per person that is visible in part (a) is not a global phenomenon.

Hong Kong, Korea, Singapore, and Taiwan were in the headlines in 1998 because, along with some other Asian countries, they experienced a recession. But as Fig. 11.3 shows, their long-term growth has been spectacular. In 1960, these countries had levels of real GDP per person that ranged from one tenth to one quarter that in the United States. By 1998, two of them (Hong Kong and Singapore) had caught the United States and the other two were close behind.

FIGURE 11.3
Catch-Up in Asia

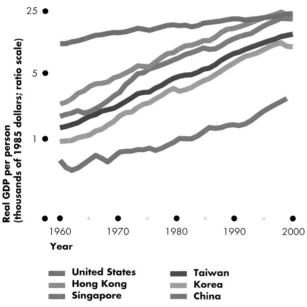

The clearest examples of catch-up have occurred in five economies in Asia. After starting out in 1960 with real GDP per person as little as one tenth of that in the United States, Hong Kong, Korea, Singapore, and Taiwan have substantially narrowed the gap on the United States. And from being a very poor developing country in 1960, China's real GDP per person now exceeds that of Hong Kong in 1960. China is growing at a rate that is enabling it to continue to catch up with the United States.

Sources: 1960–1992, Robert Summers and Alan Heston, New Computer Diskette (Mark 5.5), June 15, 1993, distributed by the National Bureau of Economic Research to update "The Penn World Table (Mark 5): An Expanded Set of International Comparisons, 1950–1988," Quarterly Journal of Economics, May 1991, 327–368; 1993–1998, World Economic Outlook, International Monetary Fund, Washington D.C., October, 1998.

Figure 11.3 also shows that China is catching up, but more slowly and from a very long way behind. In 1960, China's real GDP per person was one twentieth that of the United States, but by 1998 it was one eighth.

The four small Asian countries shown in Fig. 11.3 are like fast trains running on the same track at similar speeds and with a roughly constant gap between them. Hong Kong is the lead train and runs about 10 years in front of Taiwan, which is the last train. Real GDP per person in Taiwan in 1990 was similar to that in Hong Kong in 1980, ten years earlier. Between 1960 and 1999, Hong Kong transformed itself from a poor developing country into one of the world's richest countries.

China is now doing what Hong Kong has done. If China continues its rapid growth, the world economy will become a dramatically different place—China is equivalent to more than 200 countries the size of Hong Kong. Whether China will continue on its current path of rapid growth is impossible to predict.

R E V I E W   Q U I Z

- What is the average rate of economic growth in the United States over the past 100 years? In which periods was growth the most rapid and in which was it the slowest?

- Describe the gaps between real GDP per person in the United States and other countries. For which countries are the gaps narrowing? For which countries are the gaps widening? And for which countries are the gaps remaining unchanged?

- Compare the growth rates and levels of real GDP per person in Hong Kong, Korea, Singapore, Taiwan, China, and the United States. How far is China behind the other Asian economies?

The facts about economic growth in the United States and around the world raise some big questions that we're now going to answer. We'll study the causes of economic growth in three stages. First, we'll look at the preconditions for growth and the activities that sustain it. Second, we'll learn how economists measure the relative contributions of the sources of growth—an activity called *growth accounting*. And third, we'll study three theories of economic growth that seek to explain how the influences on growth interact to determine the growth rate.

The Causes of Economic Growth: A First Look

MOST HUMAN SOCIETIES HAVE LIVED FOR centuries and even thousands of years like Songman Yang, with no economic growth. The key reason is that they have lacked some fundamental social institutions and arrangements that are essential preconditions for economic growth. Let's see what these preconditions are.

Preconditions for Economic Growth

The most basic precondition for economic growth is an appropriate *incentive* system. Three institutions are crucial to the creation of incentives. They are:

1. Markets
2. Property rights
3. Monetary exchange

Markets enable buyers and sellers to get information and to do business with each other, and market prices send signals to buyers and sellers that create incentives to increase or decrease the quantities demanded and supplied. Markets enable people to specialize and trade and to save and invest. But for markets to work, we need property rights and monetary exchange.

Property rights are the social arrangements that govern the ownership, use, and disposal of resources and goods and services. They include the rights to physical property (land, buildings, and capital equipment), to financial property (claims by one person against another), and to intellectual property (such as inventions). Clearly established and enforced property rights give people an assurance that a capricious government will not confiscate their income or savings.

Monetary exchange facilitates transactions of all kinds, including the orderly transfer of private property from one person to another. Property rights and monetary exchange create incentives for people to specialize and trade, to save and invest, and to discover new technologies.

No unique political system is necessary to deliver the preconditions for economic growth. Liberal democracy, founded on the fundamental principle of the rule of law, is the system that does the best job. It provides a solid base on which property rights can be established and enforced. But authoritarian political systems have sometimes provided an environment in which economic growth has occurred.

Early human societies, based on hunting and gathering, did not experience economic growth because they lacked these preconditions. Economic growth began when societies evolved the three key institutions that create incentives. But the presence of an incentive system and the institutions that create it does not guarantee that economic growth will occur. It permits economic growth but does not make that growth inevitable.

The simplest way in which growth happens when the appropriate incentive system exists is that people begin to specialize in the activities at which they have a comparative advantage and trade with each other. You saw in Chapter 3 how everyone can gain from such activity. By specializing and trading, everyone can acquire goods and services at the lowest possible cost. Equivalently, people can obtain a greater volume of goods and services from their labor.

As an economy moves from one with little specialization to one that reaps the gains from specialization and exchange, its production and consumption grow. Real GDP per person increases, and the standard of living rises.

But for growth to be persistent, people must face incentives that encourage them to pursue three activities that generate ongoing economic growth. These activities are:

- Saving and investment in new capital
- Investment in human capital
- Discovery of new technologies

These three sources of growth, which interact with each other, are the primary sources of the extraordinary growth in productivity during the past 200 years. Let's look at each in turn.

Saving and Investment in New Capital

Saving and investment in new capital increase the amount of capital per worker and increase real GDP per hour of labor—labor productivity. Labor productivity took the most dramatic upturn when the amount of capital per worker increased during the Industrial Revolution. Production processes that use hand tools can create beautiful objects, but production methods that use large amounts of capital per worker, such as auto plant assembly lines, are much more productive.

The accumulation of capital on farms, in textile factories, in iron foundries and steel mills, in coal mines, on building sites, in chemical plants, in auto plants, in banks and insurance companies, and in shopping malls has added incredibly to the productivity of our economy. The next time you see a movie that's set in the Old West, look carefully at the small amount of capital around. Try to imagine how productive you would be in such circumstances compared with your productivity today.

Investment in Human Capital

Human capital—the accumulated skill and knowledge of human beings—is the most fundamental source of economic growth. It is a source of both increased productivity and technological advance.

The development of one of the most basic human skills—writing—was the source of some of the earliest major gains in productivity. The ability to keep written records made it possible to reap ever-larger gains from specialization and exchange. Imagine how hard it would be to do any kind of business if all the accounts, invoices, and agreements existed only in people's memories.

Later, the development of mathematics laid the foundation for the eventual extension of knowledge about physical forces and chemical and biological processes. This base of scientific knowledge was the foundation for the technological advances of the Industrial Revolution 200 years ago and of today's Information Revolution.

But much human capital that is extremely productive is much more humble. It takes the form of millions of individuals learning and repetitively doing simple production tasks and becoming remarkably more productive in the tasks.

One carefully studied example illustrates the importance of this kind of human capital. Between 1941 and 1944 (during World War II), U.S. shipyards produced some 2,500 units of a cargo ship, called the Liberty Ship, to a standardized design. In 1941, it took 1.2 million person-hours to build a ship. By 1942, it took 600,000, and by 1943, it took only 500,000. Not much change occurred in the capital employed during these years. But an enormous amount of human capital was accumulated. Thousands of workers and managers learned from experience and accumulated human capital that more than doubled their productivity in 2 years.

Discovery of New Technologies

Saving and investment in new capital and the accumulation of human capital have made a large contribution to economic growth. But the contribution of technological change—of the discovery and the application of new technologies and new goods—has made an even greater contribution.

People are many times more productive today than they were a hundred years ago. We are not more productive because we have more steam engines per person and more horse-drawn carriages per person. Rather, it is because we have the engines and transportation equipment that use technologies that were unknown a hundred years ago and that are more productive than the old technologies were. Technological change makes an enormous contribution to our increased productivity. It arises from formal research and development programs and from informal trial and error, and it involves discovering new ways of getting more out of our resources.

To reap the benefits of technological change, capital must increase. Some of the most powerful and far-reaching fundamental technologies are embodied in human capital—for example, language, writing, and mathematics. But most technologies are embodied in physical capital. For example, to reap the benefits of the internal combustion engine, millions of horse-drawn carriages and horses had to be replaced by automobiles; more recently, to reap the benefits of computerized word processing, millions of typewriters had to be replaced by PCs and printers.

REVIEW QUIZ

- What economic activities that lead to economic growth do markets, property rights, and monetary exchange facilitate?
- What are the roles of saving and investment in new capital, the growth of human capital, and the discovery of new technologies in economic growth?
- Provide some examples of how human capital has created new technologies that are embodied in both human and physical capital.

What is the quantitative contribution of the sources of economic growth? To answer this question, economists use growth accounting.

Growth Accounting

THE QUANTITY OF REAL GDP SUPPLIED (Y) depends on three factors:

1. The quantity of labor (N)
2. The quantity of capital (K)
3. The state of technology (T)

The purpose of **growth accounting** is to calculate how much real GDP growth results from growth of labor and capital and how much is attributable to technological change.

The key tool of growth accounting is the **aggregate production function**, which is written as the equation:

$$Y = F(N, K, T).$$

In words, the quantity of real GDP supplied is determined by (is a function F of) the quantities of labor and capital and of the state of technology. The larger N, K, or T, the greater is Y. And the faster N and K grow and the faster T advances, the faster Y grows.

So understanding what makes labor and capital grow and technology advance is the key to understanding economic growth. Labor growth depends primarily on population growth. And the growth rate of capital and the pace of technological advance determine the growth rate of labor productivity.

Labor Productivity

Labor productivity is real GDP per hour of work. It is calculated by dividing real GDP by aggregate labor hours. That is, labor productivity equals Y divided by N.

Labor productivity determines how much income an hour of labor generates. Figure 11.4 shows labor productivity for the period 1960–1998. You can see in this figure that productivity growth was most rapid during the 1960s and that it slowed down in 1973. You can also see that it speeded up again after 1983, but not to the pace of the 1960s.

Why did productivity grow fastest during the 1960s? Why did it slow down during the 1970s and then speed up again after 1983? Growth accounting answers these questions by dividing the growth in

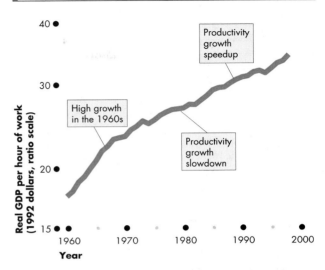

FIGURE 11.4
Real GDP per Hour of Work

Real GDP divided by aggregate hours equals real GDP per hour of work, which is a broad measure of productivity. During the 1960s, the productivity growth rate was high. It slowed during the 1970s and speeded up again after 1983.

Sources: U.S. Department of Commerce, *National Income and Product Accounts of the United States* (Washington, D.C.: U.S. Government Printing Office); U.S. Department of Labor, *Current Population Survey* (Washington, D.C.: U.S. Government Printing Office).

labor productivity into two components and then measuring the contribution of each. The components are:

- Growth in capital per hour of work
- Technological change

Technological change includes everything that contributes to labor productivity growth that is not included in growth in capital per hour. In particular, it includes human capital growth. Human capital growth and technological change are intimately related. Technology advances because knowledge advances. And knowledge is part of human capital. So "technological change" is a broad catchall concept.

The analytical engine of growth accounting is a relationship called the productivity function. Let's learn about this relationship and see how it is used.

The Productivity Function

The **productivity function** is a relationship that shows how real GDP per hour of labor changes as the amount of capital per hour of labor changes with a given state of technology. Figure 11.5 illustrates the productivity function. Capital per hour of work is measured on the *x*-axis, and real GDP per hour of work is measured on the *y*-axis. The figure shows *two* productivity functions. One is the curve labeled PF_0, and the other is the curve labeled PF_1.

An increase in the quantity of capital per hour of labor increases real GDP per hour of labor, which is shown by a movement along a productivity function. For example, on PF_0, when capital per hour of labor is $30, real GDP per hour of labor is $20. If capital per hour of labor increases to $60, real GDP per hour of labor increases to $25.

Technological change increases the amount of GDP per hour of labor that can be produced by a given amount of capital per hour of labor. It is shown by an upward shift of the productivity function. For example, if capital per hour of work is $30 and a technological change increases real GDP per hour of work from $20 to $25, the productivity function shifts upward from PF_0 to PF_1 in Fig. 11.5. Similarly, if capital per hour of work is $60, the same technological change increases real GDP per hour of work from $25 to $32 and shifts the productivity function upward from PF_0 to PF_1.

To calculate the contributions of capital growth and technological change to productivity growth, we need to know the shape and slope of the productivity function. The shape of the productivity function reflects a fundamental economic law—the law of diminishing returns. The **law of diminishing returns** states that as the quantity of one input increases with the quantities of all other inputs remaining the same, output increases but by ever smaller increments. For example, in a factory that has a given amount of capital, as more labor is hired, production increases. But each *additional* hour of labor produces less *additional* output than the previous hour produced. Two typists working with one computer type fewer than twice as many pages per day as one typist working with one computer.

Applied to capital, the law of diminishing returns states that if a given number of hours of labor use more capital (with the same technology), the *additional* output that results from the *additional* capital gets smaller as the amount of capital increases. One

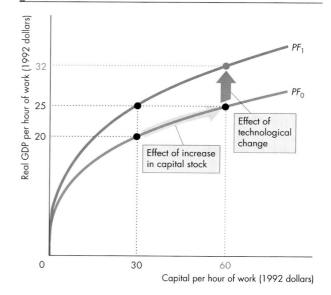

FIGURE 11.5

How Productivity Grows

Productivity is measured by real GDP per hour of work, and it can grow for two reasons: (1) Capital per hour of work increases, and (2) technological advances occur. The productivity function, PF_0, shows the effects of an increase in capital per hour of work on productivity. Here, when capital per hour of work increases from $30 to $60, real GDP per hour of work increases from $20 to $25 along the productivity curve PF_0. Technological advance shifts the productivity function upward. Here, an advance in technology shifts the productivity function from PF_0 to PF_1. With this technological advance, real GDP per hour of work increases from $25 to $32 when there is $60 of capital per hour of work.

typist working with two computers types fewer than twice as many pages per day as one typist working with one computer. More generally, one hour of labor working with $60 of capital produces less than twice the output of one hour of labor working with $30 of capital. But how much less? The answer is given by the *one third rule*.

The One Third Rule Robert Solow of MIT estimated a production function from U.S. data. He discovered that on the average, with no change in technology, a 1 percent increase in capital per hour of labor brings a *one third of 1 percent* increase in real GDP per hour of labor. This one third rule is used to calculate the contributions of an increase in capital per hour of work and technological change to the growth of real GDP. Let's do such a calculation.

Suppose that capital per hour of work grows by 3 percent a year and real GDP per hour of work grows by 2.5 percent a year. The one third rule tells us that capital growth has contributed one third of 3 percent, which is 1 percent. The rest of the 2.5 percent growth of real GDP comes from technological change. That is, technological change has contributed 1.5 percent, which is the 2.5 percent growth of real GDP per hour of work minus the estimated 1 percent contribution of capital growth.

Accounting for the Productivity Growth Slowdown and Speedup

We can use the one third rule to study U.S. productivity growth and the productivity growth slowdown. Figure 11.6 tells the story, starting in 1960.

1960 to 1973 In 1960, capital per hour of work was $56 and real GDP per hour of work was $18 at the point marked 60 on PF_0. During the next 13 years, real GDP per hour of work expanded by 40 percent to $25. At the same time, capital per hour of work increased by 30 percent to $74. With no change in technology, the economy would have moved to point a on PF_0 in Fig. 11.6, where real GDP per hour of work has increased by 10 percent (1/3 of 30 percent). But rapid technological change shifted the productivity curve upward to PF_1 and the economy moved to the point marked 73 on that curve.

1973 to 1983 During the 11 years from 1973 to 1983, real GDP per hour of work expanded by 8 percent to $27. At the same time, capital per hour of work increased by 15 percent to $86. With no change in technology, the economy would have moved to point b on PF_1 in Fig. 11.6, where real GDP per hour of work has increased by 5 percent (1/3 of 15 percent). But a tiny amount of technological change shifted the productivity curve upward to PF_2 and the economy moved to the point marked 83 on that curve.

We've now isolated the reason for the productivity growth slowdown. It occurred because the contribution of technological change to real GDP growth slowed.

1983 to 1998 During the 16 years from 1983 to 1998, real GDP per hour of work expanded by 22 percent to $33. At the same time, capital per hour of work increased by 14 percent to $98. With no change

FIGURE 11.6

Growth Accounting and the Productivity Growth Slowdown

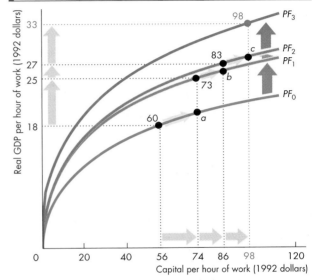

Between 1960 and 1973, which was a period of rapid productivity growth, capital per hour of work increased from $56 to $74, and technological progress shifted the productivity function upward from PF_0 to PF_1. Between 1973 and 1983, when potential GDP grew slowly, capital per hour of work increased from $74 to $86 and the productivity function barely shifted to PF_2. The effect of technological change was offset by oil price shocks. Between 1983 and 1998, capital per hour of work increased from $86 to $98, and technological progress shifted the productivity function upward from PF_2 to PF_3. Although productivity growth was not as rapid as in the 1960s, the productivity growth rate did increase.

Sources: U.S. Department of Commerce, *National Income and Product Accounts of the United States* (Washington, D.C.: U.S. Government Printing Office); U.S. Department of Labor, *Current Population Survey* (Washington, D.C.: U.S. Government Printing Office); and the author's calculations.

in technology, the economy would have moved to point c on PF_2 in Fig. 11.6, where real GDP per hour of work has increased by 4.5 percent (1/3 of 14 percent). But a return of more rapid technological change shifted the productivity curve upward to PF_3 and the economy moved to the point marked 98 on that curve. Although technological change resumed, its pace was slower than during the 1960s.

Technological Change During the Productivity Growth Slowdown

Technological change did not stop during the productivity growth slowdown. But its focus changed from increasing productivity to coping with:

- Energy price shocks
- The environment

Energy Price Shocks   Energy price increases that occurred in 1973–1974 and in 1979–1980 diverted research efforts toward saving energy rather than increasing productivity. Airplanes became more fuel efficient, but they didn't operate with smaller crews. Real GDP per gallon of fuel increased faster, but real GDP per hour of labor increased more slowly.

The Environment   The 1970s saw an expansion of laws and resources devoted to protecting the environment and improving the quality of the workplace. The benefits of these actions—cleaner air and water and safer factories—are not counted as real GDP. So the growth of these benefits is not measured as part of productivity growth.

Achieving Faster Growth

Growth accounting tells us that to achieve faster economic growth, we must either increase the growth rate of capital per hour of work or increase the pace of technological advance (which includes improving human capital). The main suggestions for achieving these objectives are:

- Stimulate saving
- Stimulate research and development
- Target high-technology industries
- Encourage international trade
- Improve the quality of education

Stimulate Saving   Saving finances investment, which brings capital accumulation. So stimulating saving can stimulate economic growth. The East Asian economies have the highest growth rates and saving rates. Some African economies have the lowest growth rates and saving rates.

Tax incentives can increase saving. Individual Retirement Accounts (IRAs) are an example of a tax incentive to save. Economists claim that a tax on consumption rather than on income provides the best saving incentive.

Stimulate Research and Development   Everyone can use the fruits of *basic* research and development efforts. For example, all biotechnology firms can use advances in gene-splicing technology. Because basic inventions can be copied, the inventor's profit is limited, and the market allocates too few resources to this activity.

Governments can direct public funds toward financing basic research, but this solution is not foolproof. It requires a mechanism for allocating the public funds to their highest-valued use. The National Science Foundation is one possibly efficient channel for allocating public funds to the universities to finance and stimulate basic research.

Target High-Technology Industries   Some people say that by providing public funds to high-technology firms and industries, a country can become the first to exploit a new technology and can earn above-average profits for a period while others are busy catching up. This strategy is risky and just as likely to use resources inefficiently as to speed growth.

Encourage International Trade   Free international trade stimulates growth by extracting all the available gains from specialization and exchange. The fastest-growing nations today are those with the fastest-growing exports and imports.

Improve the Quality of Education   The free market produces too little education because it brings benefits beyond those valued by the people who receive the education. By funding basic education and by ensuring high standards in basic skills such as language, mathematics, and science, governments can contribute to a nation's growth potential. Education can also be stimulated and improved by using tax incentives to encourage improved private provision.

R E V I E W   Q U I Z

- Explain the *one third* rule, and explain how it is used in growth accounting to isolate the contributions of capital growth and technological change to productivity growth.
- Explain how growth accounting can be used to provide information about the factors that contributed to the productivity growth slowdown of the 1970s. What does growth accounting tell us about why the slowdown occurred?

Growth Theories

WE'VE SEEN THAT REAL GDP GROWS WHEN THE quantities of labor and capital (which includes human capital) grow and when technology advances. Does this mean that the growth of labor and capital and technological advances *cause* economic growth? It might. But there are other possibilities. *One* of these factors might be the cause of real GDP growth and the others, the *effect*. We must try to discover how the influences on economic growth interact with each other to make some economies grow quickly and others grow slowly. And we must probe the reasons why a country's long-term growth rate sometimes speeds up and sometimes slows.

Growth theories are designed to study the interactions among the several factors that contribute to growth and to disentangle cause and effect. They are also designed to enable us to study the way in which the different factors influence each other.

Growth theories are also designed to be universal. They are not theories about the growth of poor countries only or rich countries only. They are theories about why and how poor countries become rich and rich countries continue to get richer.

We're going to study three theories of economic growth, each of which gives some insights about the process of economic growth. But none provides a definite answer to the basic questions: What causes economic growth and why do growth rates vary? Economics has some way to go before it can provide a definite answer to these most important of questions. The three growth theories that we study are:

- Classical growth theory
- Neoclassical growth theory
- New growth theory

Classical Growth Theory

Classical growth theory is the view that real GDP growth is temporary and that when real GDP per person rises above the subsistence level, a population explosion eventually brings real GDP per person back to the subsistence level. Adam Smith, Thomas Robert Malthus, and David Ricardo, the leading economists of the late eighteenth century and early nineteenth century, proposed this theory, but the view is most closely associated with the name of Malthus and is sometimes called the *Malthusian theory*.

Many people today are Malthusians! They say that if today's global population of 5 billion explodes to 11 billion by 2200, we will run out of resources and return to a primitive standard of living. We must act, say the Malthusians, to contain the population growth.

The Basic Idea To understand the basic idea of classical growth theory, let's transport ourselves back to the world of 1776, when Adam Smith is first explaining the idea. Most of the 2.5 million people who live in the newly independent United States of America work on farms or on their own land and perform their tasks using simple tools and animal power. They earn an average of 2 shillings (a bit less than $12 dollars in today's money) for working a 10-hour day.

Then advances in farming technology bring new types of plows and seeds that increase farm productivity. As farm productivity increases, farm production increases and some farm workers move from the land to the cities, where they get work producing and selling the expanding range of farm equipment. Incomes rise, and the people seem to be prospering. But will the prosperity last? Classical growth theory says that it will not.

Advances in technology—in both agriculture and industry—lead to an investment in new capital, which makes labor more productive. More and more businesses start up and hire the now more productive labor. The greater demand for labor raises the real wage rate and increases employment.

At this stage, economic growth has occurred and everyone has benefited from it. Real GDP has increased, and the real wage rate has increased. But the classical economists believe that this new situation can't last because it will induce a population explosion.

Classical Theory of Population Growth When the classical economists were developing their ideas about population growth, an unprecedented population explosion was under way. In Britain and other Western European countries, improvements in diet and hygiene had lowered the death rate while the birth rate remained high. For several decades, population growth was extremely rapid. For example, after being relatively stable for several centuries, the population of Britain increased by 40 percent between 1750 and 1800 and by a further 50 percent between 1800 and 1830. At the same time, an estimated 1 million people (about 20 percent of the 1750 population) left

Britain for America and Australia before 1800, and outward migration continued on a similar scale through the nineteenth century. These facts are the empirical basis for the classical theory of population growth.

To explain the high rate of population growth, the classical economists used the idea of a **subsistence real wage rate**, which is the minimum real wage rate needed to maintain life. If the actual real wage rate is less than the subsistence real wage rate, some people cannot survive and the population decreases. In classical theory, when the real wage rate exceeds the subsistence real wage rate, the population grows. But an increasing population increases the quantity of labor and brings diminishing returns to labor. So labor productivity eventually decreases. This dismal implication led to economics being called the *dismal science*. The dismal implication is that no matter how much technological change occurs, real wage rates are always pushed back toward the subsistence level.

Figure 11.7 illustrates the classical growth theory. Part (a) shows the situation before growth begins. The labor demand curve is LD_0, and the labor supply curve is LS_0. There is equilibrium in the labor market: The quantity of labor demanded equals the quantity supplied at a real wage rate of 2 shillings a day and 2 million people are employed. The subsistence real wage rate is (by assumption) 2 shillings a day. (We will use constant 1776 prices to keep this example in its historical context.)

Figure 11.7(a) also shows what happens when growth begins. Technological change and investment in new capital that make labor more productive increase the demand for labor, and the demand curve shifts rightward to LD_1. With this greater demand for labor, the real wage rate rises to 4 shillings a day, and this higher wage rate brings an increase in the quantity of labor supplied (a movement along the labor supply curve). Now 3 million people are employed.

Figure 11.7(b) shows what happens next, according to the Malthusians. The actual real wage rate, at the intersection of LS_0 and LD_1, is now 4 shillings a day. Because the actual real wage rate exceeds the subsistence real wage rate of 2 shillings a day, the population grows and the labor supply increases. The labor supply curve shifts rightward to LS_1. As it does so, the real wage rate falls and the quantity of labor demanded increases. Eventually, in the absence of further technological change, the economy comes to rest at the subsistence real wage rate of 2 shillings a day and 5 million people are employed.

FIGURE 11.7

Classical Growth Theory

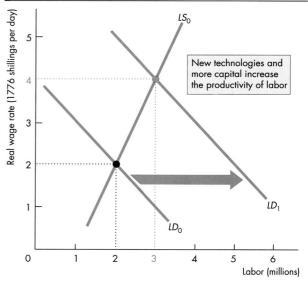

(a) Growth begins

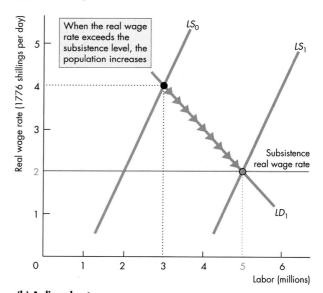

(b) A dismal outcome

Initially, 2 million people earn 2 shillings a day. The demand for labor increases to LD_1. The real wage rate rises to 4 shillings a day, and employment increases to 3 million (part a). With above subsistence real wages, the population increases. The labor supply curve shifts rightward toward LS_1. The real wage falls and the quantity of labor employed increases. Population growth stops when the subsistence real wage returns.

The economy has grown, real GDP has increased, but a larger population is earning only the subsistence real wage rate.

The classical growth theory, with its focus on the labor market and population, makes technological change and capital accumulation the engines of growth. But the classical theory ignores any influences that real GDP growth might have on the capital stock, investment, saving, and interest rates. The neoclassical theory corrects this omission. It demotes the labor market and places it in the background. Instead, it puts capital, investment, saving, and the interest rate at center stage. It explores the interactions among these capital market variables and the level and growth rate of real GDP. Let's now study neoclassical growth theory.

Neoclassical Growth Theory

Neoclassical growth theory is the proposition that that real GDP per person grows because technological change induces a level of saving and investment that makes capital per person grow. Growth ends if technological change stops.

Robert Solow of MIT suggested the most popular version of neoclassical growth theory during the 1950s. But Frank Ramsey of Cambridge University in England first developed this theory during the 1920s.

Neoclassical theory's big break with its classical predecessor is its view about population growth. So we'll begin our account of neoclassical theory by examining its views about population growth.

The Neoclassical Economics of Population Growth

The population explosion of eighteenth century Europe that created the classical theory of population eventually ended. The birth rate fell, and while the population continued to increase, its rate of increase became moderate. This slowdown in population growth seemed to make the classical theory increasingly less relevant. It also eventually led to the development of a modern economic theory of population growth.

The modern view is that although the population growth rate is influenced by economic factors, the influence is not a simple and mechanical one like that proposed by the classical economists. Key among the economic influences on population growth is the opportunity cost of a woman's time. As women's wage rates increase and their job opportunities expand, the opportunity cost of having children

increases. Faced with a higher opportunity cost, families choose to have a smaller number of children and the birth rate falls.

A second economic influence works on the death rate. The technological advance that brings increased productivity and increased incomes brings advances in health care that extends lives.

So two opposing economic forces influence population growth. As incomes increase, the birth rate decreases and the death rate decreases. It turns out that these opposing forces are almost offsetting, so to a good approximation, the rate of population growth is independent of the rate of economic growth.

This modern view of population growth and the historical trends that support it contradict the views of the classical economists. It also calls into question the modern doomsday conclusion that we will be one day swamped with too many people for the planet to feed.

Neoclassical growth theory adopts this modern view of population growth. Forces other than real GDP and its growth rate determine population growth.

Technological Change   In the neoclassical theory, the rate of technological change influences the rate of economic growth, but economic growth does not influence the pace of technological change. It is assumed that technological change results from chance. When we get lucky, we have rapid technological change, and when bad luck strikes, the pace of technological advance slows.

The Basic Idea   To understand the basic ideal of neoclassical growth theory, imagine the world of the mid-1950s, when Robert Solow is explaining his idea. Americans are enjoying post World War II prosperity. Income per person is around $12,000 a year in today's money. The population is growing at about 1 percent a year. People are saving and investing about 20 percent of their incomes. But income per person is not growing much.

Then technology begins to advance at a more rapid pace across a range of activities. The transistor revolutionizes an emerging electronics industry. New plastics revolutionize the manufacture of household appliances. Jet airliners start to replace piston-engine airplanes and speed transportation. Elvis revolutionizes popular music by inventing rock!

These technological advances bring new profit opportunities. Businesses expand, and new businesses are created to exploit the newly available profitable technologies. Investment and saving increase. The economy enjoys new levels of prosperity and growth. But will the prosperity last? And will the growth last? Neoclassical growth theory says that the prosperity will last but the growth will not unless technology keeps advancing.

According to the neoclassical growth theory, the prosperity will persist because there is no classical population growth induced to lower wages.

But growth will stop if technology stops advancing for two related reasons. First, high profit rates that result from technological change bring increased investment and capital accumulation. But second, capital accumulation eventually results in diminishing returns that lower the return on capital, and that eventually decreases saving and slows the rate of capital accumulation.

Figure 11.8 illustrates neoclassical growth theory. In part (a), the investment demand curve is ID_0 and the saving supply curve is SS_0. (See Chapter 10, pp. 208 and 211 for a refresher.) Equilibrium occurs at the point of intersection of ID_0 and SS_0 where the real interest rate is 4 percent a year and saving and investment equal $1 trillion a year. Suppose that this amount of investment is sufficient to replace depreciated capital. Net investment is zero, and the capital stock is constant. Real GDP per person is also constant.

Now a technological advance increases the productivity of capital and increases the expected profit rate. So investment demand increases, and the investment demand curve shifts rightward to ID_1. The real interest rate rises to 6 percent a year, and saving and investment increase to $1.5 trillion. Net investment is now positive, the capital stock is increasing, and real GDP is growing.

Now that real GDP is growing, rising disposable income and an increasing capital stock induce changes in saving and investment— the saving supply curve and the investment demand curve shift. We cannot keep track of all these changes by using the investment demand–saving supply figure. Instead, we look at two related demand and supply curves: the demand for and the supply of the *stock* of capital.

Investment demand is the demand for *newly produced* capital during a given time period. The demand for the *stock* of capital is the quantity of capital that people and businesses would like to have available for use at the end of a period. It is equal to the capital stock at the beginning of a period *plus* investment demand during the period.

Similarly, saving supply is the supply of funds to buy newly produced capital in a given time period. And the supply of the *stock* of capital is the quantity of funds (wealth) that people and businesses plan to

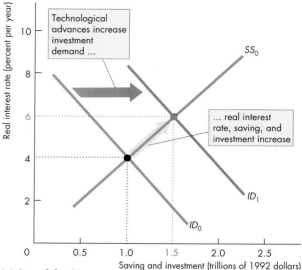

FIGURE 11.8

Neoclassical Growth Theory

(a) **Growth begins**

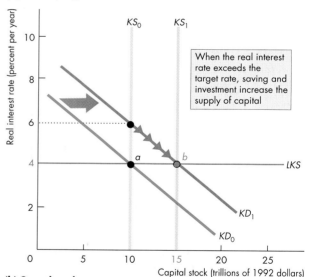

(b) **Growth ends**

Initially, investment is $1 trillion a year, the real interest rate is 4 percent a year, and the capital stock is $10 trillion. A technological advance increases investment demand to ID_1 and increases the demand for capital to KD_1. The real interest rate rises to 6 percent a year, investment increases to $1.5 trillion (part a), and the capital stock grows (part b). The KS curve shifts rightward toward KS_1 and the real interest rate falls. When the real interest rate equals the target rate, the capital stock is $15 trillion and growth ends.

own at the end of a period. It is equal to the quantity at the beginning of a period *plus* saving supply during the period.

Figure 11.8(b) shows the demand for the stock of capital KD_0. The lower the real interest rate, the greater is the quantity of capital demanded. This demand curve slopes downward for the same reason that the investment demand curve slopes downward.

At a given moment, the quantity of capital is given. It is the vertical line KS_0. In the long run, the supply of capital depends on saving decision.

Target Rate and Long-Run Saving   The neoclassical theory holds that if the real interest rate exceeds a *target rate*, the supply of capital increases; if the real interest rate is less than a target rate, the supply of capital decreases; and if the real interest rate equals a target rate, the supply of capital is constant. In Fig. 11.8(b), the target real interest rate is 4 percent a year and the long-run capital supply curve is LKS. If the real interest rate exceeds 4 percent a year, saving is positive, and the quantity of capital supplied persistently increases. And if the real interest rate is less than 4 percent a year, saving is negative, and the quantity of capital supplied persistently decreases. (Negative saving occurs and capital decreases when capital is not replaced as it wears out.)

Initially, equilibrium is at point *a*, where KD_0 and KS_0 intersect and where the real interest rate is 4 percent a year—its target rate. The capital stock is $10 trillion. Neoclassical growth begins from this point.

A technological advance now increases the productivity of capital, and the demand for capital curve shifts rightward to KD_1. The expected rate of profit increases. As a result, investment demand increases (shown in Fig. 11.8a). With greater investment, the supply of capital increases and the KS curve begins to shift rightward. As it does so, the real interest rate falls.

The capital stock continues to increase and the real interest rate continues to fall until the economy reaches point *b* in Fig. 11.8(b). Here, the real interest rate is back at its target rate of 4 percent a year and the capital stock has grown to $15 trillion. With no further growth of the capital stock, real GDP stops growing, and in the absence of another technological advance, growth ends.

Throughout the process you've just studied, real GDP grows but the growth rate gradually decreases and eventually ends. Ongoing technology advances are constantly increasing the demand for capital, raising the real interest rate, and inducing the saving that

increases the capital stock. The process repeats as long as technology advances and creates ongoing long-term economic growth. The growth rate fluctuates because technological progress occurs at a variable rate.

A Problem with Neoclassical Growth Theory   All economies have access to the same technologies, and capital is free to roam the globe seeking the highest available real interest rate. So neoclassical growth theory implies that growth rates and income levels per person around the globe will converge. While there is some sign of convergence among the rich countries (shown in Fig. 11.2a), convergence is slow, and it does not appear to be imminent for all countries (as we saw in Fig. 11.2b).

New growth theory attempts to overcome this shortcoming of neoclassical growth theory. It also attempts to explain how the rate of technological progress is determined.

New Growth Theory

New growth theory holds that real GDP per person grows because of the choices people make in the pursuit of profit and that growth can persist indefinitely. Paul Romer of Stanford University developed this theory during the 1980s, but the ideas go back to work by Joseph Schumpeter during the 1930s and 1940s.

The theory begins with two facts about market economies:

- Discoveries result from choices.
- Discoveries bring profit and competition destroys profit.

Discoveries and Choices   When people discover a new product or technique, they think of themselves as being lucky. They are right. But the pace at which new discoveries are made—and at which technology advances—is not determined by chance. It depends on how many people are looking for a new technology and how intensively they are looking.

Discoveries and Profits   Profit is the spur to technological change. The forces of competition squeeze profits, so to increase profit, people constantly seek either lower-cost methods of production or new and better products for which people are willing to pay a higher price. Inventors can maintain a profit for several years by taking out a patent or copyright. But eventually, a new discovery is copied, and profits disappear.

Two further facts play a key role in the new growth theory. They are:

- Discoveries can be used by many people at the same time.
- Physical activities can be replicated.

Discoveries Used by All   Once a profitable new discovery has been made, everyone can use it. And one person's use of a new discovery does not prevent others from using it. This fact means that as the benefits of a new discovery spread, free resources become available. These resources are free because nothing is given up when they are used. They have a zero opportunity cost.

Replicating Activities   Production activities can be replicated. For example, there might be two, three, or fifty-three identical firms making fiber-optic cable using an identical assembly line and production technique. If one firm increases its capital and output, that firm experiences diminishing returns. But the economy can increase its capital and output by adding another identical fiber-cable factory and the economy does not experience diminishing returns.

The assumption that capital does *not* experience diminishing returns is the central novel proposition of the new growth theory. And the implication of this simple and appealing idea is astonishing. In the neoclassical theory, with its diminishing returns to capital, as capital is accumulated, the real interest rate gradually falls until it equals the target real interest rate. At this point, growth stops. But the new growth theory has no such growth-stopping mechanism. As capital accumulates, the real interest rate is unaffected. It can remain above the target real interest rate indefinitely. Real GDP per person grows indefinitely as long as people can undertake research and development that yields a higher real interest rate than the target rate.

New growth theory sees the economy as a kind of perpetual motion mechanism. Economic growth is driven by our insatiable wants, which lead us to pursue profit and innovate. The result of this process is new and better products. But new and better products result in new firms starting up and old firms going out of business. In this process, jobs are created and destroyed. The outcome is new and better jobs, more leisure, and more consumption. But our insatiable wants are still there, so the process continues, going round and round a circle of wants, profits, innovation, and new products.

The growth rate depends on people's ability to innovate and the real interest rate. Over the years, this ability has changed. The invention of language and writing (the two most basic human capital tools), and later the development of the scientific method and the establishment of universities and research institutions, brought a huge increase in the real interest rate. Today, a deeper understanding of genes is bringing profit in a growing biotechnology industry. And astonishing advances in computer technology are creating an explosion of profit opportunities in a wide range of new information age industries.

Figure 11.9 illustrates new growth theory. Like Fig. 11.8(b), it shows the demand for and supply of the *stock* of capital. But unlike Fig. 11.8(b), here the marginal product of capital does not diminish as the quantity of capital increases. The demand curve for capital is horizontal at the real interest rate that equals the expected rate of profit. This expected profit rate does not change as the stock of capital changes. The horizontal demand for capital curve captures the special feature of the new growth theory that produces its novel prediction.

The supply of capital is fixed in the short run and is shown by a vertical supply curve such as KS_0. The long-run capital supply curve is horizontal at the target real interest rate and is LKS.

Initially, the real interest rate is 2 percent a year, and the line KD_0 in Fig. 11.9 shows the demand for capital. This real interest rate is below the target rate, so no one has an incentive to save. The economy is stuck at point a.

The development of basic human capital tools such as mathematics and physics increases the return to capital and innovation, and the demand for capital curve shifts upward to KD_1. The real interest rate now exceeds the target rate, and there is an incentive to save and invest. So investment and saving increase, and the quantity of capital grows. As it does so, the supply of capital curve shifts rightward through KS_0, KS_1, KS_2, KS_3, and so on. The capital stock grows, real GDP grows, and because there are no diminishing returns to capital, the real interest rate remains constant. Economic growth continues indefinitely as long as the real interest rate exceeds the target rate.

Figure 11.9 shows the process we've just described. The target real interest rate is 4 percent a year, and the real interest rate is 6 percent a year.

FIGURE 11.9

New Growth Theory

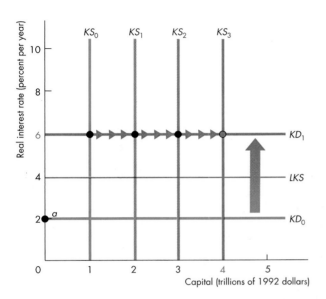

In new growth theory, economic growth results from incentives to innovate and from capital that does not experience diminishing returns. Initially, the real interest rate is 2 percent a year and the demand for capital is KD_0. The stock of capital is zero, and the economy is stuck at point a. The development of the scientific method increases the real interest rate to 6 percent a year, and the demand for capital increases to KD_1. With a real interest rate greater than the target real interest rate, saving increases and the supply of capital increases. The capital supply curve shifts rightward successively through KS_0, KS_1, KS_2, KS_3, and so on. As capital grows, real GDP grows, but the real interest rate does not fall because there are no diminishing returns. Real GDP growth continues indefinitely.

With positive saving, the capital supply curve shifts rightward indefinitely. The speed with which it shifts rightward depends on the extent to which the real interest rate exceeds the target rate. The higher the real interest rate, the more it exceeds that target rate and the faster the capital supply curve shifts rightward. So the faster the economy grows.

Sorting Out the Theories

Which theory is correct? Probably none is exactly correct. But they all teach us something of value. The classical theory reminds us that our physical resources are limited and that with no advances in technology, we must eventually hit diminishing returns. Neoclassical theory reaches essentially the same conclusion, but not because of a population explosion. Instead, it emphasizes potentially diminishing returns to capital and reminds us that we cannot necessarily keep growth going just by accumulating capital. New growth theory emphasizes the possible capacity of human resources to innovate at a pace that offsets diminishing returns.

REVIEW QUIZ

- What is the central idea of classical growth theory that leads to the dismal outcome?
- Explain the mechanism at work in the classical growth theory and describe the role played by diminishing returns.
- What, according to the neoclassical growth theory, is the fundamental cause of economic growth?
- What is the key proposition of the new growth theory that makes growth persist? Is the proposition believable? Is the conclusion believable?

◆ Economic growth is the single most decisive factor in influencing a country's living standard, but it is not the only one. Another is the extent to which the country fully employs its scarce resources, especially its labor. In recent years, the United States has enjoyed full employment and steady growth. But the business cycle is almost certainly not dead. And unemployment has become a severe problem for many countries. In Part 5, we study the fluctuations of real GDP and employment and unemployment around their long-term trends. But before embarking on this new topic, take a look at *Reading Between the Lines* on pages 242–243 and see how the Internet is contributing to the growth of our economy today.

Growth in the Internet Economy

THE NEW YORK TIMES, APRIL 5, 1999

Tech Stocks Fuel Market Gain

NEW YORK—The stock market's torrid affair with technology and Internet companies continued Monday, lifting the three main gauges of stock market performance to records, with the Dow Jones industrial average closing above 10,000 for the second time ever.

Among the biggest gainers was Internet portal Yahoo, which jumped $39.38 to $219.13 on news that the company plans to extend its reach beyond personal computers to hand-held devices and television-based Internet appliances like WebTV.

The Internet sector got an extra boost from a report that more individual investors are turning to the Internet to trade, casting aside their reliance on traditional stock brokers.

"The Internet stocks are running the show," said Barry Hyman, market strategist at Ehrenkrantz, King & Nussbaum. ...

For the most part, the biggest gains were concentrated among the largest and best-known leaders of a select group of industries, from IBM and Microsoft to Intel, Lucent and America Online. Several financial-services stocks also soared. ...

■ Stock prices increased during April 1999 to record levels, and the Dow Jones industrial average closed above 10,000.

■ The biggest gains were concentrated in technology and Internet stocks such as IBM, Microsoft, Intel, Lucent, America Online, Yahoo, and providers of financial services.

■ Yahoo had one of the biggest price increases— up $39.38 to $219.13— when the company announced plans to develop services for hand-held devices and television-based Internet appliances.

■ A report that more individual investors are switching from traditional stockbrokers to Internet trading also boosted Internet stock prices.

■ The extraordinary growth of stock prices, especially for Internet firms, is based on the equally extraordinary growth of the Internet.

■ And the growth of the Internet is one aspect of the growth of the U.S. and global economies during the 1990s.

■ Figure 1 shows the growth of the Internet on two measures. One measure is the number of host computers, which grew from 1.3 million in 1993 to 43.2 million in 1999, a growth rate of 5.0 percent *per month*. This growth rate doubles the size of the Internet every 14 months!

■ The other measure is consumer expenditure on the Internet, which increased 10-fold between 1990 and 1998.

■ The growth of the Internet is one element in overall economic growth in the United States.

■ Figure 2 shows real GDP from 1987 to 1998. The growth rate of real GDP was 2.06 percent a year between 1987 and 1992 (before the Internet took off). It was 3.26 percent a year between 1993 and 1998 (after the Internet took off).

■ Although real GDP growth increased after 1993, it is too early to tell whether potential GDP growth has increased as well. In 1992, the economy was still recovering from the 1990–1991 recession and the unemployment rate was more than 7 percent. By 1996, the unemployment rate had fallen to 5.5 percent. We will not be able to say whether the *growth rate* of potential GDP has increased until we can see the current business cycle in a longer-term perspective.

■ Although we cannot determine whether the *growth rate* of potential GDP has increased, it is undeniable that the Internet has had a positive effect on the *level* of potential GDP.

■ The new technologies that are helping the Internet to grow are available for everyone to use. And the opportunity cost of using these technologies is low.

■ Also, the human capital and physical capital that the Internet uses are probably not yet experiencing diminishing returns and perhaps will not do so for a long time.

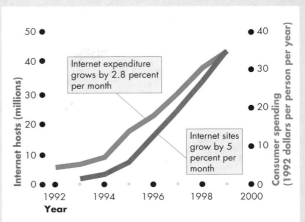

Figure 1 Growth of the Internet

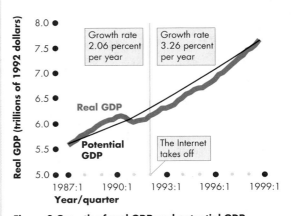

Figure 2 Growth of real GDP and potential GDP

■ It is possible that these new technologies have increased the rate of profit. If they have done so, they might have created a new growth environment in which the U.S. economy will expand at a more rapid rate than it did previously.

■ The evidence is not yet present in the GDP data. But current estimates of real GDP might understate its true growth rate.

SUMMARY

KEY POINTS

Long-Term Growth Trends (pp. 226–228)

- Between 1895 and 1998, real GDP per person in the United States grew at an average rate of 2 percent a year. Growth was fastest during the 1920s and 1960s.

- The real GDP gaps between the United States and Africa as well as Central and South America have widened. The gaps between the United States and Hong Kong, Korea, Taiwan, and China have narrowed.

The Causes of Economic Growth: A First Look (pp. 229–230)

- Economic growth requires an *incentive* system created by markets, property rights, and monetary exchange.

- Economic growth occurs when people save, invest in physical and human capital, and discover new technologies.

Growth Accounting (pp. 231–234)

- Growth accounting measures the contributions of capital accumulation and technological change to productivity growth.

- Growth accounting uses the productivity function and the *one third rule:* A 1 percent increase in capital per hour of work brings a 1/3 percent increase in real GDP per hour of work.

- During the productivity growth slowdown of the 1970s, technological change made no contribution to real GDP growth.

- It might be possible to achieve faster growth by stimulating saving, subsidizing research and development, targeting (and possibly subsidizing) high-technology industries, and encouraging more international trade.

Growth Theories (pp. 235–241)

- In classical theory, when technological advances increase real GDP per person above the *subsistence* level, a population explosion brings diminishing returns to labor and real GDP per person returns to the subsistence level.

- In neoclassical growth theory, when technological advances increase saving and investment, an increase in the capital stock brings diminishing returns to capital, and eventually, without further technological change, the capital stock and real GDP per person stop growing.

- In new growth theory, when technological advances increase saving and investment, an increase in the capital stock *does not* bring diminishing returns to capital and growth persists indefinitely.

KEY FIGURES

KEY TERMS

PROBLEMS

*1. The following information has been discovered about the economy of Longland: The economy's productivity function is:

Capital per hour of work (1997 dollars per hour)	Real GDP per hour of work (1997 dollars per hour)
10	3.80
20	5.70
30	7.13
40	8.31
50	9.35
60	10.29
70	11.14
80	11.94

Does this economy conform to the one third rule? If so, explain why. If not, explain why not and explain what rule, if any, it does conform to. Explain how you would do the growth accounting for this economy.

2. The following information has been discovered about the economy of Flatland: The economy's productivity function is:

Capital per hour of work (1997 dollars per hour)	Real GDP per hour of work (1997 dollars per hour)
10	3.00
20	3.75
30	4.22
40	4.57
50	4.86
60	5.10
70	5.31
80	5.50

Does this economy conform to the one third rule? If so, explain why. If not, explain why not and explain what rule, if any, it does conform to. Explain how you would do the growth accounting for this economy.

*3. In Longland, described in problem 1, capital per hour of work in 1999 was $40 and real GDP per hour of work was $8.31. In 2001, capital per hour of work had increased to $50 and real GDP per hour of work had increased to $10.29 an hour.
   a. Does Longland experience diminishing returns? Explain why or why not.

   b. Use growth accounting to find the contribution of the change in capital between 1999 and 2001 to the growth of productivity in Longland.
   c. Use growth accounting to find the contribution of technological change between 1999 and 2001 to the growth of productivity in Longland.

4. In Flatland, described in problem 2, capital per hour of work in 1999 was $30 and real GDP per hour of work was $4.22. In 2001, capital per hour of work had increased to $60 and real GDP per hour of work had increased to $6.37 an hour.
   a. Does Flatland experience diminishing returns? Explain why or why not.
   b. Use growth accounting to find the contribution of the change in capital between 1999 and 2001 to the growth of productivity in Flatland.
   c. Use growth accounting to find the contribution of technological change between 1999 and 2001 to the growth of productivity in Flatland.

*5. The following information has been discovered about the economy of Cape Despair. The subsistence real wage rate is $7 an hour. Whenever the real wage rate rises above this level, the population grows; when the real wage rate falls below this level, the population falls. With its current population, the demand and supply schedules for labor in Cape Despair are as follows:

Real wage rate (1992 dollars per hour)	Quantity of labor demanded (billions of hours per year)	Quantity of labor supplied (billions of hours per year)
3	8	4
5	7	5
7	6	6
9	5	7
11	4	8
13	3	9
15	2	10
17	1	11

Initially, the labor force of Cape Despair is constant, and the real wage is at its subsistence level. Then a technological advance increases the amount that firms are willing to pay for labor by $2 at each level of employment.

a. What is the initial level of employment and real wage rate in Cape Despair?
b. What happens to the real wage rate immediately following the technological advance?
c. What happens to the population growth rate following the technological advance?
d. What is the employment level when Cape Despair returns to a long-run equilibrium?

6. Martha's Island is an economy that behaves according to the neoclassical growth model. The economy is in long-run equilibrium and is described in the following table.

Real interest rate (percent per year)	Quantity of capital demanded (billions of dollars)	Quantity of capital (billions of dollars)
1	9	7
2	8	7
3	7	7
4	6	7
5	5	7
6	4	7
7	3	7
8	2	7

a. What is the real interest rate on Martha's Island?
b. What is the target rate?

A technological advance increases the demand for capital by $2 billion at each real interest rate.

c. What is the real interest rate immediately following the technological advance?
d. What is the real interest rate and quantity of capital when Martha's Island returns to a long-run equilibrium?

*7. Romeria is a country that behaves according to the predictions of new growth theory. The target real interest rate is 3 percent a year. A technological advance increases the demand for capital and raises the real interest rate to 5 percent a year. Describe the events that happen in Romeria and contrast them with the events in Martha's Island in problem 6.

8. Suppose that in Romeria, which is described in problem 7, technological advance slows and the real interest rate falls to 3 percent a year. Describe what happens in Romeria.

CRITICAL THINKING

1. After studying *Reading Between the Lines* on pp. 242–243, answer the following questions:
   a. How quickly is the Internet growing in comparison with the growth of real GDP?
   b. Are the measures of growth of the Internet in Figure 1 comparable with the measure of the growth of real GDP in Figure 2? (Hint: Think about what real GDP measures.)
   c. What information about growth of the Internet would you need to determine the contribution of the Internet to real GDP?
   d. Suppose that the arrival of the Internet increases the growth rate of potential GDP. What, according to each of the three economic growth theories—classical, neoclassical, and new—will happen in the longer term?

2. Use the link on the Parkin Web site to visit the Penn World Table and obtain data on real GDP per person for the United States, China, South Africa, and Mexico since 1960.
   a. Draw a graph of the data.
   b. Which country has the lowest real GDP per person and which has the highest?
   c. Which country has experienced the fastest growth rate since 1960 and which has experienced the slowest?
   d. Explain why the growth rates in these four countries are ranked on the order you have discovered?
   e. Return to the Penn World Table Web site and obtain data for any four other countries that interest you. Describe and explain the patterns that you find for these countries.

3. Write a memo to your member of Congress in which you set out the policies you believe the U.S. government must follow to speed up the growth rate of real GDP in the United States. Explain how each policy would work.

4. Is faster economic growth always a good thing? Argue the case for faster growth and for slower growth, and then reach a conclusion on whether growth should be increased or decreased.

Understanding Aggregate Supply and Economic Growth

Expanding the Frontier

Economics is about how we cope with scarcity. We cope by making choices that balance marginal benefits and marginal costs so that we use our scarce resources efficiently. ◆ These choices determine how much work we do, how hard we work at school to learn the mental skills that form our human capital and that determine the kinds of jobs we get and the incomes we earn; and how much we save for future big-ticket expenditures. These choices also determine how much businesses and governments spend on new capital—on auto assembly lines, computers and fiber cables for improved Internet services, shopping malls, highways, bridges, and tunnels; and how intensively existing capital and natural resources are used and therefore how quickly they wear out or are used up. Most significant of all, these choices determine the problems that scientists, engineers, and other inventors work on to develop new technologies. ◆ All the choices we've just described determine two vital measures of economic performance:

- Real GDP
- Economic growth

Real GDP is determined by the quantity of labor, the quantity of capital, and the state of technological knowledge. And economic growth—the growth rate of real GDP—is determined by growth in the quantity of labor, capital accumulation, and technological advances. ◆ Economic growth, maintained at a steady rate over a number of decades, is the single most powerful influence on any society. It brings a transformation that continues to amaze thoughtful people. Economic growth that is maintained at a rapid rate can transform a society in years, not decades. Such transformations are taking place right now in many Asian countries. These transformations are economic miracles. ◆ The three chapters in this part studied the miracle of rapid economic growth and the forces that shape our capacity to produce goods and services. ◆ Chapter 9 explained how potential GDP and the full-employment quantity of labor, employment, and unemployment are determined by equilibrium in the labor market. ◆ Chapter 10 explained how capital accumulation results from saving and investment decisions that are coordinated in a global capital market. Some countries don't save enough to pay for the capital they accumulate; others save more than they need. And the international capital market moves savings to the places in which they obtain the highest available real interest rate. ◆ Chapter 11 studied the process of economic growth in the fast-growing economies of Asia and the United States. It explained how growth is influenced by technological change and the incentives that stimulate it. ◆ Modern ideas about economic growth owe much to two economists, Joseph Schumpeter and Paul Romer, whom you can meet on the following pages.

Incentives to Innovate

> "Economic progress, in capitalist society, means turmoil."
>
> JOSEPH SCHUMPETER
> *Capitalism, Socialism, and Democracy*

Joseph Schumpeter, *the son of a textile factory owner, was born in Austria in 1883. He moved from Austria to Germany during the tumultuous 1920s when those two countries experienced hyperinflation. In 1932, in the depths of the Great Depression, he came to the United States and became a professor of economics at Harvard University.*

This creative economic thinker wrote about economic growth and development, business cycles, political systems, and economic biography. He was a person of strong opinions who expressed them strongly and delighted in verbal battles.

Schumpeter has become the unwitting founder of modern growth theory. He saw the development and diffusion of new technologies by profit-seeking entrepreneurs as the source of economic progress. But he saw economic progress as a process of creative destruction—the creation of new profit opportunities and the destruction of currently profitable businesses. For Schumpeter, economic growth and the business cycle were a single phenomenon.

When Schumpeter died, in 1950, he had achieved his self-expressed life ambition: He was regarded as the world's greatest economist.

The Issues

Technological change, capital accumulation, and population growth all interact to produce economic growth. But what is cause and what is effect? And can we expect productivity and income per person to keep growing?

The classical economists of the eighteenth and nineteenth centuries believed that technological advances and capital accumulation were the engines of growth. But they also believed that no matter how successful people were at inventing more productive technologies and investing in new capital, they were destined to live at the subsistence level. These economists based their conclusion on the belief that productivity growth causes population growth, which in turn causes productivity to decline. These classical economists believed that whenever economic growth raises incomes above the subsistence level, the population will increase. They went on to reason that the increase in population brings diminishing returns that lower productivity. As a result, incomes must always return to the subsistence level. Only when incomes are at the subsistence level is population growth held in check.

A new approach, called neoclassical growth theory, was developed by Robert Solow of MIT, during the 1950s. Solow, who was one of Schumpeter's students, received the Nobel Prize for Economic Science for this work.

Solow challenged the conclusions of the classical economists. But the new theories of economic growth developed during the 1980s and 1990s went further. They stand the classical belief on its head. Today's theory of population growth is that rising income slows the population growth rate because it increases the opportunity cost of having children and lowers the opportunity cost of investing in children and equipping them with more human capital, which makes them more productive. Productivity and income grow because technology advances, and the scope for further productivity growth, which is stimulated by the search for profit, is practically unlimited.

Now

Today's technologies are expanding our horizons beyond the confines of our planet and are expanding our minds. Geosynchronous satellites bring us global television, voice and data communication, and more accurate weather forecasts, which, incidentally, increase agricultural productivity. In the foreseeable future, we might have superconductors that revolutionize the use of electric power, virtual reality theme parks and training facilities, pollution-free hydrogen cars, wristwatch telephones, and optical computers that we can talk to. Equipped with these new technologies, our ability to create yet more dazzling technologies increases. Technological change begets technological change in an (apparently) unending process and makes us ever more productive and brings ever higher incomes.

Then

In 1830, a strong and experienced farm worker could harvest three acres of wheat in a day. The only capital employed was a scythe to cut the wheat, which had been used since Roman times, and a cradle on which the stalks were laid, which had been invented by Flemish farmers in the fifteenth century. With newly developed horse-drawn plows, harrows, and planters, farmers could plant more wheat than they could harvest. But despite big efforts, no one had been able to make a machine that could replicate the swing of a scythe. Then in 1831, 22-year-old Cyrus McCormick built a machine that worked. It scared the horse that pulled it, but it did in a matter of hours what three men could accomplish in a day. Technological change has increased productivity on farms and brought economic growth. Do the facts about productivity growth mean that the classical economists, who believed that diminishing returns would push us relentlessly back to a subsistence living standard, were wrong?

Today's revolution in the way economists think about economic growth has been led by Paul Romer, a professor of economics at Stanford University, whom you can meet on the following pages.

249

Paul Romer *is Professor of Economics at the Graduate School of Business at Stanford University and the Royal Bank Fellow of the Canadian Institute for Advanced Research. Born in 1955 in Denver, Colorado, he earned his B.S. in Mathematics (1977) and his Ph.D. in Economics (1983) from the University of Chicago. Professor Romer has transformed the way economists think about economic growth. He believes that sustained economic growth arises from competition among firms. Firms try to increase their profits by devoting resources to creating new products and developing new ways of making existing products.*

Michael Parkin talked with Professor Romer about his work, how he was influenced by Joseph Schumpeter and Robert Solow, and the insights economic growth offers us.

Professor Romer, why did you decide to become an economist?
As an undergraduate, I studied math and physics and was interested in becoming a cosmologist. During my senior year, I concluded that job prospects in physics were not very promising, so I decided to go to law school. I was an undergraduate at the University of Chicago, where the law and economics movement first emerged. In the fall of my senior year, I took my first economics course to prepare for law school. My economics professor, Sam Peltzman, presented a simple piece of economic analysis that changed my life. He argued that the demand for economists was likely to grow for decades. The government, which employs economists, would grow in size. Businesses that deal with the government would want their own economists. The legal profession that serves businesses would also need more economists. Because of all these demands, many students would want to take economics courses. This meant that there would be many job openings for economists at universities. Moreover, he claimed, being a professor of economics was a lot like being a cosmologist and far more fun than being a lawyer. I could take fragmentary bits of evidence and try to make sense of them using mathematical equations. So I tore up my law school applications, applied to graduate school in economics, and never looked back.

What are the truly important lessons about the causes of economic growth?
As a physics major, I felt that the description economists used for growth violated a basic law of physics: the conservation of mass. Economists seemed to be saying that GDP, the output of a nation, was a bunch of stuff that was "produced" and that the quantity of stuff produced has grown steadily over time and will continue to do so. But this can't be right. We have the same amount of stuff, or elements from the periodic table, that we had 100,000 years ago because there are many more

Paul Romer

people now. In terms of kilograms of matter per person, we know that we are vastly poorer than our ancestors were 100,000 years ago. Yet we clearly have a higher standard of living. How could this be? This basic question indicates that thinking about growth as a production process that generates stuff is a dead-end. Instead, economic growth has to be about rearranging the fixed amount of matter that we have to work with and making new combinations that seem a lot more valuable. The key insight is that economic growth comes from increases in value, not increases in the amount of matter.

Can you give us an example of an increase in value?

For tens of thousands of years, we treated iron oxide, ordinary rust, like dirt. When we lived in caves, we learned how to use it as a pigment for decorating cave walls. We took the low-value dirt and put it to the higher-valued use of making cave paintings. Later, we learned how to extract the iron from iron ore to make bridges and rails. Later still, we learned how to arrange the iron atoms together with carbon atoms and make steel. Recently, we learned how to take iron oxide and put it on magnetic tape and use it to store sound and pictures. The iron, oxygen, and carbon atoms have always been here. We have a higher standard of living because we have learned how to arrange these atoms in ways that we find more valuable.

What kind of policy implications does this kind of thinking lead to?

Policy makers must encourage institutions to become more efficient at discovering new recipes to rearrange matter. Consider the transistor as an example. We take silicon and mix it with a few impurities and some metal in just the right way, and we get a computer chip worth thousands of times what the raw ingredients were worth. Research grants, subsidies for education, and institutions like the nonprofit private university encourage the production of new recipes or ideas. But so do venture capitalists who help new-technology startups, competitive markets that allow the firms with better instructions or ideas to quickly displace existing firms,

> We take silicon and mix it with a few impurities and some metal in just the right way, and we get a computer chip worth thousands of times what the raw ingredients were worth.

and labor laws that let inefficient firms lay off workers when more efficient new firms come on the scene. We must let firms like Digital Electronics or Wang Computers shrink, maybe even fail, if we want to make room for new firms like Intel to enter the scene and thrive.

Were the classical economists wrong in their view that population growth and diminishing returns are the dominant long-term influences on production and incomes? Or is the current global population explosion part of a process that will ultimately prove them correct?

Classical economists like Malthus and Ricardo were right when they argued that we have a fixed amount of natural resources to work with. Malthus pointed out that resource scarcity will lead to falling standards of living if we continue to work with the same set of recipes or instructions for using our resources. Where he went wrong was in assuming that there was little scope for us to find new recipes for taking resources such as land, water, carbon dioxide, nitrogen, and sunshine and converting them into carbohydrates and proteins that we can eat.

The classical economists got half of the story right. We do live in a world with scarce resources. They missed the other half. There is an incomprehensibly large number of different formulas we can use to recombine these scarce resources into things we value, such as protein or entertainment.

Scarcity is a very important part of economics and our lives. For example, we know that there is an absolute limit on the number of people who can live on the earth. One way or another, we know that the rate of population growth will slow down. It's only a question of how and when. But will this ultimately lead to a period when standards of living fall as Malthus predicted? I doubt it. As countries get rich, population growth slows. As a larger fraction of the worldwide population becomes educated, these people will help us to discover new things, like plants that are more efficient at taking carbon dioxide out of the atmosphere, and more efficient distribution systems. Thus standards of living for all humans will continue to improve.

During the past decade, China and several other economies in East Asia have experienced rapid, unheralded growth rates. Why?
These countries took some of the recipes, formulas, and instructions for generating value that already existed in the advanced countries of the world and put them to use within their borders. It's the same process that the Japanese followed after the Meiji restoration at the end of the last century. These countries noticed that other people in the world knew a lot about how to create value and realized that by trading with these people, they could share in the gains.

What lessons from East Asia can, in principle, be applied in Africa and Central Europe?
The basic insight is that there are huge potential gains from trade. Poor countries can supply their natural and human resources. Rich countries can supply their know-how. When these are combined, everyone can be better off. The challenge is for a country to arrange its laws and institutions so that both sides can profitably engage in trade. If there are barriers to trade or if the government cannot protect basic property rights and prevent crime, trade can't take place. For example, the Japanese have been able to borrow many ideas about manufacturing and design and even to improve on some of these ideas. But because they have barriers that limit entry of foreign firms into the retail sector, they still waste vast quantities of resources on a very inefficient distribution system.

What does today's thinking about economic growth owe to Joseph Schumpeter and Robert Solow?
Schumpeter worked at a time before most economists had learned to work with equations. He coined the phrase "creative destruction," which describes the process by which companies like Wang shrink or go out of business when new firms come in. He also described in words how important monopoly profits are in the process of innovation. There were many other economists, including Alfred Marshall, who described these same issues in verbal terms and also struggled to express these ideas in terms of equations.

Robert Solow was part of the post–World War II generation of economists who truly mastered the use of equations and wrote eloquently using both words and equations. As a result, his ideas have been far more influential than Schumpeter's. Many economists in the 1950s were trying to get a grasp on the economic effects of knowledge, formulas, recipes, and instructions. Solow called these things "technology" and gave us a wonderfully concise and workable way to think about how technology interacts with other economic inputs such as capital and labor. He also linked the methods that he and several economists were using to measure technology with this framework for thinking about the behavior of the economy as a whole. His work on growth was a masterful piece of invention, synthesis, and exposition.

Recent economists have taken Solow's mathematical framework and extended it to bring in some of the elements that Schumpeter described in words, like creative destruction and monopoly power. One of the great things about ideas is that they build on each other. In Isaac Newton's famous phrase, those of us working on growth today are "able to see farther because we stand on the shoulders of giants." Newton was another person who was pretty good with equations and could turn a good phrase.

Is economics a worthwhile subject to major in? What can one do with an economics degree?
Economics is an excellent training ground for developing mathematical and verbal skills. But students should supplement the courses in

> If you can learn how to write readable prose and use the basic tools of mathematics, you can do almost anything.

economics with courses in mathematics and science that force them to practice working with equations, graphs, and numbers. There is no substitute for such practice. Innate ability is far less important than most students think.

They should also take courses that force them to write, revise, and edit. I took an English course in college that taught me the basics of how to edit, and it is one of the best investments I made. You can't tell what you will end up doing or what skills you will need later in life. But if you can learn how to write readable prose and use the basic tools of mathematics, you can do almost anything.

Chapter 12

Expenditure Multipliers

In the Red Rocks Amphitheater in Denver, Bonnie Raitt sings into a microphone in a barely audible whisper. Moving to a louder passage, she increases the volume of her voice and now, through the magic of electronic amplification, booms across the stadium, drowning out every other sound. ◆ Dennis Archer, the mayor of Detroit, and a secretary are being driven to a business meeting along one of the city's less well-repaired highways. (There are some badly potholed highways in Detroit.) The car's wheels are bouncing and vibrating over some of the worst highways in the nation, but its passengers are completely undisturbed and the secretary's notes are written without a ripple, thanks to the car's efficient shock absorbers. ◆ Investment and exports fluctuate like the volume of Bonnie Raitt's voice and the uneven surface of a Detroit highway. How does the economy react to those fluctuations? Does it react like Dennis Archer's limousine, absorbing the shocks and providing a smooth ride for the economy's passengers? Or does it behave like Bonnie Raitt's amplifier, blowing up the fluctuations and spreading them out to affect the many millions of participants in an economic rock concert?

Amplifier or Shock Absorber?

◆ You will explore these questions in this chapter. You will learn how a recession or a recovery begins when a change in investment or exports triggers a larger change in *aggregate* expenditure and real GDP—like Bonnie Raitt's amplifier. You will also learn how imports and income taxes have lowered the power of the amplifier. Finally, you will discover that in contrast to the initial amplification effect, the economy's shock absorbers, which are price and wage changes, pull real GDP back toward potential GDP. ◆ To achieve these objectives, we use a model called the *aggregate expenditure model*. This model explains changes in aggregate expenditure in a very short time frame during which prices do not change.

After studying this chapter, you will be able to:

- Explain how expenditure plans are determined

- Explain how real GDP is determined when the price level is fixed

- Explain the multiplier

- Explain how imports and taxes influence the multiplier

- Explain how recessions and expansions begin

- Explain the relationship between aggregate expenditure and aggregate demand

- Explain how the multiplier gets smaller as the price level changes

Fixed Prices and Expenditure Plans

MOST FIRMS ARE LIKE YOUR LOCAL SUPERMARKET. They set their prices, advertise their products and services, and sell the quantities their customers are willing to buy. If firms persistently sell a greater quantity than they plan to and are constantly running out of inventory, they eventually raise their prices. And if firms persistently sell a smaller quantity than they plan to and have inventories piling up, they eventually cut their prices. But in the very short term, their prices are fixed. They hold the prices they have set, and the quantities they sell depend on demand, not supply.

The Aggregate Implications of Fixed Prices

Fixed prices have two immediate implications for the economy as a whole:

1. Because each firm's price is fixed, the *price level* is fixed.
2. Because demand determines the quantities that each firm sells, *aggregate demand* determines the aggregate quantity of goods and services sold, which equals real GDP.

So to understand the fluctuations in real GDP when the price level is fixed, we must understand aggregate demand fluctuations. The aggregate expenditure model explains fluctuations in aggregate demand by identifying the forces that determine expenditure plans.

Expenditure Plans

The components of aggregate expenditure are:

- Consumption expenditure
- Investment
- Government purchases of goods and services
- Net exports (exports *minus* imports)

These four components of aggregate expenditure sum to real GDP (see Chapter 6, pp. 118–119).

Aggregate planned expenditure is equal to *planned* consumption expenditure plus *planned* investment plus *planned* government purchases plus *planned* exports minus *planned* imports.

In the very short term, *planned* investment, *planned* government purchases, and *planned* exports are fixed. But *planned* consumption expenditure and *planned* imports are not fixed. They depend on the level of real GDP itself.

A Two-Way Link Between Aggregate Expenditure and GDP Because real GDP influences consumption expenditure and imports and because consumption expenditure and imports are components of aggregate expenditure, there is a two-way link between aggregate expenditure and GDP. Other things remaining the same:

- An increase in real GDP increases aggregate planned expenditure.
- An increase in aggregate expenditure increases real GDP.

You are going to learn how this two-way link between aggregate expenditure and real GDP determines real GDP when the price level is fixed. The starting point is to consider the first piece of the two-way link: the influence of real GDP on planned consumption expenditure and saving.

Consumption Function and Saving Function

Several factors influence consumption expenditure and saving. The more important ones are:

- Real interest rate
- Disposable income
- Purchasing power of net assets
- Expected future income

Chapter 10 (see p. 212) explains how these factors influence consumption expenditure and saving. The second factor, **disposable income**, is aggregate income minus taxes plus transfer payments. And aggregate income equals real GDP. So to explore the two-way link between real GDP and planned consumption expenditure, our focus here is on the relationship between consumption expenditure and disposable income when the other factors are constant.

Consumption and Saving Plans The table in Fig. 12.1 shows an example of the relationship among planned consumption expenditure, planned saving, and disposable income. It lists the consumption expenditure and the saving that people plan to undertake at each level of disposable income. Notice that at each level of disposable income, consumption expenditure plus saving always equals disposable income. The reason is that households can only consume or save their disposable income. So planned consumption plus planned saving always equals disposable income.

The relationship between consumption expenditure and disposable income, other things remaining the same, is called the **consumption function.** The relationship between saving and disposable income, other things remaining the same, is called the **saving function**. Let's begin by studying the consumption function.

FIGURE 12.1

Consumption Function and Saving Function

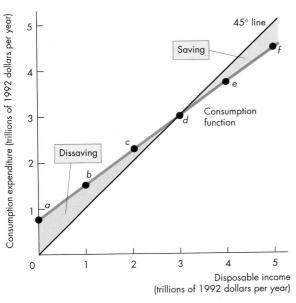

(a) Consumption function

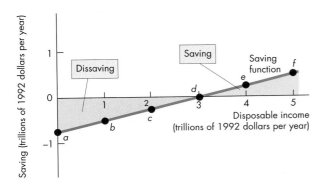

(b) Saving function

	Disposable income	Planned consumption expenditure	Planned saving
		(trillions of 1992 dollars per year)	
a	0	0.75	−0.75
b	1	1.50	−0.50
c	2	2.25	−0.25
d	3	3.00	0
e	4	3.75	0.25
f	5	4.50	0.50

The table shows consumption expenditure and saving plans at various levels of disposable income. Part (a) of the figure shows the relationship between consumption expenditure and disposable income (the consumption function). The height of the consumption function measures consumption expenditure at each level of disposable income. Part (b) shows the relationship between saving and disposable income (the saving function). The height of the saving function measures saving at each level of disposable income. Points a through f on the consumption and saving functions correspond to the rows of the table. The height of the 45° line in part (a) measures disposable income. So, along the 45° line, consumption expenditure equals disposable income. Consumption expenditure plus saving equals disposable income. When the consumption function is above the 45° line, saving is negative (dissaving occurs). When the consumption function is below the 45° line, saving is positive. At the point where the consumption function intersects the 45° line, all disposable income is consumed and saving is zero.

Consumption Function   Figure 12.1(a) shows a consumption function. The *y*-axis measures consumption expenditure, and the *x*-axis measures disposable income. Along the consumption function, the points labeled *a* through *f* correspond to the rows of the table. For example, point *e* shows that when disposable income is $4 trillion, consumption expenditure is $3.75 trillion. Along the consumption function, as disposable income increases, consumption expenditure also increases.

At point *a* on the consumption function, consumption expenditure is $0.75 trillion even though disposable income is zero. This consumption expenditure is called *autonomous consumption*, and it is the amount of consumption expenditure that would take place in the short run, even if people had no current income. Consumption expenditure in excess of this amount is called *induced consumption*, which is expenditure that is induced by an increase in disposable income.

45° Line   Figure 12.1(a) also contains a 45° line, the height of which measures disposable income. At each point on this line, consumption expenditure equals disposable income. In the range over which the consumption function lies above the 45° line—between *a* and *d*—consumption expenditure exceeds disposable income. In the range over which the consumption function lies below the 45° line—between *d* and *f*—consumption expenditure is less than disposable income. And at the point at which the consumption function intersects the 45° line—at point *d*—consumption expenditure equals disposable income.

Saving Function   Figure 12.1(b) shows a saving function. The *x*-axis is exactly the same as that in part (a). The *y*-axis measures saving. Again, the points marked *a* through *f* correspond to the rows of the table. For example, point *e* shows that when disposable income is $4 trillion, saving is $0.25 trillion. Along the saving function, as disposable income increases, saving also increases. At disposable income less than $3 trillion (point *d*), saving is negative. Negative saving is called *dissaving*. At disposable income greater than $3 trillion, saving is positive, and at $3 trillion, saving is zero.

Notice the connection between the two parts of Fig. 12.1. When consumption expenditure exceeds disposable income in part (a), saving is negative in part (b). When disposable income exceeds consumption expenditure in part (a), saving is positive in part (b). And when consumption expenditure equals disposable income in part (a), saving is zero in part (b).

When saving is negative (when consumption expenditure exceeds disposable income), past savings are used to pay for current consumption. Such a situation cannot last forever, but it can occur if disposable income falls temporarily.

Marginal Propensities to Consume and Save

The extent to which consumption expenditure changes when disposable income changes depends on the marginal propensity to consume. The **marginal propensity to consume** (*MPC*) is the fraction of a *change* in disposable income that is consumed. It is calculated as the *change* in consumption expenditure (ΔC) divided by the *change* in disposable income (ΔYD) that brought it about. That is,

$$MPC = \frac{\Delta C}{\Delta YD}.$$

In the table in Fig. 12.1, when disposable income increases from $3 trillion to $4 trillion, consumption expenditure increases from $3 trillion to $3.75 trillion. The $1 trillion increase in disposable income increases consumption expenditure by $0.75 trillion. The *MPC* is $0.75 trillion divided by $1 trillion, which equals 0.75.

The **marginal propensity to save** (*MPS*) is the fraction of a *change* in disposable income that is saved. It is calculated as the *change* in saving (ΔS) divided by the *change* in disposable income (ΔYD) that brought it about. That is,

$$MPS = \frac{\Delta S}{\Delta YD}.$$

In the table in Fig. 12.1, an increase in disposable income from $3 trillion to $4 trillion increases saving from zero to $0.25 trillion. The $1 trillion increase in disposable income increases saving by $0.25 trillion. The *MPS* is $0.25 trillion divided by $1 trillion, which equals 0.25.

The marginal propensity to consume plus the marginal propensity to save always equals 1. They sum to 1 because consumption expenditure and saving exhaust disposable income. Part of each dollar increase in disposable income is consumed, and the remaining part is saved. You can see that these two marginal propensities sum to 1 by using the equation

$$\Delta C + \Delta S = \Delta YD.$$

Divide both sides of the equation by the change in disposable income to obtain

$$\frac{\Delta C}{\Delta YD} + \frac{\Delta S}{\Delta YD} = 1.$$

$\Delta C/\Delta YD$ is the *marginal propensity to consume* (*MPC*), and $\Delta S/\Delta YD$ is the *marginal propensity to save* (*MPS*), so

$$MPC + MPS = 1.$$

Slopes and Marginal Propensities

The slopes of the consumption function and the saving function are the marginal propensities to consume and save. Figure 12.2(a) shows the *MPC* as the slope of the consumption function. A $1 trillion increase in disposable income from $3 trillion to $4 trillion is the base of the red triangle. The increase in consumption expenditure that results from this increase in income is $0.75 trillion and is the height of the triangle. The slope of the consumption function is given by the formula "slope equals rise over run" and is $0.75 trillion divided by $1 trillion, which equals 0.75—the *MPC*.

Figure 12.2(b) shows the *MPS* as the slope of the saving function. A $1 trillion increase in disposable income from $3 trillion to $4 trillion (the base of the red triangle) increases saving by $0.25 trillion (the height of the triangle). The slope of the saving function is $0.25 trillion divided by $1 trillion, which equals 0.25—the *MPS*.

Other Influences on Consumption Expenditure and Saving

You've seen that a change in disposable income leads to changes in consumption expenditure and saving. A change in disposable income brings movements along the consumption function and saving function.

FIGURE 12.2

Marginal Propensities to Consume and Save

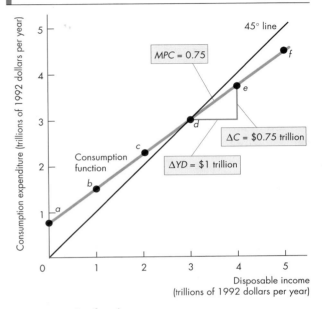

(a) Consumption function

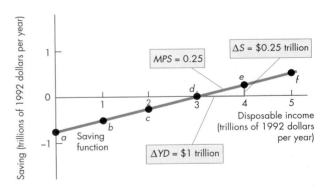

(b) Saving function

The marginal propensity to consume, *MPC*, is equal to the change in consumption expenditure divided by the change in disposable income, other things remaining the same. It is measured by the slope of the consumption function. In part (a), the *MPC* is 0.75. The marginal propensity to save, *MPS*, is equal to the change in saving divided by the change in disposable income, other things remaining the same. It is measured by the slope of the saving function. In part (b), the *MPS* is 0.25.

Along the consumption function and saving function, all other influences on consumption expenditure and saving (such as the real interest rate, expected future income, and the purchasing power net assets) are fixed. A change in any of these other influences shifts both the consumption function and the saving function.

When the real interest rate falls or when the purchasing power of net assets or expected future income increases, consumption expenditure increases and saving decreases. Figure 12.3 shows the effects of these changes on the consumption function and the saving function. The consumption function shifts upward from CF_0 to CF_1, and the saving function shifts downward from SF_0 to SF_1. Such shifts commonly occur during the expansion phase of the business cycle because, at such times, expected future income increases.

When the real interest rate rises or when the purchasing power of net assets or expected future income decreases, consumption expenditure decreases and saving increases. Figure 12.3 also shows the effects of these changes on the consumption function and the saving function. The consumption function shifts downward from CF_0 to CF_2, and the saving function shifts upward from SF_0 to SF_2. Such shifts often occur when a recession begins because at such a time, expected future income decreases.

We've studied the theory of the consumption function. Let's now see how that theory applies to the U.S. economy.

The U.S. Consumption Function

Figure 12.4 shows the U.S. consumption function. Each point identified by a blue dot represents consumption expenditure and disposable income for a particular year. (The dots are for the years 1970–1998, and the even-numbered years are identified in the figure.) The line labeled CF_0 is an estimate of the U.S. consumption function in 1970, and the line labeled CF_1 is an estimate of the U.S. consumption function in 1998.

The slope of the consumption function in Fig. 12.4 is 0.75, which means that a $1 trillion increase in disposable income brings a $0.75 trillion increase in consumption expenditure. This slope, which is an estimate of the marginal propensity to consume, is an assumption that is in the middle of the range of values that economists have estimated for the marginal propensity to consume.

FIGURE 12.3

Shifts in the Consumption and Saving Functions

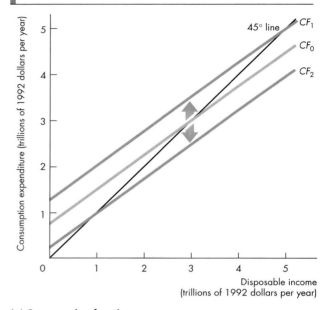

(a) Consumption function

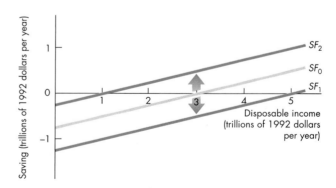

(b) Saving function

A fall in the real interest rate, an increase in the purchasing power of net assets, or an increase in expected future income increases consumption expenditure and decreases saving. It shifts the consumption function upward from CF_0 to CF_1 and shifts the saving function downward from SF_0 to SF_1. A rise in the real interest rate or a decrease in either the purchasing power of net assets or expected future income shifts the consumption function downward from CF_0 to CF_2 and shifts the saving function upward from SF_0 to SF_2.

and real GDP to determine equilibrium expenditure. But before we do so, we need to look at one further component of aggregate expenditure: imports. Like consumption expenditure, imports are influenced by real GDP.

FIGURE 12.4

The U.S. Consumption Function

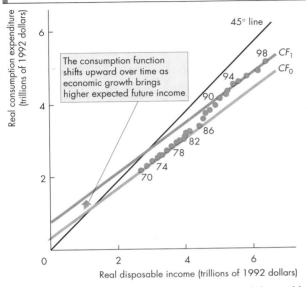

Each blue dot shows consumption expenditure and disposable income for a particular year. The lines CF_0 and CF_1 are estimates of the U.S. consumption function in 1970 and 1998, respectively. Here, the (assumed) marginal propensity to consume is 0.75.

The consumption function shifts upward over time as other influences on consumption expenditure. Of these other influences, the real interest rate and the purchasing power of net assets fluctuate and so bring upward and downward shifts in the consumption function. But rising expected future income brings a steady upward shift in the consumption function. As the consumption function shifts upward, autonomous consumption expenditure increases.

Consumption as a Function of Real GDP

You've seen that consumption expenditure changes when disposable income changes. Disposable income changes when either real GDP changes or net taxes change. If tax rates don't change, real GDP is the only influence on disposable income. So consumption depends not only on disposable income but also on real GDP. We use this link between consumption

and real GDP to determine equilibrium expenditure. But before we do so, we need to look at one further component of aggregate expenditure: imports. Like consumption expenditure, imports are influenced by real GDP.

Import Function

U.S. imports are determined by many factors, but in the short run, one factor dominates: U.S. real GDP. Other things remaining the same, the greater the U.S. real GDP, the larger is the quantity of U.S. imports.

The relationship between imports and real GDP is determined by the marginal propensity to import. The **marginal propensity to import** is the fraction of an increase in real GDP that is spent on imports. It is calculated as the change in imports divided by the change in real GDP that brought it about, other things remaining the same. For example, if a $1 trillion increase in real GDP increases imports by $0.25 trillion, the marginal propensity to import is 0.25.

In recent years, since the North American Free Trade Agreement was implemented, U.S. imports have surged. For example, in 1998, real GDP increased by $280 billion and imports increased by $120 billion. Other factors also influenced imports in 1998, but the marginal propensity to import in that year was probably larger than 0.2. The U.S. marginal propensity to import has been increasing.

R E V I E W Q U I Z

- Which components of aggregate expenditure are influenced by real GDP?
- Define the marginal propensity to consume. What is your estimate of your own marginal propensity to consume? After you graduate, will it change? Why?
- How do we calculate the effects of real GDP on consumption expenditure and imports by using the marginal propensity to consume and the marginal propensity to import?

Real GDP influences consumption and imports. But consumption and imports along with investment, government purchases, and exports influence real GDP. Your next task is to study this second piece of the two-way link between aggregate expenditure and real GDP and see how all the components of aggregate planned expenditure interact to determine real GDP.

Real GDP with a Fixed Price Level

YOU ARE NOW GOING TO DISCOVER HOW AGGRE-
gate expenditure plans interact to determine real
GDP when the price level is fixed. First, we will study
the relationship between aggregate planned expenditure and real GDP. Second, we'll learn about the key
distinction between *planned* expenditure and *actual*
expenditure. And third, we'll study equilibrium expenditure, a situation in which aggregate planned
expenditure and actual expenditure are equal.

The relationship between aggregate planned
expenditure and real GDP can be described by either
an aggregate expenditure schedule or an aggregate
expenditure curve. The *aggregate expenditure schedule*
lists aggregate planned expenditure generated at each
level of real GDP. The *aggregate expenditure curve* is a
graph of the aggregate expenditure schedule.

FIGURE 12.5

Aggregate Planned Expenditure

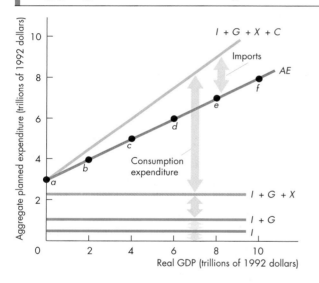

The aggregate expenditure schedule shows the relationship
between aggregate planned expenditure and real GDP.
Aggregate planned expenditure is the sum of planned consumption expenditure, investment, government purchases of
goods and services, and exports minus imports. For example,
in row b of the table, when real GDP is $2 trillion, planned
consumption expenditure is $2.25 trillion, planned investment
is $0.5 trillion, planned government purchases of goods and
services are $0.55 trillion, planned exports are $1.2 trillion,
and planned imports are $0.5 trillion. Thus when real GDP is
$2 trillion, aggregate planned expenditure is $4 trillion ($2.25
+ $0.5 + $0.55 + $1.2 − $0.5). The schedule shows that aggregate planned expenditure increases as real GDP increases.
This relationship is graphed as the aggregate expenditure
curve AE, the line af. The components of aggregate expenditure that increase with real GDP are consumption expenditure and imports. The other components—investment, government purchases, and exports—do not vary with real GDP.

| | | Planned expenditure | | | | | Aggregate planned expenditure |
	Real GDP (Y)	Consumption expenditure (C)	Investment (I)	Government purchases (G)	Exports (X)	Imports (M)	(AE = C + I + G + X − M)
				(trillions of 1992 dollars)			
a	0	0.75	0.5	0.55	1.2	0.0	3
b	2	2.25	0.5	0.55	1.2	0.5	4
c	4	3.75	0.5	0.55	1.2	1.0	5
d	6	5.25	0.5	0.55	1.2	1.5	6
e	8	6.75	0.5	0.55	1.2	2.0	7
f	10	8.25	0.5	0.55	1.2	2.5	8

Aggregate Planned Expenditure and Real GDP

The table in Fig. 12.5 sets out an aggregate expenditure schedule together with the components of aggregate planned expenditure. To calculate aggregate planned expenditure at a given real GDP, we add the various components together. The first column of the table shows real GDP, and the second column shows the consumption expenditure generated by each level of real GDP. A $2 trillion increase in real GDP generates a $1.50 trillion increase in consumption expenditure—the MPC is 0.75.

The next two columns show investment and government purchases of goods and services. Investment depends on the real interest rate and the expected rate of profit (see Chapter 10, p. 209). At a given point in time, these factors generate a particular level of investment. Suppose this level of investment is $0.5 trillion. Also, suppose that government purchases of goods and services are $0.55 trillion.

The next two columns show exports and imports. Exports are influenced by events in the rest of the world, prices of foreign-made goods and services relative to the prices of similar U.S.-made goods and services, and foreign exchange rates. But exports are not directly affected by real GDP in the United States. Exports are a constant $1.2 trillion. Imports increase as real GDP increases. A $2 trillion increase in real GDP generates a $0.5 trillion increase in imports—the marginal propensity to import is 0.25.

The final column shows aggregate planned expenditure—the sum of planned consumption expenditure, investment, government purchases of goods and services, and exports minus imports.

Figure 12.5 plots an aggregate expenditure curve. Real GDP is shown on the x-axis, and aggregate planned expenditure is shown on the y-axis. The aggregate expenditure curve is the red line AE. Points a through f on that curve correspond to the rows of the table. The AE curve is a graph of aggregate planned expenditure (the last column) plotted against real GDP (the first column).

Figure 12.5 also shows the components of aggregate expenditure. The constant components—investment (I), government purchases of goods and services (G), and exports (X)—are shown by the horizontal lines in the figure. Consumption expenditure (C) is the vertical gap between the lines labeled $I + G + X$ and $I + G + X + C$.

To construct the AE curve, subtract imports (M) from the $I + G + X + C$ line. Aggregate expenditure is expenditure on U.S.-made goods and services. But the components of aggregate expenditure—C, I, and G—include expenditure on imported goods and services. For example, a student's purchase of a new motor bike is part of consumption expenditure. But if that motor bike is a Honda made in Japan, expenditure on it must be subtracted from consumption expenditure to find out how much is spent on goods and services produced in the United States—on U.S. real GDP. Money paid to Honda for motor bike imports from Japan does not add to aggregate expenditure on U.S.-made goods and services.

Figure 12.5 shows that aggregate planned expenditure increases as real GDP increases. But as real GDP increases, only some of the components of aggregate planned expenditure increase. These components are consumption expenditure and imports. The sum of the components of aggregate expenditure that vary with real GDP is called **induced expenditure**. The sum of the components of aggregate expenditure that are not influenced by real GDP is called **autonomous expenditure**. The components of autonomous expenditure are investment, government purchases, exports, and autonomous consumption—that part of consumption expenditure that does not vary with real GDP. That is, autonomous expenditure is equal to the level of aggregate planned expenditure when real GDP is zero. In Fig. 12.5, autonomous expenditure is $3 trillion. And as real GDP increases from zero to $2 trillion, aggregate expenditure increases from $3 trillion to $4 trillion. Induced expenditure is $1 trillion—$4 trillion minus $3 trillion.

The aggregate expenditure curve summarizes the relationship between aggregate *planned* expenditure and real GDP. But what determines the point on the aggregate expenditure curve at which the economy operates? What determines *actual* aggregate expenditure?

Actual Expenditure, Planned Expenditure, and Real GDP

Actual aggregate expenditure is always equal to real GDP, as we saw in Chapter 6 (p. 117). But aggregate *planned* expenditure is not necessarily equal to actual aggregate expenditure and therefore is not necessarily equal to real GDP. How can actual expenditure and planned expenditure differ from each other? Why don't expenditure plans get implemented? The main reason is that firms might end up with more inventories than planned or with less inventories than planned. People carry out their consumption expenditure plans, the government implements its planned purchases of goods and services, and net exports are as planned. Firms carry out their plans to purchase new buildings, plant, and equipment. But one component of investment is the change in firms' inventories of goods. If aggregate planned expenditure is less than real GDP, firms don't sell all the goods they produce and they end up with inventories they hadn't planned. If aggregate planned expenditure exceeds real GDP, firms sell more than they produce and inventories decrease below the level that firms had planned.

FIGURE 12.6

Equilibrium Expenditure

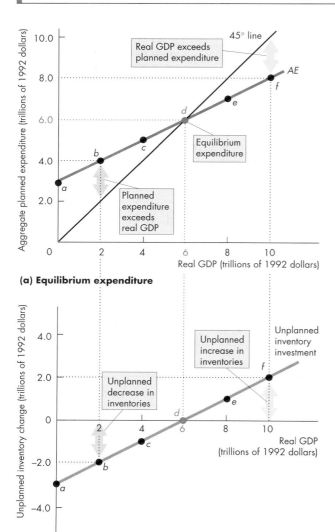

(a) Equilibrium expenditure

(b) Unplanned inventory changes

	Real GDP (Y)	Aggregate planned expenditure (AE)	Unplanned inventory change (Y − AE)
		(trillions of 1992 dollars)	
a	0	3	−3
b	2	4	−2
c	4	5	−1
d	6	6	0
e	8	7	1
f	10	8	2

The table shows expenditure plans at different levels of real GDP. When real GDP is $6 trillion, aggregate planned expenditure equals real GDP. Part (a) of the figure illustrates equilibrium expenditure, which occurs when aggregate planned expenditure equals real GDP at the intersection of the 45° line and the AE curve. Part (b) of the figure shows the forces that bring about equilibrium expenditure. When aggregate planned expenditure exceeds real GDP, inventories decrease—for example, point b in both parts of the figure. Firms increase production, and real GDP increases. When aggregate planned expenditure is less than real GDP, inventories increase—for example, point f in both parts of the figure. Firms decrease production, and real GDP decreases. When aggregate planned expenditure equals real GDP, there are no unplanned inventory changes and real GDP remains constant at equilibrium expenditure.

Equilibrium Expenditure

Equilibrium expenditure is the level of aggregate expenditure that occurs when aggregate *planned* expenditure equals real GDP. It is a level of aggregate expenditure and real GDP at which everyone's spending plans are fulfilled. When the price level is fixed, equilibrium expenditure determines real GDP. When aggregate planned expenditure and actual aggregate expenditure are unequal, a process of convergence toward equilibrium expenditure occurs. And throughout this convergence process, real GDP adjusts. Let's examine equilibrium expenditure and the process that brings it about.

Figure 12.6(a) illustrates equilibrium expenditure. The table sets out aggregate planned expenditure at various levels of real GDP. These values are plotted as points *a* through *f* along the *AE* curve. The 45° line shows all the points at which aggregate planned expenditure equals real GDP. Thus where the *AE* curve lies above the 45° line, aggregate planned expenditure exceeds real GDP; where the *AE* curve lies below the 45° line, aggregate planned expenditure is less than real GDP; and where the *AE* curve intersects the 45° line, aggregate planned expenditure equals real GDP. Point *d* illustrates equilibrium expenditure. At this point, real GDP is $6 trillion.

Convergence to Equilibrium

What are the forces that move aggregate expenditure toward its equilibrium level? To answer this question, we must look at a situation in which aggregate expenditure is away from its equilibrium level. Suppose that in Fig. 12.6, real GDP is $2 trillion. With real GDP at $2 trillion, actual aggregate expenditure is also $2 trillion. But aggregate *planned* expenditure is $4 trillion (point *b* in Fig. 12.6a). Aggregate planned expenditure exceeds *actual* expenditure. When people spend $4 trillion and firms produce goods and services worth $2 trillion, firms' inventories fall by $2 trillion (point *b* in Fig. 12.6b). Because the change in inventories is part of investment, *actual* investment is $2 trillion less than *planned* investment.

Real GDP doesn't remain at $2 trillion for very long. Firms have inventory targets based on their sales. When inventories fall below target, firms increase production to restore inventories to the target level. To increase inventories, firms hire additional labor and increase production. Suppose that they

increase production in the next period by $2 trillion. Real GDP increases by $2.0 trillion to $4.0 trillion. But again, aggregate planned expenditure exceeds real GDP. When real GDP is $4.0 trillion, aggregate planned expenditure is $5 trillion (point *c* in Fig. 12.6a). Again, inventories decrease, but this time by less than before. With real GDP of $4.0 trillion and aggregate planned expenditure of $5 trillion, inventories decrease by $1 trillion (point *c* in Fig. 12.6b). Again, firms hire additional labor, and production increases; real GDP increases yet further.

The process that we have just described—planned expenditure exceeds real GDP, inventories decrease, and production increases—ends when real GDP has reached $6 trillion. At this real GDP, there is an equilibrium. There are no unplanned inventory changes, and firms do not change their production.

You can do an experiment similar to the one we've just done but starting with a level of real GDP greater than equilibrium expenditure. In this case, planned expenditure is less than actual expenditure, inventories pile up, and firms cut production. As before, real GDP keeps on changing (decreasing this time) until it reaches its equilibrium level of $6.0 trillion.

R E V I E W   Q U I Z

- What is the relationship between aggregate planned expenditure and real GDP in expenditure equilibrium?
- How does equilibrium expenditure come about? What adjusts to achieve equilibrium?
- If real GDP and aggregate expenditure are less than their equilibrium levels, what happens to firms' inventories? How do firms change their production? And what happens to real GDP?
- If real GDP and aggregate expenditure are greater than their equilibrium levels, what happens to firms' inventories? How do firms change their production? And what happens to real GDP?

We've learned that when the price level is fixed, real GDP is determined by equilibrium expenditure. And we have seen how unplanned changes in inventories and the production response they generate bring a convergence toward equilibrium. We're now going to study *changes* in equilibrium and discover an economic amplifier called the *multiplier*.

The Multiplier

INVESTMENT AND EXPORTS CAN CHANGE FOR many reasons. A fall in the real interest rate might induce firms to increase their planned investment. A wave of innovation, such as occurred with the spread of multimedia computers in the 1990s, might increase expected future profits and lead firms to increase their planned investment. An economic boom in Western Europe and Japan might lead to a large increase in their expenditure on U.S.-produced goods and services—on U.S. exports. These are all examples of increases in autonomous expenditure.

When autonomous expenditure increases, aggregate expenditure increases, and so does equilibrium expenditure and real GDP. But the increase in real GDP is *larger* than the change in autonomous expenditure. The **multiplier** is the amount by which a change in autonomous expenditure is magnified or multiplied to determine the change in equilibrium expenditure and real GDP.

It is easiest to get the basic idea of the multiplier if we work with an example economy in which there are no income taxes and no imports. So we'll first assume that these factors are absent. Then, when you understand the basic idea, we'll bring these factors back into play and see what difference they make to the multiplier.

The Basic Idea of the Multiplier

Suppose that investment increases. The additional expenditure by businesses means that aggregate expenditure and real GDP increase. The increase in real GDP increases disposable income and with no income taxes, real GDP and disposable income increase by the same amount. The increase in disposable income brings an increase in consumption expenditure. And the increased consumption expenditure adds even more to aggregate expenditure. Real GDP and disposable income increase further, and so does consumption expenditure. The initial increase in investment brings an even bigger increase in aggregate expenditure because it induces an increase in consumption expenditure. The magnitude of the increase in aggregate expenditure that results from an increase in autonomous expenditure is determined by the *multiplier*.

The table in Fig. 12.7 sets out aggregate planned expenditure. Initially, when real GDP is $5 trillion,

aggregate planned expenditure is $5.25 trillion. For each $1 trillion increase in real GDP, aggregate planned expenditure increases by $0.75 trillion. This aggregate expenditure schedule is shown in the figure as the aggregate expenditure curve AE_0. Initially, equilibrium expenditure is $6 trillion. You can see this equilibrium in row b of the table and in the figure where the curve AE_0 intersects the 45° line at the point marked b.

Now suppose that autonomous expenditure increases by $0.5 trillion. What happens to equilibrium expenditure? You can see the answer in Fig. 12.7. When this increase in autonomous expenditure is added to the original aggregate planned expenditure, aggregate planned expenditure increases by $0.5 trillion at each level of real GDP. The new aggregate expenditure curve is AE_1. The new equilibrium expenditure, highlighted in the table (row d'), occurs where AE_1 intersects the 45° line and is $8 trillion (point d'). At this real GDP, aggregate planned expenditure equals real GDP.

The Multiplier Effect

In Fig. 12.7, the increase in autonomous expenditure of $0.5 trillion increases equilibrium expenditure by $2 trillion. That is, the change in autonomous expenditure leads, like Bonnie Raitt's music-making equipment, to an amplified change in equilibrium expenditure. This amplified change is the *multiplier effect*—equilibrium expenditure increases by *more than* the increase in autonomous expenditure. The multiplier is greater than 1.

Initially, when autonomous expenditure increases, aggregate planned expenditure exceeds real GDP. As a result, inventories decrease. Firms respond by increasing production so as to restore their inventories to the target level. As production increases, so does real GDP. With a higher level of real GDP, *induced expenditure* increases. Thus equilibrium expenditure increases by the sum of the initial increase in autonomous expenditure and the increase in induced expenditure. In this example, induced expenditure increases by $1.5 trillion, so equilibrium expenditure increases by $2 trillion.

Although we have just analyzed the effects of an *increase* in autonomous expenditure, the same analysis applies to a decrease in autonomous expenditure. If initially the aggregate expenditure curve is AE_1, equilibrium expenditure and real GDP are $8

Why Is the Multiplier Greater Than 1?

We've seen that equilibrium expenditure increases by more than the increase in autonomous expenditure. This makes the multiplier greater than 1. How come? Why does equilibrium expenditure increase by more than the increase in autonomous expenditure?

The multiplier is greater than 1 because of induced expenditure—an increase in autonomous expenditure *induces* further increases in expenditure. If General Motors spends $10 million on a new car assembly line, aggregate expenditure and real GDP immediately increase by $10 million. But that is not the end of the story. Engineers and construction workers now have more income, and they spend part of the extra income on cars, microwave ovens, vacations, and a host of other goods and services. Real GDP now rises by the initial $10 million plus the extra consumption expenditure induced by the $10 million increase in income. The producers of cars, microwave ovens, vacations, and other goods now have increased incomes, and they, in turn, spend part of the increase in their incomes on consumption goods and services. Additional income induces additional expenditure, which creates additional income.

We have seen that a change in autonomous expenditure has a multiplier effect on real GDP. But how big is the multiplier effect?

The Size of the Multiplier

Suppose that the economy is in a recession. Profit prospects start to look better, and firms are making plans for large increases in investment. The world economy is also heading toward expansion, and exports are increasing. The question on everyone's lips is: How strong will the expansion be? This is a hard question to answer. But an important ingredient in the answer is working out the size of the multiplier.

The *multiplier* is the amount by which a change in autonomous expenditure is multiplied to determine the change in equilibrium expenditure that it generates. To calculate the multiplier, we divide the change in equilibrium expenditure by the change in autonomous expenditure. Let's calculate the multiplier for the example in Fig. 12.7. Initially, equilibrium expenditure is $6 trillion. Then autonomous expenditure increases by $0.5 trillion, and equilibrium expenditure increases by $2 trillion to $8 trillion.

FIGURE 12.7
The Multiplier

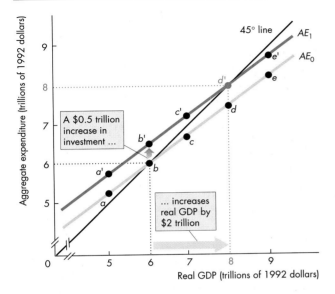

Real GDP (Y)	Aggregate planned expenditure			
		Original (AE₀)		New (AE₁)
		(trillions of 1992 dollars)		
5	a	5.25	a'	5.75
6	b	6.00	b'	6.50
7	c	6.75	c'	7.25
8	d	7.50	d'	8.00
9	e	8.25	e'	8.75

A $0.5 trillion increase in autonomous expenditure shifts the AE curve upward by $0.5 trillion from AE₀ to AE₁. Equilibrium expenditure increases by $2 trillion, from $6 trillion to $8 trillion. The increase in equilibrium expenditure is 4 times the increase in autonomous expenditure, so the multiplier is 4.

trillion. A decrease in autonomous expenditure of $0.5 trillion shifts the aggregate expenditure curve downward by $0.5 trillion to AE₀. Equilibrium expenditure decreases from $8 trillion to $6 trillion. The decrease in equilibrium expenditure ($2 trillion) is larger than the decrease in autonomous expenditure that brought it about ($0.5 trillion). The multiplier is 4.

The multiplier is

$$\text{Multiplier} = \frac{\text{Change in equilibrium expenditure}}{\text{Change in autonomous expenditure}}$$

$$= \frac{\$2 \text{ trillion}}{\$0.5 \text{ trillion}} = 4.$$

The Multiplier and the Marginal Propensity to Consume and Save

What determines the magnitude of the multiplier? The answer is the marginal propensity to consume. The larger is the marginal propensity to consume, the larger is the multiplier. To see why, let's do a calculation.

Aggregate expenditure and real GDP change because consumption expenditure changes and investment changes. The change in real GDP (ΔY) equals the change in consumption expenditure (ΔC) plus the change in investment (ΔI). That is,

$$\Delta Y = \Delta C + \Delta I.$$

But the change in consumption expenditure is determined by the change in real GDP and the marginal propensity to consume. It is

$$\Delta C = MPC \times \Delta Y.$$

Now substitute $MPC \times \Delta Y$ for ΔC in the previous equation to give

$$\Delta Y = (MPC \times \Delta Y) + \Delta I.$$

Now solve for ΔY as

$$(1 - MPC) \times \Delta Y = \Delta I.$$

and rearranging gives

$$\Delta Y = \frac{\Delta I}{(1 - MPC)}$$

Finally, divide both sides of the previous equation by ΔI to give

$$\text{Multiplier} = \frac{\Delta Y}{\Delta I} = \frac{1}{(1 - MPC)}.$$

Using the numbers for Fig. 12.7, the MPC is 0.75 so the multiplier is

$$\text{Multiplier} = \frac{1}{(1 - 0.75)} = \frac{1}{0.25} = 4.$$

There is another formula for the multiplier. Because the marginal propensity to consume (MPC) plus the marginal propensity to save (MPS) sum to 1, the term ($1 - MPC$) equals MPS. Therefore another formula for the multiplier is

$$\text{Multiplier} = \frac{1}{MPS}.$$

Again using the numbers in Fig. 12.7, we have

$$\text{Multiplier} = \frac{1}{0.25} = 4.$$

Because the marginal propensity to save (MPS) is a fraction—a number between 0 and 1—the multiplier is greater than 1.

Figure 12.8 illustrates the multiplier process. In round 1, autonomous expenditure increases by $0.5 trillion (shown by the green bar). At this time, induced expenditure does not change, so aggregate expenditure and real GDP increase by $0.5 trillion. In round 2, the larger real GDP induces more consumption expenditure. Induced expenditure increases by 0.75 times the increase in real GDP, so the increase in real GDP of $0.5 trillion induces a further increase in expenditure of $0.375 trillion. This change in induced expenditure (the green bar in round 2), when added to the previous increase in expenditure (the blue bar in round 2), increases aggregate expenditure and real GDP by $0.875 trillion. The round 2 increase in real GDP induces a round 3 increase in expenditure. The process repeats through successive rounds. Each increase in real GDP is 0.75 times the previous increase. The cumulative increase in real GDP gradually approaches $2 trillion.

So far, we've ignored imports and income taxes. Let's now see how these two factors influence the multiplier.

Imports and Income Taxes

The multiplier is determined, in general, not only by the marginal propensity to consume but also by the marginal propensity to import and by the marginal tax rate. Imports make the multiplier smaller than it otherwise would be. To see why, think about what

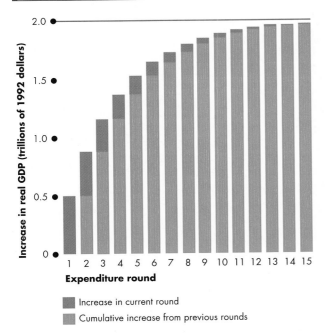

FIGURE 12.8

The Multiplier Process

Autonomous expenditure increases in round 1 by $0.5 trillion. As a result, real GDP increases by the same amount. With a marginal propensity to consume of 0.75, each additional dollar of real GDP induces an additional 0.75 of a dollar of aggregate expenditure. The round 1 increase in real GDP induces an increase in consumption expenditure of $0.375 trillion in round 2. At the end of round 2, real GDP has increased by $0.875 trillion. The extra $0.375 trillion of real GDP in round 2 induces a further increase in consumption expenditure of $0.281 trillion in round 3. Real GDP increases yet further to $1.156 trillion. This process continues with real GDP increasing by ever-smaller amounts. When the process comes to an end, real GDP has increased by a total of $2 trillion.

happens following an increase in investment. An increase in investment increases real GDP, which in turn increases consumption expenditure. But part of the increase in investment and consumption expenditure is expenditure on imported goods and services, not U.S.-produced goods and services. Only expenditure on U.S.-produced goods and services increases U.S. real GDP. The larger the marginal propensity to import, the smaller is the change in U.S. real GDP.

Income taxes also make the multiplier smaller than it otherwise would be. Again, think about what happens following an increase in investment. An increase in investment increases real GDP. But because income taxes increase, disposable income increases by less than the increase in real GDP. Consequently, consumption expenditure increases by less than it would do if taxes had not changed. The larger is the marginal tax rate, the smaller is the change in disposable income and real GDP.

The marginal propensity to import and the marginal tax rate together with the marginal propensity to consume determine the multiplier. And their combined influence depends on the slope of the *AE* curve. The multiplier is equal to 1 divided by 1 minus the slope of the *AE* curve. Figure 12.9 compares two situations. In Fig. 12.9(a), there are no imports and no taxes. The slope of the *AE* curve equals the marginal propensity to consume, which is 0.75, and the multiplier is 4. In Fig. 12.9(b), imports and income taxes decrease the slope of the *AE* curve to 0.5. In this case, the multiplier is 2.

Over time, the value of the multiplier changes as tax rates change and as the marginal propensity to consume and the marginal propensity to import change. These ongoing changes make the multiplier hard to predict. But they do not change the fundamental fact that an initial change in autonomous expenditure leads to a magnified change in aggregate expenditure and real GDP.

Now that we've studied the multiplier and the factors that influence its magnitude, let's use what we've learned to gain some insights into business cycle turning points.

Business Cycle Turning Points

At business cycle turning points, the economy moves from expansion to recession or from recession to expansion. Economists understand these turning points as seismologists understand earthquakes. They know quite a lot about the forces and mechanisms that produce them, but they can't predict them. The forces that bring business cycle turning points are the swings in autonomous expenditure such as investment and exports. The mechanism that gives momentum to the economy's new direction is the multiplier. Let's use what we've now learned to examine these turning points.

FIGURE 12.9

The Multiplier and the Slope of the *AE* Curve

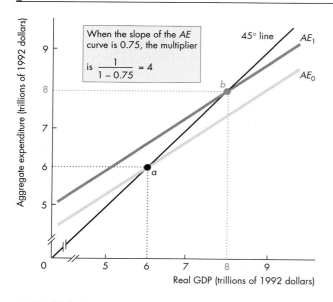

(a) Multiplier is 4

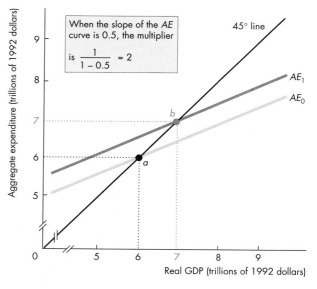

(b) Multiplier is 2

Imports and income taxes make the *AE* curve less steep and reduce the value of the multiplier. In part (a), with no imports and income taxes, the slope of the *AE* curve is 0.75 (the marginal propensity to consume) and the multiplier is 4. But with

imports and income taxes, the slope of the *AE* curve is less than the marginal propensity to consume. In part (b), the slope of the *AE* curve is 0.5. In this case, the multiplier is 2.

An Expansion Begins An expansion is triggered by an increase in autonomous expenditure that increases aggregate planned expenditure. At the moment the economy turns the corner into expansion, aggregate planned expenditure exceeds real GDP. In this situation, firms see their inventories taking an unplanned dive. The expansion now begins. To meet their inventory targets, firms increase production, and real GDP begins to increase. This initial increase in real GDP brings higher incomes that stimulate consumption expenditure. The multiplier process kicks in, and the expansion picks up speed.

A Recession Begins The process we've just described works in reverse at a business cycle peak. A recession is triggered by a decrease in autonomous expenditure that decreases aggregate planned expenditure. At the moment the economy turns the corner into recession, real GDP exceeds aggregate planned

expenditure. In this situation, firms see unplanned inventories piling up. The recession now begins. To reduce their inventories, firms cut production, and real GDP begins to decrease. This initial decrease in real GDP brings lower incomes that cut consumption expenditure. The multiplier process reinforces the initial cut in autonomous expenditure, and the recession takes hold.

The Next U.S. Recession? Since 1991, the U.S. economy has been in a business cycle expansion. The last real GDP trough was in the first quarter of 1991. The science of macroeconomics cannot predict when the next recession will begin. A recession seemed possible in 1995 following a rapid buildup of inventories during 1994. But firms planned this inventory buildup. At the beginning of 1999, there was still no immediate prospect of the next recession. But it will surely come. And when it does, the mechanism you've just studied will operate.

- What is the multiplier? What does it determine? Why does it matter?
- How do the marginal propensity to consume, the marginal propensity to import, and the marginal tax rate influence the multiplier?
- How do fluctuations in autonomous expenditure influence real GDP? If autonomous expenditure decreases, which phase of the business cycle does the economy enter?

The economy's potholes are changes in investment and exports. And the economy does not operate like the shock absorbers on Dennis Archer's car. While the price level is fixed, the effects of the economic potholes are not smoothed out. Instead, they are amplified like Bonnie Raitt's voice. But we've considered only the adjustments in spending that occur in the very short term when the price level is fixed. What happens after a long enough time lapse for the price level to change? Let's answer this question.

The Multiplier and the Price Level

WHEN FIRMS CAN'T KEEP UP WITH SALES AND their inventories fall below target, they increase production, but at some point, they raise their prices. Similarly, when firms find unwanted inventories piling up, they decrease production, but eventually, they cut their prices. So far, we've studied the macroeconomic consequences of firms changing their production levels when their sales change, but we haven't looked at the effects of price changes. When individual firms change their prices, the economy's price level changes.

To study the simultaneous determination of real GDP and the price level, we use the *aggregate supply–aggregate demand model*, which is explained in Chapter 8. But to understand how aggregate demand adjusts, we need to work out the connection between the aggregate supply–aggregate demand model and the equilibrium expenditure model that we've used in this chapter. The key to understanding the relationship between these two models is the distinction between the aggregate *expenditure* and aggregate *demand*.

Aggregate Expenditure and Aggregate Demand

The aggregate expenditure curve is the relationship between the aggregate planned expenditure and real GDP, all other influences on aggregate planned expenditure remaining the same. The aggregate demand curve is the relationship between the aggregate quantity of goods and services demanded and the price level, all other influences on aggregate demand remaining the same. Let's explore the links between these two relationships.

Aggregate Expenditure and the Price Level

When the price level changes, aggregate planned expenditure changes and the quantity of real GDP demanded changes. The aggregate demand curve slopes downward. Why? There are two main reasons:

1. Wealth effect
2. Substitution effects

Wealth Effect   Other things remaining the same, the higher the price level, the smaller is the purchasing power of people's assets. For example, suppose you have $100 in the bank and the price level is 110. If the price level rises to 130, your $100 buys fewer goods and services. You are less wealthy. With less wealth, you will probably want to try to spend a bit less and save a bit more. Aggregate planned expenditure is lower the higher the price level, other things remaining the same.

Substitution Effects   A rise in the price level today, other things remaining the same, makes current goods and services more costly relative to future goods and services and results in a delay in purchases—an *intertemporal substitution*. A rise in the price level, other things remaining the same, makes U.S.-produced goods more expensive relative to foreign-produced goods and services and increases imports and decreases exports—an *international substitution*.

When the price level rises, each of these effects reduces aggregate planned expenditure at each level of real GDP. As a result, when the price level rises, the aggregate expenditure curve shifts downward. A fall in the price level has the opposite effect. When the price level falls, the aggregate expenditure curve shifts upward.

Figure 12.10(a) shows the shifts of the *AE* curve. When the price level is 110, the aggregate expenditure curve is AE_0, which intersects the 45° line at point *b*. Equilibrium expenditure is $7 trillion. If the price level increases to 130, the aggregate expenditure curve shifts downward to AE_1, which intersects the 45° line at point *a*. Equilibrium expenditure is $6 trillion. If the price level decreases to 90, the aggregate expenditure curve shifts upward to AE_2, which intersects the 45° line at point *c*. Equilibrium expenditure is $8 trillion.

We've just seen that when the price level changes, other things remaining the same, the aggregate expenditure curve shifts and the equilibrium expenditure changes. And when the price level changes, other things remaining the same, there is a movement along the aggregate demand curve. Figure 12.10(b) shows these movements along the aggregate demand curve. At a price level of 110, the aggregate quantity of goods and services demanded is $7 trillion—point *b* on the aggregate demand curve *AD*. If the price level rises to 130, the aggregate quantity of goods and services demanded decreases to $6 trillion. There is a movement along the aggregate demand curve to point *a*. If the price level falls to 90, the aggregate quantity of goods and services demanded increases to $8 trillion. There is a movement along the aggregate demand curve to point *c*.

Each point on the aggregate demand curve corresponds to a point of equilibrium expenditure. The equilibrium expenditure points *a*, *b*, and *c* in Fig. 12.10(a) correspond to the points *a*, *b*, and *c* on the aggregate demand curve in Fig. 12.10(b).

When the price level changes, other things remaining the same, the aggregate expenditure curve shifts and there is a movement along the aggregate demand curve. When any other influence on aggregate planned expenditure changes, *both* the aggregate expenditure curve and the aggregate demand curve shift. For example, an increase in investment or in exports increases both aggregate planned expenditure and aggregate demand and shifts both the *AE* curve and the *AD* curve. Figure 12.11 illustrates the effect of such an increase.

Initially, the aggregate expenditure curve is AE_0 in part (a) and the aggregate demand curve is AD_0 in part (b). The price level is 110, real GDP is $7 trillion, and the economy is at point *a* in both parts of the figure. Now suppose that investment increases by $1 trillion. At a constant price level of 110, the aggregate expenditure curve shifts upward to AE_1. This curve intersects the 45° line at an equilibrium

FIGURE 12.10

Aggregate Demand

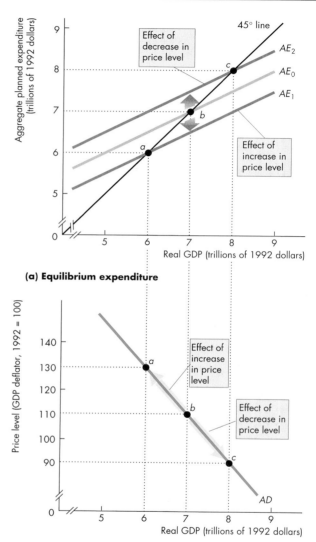

(a) Equilibrium expenditure

(b) Aggregate demand

A change in the price level shifts the *AE* curve and results in a *movement along* the *AD* curve. When the price level is 110, the *AE* curve is AE_0, and equilibrium expenditure is $7 trillion at point *b*. When the price level rises to 130, the *AE* curve is AE_1, and equilibrium expenditure is $6 trillion at point *a*. When the price level falls to 90, the *AE* curve is AE_2, and equilibrium expenditure is $8 trillion at point *c*. Points *a*, *b*, and *c* on the *AD* curve in part (b) correspond to the equilibrium expenditure points *a*, *b*, and *c* in part (a).

FIGURE 12.11

A Change in Aggregate Demand

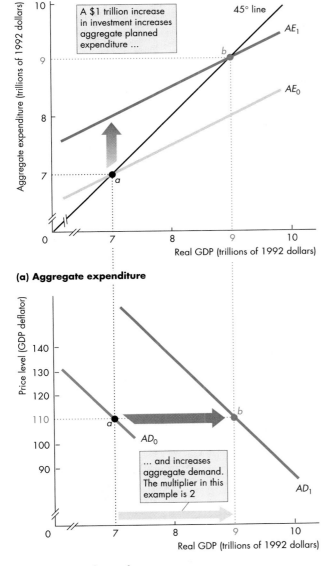

(a) Aggregate expenditure

(b) Aggregate demand

The price level is 110. When the aggregate expenditure curve is AE_0 (part a), the aggregate demand curve is AD_0 (part b). An increase in autonomous expenditure shifts the AE curve upward to AE_1. In the new equilibrium, real GDP is $9 trillion (at b). Because the quantity of real GDP demanded at a price level of 110 increases to $9 trillion, the AD curve shifts rightward to AD_1.

expenditure of $9 trillion (point b). This equilibrium expenditure of $9 trillion is the aggregate quantity of goods and services demanded at a price level of 110, as shown by point b in part (b). Point b lies on a new aggregate demand curve. The aggregate demand curve has shifted rightward to AD_1.

But how do we know by how much the AD curve shifts? The multiplier determines the answer. The larger the multiplier, the larger is the shift in the aggregate demand curve that results from a given change in autonomous expenditure. In this example, the multiplier is 2. A $1 trillion increase in investment produces a $2 trillion increase in the aggregate quantity of goods and services demanded at each price level. That is, a $1 trillion increase in autonomous expenditure shifts the aggregate demand curve rightward by $2 trillion.

A decrease in autonomous expenditure shifts the aggregate expenditure curve downward and shifts the aggregate demand curve leftward. You can see these effects by reversing the change that we've just studied. Suppose that the economy is initially at point b on the aggregate expenditure curve AE_1 and the aggregate demand curve AD_1. A decrease in autonomous expenditure shifts the aggregate planned expenditure curve downward to AE_0. The aggregate quantity of goods and services demanded falls from $9 trillion to $7 trillion, and the aggregate demand curve shifts leftward to AD_0.

Let's summarize what we have just discovered:

If some factor other than a change in the price level increases autonomous expenditure, the AE curve shifts upward and the AD curve shifts rightward.

The size of the AD curve shift depends on the change in autonomous expenditure and the multiplier.

Equilibrium Real GDP and the Price Level

In Chapter 8, we learned that aggregate demand and short-run aggregate supply determine equilibrium real GDP and the price level. We've now put aggregate demand under a more powerful microscope and have discovered that a change in investment (or in any component of autonomous expenditure) changes aggregate demand and shifts the aggregate demand curve. The magnitude of the shift depends on the multiplier. But whether a change in autonomous expenditure results ultimately in a change in real

GDP, a change in the price level, or a combination of the two depends on aggregate supply. There are two time frames to consider, the short run and the long run. First we'll see what happens in the short run.

An Increase in Aggregate Demand in the Short Run
Figure 12.12 describes the economy. In part (a), the aggregate expenditure curve is AE_0, and equilibrium expenditure is $7 trillion—point *a*. In part (b), aggregate demand is AD_0, and the short-run aggregate supply curve is *SAS*. (Look at Chapter 8 if you need to refresh your understanding of this curve.) Equilibrium is at point *a*, where the aggregate demand and short-run aggregate supply curves intersect. The price level is 110, and real GDP is $7 trillion.

Now suppose that investment increases by $1 trillion. With the price level fixed at 110, the aggregate expenditure curve shifts upward to AE_1. Equilibrium expenditure increases to $9 trillion—point *b* in part (a). In part (b), the aggregate demand curve shifts rightward by $2 trillion, from AD_0 to AD_1. How far the aggregate demand curve shifts is determined by the multiplier when the price level is fixed. But with this new aggregate demand curve, the price level does not remain fixed. The price level rises, and as it does so, the aggregate expenditure curve shifts downward. The short-run equilibrium occurs when the aggregate expenditure curve has shifted downward to AE_2 and the new aggregate demand curve, AD_1, intersects the short-run aggregate supply curve. Real GDP is $8.6 trillion, and the price level is 116 (at point *c*).

When price level effects are taken into account, the increase in investment still has a multiplier effect on real GDP, but the effect is smaller than it would be if the price level were fixed. The steeper the slope of the short-run aggregate supply curve, the larger is the increase in the price level and the smaller is the multiplier effect on real GDP.

An Increase in Aggregate Demand in the Long Run
Figure 12.13 illustrates the long-run effect of an increase in aggregate demand. In the long run, real GDP equals potential GDP and there is full employment. Potential GDP is $7 trillion, and the long-run aggregate supply curve is *LAS*. Initially, the economy is at point *a* (parts a and b).

Investment increases by $1 trillion. The aggregate expenditure curve shifts to AE_1, and the aggregate demand curve shifts to AD_1. With no change in the price level, the economy would move to point *b*

FIGURE 12.12

The Multiplier in the Short Run

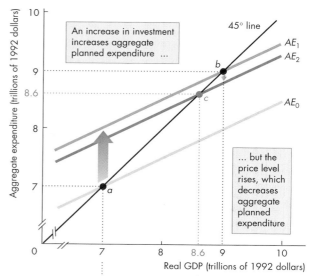

(a) Aggregate expenditure

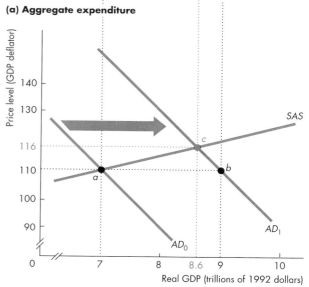

(b) Aggregate demand

An increase in investment shifts the *AE* curve from AE_0 to AE_1 (part a) and the *AD* curve from AD_0 to AD_1 (part b). The price level does not remain at 110 but rises. The higher price level shifts the *AE* curve downward from AE_1 to AE_2. The economy moves to point *c* in both parts. In the short run, the multiplier effect is smaller than when the price level is fixed.

and real GDP would increase to $9 trillion. But in the short run, the price level rises to 116 and real GDP increases to only $8.6 trillion. With the higher price level, the *AE* curve shifts from AE_1 to AE_2. The economy is now in a short-run equilibrium at point *c*. Real GDP is now above potential GDP. The labor force is more than fully employed, and shortages of labor increase the money wage rate. The higher money wage rate increases costs, which decreases short-run aggregate supply and shifts the *SAS* curve leftward to SAS_1. The price level rises further, and real GDP decreases. There is a movement along AD_1, and the *AE* curve shifts downward from AE_2 toward AE_0. When the money wage rate and the price level have increased by the same percentage, real GDP is again equal to potential GDP and the economy is at point *a'*. In the long run, the multiplier is zero.

FIGURE 12.13

The Multiplier in the Long Run

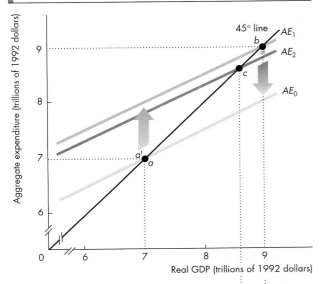

(a) Aggregate expenditure

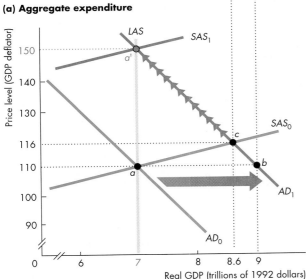

(b) Aggregate demand

Starting from point *a*, an increase in investment shifts the *AE* curve to AE_1 and the *AD* curve to AD_1. In the short run, the economy moves to point *c*. In the long run, the money wage rate rises, the *SAS* curve shifts to SAS_1, the *AE* curve shifts back to AE_0, the price level rises, and real GDP falls. The economy moves to point *a'*, and in the long run, the multiplier is zero.

R E V I E W   Q U I Z

- How does a change in the price level influence the *AE* curve and the *AD* curve?
- If autonomous expenditure increases with no change in the price level, what happens to the *AE* curve and the *AD* curve? Which curve shifts by an amount that is determined by the multiplier and why?
- How does real GDP change in the short run when autonomous expenditure increases? Does real GDP change by the same amount as the change in aggregate demand? Why or why not?
- How does real GDP change in the long run when autonomous expenditure increases? Does real GDP change by the same amount as the change in aggregate demand? Why or why not?

You are now ready to build on what you've learned about expenditure fluctuations and study the roles of fiscal policy and monetary policy in smoothing the business cycle. In Chapter 13, we study fiscal policy—government purchases, taxes, and the surplus or deficit on the government's budget— and in Chapters 14 and 15, we study monetary policy—interest rates and the quantity of money. But before you leave the current topic, look at *Reading Between the Lines* on pages 274–275 and see the expenditure multiplier you've studied in this chapter at work in the U.S. economy.

A Local Multiplier

THE SEATTLE TIMES, DECEMBER 4, 1998

Will Cuts at Boeing Multiply Hard Times for Area?

MICHELE MATASSA FLORES

We hear it all the time, a refrain that sounds as much like a prep-school cheer as solid economic analysis.

"For every Boeing job, 2.8 more are created around Washington state."

"Seattle will lose 1,800 jobs if the Mariners leave town."

"Cultural/arts organizations create more than 8,800 jobs in the county each year."

Such numbers, called "multipliers," typically are cited with precision and certainty, as if they're sure-fire ways to measure economic impact. In fact, they are inexact and controversial, a fact that could be underscored next year when Boeing begins laying off thousands of workers.

One of the most debatable things about so-called multiplier effects is whether they work in reverse, as a company cuts jobs instead of adding them.

If multipliers do work in reverse, then Boeing's imminent elimination of an estimated 30,000 Puget Sound jobs in the next two years will cost the state more than 114,000 jobs. Everyone from a line worker at an airplane-parts supplier to a clerk at the corner Safeway could be at risk.

But there's a catch.

"They are just numbers. It ought to work the same way going down as it does going up," said Paul Sommers, a regional economist and head of the Northwest Policy Center at the University of Washington. "But there seems to be some stickiness on the way down."

Here's why:

— Some employees facing layoffs will instead take early retirement, maintaining enough income to continue making house payments, buying food and clothing and eating out, supporting the spin-off jobs cited in multiplier studies.

— Laid-off workers are eligible for unemployment compensation, so they, too, can continue spending money. Some live off their savings for a while instead of cutting back their spending.

— Companies that do lose business often postpone or avoid their own layoffs, hoping instead to ride out the slump.

— Often, there are hiring booms under way in other industries, smoothing the ripples caused by the layoffs. ...

Essence of the Story

■ A claim in Washington State is that one Boeing job creates 2.8 additional jobs in the state—a multiplier effect.

■ If the Boeing multiplier works in reverse, then Boeing's elimination of 30,000 jobs will cost the state more than 114,000 jobs.

■ According to economist Paul Sommers of the University of Washington, the multiplier is smaller on the way down. Spending levels are maintained because:
- Some employees facing layoffs take early retirement.
- Laid-off workers receive unemployment compensation.
- Companies that lose business postpone or avoid layoffs.
- Hiring booms in other industries counteract layoffs in other industries.

Economic Analysis

■ This news article highlights several confusions about multipliers.

■ The first confusion is about what initiates an economic change and what gets multiplied.

■ In the expenditure model, the initiator of change is a change in *autonomous* expenditure. The change in autonomous expenditure is multiplied to determine the change in aggregate expenditure.

■ Figure 1 shows the autonomous expenditure multiplier for the state of Washington on the assumption that the multiplier is 2.8, the value in the news article for the so-called Boeing multiplier.

■ In Fig. 1, the Washington state aggregate expenditure curve is initially AE_0 and gross state product (GSP) is $160 billion, where the AE_0 curve intersects the 45° line.

■ A $10 billion decrease in autonomous expenditure shifts the AE curve downward to AE_1. Equilibrium expenditure decreases to $132 billion, a decrease of $28 billion.

■ The decrease in equilibrium expenditure is 2.8 times the decrease in autonomous expenditure. An AE curve with a slope of 0.643 delivers this multiplier. (Check that $1/(1 − 0.643) = 2.8$.)

■ As Washington's GSP is decreasing, firms are laying off workers. One of these firms might be Boeing. And the change in employment in Washington divided by the change in employment at Boeing is the "Boeing multiplier."

■ If the change in expenditure that brings the change in the Boeing labor force is *autonomous*, then the Boeing multiplier is relevant for determining the change in total employment. But if the change in expenditure that brings the change in the Boeing labor force is *induced*, then the Boeing multiplier is irrelevant.

■ The news article asks whether the multiplier is the same in both directions.

■ The answer for the autonomous expenditure multiplier is that it is the same in both directions because the slope of the AE curve determines the outcome. And this slope is the same for an increase as it is for a decrease in expenditure.

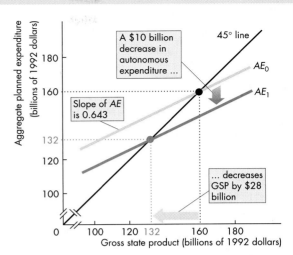

Figure 1 A multiplier of 2.8

■ The reasons attributed to economist Paul Sommers of the University of Washington why the multiplier is smaller on the way down apply with equal force on the way up.

■ In bad times, some employees facing layoffs take early retirement; and in good times some employees considering retirement postpone it.

■ In bad times, laid-off workers receive unemployment compensation; and in good times, previously laid off workers go back to work.

■ In bad times, companies that lose business postpone or avoid layoffs; and in good times, companies that gain business first use the slack in their existing work force before hiring again.

■ In both bad times and good times, hiring booms in some industries counteract layoffs in other industries.

■ These are all reasons why the multiplier is small, not reasons why its value is different for expansions and recessions. And for these reasons, it is most unlikely that the Washington state multiplier is as large as 2.8.

MATHEMATICAL NOTE
The Algebra of the Multiplier

THIS NOTE EXPLAINS THE MULTIPLIER IN GREATER detail than that presented on p. 266. We begin by defining the symbols we need:

- Aggregate planned expenditure, AE
- Real GDP, Y
- Consumption expenditure, C
- Investment, I
- Government purchases, G
- Exports, X
- Imports, M
- Net taxes, T
- Disposable income, YD
- Autonomous consumption expenditure, a
- Marginal propensity to consume, b
- Marginal propensity to import, m
- Marginal tax rate, t
- Autonomous expenditure, A

Aggregate Expenditure

Aggregate planned expenditure (AE) is the sum of the planned amounts of consumption expenditure (C), investment (I), government purchases (G), and exports (X) minus the planned amount of imports (M). That is

$$AE = C + I + G + X - M.$$

Consumption Function   Consumption expenditure (C) depends on disposable income (YD), and we write the consumption function as

$$C = a + bYD.$$

Disposable income (YD) equals real GDP minus net taxes ($Y - T$). So by replacing YD with ($Y - T$), the consumption function becomes

$$C = a + b(Y - T).$$

Net taxes equal real GDP (Y) multiplied by the marginal tax rate (t). That is,

$$T = tY.$$

Use this equation in the previous one to obtain

$$C = a + b(1 - t)Y.$$

This equation describes consumption expenditure as a function of real GDP.

Import Function   Imports depend on real GDP, and the import function is

$$M = mY.$$

Aggregate Expenditure Curve   Use the consumption function and the import function to replace C and M in the aggregate planned expenditure equation. That is,

$$AE = a + b(1 - t)Y + I + G + X - mY.$$

Collect the terms on the right side of the equation that involve Y to obtain

$$AE = [a + I + G + X] + [b(1 - t) - m]Y.$$

Autonomous expenditure (A) is $[a + I + G + X]$, and the slope of the AE curve is $[b(1 - t)) - m]$. So the equation for the AE curve, which is shown in the following figure, is

$$AE = A + [b(1 - t) - m]Y.$$

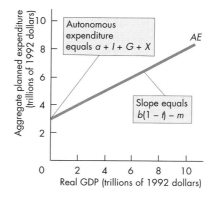

Equilibrium Expenditure

Equilibrium expenditure occurs when aggregate planned expenditure (AE) equals real GDP (Y). That is,

$$AE = Y.$$

In the figure below, the scales of the x-axis (real GDP) and the y-axis (aggregate planned expenditure) are identical, so the 45° line shows the points at which aggregate planned expenditure equals real GDP. That is, the 45° line is the line along which $AE = Y$.

The figure shows the point of equilibrium expenditure at the intersection of the AE curve and the 45° line.

To calculate equilibrium expenditure and real GDP, we solve the equations for the AE curve and the 45° line for the two unknown quantities AE and Y. So, starting with

$$AE = A + [b(1 - t) - m]Y$$

$$AE = Y,$$

replace AE with Y in the AE equation to obtain

$$Y = A + [b(1 - t) - m]Y.$$

The solution for Y is

$$Y = \frac{1}{1 - [b(1 - t) - m]} A.$$

The Multiplier

The multiplier equals the change in equilibrium expenditure and real GDP (Y) that results from a change in autonomous expenditure (A) divided by the change in autonomous expenditure.

A change in autonomous expenditure (ΔA) leads to a change in equilibrium expenditure and real GDP (ΔY), which is given by

$$\Delta Y = \frac{1}{1 - [b(1 - t) - m]} \Delta A.$$

$$\text{Multiplier} = \frac{1}{1 - [b(1 - t) - m]}.$$

The size of the multiplier depends on the slope of the AE curve $b(1 - t) - m$. The larger the slope, the larger is the multiplier. So the multiplier is larger,

- The greater the marginal propensity to consume (b)
- The smaller the marginal tax rate (t)
- The smaller the marginal propensity to import (m)

An economy with no imports and no marginal taxes has $m = 0$ and $t = 0$. In this special case, the multiplier equals $1/(1 - b)$. If b is 0.75, then the multiplier is 4, as shown in the following figure. In an economy with $b = 0.75$, $t = 0.2$, and $m = 0.1$, the multiplier is 1 divided by 1 minus $0.75(1 - 0.2) - 0.1$, which equals 2. Make up some more examples to show the effects of b, t, and m on the multiplier.

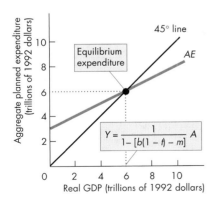

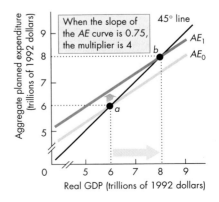

KEY POINTS

Fixed Prices and Expenditure Plans
(pp. 254–259)

■ When the price level is fixed, expenditure plans determine real GDP.

■ Consumption expenditure is determined by disposable income, and the marginal propensity to consume (*MPC*) determines the change in consumption expenditure brought about by a change in disposable income. Real GDP determines disposable income.

■ Imports are determined by real GDP, and the marginal propensity to import determines the change in imports brought about by a change in real GDP.

Real GDP with a Fixed Price Level
(pp. 260–263)

■ Aggregate *planned* expenditure depends on real GDP.

■ Equilibrium expenditure occurs when aggregate planned expenditure equals actual expenditure and real GDP.

The Multiplier (pp. 264–269)

■ The multiplier is the magnified effect of a change in autonomous expenditure on real GDP.

■ The multiplier is influenced by the marginal propensity to consume, the marginal propensity to import, and the marginal income tax rate.

The Multiplier and the Price Level
(pp. 269–273)

■ The aggregate demand curve is the relationship between the quantity of real GDP demanded and the price level, other things remaining the same.

■ The aggregate expenditure curve is the relationship between aggregate planned expenditure and real GDP, other things remaining the same.

■ At a given price level, there is a given aggregate expenditure curve. A change in the price level changes aggregate planned expenditure and shifts the aggregate expenditure curve. A change in the price level also creates a movement along the aggregate demand curve.

■ A change in autonomous expenditure that is not caused by a change in the price level shifts the aggregate expenditure curve and shifts the aggregate demand curve. The magnitude of the shift of the aggregate demand curve depends on the multiplier and on the change in autonomous expenditure.

■ The multiplier decreases as the price level changes, and in the long run the multiplier is zero.

KEY FIGURES ◆

KEY TERMS

PROBLEMS

💻 *1. You are given the following information about the economy of Heron Island:

Disposable income (millions of dollars per year)	Consumption expenditure (millions of dollars per year)
0	5
10	10
20	15
30	20
40	25

Calculate Heron Island's:
a. Marginal propensity to consume.
b. Saving at each level of disposable income.
c. Marginal propensity to save.

2. You are given the following information about the economy of Spendthrift Island:

Disposable income (millions of dollars per year)	Saving (millions of dollars per year)
0	−100
500	−50
1,000	0
1,500	50
2,000	100
2,500	150
3,000	200

Calculate Spendthrift Island's:
a. Marginal propensity to save.
b. Consumption at each level of disposable income.
c. Marginal propensity to consume.
d. Why is the island called Spendthrift?

*3. Turtle Island has no imports or exports, the people of Turtle Island pay no incomes taxes, and the price level is fixed. The figure illustrates the components of aggregate planned expenditure on Turtle Island.

On Turtle Island, what is:
a. Autonomous expenditure?
b. The marginal propensity to consume?
c. Aggregate planned expenditure when real GDP is $6 billion?
d. Happening to inventories if real GDP is $4 billion?
e. Happening to inventories if real GDP is $6 billion?
f. The multiplier?

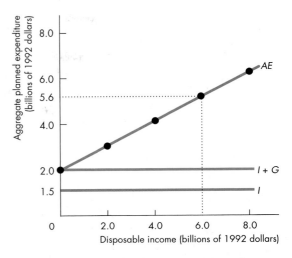

4. The spreadsheet lists the components of aggregate planned expenditure in Spice Bay. The numbers are in billions of cloves, the currency of the Bay.

	A	B	C	D	E	F	G
1		Y	C	I	G	X	M
2	a	100	110	50	60	60	15
3	b	200	170	50	60	60	30
4	c	300	230	50	60	60	45
5	d	400	290	50	60	60	60
6	e	500	350	50	60	60	75
7	f	600	410	50	60	60	90

In Spice Bay, what is:
a. Autonomous expenditure?
b. The marginal propensity to consume?
c. Aggregate planned expenditure when real GDP is 200 billion cloves?
d. Happening to inventories if real GDP is 200 billion cloves?
e. Happening to inventories if real GDP is 500 billion cloves?
f. The multiplier in Spice Bay?

💻 *5. In the economy of Zeeland: Autonomous consumption expenditure is $100 billion, and the marginal propensity to consume is 0.9. Investment is $460 billion, government purchases of goods and services are $400 billion, and net taxes are a constant $400 billion—they do not vary with income. Zeeland has no imports or exports.
a. What is the consumption function?
b. What is the equation that describes the aggregate expenditure curve?

c. Calculate equilibrium expenditure.

d. If investment falls to $360 billion, what is the change in equilibrium expenditure and what is the size of the multiplier?

6. You are given the following information about the economy of Antarctica: Autonomous consumption expenditure is $1 billion, and the marginal propensity to consume is 0.95. Investment is $4 billion, government purchases of goods and services are $4 billion, and net taxes are a constant $4 billion—they do not vary with income.

a. What is the consumption function?

b. What is the equation that describes the aggregate expenditure curve?

c. Calculate equilibrium expenditure.

d. If investment falls to $3 billion, what is the change in equilibrium expenditure and what is the size of the multiplier?

*7. Suppose that in problem 5 the price level is 100 and real GDP equals potential GDP. If investment increases by $100 billion,

a. What happens to the quantity of real GDP demanded?

b. In the short run, does equilibrium real GDP increase by more than, less than, or the same amount as the increase in the quantity of real GDP demanded?

c. In the long run, does equilibrium real GDP increase by more than, less than, or the same amount as the increase in the quantity of real GDP demanded?

d. In the short run, does the price level in Zeeland rise, fall, or remain unchanged? In the long run, does the price level in Zeeland rise, fall, or remain unchanged?

8. Suppose that in problem 6 the price level is 100 and real GDP equals potential GDP. If investment increases by $1 billion,

a. What happens to the quantity of real GDP demanded?

b. In the long run, does equilibrium real GDP increase by more than, less than, or the same amount as the increase in the quantity of real GDP demanded?

c. In the short run, does the price level in Antarctica rise, fall, or remain unchanged?

CRITICAL THINKING

1. Study *Reading Between the Lines* on pp. 274–275, and then answer the following questions:

a. What does the news article say about the magnitude and stability of the Boeing multiplier?

b. What is the distinction between autonomous expenditure and induced expenditure?

c. Do you think the changes in expenditure that change employment at Boeing are typically changes in autonomous expenditure, changes in induced expenditure, or a mixture of the two. (Hint: Think about what Boeing produces and who its customers are.)

d. Why does it matter whether the change in expenditure that changes Boeing's employment is autonomous or induced?

e. What information do you need to be able to predict the Boeing multiplier?

f. Think of other big firms in other regions that might have a multiplier effect.

2. Use the link on the Parkin Web site to visit the Penn World Table and obtain data on real GDP per person and consumption as a percentage of real GDP for the United States, China, South Africa, and Mexico since 1960.

a. In a spreadsheet, multiply your real GDP data by the consumption percentage and divide by 100 to obtain data on real consumption expenditure per person.

b. Make graphs like Fig. 12.4 on p. 259 that show the relationship between consumption and real GDP for these four countries.

c. On the basis of the numbers you've obtained, in which country do you expect the multiplier to be largest (other things remaining the same)?

d. What other data would you need to be able to calculate the multipliers for these countries?

e. You are a research assistant in the office of the President's Council of Economic Advisors. The President wants only 250 words of crisp, clear, jargon-free explanation together with a lively example of the power and limitations of the multiplier. You are asked to draft this note.

Chapter 13

Fiscal Policy

Balancing Acts on Capitol Hill

In 1999, the federal government planned to spend $1,868 billion, or 23 cents of every dollar that Americans earn. What are the effects of government spending on the economy? Does it create jobs? Or does it destroy them? And does a dollar spent by the government on goods and services have the same effect as a dollar spent by someone else? ◆ Although the federal government planned to *spend* 23 cents of every dollar earned, it did not plan to tax us by that amount. Its plans were for tax revenues of $1,987 billion or 24 cents of every dollar earned. What are the effects of taxes on the economy? Do taxes harm employment and economic growth? ◆ The plan to have tax revenues fall short of expenditures is not new on Capitol Hill. The last time the federal government budget was in surplus was 1969. Over the 30 years since then, and using constant 1992 dollars, the federal government's debt has increased from $1,000 billion to $3,250 billion. If these numbers are too big to mean anything, divide them by the U.S. population to find *your* share. Government debt per person was more than $12,000 in 1999. Does it matter if the government doesn't balance its books? What are the effects of an ongoing government deficit and accumulating debt? Does it slow economic growth? Does it impose a burden on future generations—on you and your children? What must be done to balance the budget? Can spending cuts do it? Or must taxes be increased? Or can spending be cut so severely that taxes can also be cut?

◆ These are the fiscal policy issues that you will study in this chapter. We'll begin by describing the federal budget and the process of creating it. We'll also look at the recent history of the budget. We'll then use the multiplier analysis of Chapter 12 and the aggregate supply–aggregate demand model of Chapter 8 to study the effects of the budget on the economy.

After studying this chapter, you will be able to:

- **Describe the federal budget process**
- **Describe the recent history of federal expenditures, tax revenues, and the budget deficit**
- **Distinguish between automatic and discretionary fiscal policy**
- **Define and explain the fiscal policy multipliers**
- **Explain the effects of fiscal policy in the short run and in the long run**
- **Distinguish between and explain the demand-side and supply-side effects of fiscal policy**

The Federal Budget

T HE ANNUAL STATEMENT OF THE EXPENDITURES and tax revenues of the government of the United States together with the laws and regulations that approve and support those expenditures and taxes make up the **federal budget**. The federal budget has two purposes:

1. To finance the activities of the federal government
2. To stabilize the economy

The first purpose of the federal budget was its only purpose before the Great Depression years of the 1930s. The second purpose of the federal budget arose as a reaction to the Great Depression. The use of the federal budget to achieve macroeconomic objectives such as full employment, sustained economic growth, and price level stability is called **fiscal policy**. It is on this second purpose that we focus in this chapter.

The Institutions and Laws

Fiscal policy is made by the President and Congress on an annual time line that is shown in Figure 13.1.

The Roles of the President and Congress The President *proposes* a budget to Congress each February and, after Congress has passed the budget acts in September, either signs those acts into law or vetoes them. The President approves or vetoes the *entire* budget bill. He does not have the veto power to eliminate specific items in a budget bill and approve others—known as a *line-item veto*. Many state governors have a line-item veto authority, and Congress attempted to grant this power to the President in 1996. But a Supreme Court ruling of 1998 declared the line-item veto for the President unconstitutional. Although the President proposes and ultimately approves the budget, the task of making the tough decisions on spending and taxes rests with Congress.

Congress begins its work on the budget with the President's proposal. The House of Representatives and the Senate develop their own budget ideas in their respective House and Senate Budget Committees. Formal conferences between the two houses eventually resolve differences of view, and a series of spending acts and an overall budget act are usually passed by both houses before the start of the fiscal year. A *fiscal*

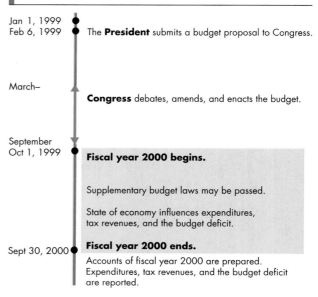

FIGURE 13.1

The Federal Budget Time Line in Fiscal 2000

Jan 1, 1999
Feb 6, 1999 ● The **President** submits a budget proposal to Congress.

March– **Congress** debates, amends, and enacts the budget.

September
Oct 1, 1999 ● **Fiscal year 2000 begins.**

Supplementary budget laws may be passed.

State of economy influences expenditures, tax revenues, and the budget deficit.

Sept 30, 2000 ● **Fiscal year 2000 ends.**
Accounts of fiscal year 2000 are prepared. Expenditures, tax revenues, and the budget deficit are reported.

The federal budget process begins with the President's proposals in February. Congress debates and amends these proposals and enacts a budget before the start of the fiscal year on October 1. The President signs the budget acts into law or vetoes them. Throughout the fiscal year, Congress might pass supplementary budget laws. The budget outcome is calculated after the fiscal year ends on September 30.

year is a year that runs from October 1 to September 30 in the next calendar year. *Fiscal 2000* is the fiscal year that *begins* on October 1, 1999.

During a fiscal year, Congress often passes supplementary budget laws, and the budget outcome is influenced by the evolving state of the economy. For example, if a recession begins, tax revenues fall and welfare payments increase.

The Employment Act of 1946 Fiscal policy operates within the framework of the **Employment Act of 1946**, in which Congress declared that

it is the continuing policy and responsibility of the Federal Government to use all practicable means ... to coordinate and utilize all its plans, functions, and resources ... to promote maximum employment, production, and purchasing power.

This act recognized a role for government actions to keep unemployment low, keep the economy expanding, and keep inflation in check. The *Full Employment and Balanced Growth Act of 1978*, more commonly known as the *Humphrey-Hawkins Act*, went further than the 1946 employment act and set a specific target of 4 percent for the unemployment rate. But this target has never been treated as an unwavering policy goal. Under the 1946 Act, the President must describe the current economic situation and the policies he believes are needed in an annual *Economic Report of the President*, which is written by the Council of Economic Advisers.

The Council of Economic Advisers The President's **Council of Economic Advisers** (CEA) was established in 1946 by the Employment Act. The Council consists of a Chair and two other members, all of whom are economists on a 1- or 2-year leave from their regular university or public service jobs. In 1999, the Chair of President Clinton's Council of Economic Advisers was Janet Yellen of the University of California at Berkeley. The Council monitors the economy and keeps the President and the public well informed about the current state of the economy and

the best available forecasts of where it is heading. This economic intelligence activity is one source of data that informs the budget-making process.

Let's look at the most recent federal budget.

Highlights of the 2000 Budget

Table 13.1 shows the main items in the federal budget proposed by President Clinton for 2000. The numbers are projected amounts for the fiscal year beginning on October 1, 1999—fiscal 2000. Notice the three main parts of the table: *tax revenues* are the government's receipts, *expenditures* are the government's outlays, and the *surplus* is the amount by which the government's tax revenues exceed its expenditures.

Tax Revenues Tax revenues were projected to be $1,987 billion in fiscal 2000. These revenues come from four sources:

1. Personal income taxes
2. Social insurance taxes
3. Corporate income taxes
4. Indirect taxes

The largest source of revenue is *personal income taxes*, which in 2000 are expected to be $926 billion. These are the taxes paid by individuals on their incomes. The second largest source is *social insurance taxes*. These are the taxes paid by workers and their employers to finance the government's social insurance programs. Third in size are *corporate income taxes*. These are the taxes paid by companies on their profits. Finally, the smallest source of federal revenue comes from what are called *indirect taxes*. These are taxes on the sale of gasoline, alcoholic drinks, and a few other items.

Expenditures Expenditures are classified in three categories:

1. Transfer payments
2. Purchases of goods and services
3. Debt interest

The largest item of expenditure, *transfer payments*, are payments to individuals, businesses, other levels of government, and the rest of the world. In 2000, this item is expected to be $1,868 billion. It includes Social Security benefits, Medicare and Medicaid, unemployment checks, welfare payments, farm

TABLE 13.1

Federal Budget in Fiscal 2000

Item	Projections (billions of dollars)	
Tax Revenues	**1,987**	
Personal income taxes		926
Social insurance taxes		738
Corporate income taxes		211
Indirect taxes		112
Expenditures	**1,868**	
Transfer payments		1,189
Purchases of goods and services		477
Debt interest		202
Surplus	**119**	

Source: Budget of the United States Government, Fiscal Year 2000, Table 14.1, Federal Transactions in the National Income and Product Accounts.

subsidies, grants to state and local governments, aid to developing countries, and dues to international organizations such as the United Nations. Transfer payments, especially those on Medicare and Medicaid, are sources of persistent growth in government expenditures and are a major source of concern and political debate.

Purchases of goods and services are expenditures on final goods and services, and in 2000, they are expected to total $477 billion. These expenditures, which include those on national defense, the NASA space program, research on cures for AIDS, computers for the Internal Revenue Service, government cars and trucks, federal highways, and dams, have decreased in recent years. This component of the federal budget is *government purchases of goods and services* that appears in the circular flow of expenditure and income and in the National Income and Product Accounts (see Chapter 6, pp. 118–119).

Debt interest is the interest on the government debt. In 2000, this item is expected to be $202 billion—some 11 percent of total expenditure. This interest payment is large because the government has a debt of more $3 trillion, which has arisen from many years of budget deficits during the 1970s, 1980s, and 1990s.

Surplus   The government's budget balance is equal to its tax revenues minus its expenditures. That is,

Budget balance = Tax revenues − Expenditures.

If tax revenues exceed expenditures, the government has a **budget surplus**. If expenditures exceed tax revenues, the government has a **budget deficit**. If tax revenues equal expenditures, the government has a **balanced budget**. In fiscal 2000, with projected expenditures of $1,868 billion and tax revenues of $1,987 billion, the government projected a budget surplus of $119 billion.

Big numbers like these are hard to visualize and hard to compare over time. To get a better sense of the magnitude of taxes, spending, and the surplus, we often express them as percentages of GDP. Expressing them in this way lets us to see how large government is relative to the size of the economy and also helps us to study *changes* in the scale of government over time.

How typical is the federal budget of 2000? Let's look at its recent history.

The Budget in Historical Perspective

Figure 13.2 shows the government's tax revenues, expenditures, and budget surplus or deficit since 1980. Through 1997, there was a budget deficit. The deficit was about 2 percent of GDP in 1980 and

FIGURE 13.2
The Budget Deficit

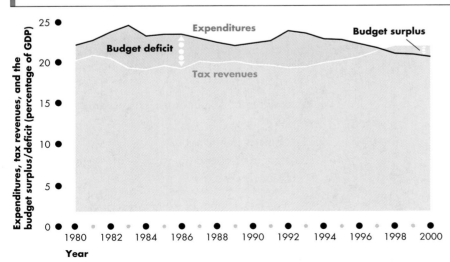

The figure records the federal government's expenditures, tax revenues, and budget surplus/deficit from 1980 through 2000. During the 1980s, a large and persistent budget deficit arose from the combination of a decrease in tax revenues and an increase in expenditures. In 1998, rising revenues and falling expenditures (as percentages of GDP) created a budget surplus.

Source: *Budget of the United States Government, Fiscal Year 2000*, Table 14.2, Federal Transactions in the National Income and Product Accounts.

1981, but it then increased and reached a peak in 1983 of 5.2 percent of GDP. It declined from 1983 through 1989 but climbed again during the 1990–1991 recession. During the 1990s expansion, the deficit gradually shrank and in 1998, the first surplus since 1969 emerged.

Why did the budget deficit grow during the 1980s and eventually vanish in the late 1990s? The answer lies in the changes in expenditures and tax revenues. But which components of expenditures and tax revenues changed to swell and then shrink the deficit? Let's look at tax revenues and expenditures in a bit more detail.

Tax Revenues   Figure 13.3(a) shows the components of tax revenues as percentages of GDP between 1980 and 2000. Cuts in corporate and personal income taxes lowered total tax revenues between 1981 and 1986. The decline resulted from tax cuts passed during 1981. From 1986 through 1991, tax

FIGURE 13.3

Federal Government Tax Revenues and Expenditures

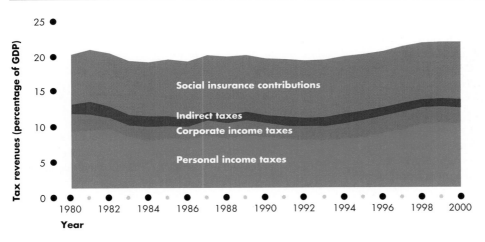

(a) Tax revenues

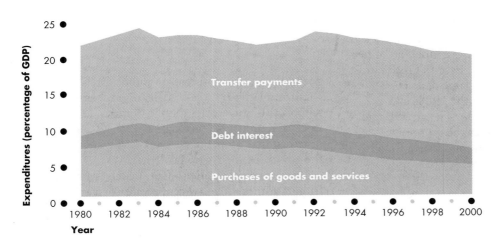

(b) Expenditures

In part (a), revenues from personal and corporate income taxes decreased during the early 1980s and revenues from personal income taxes increased during the 1990s. The other components of tax revenues remained steady.

In part (b), purchases of goods and services increased during the early 1980s and decreased through the 1990s. Transfer payments increased during the early 1980s. Debt interest increased steadily during the 1980s as the budget deficit fed on itself and then decreased during the 1990s as the deficit shrank and interest rates fell.

Source: *Budget of the United States Government, Fiscal Year 2000*, Table 14.2, Federal Transactions in the National Income and Product Accounts.

revenues did not change much as a percentage of GDP. But rising personal income taxes increased total tax revenues through the 1990s.

Expenditures   Figure 13.3(b) shows the components of government expenditures as percentages of GDP between 1980 and 2000. Total expenditures increased sharply between 1980 and 1983 and then declined slightly through 1989 before increasing again through 1992. After 1992, total expenditures decreased steadily. Purchases of goods and services decreased most during the 1990s. Debt interest increased most during the 1980s and contributed to the decrease in expenditures during the 1990s. To understand why, we need to see the connection between the government budget surplus or deficit and government debt.

Surplus, Deficit, and Debt   The government borrows when it has a budget deficit and makes repayments when it has a budget surplus. **Government debt** is the total amount that the government has borrowed. It is the sum of past deficits minus the sum of past surpluses. When the government has a budget deficit, its debt increases. And if a budget deficit persists, as it did during the 1980s, the deficit feeds itself. The deficit leads to increased borrowing; increased borrowing leads to larger interest payments; and larger interest payments lead to a larger deficit. That is the story of the increasing deficit of the 1980s.

Figure 13.4 shows the history of government debt since 1940. At the end of World War II, debt (as a percentage of GDP) was at an all-time high of 109 percent. Huge wartime deficits had increased debt to the point that it exceeded real GDP. Budget surpluses and rapid economic growth lowered the debt to GDP ratio through 1974, by which time it stood at 24 percent. Small deficits increased the debt to GDP ratio slightly through the 1970s, and large deficits increased it dramatically during the 1980s and through the 1990–1991 recession. The growth rate of the debt to GDP ratio slowed as the economy expanded during the mid-1990s and began to fall when the government budget went into surplus in the late 1990s.

Debt and Capital   Businesses and individuals incur debts to buy capital—assets that yield a return. In fact, the main point of debt is to enable people to buy assets that will earn a return that exceeds the interest paid on the debt. The government is similar to individuals and businesses in this regard. Much

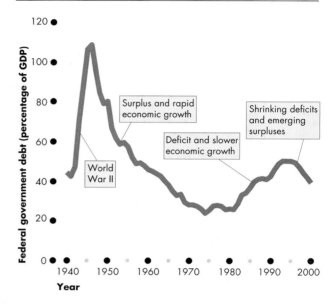

FIGURE 13.4

The Federal Government Debt

Federal government debt (the accumulation of past budget deficits less past budget surpluses) was more than 100 percent of GDP at the end of World War II. Debt as a percentage of GDP fell through 1974 but then started to increase. After a further brief decline during the late 1970s, it exploded during the 1980s and continued to increase through 1995, after which it began to fall.

Source: Budget of the United States Government, Fiscal Year 2000, Table 7.1, Federal Debt.

government expenditure is on public assets that yield a return. Highways, major irrigation schemes, public schools and universities, public libraries, and the stock of national defense capital all yield a social rate of return that probably far exceeds the interest rate the government pays on its debt.

But total government debt, which is almost $4 trillion, is more than twice the value of the public capital stock. So some government debt has been incurred to finance public consumption expenditure (such as foreign travel for diplomats). This expenditure does not have an ongoing social return.

How does the U. S. government budget balance compare with those in other countries?

The Budget Surplus in Global Perspective

Is the United States unusual in running a budget surplus? Do other countries have budget surpluses or do they have budget deficits? Figure 13.5 answers these questions. In today's world, almost all countries have budget deficits. To compare countries, we measure the budget surplus or deficit as a percentage of GDP. The biggest deficit relative to GDP is found in Japan, where the budget deficit exceeds 5 percent of GDP. The rest of Asia and the Middle East also have large deficits. The smallest deficits relative to GDP are found in the European Union.

The United States and a small group of other countries that include Canada, Australia, Ireland, and some Scandinavian countries are relatively unusual in having budget *surpluses*.

State and Local Budgets

The *total government* sector of the United States includes state and local governments as well as the federal government. In 1998, when federal government expenditures were $1,750 billion, state and local expenditures were more than $1,000 billion. Most of these expenditures were on public schools, colleges, and universities ($350 billion); local police and fire services; and roads.

It is the total government sector that influences the aggregate economy. But state and local budgets are not designed, as the federal budget is, with the specific goal of stabilizing the aggregate economy. On the contrary, sometimes, when the aggregate economy needs an injection of additional expenditures, state and local governments cut their expenditures and deficits. Such changes in expenditures occurred during the 1990–1991 recession when many states both cut their expenditures and increased taxes.

FIGURE 13.5

Government Budgets Around the World in 1999

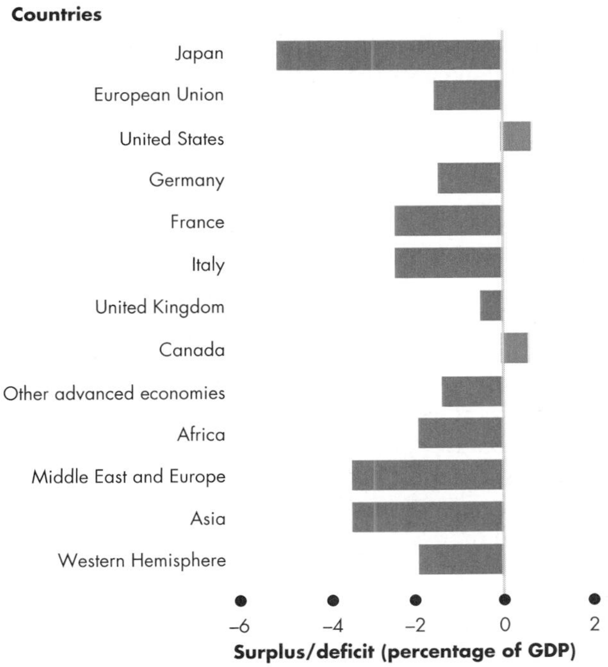

Governments in most countries have budget deficits. The largest ones are in Japan followed by the Middle East and the rest of Asia. The United States, Canada, and a few other advanced economies have surpluses.

Source: World Economic Outlook, October 1998, International Monetary Fund, Washington, D.C., Tables A15 and A20.

R E V I E W   Q U I Z

- What is fiscal policy, who makes it, and what is it designed to influence?
- What special role does the President play in creating fiscal policy?
- What is the time line for the U.S. federal budget each year? When does a fiscal year begin and end?
- Is the U.S. federal government budget today in surplus or deficit?

Now that you know what the federal budget is and what the main items of revenue and expenditure are, it is time to study the *effects* of fiscal policy. We'll begin by learning about its effects on expenditure plans when the price level is fixed. You will see that fiscal policy has multiplier effects like the expenditure multipliers explained in Chapter 12. Then we'll study the influences of fiscal policy on both aggregate demand and aggregate supply and look at its short-run and long-run effects on real GDP and the price level.

Fiscal Policy Multipliers

FISCAL POLICY ACTIONS CAN BE EITHER AUTOMATIC or discretionary. **Automatic fiscal policy** is a change in fiscal policy that is triggered by the state of the economy. For example, an increase in unemployment triggers an *automatic* increase in payments to the unemployed. A fall in income triggers an *automatic* decrease in tax receipts. That is, this type of fiscal policy adjusts automatically. **Discretionary fiscal policy** is a policy action that is initiated by an act of Congress. It requires a change in tax laws or in some spending program. For example, an increase in the income tax rate and an increase in defense spending are discretionary fiscal policy actions. That is, discretionary fiscal policy is a deliberate policy action.

We begin by studying the effects of *discretionary* changes in government spending and taxes. To focus on the essentials, we'll initially study a model economy that is simpler than the one in which we live. In our model economy, there is no international trade and the taxes are all lump sum. **Lump-sum taxes** are taxes that do not vary with real GDP. The government fixes them, and they change when the government changes them. But they do not vary automatically with the state of the economy.

The main example of a lump-sum tax is the *property tax*. This tax varies across individuals and depends on the value of the property a person occupies. But unlike the income tax, it does not change simply because a person's income changes.

We use lump-sum taxes in our model economy because they make the principles we are studying easier to understand. Once we've grasped the principles, we'll explore our real economy with its international trade and income taxes—taxes that *do* vary with real GDP.

Like our real economy, the model economy we study is bombarded by spending fluctuations. Business investment in new building, plant and equipment, and inventories fluctuates because of swings in profit expectations and interest rates. These fluctuations set up multiplier effects that start a recession or an expansion. If a recession takes hold, unemployment increases and incomes fall. If an expansion becomes too strong, inflationary pressures build up. To minimize the effects of these swings in spending, the government might change either its purchases of goods and services or taxes. By changing either of these items, the government can influence aggregate expenditure and real GDP. But it also changes its budget deficit or surplus. An alternative fiscal policy action is to change both purchases and taxes together so that the budget balance does not change. We are going to study the initial effects of these discretionary fiscal policy actions in the very short run when the price level is fixed. Each of these actions creates a multiplier effect on real GDP. These multipliers are:

- The government purchases multiplier
- The lump-sum tax multiplier

The Government Purchases Multiplier

The **government purchases multiplier** is the magnification effect of a change in government purchases of goods and services on equilibrium expenditure and real GDP.

Government purchases are a component of aggregate expenditure. So when government purchases change, aggregate expenditure and real GDP change. The change in real GDP induces a change in consumption expenditure, which brings a further change in aggregate expenditure. A multiplier process ensues. This multiplier process is like the one described in Chapter 12 (pp. 264–269). Let's look at an example.

Cape Canaveral Multiplier Before the National Aeronautics and Space Administration (NASA) built a major space launching facility at Cape Canaveral in Florida in the 1960s, the Cape was a quiet place. The injection of government purchases to build the space launching and research facility created jobs in the region. Because construction workers and NASA workers spent most of their incomes locally, consumption expenditure increased. Retail stores and hotels and motels opened and hired yet more people and, in the process, created yet bigger incomes. These incomes were also spent in the area, so spending and incomes rose still further. Eventually, expenditures and incomes stopped rising but remained at their new higher levels.

The Size of the Multiplier Table 13.2 illustrates the government purchases multiplier with a numerical example. The first column lists various possible levels of real GDP. Our task is to find equilibrium expenditure and the change in real GDP when government purchases change. The second column shows taxes.

TABLE 13.2

The Government Purchases Multiplier

	Real GDP (Y)	Taxes (T)	Disposable income (Y – T)	Consumption expenditure (C)	Investment (I)	Initial government purchases (G)	Initial aggregate planned expenditure (C + I + G)	Increase in government purchases (ΔG)	New aggregate planned expenditure (C + I + G + ΔG)
					(trillions of dollars)				
a	5.0	0.5	4.5	3.75	1.0	0.5	5.25	0.5	5.75
b	6.0	0.5	5.5	4.50	1.0	0.5	6.00	0.5	6.50
c	7.0	0.5	6.5	5.25	1.0	0.5	6.75	0.5	7.25
d	8.0	0.5	7.5	6.00	1.0	0.5	7.50	0.5	8.00
e	9.0	0.5	8.5	6.75	1.0	0.5	8.25	0.5	8.75

They are fixed at $0.5 trillion, regardless of the level of real GDP. (This is an assumption that keeps your attention on the key idea and makes the calculations easier to do.) The third column calculates disposable income. Because taxes are a lump sum, disposable income equals real GDP minus the $0.5 trillion of taxes. For example, in row *b*, real GDP is $6 trillion and disposable income is $5.5 trillion. The next column shows consumption expenditure. In this example, the *marginal propensity to consume* is 0.75. That is, a $1 increase in disposable income brings a 75-cent increase in consumption expenditure. Check this fact by calculating the increase in consumption expenditure when disposable income increases by $1 trillion from row *b* to row *c*. Consumption expenditure increases by $0.75 trillion. The next column shows investment, which is a constant of $1 trillion. The next column shows the initial level of government purchases, which is $0.5 trillion. Aggregate planned expenditure is the sum of consumption expenditure, investment, and government purchases.

Equilibrium expenditure and real GDP occur when aggregate planned expenditure equals actual expenditure. In this example, equilibrium expenditure is $6 trillion (highlighted in row *b* of the table.)

The final two columns of the table show what happens when government purchases increase by $0.5 trillion to $1 trillion. Aggregate planned expenditure increases by $0.5 trillion at each level of real GDP. At the initial real GDP of $6 trillion (row *b*), aggregate planned expenditure increases to $6.5 trillion.

Because aggregate planned expenditure now exceeds real GDP, inventories decrease and firms increase production. Output, incomes, and expenditure increase. Increased incomes induce a further increase in expenditure. But the induced increase in aggregate planned expenditure is less than the increase in income, and eventually a new equilibrium is reached. The new equilibrium is at a real GDP of $8 trillion (highlighted in row *d*).

A $0.5 trillion increase in government purchases has increased equilibrium expenditure and real GDP by $2 trillion. Therefore the government purchases multiplier is 4. The size of the multiplier depends on the marginal propensity to consume, which in this example is 0.75. The following formula shows the connection between the government purchases multiplier and the marginal propensity to consume (*MPC*):

$$\text{Government purchases multiplier} = \frac{1}{1 - MPC}.$$

Let's check this formula by using the numbers in the above example. The marginal propensity to consume is 0.75, so the government purchases multiplier is 4.

Figure 13.6 illustrates the government purchases multiplier. Initially, aggregate planned expenditure is shown by the curve labeled AE_0. The points on this curve, labeled *a* through *e*, correspond with the rows of Table 13.2. This aggregate expenditure curve intersects the 45° line at the equilibrium level of real GDP, which is $6 trillion.

FIGURE 13.6

The Government
Purchases Multiplier

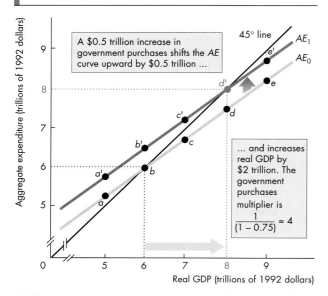

Initially, the aggregate expenditure curve is AE_0 and real GDP is $6 trillion (at point *b*). An increase in government purchases of $0.5 trillion increases aggregate planned expenditure at each level of real GDP by $0.5 trillion. The aggregate expenditure curve shifts upward from AE_0 to AE_1—a parallel shift. At the initial real GDP of $6 trillion, aggregate planned expenditure is now $6.5 trillion. Because aggregate planned expenditure is greater than real GDP, real GDP increases. The new equilibrium is reached when real GDP is $8 trillion—the point at which the AE_1 curve intersects the 45° line (at *d′*). In this example, the government purchases multiplier is 4.

When government purchases increase by $0.5 trillion, the aggregate expenditure curve shifts upward by that amount to AE_1. With this new aggregate expenditure curve, equilibrium real GDP increases to $8 trillion. The increase in real GDP is 4 times the increase in government purchases. The government purchases multiplier is 4.

You've seen that in the very short term, when the price level is fixed, an increase in government purchases increases real GDP. But to produce more output, more people must be employed. So in the short term, an increase in government purchases can create jobs.

Increasing its purchases of goods and services is one way in which the government can try to stimulate the economy. A second way in which the government might act to increase real GDP in the very short run is by decreasing lump-sum taxes. Let's see how this action works.

The Lump-Sum Tax Multiplier

The **lump-sum tax multiplier** is the magnification effect of a change in lump-sum taxes on equilibrium expenditure and real GDP. An *increase* in taxes *decreases* disposable income, which *decreases* consumption expenditure. The amount by which consumption expenditure initially changes is determined by the marginal propensity to consume. In our example, the marginal propensity to consume is 0.75, so a $1 tax cut increases disposable income by $1 and increases aggregate expenditure initially by 75 cents.

This initial change in aggregate expenditure has a multiplier just like the government purchases multiplier. We've seen that the government purchases multiplier is $1/(1 - MPC)$. Because a tax *increase* leads to a *decrease* in expenditure, the lump-sum tax multiplier is *negative*. And because a change in lump-sum taxes changes aggregate expenditure initially by only MPC multiplied by the tax change, the lump-sum tax multiplier is equal to

$$\text{Lump-sum tax multiplier} = \frac{-MPC}{1 - MPC}.$$

In our example, the marginal propensity to consume is 3/4, so the lump-sum tax multiplier is

$$\text{Lump-sum tax multiplier} = \frac{-\dfrac{3}{4}}{1 - \dfrac{3}{4}} = -3.$$

Figure 13.7 illustrates the lump-sum tax multiplier. Initially, the aggregate expenditure curve is AE_0, and equilibrium expenditure is $8 trillion. Taxes increase by $1 trillion, and disposable income falls by that amount. With a marginal propensity to consume of 3/4, aggregate expenditure decreases initially by $0.75 trillion and the aggregate expenditure curve shifts downward by that amount to AE_1. Equilibrium expenditure and real GDP fall by $3 trillion to $5 trillion. The lump-sum tax multiplier is −3.

FIGURE 13.7

The Lump-Sum Tax Multiplier

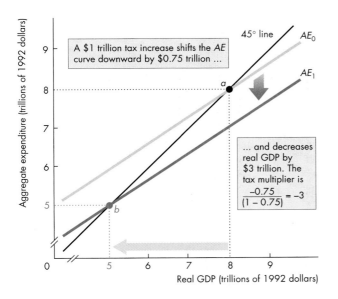

Initially, the aggregate expenditure curve is AE_0 and equilibrium expenditure is $8 trillion. The marginal propensity to consume is 0.75. Lump-sum taxes increase by $1 trillion, so disposable income falls by $1 trillion. The decrease in aggregate expenditure is found by multiplying this change in disposable income by the marginal propensity to consume and is $1 trillion × 0.75 = $0.75 trillion. The aggregate expenditure curve shifts *downward* by this amount to AE_1. Equilibrium expenditure decreases by $3 trillion, from $8 trillion to $5 trillion. The lump-sum tax multiplier is −3.

Lump-Sum Transfer Payments The lump-sum tax multiplier also tells us the effects of a change in lump-sum transfer payments. Transfer payments are like negative taxes, so an increase in transfer payments works like a decrease in taxes. Because the tax multiplier is negative, a decrease in taxes increases expenditure. An increase in transfer payments also increases expenditure. So the lump-sum transfer payments multiplier is positive. It is

$$\frac{\text{Lump-sum transfer}}{\text{payments multiplier}} = \frac{MPC}{1 - MPC}.$$

Induced Taxes and Entitlement Spending

In the examples we've studied so far, taxes are lump-sum taxes. But in reality, net taxes (taxes minus transfer payments) vary with the state of the economy.

On the revenue side of the budget, tax laws define tax *rates* to be paid, not tax *dollars* to be paid. Tax *dollars* paid depend on tax *rates* and incomes. But incomes vary with real GDP, so tax *revenues* depend on real GDP. Taxes that vary with real GDP are called **induced taxes.** When the economy expands, induced taxes increase because real GDP increases. When the economy is in a recession, induced taxes decrease because real GDP decreases.

On the outlay side of the budget, the government creates programs that entitle suitably qualified people and businesses to receive benefits. The spending on such programs is called **entitlement spending,** and it results in transfer payments that depend on the economic state of individual citizens and businesses. When the economy is in a recession, unemployment is high, the number of people experiencing economic hardship increases, and a larger number of firms and farms experience hard times. Entitlement spending increases. When the economy expands, entitlement spending decreases.

Induced taxes and entitlement payments decrease the multiplier effects of changes in government purchases and lump-sum taxes. The reason is that they weaken the link between real GDP and disposable income and so dampen the effect of a change in real GDP on consumption expenditure. When real GDP increases, induced taxes increase and entitlement payments decrease, so disposable income does not increase by as much as the increase in real GDP. As a result, consumption expenditure does not increase by as much as it otherwise would have done and the multiplier effect is reduced.

The extent to which induced taxes and entitlement payments decrease the multiplier depends on the *marginal tax rate*. The marginal tax rate is the proportion of an additional dollar of real GDP that flows to the government in net taxes (taxes minus transfer payments). The higher the marginal tax rate, the larger is the proportion of an additional dollar of real GDP that is paid to the government and the smaller is the induced change in consumption expenditure. The smaller the change in consumption expenditure induced by a change in real GDP, the smaller is the multiplier effect of a change in government purchases or lump-sum taxes.

International Trade and Fiscal Policy Multipliers

Not all expenditure in the United States is on U.S.-produced goods and services. Some of it is on imports—on foreign-produced goods and services. Imports affect the fiscal policy multipliers in exactly the same way that they influence the expenditure multiplier, as explained in Chapter 12 (see pp. 266–267), and there is no new principle involved. The extent to which an additional dollar of real GDP is spent on imports is determined by the *marginal propensity to import.* Expenditure on imports does not generate U.S. real GDP and does not lead to an increase in U.S. consumption expenditure. The larger the marginal propensity to import, the smaller is the increase in consumption expenditure induced by an increase in real GDP and the smaller are the government purchases and lump-sum tax multipliers.

So far, we've studied *discretionary* fiscal policy. Let's now look at *automatic* stabilizers.

Automatic Stabilizers

Automatic stabilizers are mechanisms that stabilize real GDP without explicit action by the government. Their name is borrowed from engineering and conjures up images of shock absorbers, thermostats, and sophisticated devices that keep airplanes and ships steady in turbulent air and seas. Automatic fiscal stabilizers are a consequence of income taxes and transfer payments that automatically fluctuate with real GDP. If real GDP begins to decrease, tax revenues fall and transfer payments rise. These changes in taxes and transfer payments affect the economy and the government's budget deficit. Let's study the budget deficit over the business cycle.

Budget Deficit Over the Business Cycle   Figure 13.8 shows the business cycle and fluctuations in the budget deficit since 1975. Part (a) shows the fluctuations of real GDP around potential GDP. Part (b) shows the federal budget deficit. Both parts highlight recessions by shading those periods. By comparing the two parts of the figure, you can see the relationship between the business cycle and the budget deficit. As a rule, when the economy is in the expansion phase of a business cycle, the budget deficit declines. (In the figure, a declining deficit means a deficit that is getting closer to zero.) As the expansion slows before the recession begins, the budget deficit

FIGURE 13.8

The Business Cycle and the Budget Deficit

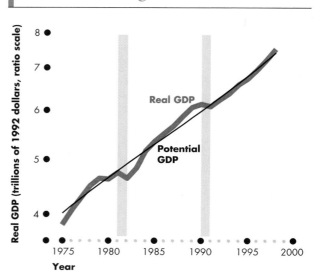

(a) Growth and recessions

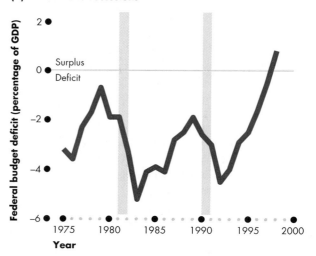

(b) Federal budget deficit

As real GDP fluctuates around potential GDP (part a), the budget deficit fluctuates (part b). During a recession (shaded years), tax revenues decrease, transfer payments increase, and the budget deficit increases. The deficit also increases *before* a recession as real GDP growth slows and *after* a recession before real GDP growth speeds up.

Source: Economic Report of the President, 1999, and the author's calculations.

increases. It continues to increase during the recession and for a further period after the recession is over. Then, when the expansion is well under way, the budget deficit declines again.

The budget deficit fluctuates with the business cycle because both tax revenues and expenditures fluctuate with real GDP. As real GDP increases during an expansion, tax revenues increase and transfer payments decrease, so the budget deficit automatically decreases. As real GDP decreases during a recession, tax revenues decrease and transfer payments increase, so the budget deficit automatically increases.

Fluctuations in investment and exports have a multiplier effect on real GDP. But automatic fluctuations in tax revenues (and the budget deficit) act as an automatic stabilizer. They decrease the swings in disposable income and make the multiplier effect smaller. They dampen both expansions and recessions.

Cyclical and Structural Balances   Because the government budget balance fluctuates with the business cycle, we need a method of measuring the balance that tells us whether it is a temporary cyclical phenomenon or a persistent phenomenon. A temporary and cyclical surplus or deficit vanishes when full employment returns. A persistent surplus or deficit requires government action to remove it.

To determine whether the budget balance is temporary and cyclical or persistent, economists have developed the concepts of the structural budget balance and the cyclical budget balance. The **structural surplus or deficit** is the budget balance that would occur if the economy were at full employment and real GDP equalled potential GDP. The **cyclical surplus or deficit** is the actual surplus or deficit minus the structural surplus or deficit. That is, the cyclical surplus or deficit is the part of the budget balance that arises purely because real GDP does not equal potential GDP.

For example, suppose there is a budget deficit of $100 billion. And suppose that economists have determined that there is a structural deficit of $25 billion. Then there is a cyclical deficit of $75 billion.

Figure 13.9 illustrates the concepts of cyclical surplus or deficit and structural surplus or deficit. The blue curve shows government expenditures. The expenditures curve slopes downward because the higher the level of real GDP, the smaller is the level of transfer payments and so the smaller is the level of government expenditures. The green curve shows tax revenues. The tax revenues curve slopes upward

FIGURE 13.9

Cyclical and Structural Surpluses and Deficits

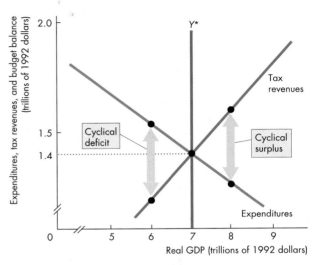

(a) Cyclical deficit and cyclical surplus

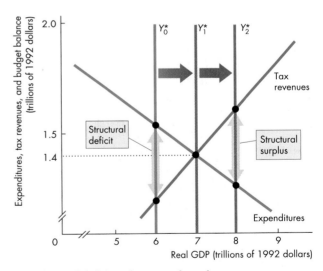

(b) Structural deficit and structural surplus

In part (a), potential GDP is $7 trillion. When real GDP is less than potential GDP, the budget is in a *cyclical deficit*. When real GDP exceeds potential GDP, the budget is in a *cyclical surplus*. The government has a *balanced budget* when real GDP equals potential GDP. In part (b), when potential GDP is $6 trillion, there is a *structural deficit*. But when potential GDP is $8 trillion, there is a *structural surplus*.

because most components of tax revenues increase as incomes and real GDP increase.

In Fig. 13.9(a), potential GDP is $7 trillion. If real GDP equals potential GDP, the government has a *balanced budget*. Expenditures and tax revenues each equal $1.4 trillion. If real GDP is less than potential GDP, expenditures exceed tax revenues and there is a *cyclical deficit*. If real GDP is greater than potential GDP, expenditures are less than tax revenues and there is a *cyclical surplus*.

In Fig. 13.9(b), potential GDP grows but the tax revenue curve and the expenditure curve do not change. When potential GDP is $6 trillion, there is a *structural deficit*. When potential GDP grows to $7 trillion, there is a *structural balance* of zero (neither a deficit nor a surplus). And when potential GDP grows to $8 trillion, there is a *structural surplus*.

The U.S. federal budget was in a structural deficit starting in the mid-1970s and through the mid-1990s. That is, even if the economy had been at full employment, the budget would have been in deficit. Worse, the structural deficit was so large that even at the peak of a business cycle, the budget was in deficit.

At the end of the 1990s, a budget surplus was emerging. But it is not yet clear that this surplus is structural. The economy was above full employment, so the surplus could be cyclical.

R E V I E W   Q U I Z

- What are the government purchases multiplier and the lump-sum tax multiplier? How do these multiplier effects work?
- Which multiplier effect is larger, that of a change in government purchases or that of a change in lump-sum taxes? Why is one larger than the other?
- How do income taxes and international trade influence the size of the fiscal policy multipliers?
- How do income taxes and entitlement programs work as automatic stabilizers to dampen the business cycle?
- How do we tell whether a budget deficit needs government action to remove it?

Your next task is to see how, with the passage of more time and with some price level adjustments, these multiplier effects change.

Fiscal Policy Multipliers and the Price Level

WE'VE SEEN HOW REAL GDP RESPONDS TO changes in fiscal policy when the price level is fixed and all the adjustments that take place are in spending, income, and production. The period over which this response occurs is very short. Once production starts to change, regardless of whether it increases or decreases, prices also start to change. The price level and real GDP change together, and the economy moves to a new short-run equilibrium.

To study the simultaneous changes in real GDP and the price level that result from fiscal policy, we use the aggregate supply–aggregate demand model of Chapter 8. In the long run, both the price level and the money wage rate respond to fiscal policy. As these further changes take place, the economy gradually moves toward a new long-run equilibrium. We also use the aggregate supply–aggregate demand model to study these adjustments.

We begin by looking at the effects of fiscal policy on aggregate demand and the aggregate demand curve.

Fiscal Policy and Aggregate Demand

You learned about the relationship between aggregate demand, aggregate expenditure, and equilibrium expenditure in Chapter 12. You are now going to use what you learned there to work out what happens to aggregate demand, the price level, real GDP, and jobs when fiscal policy changes. We'll start by looking at the effects of a change in fiscal policy on aggregate demand.

Figure 13.10 shows the effects of an increase in government purchases on aggregate demand. Initially, the aggregate expenditure curve is AE_0 in part (a), and the aggregate demand curve is AD_0 in part (b). The price level is 110, real GDP is $7 trillion, and the economy is at point a in both parts of the figure. Now suppose that government purchases increase by $0.5 trillion. At a constant price level of 110, the aggregate expenditure curve shifts upward to AE_1. This curve intersects the 45° line at an equilibrium expenditure of $9 trillion at point b. This amount is the aggregate quantity of goods and services demanded at a price level of 110, as shown by point b in part (b). Point b

FIGURE 13.10

Government Purchases and Aggregate Demand

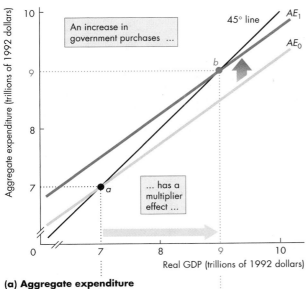

(a) Aggregate expenditure

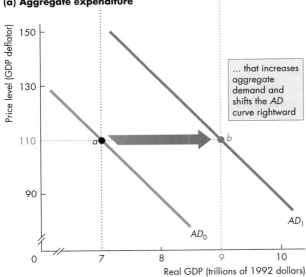

(b) Aggregate demand

The price level is 110, aggregate planned expenditure is AE_0 (part a), and aggregate demand is AD_0 (part b). An increase in government purchases shifts the AE curve to AE_1 and equilibrium real GDP increases to $9 trillion. The aggregate demand curve shifts rightward to AD_1.

lies on a new aggregate demand curve. The aggregate demand curve has shifted rightward to AD_1.

The government purchases multiplier determines the distance by which the aggregate demand curve shifts rightward. The larger the multiplier, the larger is the shift in the aggregate demand curve resulting from a given change in government purchases. In this example, a $0.5 trillion increase in government purchases produces a $2 trillion increase in the aggregate quantity of goods and services demanded at each price level. The multiplier is 4. So the $0.5 trillion increase in government purchases shifts the aggregate demand curve rightward by $2 trillion.

Figure 13.10 shows the effects of an increase in government purchases. But a similar effect occurs for *any* expansionary fiscal policy. An **expansionary fiscal policy** is an increase in government purchases or a decrease in tax revenues. But the distance the AD curve shifts is smaller for a tax cut than for a government purchases increase of the same size.

Figure 13.10 can also be used to illustrate the effects of a **contractionary fiscal policy**—a decrease in government purchases or an increase in tax revenues. In this case, start at point *b* in each part of the figure and decrease government purchases or increase taxes. Aggregate demand decreases from AD_1 to AD_0.

Equilibrium GDP and the Price Level in the Short Run   We've seen how an increase in government purchases increases aggregate demand. Let's now see how it changes real GDP and the price level. Figure 13.11(a) describes the economy. Aggregate demand is AD_0, and the short-run aggregate supply curve is *SAS*. (Check back to Chapter 8 if you need to refresh your understanding of the *SAS* curve.) Equilibrium is at point *a*, where the aggregate demand and short-run aggregate supply curves intersect. The price level is 110, and real GDP is $7 trillion.

An increase in government purchases of $0.5 trillion shifts the aggregate demand curve rightward from AD_0 to AD_1. While the price level is fixed at 110, the economy moves toward point *b* and real GDP increases toward $9 trillion. But during the adjustment process, the price level does not remain constant. It gradually rises, and the economy moves along the short-run aggregate supply curve to the point of intersection of the short-run aggregate supply curve and the new aggregate demand curve—point *c*. The price level rises to 116, and real GDP increases to only $8.6 trillion.

FIGURE 13.11

Fiscal Policy, Real GDP, and the Price Level

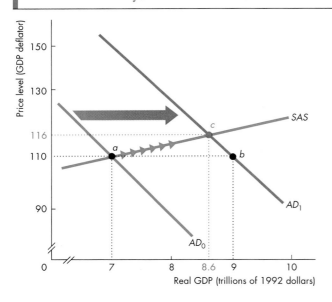

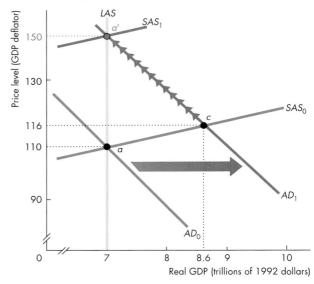

(a) Fiscal policy with unemployment

An increase in government purchases shifts the *AD* curve from *AD₀* to *AD₁*. With a fixed price level, the economy would have moved to point *b*. But the price level rises, and in the short run, the economy moves to point *c*. The price level increases to 116, and real GDP increases to $8.6 trillion.

(b) Fiscal policy with full employment

At point *c*, real GDP exceeds potential GDP and unemployment is below the natural rate. The wage rate rises, and short-run aggregate supply decreases. The *SAS* curve shifts leftward to *SAS₁*, and in the long run, the economy moves to point *a'*. The price level rises to 150, and real GDP returns to $7 trillion.

When we take the price level effect into account, the increase in government purchases still has a multiplier effect on real GDP, but the effect is smaller than it would be if the price level remained constant. Also, the steeper the slope of the short-run aggregate supply curve, the larger is the increase in the price level, the smaller is the increase in real GDP, and the smaller is the government purchases multiplier. But the multiplier is not zero.

In the long run, real GDP equals potential GDP—the economy is at full-employment equilibrium. When real GDP equals potential GDP, an increase in aggregate demand has the same short-run effect as we've just worked out, but its long-run effect is different. The increase in aggregate demand raises the price level, but in the long run, it leaves real GDP unchanged at potential GDP.

To study this case, let's see what happens if the government embarks on an expansionary fiscal policy when real GDP equals potential GDP.

Fiscal Expansion at Potential GDP

Suppose that real GDP is equal to potential GDP, which means that unemployment is equal to the natural rate of unemployment. But suppose also that the unemployment rate and the natural rate are high and that most people, including the government, mistakenly think that the unemployment rate exceeds the natural rate. In this situation, the government tries to lower the unemployment rate by using an expansionary fiscal policy.

Figure 13.11(b) shows the effect of an expansionary fiscal policy when real GDP equals potential GDP. In this example, potential GDP is $7 trillion. Aggregate demand increases, and the aggregate demand curve shifts rightward from *AD₀* to *AD₁*. The short-run equilibrium, point *c*, is an above full-employment equilibrium. The labor force is more than fully employed, and there are shortages of labor.

Money wage rates begin to increase. Higher money wage rates increase costs, and short-run aggregate supply decreases. The *SAS* curve begins to shift leftward from SAS_0 to SAS_1. The economy moves up the aggregate demand curve AD_1 toward point a'.

Eventually, when all adjustments to wage rates and the price level have been made, the price level is 150 and real GDP is again at potential GDP of $7 trillion. The multiplier in the long run is zero. There has been a temporary decrease in the unemployment rate during the process you've just looked at, but not a permanent decrease. But the price level rise is permanent.

Limitations of Fiscal Policy

Because the short-run fiscal policy multipliers are not zero, expansionary fiscal policy can be used to increase real GDP and decrease the unemployment rate in a recession. Contractionary fiscal policy can also be used if the economy is overheating to decrease real GDP and help to keep inflation in check. But the use of fiscal policy is limited by two factors.

First, the legislative process is slow, which means that it is difficult to take fiscal policy actions in a timely way. The economy might be able to benefit from fiscal stimulation right now, but it will take Congress many months to act. By then, the economy might need an entirely different fiscal medicine.

Second, it is not always easy to tell whether real GDP is below (or above) potential GDP. A change in aggregate demand can move real GDP away from potential GDP, or a change in aggregate supply can change real GDP and change potential GDP. This difficulty is a serious one because, as you've seen, fiscal stimulation at full employment leads to a rise in the price level and has no long-run effect on real GDP.

R E V I E W   Q U I Z

- How do changes in the price level influence the multiplier effects of fiscal policy on real GDP?
- What are the long-run effects of fiscal policy on real GDP and the price level when initially real GDP equals potential GDP?

So far in this chapter, we've ignored any potential effects of fiscal policy on aggregate supply. Yet many economists believe that the supply-side effects of fiscal policy are large. Let's now look at these effects.

Fiscal Policy and Aggregate Supply

DURING THE 1980S, WHEN RONALD REAGAN WAS President, a group of economists known as *supply-siders* became prominent. Supply-siders believed that tax cuts would strengthen incentives and increase aggregate supply. George Bush called their ideas "voodoo economics," and many other people are skeptical about supply-siders' claims. But these claims remain part of the political debate today. They are the main rationale for a flat tax that some economists and politicians have advocated.

Using the concepts of the *AS-AD* model, the supply-siders' claim is that tax cuts increase potential GDP. Is this claim correct?

There is no disagreement among economists that taxes create disincentives and decrease potential GDP. The disagreements are about numbers. Supply-siders say the effects are large. Others suspect that the effects are small, possibly too small to bother about.

Let's study the effects of taxes on potential GDP and then see how the supply effects and demand effects together influence real GDP and the price level.

Fiscal Policy and Potential GDP

Potential GDP depends on the full-employment quantity of labor, the quantity of capital, and the state of technology. Taxes can influence all three of these factors. The main tax to consider is the income tax. By taxing the incomes people earn when they work or save, the government weakens the incentives to work and save. The result is a smaller quantity of labor and capital and a lower potential GDP. Also, the income tax weakens the incentive to develop new technologies that increase income. So the pace of technological change might be slowed, which slows the growth rate of potential GDP. Let's look at the effect of the income tax on both the quantity of labor and the quantity of capital.

Labor and the Income Tax   The quantity of labor is determined by demand and supply in the labor market (see Chapter 9, pp. 190–191). Figure 13.12(a) shows a labor market. The demand for labor is *LD*, and the supply is *LS*. With no income tax, this labor market achieves equilibrium at a real wage rate of $14 an hour and 230 billion hours of labor per year are employed.

FIGURE 13.12

Supply-Side Effects of the Income Tax

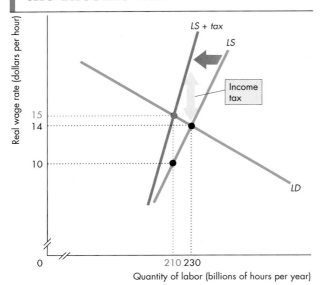

(a) The labor market

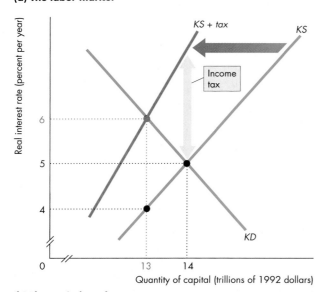

(b) The capital market

In part (a), the income tax shifts the supply of labor curve, LS, leftward to LS + tax. The before-tax wage rate rises, the after-tax wage rate falls, and the quantity of labor employed decreases. In part (b), the income tax shifts the supply of capital curve, KS, leftward to KS + tax. The before-tax interest rate rises, the after-tax interest rate falls, and the quantity of capital decreases. With less labor and less capital, potential GDP falls.

Now suppose an income tax is introduced. The income tax weakens the incentive to work and decreases the supply of labor. The supply curve shifts leftward to LS + tax. With this new lower supply of labor, the *before-tax* wage rate rises to $15 an hour and the quantity of labor employed decreases to 210 billion hours a year. The before-tax wage rate rises, but the *after-tax* wage rate falls. In Fig. 13.12(a), it falls to $10 an hour.

Capital and the Income Tax   The quantity of capital is determined by demand and supply in the capital market (see Chapter 10, pp. 213–215). Figure 13.12(b) shows the capital market. The demand for capital is *KD*, and the supply is *KS*. With no income tax, the capital market achieves equilibrium at a real interest rate of 5 percent a year and $14 trillion of capital is available.

Now consider the effects of a tax on income from capital. The income tax, which weakens the incentive to save, decreases the supply of capital. The supply curve shifts leftward to *KS + tax*. The *before-tax* interest rate rises to 6 percent a year, and the quantity of capital decreases to $13 trillion. The before-tax interest rate rises, but the *after-tax* interest rate falls. In Fig. 13.12, it falls to 4 percent a year.

Potential GDP and *LAS*   Because the income tax decreases the equilibrium quantities of labor and capital, it also decreases potential GDP. But potential GDP determines long-run aggregate supply. So the income tax decreases long-run aggregate supply and shifts the *LAS* curve leftward.

Supply Effects and Demand Effects

Let's now bring the supply effects and demand effects of fiscal policy together. Figure 13.13(a) shows the most likely effects of a tax cut. The tax cut increases aggregate demand and shifts the *AD* curve rightward, just as before. But a tax cut that increases the incentive to work and save also increases aggregate supply. It shifts the long-run and short-run aggregate supply curves rightward. Here we focus on the short-run and show the effect on the *SAS* curve, which shifts rightward to *SAS*₁. In this example, the tax cut has a large effect on aggregate demand and a small effect on aggregate supply. The aggregate demand curve shifts rightward by a larger amount than the rightward shift in the short-run aggregate supply curve. The outcome is a rise in the price level and an increase in real GDP.

FIGURE 13.13

Two Views of the Supply-Side Effects of Fiscal Policy

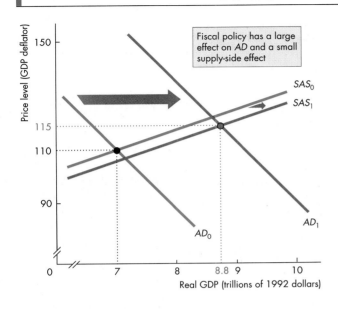

(a) The traditional view

A tax cut increases aggregate demand and shifts the AD curve rightward from AD_0 to AD_1 (both parts). Such a policy change also has a supply-side effect. If the supply-side effect is small, the SAS curve shifts rightward from SAS_0 to SAS_1 in part (a). The demand-side effect dominates the supply-side effect, real GDP increases, and the price level rises.

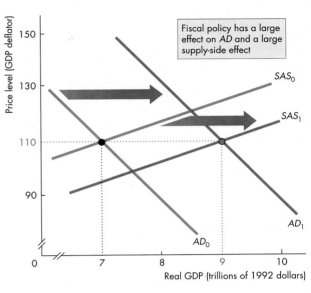

(b) The supply-side view

If the supply-side effect of a tax cut is large, the SAS curve shifts to SAS_1 in part (b). In this case, the supply-side effect is as large as the demand-side effect. Real GDP increases, and the price level remains constant. But if the supply-side effect were larger than the demand-side effect, the price level would actually fall.

But notice that the price level rises by *less* and real GDP increases by *more* than would occur if there were no supply-side effects.

Figure 13.13(b) shows the effects that supply-siders believe to occur. A tax cut still has a large effect on aggregate demand, but it has a similarly large effect on aggregate supply. The aggregate demand curve and the short-run aggregate supply curve shift rightward by similar amounts. In this particular case, the price level remains constant and real GDP increases. A slightly larger increase in aggregate supply would have brought a fall in the price level, a possibility that some supply-siders believe could occur.

The general point that everyone agrees with is that a tax cut that strengthens incentives increases real GDP by more and is less inflationary than an equal-sized expansionary fiscal policy that does not change incentives or that weakens them.

REVIEW QUIZ

- What are the incentive effects that the income tax has on the supply of labor and the supply of capital and how would a cut in the income tax rate affect potential GDP?
- Because a tax cut increases both aggregate supply and aggregate demand, can we tell whether a tax cut increases or decreases real GDP and the price level?

◆ You've seen how fiscal policy influences real GDP and potential GDP. *Reading Between the Lines* on pp. 300–301 looks at U.S. fiscal policy in 1999. Your next task is to study monetary policy. We begin by describing the monetary system of a modern economy.

Deficit and Debts

THE NEW YORK TIMES, JANUARY 31, 1999

The Deficit's Gone, but Not the National Debt

By Richard W. Stevenson

WASHINGTON—The Federal budget deficit is gone, transformed by a strong economy into a string of projected surpluses that should grow larger for years to come—at least by the reckoning that passes for fiscal forecasting in Washington.

Eliminating the deficit is hardly the end of the Government's financial troubles, however, and it marks the beginning of a new debate over how fiscal policy should be used to shape the nation's future.

It's like a family that after spending more than it earns month after month suddenly finds itself bringing in more than it spends—great news, to be sure, but a turnaround that still leaves the family with the debt it ran up during the hard times and the choice of whether to pay it off.

Washington was never in much danger of maxing out its credit cards. But the national debt was built up over decades of deficit spending—the Federal Government has not run steady surpluses since the 1920's—and it remains an economic millstone of considerable proportions. Only now do Congress and the White House have the luxury of debating what to do about it. ...

"Debt reduction ultimately gets trumped in a political process by Government spending," said John F. Cogan, a senior fellow at the Hoover Institution and a former budget official in the Reagan and Bush Administrations. "Achieving a sustained policy of debt reduction is very difficult, to say the least."

There are several ways to measure the national debt, but the most meaningful is to look at the debt held by the public—the individuals, Wall Street firms and banks from around the world that bought bonds sold by the Treasury Department. There is currently $3.7 trillion in public debt outstanding, which is equal to 45 percent of the economy's total output. ...

In economic terms, the question of whether debt reduction should be a higher priority than tax cuts or spending increases is an easy call. Most economists agree that paying down the national debt is the surest way to spur more savings and investment, create more jobs, improve productivity and generally enable the economy to grow faster. ...

Essence of the Story

■ The federal budget is in surplus, but the federal government has a large debt.

■ The debt held by the public was $3.7 trillion or 45 percent of GDP in January 1999.

■ The national debt was built up over decades of deficit spending, and it is a large economic millstone.

■ Most economists agree that decreasing the national debt will increase saving and investment, create jobs, increase productivity, and increase the economic growth rate.

■ But politically, it is difficult to achieve a sustained commitment to deficit reduction.

Economic Analysis

■ To increase the pace at which we pay down the national debt, the government must either increase taxes or cut purchases of goods and services.

■ The short-run effects of paying down the debt work in the opposite direction to the long-run effects.

■ Figure 1 shows the short-run effects. Initially, the aggregate planned expenditure curve is AE_0. Equilibrium expenditure and real GDP are $7.6 trillion, where the AE curve intersects the 45° line. Potential GDP is also $7.6 trillion (an assumption).

■ Now the federal government decides to step up the pace at which it pays down the debt. It raises taxes and cuts its purchases of goods and services. The AE curve shifts downward to AE_1. Real GDP decreases, and the economy moves to below full employment.

■ The outcome in Fig. 1 is temporary. The price level rises less quickly, the real interest rate falls, and the economy returns to full employment.

■ With a lower real interest rate, investment increases and economic growth increases.

■ Figure 2 shows the long-run effect after 10 years—in 2009—if the economic growth rate increases from 3 percent a year to 4 percent a year.

■ With growth at 3 percent a year, potential GDP increases to $10.2 trillion by 2009. With growth at 4 percent a year, potential GDP increases to $11.2 trillion by 2009.

■ To be at full employment in 2009, aggregate expenditure must be AE_0 if potential GDP is $10.2 trillion and AE_1 if potential GDP is $11.2 trillion.

■ The level of investment is greater on AE_1 than on AE_0 and it is this fact that enables the economy to expand more rapidly and achieve the greater level of potential GDP.

■ The effect of the deficit on growth is probably small. Economists are not as much in agreement on the relationship between the deficit and growth as the news article suggests. And most economists do not think the debt is a millstone.

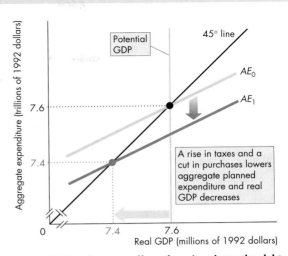

Figure 1 **The short-run effect of paying down the debt**

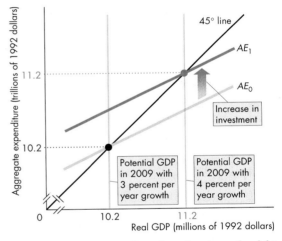

Figure 2 **The long-run effect of paying down the debt**

You're The Voter

■ Do you think that the debt should be paid down faster than the government plans? Why or why not?

■ Do you think that the debt should be paid down more slowly than the government plans? Why or why not?

■ Do you think that the debt should be paid down with a greater emphasis on tax increases than on spending cuts? Why or why not?

301

MATHEMATICAL NOTE
The Algebra of the Fiscal Policy Multipliers

THIS MATHEMATICAL NOTE DERIVES FORMULAS FOR the fiscal policy multipliers. We begin by defining the symbols we need:

- Aggregate planned expenditure, AE
- Real GDP, Y
- Consumption expenditure, C
- Investment, I
- Government purchases, G
- Exports, X
- Imports, M
- Net taxes, T
- Autonomous consumption expenditure, a
- Lump-sum taxes, T_a
- Lump-sum transfer payments, T_r
- Marginal propensity to consume, b
- Marginal propensity to import, m
- Marginal tax rate, t
- Autonomous expenditure, A

Equilibrium Expenditure

Aggregate planned expenditure is

$$AE = C + I + G + X - M.$$

The consumption function is

$$C = a + b(Y - T).$$

Net taxes equals lump-sum taxes minus lump-sum transfer payments plus induced taxes, which is

$$T = T_a - T_r + tY.$$

Use the last equation in the consumption function to give consumption expenditure as a function of GDP

$$C = a - bT_a + bT_r + b(1 - t)Y.$$

The import function is

$$M = mY.$$

Use the consumption function and the import function to replace C and M in the aggregate planned expenditure equation to obtain

$$AE = a - bT_a + bT_r + b(1 - t)Y + I + G + X - mY.$$

Collect the terms on the right side of the equation that involve Y to obtain

$$AE = [a - bT_a + bT_r + I + G + X] + [b(1 - t) - m]Y.$$

Autonomous expenditure (A) is given by

$$A = a - bT_a + bT_r + I + G + X,$$

so

$$AE = A + [b(1 - t) - m]Y.$$

Equilibrium expenditure occurs when aggregate planned expenditure (AE) equals real GDP (Y). That is,

$$AE = Y.$$

To calculate equilibrium expenditure, we solve the equation

$$Y = A + [b(1 - t) - m]Y$$

to obtain

$$Y = \frac{1}{1 - [b(1 - t) - m]} A.$$

Government Purchases Multiplier

The government purchases multiplier equals the change in equilibrium expenditure (Y) that results from a change in government purchases (G) divided by the change in government purchases. Because autonomous expenditure is equal to

$$A = a - bT_a + bT_r + I + G + X,$$

the change in government purchases changes autonomous expenditure such that

$$\Delta A = \Delta G.$$

The government purchases multiplier is found by working out the change in Y that results from the change in A. You can see from the solution for Y that

$$\Delta Y = \frac{1}{1 - [b(1 - t) - m]} \Delta G.$$

The government purchases multiplier equals

$$\frac{1}{1 - [b(1 - t) - m]}.$$

In an economy in which $t = 0$ and $m = 0$, the government purchases multiplier is $1/(1 - b)$. With $b = 0.75$, the government purchases multiplier equals 4, as part (a) of the figure shows. Make up some examples and use the above formula to show how b, m, and t influence the government purchases multiplier.

Lump-Sum Taxes Multiplier

The lump-sum taxes multiplier equals the change in equilibrium expenditure (Y) that results from a change in lump-sum taxes (T_a) divided by the change in lump-sum taxes. Because autonomous expenditure is equal to

$$A = a - bT_a + bT_r + I + G + X,$$

the change in lump-sum taxes changes autonomous expenditure such that

$$\Delta A = -b\Delta T_a.$$

You can see from the solution for equilibrium expenditure Y that

$$\Delta Y = \frac{-b}{1 - [b(1 - t) - m]}\Delta T_a.$$

The lump-sum taxes multiplier equals

$$\frac{-b}{1 - [b(1 - t) - m]}.$$

In an economy in which $t = 0$ and $m = 0$, the lump-sum taxes multiplier is $-b/(1 - b)$. With $b = 0.75$, the lump-sum tax multiplier equals -3, as part (b) of the

figure shows. Make up some examples and use the above formula to show how b, m, and t influence the lump-sum tax multiplier.

Lump-Sum Transfer Payments Multiplier

The lump-sum transfer payments multiplier equals the change in equilibrium expenditure (Y) that results from a change in lump-sum transfer payments (T_r) divided by the change in lump-sum transfer payments. Because autonomous expenditure is equal to

$$A = a - bT_a + bT_r + I + G + X,$$

the change in lump-sum transfer payments changes autonomous expenditure such that

$$\Delta A = b\Delta T_r.$$

This amount equals minus the change in autonomous expenditures when $\Delta T_a = \Delta T_r$. So the lump-sum transfer payments multiplier equals minus the lump-sum taxes multiplier. The lump-sum transfer payments multiplier equals

$$\frac{b}{1 - [b(1 - t) - m]}.$$

In an economy in which $t = 0$ and $m = 0$, the lump-sum transfer payments multiplier is $b/(1 - b)$. With $b = 0.75$, the lump-sum transfer payments multiplier equals 3, as part (c) of the figure shows. Make up some examples and use the above formula to show how b, m, and t influence the lump-sum transfer payments multiplier.

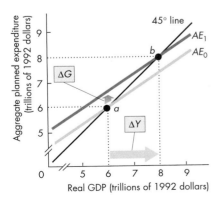

(a) Government purchases multiplier

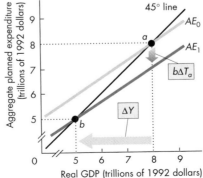

(b) Lump-sum tax multiplier

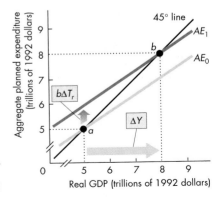

(c) Lump-sum transfer payments multiplier

SUMMARY

KEY POINTS

The Federal Budget (pp. 282–287)

- The federal budget finances the activities of the government and is used to stabilize real GDP.
- Federal tax revenues come from personal income taxes, social insurance taxes, corporate income taxes, and indirect taxes. Federal expenditures include transfer payments, purchases of goods and services, and debt interest.
- When tax revenues exceed government expenditures, the government has a budget surplus.

Fiscal Policy Multipliers (pp. 288–294)

- Fiscal policy actions are discretionary or automatic.
- The government purchases multiplier equals $1/(1 - MPC)$. The lump-sum tax multiplier equals $-MPC/(1 - MPC)$. The transfer payments multiplier is equal in magnitude to the lump-sum tax multiplier but is positive.
- Income taxes and entitlement payments bring fluctuations in tax revenues and transfer payments over the business cycle and act as automatic stabilizers.

Fiscal Policy Multipliers and the Price Level (pp. 294–297)

- An expansionary fiscal policy increases aggregate demand and shifts the aggregate demand curve rightward. It increases real GDP and raises the price level. (A contractionary fiscal policy has the opposite effects.)
- Price level changes dampen fiscal policy multiplier effects.
- At potential GDP, an expansionary fiscal policy raises the price level and in the long run leaves real GDP unchanged. The fiscal policy multipliers in the long run are zero.

Fiscal Policy and Aggregate Supply (pp. 297–299)

- Fiscal policy has supply-side effects because the increases in taxes weaken the incentives to work, save, and invest.
- A tax cut increases both aggregate demand and aggregate supply. It increases real GDP but has an ambiguous effect on the price level.

KEY FIGURES

KEY TERMS

PROBLEMS

*1. In the economy of Zap, the marginal propensity to consume is 0.9. Investment is $50 billion, government purchases of goods and services are $40 billion, and lump-sum taxes are $40 billion. Zap has no exports and no imports.
   a. The government cuts its purchases of goods and services to $30 billion. What is the change in equilibrium expenditure?
   b. What is the value of the government purchases multiplier?
   c. The government continues to purchase $40 billion worth of goods and services and cuts lump-sum taxes to $30 billion. What is the change in equilibrium expenditure?
   d. What is the value of the tax multiplier?
   e. The government simultaneously cuts both its purchases of goods and services and taxes to $30 billion. What is the change in equilibrium expenditure? Why does equilibrium expenditure decrease?

2. In the economy of Zip, the marginal propensity to consume is 0.8. Investment is $60 billion, government purchases of goods and services are $50 billion, and lump-sum taxes are $60 billion. Zip has no exports and no imports.
   a. The government increases its purchases of goods and services to $60 billion. What is the change in equilibrium expenditure?
   b. What is the value of the government purchases multiplier?
   c. The government continues to purchase $60 billion worth of goods and services and increases lump-sum taxes to $70 billion. What is the change in equilibrium expenditure?
   d. What is the value of the tax multiplier?
   e. The government simultaneously increases its purchases of goods and services and taxes by $10 billion. What is the change in equilibrium expenditure? Why does equilibrium expenditure increase?

*3. Suppose that the price level in the economy of Zap, as described in problem 1, is 100. The economy is also at full employment.
   a. If the government of Zap increases its purchases of goods and services by $10 billion, what happens to the quantity of real GDP demanded?
   b. How does Zap's aggregate demand curve change? Draw a two-part diagram that is similar to Fig. 13.10 to illustrate the change in both the *AE* curve and the *AD* curve.
   c. In the short run, does equilibrium real GDP increase by more than, less than, or the same amount as the increase in the quantity of real GDP demanded?
   d. In the long run, does equilibrium real GDP increase by more than, less than, or the same amount as the increase in the quantity of real GDP demanded?
   e. In the short run, does the price level in Zap rise, fall, or remain unchanged?
   f. In the long run, does the price level in Zap rise, fall, or remain unchanged?

4. Suppose that the price level in the economy of Zip, as described in problem 1, is 100. The economy is also at full employment.
   a. If the government of Zip decreases its purchases of goods and services by $5 billion, what happens to the quantity of real GDP demanded?
   b. How does Zip's aggregate demand curve change? Draw a two-part diagram that is similar to Fig. 13.10 to illustrate the change in both the *AE* curve and the *AD* curve.
   c. In the short run, does equilibrium real GDP decrease by more than, less than, or the same amount as the increase in the quantity of real GDP demanded?
   d. In the short run, does the price level in Zip rise, fall, or remain unchanged?
   e. Why does real GDP in the short term decrease by a smaller amount than the decrease in aggregate demand?

*5. The figure shows expenditures and tax revenues of the government of Dreamland. Potential GDP is $40 million.

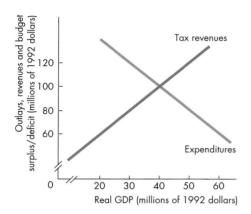

a. What is the government's budget balance if real GDP is $40 million?
b. Does Dreamland have a structural surplus or deficit if its real GDP is $40 million? What is its size? Explain why.
c. What is the government's budget balance if real GDP is $30 million?
d. If Dreamland's real GDP is $30 million, does Dreamland have a structural surplus or deficit? What is its size? Explain why.
e. If Dreamland's real GDP is $50 million, does Dreamland have a structural surplus or deficit? What is its size? Explain why.

6. In problem 5, if Dreamland's real GDP is $50 million,
a. What is the government's budget balance?
b. Does Dreamland have a structural surplus? What is its size? Explain why.
c. What is the government's budget balance if potential GDP is $30 million?
d. If Dreamland's potential GDP is $30 million, does Dreamland have a structural surplus or deficit? What is its size? Explain why.
e. What would Dreamland's real GDP have to be for it to have neither a structural deficit/surplus nor a cyclical deficit/surplus if its potential GDP is $40 million.

CRITICAL THINKING

1 Study *Reading Between the Lines* on pp. 300–301 and then:
a. Explain the short-run effects of paying down the national debt at a more rapid pace.
b. Explain the long-run effects of paying down the national debt at a more rapid pace.
c. Use the link on the Parkin Web site to obtain data on the federal government's more recent budget and compare the projected deficit with the projection one year earlier. Do the data support or reject the views of John Cogan reported in the news article?
d. Use the link on the Parkin Web site to obtain data on the federal government's debt and economic growth. Do the data support or reject the view that is attributed to "most economists" in the news article: That the debt is a millstone and cutting it will speed economic growth?

2. Thinking about the supply-side effects of tax cuts:
a. What would be the main effects of lower income tax rates on the level of potential GDP?
b. How would lower income taxes influence the real wage rate and the real interest rate?
c. What are the main costs of lower income taxes?

3. Use the links of the Parkin Web site to visit the National Center for Policy Analysis Idea House and study any two flat tax plans that are described there. When you have studied these plans, answer the following questions:
a. What are the main features of the two plans?
b. What do you predict would be the main effects of each proposal?
c. Which proposal appeals most to you and why?

4. Use the link on the Parkin Web site to obtain data on the amounts of government expenditure in the main industrial countries. Then use the fiscal policy multiplier analysis that you've learned about in this chapter to predict which countries have strong automatic stabilizers and which have a weak one. Explain the reasons for your predictions.

14

Money

Money, like fire and the wheel, has been around for a very long time. An incredible array of items have served as money. Wampum (beads made from shells) was used by North American Indians, whale's teeth were used by Fijians, and tobacco was used by early American colonists. Cakes of salt served as money in Ethiopia and Tibet. Today, when we want to buy something, we use coins or bills, write a check, or present a credit card. Tomorrow, we'll use a "smart card" that keeps track of spending and that our pocket computer can read. Are all these things money? ◆ When we deposit some coins or notes into a bank, is that still money? And what happens when the bank lends the money in our deposit account to someone else? How can we get our money back if it's been lent out? Does lending by banks create money—out of thin air? ◆ In the 1970s, you had either a savings deposit that earned interest or a checking deposit that did not. Today, there are accounts that provide the convenience of a checking deposit and the income of a savings deposit. Why were these new kinds of bank deposits introduced? ◆ During the 1970s, the quantity of money in the United States increased quickly, but during the 1980s and 1990s, it increased at a slower pace. In Russia and in some Latin American countries, the quantity of money increased at an extremely rapid pace during the early 1990s, but the pace has slowed in recent years. Does the rate of increase in the quantity of money matter? What are the effects of an increasing quantity of money on our economy?

◆ In this chapter, we'll study that useful invention: money. We'll look at its functions and the way it is measured in the United States today. We'll explain how banks and other financial institutions create money. Finally, we'll examine the effects of money on the economy.

Money Makes the World Go Around

After studying this chapter, you will be able to:

■ Define money and describe its functions

■ Explain the economic functions of banks and other financial institutions

■ Describe the financial innovations of the 1980s and 1990s

■ Explain how banks create money

■ Explain why the quantity of money is an important economic magnitude

■ Explain the quantity theory of money

What Is Money?

WHAT DO WAMPUM, TOBACCO, AND NICKELS AND dimes have in common? Why are they all examples of money? To answer these questions, we need a definition of money. **Money** is any commodity or token that is generally acceptable as the means of payment. A **means of payment** is a method of settling a debt. When a payment has been made, there is no remaining obligation between the parties to a transaction. So what wampum, tobacco, and nickels and dimes have in common is that they have served (or still do serve) as the means of payment. But money has three other functions:

- Medium of exchange
- Unit of account
- Store of value

Medium of Exchange

A *medium of exchange* is an object that is generally accepted in exchange for goods and services. Money acts as such a medium. Without money, it would be necessary to exchange goods and services directly for other goods and services—an exchange called **barter**. For example, if you want to buy a hamburger, you offer the paperback novel you've just finished reading in exchange for it. Barter requires a *double coincidence of wants*, a situation that occurs when Erika wants to buy what Kazia wants to sell and Kazia wants to buy what Erika wants to sell. To get your hamburger, you must find someone who's selling hamburgers and who wants your paperback novel. Money guarantees that there is a double coincidence of wants because people with something to sell will always accept money in exchange for it. Money acts as a lubricant that smoothes the mechanism of exchange.

Unit of Account

A *unit of account* is an agreed measure for stating the prices of goods and services. To get the most out of your budget, you have to figure out whether seeing one more movie is worth its opportunity cost. But that cost is not dollars and cents. It is the number of ice-cream cones, sodas, and cups of coffee that you must give up. It's easy to do such calculations when all these goods have prices in terms of dollars and cents (see Table 14.1). If a movie costs $6 and a six-pack of soda costs $3, you know right away that seeing one movie costs you 2 six-packs of soda. If jelly beans are 50¢ a pack, a movie costs 12 packs of jelly beans. You need only one calculation to figure out the opportunity cost of any pair of goods and services.

But imagine how troublesome it would be if your local movie theater posted its price as 2 six-packs of soda, and if the convenience store posted the price of a six-pack of soda as 2 ice-cream cones, and if the ice-cream shop posted the price of a cone as 3 packs of jelly beans, and if the candy store priced a pack of jelly beans as 2 cups of coffee! Now how much running around and calculating do you have to do to figure out how much that movie is going to cost you

---

TABLE 14.1

The Unit of Account Function of Money Simplifies Price Comparisons

Good	Price in money units	Price in units of another good
Movie	$6.00 each	2 six-packs of soda
Soda	$3.00 per six-pack	2 ice-cream cones
Ice cream	$1.50 per cone	3 packs of jelly beans
Jelly beans	$0.50 per pack	2 cups of coffee
Coffee	$0.25 per cup	1 local phone call

Money as a unit of account: The price of a movie is $6 and the price of a cup of coffee is 25¢, so the opportunity cost of a movie is 24 cups of coffee ($6.00 ÷ 25¢ = 24).

No unit of account: You go to a movie theater and learn that the price of a movie is 2 six-packs of soda. You go to a candy store and learn that a pack of jelly beans costs 2 cups of coffee. But how many cups of coffee does seeing a movie cost you? To answer that question, you go to the convenience store and find that a six-pack of soda costs 2 ice-cream cones. Now you head for the ice-cream shop, where an ice-cream cone costs 3 packs of jelly beans. Now you get out your pocket calculator: 1 movie costs 2 six-packs of soda, or 4 ice-cream cones, or 12 packs of jelly beans, or 24 cups of coffee!

in terms of the soda, ice cream, jelly beans, or coffee that you must give up to see it? You get the answer for soda right away from the sign posted on the movie theater. But for all the other goods, you're going to have to visit many different stores to establish the price of each commodity in terms of another and then calculate prices in units that are relevant for your own decision. Cover up the column labeled "price in money units" in Table 14.1 and see how hard it is to figure out the number of local phone calls it costs to see one movie. It's enough to make a person swear off movies! How much simpler it is if all the prices are expressed in dollars and cents.

Store of Value

Any commodity or token that can be held and exchanged later for goods and services is called a *store of value*. Money acts as a store of value. If it did not, it would not be acceptable in exchange for goods and services. The more stable the value of a commodity or token, the better it can act as a store of value, and the more useful it is as money. No store of value is completely safe. The value of a physical object, such as a house, a car, or a work of art, fluctuates over time. The value of commodities and tokens used as money also fluctuate, and when there is inflation, they persistently fall in value.

Money in the United States Today

In the United States today, money consists of:

■ Currency
■ Deposits at banks and other financial institutions

Currency   The bills and coins that we use in the United States today are known as **currency**. Bills are money because the government declares them so with the words "This note is legal tender for all debts, public and private." You can see these words on every dollar bill.

Deposits   Deposits at banks and other financial institutions such as savings and loan associations (S&Ls) are also money. Deposits are money because they can be converted into currency and because they are used to settle debts.

Official Measures of Money   The two main official measures of money in the United States today are known as M1 and M2. Figure 14.1 shows the items that make up these two measures. **M1** consists of currency and traveler's checks plus checking deposits owned by individuals and businesses. M1 does *not* include currency held by banks, and it does not include currency and checking deposits owned by the U.S. government. **M2** consists of M1 plus savings deposits, time deposits, money market mutual funds, and other deposits. (There is a third official measure of money, M3, which consists of M2 plus large-scale time deposits and term deposits.)

FIGURE 14.1
Two Measures of Money

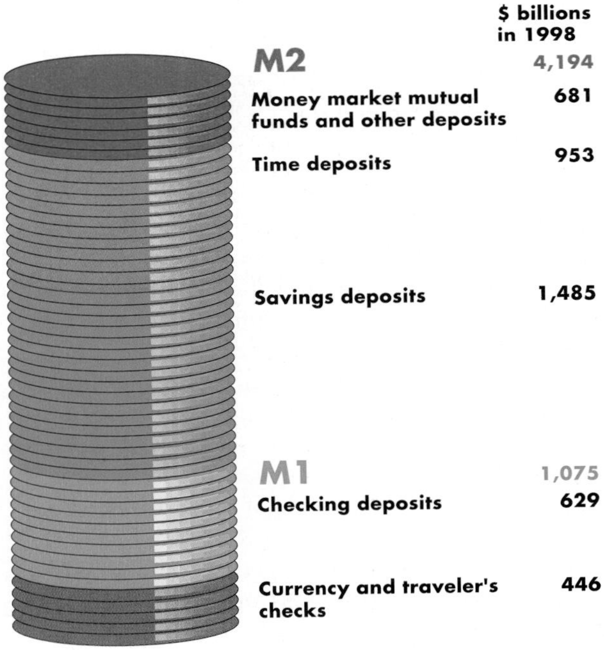

	$ billions in 1998
M2	4,194
Money market mutual funds and other deposits	681
Time deposits	953
Savings deposits	1,485
M1	1,075
Checking deposits	629
Currency and traveler's checks	446

M1 ■ Currency held outside banks and traveler's checks
    ■ Checking deposits at commercial banks, S&Ls, savings banks, and credit unions

M2 ■ M1
    ■ Savings deposits
    ■ Time deposits
    ■ Money market mutual funds and other deposits

Source: Economic Report of the President, 1999.

Are M1 and M2 Really Money? Money is the means of payment. So the test of whether an asset is money is whether it serves as a means of payment. Currency passes the test. But what about deposits? Checking deposits are money because they can be transferred from one person to another by writing a check. Such a transfer of ownership is equivalent to handing over currency. Because M1 consists of currency plus checking deposits and each of these is a means of payment, *M1 is money.*

But what about M2? Some of the savings deposits in M2 are just as much a means of payment as the checking deposits in M1. You can use the ATM at the grocery store checkout or gas station and transfer funds directly from your saving account to pay for your purchase. But other saving deposits are not means of payment. These deposits are known as *liquid assets.* **Liquidity** is the property of being instantly convertible into a means of payment with little loss in value. Because most of the deposits in M2 are quickly and easily converted into currency or checking deposits, they are operationally similar to M1, but they are not means of payment.

Deposits Are Money but Checks Are Not In defining money, we include, along with currency, deposits at banks and other financial institutions. But we do not count the checks that people write as money. Why are deposits money and checks not?

To see why deposits are money but checks are not, think about what happens when Colleen buys some roller blades for $200 from Rocky's Rollers. When Colleen goes to Rocky's shop, she has $500 in her deposit account at the Laser Bank. Rocky has $1,000 in his deposit account—at the same bank, as it happens. The total deposits of these two people is $1,500. Colleen writes a check for $200. Rocky takes the check to the bank right away and deposits it. Rocky's bank balance rises from $1,000 to $1,200, and Colleen's balance falls from $500 to $300. The total deposits of Colleen and Rocky are still the same as before: $1,500. Rocky now has $200 more, and Colleen has $200 less than before.

This transaction has transferred money from Colleen to Rocky. The check itself was never money. There wasn't an extra $200 worth of money while the check was in circulation. The check instructs the bank to transfer money from Colleen to Rocky.

In the example, Colleen and Rocky use the same bank. The same story, but with additional steps, describes what happens if Colleen and Rocky use

different banks. Rocky's bank credits the check to Rocky's account and then takes the check to a check-clearing center. The check is then sent to Colleen's bank, which pays Rocky's bank $200 and then debits Colleen's account $200. This process can take a few days, but the principles are the same as when two people use the same bank.

Credit Cards Are Not Money So checks are not money. But what about credit cards? Isn't having a credit card in your wallet and presenting the card to pay for your roller blades the same thing as using money? Why aren't credit cards somehow valued and counted as part of the quantity of money?

When you pay by check, you are frequently asked to prove your identity by showing your driver's license. It would never occur to you to think of your driver's license as money. It's just an ID card. A credit card is also an ID card but one that lets you take a loan at the instant you buy something. When you sign a credit card sales slip, you are saying, "I agree to pay for these goods when the credit card company bills me." Once you get your statement from the credit card company, you must make the minimum payment due (or clear your balance). To make that payment, you need money—you need to have currency or a checking deposit to pay the credit card company. So although you use a credit card when you buy something, the credit card is not the *means of payment*, and it is not money.

REVIEW QUIZ

- What makes something money? What functions does money perform? Why do you think packets of chewing gum don't serve as money?
- What are the problems that arise when a commodity is used as money?
- What are the main components of money in the United States today?
- What are the official measures of money? Are all the measures really money?
- Why are checks and credit cards not money?

We've seen that the main component of money in the United States is deposits at banks and other financial institutions. Let's take a closer look at these institutions.

Financial Intermediaries

A FIRM THAT TAKES DEPOSITS FROM HOUSEHOLDS and firms and makes loans to other households and firms is called a **financial intermediary**. The deposits of three types of financial intermediaries make up the nation's money:

- Commercial banks
- Thrift institutions
- Money market mutual funds

Commercial Banks

A **commercial bank** is a firm, licensed by the Comptroller of the Currency (in the U.S. Treasury) or by a state agency to receive deposits and make loans. Close to 13,000 commercial banks operate in the United States today. A commercial bank's business is summarized in its balance sheet.

A bank's *balance sheet* lists its assets, liabilities, and net worth. *Assets* are what the bank *owns*, *liabilities* are what the bank *owes*, and *net worth*, which is equal to assets minus liabilities, is the value of the bank to its stockholders—its owners. A bank's balance sheet is described by the equation

$$\text{Assets} = \text{Liabilities} + \text{Net worth.}$$

Among a bank's liabilities are the deposits that are part of the nation's money. Your deposit at the bank is a liability to your bank (and an asset to you) because the bank must repay your deposit (and sometimes the interest on it, too) whenever you decide to take your money out of the bank.

Profit and Prudence: A Balancing Act

The aim of a bank is to maximize the net worth of its stockholders. To achieve this objective, the interest rate at which a bank lends exceeds the interest rate at which it borrows. But a bank must perform a delicate balancing act. Lending is risky, and the more deposits a bank ties up in high-risk, high-interest rate loans, the bigger is its chance of not being able to repay its depositors. And if depositors perceive a high risk of not being repaid, they withdraw their funds and create a crisis for the bank. So a bank must be prudent in the way it uses its deposits, balancing security for the depositors against profit for its stockholders.

Reserves and Loans

To achieve security for its depositors, a bank divides its funds into two parts: reserves and loans. **Reserves** are cash in a bank's vault plus its deposits at Federal Reserve banks. (We'll study the Federal Reserve banks in Chapter 15.) The cash in a bank's vaults is a reserve to meet its depositor's demand for currency. It keeps the ATM replenished every time you and your friends have raided it for cash for a midnight pizza. The account of a bank at the Federal Reserve is similar to your own bank account. Commercial banks use these accounts to receive and make payments. A commercial bank deposits cash into or draws cash out of its account at the Federal Reserve and writes checks on that account to settle debts with other banks.

If a bank kept all its deposits as reserves, it wouldn't make any profit. In fact, it keeps only a small fraction of its funds in reserves and lends the rest. A bank has three types of assets. They are as follows:

1. *Liquid assets* are U.S. government Treasury bills and commercial bills. These assets are the banks' first line of defense if they need cash. They can be sold and instantly converted into cash with virtually no risk of loss. Because liquid assets are virtually risk free, they have a low interest rate.

2. *Investment securities* are longer-term U.S. government bonds and other bonds. These assets can be sold quickly and converted into cash but at prices that fluctuate. Because their prices fluctuate, these assets are riskier than liquid assets, but they also have a higher interest rate.

3. *Loans* are commitments of fixed amounts of money for agreed-upon periods of time. Most banks' loans are made to corporations to finance the purchase of capital equipment and inventories and to households—personal loans—to finance consumer durable goods, such as cars or boats. The outstanding balances on credit card accounts are also bank loans. Loans are the riskiest assets of a bank because they cannot be converted into cash until they are due to be repaid. And some borrowers default and never repay. Because they are the riskiest of a bank's assets, they also carry the highest interest rate.

Commercial bank deposits are one component of the nation's money. But thrift institutions and money market mutual funds also take deposits that form part—an increasing part—of the nation's money. We'll now describe the other institutions whose deposits form part of the nation's money.

Thrift Institutions

The **thrift institutions** are:

- Savings and loan associations
- Savings banks
- Credit unions

Savings and Loan Associations   A **savings and loan association** (S&L) is a financial intermediary that receives checking deposits and savings deposits and that makes personal, commercial, and home-purchase loans.

Savings Banks   A **savings bank** is a financial intermediary that accepts savings deposits and makes mostly mortgage loans. Some savings banks (called *mutual* savings banks) are owned by their depositors.

Credit Unions   A **credit union** is a financial intermediary owned by a social or economic group, such as a firm's employees, that accepts savings deposits and makes mostly consumer loans.

Money Market Mutual Funds

A **money market mutual fund** is a financial institution that obtains funds by selling shares and uses these funds to buy liquid assets such as U.S. Treasury bills. Money market mutual fund shares act like bank deposits. Shareholders can write checks on their money market mutual fund accounts. But there are restrictions on most of these accounts. For example, the minimum deposit accepted might be $2,500, and the smallest check a depositor is permitted to write might be $500.

The Economic Functions of Financial Intermediaries

All financial intermediaries make a profit from the spread between the interest rate they pay on deposits and the interest rate at which they lend. Why can financial intermediaries get deposits at a low interest rate and lend at a higher one? What services do they perform that make their depositors willing to put up with a low interest rate and their borrowers willing to pay a higher one?

Financial intermediaries provide four main services that people are willing to pay for:

- Creating liquidity
- Minimizing the cost of obtaining funds
- Minimizing the cost of monitoring borrowers
- Pooling risk

Creating Liquidity   Financial intermediaries create liquidity. *Liquid* assets are those that are easily and with certainty convertible into money. Some of the liabilities of financial intermediaries are themselves money; others are highly liquid assets that are easily converted into money.

Financial intermediaries create liquidity by borrowing short and lending long. Borrowing short means taking deposits but standing ready to repay them on short notice (and on even no notice in the case of checking deposits). Lending long means making loan commitments for a prearranged, and often quite long, period of time. For example, when a person makes a deposit with a savings and loan association, that deposit can be withdrawn at any time. But the S&L makes a lending commitment for perhaps more than 20 years to a homebuyer.

Minimizing the Cost of Borrowing   Finding someone from whom to borrow can be a costly business. Imagine how troublesome it would be if there were no financial intermediaries. A firm that was looking for $1 million to buy a new production plant would probably have to hunt around for several dozen people from whom to borrow in order to acquire enough funds for its capital project. Financial intermediaries lower those costs. The firm needing $1 million can go to a single financial intermediary to obtain those funds. The financial intermediary has to borrow from a large number of people, but it's not doing that just for this one firm and the million dollars it wants to borrow. The financial intermediary can establish an organization that is capable of raising funds from a large number of depositors and can spread the cost of this activity over a large number of borrowers.

Minimizing the Cost of Monitoring Borrowers
Lending money is a risky business. There's always a danger that the borrower might not repay. Most of the money lent gets used by firms to invest in projects that they hope will return a profit. But sometimes those hopes are not fulfilled. Checking up on the activities of a borrower and ensuring that the best possible decisions are being made for making a profit and avoiding a loss are costly and specialized activities. Imagine how costly it would be if each

household that lent money to a firm had to incur the costs of monitoring that firm directly. By depositing funds with a financial intermediary, households avoid those costs. The financial intermediary performs the monitoring activity by using specialized resources that have a much lower cost than what each household would incur if it had to undertake the activity individually.

Pooling Risk As we noted above, lending money is risky. There is always a chance of not being repaid—of default. Lending to a large number of different individuals can reduce the risk of default. In such a situation, if one person defaults on a loan, it is a nuisance but not a disaster. In contrast, if only one person borrows and that person defaults on the loan, the entire loan is a write-off. Financial intermediaries enable people to pool risk in an efficient way. Thousands of people lend money to any one financial intermediary, and, in turn, the financial intermediary re-lends the money to hundreds, perhaps thousands, of individual firms. If any one firm defaults on its loan, that default is spread across all the depositors with the intermediary, and no individual depositor is left exposed to a high degree of risk.

R E V I E W   Q U I Z

- What are the functions of commercial banks, savings and loan associations, savings banks and credit unions, and money market mutual funds? What functions do they have in common and how do they differ from each other?
- What is liquidity and how do financial intermediaries create it?
- How do financial intermediaries lower the cost of borrowing and lending and of monitoring borrowers?
- How do financial intermediaries pool risks?

We are interested in banks and other financial intermediaries because they create money. But these firms are highly regulated, and this regulation limits their ability to create money. So next, we'll examine these regulations. We'll also look at the deregulation and innovation that have occurred in the financial sector during the past 20 years.

Financial Regulation, Deregulation, and Innovation

FINANCIAL INTERMEDIARIES ARE HIGHLY REGULATED institutions. But regulation is not static, and in the 1980s, some important changes in their regulation as well as deregulation took place. Also, the institutions are not static. In their pursuit of profit, they constantly seek lower-cost ways of obtaining funds, monitoring borrowers, pooling risk, and creating liquidity. They also are inventive in seeking ways to avoid the costs imposed on them by financial regulation. Let's look at regulation, deregulation, and innovation in the financial sector in recent years.

Financial Regulation

Financial intermediaries face two types of regulation:

- Deposit insurance
- Balance sheet rules

Deposit Insurance The deposits of most financial intermediaries are insured by the Federal Deposit Insurance Corporation (FDIC). The FDIC is a federal agency that receives its income from compulsory insurance premiums paid by commercial banks and other financial intermediaries. The FDIC operates two separate insurance funds: the Bank Insurance Fund (BIF), which insures deposits in commercial banks, and the Saving Association Insurance Fund (SAIF), which insures the deposits of S&Ls, savings banks, and credit unions. Each of these funds insures deposits of up to $100,000.

The existence of deposit insurance provides protection for depositors in the event that a financial intermediary fails. But it also limits the incentive for the owner of a financial intermediary to make safe investments and loans. Some economists believe that deposit insurance played an important role in creating a crisis for S&Ls during the 1980s. Depositors did not worry about risk because their deposits were insured. The S&L owners made high-risk loans because they knew they were making a one-way bet. If their loans paid off, they made a high rate of return. If they failed and could not meet their obligations to the depositors, the insurance fund would step in. Bad loans were good business!

Because of this type of problem, all financial intermediaries face regulation of their balance sheets.

Balance Sheet Rules   The most important balance sheet regulations are:

■ Capital requirements
■ Reserve requirements
■ Deposit rules
■ Lending rules

Capital requirements are the minimum amount of an owner's own financial resources that must be put into an intermediary. This amount must be sufficiently large to discourage owners from making loans that are too risky.

Reserve requirements are rules setting out the minimum percentages of deposits that must be held in currency or other safe, liquid assets. These minimum percentages vary across the different types of intermediaries and deposits; they are largest for checking deposits and smallest for long-term savings deposits.

Deposit rules are restrictions on the different types of deposits that an intermediary can accept. These are the rules that historically have created the sharpest distinctions between the various institutions. For example, in the past, commercial banks provided checking accounts while other institutions provided only savings accounts.

Lending rules are restrictions on the proportions of different types of loans that an intermediary may make. Like deposit rules, these rules also helped to create sharp distinctions between the various institutions. Before 1980, commercial banks were the only intermediaries that were permitted to make commercial loans, and S&Ls and savings banks were restricted to making mostly mortgage loans to home buyers.

Deregulation in the 1980s

In 1980, Congress passed the Depository Institutions' Deregulation and Monetary Control Act (DIDMCA). The DIDMCA removed many of the distinctions between commercial banks and other financial intermediaries. It permitted nonbank financial intermediaries to compete with commercial banks in a wider range of lending business. At the same time, it permitted the payment of interest on checking deposits so that NOW accounts and ATS accounts could be offered by all deposit-taking institutions—

banks and nonbanks.[1] It also extended the powers of the Federal Reserve to place reserve requirements on *all* depository institutions. Despite the general direction of deregulation, this move brought a greater measure of central control over the financial system than had previously existed and represented a strengthening of the Fed's control.

The ability of S&Ls and savings banks to compete for lending business with commercial banks was further strengthened in 1982 with the passage of the Garn–St. Germain Depository Institutions Act. This legislation further eased restrictions on the scale of commercial lending that S&Ls and savings banks could undertake.

Deregulation in the 1990s

The most significant deregulation during the 1990s is the Riegle–Neal Interstate Banking and Branching Efficiency Act of 1994. This law permits U.S. banks for the first time to establish branches in any state.

Large changes have occurred in the structure of the banking industry because of this new law. The most visible are the wave of mergers of large banks and the appearance on the American banking scene of some major international banks. These changes will make the U.S. banking industry more efficient.

Financial Innovation

The development of new financial products—of new ways of borrowing and lending—is called **financial innovation**. The aim of financial innovation is to lower the cost of deposits or to increase the return from lending or, more simply, to increase the profit from financial intermediation. There are three main influences on financial innovation:

■ Economic environment
■ Technology
■ Regulation

The pace of financial innovation was remarkable during the 1980s and 1990s, and all three of these forces played a role.

---

[1] A NOW account is a Negotiable Order of Withdrawal account; "negotiable order of withdrawal" is another name for a check. An ATS account is an Automatic-Transfer Savings account—a savings account that is linked to a checking account. Funds are automatically transferred between the two accounts.

Economic Environment   Some of the innovation was a response to high inflation and high interest rates of the late 1970s and early 1980s. An important example is the development of variable interest rate mortgages. Traditionally, house purchases have been financed by mortgage loans at a guaranteed interest rate. Rising interest rates brought rising borrowing costs for S&Ls, and because they were committed to fixed interest rates on their mortgages, the industry incurred severe losses. The creation of variable interest rate mortgages has taken some of the risk out of long-term lending for house purchases.

Technology   Other financial innovations resulted from technological change, most notably that associated with the decreased cost of computing and long-distance communication. The spread in the use of credit cards and the development of international financial markets—for example, the increased importance of Eurodollars—are consequences of technological change.[2]

Regulation   A good deal of financial innovation takes place to avoid regulation. For example, Regulation Q, which prevented banks from paying interest on checking deposits, gave the impetus to devising new types of deposits on which checks could be written and interest paid, thereby getting around the regulation.

Deregulation, Innovation, and Money

Deregulation and financial innovation that have led to the development of new types of deposit accounts have brought important changes in the composition of the nation's money. In 1960, M1 consisted of only currency and checking deposits at commercial banks. In the 1990s, other new types of checking deposits have expanded while traditional checking deposits have declined. Similar changes have taken place in the composition of M2. Savings deposits have declined, while time deposits and money market mutual funds have expanded.

---

[2]Eurodollars are U.S. dollar bank accounts held in other countries, mainly in Europe. They were "invented" during the 1960s when the Soviet Union wanted the security and convenience of holding funds in U.S. dollars but were unwilling to place deposits in U.S. banks.

R E V I E W   Q U I Z

- Is everyone free to open a bank, take deposits, and make loans with no restrictions on these activities? What are the main restrictions that regulators impose on banks? Why?
- Did the financial deregulation of the 1980s make commercial banks more like or less like other financial institutions?
- What are the main factors that constantly stimulate financial intermediaries to develop new financial products and services?
- What have deregulation and financial innovation done to the composition of the nation's money?

We're now ready to learn how banks create money. In the following section, we'll use the term *banks* to refer to all the depository institutions whose deposits are part of the money supply. Let's see how money gets created.

How Banks Create Money

BANKS CREATE MONEY. BUT THIS DOESN'T MEAN that they have smoke-filled back rooms in which counterfeiters are busily working. Remember, most money is deposits, not currency. What banks create is deposits, and they do so by making loans. But the amount of deposits they can create is limited by their reserves.

Reserves: Actual and Required

We've seen that banks don't have $100 in bills for every $100 that people have deposited with them. In fact, a typical bank today has reserves of $6.00 for every $100 of deposits. No need for panic. These reserve levels are adequate for ordinary business needs.

The fraction of a bank's total deposits that are held in reserves is called the **reserve ratio**. The reserve ratio changes when a bank's customers make a deposit or withdrawal. Making a deposit increases the reserve ratio, and making a withdrawal decreases the reserve ratio.

The **required reserve ratio** is the ratio of reserves to deposits that banks are required, by regulation, to hold. A bank's *required reserves* are equal to its deposits multiplied by the required reserve ratio. Actual reserves minus required reserves are **excess reserves**. Whenever banks have excess reserves, they are able to create money.

To see how banks create money, we'll look at two model banking systems. In the first, there is only one bank; in the second, there are many banks.

Creating Deposits by Making Loans in a One-Bank Economy

In the model banking system that we'll study first, there is only one bank and its required reserve ratio is 25 percent. That is, for each dollar deposited, the bank keeps 25¢ in reserves and lends the rest. The balance sheet of One-and-Only Bank is shown in Fig. 14.2(a). On January 1, its deposits are $400 million and its reserves are 25 percent of this amount—$100 million. Its loans are equal to deposits minus reserves and are $300 million.

The story begins with Al Capone, who has decided to end his career of crime. He has been holding all his money in currency and has a nest egg of $1 million. On January 2, Al decides to put his $1 million on deposit at the One-and-Only Bank. On the day that Al makes his deposit, the One-and-Only Bank's balance sheet changes. The new situation is shown in Fig. 14.2(b). The bank now has $101 million in reserves and $401 million in deposits. It still has loans of $300 million.

The bank now has *excess reserves*. With reserves of $101 million, the bank would like to have deposits of $404 million and loans of $303 million. Because it is the One-and-Only Bank, the manager knows that the reserves will remain at $101 million. That is, she knows that when she makes a loan, the amount lent remains on deposit at the One-and-Only Bank. She knows, for example, that all the suppliers of Sky's-the-Limit Construction are also depositors of One-and-Only. So she knows that if she makes the loan that Sky's-the-Limit has just requested, the deposit she lends will never leave One-and-Only. When Sky's-the-Limit uses part of its new loan to pay $100,000 to I-Dig-It Excavating Company for some excavations, the One-and-Only Bank simply moves the funds from Sky's-the-Limit's checking account to I-Dig-It's checking account.

So on January 3, the manager of One-and-Only calls Sky's-the-Limit's accountant and offers to lend the maximum that she can. How much does she lend? She lends $3 million. By lending $3 million, One-and-Only's balance sheet changes to the one shown in Fig. 14.2(c). Loans increase by $3 million to $303 million. The loan shows up in Sky's-the-Limit's deposit initially, and total deposits increase to $404 million—$400 million plus Al Capone's deposit of $1 million plus the newly created deposit of $3 million. The bank now has no excess reserves and has reached the limit of its ability to create money.

FIGURE 14.2

Creating Money at the One-and-Only Bank

(a) Balance sheet on January 1

Assets (millions of dollars)		Liabilities (millions of dollars)	
Reserves	$100	Deposits	$400
Loans	$300		
Total	$400	Total	$400

(b) Balance sheet on January 2

Assets (millions of dollars)		Liabilities (millions of dollars)	
Reserves	$101	Deposits	$401
Loans	$300		
Total	$401	Total	$401

(c) Balance sheet on January 3

Assets (millions of dollars)		Liabilities (millions of dollars)	
Reserves	$101	Deposits	$404
Loans	$303		
Total	$404	Total	$404

In part (a) the One-and-Only Bank has deposits of $400 million, loans of $300 million, and reserves of $100 million. The bank's required reserve ratio is 25 percent. When the bank receives a deposit of $1 million (part b), it has excess reserves. It lends $3 million and creates a further $3 million of deposits. Deposits increase by $3 million, and loans increase by $3 million (in part c).

The Deposit Multiplier

The **deposit multiplier** is the amount by which an increase in bank reserves is multiplied to calculate the increase in bank deposits. That is,

$$\text{Deposit multiplier} = \frac{\text{Change in deposits}}{\text{Change in reserves}}.$$

In the example we've just worked through, the deposit multiplier is 4. The $1 million increase in reserves created a $4 million increase in deposits. The deposit multiplier is linked to the required reserve ratio by the following equation:

$$\text{Deposit multiplier} = \frac{1}{\text{Required reserve ratio}}.$$

In the example, the required reserve ratio is 25 percent, or 0.25. That is,

$$\text{Deposit multiplier} = \frac{1}{0.25}$$

$$= 4.$$

Creating Deposits by Making Loans with Many Banks

If you told the loan officer at your own bank that she creates money, she wouldn't believe you. Bankers see themselves as lending the money they receive from others, not creating money. But in fact, even though each bank lends only what it receives, the banking *system* creates money. To see how, let's look at another example.

Figure 14.3 is going to keep track of what is happening in the process of money creation by a banking system in which each bank has a required reserve ratio of 25 percent. The process begins when Art decides to decrease his currency holding and put $100,000 on deposit. Now Art's bank has $100,000 of new deposits and $100,000 of additional reserves. With a required reserve ratio of 25 percent, the bank keeps $25,000 on reserve and lends $75,000 to Amy. Amy writes a check for $75,000 to buy a copy-shop franchise from Barb. At this point, Art's bank has a new deposit of $100,000, new loans of $75,000, and new reserves of $25,000. You can see this situation in Fig. 14.3 as the first row of the "running tally."

For Art's bank, that is the end of the story. But it's not the end of the story for the entire banking system. Barb deposits her check for $75,000 in another bank, which has an increase in deposits and reserves of $75,000. This bank puts 25 percent of its increase in deposits ($18,750) into reserve and lends $56,250 to Bob. And Bob writes a check to Carl to pay off a business loan. The current state of play is seen in the second row of the "running tally" in Fig. 14.3. Now total bank reserves have increased by $43,750 ($25,000 plus $18,750), total loans have increased by $131,250 ($75,000 plus $56,250), and total deposits have increased by $175,000 ($100,000 plus $75,000).

When Carl takes his check to his bank, its deposits and reserves increase by $56,250, $14,063 of which it keeps in reserve and $42,187 of which it lends. This process continues until there are no excess reserves in the banking system. But the process takes a lot of further steps. One additional step is shown in Fig. 14.3. The figure also shows the final tallies—reserves increase by $100,000, loans increase by $300,000, and deposits increase by $400,000.

The sequence in Fig. 14.3 is the first four stages of the process. To figure out the entire process, look closely at the numbers in the figure. At each stage, the loan is 75 percent (0.75) of the previous loan and the deposit is 0.75 of the previous deposit. Call that proportion L ($L = 0.75$). The complete sequence is

$$1 + L + L^2 + L^3 + \dots .$$

Remember, L is a fraction, so at each stage in this sequence, the amount of new loans gets smaller. The total number of loans made at the end of the process is the above sum, which is[3]

$$\frac{1}{(1 - L)}.$$

---

[3]Both here and in the expenditure multiplier process in Chapter 12, the sequence of values is called a convergent geometric series. To find the sum of a series such as this, begin by calling the sum S. Then write out the sum as

$$S = 1 + L + L^2 + L^3 + \dots.$$

Multiply by L to get

$$LS = L + L^2 + L^3 + \dots$$

and then subtract the second equation from the first to get

$$S(1 - L) = 1$$

or

$$S = \frac{1}{(1 - L)}.$$

FIGURE 14.3

The Multiple Creation of Bank Deposits

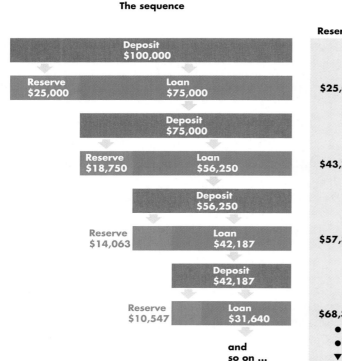

	The sequence		The running tally		
			Reserves	**Loans**	**Deposits**
	Deposit $100,000				
Reserve $25,000		Loan $75,000	$25,000	$75,000	$100,000
	Deposit $75,000				
Reserve $18,750		Loan $56,250	$43,750	$131,250	$175,000
	Deposit $56,250				
Reserve $14,063		Loan $42,187	$57,813	$173,437	$231,250
	Deposit $42,187				
Reserve $10,547		Loan $31,640	$68,360	$205,077	$273,437
	and so on ...		• • ▼	• • ▼	• • ▼
			$100,000	$300,000	$400,000

When a bank receives deposits, it keeps 25 percent in reserves and lends 75 percent. The amount lent becomes a new deposit at another bank. The next bank in the sequence keeps 25 percent and lends 75 percent, and the process continues until the banking system has created enough deposits to eliminate its excess reserves. The running tally tells us the amounts of deposits and loans created at each stage. At the end of the process, an additional $100,000 of reserves creates an additional $400,000 of deposits.

If we use the numbers from the example, the total increase in deposits is

$100,000 + 75,000 + 56,250 + 42,190 + ...$

$= \$100,000 \ (1 + 0.75 + 0.5625 + 0.4219 + ...)$

$= \$100,000 \ (1 + 0.75 + 0.75^2 + 0.75^3 + ...)$

$= \$100,000 \times \dfrac{1}{(1 - 0.75)}$

$= \$100,000 \times \dfrac{1}{(0.25)}$

$= \$100,000 \times 4$

By using the same method, you can check that the totals for reserves and loans are the ones shown in Fig. 14.3.

So even though each bank lends only the money it receives, the banking system as a whole does create money by making loans. The amount created is exactly the same in a multibank system as in a one-bank system.

The Deposit Multiplier in the United States The deposit multiplier in the United States works in the same way as the deposit multiplier we've just worked out for a model economy. But the deposit multiplier in the United States differs from the one we've just calculated for three reasons. First, the required reserve ratio of U.S. banks is smaller than the 25 percent we used here. Second, U.S. banks sometimes choose to hold excess reserves. Third, not all the loans made by banks return to them in the form of reserves. Some of the loans remain outside the banks and are held as currency. The smaller required reserve ratio makes the U.S. multiplier larger than the multiplier in the above example. But the other two factors make the U.S. multiplier smaller.

R E V I E W   Q U I Z

- How do banks create deposits by making loans, and what are the factors that limit the amount of deposits and loans they can create?
- A bank manager tells you that he doesn't create money. He just lends the money that people deposit in the bank. How do you explain to him that he's wrong and that he does create money?
- If the banks receive new deposits of $100 million, what determines the total change in deposits that the banking system can create?

Now that we know what money is and how banks create it, let's see how the amount of money created by the banks influences the economy. We'll discover that this influence is powerful.

Money, Real GDP, and the Price Level

YOU NOW KNOW THAT IN A MODERN ECONOMY such as that of the United States today, most of the money is bank deposits. You've seen that banks actually create money by making loans. Does the quantity of money created by the banking and financial system matter? What effect does money have? Does it matter whether the quantity of money increases quickly or slowly? How does the quantity of money influence real GDP, the price level, and the inflation rate? Can a country increase its real GDP just by increasing the quantity of money?

We're going to answer these questions first by using the aggregate supply–aggregate demand model, which explains how money affects real GDP and the price level in the short run. Then we're going to study a theory called the quantity theory of money, which explains how money growth influences inflation in the long run. We'll also look at some historical and international evidence on the relationship between money growth and inflation.

The Short-Run Effects of a Change in the Quantity of Money

Figure 14.4 illustrates the *AS-AD* model that explains how real GDP and the price level are determined in the short run. (For a full explanation of the *AS-AD* model, see Chapter 8, pp. 162–163.) We are going to use this model to study the short-run effects of a change in the quantity of money on real GDP and the price level. Potential GDP is $7 trillion, and the long-run aggregate supply curve is *LAS*. The short-run aggregate supply curve is *SAS*. Initially, the aggregate demand curve is AD_0. Equilibrium real GDP is $6.8 trillion, and the price level is 107 at the intersection of the *AD* curve and the *SAS* curve.

FIGURE 14.4

Short-Run Effects of Change in Quantity of Money

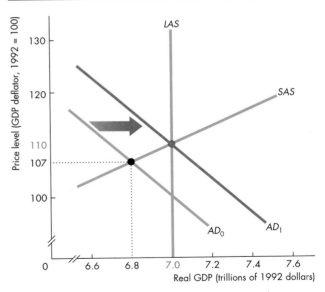

Real GDP is less than potential GDP. An increase in the quantity of money increases aggregate demand and shifts the aggregate demand curve rightward from AD_0 to AD_1. The price level rises to 110, and real GDP expands to $7 trillion. The increase in the quantity of money increases real GDP to potential GDP.

Banks, flush with excess reserves, make loans, and the loans create money. This increase results from the process of money creation we've just studied. With more money in their bank accounts and more loans, people plan to increase their consumption expenditure and businesses plan to increase their investment. Aggregate demand increases, and the aggregate demand curve shifts rightward to AD_1. A new equilibrium emerges at the intersection point of AD_1 and SAS. Real GDP expands to $7 trillion, and the price level rises to 110. Real GDP now equals potential GDP, and there is full employment. This increase in the quantity of money has increased both real GDP and the price level.

Now imagine the reverse situation. Real GDP is initially $7 trillion, and the price level is 110 at the intersection point of AD_1 and SAS. The quantity of money *decreases*. With *less* money in their bank accounts, people and businesses plan to decrease their expenditures. Aggregate demand decreases, and the aggregate demand curve shifts leftward to AD_0. A recession occurs as real GDP shrinks to $6.8 trillion, and the price level falls to 107.

These influences of the quantity of money on real GDP and the price level are *short-run* effects. In the long run, a change in the quantity of money, perhaps surprisingly, has no effect on real GDP. All its effects are on the price level. Let's see why this outcome occurs.

The Long-Run Effects of a Change in the Quantity of Money

Figure 14.5 explains how real GDP and the price level are determined in both the short run and the long run. Again, potential GDP is $7 trillion and the long-run aggregate supply curve is *LAS*. The short-run aggregate supply curve is SAS_1. Initially, the aggregate demand curve is AD_1. Equilibrium real GDP is $7 trillion, and the price level is 110. So real GDP equals potential GDP, and there is full employment.

Now suppose the quantity of money increases. Aggregate demand increases, and the aggregate demand curve shifts rightward to AD_2. The new short-run equilibrium is at the intersection point of AD_2 and SAS_1. The price level rises to 113, and real GDP expands to $7.2 trillion. This short-run adjustment has put real GDP above potential GDP and has decreased unemployment below the natural rate. A

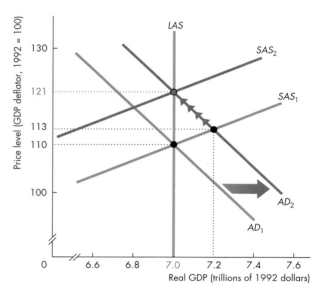

FIGURE 14.5

Long-Run Effects of Change in Quantity of Money

Real GDP equals potential GDP. An increase in the quantity of money shifts the aggregate demand curve from AD_1 to AD_2. In the short run, the price level rises to 113, and real GDP increases to $7.2 trillion. Real GDP exceeds potential GDP, and the money wage rate rises. Short-run aggregate supply decreases, and the SAS curve shifts leftward from SAS_1 to SAS_2. Real GDP returns to potential GDP, and the price level rises to 121. In the long run, the increase in the quantity of money increases the price level and has no effect on real GDP.

shortage of labor makes the money wage rate rise. As the money wage rate rises, short-run aggregate supply decreases and the *SAS* curve shifts leftward toward SAS_2. As short-run aggregate supply decreases, the price level rises to 121 and real GDP decreases back to potential GDP at $7 trillion.

Thus from one full-employment equilibrium to another, an increase in the quantity of money increases the price level and has no effect on real GDP. This relationship between the quantity of money and the price level at full employment is made more precise by the quantity theory of money, which tells us about the quantitative link between money growth and inflation.

The Quantity Theory of Money

The **quantity theory of money** is the proposition that in the long run, an increase in the quantity of money brings an equal percentage increase in the price level. The original basis of the quantity theory of money is a concept known as *the velocity of circulation* and an equation called *the equation of exchange*.

The **velocity of circulation** is the average number of times a dollar of money is used annually to buy the goods and services that make up GDP. GDP is equal to the price level (*P*) multiplied by real GDP (*Y*); that is,

$$GDP = PY.$$

Call the quantity of money *M*. The velocity of circulation, *V*, is determined by the equation

$$V = PY/M.$$

For example, if GDP is $6.0 trillion and the quantity of money is $3 trillion, the velocity of circulation is

2. On the average, each dollar of money circulates twice in its use to purchase the final goods and services that make up GDP; that is, each dollar of money is used twice in a year to buy GDP.

Figure 14.6 shows the velocity of circulation of both M1 and M2, the two main official definitions of money since 1960. You can see that the velocity of circulation of M1 increased through 1980 and fluctuated during the 1980s and 1990s. In contrast, the velocity of circulation of M2 has been remarkably stable. The reason why the velocity of M1 has increased is that deregulation and financial innovation have created new types of deposits and payments technologies that are substitutes for M1. As a result, the quantity of M1 per dollar of GDP has decreased, and equivalently, the velocity of circulation of M1 has increased. The reason why the velocity of M2 has been almost constant is that the new types of deposits that have replaced M1 are part of M2. So the ratio of M2 to GDP and the velocity of circulation of M2 have been much more stable.

FIGURE 14.6

The Velocity of Circulation in the United States: 1960–1998

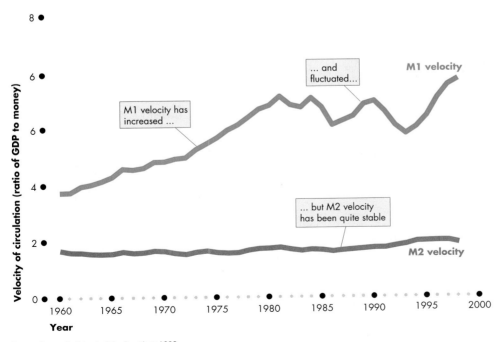

The velocity of circulation of M1 has increased over the years because financial innovation has developed M1 substitutes. The velocity of circulation of M2 has been relatively stable because the M1 substitutes that have resulted from financial innovation are new types of deposits that are part of M2.

Source: *Economic Report of the President*, 1999.

The **equation of exchange** states that the quantity of money (M) multiplied by the velocity of circulation (V) equals GDP, or

$$MV = PY.$$

Given the definition of the velocity of circulation, this equation is always true—it is true by definition. With M equal to $3 trillion and V equal to 2, MV is equal to $6.0 trillion, the value of GDP.

The equation of exchange becomes the quantity theory of money by making two assumptions:

1. The velocity of circulation is not influenced by the quantity of money.
2. Potential GDP is not influenced by the quantity of money.

If these two assumptions are true, the equation of exchange tells us that a change in the quantity of money brings about an equal proportional change in the price level. You can see why by solving the equation of exchange for the price level. Dividing both sides of the equation by real GDP (Y) gives

$$P = (V/Y)M.$$

In the long run, real GDP (Y) equals potential GDP, so if potential GDP and velocity are not influenced by the quantity of money, the relationship between the change in the price level (ΔP) and the change in the quantity of money (ΔM) is

$$\Delta P = (V/Y)\,\Delta M.$$

Divide this equation by the previous one, $P = (V/Y)M$, to get

$$\Delta P/P = \Delta M/M.$$

($\Delta P/P$) is the proportional increase in the price level, and ($\Delta M/M$) is the proportional increase in the quantity of money. So this equation is the quantity theory of money: In the long run, the percentage increase in the price level equals the percentage increase in the quantity of money.

The Quantity Theory and the AS-AD Model

The quantity theory of money can be interpreted in terms of the *AS-AD* model. The aggregate demand curve is a relationship between the quantity of real GDP demanded (Y) and the price level (P), other things remaining constant. We can obtain such a

relationship from the equation of exchange,

$$MV = PY.$$

Dividing both sides of this equation by real GDP (Y) gives

$$P = MV/Y.$$

This equation may be interpreted as describing an aggregate demand curve. In Chapter 8 (pp. 159–160), you saw that the aggregate demand curve slopes downward: As the price level increases, the quantity of real GDP demanded decreases. The above equation also shows such a relationship between the price level and the quantity of real GDP demanded. For a given quantity of money (M) and a given velocity of circulation (V), the higher the price level (P), the smaller is the quantity of real GDP demanded (Y).

In general, when the quantity of money changes, the velocity of circulation might also change. But the quantity theory asserts that velocity is not influenced by the quantity of money. If this assumption is correct, an increase in the quantity of money increases aggregate demand and shifts the aggregate demand curve upward by the same amount as the percentage change in the quantity of money.

The quantity theory of money also asserts that real GDP, which in the long run equals potential GDP, is not influenced by the quantity of money. This assertion is true in the *AS-AD* model in the long run when the economy is on its long-run aggregate supply curve. Figure 14.5 shows the quantity theory result in the *AS-AD* model. Initially, the economy is on the long-run aggregate supply curve *LAS* and at the intersection of the aggregate demand curve AD_1 and the short-run aggregate supply curve SAS_1. A 10 percent increase in the quantity of money shifts the aggregate demand curve from AD_1 to AD_2. This shift, measured by the vertical distance between the two demand curves, is 10 percent. In the long run, wages rise (also by 10 percent) and shift the *SAS* curve leftward to SAS_2. A new long-run equilibrium occurs at the intersection of AD_2 and SAS_2. Real GDP remains at potential GDP of $7 trillion, and the price level rises to 121. The new price level is 10 percent higher than the initial one ($121 - 110 = 11$, which is 10 percent of 110).

So the *AS-AD* model predicts the same outcome as the quantity theory of money. The *AS-AD* model also predicts a less precise relationship between the quantity of money and the price level in the short run than in the long run. For example, Fig. 14.4 shows that if we start out at a below-full employment equilibrium, an increase in the quantity of money increases real GDP. In this case, a 10 percent increase in the money supply increases the price level from 107 to 110—a 2.8 percent increase. That is, the price level increases by a smaller percentage than the percentage increase in the quantity of money.

How good a theory is the quantity theory of money? Let's answer this question by looking at the relationship between money and the price level, both historically and internationally.

Historical Evidence on the Quantity Theory of Money

The percentage increase in the price level is the inflation rate, and the percentage increase in the quantity of money is the money supply growth rate. So the quantity theory predictions can be cast in terms of money growth and inflation. The quantity theory predicts that at a given level of potential GDP and in the long run, the inflation rate will equal the money growth rate. But over time, potential GDP expands. Taking this expansion into account, the quantity theory predicts that in the long run, the inflation rate will equal the money growth rate minus the growth rate of potential GDP.

We can test the quantity theory of money by looking at the historical relationship between money growth and inflation in the United States. Figure 14.7 shows two views of this relationship for the years between 1930 and 1998. In both parts of the figure, the inflation rate is the percentage change in the GDP deflator, and the two alternative money growth rates are based on M1 and M2. Part (a) shows year-to-year changes in money and the price level. These changes show the short-run relationship between money growth and inflation. Part (b) shows decade average changes. These changes average out the year-to-year fluctuations and enable us to see the long-run relationship between the variables. If the quantity theory is a reasonable guide to reality, there should be a strong correlation between inflation and money growth in the decade average data and a weak correlation in the year-to-year data.

The data are broadly consistent with the quantity theory. The money growth rate and the inflation rate are correlated, but the relationship is not precise. During World War II, money growth increased sharply while inflation remained low. After the war, inflation exploded while money growth remained

steady. Between 1950 and 1998, the inflation rate fluctuated less than the fluctuations in the money growth rate. The year-to-year fluctuations in money growth and inflation, which contain short-run influences (in part a), show a weak correlation, and the decade average fluctuations in money growth and inflation (in part b) show a stronger correlation.

International Evidence on the Quantity Theory of Money

Another way to test the quantity theory of money is to look at the cross-country relationship between money growth and inflation. Figure 14.8 shows this relationship for 60 countries during the 1980s. By looking at a decade average, we again are smoothing out the short-run effects of money growth and focusing on the long-run effects. There is in these data an unmistakable tendency for high money growth to be associated with high inflation. The evidence is strongest for the high-inflation countries, which are shown in Fig. 14.8(a), but it is also present for the low-inflation countries, which are shown in Fig. 14.8(b).

Correlation, Causation, and Other Influences

Both the historical evidence for the United States and the international data tell us that in the long run, money growth and inflation are correlated. But the correlation between money growth and inflation does not tell us that money growth causes inflation. Money growth might cause inflation; inflation might cause money growth; or some third variable might simultaneously cause inflation and money growth.

According to the quantity theory and according to the *AS-AD* model, causation runs from money growth to inflation. But neither theory denies the possibility that at different times and places, causation might run in the other direction or that some third factor might be the root cause of both rapid money growth and inflation. One possible third factor is a large and persistent government budget deficit that gets financed by creating money.

But some occasions give us an opportunity to test our assumptions about causation. One of these is World War II and the years immediately following it. Rapid money growth during the war years was accompanied by controls that held prices down during

FIGURE 14.7

Money Growth and Inflation in the United States

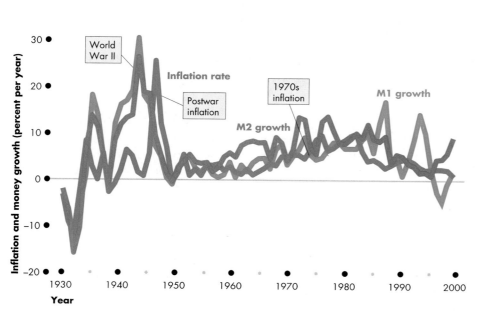

(a) Year-to-year change in money supply and the price level

Year-to-year fluctuations in money growth and inflation (part a) are loosely correlated, but decade average fluctuations in money growth and inflation (part b) are closely correlated. The burst of postwar inflation was caused by rapid money growth during World War II, and the rise in inflation during the 1970s was caused by more rapid money growth during the 1960s.

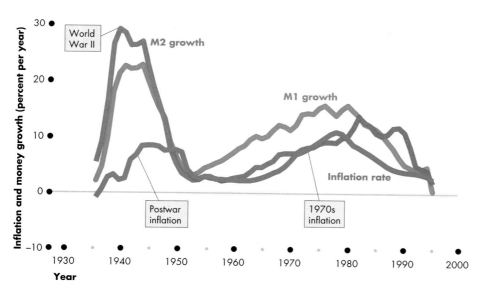

(b) Decade average change in money supply and the price level

Sources: *Historical Statistics of the United States, Economic Report of the President*, 1999, and the author's calculations.

FIGURE 14.8
Money Growth and Inflation in the World Economy

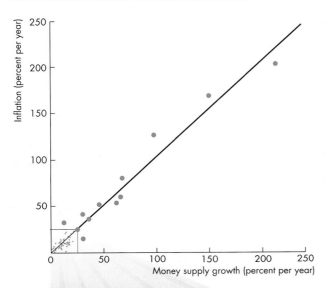

(a) All countries

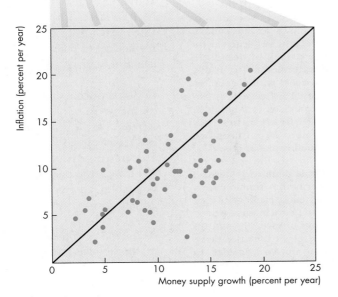

(b) Low-inflation countries

Inflation and money growth in 60 countries (in part a) and low-inflation countries (in part b) show a clear positive relationship between money growth and inflation.

Source: Federal Reserve Bank of St. Louis, *Review*, May/June 1988, p. 15.

the war but allowed them to rise immediately after the war. The inflationary consequences of wartime money growth were delayed by price controls but not removed. It is inconceivable that this was an example of reverse causation—of postwar inflation causing wartime money growth. Another is the late 1960s and 1970s. Rapid money growth that began during the 1960s almost certainly caused the high and persistent inflation of the 1970s. The combination of historical and international correlations between money growth and inflation and independent evidence about the direction of causation leads to the conclusion that the quantity theory is correct in the long run. It explains the long-term fundamental source of inflation. But the quantity theory is not correct in the short run. To understand the short-term fluctuations in inflation, the joint effects of a change in the quantity of money on real GDP, the velocity of circulation, and the price level must be explained. The *AS-AD* model provides this explanation. It also points to the possibility of other factors that influence both aggregate supply and aggregate demand influencing the inflation rate independently of the money growth rate in the short run.

R E V I E W Q U I Z

- Do the short-run effects of an increase in the quantity of money on the price level and real GDP differ from the long-run effects? If so, what are the differences? Why are there different effects?
- What is the quantity theory of money? Are the predictions of the quantity theory in conflict with the predictions of the *AS-AD* model?
- Do the long-run historical evidence and the international evidence on the relationship between money growth and inflation support the quantity theory?

Before you leave the subject of this chapter, look at *Reading Between the Lines* on pp. 326–327 and see the quantity theory in action in Brazil. In the next chapter, we'll learn how the Fed influences the quantity of money and interest rates in its attempt to steer the course of the economy. Then, in Chapter 16, we'll return to the problem of inflation and explore more deeply its causes and consequences and ways of keeping it under control.

The Quantity Theory in Action

THE WALL STREET JOURNAL, JANUARY 22, 1999

Brazilians Brace Again for Inflation ...

BY WALL STREET JOURNAL STAFF REPORTERS PETER FRITSCH IN SAO PAULO AND MATT MOFFETT IN RIO DE JANEIRO

Campaigning for re-election last year, Brazilian President Fernando Henrique Cardoso popped in on the Peres Bakery, outside Brasilia, and noted with deep satisfaction that the price of a French roll had barely budged since his last visit three years earlier.

But next week, bakery owner Arnaldo Peres will raise the price of that French roll somewhere between 20% and 50%, saying that half the flour he uses comes from Argentina and is more expensive since last week's devaluation of the Brazilian real.

Mr. Cardoso's hard-won victory over inflation—which relied on an artificially inflated local currency—is being put to the test like never before. Vendors are giving in to old temptations, and bread winners are bracing for the effects of higher prices and climbing interest rates, already the world's most severe. And Mr. Peres isn't alone out there.

Already, memories of the Brazilian hyperinflation of the early 1990s—rivaling in ferocity that of Germany's Weimar Republic in the 1920s—appear to be stirring some shopkeepers to action. In local supermarkets, the price of Chilean salmon fillets are up nearly 30% this week. The cost of a bus ticket in São Paulo went up 15% the very day Brazil first moved to devalue its currency on Jan. 13. At São Paulo's vast produce market known as Ceagesp, the prices of domestic papaya and watermelon are up 8% over the past week, with vegetables up an average 24%. Ceagesp attributes the sudden rises to a pinch in supply due to heavy rains this month, but most Brazilians are skeptical of such explanations.

Stopping by the Rio Sul supermarket in Rio de Janeiro yesterday, housewife Fernanda Almeida says she tucked an extra package of rice in her shopping cart in case prices rise in the near future. "It said on the television news that the price could be going up, so I decided to be prepared," she said. In one São Paulo market, the price of a bag of black beans is up 33% from last week. ...

Essence of the Story

- During the early 1990s, Brazil had a hyperinflation that rivaled that of Germany during the 1920s.

- President Cardoso lowered Brazil's inflation, and price increases have been modest for the past three years. But inflation seemed set to take off again in January 1999.

- Some price increases in one week: salmon fillets, almost 30 percent; a bus ticket in São Paulo, 15 percent; papaya and watermelon, 8 percent; vegetables, an average of 24 percent.

- A São Paolo produce market official says that prices have increased because heavy rains have decreased supply. Most Brazilians do not believe this explanation.

- Shoppers are buying larger quantities than normal in anticipation of higher prices.

■ Brazil had a serious inflation during the early 1990s. But it was not a hyperinflation and was not even close to the inflation that Germany experienced during the 1920s.

■ Figure 1 shows the inflation rate in Brazil between 1975 and 1999.

■ Note that the numbers for the growth rates are *thousands* of percent per year!

■ Hyperinflation is defined as an inflation rate greater than 50 percent per month, or 12,875 percent per year. Germany's inflation during the 1920s *exceeded* this rate!

■ Brazil has not had hyperinflation, but its inflation rate has been high and reached almost 3,000 percent a year in 1993.

■ Also, as you can see from the figure, money growth and inflation tend to move in a similar direction.

■ The quantity theory of money can be used to explain the movements in money growth and inflation.

■ When inflation is as high and variable as it was in Brazil during the early 1990s and people fear that such inflation

might occur again, money ceases to work well as a medium of exchange, a unit of account, or a store of value.

■ As a result, people don't want to hold money. They prefer to hold goods like the rice that Fernanda Almeida bought in the news article. So the velocity of circulation increases.

■ The higher the inflation rate, the more quickly people try to spend their income and the higher is the velocity of circulation. Figure 2 shows that in low-inflation Japan, the velocity of circulation is lower than that in high-inflation Brazil. And in hyperinflation Zaire, the velocity of circulation is even higher than in Brazil.

■ Brazil's money supply grows rapidly in some years not because the government is trying to cause inflation but because it has no other way of getting the funds that it needs to meet its expenditures. The government deficit is financed by printing money.

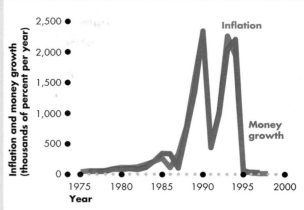

Figure 1 Inflation and money growth in Brazil

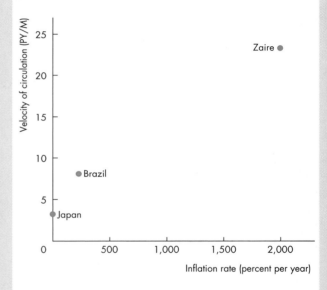

Figure 2 Inflation and velocity

KEY POINTS

What Is Money? (pp. 308–310)

- Money is the means of payment, a medium of exchange, a unit of account, and a store of value.
- M1 consists of currency, travelers' checks, and checking deposits), and M2 consists of M1 plus savings deposits, time deposits, and money market mutual funds.

Financial Intermediaries (pp. 311–313)

- Commercial banks, thrift institutions (S&Ls, savings banks, and credit unions) and money market mutual funds are financial intermediaries whose liabilities are money.
- Financial intermediaries provide four main economic services: They create liquidity, minimize the cost of obtaining funds, minimize the cost of monitoring borrowers, and pool risks.

Financial Regulation, Deregulation, and Innovation (pp. 313–315)

- Financial regulation to protect depositors includes deposit insurance, minimum capital rules, and required reserves.
- Deregulation during the 1980s removed the distinctions between banks and nonbank intermediaries.
- The search for profit leads to the creation of new types of deposits and loans, which change the composition of the nation's money supply.

How Banks Create Money (pp. 315–319)

- Banks create money by making loans.
- The total quantity of deposits that can be supported by a given amount of reserves (the deposit multiplier) is determined by the required reserve ratio.

Money, Real GDP, and the Price Level (pp. 319–325)

- An increase in the quantity of money increases aggregate demand and, in the short run, increases both the price level and real GDP.
- In the long run, an increase in the quantity of money brings increases in the price level and no change in real GDP.
- Like the *AS-AD* model, the quantity theory of money predicts no long-run relationship between money and real GDP.

KEY FIGURES

KEY TERMS

PROBLEMS

*1. In the United States today, money includes which of the following items?
   a. Federal Reserve banknotes in the Bank of America's cash machines
   b. Your Visa card
   c. The quarters inside public phones
   d. U.S. dollar bills in your wallet
   e. The check you have just written to pay for your rent
   f. The loan you took out last August to pay for your school fees

2. Which of the following items are money? Which are deposit money?
   a. Checking deposits at Citicorp
   b. IBM stock held by individuals
   c. The Susan B. Anthony dollar coin
   d. U.S. government securities
   e. NOW accounts

   Explain your answer by referring to the three basic functions of money.

*3. Sara withdraws $1,000 from her savings account at the Lucky S&L, keeps $50 in cash, and deposits the balance in her checking account at the Bank of Illinois. What is the immediate change in M1 and M2?

4. Monica takes $10,000 from her savings account at the Bank of Alaska and puts the funds into her money market mutual fund. What is the immediate change in M1 and M2?

*5. The commercial banks in Zap have:

Reserves	$250 million
Loans	$1,000 million
Deposits	$2,000 million
Total assets	$2,500 million

   a. Construct the commercial banks' balance sheet. If you are missing any assets, call them "other assets"; if you are missing any liabilities, call them "other liabilities."
   b. Calculate the banks' reserve ratio.
   c. If banks hold no excess reserves, calculate the deposit multiplier.

6. The commercial banks in Zip have:

Reserves	$125 million
Loans	$1,875 million
Deposits	$2,000 million
Total assets	$2,100 million

   a. Construct the commercial banks' balance sheet. If you are missing any assets, call them "other assets"; if you are missing any liabilities, call them "other liabilities."
   b. Calculate the banks' reserve ratio.
   c. If banks hold no excess reserves, calculate the deposit multiplier.

*7. An immigrant arrives in New Transylvania with $1,200. The $1,200 is deposited in a bank. All the banks in Transylvania have a required reserve ratio of 10 percent, and they have no excess reserves when the immigrant arrives.
   a. What is the initial increase in the quantity of money in New Transylvania?
   b. What is the initial increase in the quantity of bank deposits when the immigrant arrives?
   c. How much does the immigrant's bank lend out initially?
   d. Calculate the amount lent and the amount of deposits created if all the funds lent in (c) are returned to the banking system in the form of deposits.
   e. By how much has the quantity of money increased after the banks have made 20 loans?
   f. What is the total increase in the quantity of money, in bank loans, and in bank deposits when the process comes to an end?

8. An Internet thief in Chicago steals $100,000 from a bank in Buenos Aires, Argentina. He transfers the funds to a bank account in Chicago. The Chicago bank has a required reserve ratio of 5 percent, and it has no excess reserves when the transfer occurs.
   a. What is the initial increase in the quantity of money in the United States?
   b. What is the initial increase in the quantity of bank deposits when the theft occurs?
   c. How much does the thief's bank lend out?
   d. Calculate the amount lent and the amount of deposits created if all the funds lent in (c) are returned to the banking system in the form of deposits.
   e. By how much has the quantity of money increased after the banks have made 2 rounds of loans?
   f. What is the total increase in the quantity of money, in bank loans, and in bank deposits when the process comes to an end?

*9. Slowcon is a country in which the quantity theory of money operates in the long run but not in the short run. Slowcon has some unemployment when banks begin to make new loans and increase the quantity of money.
   a. What is the effect of the banks' actions on aggregate demand?
   b. What are the effects of the banks' actions on real GDP and the price level in the short run?
   c. What are the effects of the banks' actions on real GDP and the price level in the long run?

10. Banks in Indonesia make bad loans that don't get repaid, and several banks fail. The banks' customers lose their deposits.
   a. What is the effect of the bank failures on the quantity of money?
   b. What is the effect of the bank failures on aggregate demand?
   c. What are the effects of the bank failures on real GDP and the price level in the short run?
   d. What are the effects of the bank failures on real GDP and the price level in the long run?

*11. Quantecon is a country in which the quantity theory of money operates. The country has a constant population, capital stock, and technology. In year 1, real GDP was $400 million, the price level was 200, and the velocity of circulation of money was 20. In year 2, the quantity of money was 20 percent higher than in year 1.
   a. What was the quantity of money in year 1?
   b. What was the quantity of money in year 2?
   c. What was the price level in year 2?
   d. What was the level of real GDP in year 2?
   e. What was the velocity of circulation in year 2?

12. In Quantecon, described in problem 11, in year 3, the quantity of money falls to one fifth of its year 2 level.
   a. What is the quantity of money in year 3?
   b. What is the price level in year 3?
   c. What is the level of real GDP in year 3?
   d. What is the velocity of circulation in year 3?
   e. If it takes more than one year for the full quantity theory effect to occur, what do you predict happens to real GDP in Quantecon in year 3? Why?

CRITICAL THINKING

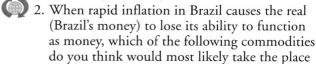

1. Study *Reading Between the Lines* on pp. 326–327 and then answer the following questions:
   a. What, according to the news article, were Brazilians expecting to happen to the inflation rate in January 1999?
   b. Use the link on the Parkin Web site to obtain data on Brazil's inflation since January 1999. Were the people's expectations correct?
   c. How do Brazilians protect themselves from a falling value of the real (Brazil's money)?
   d. Why has Brazil's inflation rate been higher than its money supply growth rate in some years? Does this fact contradict the quantity theory of money?

2. When rapid inflation in Brazil causes the real (Brazil's money) to lose its ability to function as money, which of the following commodities do you think would most likely take the place of the real in the Brazilian economy and why?
   a. Tractor parts
   b. Packs of cigarettes
   c. Loaves of bread
   d. Impressionist paintings
   e. Baseball trading cards

3. Use the link on the Parkin Web site to visit Mark Bernkopf's Central Banking Resource Center. Read the short article on Electronic Cash and also read "The End of Cash" by James Gleick (first published in the *New York Times Magazine* on June 16, 1996). Then answer the following questions:
   a. What is e-cash?
   b. Mark Bernkopf asks: "Will 'e-cash' enable private currencies to overturn the ability of governments to make monetary policy?" Will it? Why or why not?
   c. When you buy an item on the Internet and pay by using a form of e-cash, are you using money? Explain why or why not.
   d. In your opinion, is the concern about e-cash a real concern or hype?

Chapter 15

Monetary Policy

In 1987, William Greider's *Secrets of the Temple: How the Federal Reserve Runs the Country* made the *New York Times* best-seller list. This book was popular partly because it was (and is) a good read and partly because it let its reader in on some secrets— the secrets of the mysterious Fed. What exactly is the Fed? What tools does it possess? And how does it use them? ◆ One thing the Fed does is to manage the nation's money. The amount of money in existence is surprisingly large. An unknown quantity of U.S. bills circulates abroad, especially in Russia and the rest of Eastern Europe. But there are enough coins and bills circulating in the United States today for every person to have a wallet stuffed with more than $1,000. In addition, enough money is deposited in banks and other financial institutions for every person to have a deposit of more than $12,500. What determines the amount of currency and bank deposits in existence? How does the Fed change the amount of money floating around the economy? And why do individuals and businesses hold so much money? ◆ In 1997 and 1998, financial markets in some Asian economies were under stress. Banks collapsed and currencies sank. People feared contagion. Would the Asian problems spread to the United States? Anxious to maintain calm and keep the economy expanding, the Fed gradually lowered interest rates through 1998. Would the Fed keep on lowering interest rates through 1999 or would it increase interest rates to choke off inflation? How does the Fed change interest rates? How do interest rates influence the economy? How do higher interest rates keep inflation in check?

◆ In this chapter, you will learn about the Fed and monetary policy. You will learn how the Fed influences interest rates and how interest rates influence the economy. You'll discover that interest rates depend, in part, on the amount of money in existence. You will also discover how the Fed influences the quantity of money to influence interest rates as it attempts to smooth the business cycle and keep inflation in check.

Temple of Secrets

After studying this chapter, you will be able to:

■ Describe the structure of the Federal Reserve System (the Fed)

■ Describe the tools used by the Fed to conduct its monetary policy

■ Explain what an open market operation is and how it works

■ Explain how an open market operation changes the money supply

■ Explain what determines the demand for money

■ Explain how the Fed influences interest rates

■ Explain how interest rates influence the economy

The Federal Reserve System

THE CENTRAL BANK OF THE UNITED STATES IS the **Federal Reserve System**. A **central bank** is a bank's bank and a public authority that regulates a nation's financial institutions and markets. As the banks' bank, the Fed provides banking services to commercial banks such as Citibank and the Bank of America. A central bank is not a citizens' bank. That is, the Fed does not provide general banking services for businesses and individual citizens.

The Fed conducts the nation's **monetary policy**, which means that it adjusts the quantity of money in circulation. The Fed's goals are to keep inflation in check, maintain full employment, moderate the business cycle, and contribute toward achieving long-term growth. Complete success in the pursuit of these goals is impossible, and the Fed's more modest goal is to improve the performance of the economy and to get closer to the goals than a "hands off" approach would achieve. Whether the Fed succeeds in improving economic performance is a matter on which there is a range of opinion.

This chapter examines the tools available to the Fed in its conduct of monetary policy and looks at the effects of the Fed's actions on the economy. We begin by describing the structure of the Fed.

The Structure of the Federal Reserve System

The key elements in the structure of the Federal Reserve System are:
- The Board of Governors
- The Regional Federal Reserve Banks
- The Federal Open Market Committee

The Board of Governors   The Board of Governors has seven members, who are appointed by the President of the United States and confirmed by the Senate, each for a 14-year term. The terms are staggered so that one seat on the board becomes vacant every two years. The President appoints one of the board members as Chairman for a term of four years, which is renewable.

The Federal Reserve Banks   There are 12 Federal Reserve banks, one for each of 12 Federal Reserve districts shown in Fig. 15.1. Each Federal Reserve bank has nine directors. Three of the directors are appointed by the Board of Governors and each of the other six are elected by the commercial banks in their Federal Reserve district. The directors of the regional Federal Reserve banks appoint the bank's president, and the Board of Governors approves this appointment.

The Federal Reserve Bank of New York (known as the New York Fed) occupies a special place in the Federal Reserve System because it implements some of the Fed's most important policy decisions.

The Federal Open Market Committee   The **Federal Open Market Committee** (FOMC) is the main policy-making organ of the Federal Reserve System. The FOMC consists of the following voting members:
- The chairman and other six members of the Board of Governors
- The president of the Federal Reserve Bank of New York
- The presidents of the other regional Federal Reserve banks (of whom, on a yearly rotating basis, only four vote)

The FOMC meets approximately every six weeks to review the state of the economy and to decide the actions to be carried out by the New York Fed.

The Fed's Power Center

A description of the formal structure of the Fed gives the impression that power in the Fed resides with the Board of Governors. In practice, it is the chairman of the Board of Governors who has the largest influence on the Fed's monetary policy actions, and some remarkable individuals have held this position. One of these is Paul Volcker, who was appointed in 1979 by President Carter and reappointed in 1983 by President Reagan. Volcker eradicated inflation but helped to create one of the most severe postwar recessions. Another is Alan Greenspan, who was appointed by President Reagan in 1987 and reappointed by President Bush in 1992 and again for another term by President Clinton in 1996.

The chairman's power and influence stem from three sources. First, it is the chairman who controls the agenda and who dominates the meetings of the FOMC. Second, day-to-day contact with a large staff of economists and other technical experts provides the chairman with detailed background briefings on monetary policy issues. Third, the chairman is the spokesperson for the Fed and the Fed's

FIGURE 15.1

The Federal Reserve System

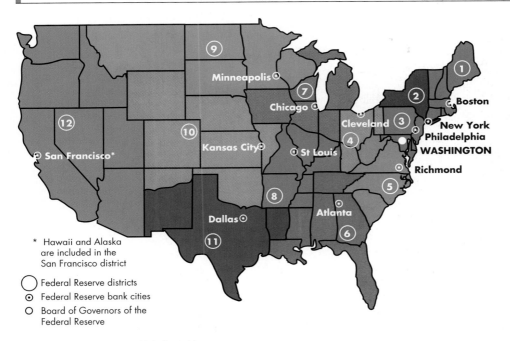

The nation is divided into 12 Federal Reserve districts, each having a Federal Reserve bank. (Some of the larger districts also have branch banks.) The Board of Governors of the Federal Reserve System is located in Washington, D.C.

* Hawaii and Alaska are included in the San Francisco district

◯ Federal Reserve districts
◉ Federal Reserve bank cities
◯ Board of Governors of the Federal Reserve

Source: Federal Reserve Bulletin, published monthly.

main point of contact with the President and government and with foreign central banks and governments.

The Fed's Policy Tools

The Federal Reserve System has many responsibilities, but we'll examine its single most important one: regulating the amount of money floating around in the United States. How does the Fed control the money supply? It does so by adjusting the reserves of the banking system. It is also by adjusting the reserves of the banking system and by standing ready to make loans to banks that the Fed is able to prevent bank failures. The Fed uses three main policy tools to achieve its objectives:

- Required reserve ratios
- Discount rate
- Open market operations

Required Reserve Ratios   All depository institutions in the United States are required to hold a minimum

percentage of deposits as reserves. This minimum percentage is known as a *required reserve ratio*. The Fed determines a required reserve ratio for each type of deposit. In 1997, banks were required to hold minimum reserves equal to 3 percent of checking deposits up to $49 million and 10 percent of these deposits in excess of $49 million. The required reserves on other types of deposits were zero.

Discount Rate   The **discount rate** is the interest rate at which the Fed stands ready to lend reserves to commercial banks. A change in the discount rate is proposed to the FOMC by the Board of Directors of at least one of the 12 Federal Reserve banks and is approved by the Board of Governors.

Open Market Operations   An **open market operation** is the purchase or sale of government securities—U.S. Treasury bills and bonds—by the Federal Reserve System in the open market. When the Fed conducts an open market operation, it makes a transaction with a bank or some other business but it does not transact with the federal government.

The structure and policy tools of the Federal Reserve System are summarized in Fig. 15.2. To understand how open market operations work, we need to know about the Fed's balance sheet.

The Fed's Balance Sheet

The balance sheet of the Federal Reserve System for December 1998 is set out in Table 15.1. The assets on the left side are what the Fed owns, and the liabilities on the right side are what it owes. The Fed's three main assets are:

1. Gold and foreign exchange
2. U.S. government securities
3. Loans to banks

The Fed's holdings of gold and foreign exchange are its international reserves. Most of the Fed's foreign exchange consists of deposits by the Fed at other central banks. The Fed's holdings of U.S. government securities are the backing for dollar bills and banks' deposits at the Fed. The Fed sometimes makes loans to banks on which the Fed charges them the discount rate. (These loans were negligible in December 1998.)

The Fed's two main liabilities are:

1. Federal Reserve notes in circulation
2. Banks' deposits

The Federal Reserve notes in circulation are the dollar bills that we use in our daily transactions. Some of these bills are in circulation with the public; others are in the tills and vaults of banks and other financial institutions. Banks' deposits are the deposits of commercial banks, which are part of the reserves of those banks.

You might be wondering why Federal Reserve notes are considered a liability of the Fed. When bank notes were invented, they gave their owner a claim on the gold reserves of the issuing bank. Such notes were *convertible paper money*. The holder of such a note could convert the note on demand into gold (or some other commodity such as silver) at a guaranteed price. Thus when a bank issued a note, it was holding itself liable to convert that note into gold or silver. Modern bank notes are nonconvertible. A *nonconvertible note* is a bank note that is not convertible into any commodity and that obtains its value by government fiat—hence the term "fiat money." Such notes are the legal liability of the bank that issues them, and they are backed by holdings of securities and loans. Federal Reserve notes are backed by the Fed's holdings of U.S. government securities.

FIGURE 15.2
The Structure of the Fed

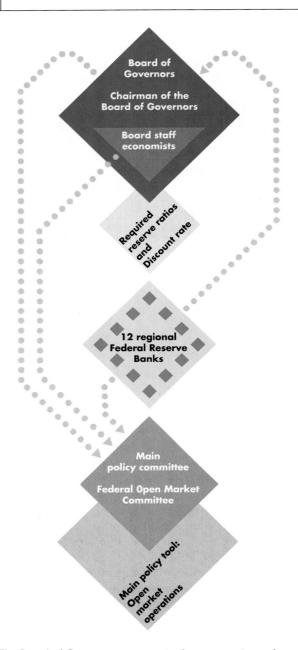

The Board of Governors sets required reserve ratios and, on the proposal of the 12 Federal Reserve banks, sets the discount rate. The Board of Governors and presidents of the regional Federal Reserve banks sit on the FOMC to determine open market operations.

TABLE 15.1

The Fed's Balance Sheet, December 1998

Assets (billions of dollars)		Liabilities (billions of dollars)	
Gold and foreign exchange	65	Federal Reserve notes	481
U.S. government securities	463	Banks' deposits	27
Loans to banks	0	Other liabilities (net)	20
Total assets	528	Total liabilities	528

Source: Federal Reserve Bulletin (March 1999).

The Fed's liabilities, together with coins in circulation (coins are issued by the Treasury and are not liabilities of the Fed), make up the monetary base. That is, the **monetary base** is the sum of Federal Reserve notes, coins, and banks' deposits at the Fed. The monetary base is so called because it acts like a base that supports the nation's money supply. The larger the monetary base, the greater is the quantity of money.

R E V I E W   Q U I Z

- What is the central bank of the United States and what functions does it perform?
- Who appoints the Fed board members and chairman and for how long do they serve?
- What is special about the Federal Reserve Bank of New York?
- Can you name the three policy tools that the Fed uses?
- What is the Federal Open Market Committee and what are its main functions?
- How often does the FOMC meet?

Next, we're going to see how the Fed controls the money supply. We'll see how the Fed's monetary policy instruments change the monetary base and how changes in the monetary base change the quantity of money in circulation.

Controlling the Money Supply

THE FED CONSTANTLY MONITORS AND ADJUSTS the quantity of money in the economy. To change the quantity of money, the Fed can use any of its three tools: required reserve ratios, the discount rate, and open market operations. Required reserve ratios are changed infrequently. The discount rate and open market operations are used more frequently. Let's see how these tools work.

How Required Reserve Ratios Work

When the Fed *increases* the required reserve ratio, the banks must hold more reserves. To increase their reserves, the banks must *decrease* their lending, which *decreases* the quantity of money. When the Fed *decreases* the required reserve ratio, the banks may hold less reserves. To decrease their reserves, the banks *increase* their lending, which *increases* the quantity of money.

How the Discount Rate Works

When the Fed *increases* the discount rate, the banks must pay a higher price for any reserves that they borrow from the Fed. Faced with higher cost of reserves, the banks try to get by with smaller reserves. But with a given required reserve ratio, the banks must also *decrease* their lending to decrease their borrowed reserves. So the quantity of money *decreases*. When the Fed *decreases* the discount rate, the banks pay a lower price for any reserves that they borrow from the Fed. Faced with lower cost of reserves, the banks are willing to borrow more reserves and *increase* their lending. So the quantity of money *increases*.

How an Open Market Operation Works

When the Fed *buys* securities in an open market operation, bank reserves *increase,* banks *increase* their lending, and the quantity of money *increases*. When the Fed *sells* securities in an open market operation, bank reserves *decrease,* banks *decrease* their lending, and the quantity of money *decreases*. Open market operations are used more frequently than the other two tools and are the most complex in their operation. So we'll study this tool in greater detail than the other two.

The key to understanding how an open market operation works is to see how it changes the reserves of the banking system. We'll trace the effects of an open market operation when the Fed *buys* securities. (The effects of a sale of securities are the reverse of what we'll see here.)

The Fed Buys Securities   Suppose the Fed buys $100 million of U.S. government securities in the open market. There are two cases to consider: when the Fed buys from a commercial bank and when it buys from the public (a person or business that is not a commercial bank). The outcome is essentially the same in either case, but you might need to be convinced of this fact, so we'll study the two cases, starting with the simplest case, in which the Fed buys from a commercial bank.

Buys from Commercial Bank   When the Fed buys $100 million of securities from the Manhattan Commercial Bank, two things happen:

1. The Manhattan Commercial Bank has $100 million less securities, and the Fed has $100 million more securities.
2. The Fed pays for the securities by crediting the Manhattan Commercial Bank's deposit account at the Fed with $100 million.

Figure 15.3(a) shows the effects of these actions on the balance sheets of the Fed and the Manhattan Commercial Bank. Ownership of the securities passes from the commercial bank to the Fed, so the bank's assets decrease by $100 million and the Fed's assets increase by $100 million, as shown by the blue arrow running from the Manhattan Commercial Bank to the Fed. The Fed pays for the securities by crediting the Manhattan Commercial Bank's deposit account— its reserves—at the Fed with $100 million, as shown by the green arrow running from the Fed to the Manhattan Commercial Bank. This action increases the monetary base and increases the reserves of the banking system.

The Fed's assets increase by $100 million, and its liabilities also increase by $100 million. The commercial bank's total assets remain constant, but their composition changes. Its holdings of government securities decrease by $100 million, and its deposits at the Fed increase by $100 million. So the bank has additional reserves, which it can use to make loans.

FIGURE 15.3

The Fed Buys Securities in the Open Market

(a) The Fed buys securities from a commercial bank

The Federal Reserve Bank of New York

Assets	Liabilities
Securities +$100	Reserves of Manhattan Commercial Bank +$100

The Fed buys securities from a commercial bank …

… and pays for the securities by increasing the reserves of the commercial bank

The Manhattan Commercial Bank

Assets	Liabilities
Securities −$100	
Reserves +$100	

(b) The Fed buys securities from the public

The Federal Reserve Bank of New York

Assets	Liabilities
Securities +$100	Reserves of Manhattan Commercial Bank +$100

The Fed buys securities from Goldman Sachs, a member of the general public …

Goldman Sachs

Assets	Liabilities
Securities −$100	… and pays for the securities by writing a check that is deposited to Goldman Sachs's account at the Manhattan Commercial Bank and that increases the reserves of the commercial banks
Deposits at Manhattan Commercial Bank +$100	

The Manhattan Commercial Bank

Assets	Liabilities
Reserves +$100	Goldman Sachs's deposit +$100

We've just seen that when the Fed buys government securities from a bank, the bank's reserves increase. But what happens if the Fed buys government securities from the public—say, from Goldman Sachs, a financial services company?

Buys from Public   When the Fed buys $100 million of securities from Goldman Sachs, three things happen:

1. Goldman Sachs has $100 million less securities, and the Fed has $100 million more securities.
2. The Fed pays for the securities with a check for $100 million drawn on itself, which Goldman Sachs deposits in its account at the Manhattan Commercial Bank.
3. The Manhattan Commercial Bank collects payment of this check from the Fed, and $100 million is deposited in Manhattan's deposit account at the Fed.

Figure 15.3(b) shows the effects of these actions on the balance sheets of the Fed, Goldman Sachs, and the Manhattan Commercial Bank. Ownership of the securities passes from Goldman Sachs to the Fed, so Goldman Sachs's assets decrease by $100 million and the Fed's assets increase by $100 million, as shown by the blue arrow running from Goldman Sachs to the Fed. The Fed pays for the securities with a check payable to Goldman Sachs, which Goldman Sachs deposits in the Manhattan Commercial Bank. This payment increases Manhattan's reserves by $100 million, as shown by green arrow running from the Fed to Manhattan Commercial Bank. It also increases Goldman Sachs's deposit at the Manhattan Commercial Bank by $100 million, as shown by the red arrow running from the Manhattan Commercial Bank to Goldman Sachs. Just as when the Fed buys from a bank, this action increases the monetary base and increases the reserves of the banking system.

Again, the Fed's assets increase by $100 million, and its liabilities also increase by $100 million. Goldman Sachs has the same total assets as before, but their composition has changed. It now has more money and fewer securities. The Manhattan Commercial Bank's total assets increase, and so do its liabilities. Its deposits at the Fed—its reserves—increase by $100 million, and its deposit liability to Goldman Sachs increases by $100 million. Because its reserves have increased by the same amount as its deposits, the bank has excess reserves, which it can use to make loans.

We've studied what happens when the Fed *buys* government securities from either a bank or the public. When the Fed *sells* securities, all the transactions and events you've just studied work in reverse. (Trace the process again but with the Fed selling and the banks or public buying securities.)

The effects of an open market operation on the balance sheets of the Fed and the banks that we've just described are not the end of the story—they are just the beginning.

A change in bank reserves that results from an open market operation has ripple effects through the economy. First, it has a multiplier effect on the quantity of money. Second, it changes interest rates. Third, it changes aggregate expenditure and real GDP.

We are going to study these ripple effects in the rest of this chapter. We begin by studying the multiplier effect of an open market operation on the quantity of money. To do so, we build on the link between bank reserves and bank deposits that you studied in Chapter 14. But first we must learn about a related link between bank reserves and the monetary base.

Bank Reserves, the Monetary Base, and the Money Multiplier

An open market purchase that increases bank reserves also increases the monetary base. The increase in the monetary base equals the amount of the open market purchase and, initially it equals the increase in bank reserves. To see why, recall that the *monetary base* is the sum of Federal Reserve notes, coins, and banks' deposits at the Fed. An open market purchase increases the banks' deposits at the Fed—part of banks' reserves—by the amount of the open market purchase. Nothing else changes, so the monetary base increases by the amount of the open market purchase.

But when the banks use the new reserves to make loans, bank deposits and currency held outside the banks increase. An increase in currency held outside the banks is called a **currency drain**. A currency drain does not change the monetary base. Bank reserves decrease, currency increases, and the monetary base remains the same. But a currency drain decreases the amount of money that banks can create from a given increase in the monetary base.

The amount of money that banks can create from a given increase in the monetary base is determined by the **money multiplier**, which is the amount by which a change in the monetary base is multiplied to determine the resulting change in the quantity of money. Let's now look at the money multiplier.

The Multiplier Effect of an Open Market Operation

Figure 15.4 shows the multiplier effect of an open market purchase of securities from the banks. Initially, the banks' reserves increase but the quantity of money does not change. The banks have excess reserves, and the following sequence of events takes place:

■ Banks lend excess reserves.
■ The money supply increases.
■ New deposits are used to make payments.
■ Some of the new money is held as currency— a *currency drain*.
■ Some of the new money remains on deposit in banks.
■ Banks' required reserves increase.
■ Excess reserves decrease but remain positive.

The sequence repeats in a series of rounds, but each round begins with a smaller quantity of excess reserves than did the previous one. The process continues until excess reserves have finally been eliminated.

Figure 15.5 keeps track of the increases in reserves, loans, deposits, currency, and money that results from an open market operation of $100,000. In this figure, the *currency drain* is 33.33 percent and the *required reserve ratio* is 10 percent. These numbers are assumed to keep the arithmetic simple.

The Fed buys $100,000 of securities from the banks. The banks' reserves increase by this amount, but deposits do not change. The banks have excess reserves of $100,000, and they lend those reserves. When the banks lend $100,000 of excess reserves, $66,667 remains in the banks as deposits and $33,333 drains off and is held outside the banks as currency. The quantity of money has now increased by $100,000—the increase in deposits plus the increase in currency holdings.

The increased bank deposits of $66,667 generates an increase in required reserves of 10 percent of that amount, which is $6,667. Actual reserves have

---

FIGURE 15.4

A Round in the Multiplier Process Following an Open Market Operation

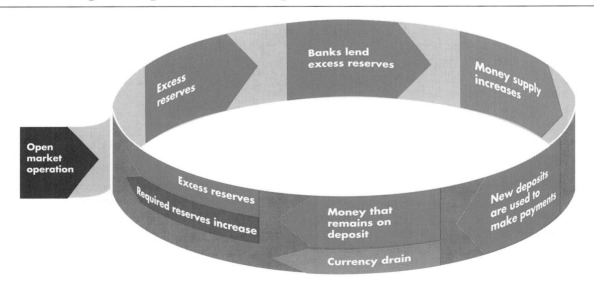

An open market operation increases bank reserves and creates excess reserves. Banks lend the excess reserves, and new loans are used to make payments. Households and firms receiving payments keep some of the receipts in the form of currency— a currency drain—and place the rest on deposit in banks. The increase in bank deposits increases banks' reserves but also increases banks' required reserves. Required reserves increase by less than actual reserves, so the banks still have some excess reserves, though less than before. The process repeats until excess reserves have been eliminated.

FIGURE 15.5

The Multiplier Effect of an Open Market Operation

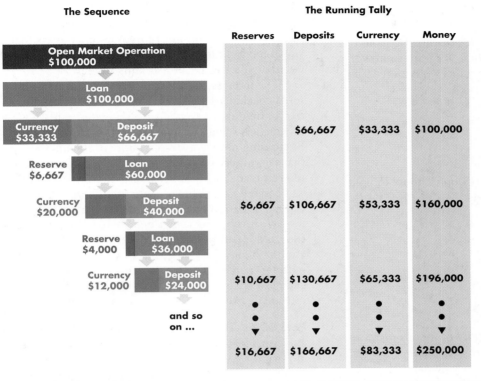

When the Fed provides the banks with $100,000 of additional reserves in an open market operation, the banks lend those reserves. Of the amount lent, $33,333 (33.33 percent) leaves the banks in a currency drain and $66,667 remains on deposit. With additional deposits, required reserves increase by $6,667 (10 percent required reserve ratio) and the banks lend $60,000. Of this amount, $20,000 leaves the banks in a currency drain and $40,000 remains on deposit. The process repeats until the banks have created enough deposits to eliminate their excess reserves. An additional $100,000 of reserves creates $250,000 of money.

increased by the same amount as the increase in deposits—$66,667. So the banks now have excess reserves of $60,000. At this stage, we have gone once around the circle shown in Fig. 15.4. The process we've just described repeats but begins with excess reserves of $60,000. Figure 15.5 shows the next two rounds. At the end of the process, the quantity of money has increased by a multiple of the increase in the monetary base. In this case, the increase is $250,000, which is 2.5 times the increase in the monetary base.

An open market *sale* works similarly to an open market purchase, but it *decreases* the quantity of money. (Trace the process again but with the Fed selling and the banks or public buying securities.)

When the Fed undertakes an open market operation, it is trying to influence the course of the economy. But the Fed's influence is indirect. You've now studied the initial effect of the Fed's actions, which is to change the quantity of money.

R E V I E W   Q U I Z

- What happens when the Fed buys securities in the open market?
- What happens when the Fed sells securities in the open market?
- What do the banks do when they have excess reserves and how do their actions influence the quantity of money?
- What do the banks do when they are short of reserves and how do their actions influence the quantity of money?

When the Fed changes the quantity of money, interest rates change. To see why, we must study the demand for money.

The Demand for Money

THE AMOUNT OF MONEY WE RECEIVE EACH WEEK in payment for our labor is income—a flow. The amount of money that we hold in our wallet or in a deposit account at the bank is an inventory—a stock. There is no limit to how much income we would like to receive each week. But there is a limit to how big an inventory of money each of us would like to hold on to and not spend.

The Influences on Money Holding

The quantity of money that people choose to hold depends on four main factors:

- The price level
- The interest rate
- Real GDP
- Financial innovation

Let's look at each of them.

The Price Level   The quantity of money measured in dollars is called the quantity of *nominal money*. The quantity of nominal money demanded is proportional to the price level, other things remaining the same. That is, if the price level (GDP deflator) increases by 10 percent, people will want to hold 10 percent more nominal money than before, other things being equal. What matters is not the number of dollars that you hold but their buying power. If you hold $20 to buy your weekly movies and soda, you will increase your money holding to $22 if the prices of movies and soda—and your wage rate—increase by 10 percent.

The quantity of money measured in constant dollars (for example, in 1992 dollars) is called *real money*. Real money is equal to nominal money divided by the price level. It is the quantity of money measured in terms of what it will buy. In the above example, when the price level rises by 10 percent and you increase your average cash holding by 10 percent, you are keeping your *real* cash holding constant. Your $22 at the new price level buys the same quantity of goods and is the same quantity of *real money* as your $20 at the original price level. The quantity of real money held does not depend on the price level.

The Interest Rate   A fundamental principle of economics is that as the opportunity cost of something increases, people try to find substitutes for it. Money is no exception. The higher the opportunity cost of holding money, other things being equal, the lower is the quantity of real money demanded. But what is the opportunity cost of holding money? It is the interest rate that you must forgo on other assets that you could hold instead of money minus the interest rate that you can earn by holding money.

The interest rate that you earn on currency and some checking deposits is zero. So the opportunity cost of holding these items is the interest rate on other assets such as a savings bond or Treasury bill. By holding money instead, you forgo the interest that you otherwise would have received. This forgone interest is the opportunity cost of holding money.

Money loses value because of inflation. So why isn't the inflation rate part of the cost of holding money? It is: Other things being equal, the higher the expected inflation rate, the higher are interest rates and the higher, therefore, is the opportunity cost of holding money. (The forces that make interest rates change to reflect changes in the expected inflation rate are described in Chapter 16 on pp. 370–371.)

Real GDP   The quantity of money that households and firms plan to hold depends on the amount they are spending, and the quantity of money demanded in the economy as a whole depends on aggregate expenditure—real GDP.

Again, suppose that you hold an average of $20 to finance your weekly purchases of movies and soda. Now imagine that the prices of these goods and of all other goods remain constant but that your income increases. As a consequence, you now spend more, and you also keep a larger amount of money on hand to finance your higher volume of expenditure.

Financial Innovation   Technological change and the arrival of new financial products change the quantity of money held. The major financial innovations are the widespread use of:

1. Daily interest checking deposits
2. Automatic transfers between checking and savings deposits
3. Automatic teller machines
4. Credit cards

These innovations have occurred because of the development of computing power that has lowered the cost of calculations and record keeping.

We summarize the effects of the influences on money holding by using the demand for money curve.

The Demand for Money Curve

The *demand for money* is the relationship between the quantity of real money demanded and the interest rate, when all other influences on the amount of money that people wish to hold remain the same. Figure 15.6 shows a demand for money curve, *MD*. When the interest rate rises, everything else remaining the same, the opportunity cost of holding money rises and the quantity of money demanded decreases—there is a movement along the demand for money curve. Similarly, when the interest rate falls, the opportunity cost of holding money falls and the quantity of money demanded increases—there is a downward movement along the demand for money curve.

Shifts in the Demand Curve for Real Money

A change in real GDP or financial innovation changes the demand for money and shifts the demand curve for real money. Figure 15.7 illustrates the change in the demand for money. A decrease in real GDP decreases the demand for money and shifts the demand curve leftward from MD_0 to MD_1. An increase in real GDP has the opposite effect. It increases the demand for money and shifts the demand curve rightward from MD_0 to MD_2.

The influence of financial innovation on the demand for money curve is more complicated. It might increase the demand for some types of deposits, decrease the demand for others, and decrease the demand for currency. We'll look at the effects of financial innovation by studying the demand for money in the United States.

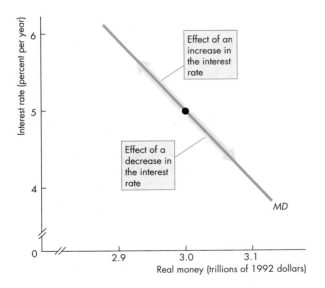

FIGURE 15.6

The Demand for Money

The demand for money curve, *MD*, shows the relationship between the quantity of money that people plan to hold and the interest rate, other things remaining the same. The interest rate is the opportunity cost of holding money. A change in the interest rate brings a movement along the demand curve.

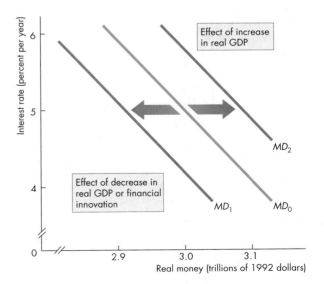

FIGURE 15.7

Changes in the Demand for Money

A decrease in real GDP decreases the demand for money and shifts the demand curve leftward from MD_0 to MD_1. An increase in real GDP increases the demand for money and shifts the demand curve rightward from MD_0 to MD_2. Financial innovation generally decreases the demand for money.

The Demand for Money in the United States

Figure 15.8 shows the relationship between the interest rate and the quantity of real money demanded in the United States between 1970 and 1998. Each dot shows the interest rate and the amount of real money held in a given year. In 1970, the demand for M1 (shown in part a) was MD_0. During the early 1970s, the spread of credit cards decreased the demand for M1 (currency and checking deposits) and shifted the demand for M1 curve leftward to MD_1. But over the years, real GDP growth increased the demand for M1 and by 1994 the demand for M1 curve had shifted rightward to MD_2. Further financial innovation arising from a continued increase in the use of credit cards and the spread of ATMs decreased the demand for M1 and shifted the demand curve leftward again.

In 1970, the demand for M2 (shown in part b) was MD_0. The spread of credit cards that decreased the demand for M1 during the period did not decrease demand for M2. The reason is that many new financial products were M2 deposits. So from 1970 through 1989, the demand for M2 increased and the demand for M2 curve shifted rightward to MD_1. But between 1989 and 1994, innovations in financial products that compete with deposits of all kinds occurred and the demand for M2 decreased. The demand for M2 curve shifted leftward to MD_2. Finally, after 1994, the expanding economy brought rising real GDP. The demand for M2 increases again and the demand curve shifted rightward to MD_3.

FIGURE 15.8

The Demand for Money in the United States

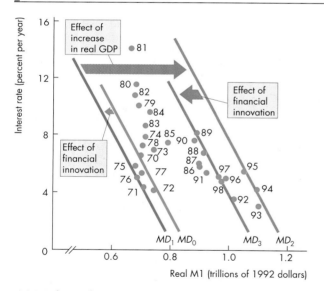

(a) M1 demand

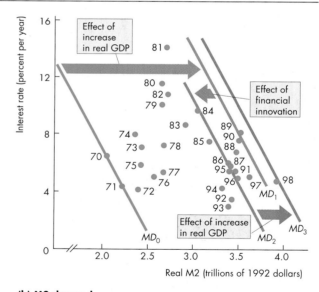

(b) M2 demand

The dots show the quantity of real money and the interest rate in each year between 1970 and 1998. In 1970, the demand for M1 was MD_0 in part (a). The demand for M1 decreased during the early 1970s because of financial innovation and the demand curve shifted leftward to MD_2. But real GDP growth increased the demand for M1 and by 1994, the demand curve had shifted rightward to MD_2. Further financial innovation decreased the demand for M1 in 1995 and 1998 and shifted the demand curve leftward again to MD_3. In 1970, the demand for M2 curve was MD_0 in part (b). The growth of real GDP increased the demand for M2 and by 1989, the demand curve had shifted rightward to MD_1. During the early 1990s, new substitutes for M2 decreased the demand for M2 and the demand curve shifted leftward to MD_2. But during the late 1990s, rapid growth of real GDP increased the demand for M2 and the demand curve shifted rightward to MD_3.

Source: Economic Report of the President, 1999, and the author's calculations and assumptions.

R E V I E W   Q U I Z

- What are the main influences on the quantity of real money that people and businesses plan to hold?

- What does the demand for money curve show?

- How does an increase in the interest rate change the quantity of money demanded and how would you use the demand curve for real money to show the effects?

- How does an increase in real GDP change the demand for money and how would you use the demand curve for real money to show the effects?

- How have financial innovations changed the demand for M1 and M2?

We now know what determines the demand for money. And we've seen that a key factor is the interest rate—the opportunity cost of holding money. But what determines the interest rate? Let's find out.

Interest Rate Determination

AN INTEREST RATE IS THE PERCENTAGE YIELD on a financial security such as a *bond* or a *stock*. The higher the price of a financial asset, other things remaining the same, the lower is the interest rate. An example will make this relationship clear. Suppose the federal government sells a bond that promises to pay $10 a year. If the price of the bond is $100, the interest rate is 10 percent per year—$10 is 10 percent of $100. If the price of the bond is $50, the interest rate is 20 percent—$10 is 20 percent of $50. And if the price of the bond is $200, the interest rate is 5 percent—$10 is 5 percent of $200.

You've just seen the link between the price of a bond and the interest rate. People divide their wealth between bonds (and other interest-bearing financial assets) and money, and the amount they hold as money depends on the interest rate. We can study the forces that determine the interest rate in either the market for bonds or the market for money. Because the Fed can influence the *supply* of money, we focus on the market for money.

Money Market Equilibrium

The interest rate is determined by the supply of and demand for money. The quantity of money supplied is determined by the actions of the banking system and the Fed. On any given day, the supply of money is a fixed quantity. The *real* quantity of money supplied is equal to the nominal quantity supplied divided by the price level. At a given moment in time, there is a particular price level, and so the quantity of real money supplied is also a fixed amount. The supply curve of real money is shown in Fig. 15.9 as the vertical line labeled *MS*. The quantity of real money supplied is $3.0 trillion.

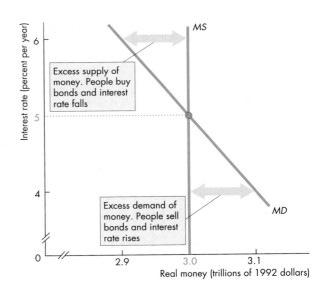

FIGURE 15.9
Money Market Equilibrium

Money market equilibrium occurs when the interest rate has adjusted to make the quantity of real money demanded equal to the quantity supplied. Here, equilibrium occurs at an interest rate of 5 percent a year. At interest rates above 5 percent a year, the quantity of real money demanded is less than the quantity supplied, so people buy bonds and the interest rate falls. At interest rates below 5 percent a year, the quantity of real money demanded exceeds the quantity supplied, so people sell bonds and the interest rate rises. Only at 5 percent a year is the quantity of real money in existence willingly held.

On any given day, all the influences on the demand for money except for the interest rate are constant. But the lower the interest rate, the greater is the quantity of real money demanded. Figure 15.9 shows a demand for real money curve, *MD*.

Equilibrium   When the quantity of real money supplied equals the quantity of real money demanded, the money market is in equilibrium. Figure 15.9 illustrates equilibrium in the money market. Equilibrium is achieved by changes in the interest rate. If the interest rate is too high, people demand a smaller quantity of money than the quantity supplied. They are holding too much money. In this situation, they try to get rid of money by buying bonds. As they do so, the price of a bond rises and the interest rate falls to the equilibrium rate. Conversely, if the interest rate is too low, people demand a larger quantity of money than the quantity supplied. They are holding too little money. In this situation, they try to get more money by selling bonds. As they do so, the price of a bond falls and the interest rate rises to the equilibrium rate. Only when the interest rate is at the level at which people are holding the quantity of money supplied do they willingly hold the money and take no actions that change the interest rate.

Changing the Interest Rate

Suppose that the economy is overheating and the Fed fears inflation. It decides to take action to decrease aggregate demand and spending. To do so, it wants to raise interest rates and discourage borrowing and expenditure on goods and services. What does the Fed do?

The Fed sells securities in the open market. As it does so, it mops up bank reserves and induces the banks to cut their lending. The banks make a smaller quantity of new loans each day until the stock of loans outstanding has fallen to a level that is consistent with the new lower level of reserves. The money supply decreases.

Suppose that the Fed undertakes open market operations on a sufficiently large scale to decrease the money supply from $3.0 trillion to $2.9 trillion. As a consequence, the supply curve of real money shifts leftward, as shown in Fig. 15.10, from MS_0 to MS_1.

The demand for money is shown by *MD*. With an interest rate of 5 percent a year and $2.9 trillion of money in the economy, firms and households are now holding less money than they wish to hold. They attempt to increase their money holding by selling financial assets. As they do so, the price of a bond

FIGURE 15.10

Interest Rate Changes

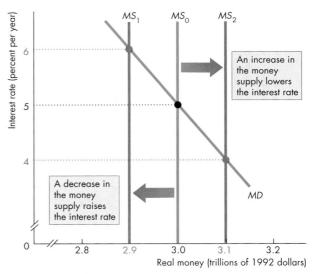

An open market sale of securities shifts the money supply curve leftward to MS_1, and the interest rate rises to 6 percent a year. An open market purchase of securities shifts the money supply curve rightward to MS_2, and the interest rate falls to 4 percent a year.

falls and the interest rate rises. When the interest rate has increased to 6 percent a year, people are willing to hold the smaller $2.9 trillion of money that the Fed and the banks have created.

Conversely, suppose that the Fed fears recession and decides to stimulate spending by increasing the money supply. If the Fed increases the real money supply to $3.1 trillion, the supply of real money curve shifts rightward from MS_0 to MS_2. The interest rate falls to 4 percent a year.

R E V I E W   Q U I Z

■ How is the short-term interest rate determined?

■ What do people do if they are holding more money than they plan to hold and what happens to the interest rate?

■ What actions does the Fed take if it wants to increase the interest rate? What actions does the Fed take if it wants to decrease the interest rate?

Monetary Policy

YOU HAVE NOW LEARNED A GREAT DEAL ABOUT the Fed, the monetary policy actions it can take, and the effects of those actions on short-term interest rates. Most of the "secrets of the temple" have been revealed. But you are possibly thinking: All this sounds nice in theory, but does it really happen? Does the Fed actually do the things we've learned about in this chapter? Indeed, it does happen, sometimes with dramatic effect.

To see the Fed in action, we'll do two things. First, we'll look at the fluctuations in short-term interest rates in the United States since 1970 and see how the Fed has influenced those fluctuations. Second, we'll focus on two episodes in the life of the Fed. One is from the turbulent years of the early 1980s when the Fed was struggling to eradicate a stubborn inflation. The other is from the period since a stock market crash of 1987 during which the Fed tried to keep inflation in check without killing economic growth.

The Fed in Action

You've seen that the immediate effect of the Fed's actions is a change in the short-term interest rate. Figure 15.11 shows the course of four short-term interest rates since 1970:

1. The 3-month Treasury bill rate, which is the interest rate paid by the federal government on 3-month loans

2. The 6-month commercial bill rate, which is the interest rate paid by large corporations on 6-month loans

3. The discount rate, which is the interest rate charged to banks by the Fed when the banks borrow reserves

4. The federal funds rate, which is the interest rate that the banks charge each other on overnight loans of reserves

Notice how closely these four interest rates move together. The interest rate that the Fed directly controls is the discount rate, and the rate that it closely

FIGURE 15.11
Short-Term Interest Rates

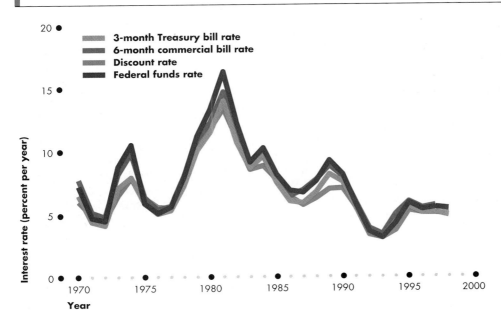

The Fed directly determines the discount rate (the rate at which the Fed lends reserves to banks) and closely monitors the federal funds rate (the rate at which banks lend reserves to each other). All short-term interest rates move up and down together, so the Fed influences all short-term rates such as the 3-month Treasury bill rate (the rate at which the federal government borrows in the short term) and the 6-month commercial bill rate (the rate at which big corporations borrow in the short term).

Source: *Economic Report of the President, 1999*

monitors is the federal funds rate, but because the short-term rates all move up and down together, the Fed is effectively able to influence all these rates.

Do short-term interest rates rise and fall in response to changes in the quantity of money, as the theory we've just studied predicts? Mostly they do, but not quite always. Figure 15.12 illustrates this connection. It shows the federal funds rate and a measure of the quantity of money. This measure of money is M2 expressed as a percentage of GDP. The reason for looking at M2 is that it is this measure of money that the Fed has placed greatest emphasis on. The reason for expressing M2 as a percentage of GDP is that we can see both the supply-side and demand-side effects on interest rates in a single measure. Interest rates rise if the quantity of money decreases. Interest rates also rise if the demand for money increases. But the demand for money increases if GDP increases. So the ratio of M2 to GDP decreases if either the supply of money decreases (M2 decreases) or the demand for money increases (GDP increases).

You can see by studying Fig. 15.12 that between 1970 and 1990, the rises and falls in the interest rate were exactly matched by decreases and increases in the ratio of M2 to GDP. An increase in the supply of money relative to the demand for money brought a fall in the interest rate (1970–1972, 1974–1977, and 1981–1986). A decrease in the supply of money relative to the demand for money brought a rise in the interest rate (1972–1974, 1977–1981, and 1986–1989).

You can also see in Fig. 15.12 that after 1990, the relationship between money and interest rates broke down. When the interest rate fell through 1993, the M2 to GDP ratio did not increase. The reason is that the demand for M2 fell because of the availability of some new substitute ways of holding wealth—bond and equity mutual funds. These funds were growing through the 1980s, but they grew more quickly during the 1990s, and their growth disturbed the traditional relationship between M2 and short-term interest rates. Consequently, after 1990, the Fed began to pay less attention to M2.

FIGURE 15.12

Money and Interest Rates

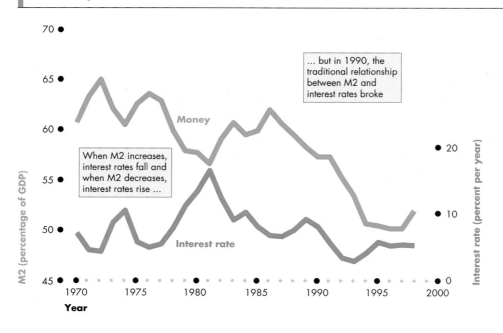

When the ratio of M2 to GDP (measured on the left scale) rises, either the supply of money increases or the demand for money decreases. The result, before 1990, is a fall in the federal funds rate (measured on the right scale). Similarly, when the ratio of M2 to GDP falls, either the supply of money has decreased or the demand for money has increased and (again before 1990) the federal funds rate rises. After 1990, the relationship between M2 and interest rates broke down because new substitutes for M2 decreased the demand for M2.

Source: *Economic Report of the President,* 1999, and the author's calculations.

You've now seen that we can explain short-term interest rate fluctuations as arising from fluctuations in the supply of money relative to the demand for money. But this relationship doesn't tell us whether actions by the Fed or fluctuations in GDP brought the fluctuations in the M2 to GDP ratio. Do the Fed's own actions move interest rates around? Let's look at the Fed in action.

Paul Volcker's Fed At the start of Paul Volcker's term of office as chairman of the Fed, which began in August 1979, the United States was locked in the grips of double-digit inflation. Volcker ended that inflation. He did so by forcing interest rates sharply upward from 1979 through 1981. This increase in interest rates resulted from the Fed using open market operations and increases in the discount rate to keep the banks short of reserves, which in turn held back the growth in the supply of loans and of money relative to the growth in their demand.

As we saw in Fig. 15.10, to increase interest rates, the Fed has to cut the real money supply. In practice, because the economy is growing and because prices are rising, a *slowdown* in nominal money supply growth is enough to increase interest rates. It is not necessary to actually *cut* the nominal money supply.

When Volcker became chairman of the Fed, the money supply was growing at more than 8 percent a year. Volcker slowed down that money supply growth to 6.5 percent in 1981. As a result, interest rates increased. The Treasury bill rate—the rate at which the government borrows—increased from 10 percent to 14 percent. The rate at which big corporations borrow increased from 9 percent to 14 percent. Mortgage rates—the rates at which homebuyers borrow—increased from 11 percent to 15 percent. The economy went into recession. The money supply growth slowdown and interest rate hike cut back the growth rate of aggregate demand. Real GDP decreased, and the inflation rate fell.

Alan Greenspan's Fed Alan Greenspan became chairman of the Fed in August 1987. In the two preceding years, the money supply had grown at a rapid pace, interest rates had tumbled, and the stock market had boomed. Then, suddenly and with no warning, stock prices fell, bringing fears of economic calamity and recession. This was Alan Greenspan's first test as Fed chairman.

The Fed's immediate reaction to the new situation was to emphasize the flexibility and sensitivity of the financial system and to make reserves plentiful to avoid any fear of a banking crisis. But as the months passed, it became increasingly clear that the economy was not heading for any kind of a recession. Unemployment continued to fall, income growth continued to be strong, and the fears that emerged were of inflation, not recession.

Seeking to avoid an upturn in inflation, the Fed slowed money growth and, just as Paul Volcker had done eight years earlier, forced interest rates sharply upward. Open market operations created a shortage of reserves and slowed the growth rate of the money supply. The slowdown in money supply growth had the effect implied by the model that you have been studying in this chapter. Interest rates increased throughout 1988. As 1989 advanced, concern about inflation remained, but renewed fears of recession returned, and interest rates were gradually lowered.

By 1990, recession had become a reality. At first, the Fed adopted a neutral position and waited for signs of recovery. But as the months passed and recovery seemed elusive, the Fed eventually began to cut interest rates. During 1991, interest rates fell by three percentage points as the Fed tried to stimulate aggregate demand.

By mid-1991, the recovery had begun and real GDP expanded. This expansion was to become one of the longest and strongest in history. The Fed helped to keep the expansion alive and to hold inflation in check. It did so by trying to anticipate unwanted deviations in either direction.

Through 1992 and 1993, the Fed permitted rapid money growth and kept interest rates low. During 1994, the Fed slowed money growth and pushed interest rates upward. It permitted interest rates to fall again during 1996 and nudged them up slightly in the first quarter of 1997.

Through most of 1997, the Fed's main concern was to hold inflation in check. But by the end of the year and throughout 1998, a different type of risk threatened. Economic growth was slowing in Asia. Japan and some other usually fast-growing economies were in deepening recession. Russia was in economic turmoil. Latin America was slowing. Even in parts of Europe, real GDP growth began to slow. At the same time, real GDP in the United States almost certainly exceeded potential GDP. So during 1998, the Fed tried to balance two opposing risks: inflation from the domestic economy and recession abroad. Eventually, the foreign risk dominated and the Fed engineered a series of interest rate cuts aimed at keeping the economy expanding.

Profiting by Predicting the Fed

Every day, the Fed influences interest rates by its open market operations. By buying securities and increasing the money supply, the Fed can lower interest rates; by selling securities and lowering the money supply, the Fed can increase interest rates. Sometimes such actions are taken to offset other influences and keep interest rates steady. At other times, the Fed moves interest rates up or down. The higher the interest rate, the lower is the price of a bond; the lower the interest rate, the higher is the price of a bond. Thus predicting interest rates is the same as predicting bond prices. Predicting that interest rates are going to fall is the same as predicting that bond prices are going to rise—a good time to buy bonds. Predicting that interest rates are going to rise is the same as predicting that bond prices are going to fall—a good time to sell bonds.

Because the Fed is the major player whose actions influence interest rates and bond prices, predicting the Fed is profitable and a good deal of effort goes into that activity. But people who anticipate that the Fed is about to increase the money supply buy bonds right away, pushing their prices upward and pushing interest rates downward *before* the Fed acts. Similarly, people who anticipate that the Fed is about to decrease the money supply sell bonds right away, pushing their prices downward and pushing interest rates upward before the Fed acts. In other words, bond prices and interest rates change as soon as the Fed's actions are foreseen. By the time the Fed actually takes its actions, if those actions are correctly foreseen, they have no effect. The effects occur in anticipation of the Fed's actions. Only changes in the money supply that are not foreseen change the interest rate at the time that those changes occur.

The Ripple Effects of Monetary Policy

You've now seen that the Fed's actions do indeed change interest rates and that the Fed tries to influence the course of the economy. These monetary policy measures work by changing aggregate demand. When the Fed slows money growth and pushes interest rates up, it decreases aggregate demand, which in turn slows both real GDP growth and inflation. When the Fed speeds money growth and lowers interest rates, it increases aggregate demand, which in turn speeds real GDP

growth and inflation. The mechanism through which aggregate demand changes involves several channels. Higher interest rates bring a decrease in consumption expenditure and investment. Tighter bank credit brings fewer loans and reinforces the effects of higher interest rates on consumption expenditure and investment.

Higher interest rates bring an increase in the exchange rate that makes U.S. exports more expensive and makes imports less costly. So net exports decrease. The decreases in consumption, investment, and net exports all combine to decrease aggregate demand, which in turn slows the growth rate of real GDP and the inflation rate. Schematically, the effects of the Fed's actions ripple through the economy in the following way:

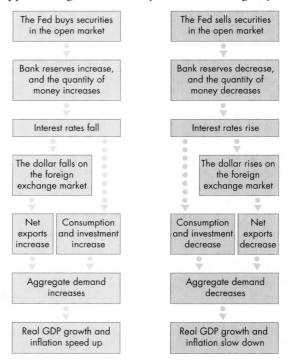

Interest Rates and the Business Cycle

You've seen the connection between the Fed's actions and interest rates in Fig. 15.12. What about the ripple effects that we've just described? Do they really occur? Do changes in interest rates ultimately influence the real GDP growth rate? Yes they do. You can see these effects in Fig. 15.13. The blue line in this figure shows the short-term interest rate minus the long-term interest rate. The short-term interest rate is influenced by the Fed in the way that you studied

FIGURE 15.13
Interest Rates and Real GDP Growth

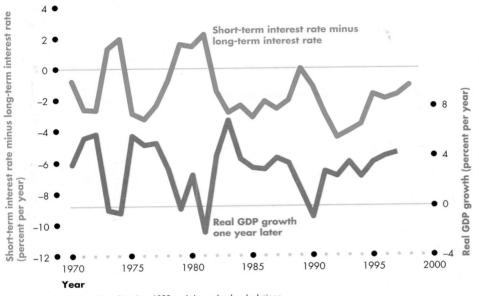

Short-term interest rate minus long-term interest rate

Real GDP growth one year later

Short-term interest rate minus long-term interest rate (percent per year)

Real GDP growth (percent per year)

Year

When the Fed increases short-term interest rates, the short-term interest rate rises above the long-term interest rate and, later, real GDP growth slows down. Similarly, when the Fed decreases short-term interest rates, the short-term interest rate falls below the long-term interest rate and, later, real GDP growth speeds up.

Source: *Economic Report of the President*, 1999, and the author's calculations.

earlier in this chapter. And changes in short-term rates have some influence on the long-term interest rate. But this influence is small, and the long-term interest rate is determined by saving and investment plans (see Chapter 10, pp. 213–215) and by long-term inflation expectations (see Chapter 16, pp. 370–371). The red line in Fig. 15.13 is the real GDP growth rate *one year later*. You can see that when short-term interest rates rise or long-term interest rates fall, the real GDP growth rate slows down in the following year. Long-term interest rates fluctuate less than short-term rates, so when short-term rates rise above long-term rates, it is because the Fed has pushed short-term rates upward. And when short-term rates fall below long-term rates, it is because the Fed has pushed short-term rates downward. So when the Fed stimulates aggregate demand (pushes short-term rates downward), the GDP growth rate speeds up, and when the Fed lowers aggregate demand (pushes short-term rates upward), the real GDP growth rate slows down. The inflation rate also increases and decreases in sympathy with these fluctuations in real GDP growth.

R E V I E W Q U I Z

- To which interest rates does the Fed pay the closest attention?
- Is there any relationship in the U.S. economy between fluctuations in short-term interest rates and fluctuations in the ratio of M2 to GDP?
- How do *un*anticipated and *anticipated* changes in the quantity of money influence interest rates?
- When the Fed lowers interest rates, what happens to aggregate demand, real GDP growth, and inflation?

Reading Between the Lines on pages 350–351 looks at the Fed in action during 1999 and its decision to hold interest rates steady. Now that you know how the Fed determines the quantity of money and interest rates, we're going to explore the influence of money (and other factors) on inflation.

The Fed in Action

THE WALL STREET JOURNAL, MARCH 31, 1999

Fed Again Holds Steady on Rates As Growth, Low Inflation Continue

BY JACOB M. SCHLESINGER STAFF REPORTER OF *THE WALL STREET JOURNAL*

WASHINGTON—Federal Reserve policy makers once again left interest rates steady Tuesday and signaled that monetary policy is likely to remain on hold for a while.

The central bank's inaction stems both from the U.S. economy's current healthy performance and its uncertain future. With growth robust and inflation low, there's little that needs fixing. The risks, meanwhile, seem evenly balanced between dangers that would invite a rate increase, such as inflation sparked by tight labor markets, and those that would dictate a cut, such as a sharp slowdown induced by weakness overseas.

The stock market's lofty levels also complicate matters: A tightening of monetary policy could trigger a sharp correction that could slash consumer spending. A policy easing could further inflate what many Fed officials fear is a bubble, which some now concede was the result of the three quarter-point rate cuts last fall.

"I don't know what adjustments to monetary policy, if any, will be needed to help the economy on a trend of sustainable growth and benign inflation," Edward Boehne, president of the Federal Reserve Bank of Philadelphia, said in a speech earlier in March.

Financial markets widely anticipated the decision to leave the target for the federal-funds rate, the rate at which banks lend to each other overnight, at 4.75%. Immediately after Tuesday's 2:15 p.m. announcement, the Dow Jones Industrial Average, which had drifted lower throughout the morning, slipped slightly. It closed down 93.52 points at 9913.26.

Fed officials issued no public comment, as is customary when the central bank takes no action. At these meetings, Fed officials also debate their so-called policy directive, a consensus statement that declares whether the next rate move is more likely to be an increase or a decrease.

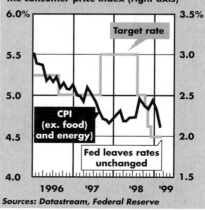

HOLDING STEADY

The Federal Reserve's target for the federal-funds rate (left axis) and inflation, or the year-to-year percentage change in the consumer-price index (right axis)

Target rate

CPI (ex. food) and energy)

Fed leaves rates unchanged

1996 '97 '98 '99

Sources: Datastream, Federal Reserve

Essence of the Story

■ The Federal Reserve decided to leave interest rates unchanged at its March 1999 meeting.

■ This decision was widely expected.

■ The Fed left interest rates unchanged because real GDP growth was strong and inflation was low, so nothing needed to be fixed.

■ But the possibility that a tight labor market might bring renewed inflation and that a weak global economy might bring a recession made the future uncertain.

■ If the Fed increased interest rates, the stock market might fall and bring a deep cut in consumer spending.

■ If the Fed decreased interest rates, the stock market might rise even further.

Economic Analysis

■ Approximately every 6 weeks, the Fed's FOMC meets to review the state of the economy and set policy guidelines for open market operations (see p. 332). During 1998, the FOMC cut interest rates.

■ Figure 1 shows the economy in 1997 and 1998.

■ In 1997, real GDP was $7.3 trillion and the price level was 112, at the intersection of the aggregate demand curve AD_{97} and the short-run aggregate supply curve SAS_{97}. Real GDP was equal to potential GDP—the economy was on the long-run aggregate supply curve LAS_{97}.

■ By 1998, real GDP had increased to $7.6 trillion and the price level had increased to 113, at the intersection of the aggregate demand curve AD_{98} and the short-run aggregate supply curve SAS_{98}. Potential GDP had increased to $7.6 trillion (an assumption but a reasonable one). So in 1998, real GDP was greater than potential GDP.

■ Looking forward through 1999, the Fed was comfortable with the state of the U.S.

economy. Figure 2 shows the Fed's forecast of aggregate demand for 1999 as AD_{99} and the short-run aggregate supply curve as SAS_{99}. The Fed expected real GDP to grow to $7.7 trillion and the price level to rise to 114.

■ If aggregate demand turned out to be AD_0, we would have an inflationary gap. Inflation and real GDP would increase. To counter such an increase, the Fed might tighten the money supply and raise interest rates.

■ If aggregate demand turned out to be AD_1, we would have a deflationary gap. Inflation and real GDP would decrease. To counter such an outcome, the Fed might loosen the money supply and lower interest rates.

■ You can see the dilemma that the Fed faces every year. If aggregate demand increases by too much, the Fed must try to dampen the economy. If aggregate demand increases by too little, the Fed must try to stimulate the economy. But to be effective, the Fed must anticipate the change in aggregate demand correctly.

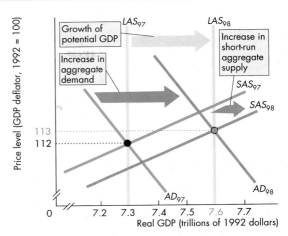

Figure 1 The economy in 1997 and 1998

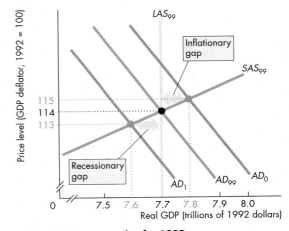

Figure 2 Some senarios for 1999

You're The Voter

■ Why did the Fed believe that no monetary policy action was needed in March 1999?

■ Did the Fed change interest rates during 1999? If so, by how much, in which direction, and why? If not, why not?

■ What, in your opinion, should the Fed do if a recession appears to be likely?

■ What, in your opinion, should the Fed do if inflation appears to be likely?

SUMMARY

KEY POINTS

The Federal Reserve System (pp. 332–335)

- The Federal Reserve System is the central bank of the United States.
- The Fed influences the economy by setting the required reserve ratio for banks, by setting the discount rate—the interest rate at which it is willing to lend reserves to the banking system—and by open market operations.

Controlling the Money Supply (pp. 335–339)

- By buying government securities in the market (an open market purchase), the Fed is able to increase the monetary base and the reserves available to banks.
- There follows an expansion of bank lending and the quantity of money increases.
- By selling government securities, the Fed is able to decrease the monetary base and bank reserves and decrease the quantity of money.

The Demand for Money (pp. 340–343)

- The quantity of money demanded is the amount of money that people plan to hold.
- The quantity of real money equals the quantity of nominal money divided by the price level.
- The quantity of real money demanded depends on the interest rate and real GDP. A higher interest rate induces a smaller quantity of real money demanded.

Interest Rate Determination (pp. 343–344)

- Changes in interest rates achieve equilibrium in the markets for money and financial assets.
- Money market equilibrium achieves an interest rate (and an asset price) that makes the quantity of real money available willingly held.
- If the quantity of real money is increased by the actions of the Fed, the interest rate falls and the prices of financial assets rise.

Monetary Policy (pp. 345–349)

- The Fed directly controls the discount rate and closely targets the federal funds rate, but all short-term rates fluctuate together and the Fed influences all short-term interest rates.
- People attempt to profit by predicting the actions of the Fed. To the extent that they can predict the Fed, interest rates and the price of financial assets move in anticipation of the Fed's actions rather than in response to them.
- Consequently, interest rates change when the Fed changes the money supply only if the Fed catches people by surprise. Anticipated changes in the money supply produce interest rate changes by themselves.
- When the Fed lowers interest rates, it increases aggregate demand, which speeds real GDP growth and inflation. And when the Fed raises interest rates, it decreases aggregate demand, which slows real GDP growth and inflation.

KEY FIGURES

KEY TERMS

PROBLEMS

1. You are given the following information about the economy of Nocoin: The banks have deposits of $300 billion. Their reserves are $15 billion, two thirds of which is in deposits with the central bank. There are $30 billion notes outside the banks. There are no coins!
   a. Calculate the monetary base.
   b. Calculate the money supply.
   c. Calculate the banks' reserve ratio as a percentage of deposits.
   d. Calculate the currency drain as a percentage of the money supply.

2. You are given the following information about the economy of Fredzone: The people and businesses in Fredzone have bank deposits of $500 billion and hold $100 billion in notes and coin. The banks hold deposits at the Fredzone Fed of $5 billion and they keep $5 billion in notes and coin in their vaults and ATM machines.
   a. Calculate the monetary base.
   b. Calculate the money supply.
   c. Calculate the banks' reserve ratio as a percentage of deposits.
   d. Calculate the currency drain as a percentage of the money supply.

*3. In problem 1, suppose that the Bank of Nocoin, the central bank, undertakes an open market purchase of securities of $1 billion. After the money multiplier process is complete, what is the new level of:
   a. The money supply?
   b. Currency in circulation?
   c. Bank deposits?
   d. Bank reserves?
   e. Why does the money supply change by more than the change in the monetary base?

4. In problem 2, suppose that the Fredzone Fed undertakes an open market sale of securities of $1 billion. After the money multiplier process is complete, what is the new level of:
   a. The money supply?
   b. Currency in circulation?
   c. Bank deposits?
   d. Bank reserves?
   e. Why does the money supply change by more than the change in the monetary base?

*5. The spreadsheet provides information about the demand for money in Miniland. Column A is the interest rate, R. Columns B, C, and D show the quantity of money demanded at three different levels of real GDP. Y_0 is $10 billion, Y_1 is $20 billion and Y_2 is $30 billion. The quantity of money supplied by the Miniland Fed is $3.0 billion. Initially, real GDP is $20 billion.

	A	B	C	D
	R	Y_0	Y_1	Y_2
1				
2	7	1.0	1.5	2.0
3	6	1.5	2.0	2.5
4	5	2.0	2.5	3.0
5	4	2.5	3.0	3.5
6	3	3.0	3.5	4.0
7	2	3.5	4.0	4.5
8	1	4.0	4.5	5.0

   What happens in Miniland if the interest rate:
   a. Exceeds 4 percent a year?
   b. Is less than 4 percent a year?
   c. Equals 4 percent a year?

6. In problem 5, Miniland experiences a severe recession. Real GDP falls to $10 billion. The Miniland Fed takes no actions to change the quantity of money.
   a. What happens if the interest rate is 4 percent a year?
   b. What is the equilibrium interest rate?
   c. Compared with the situation In problem 5, does the interest rate in Miniland rise or fall? Why?

*7. In problem 5, Miniland experiences a severe business cycle. Real GDP rises to $30 billion and then falls to $10 billion. The Miniland Fed takes no actions to change the quantity of money. What happens to the interest rate in Miniland during the:
   a. Expansion phase of the cycle?
   b. Recession phase of the cycle?

8. In problem 5, financial innovation changes the demand for money. People now plan to hold $0.5 billion less than the numbers in the spreadsheet.
   a. What happens to the interest rate if the Miniland Fed takes no actions?
   b. What happens to the interest rate if the Miniland Fed decreases the quantity of money by $0.5 billion? Explain.

*9. The figure shows the demand for real money in Upland.
 a. Draw the supply of money curve if the interest rate in Upland is 3 percent a year.
 b. If the Upland Fed wants to lower the interest rate by 1 percentage point, by how much must it change the real money supply.

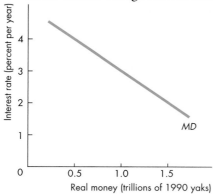

 c. Suppose that to change the quantity of money in part (b), the Upland Fed uses open market operations. Does it make an open market purchase or an open market sale of securities?

10. In Upland, a new smart card replaces currency and the demand for money changes. Also, the new smart card causes business to boom and real GDP increases.
 a. Using the figure for problem 9, draw a new demand for money curve that is consistent with the events just described.
 b. Suppose that the Upland Fed wants to prevent the interest rate from changing. What must it do to the supply of money?
 c. Does the Upland Fed make an open market purchase or an open market sale of securities?

*11. Starting from above full-employment equilibrium, briefly explain with the aid of a figure the short-run effect on the price level and real GDP of an open market purchase of securities by the Fed. Does such an action help to avoid inflation? Does such an action lower real GDP in the long run?

12. Starting from unemployment equilibrium, briefly explain with the aid of a figure the short-run effect on the price level and real GDP of an open market purchase of securities by the Fed. Does such an action help to avoid inflation? Does such an action lower real GDP in the long run?

CRITICAL THINKING

1. Study *Reading Between the Lines* on pp. 350–351 and then answer the following questions:
 a. Why did the Fed *not* change interest rates in March 1999?
 b. What does the Fed look at when it is deciding whether to change interest rates?
 c. What risks does the Fed face if it raises interest rates? What risks does it face if it does not raise interest rates? Which is the more risky in your opinion and why?
 d. When the Fed decides to raise interest rates, what actions does it take?

2. Could the Volcker Fed have brought inflation under control without creating a deep recession? If you think that the answer is "no," do you think that it was wise to lower inflation? If you think that the answer is "yes," what could the Fed have done differently?

3. Use the links on the Parkin Web site to find the latest data on M1, M2, and a short-term interest rate as well as the latest minutes of the FOMC. Then answer the following questions.
 a. Is the Fed trying to slow economic growth or speed it up? How can you tell which?
 b. What open market operations do you think the Fed has undertaken during the past month?
 c. Skim the latest minutes of the FOMC and see whether you can discover the open market operations that are planned.
 d. In light of the Fed's recent actions, what ripple effects do you expect over the coming months?
 e. What do you think the effects of the Fed's recent actions will be on bond prices and stock prices?

4. Use the link on the Parkin Web site and look at the current economic conditions described in the Beige Book for your region of the United States. On the basis of the Fed's current description of the economic conditions in your region, do you predict that the Fed will raise interest rates, lower interest rates, or hold interest rates steady? Do you think that the Fed ought to raise interest rates, lower them, or hold them steady? Write a brief summary of your predictions and prescriptions and provide your reasons.

Chapter 16

Inflation

At the end of the third century A.D., Roman Emperor Diocletian struggled to contain an inflation that raised prices by more than 300 percent a year. At the end of the twentieth century, Russian President Boris Yeltsin struggled to contain a severe inflation that raised prices at a rate of close to 1,000 percent a year. But the most rapid recent inflations have been in Brazil, where the inflation rate hit 40 percent *per month* in 1994, and in Zaire, which had an inflation rate of 75 percent *per month*. What causes rapid inflation? ◆ In comparison with the cases just described, the United States has had remarkable price stability. Nevertheless, during the 1970s, the U.S. price level more than doubled—an inflation of more than 100 percent over the decade. Today, along with the other rich industrial countries, the United States has a low inflation rate of less than 2 percent a year. Why do some countries have a low inflation

From Rome to Russia

rate? And why did a more serious inflation break out in the United States during the 1970s? ◆ Most of life's big economic decisions—whether to buy or rent a home, whether to save more for retirement—turn on what is going to happen to inflation. Will inflation increase so our savings buy less? Will inflation decrease, making our debts harder to repay? To make good decisions, we need good forecasts of inflation, and not for just next year but for many years into the future. How do people try to forecast inflation? And how do expectations of inflation influence the economy? ◆ As the inflation rate rises and falls, the unemployment rate and interest rates also fluctuate. What are the links between inflation and the economy that make unemployment and interest rates fluctuate when inflation fluctuates?

◆ In this chapter, you will learn about the forces that generate inflation, the effects of inflation, and the way in which people try to forecast inflation. You will pull together several of the threads you have been following through your study of macroeconomics. And again, you will use the *AS-AD* model of Chapter 8. But first, let's recall what inflation is and how it is measured.

After studying this chapter, you will be able to:

- ■ Distinguish between inflation and a one-time rise in the price level
- ■ Explain the different ways in which inflation can be generated
- ■ Describe how people try to forecast inflation
- ■ Explain the short-run and long-run relationships between inflation and unemployment
- ■ Explain the short-run and long-run relationships between inflation and interest rates

Inflation and the Price Level

WE DON'T HAVE MUCH INFLATION TODAY, BUT during the 1970s it was a major problem. **Inflation** is a process in which the *price level is rising* and *money is losing value.*

If the price level rises persistently, then people need more and more money to make transactions. Incomes rise, so firms must pay out more in wages and other payments to resource owners. And prices rise, so consumers must take more money with them when they go shopping. But the value of money gets smaller and smaller.

A change in one price is not inflation. For example, if the price of hot dogs jumps to $25 and all other money prices fall slightly, so the price level remains constant, there is no inflation. Instead, the relative price of hot dogs has increased. If the price of hot dogs and all other prices rise by a similar percentage, there is inflation.

But a one-time jump in the price level is not inflation. Instead, inflation is an ongoing *process.* Figure 16.1 illustrates this distinction. The red line shows the price level rising continuously. That is inflation. The blue line shows a one-time jump in the price level. This economy is not experiencing inflation. Its price level is constant most of the time.

Inflation is a serious problem, and preventing inflation is the main task of monetary policy and the actions of the Fed. We are going to learn how inflation arises and see how we can avoid the situation shown in the cartoon. But first, let's see how we calculate the inflation rate.

To measure the inflation *rate,* we calculate the annual percentage change in the price level. For

"I told you the Fed should have tightened."

Drawing by Mankoff; © 1997 *The New Yorker Magazine, Inc.*

FIGURE 16.1

Inflation Versus a One-Time Rise in the Price Level

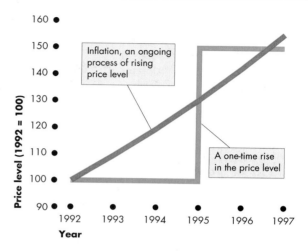

Along the red line, an economy experiences inflation because the price level is rising persistently. Along the blue line, an economy experiences a one-time rise in the price level.

example, if this year's price level is 126 and last year's price level was 120, the inflation rate is 5 percent per year. That is,

$$\text{Inflation rate} = \frac{126 - 120}{120} \times 100$$

$$= 5 \text{ percent per year.}$$

This equation shows the connection between the *inflation rate* and the *price level.* For a given price level last year, the higher the price level in the current year, the higher is the inflation rate. If the price level is *rising,* the inflation rate is *positive.* If the price level rises at a *faster* rate, the inflation rate *increases.* Also, the higher the new price level, the lower is the value of money, and the higher is the inflation rate.

Inflation can result from either an increase in aggregate demand or a decrease in aggregate supply. These two sources of impulses that can get inflation started are called:

1. Demand pull
2. Cost push

We'll first study a demand-pull inflation.

Demand-Pull Inflation

An inflation that results from an initial increase in aggregate demand is called **demand-pull inflation**. Such an inflation can arise from any factor that increases aggregate demand such as an:

1. Increase in the money supply
2. Increase in government purchases
3. Increase in exports

Initial Effect of an Increase in Aggregate Demand

Suppose that last year the price level was 110 and real GDP was $7 trillion. Potential GDP was also $7 trillion. Figure 16.2(a) illustrates this situation. The aggregate demand curve is AD_0, the short-run aggregate supply curve is SAS_0, and the long-run aggregate supply curve is LAS.

In the current year, aggregate demand increases to AD_1. Such a situation arises if, for example, the Fed loosens its grip on the money supply, or the government increases its purchases of goods and services, or exports increase.

With no change in potential GDP and no change in the money wage rate, the long-run aggregate supply curve and the short-run aggregate supply curve remain at LAS and SAS_0.

The price level and real GDP are determined at the point where the aggregate demand curve AD_1 intersects the short-run aggregate supply curve. The price level rises to 113, and real GDP increases above potential GDP to $7.5 trillion. The economy experiences a 2.7 percent rise in the price level (a price level of 113 compared with 110) and a rapid expansion of real GDP. Unemployment falls below the natural rate. The next step in the story is a rise in money wages.

FIGURE 16.2
A Demand-Pull Rise in the Price Level

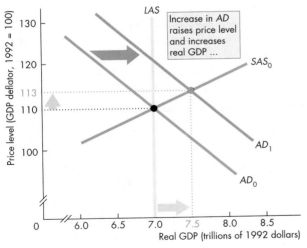

(a) Initial effect

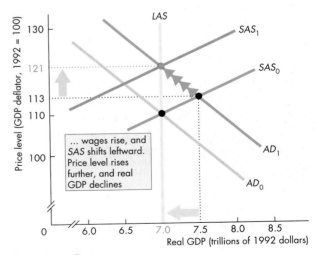

(b) Wages adjust

In part (a), the aggregate demand curve is AD_0, the short-run aggregate supply curve is SAS_0, and the long-run aggregate supply curve is LAS. The price level is 110, and real GDP is $7 trillion, its long-run level. Aggregate demand increases to AD_1 (because, for example, the Fed increases the money supply, or the government increases its purchases of goods and services, or exports increase). The new equilibrium occurs where AD_1 intersects SAS_0. The price level rises to 113, and real GDP increases to $7.5 trillion. In part (b), starting from above full employment, money wages begin to rise and the short-run aggregate supply curve shifts leftward toward SAS_1. The price level rises further, and real GDP returns to its long-run level.

Wage Response

Real GDP cannot remain above potential GDP forever. With unemployment below its natural rate, there is a shortage of labor. In this situation, the money wage rate begins to rise. As it does so, short-run aggregate supply decreases and the *SAS* curve starts to shift leftward. The price level rises further, and real GDP begins to decrease.

With no further change in aggregate demand—the aggregate demand curve remains at AD_1—this process ends when the short-run aggregate supply curve has shifted to SAS_1 in Fig. 16.2(b). At this time, the price level has increased to 121 and real GDP has returned to potential GDP of $7 trillion, the level from which it started.

A Demand-Pull Inflation Process

The process we've just studied eventually ends when, for a given increase in aggregate demand, the money wage rate has adjusted enough to restore the real wage rate to its full-employment level. We've studied a one-time rise in the price level like that described in Fig. 16.1(b). For inflation to proceed, aggregate demand must persistently increase.

The only way in which aggregate demand can persistently increase is if the quantity of money persistently increases. Suppose the government has a large budget deficit that it finances by selling bonds to the Fed. When the Fed buys these bonds, it creates more money. In this situation, aggregate demand increases year after year. The aggregate demand curve keeps shifting rightward. This persistent increase in aggregate demand puts continual upward pressure on the price level. The economy now experiences demand-pull inflation.

Figure 16.3 illustrates the process of demand-pull inflation. The starting point is the same as that shown in Fig. 16.2. The aggregate demand curve is AD_0, the short-run aggregate supply curve is SAS_0, and the long-run aggregate supply curve is *LAS*. Real GDP is $7 trillion, and the price level is 110. Aggregate demand increases, shifting the aggregate demand curve to AD_1. Real GDP increases to $7.5 trillion, and the price level rises to 113. The economy is at an above full-employment equilibrium. The money wage rate rises, shifting the short-run aggregate supply curve to SAS_1. The price level rises to 121, and real GDP returns to potential GDP.

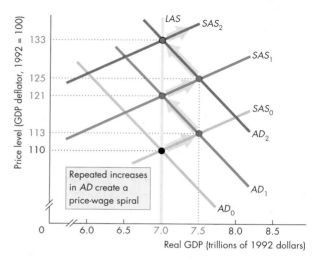

FIGURE 16.3
A Demand-Pull Inflation Spiral

Each time the money supply increases, aggregate demand increases, and the aggregate demand curve shifts rightward from AD_0 to AD_1 to AD_2, and so on. Each time real GDP goes above potential GDP and unemployment goes below the natural rate, the money wage rate rises and the short-run aggregate supply curve shifts leftward from SAS_0 to SAS_1 to SAS_2, and so on. As aggregate demand continues to increase, the price level rises from 110 through 113, 121, 125, to 133, and so on. There is a perpetual demand-pull inflation. Real GDP fluctuates between $7 trillion and $7.5 trillion.

But the money supply increases again, and aggregate demand continues to increase. The aggregate demand curve shifts rightward to AD_2. The price level rises further to 125, and real GDP again exceeds potential GDP at $7.5 trillion. Yet again, the money wage rate rises and decreases short-run aggregate supply. The *SAS* curve shifts to SAS_2, and the price level rises further to 133. As the money supply continues to grow, aggregate demand increases and the price level rises in an ongoing demand-pull inflation process.

The process you have just studied generates inflation—an ongoing process of a rising price level.

Demand-Pull Inflation in Kalamazoo You may better understand the inflation process that we've just described by considering what is going on in an individual part of the economy, such as a Kalamazoo soda-bottling plant. Initially, when aggregate demand increases, the demand for soda increases and the price of soda rises. Faced with a higher price, the soda plant works overtime and increases production. Conditions are good for workers in Kalamazoo, and the soda factory finds it hard to hang onto its best people. To do so, it has to offer higher wages. As wages increase, so do the soda factory's costs.

What happens next depends on what happens to aggregate demand. If aggregate demand remains constant (as in Fig. 16.2b), the firm's costs are increasing but the price of soda is not increasing as quickly as its costs. Production is scaled back. Eventually, wages and costs increase by the same percentage as the price of soda. In real terms, the soda factory is in the same situation as initially—before the increase in aggregate demand. The plant produces the same amount of soda and employs the same amount of labor as before the increase in demand.

But if aggregate demand continues to increase, so does the demand for soda, and the price of soda rises at the same rate as wages. The soda factory continues to operate above full employment, and there is a persistent shortage of labor. Prices and wages chase each other upward in an unending spiral.

Demand-Pull Inflation in the United States   A demand-pull inflation like the one you've just studied occurred in the United States during the 1960s. In 1960, inflation was a moderate 2 percent a year, but its rate increased slowly to 3 percent by 1966. Then, in 1967, a large increase in government purchases on the Vietnam War and an increase in spending on social programs, together with an increase in the growth rate of the money supply, increased aggregate demand more quickly. Consequently, the rightward shift of the aggregate demand curve speeded up and the price level increased more quickly. Real GDP increased above potential GDP, and the unemployment rate fell below the natural rate.

With unemployment below the natural rate, the money wage rate started to rise more quickly and the short-run aggregate supply curve shifted leftward. The Fed responded with a further increase in the money supply growth rate, and a demand-pull inflation spiral unfolded. By 1970, the inflation rate had reached 6 percent a year.

For the next three years, aggregate demand continued to grow quickly and the inflation rate remained around 6 percent a year.

REVIEW QUIZ

- How does demand-pull inflation begin? What are the initial effects of demand-pull inflation on real GDP and the price level?
- When real GDP increases to more than potential GDP, what happens to the money wage rate and short-run aggregate supply? How do real GDP and the price level respond?
- What must happen to create a demand-pull inflation spiral?

Next, let's see how shocks to aggregate supply can create cost-push inflation.

Cost-Push Inflation

AN INFLATION THAT RESULTS FROM AN INITIAL increase in costs is called **cost-push inflation**. The two main sources of increases in costs are:

1. An increase in money wage rates
2. An increase in the money prices of raw materials

At a given price level, the higher the cost of production, the smaller is the amount that firms are willing to produce. So if money wage rates rise or if the prices of raw materials (for example, oil) rise, firms decrease their supply of goods and services. Aggregate supply decreases, and the short-run aggregate supply curve shifts leftward.[1] Let's trace the effects of such a decrease in short-run aggregate supply on the price level and real GDP.

Initial Effect of a Decrease in Aggregate Supply

Suppose that last year the price level was 110 and real GDP was $7 trillion. Potential real GDP was also $7 trillion. Figure 16.4 illustrates this situation. The aggregate demand curve was AD_0, the short-run aggregate supply curve was SAS_0, and the long-run aggregate supply curve was LAS. In the current year, the

[1]Some cost-push forces, such as an increase in the price of oil accompanied by a decrease in the availability of oil, can also decrease long-run aggregate supply. We'll ignore such effects here and examine cost-push factors that change only short-run aggregate supply.

FIGURE 16.4

A Cost-Push Rise in the Price Level

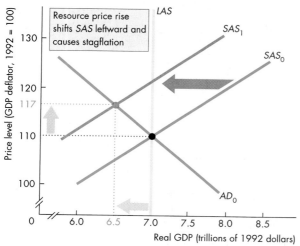

Initially, the aggregate demand curve is AD_0, the short-run aggregate supply curve is SAS_0, and the long-run aggregate supply curve is LAS. A decrease in aggregate supply (for example, resulting from an increase in the world price of oil) shifts the short-run aggregate supply curve to SAS_1. The economy moves to the point where the short-run aggregate supply curve SAS_1 intersects the aggregate demand curve AD_0. The price level rises to 117, and real GDP decreases to $6.5 trillion. The economy experiences inflation and a contraction of real GDP—*stagflation*.

world's oil producers form a price-fixing organization that strengthens their market power and increases the relative price of oil. They raise the nominal price of oil, and this action decreases short-run aggregate supply. The short-run aggregate supply curve shifts leftward to SAS_1. The price level rises to 117, and real GDP decreases to $6.5 trillion. The combination of a rise in the price level and a decrease in real GDP is called **stagflation**.

This event is a one-time rise in the price level like that in Fig. 16.1(b). It is not inflation. In fact, a supply shock on its own cannot cause inflation. Something more must happen to enable a one-time supply shock to be converted into a process of money supply growth and ongoing inflation. The money supply must persistently increase. And it often does increase, as you will now see.

Aggregate Demand Response

When real GDP falls, the unemployment rate rises above the natural rate. In such a situation, there is usually an outcry of concern and a call for action to restore full employment. Suppose that the Fed increases the money supply. Aggregate demand increases. In Fig. 16.5, the aggregate demand curve shifts rightward to AD_1. The increase in aggregate demand has restored full employment. But the price level rises to 121, a 10 percent increase over the initial price level.

A Cost-Push Inflation Process

The oil producers now see the prices of everything that they buy increase by 10 percent. So they increase the price of oil again to restore its new high relative price. Figure 16.6 continues the story.

FIGURE 16.5

Aggregate Demand Response to Cost Push

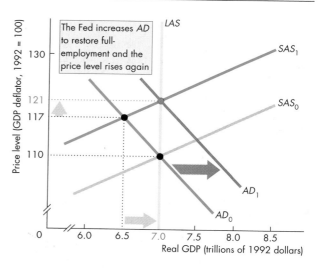

Following a cost-push increase in the price level, real GDP is below potential GDP and unemployment is above the natural rate. If the Fed responds by increasing aggregate demand to restore full employment, the aggregate demand curve shifts rightward to AD_1. The economy returns to full employment but at the expense of more inflation. The price level rises to 121.

The short-run aggregate supply curve now shifts to SAS_2, and another bout of stagflation ensues. The price level rises further to 129, and real GDP falls to $6.5 trillion. Unemployment increases above its natural rate. If the Fed responds yet again with an increase in the money supply, aggregate demand increases and the aggregate demand curve shifts to AD_2. The price level rises even higher—to 133—and full employment is again restored. A cost-push inflation spiral results. But if the Fed does not respond, the economy remains below full employment.

You can see that the Fed has a dilemma. If it increases the money supply to restore full employment, it invites another oil price hike that will call forth yet a further increase in the money supply. Inflation will rage along at a rate decided by the oil-exporting nations. If the Fed keeps the lid on money supply growth, real GDP remains below potential GDP.

Cost-Push Inflation in Kalamazoo   What is going on in the Kalamazoo soda-bottling plant when the economy is experiencing cost-push inflation? When the oil price increases, so do the costs of bottling soda. These higher costs decrease the supply of soda, increasing its price and decreasing the quantity produced. The soda plant lays off some workers. This situation will persist until either the Fed increases aggregate demand or the price of oil falls. If the Fed increases aggregate demand, as it did in the mid-1970s, the demand for soda increases and so does its price. The higher price of soda brings higher profits, and the bottling plant increases its production. The soda factory rehires the laid-off workers.

Cost-Push Inflation in the United States   A cost-push inflation like the one you've just studied occurred in the United States during the 1970s. It began in 1974 when the Organization for Petroleum Exporting Countries (OPEC) raised the price of oil fourfold. The higher oil price decreased aggregate supply, which caused the price level to rise more quickly and real GDP to shrink. The Fed then faced a dilemma. Would it increase the quantity of money and accommodate the cost-push forces or would it keep aggregate demand growth in check by limiting money growth? In 1975, 1976, and 1977, the Fed repeatedly allowed the money supply to grow quickly, and inflation proceeded at a rapid rate. In 1979 and 1980, OPEC was again able to push oil prices higher. On that occasion, the Fed decided not to respond to the oil price hike with an increase in the money supply. The result was a recession but also, eventually, a fall in inflation.

FIGURE 16.6
A Cost-Push
Inflation Spiral

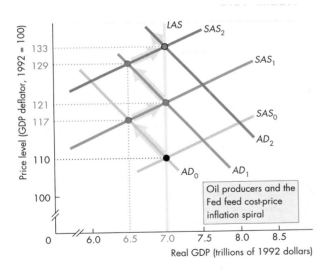

When a cost increase (for example, an increase in the world oil price) decreases short-run aggregate supply from SAS_0 to SAS_1, the price level rises to 117 and real GDP decreases to $6.5 trillion. The Fed responds with an increase in the money supply that shifts the aggregate demand curve from AD_0 to AD_1. The price level rises again to 121, and real GDP returns to $7 trillion. A further cost increase occurs, which shifts the short-run aggregate supply curve again, this time to SAS_2. Stagflation is repeated, and the price level now rises to 129. The Fed responds again, and the cost-price inflation spiral continues.

R E V I E W   Q U I Z

- How does cost-push inflation begin? What are the initial effects of cost-push inflation on real GDP and the price level?
- What is *stagflation* and why does cost-push inflation cause stagflation?
- What must the Fed do to convert a one-time rise in the price level into a freewheeling cost-push inflation?

Effects of Inflation

REGARDLESS OF WHETHER INFLATION IS DEMAND-pull or cost-push, the failure to correctly *anticipate* it results in unintended consequences. These unintended consequences impose costs in both labor markets and capital markets. Let's examine these costs.

Unanticipated Inflation in the Labor Market

Unanticipated inflation has two main consequences for the operation of the labor market:

- Redistribution of income
- Departure from full employment

Redistribution of Income   Unanticipated inflation redistributes income between employers and workers. Sometimes employers gain at the expense of workers, and sometimes they lose. If an unexpected increase in aggregate demand increases the inflation rate, then wages will not have been set high enough. Profits will be higher than expected, and wages will buy fewer goods than expected. In this case, employers gain at the expense of workers. But if aggregate demand is expected to increase at a rapid rate and it fails to do so, workers gain at the expense of employers. With a high inflation rate anticipated, wages are set too high and profits are squeezed. Redistribution between employers and workers creates an incentive for both firms and workers to try to forecast inflation correctly.

Departures from Full Employment   Redistribution brings gains to some and losses to others. But departures from full employment impose costs on everyone. To see why, let's return to the soda-bottling plant in Kalamazoo.

If the bottling plant and its workers do not anticipate inflation, but inflation occurs, the money wage rate does not rise to keep up with inflation. The real wage rate falls, and the firm tries to hire more labor and increase production. But because the real wage rate has fallen, the firm has a hard time attracting the labor it wants to employ. It pays overtime rates to its existing work force, and because it runs its plant at a faster pace, it incurs higher plant maintenance and parts replacement costs. But also, because the real wage rate has fallen, workers begin to quit the bottling plant to find jobs that pay a real wage rate that is closer to one that prevailed before the outbreak of inflation. This labor turnover imposes additional costs on the firm. So even though its production increases, the firm incurs additional costs, and its profits do not increase as much as they otherwise would. The workers incur additional costs of job search, and those who remain at the bottling plant wind up feeling cheated. They've worked overtime to produce the extra output, and when they come to spend their wages, they discover that prices have increased, so their wages buy a smaller quantity of goods and services than expected.

If the bottling plant and its workers anticipate a high inflation rate that does not occur, they increase the money wage rate by too much, and the real wage rate rises. At the higher real wage rate, the firm lays off some workers and the unemployment rate increases. Those workers who keep their jobs gain, but those who become unemployed lose. Also, the bottling plant loses because its output and profits fall.

Unanticipated Inflation in the Capital Market

Unanticipated inflation has two consequences for the operation of the capital market. They are:

- Redistribution of income
- Too much or too little lending and borrowing

Redistribution of Income   Unanticipated inflation redistributes income between borrowers and lenders. Sometimes borrowers gain at the expense of lenders, and sometimes they lose. When inflation is unexpected, interest rates are not set high enough to compensate lenders for the falling value of money. In this case, borrowers gain at the expense of lenders. But if inflation is expected and then fails to occur, interest rates are set too high. In this case, lenders gain at the expense of borrowers. Redistributions of income between borrowers and lenders create an incentive for both groups to try to forecast inflation correctly.

Too Much or Too Little Lending and Borrowing
If the inflation rate turns out to be either higher or lower than expected, the interest rate does not incorporate a correct allowance for the falling value of money and the real interest rate is either lower or higher than it otherwise would be. When the real

interest rate turns out to be too low, which occurs when inflation is *higher* than expected, borrowers wish they had borrowed more and lenders wish they had lent less. Both groups would have made different lending and borrowing decisions with greater foresight about the inflation rate. When the real interest rate turns out to be too high, which occurs when inflation is *lower* than expected, borrowers wish they had borrowed less and lenders wish they had lent more. Again, both groups would have made different lending and borrowing decisions with greater foresight about the inflation rate.

So unanticipated inflation imposes costs regardless of whether the inflation turns out to be higher or lower than anticipated. The presence of these costs gives everyone an incentive to forecast inflation correctly. Let's see how people go about this task.

Forecasting Inflation

Inflation is difficult to forecast. The reasons are, first, there are several sources of inflation—the demand-pull and cost-push sources you've just studied. Second, the speed with which a change in either aggregate demand or aggregate supply translates into a change in the price level varies. This speed of response also depends, as you will see below, on the extent to which the inflation is anticipated.

Because inflation is costly and difficult to forecast, people devote considerable resources to improving inflation forecasts. Some people specialize in forecasting, and others buy forecasts from specialists. The specialist forecasters are economists who work for public and private macroeconomic forecasting agencies and for banks, insurance companies, labor unions, and large corporations. The returns these specialists make depend on the quality of their forecasts, so they have a strong incentive to forecast as accurately as possible. The most accurate forecast possible is the one that is based on all the relevant information and is called a **rational expectation**.

A rational expectation is not necessarily a correct forecast. It is simply the best forecast available. It will often turn out to be wrong, but no other forecast that could have been made with the information available could be predicted to be better.

You've seen the effects of inflation when people fail to anticipate it. And you've seen why it pays to try to anticipate inflation. Let's now see what happens if inflation is correctly anticipated.

Anticipated Inflation

In the demand-pull and cost-push inflations that we studied earlier in this chapter, money wages are sticky. When aggregate demand increases, either to set off a demand-pull inflation or to accommodate cost-push inflation, the money wage does not change immediately. But if people correctly anticipate increases in aggregate demand, they will adjust money wage rates so as to keep up with anticipated inflation.

In this case, inflation proceeds with real GDP equal to potential GDP and unemployment equal to the natural rate. Figure 16.7 explains why. Suppose that last year the price level was 110 and real GDP was \$7 trillion, which is also potential GDP. The aggregate demand curve was AD_0, the aggregate supply curve was SAS_0, and the long-run aggregate supply curve was LAS.

Suppose that potential GDP does not change, so the LAS curve does not shift. Also suppose that aggregate demand is expected to increase and that the expected aggregate demand curve for this year is AD_1. In anticipation of this increase in aggregate demand, money wage rates rise and the short-run aggregate supply curve shifts leftward. If the money wage rate rises by the same percentage as the price level rises, the short-run aggregate supply curve for next year is SAS_1.

If aggregate demand turns out to be the same as expected, the aggregate demand curve is AD_1, and with the short-run aggregate supply curve SAS_1 the actual price level is 121. Between last year and this year the price level increased from 110 to 121 and the economy experienced an inflation rate of 10 percent, the same as the inflation rate that was anticipated. If this anticipated inflation continues, in the following year aggregate demand increases (as anticipated) and the aggregate demand curve shifts to AD_2. The money wage rate rises to reflect the anticipated inflation, and the short-run aggregate supply curve shifts to SAS_2. The price level rises by a further 10 percent to 133.

What has caused this inflation? The immediate answer is that because people expected inflation, wages were increased and prices increased. But the expectation was correct. Aggregate demand was expected to increase, and it did increase. Because aggregate demand was *expected* to increase from AD_0 to AD_1, the short-run aggregate supply curve shifted from SAS_0 to SAS_1. Because aggregate demand actually did increase by the amount that was expected, the actual aggregate demand curve shifted from AD_0

to AD_1. The combination of the anticipated and actual increases in aggregate demand produced an increase in the price level that was anticipated.

Only if aggregate demand growth is correctly forecasted does the economy follow the course described in Fig. 16.7. If the expected growth rate of aggregate demand is different from its actual growth rate, the expected aggregate demand curve shifts by an amount that is different from the actual aggregate demand curve. The inflation rate departs from its expected level, and to some extent, there is unanticipated inflation.

FIGURE 16.7
Anticipated Inflation

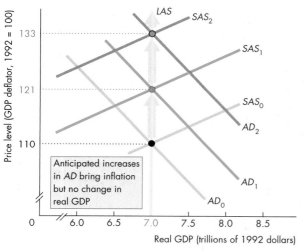

Potential real GDP is $7 trillion. Last year, aggregate demand was AD_0, and the short-run aggregate supply curve was SAS_0. The actual price level was the same as the expected price level—110. This year, aggregate demand is expected to increase to AD_1. The rational expectation of the price level changes from 110 to 121. As a result, wages rise and the short-run aggregate supply curve shifts to SAS_1. If aggregate demand actually increases as expected, the actual aggregate demand curve AD_1 is the same as the expected aggregate demand curve. Equilibrium occurs at a real GDP of $7 trillion and an actual price level of 121. The inflation is correctly anticipated. Next year the process continues with aggregate demand increasing as expected to AD_2 and wages rising to shift the short-run aggregate supply curve to SAS_2. Again, real GDP remains at $7 trillion, and the price level rises, as anticipated, to 133.

Unanticipated Inflation

When aggregate demand increases by *more* than expected, there is some unanticipated inflation that looks just like the demand-pull inflation that you studied earlier. Some inflation is expected, and the money wage rate is set to reflect that expectation. The SAS curve intersects the LAS curve at the expected price level. Aggregate demand then increases, but by more than expected. So the AD curve intersects the SAS curve at a level of real GDP that exceeds potential GDP. With real GDP above potential GDP and unemployment below the natural rate, the money wage rate rises. So the price level rises further. If aggregate demand increases again, a demand-pull inflation spiral unwinds.

When aggregate demand increases by *less* than expected, there is some unanticipated inflation that looks like the cost-push inflation that you studied earlier. Again, some inflation is expected, and the money wage rate is set to reflect that expectation. The SAS curve intersects the LAS curve at the expected price level. Aggregate demand then increases, but by less than expected. So the AD curve intersects the SAS curve at a level of real GDP below potential GDP. Aggregate demand increases to restore full employment. But if aggregate demand is expected to increase by more than it actually does, wages again rise, short-run aggregate supply again decreases, and a cost-push spiral unwinds.

We've seen that only when inflation is unanticipated does real GDP depart from potential GDP. When inflation is anticipated, real GDP remains at potential GDP. Does this mean that an anticipated inflation has no costs?

The Costs of Anticipated Inflation

The costs of an anticipated inflation depend on its rate. At a moderate rate of 2 or 3 percent a year, the cost is probably small. But as the anticipated inflation rate rises, so do its costs, and an anticipated inflation at a rapid rate can be extremely costly.

Anticipated inflation decreases potential GDP and slows economic growth. These adverse consequences arise for three major reasons:

■ Transactions costs

■ Tax effects

■ Increased uncertainty

Transactions Costs   The first transactions costs are known as the "boot leather costs." These are costs that arise from an increase in the velocity of circulation of money and an increase in the amount of running around that people do to try to avoid incurring losses from the falling value of money.

When money loses value at a rapid anticipated rate, it does not function well as a store of value and people try to avoid holding money. They spend their incomes as soon as they receive them, and firms pay out incomes—wages and dividends—as soon as they receive revenue from their sales. The velocity of circulation increases. During the 1920s, when inflation in Germany reached *hyperinflation* levels (rates more than 50 percent a month), wages were paid and spent twice in a single day!

The range of estimates of the boot leather costs is large. Some economists put the cost at close to zero. Others estimate it to be as much 2 percent of GDP for a 10 percent inflation. For a rapid inflation, these costs are much more.

The boot leather costs of inflation are just one of several transactions costs that are influenced by the inflation rate. At high anticipated inflation rates, people seek alternatives to money as a means of payment and use tokens and commodities or even barter, all of which are less efficient than money as a means of payment. For example, in Israel during the 1980s, when inflation reached 1,000 percent a year, the U.S. dollar started to replace the increasingly worthless shekel. Consequently, people had to keep track of the exchange rate between the shekel and the dollar hour by hour and had to engage in many additional and costly transactions in the foreign exchange market.

Because anticipated inflation increases transactions costs, it diverts resources from producing goods and services and it decreases potential GDP. The faster the anticipated inflation rate, the greater is the decrease in potential GDP and the further leftward does the *LAS* curve shift.

Tax Effects   Anticipated inflation interacts with the tax system and creates serious distortions in incentives. Its major effect is on real interest rates.

Anticipated inflation swells the dollar returns on investments. But dollar returns are taxed, so the effective tax rate rises. This effect becomes serious at even modest inflation rates. Let's consider an example.

Suppose the real interest rate is 4 percent a year and the tax rate is 50 percent. With no inflation, the nominal interest rate is also 4 percent a year and 50 percent of this rate is taxable. The real *after-tax* interest rate is 2 percent a year (50 percent of 4 percent). Now suppose the inflation rate is 4 percent a year, so the nominal interest rate is 8 percent a year. The nominal *after-tax* rate is 4 percent a year (50 percent of 8 percent). Now subtract the 4 percent inflation rate from this amount, and you see that the *real after-tax interest rate* is zero! The true tax rate on interest income is 100 percent.

The higher the inflation rate, the higher is the effective tax rate on income from capital. And the higher the tax rate, the higher is the interest rate paid by borrowers and the lower is the after-tax interest rate received by lenders (see Chapter 13, p. 298).

With a low after-tax real interest rate, the incentive to save is weakened and the saving rate falls. With a high cost of borrowing, the amount of investment decreases. And with a fall in saving and investment, the pace of capital accumulation slows and so does the long-term growth rate of real GDP.

Increased Uncertainty   When the inflation rate is high, there is increased uncertainty about the long-term inflation rate. Will inflation remain high for a long time or will price stability be restored? This increased uncertainty makes long-term planning difficult and gives people a shorter-term focus. Investment falls, and so the growth rate slows.

But this increased uncertainty also misallocates resources. Instead of concentrating on the activities at which they have a comparative advantage, people find it more profitable to search for ways of avoiding the losses that inflation inflicts. As a result, inventive talent that might otherwise work on productive innovations works on finding ways of profiting from the inflation instead.

The implications of inflation for economic growth have been estimated to be enormous. Peter Howitt of Ohio State University, building on work by Robert Barro of Harvard University, has estimated that if inflation is lowered from 3 percent a year to zero, the growth rate of real GDP will rise by between 0.06 and 0.09 percentage points a year. These numbers might seem small. But they are growth rates. After 30 years, real GDP would be 2.3 percent higher and the present value of all the future output would be 85 percent of current GDP—almost $6 trillion! In the rapid anticipated inflations of Brazil and Russia, the costs are much greater than the numbers given here.

R E V I E W   Q U I Z

- What is a *rational expectation*? Are people who form rational expectations ever wrong?
- Why do people forecast inflation and what information do they use to do so?
- How does anticipated inflation occur?
- What are the effects of a rapid anticipated inflation? Does anticipated inflation bring an increase in real GDP?

You've seen that an increase in aggregate demand that is not fully anticipated increases both the price level and real GDP. It also decreases unemployment. Similarly, a decrease in aggregate demand that is not fully anticipated decreases the price level and real GDP. It also increases unemployment. Do these relationships mean that there is a tradeoff between inflation and unemployment? That is, does low unemployment always bring inflation and does low inflation bring high unemployment? We explore these questions next.

Inflation and Unemployment: The Phillips Curve

THE AGGREGATE SUPPLY–AGGREGATE DEMAND model focuses on the price level and real GDP. Knowing how these two variables change, we can work out what happens to the inflation rate and the unemployment rate. But the model does not place inflation and unemployment at the center of the stage.

A more direct way of studying inflation and unemployment uses a relationship called the Phillips curve. The Phillips curve approach uses the same basic ideas as the *AS-AD* model, but it focuses directly on inflation and unemployment. The Phillips curve is so named because New Zealand economist A.W. Phillips popularized it. A **Phillips curve** is a curve that shows a relationship between inflation and unemployment. There are two time frames for Phillips curves:

- The short-run Phillips curve
- The long-run Phillips curve

The Short-Run Phillips Curve

The **short-run Phillips curve** is a curve that shows the tradeoff between inflation and unemployment, holding constant:

1. The expected inflation rate
2. The natural unemployment rate

You've just seen what determines the expected inflation rate. The natural rate of unemployment and the factors that influence it are explained in Chapter 7 p. 146 and Chapter 9 pp. 195–197.

Figure 16.8 shows a short-run Phillips curve, *SRPC.* Suppose that the expected inflation rate is 10 percent a year and the natural unemployment rate is

FIGURE 16.8

A Short-Run Phillips Curve

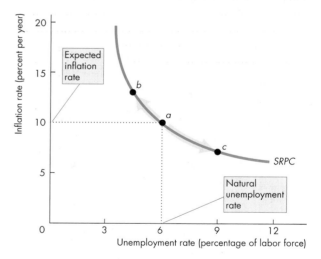

The short-run Phillips curve (*SRPC*) shows the relationship between inflation and unemployment at a given expected inflation rate and given natural unemployment rate. With an expected inflation rate of 10 percent a year and a natural unemployment rate of 6 percent, the short-run Phillips curve passes through point *a*. An unanticipated increase in aggregate demand lowers unemployment and increases inflation—a movement up the short-run Phillips curve. An unanticipated decrease in aggregate demand increases unemployment and lowers inflation—a movement down the short-run Phillips curve.

6 percent, point *a* in the figure. A short-run Phillips curve passes through this point. If inflation rises above its expected rate, unemployment falls below its natural rate. This joint movement in the inflation rate and the unemployment rate is illustrated as a movement up the short-run Phillips curve from point *a* to point *b* in the figure. Similarly, if inflation falls below its expected rate, unemployment rises above the natural rate. In this case there is movement down the short-run Phillips curve from point *a* to point *c*.

This negative relationship between inflation and unemployment along the short-run Phillips curve is explained by the aggregate supply–aggregate demand model. Figure 16.9 shows the connection between the two approaches. Initially, the aggregate demand curve is AD_0, the short-run aggregate supply curve is SAS_0, and the long-run aggregate supply curve is *LAS*. Real GDP is $7 trillion, and the price level is 100. Aggregate demand is expected to increase, and the aggregate demand curve is expected to shift right-ward to AD_1. Anticipating this increase in aggregate demand, the money wage rate rises, which shifts the short-run aggregate supply curve to SAS_1. What happens to actual inflation and real GDP depends on the *actual* change in aggregate demand.

First, suppose that aggregate demand actually increases by the amount expected, so the aggregate demand curve shifts to AD_1. The price level rises from 100 to 110, and the inflation rate is an anticipated 10 percent a year. Real GDP remains at potential GDP, and unemployment remains at the natural rate. The economy moves to point *a* in Fig. 16.9, and it can equivalently be described as being at point *a* on the short-run Phillips curve in Fig. 16.8.

Alternatively, suppose that aggregate demand is expected to increase to AD_1 but actually increases by more than expected to AD_2. The price level now rises to 113, a 13 percent inflation rate. Real GDP increases above potential GDP, and unemployment falls below the natural rate. We can now describe the economy as moving to point *b* in Fig. 16.9 or at point *b* on the short-run Phillips curve in Fig. 16.8.

Finally, suppose that aggregate demand is expected to increase to AD_1 but actually remains at AD_0. The price level now rises to 107, a 7 percent inflation rate. Real GDP falls below potential GDP, and unemployment rises above the natural rate. We can now describe the economy as moving to point *c* in Fig. 16.9 or at point *c* on the short-run Phillips curve in Fig. 16.8.

FIGURE 16.9

AS-AD and the Short-Run Phillips Curve

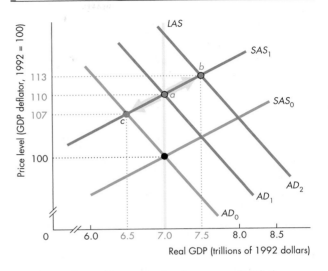

If aggregate demand is expected to increase and shift the aggregate demand curve from AD_0 to AD_1, then the money wage rate rises by an amount that shifts the short-run aggregate supply curve from SAS_0 to SAS_1. The price level rises to 110, a 10 percent rise, and the economy is at point *a* in this figure and at point *a* on the short-run Phillips curve in Fig. 16.8. If, with the same expectations, aggregate demand increases and shifts the aggregate demand curve from AD_0 to AD_2, the price level rises to 113, a 13 percent rise, and the economy is at point *b* in this figure and at point *b* on the short-run Phillips curve in Fig. 16.8. If, with the same expectations, aggregate demand does not change, the price level rises to 107, a 7 percent rise, and the economy is at point *c* in this figure and at point *c* on the short-run Phillips curve in Fig. 16.8.

The short-run Phillips curve is like the short-run aggregate supply curve. A movement along the *SAS* curve that brings a higher price level and an increase in real GDP is equivalent to a movement along the short-run Phillips curve that brings an increase in the inflation rate and a decrease in the unemployment rate. (Similarly, a movement along the *SAS* curve that brings a lower price level and a decrease in real GDP is equivalent to a movement along the short-run Phillips curve that brings a decrease in the inflation rate and an increase in the unemployment rate.)

The Long-Run Phillips Curve

The **long-run Phillips curve** shows the relationship between inflation and unemployment when the actual inflation rate equals the expected inflation rate. The long-run Phillips curve is vertical at the natural unemployment rate. In Fig. 16.10, it is the vertical line *LRPC*. The long-run Phillips curve tells us that any anticipated inflation rate is possible at the natural unemployment rate. This proposition is consistent with the *AS-AD* model, which predicts that when inflation is anticipated, real GDP equals potential GDP and unemployment is at the natural rate.

When the expected inflation rate changes, the short-run Phillips curve shifts but the long-run Phillips curve does not shift. If the expected inflation rate is 10 percent a year, the short-run Phillips curve is $SRPC_0$. If the expected inflation rate falls to 7

FIGURE 16.10
Short-Run and Long-Run Phillips Curves

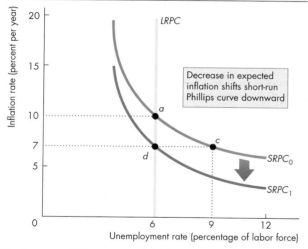

The long-run Phillips curve is *LRPC*, a vertical line at the natural unemployment rate. A fall in expected inflation shifts the short-run Phillips curve downward. For example, when the expected inflation rate falls from 10 percent a year to 7 percent a year, the short-run Phillips curve shifts downward from $SRPC_0$ and $SRPC_1$. The new short-run Phillips curve intersects the long-run Phillips curve at the new expected inflation rate—point *d*. With the original expected inflation rate (of 10 percent), an actual inflation rate of 7 percent a year would occur at an unemployment rate of 9 percent, at point *c*.

percent a year, the short-run Phillips curve shifts downward to $SRPC_1$. The distance by which the short-run Phillips curve shifts downward when the expected inflation rate falls is equal to the change in the expected inflation rate.

To see why the short-run Phillips curve shifts when the expected inflation rate changes, let's do a thought experiment. There is full employment, and a 10 percent a year anticipated inflation is raging. The Fed now begins an attack on inflation by slowing money supply growth. Aggregate demand growth slows, and the inflation rate falls to 7 percent a year. At first, this decrease in inflation is *un*anticipated, so wages continue to rise at their original rate. The short-run aggregate supply curve shifts leftward at the same pace as before. Real GDP falls, and unemployment increases. In Fig. 16.10, the economy moves from point *a* to point *c* on $SRPC_0$.

If the actual inflation rate remains steady at 7 percent a year, this rate eventually comes to be expected. As this happens, wage growth slows and the short-run aggregate supply curve shifts leftward less quickly. Eventually, it shifts leftward at the same pace at which the aggregate demand curve is shifting rightward. The actual inflation rate equals the expected inflation rate, and full employment is restored. Unemployment is back at its natural rate. In Fig. 16.10, the short-run Phillips curve has shifted from $SRPC_0$ to $SRPC_1$ and the economy is at point *d*.

An increase in the expected inflation rate has the opposite effect to that shown in Fig. 16.10. Another important source of shifts in the Phillips curve is a change in the natural rate of unemployment.

Changes in the Natural Unemployment Rate

The natural unemployment rate changes for many reasons (see Chapter 9, pp. 195–197). A change in the natural unemployment rate shifts both the short-run and long-run Phillips curves. Figure 16.11 illustrates such shifts. If the natural unemployment rate increases from 6 percent to 9 percent, the long-run Phillips curve shifts from $LRPC_0$ to $LRPC_1$, and if expected inflation is constant at 10 percent a year, the short-run Phillips curve shifts from $SRPC_0$ to $SRPC_1$. Because the expected inflation rate is constant, the short-run Phillips curve $SRPC_1$ intersects the long-run curve $LRPC_1$ (point *e*) at the same inflation rate at which the short-run Phillips curve $SRPC_0$ intersects the long-run curve $LRPC_0$ (point *a*).

The U.S. Phillips Curve

Figure 16.12(a) is a scatter diagram of inflation and unemployment since 1960. The Phillips curve does not jump out of this figure. But we can interpret the data in terms of a shifting short-run Phillips curve as in Fig. 16.12(b). During the 1960s, the natural rate of unemployment was 5 percent and the expected inflation rate was 2 percent a year (point *a*), so the short-run Phillips curve was $SRPC_0$. During the 1970s and through 1981, the expected inflation rate and the natural unemployment rate increased and the short-run Phillips curve shifted rightward to $SRPC_1$, $SRPC_2$, and $SRPC_3$. During the 1980s and 1990s, the expected inflation rate and the natural unemployment rate decreased and the short-run Phillips curve shifted leftward. By the early 1990s, the curve was back at $SRPC_1$. And by 1996, the natural unemployment rate and the expected inflation rate were back around their 1960s levels, so the short-run Phillips curve was back at $SRPC_0$.

FIGURE 16.12

Phillips Curves in the United States

(a) Time sequence

FIGURE 16.11

A Change in the Natural Unemployment Rate

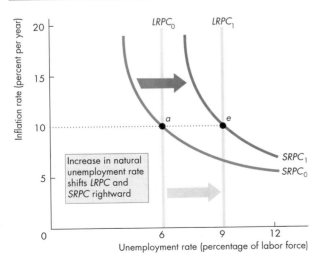

A change in the natural unemployment rate shifts both the short-run and long-run Phillips curves. Here the natural unemployment rate increases from 6 percent to 9 percent, and the two Phillips curves shift right to $SRPC_1$ and $LRPC_1$. The new long-run Phillips curve intersects the new short-run Phillips curve at the expected inflation rate—point *e*.

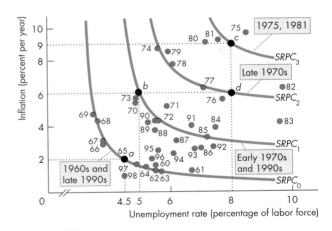

(b) Four Phillips curves

In part (a), each dot represents the combination of inflation and unemployment for a particular year in the United States. Part (b) interprets the data with a shifting short-run Phillips curve. The black dots *a*, *b*, *c*, and *d*, show the combination of the natural rate of unemployment and the expected inflation rate in different periods. The short-run Phillips curve was $SRPC_0$ during the 1960s and late 1990s. It was $SRPC_1$ during the early 1970s and 1990s, $SRPC_2$ during the late 1970s, and $SRPC_3$ (briefly) in 1975 and 1981.

Source: Economic Report of the President, 1999, and the author's calculations and assumptions.

REVIEW QUIZ

- How would you illustrate an unanticipated change in the inflation rate by using the Phillips curve?
- What are the effects of an unanticipated increase in the inflation rate on the unemployment rate?
- If the expected inflation rate increases by 10 percentage points, how does the short-run Phillips curve change and how does the long-run Phillips curve change?
- If the natural unemployment rate increases, what happens to the short-run Phillips curve? What happens to the long-run Phillips curve? What happens to the expected inflation rate?
- Does the United States have a short-run Phillips curve? If so, has the U.S. short-run Phillips curve remained stable?
- Does the United States have a stable long-run Phillips curve?

So far, we've studied the effects of inflation on real GDP, real wages, employment, and unemployment. But inflation lowers the value of money and changes the real value of the amounts borrowed and repaid. As a result, interest rates are influenced by inflation. Let's see how.

Interest Rates and Inflation

TODAY, BUSINESSES IN THE UNITED STATES CAN borrow at interest rates of around 6 percent a year. Businesses in Russia pay interest rates of 60 percent a year and in Turkey, 80 percent a year. Although U.S. interest rates have never been as high as these two cases, during the 1980s, U.S. businesses faced interest rates of 16 percent a year or higher. Why do interest rates vary so much both across countries and over time? Part of the answer is because risk differences make *real interest rates* vary across countries (see Chapter 10, p. 213). But another part of the answer is that the inflation rate varies.

You can see in Fig. 16.13 that the higher the inflation rate, the higher is the nominal interest rate. This proposition is true for the United States over time (Fig. 16.13a) and for the world at a given time (Fig. 16.13b).

FIGURE 16.13

Inflation and the Interest Rate

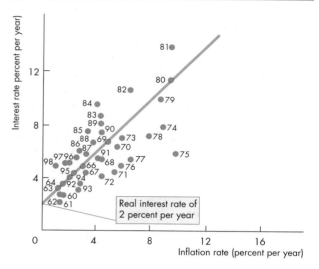

(a) United States

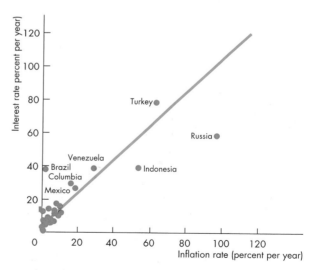

(b) Around the world

Other things remaining the same, the higher the inflation rate, the higher is the nominal interest rate. Part (a) shows this relationship between nominal interest rates and the inflation rate in the United States, and part (b) shows the relationship across a number of countries in 1999.

Source: Economic Report of the President, 1999 and The Economist, March 6, 1999.

How Interest Rates Are Determined

The *real* interest rate is determined by investment demand and saving supply in the global capital market. Investment demand and saving supply depend on the real interest rate. And the real interest rate adjusts to make investment plans and saving plans equal. (Chapter 10, pp. 213–215 explains the forces that determine the equilibrium real interest rate. National real interest rates vary around the world-average real interest rate because of national differences in risk.)

A *nominal* interest rate is determined by the demand for money and the supply of money in each nation's money market. The demand for money depends on the nominal interest rate and the supply of money is determined by the central bank's monetary policy—the Fed's monetary policy in the United States. And the nominal interest rate adjusts to make the quantity of money demanded equal to the quantity supplied. (Chapter 15, pp. 343–344 explains the forces that determine the equilibrium nominal interest rate.)

Why Inflation Influences the Nominal Interest Rate

Because the real interest rate is determined in the global capital market and nominal interest rates are determined in each nation's money market, there is no tight and mechanical link between the two interest rates. But, on the average, and other things remaining the same, a 1 percentage point rise in the inflation rate leads to a 1 percentage point rise in the nominal interest rate. Why? The answer is that the capital market and the money market are closely interconnected. The investment, saving, and demand for money decisions that people make are connected and the result is that the equilibrium nominal interest rate approximately equals the real interest rate plus the expected inflation rate.

To see why this relationship between the real interest rate and the nominal interest rate arises, think about the investment, saving, and demand for money decisions that people make. Imagine first that there is no inflation. Investment equals saving at a real interest rate of 6 percent a year. The demand for money equals the supply of money at a nominal interest rate of 6 percent a year. Walt Disney Corporation is willing to pay an interest rate of 6 percent a year to get the funds it needs to pay for its global investment in new theme parks. Sue and thousands of people like her are willing to save and lend Disney the amount it

needs for its theme parks if they can get a *real* return of 6 percent a year. (Sue is saving to buy a new car.) And Disney, Sue, and everyone else are willingly holding the quantity of (real) money supplied by the Fed.

Now imagine the inflation rate is a steady and expected 4 percent a year. All dollar amounts, including theme park profits and car prices are rising by 4 percent a year. If Disney was willing to pay a 6 percent interest rate when there was no inflation, it is now willing to pay 10 percent interest. Its profits are rising by 4 percent a year, so it is *really* paying only 6 percent. Similarly, if Sue was willing to lend at a 6 percent interest rate when there was no inflation, she is now willing to lend only if she gets a 10 percent interest rate. The price of the car Sue is planning on buying is rising by 4 percent a year, so she is *really* getting only a 6 percent interest rate.

Because borrowers are willing to pay the higher rate and lenders are willing to lend only if they receive the higher rate when inflation is anticipated, the *nominal interest rate* increases by an amount equal to the expected inflation rate. The *real interest rate* remains constant.

At a nominal interest rate of 10 percent a year, people are willingly holding the quantity of (real) money supplied by the Fed. This quantity is less than with zero inflation. The price level rises by more than the quantity of money and the real quantity of money decreases because of the increase in inflation.

R E V I E W   Q U I Z

- What is the relationship among the real interest rate, the nominal interest rate, and the inflation rate?
- Why does inflation change the nominal interest rate?

Reading Between the Lines on pages 372–373 looks at the current low inflation in the United States and the Fed's actions to keep it that way.

You have now completed your study of inflation. This material, together with that on economic growth (Chapter 11), gives a good overview of the long-term problems that confront a modern economy such as that of the United States. Our task in the following chapter is to focus more sharply on the problems of short-term fluctuations and the business cycle.

Keeping Inflation Down

THE WALL STREET JOURNAL, APRIL 5, 1999

Unemployment Data Hints At a Slowing U.S. Economy

BY GLENN BURKINS STAFF REPORTER OF *THE WALL STREET JOURNAL*

WASHINGTON—The economy, which has been expanding at a rapid rate in recent years, may be slowing somewhat, the government's latest employment report suggests.

The jobless rate in March fell to 4.2%, its lowest level since 1970, from 4.4% in February, the Labor Department said Friday. But other signs suggest that the economy may finally be leveling off, vindicating the Federal Reserve's decision last week to leave interest rates alone. (All figures are seasonally adjusted.)

Only 46,000 nonfarm jobs were created in March, down from 297,000 in February, according to the government's employer survey. The index of aggregate hours worked, a rough indicator of gross domestic product, fell 0.5% in March after rising 0.5% in February. And manufacturing,

PAYROLL PARADOX

Joblessness Hits 29-Year Low, but Wages Rise More Slowly

Monthly unemployment rate (left axis) and year-to-year change in inflation-adjusted average hourly wages* (right axis)

In constant 1982 dollars   *Source: Bureau of Labor Statistics*

after briefly showing signs of recovery, resumed its longer-term employment decline. ...

Despite the continuing tight labor market, wage gains remained moderate. Average hourly earnings of production or nonsupervisory workers on private nonfarm payrolls rose 0.2%, just three cents, in March to $13.09. Over the last 12 months, average hourly wages have risen 3.6%.

Rosanne Cahn, chief economist in the equity department at Credit Suisse First Boston, said she isn't surprised wage gains have come slowly. In part, she says, workers are putting in fewer overtime hours; that holds down the government's hourly wage figure. And despite a tight labor market, "workers are not organized to take advantage of their scarcity" by demanding higher pay, she added.

Ms Cahn says the unemployment rate would have to drop to at least 4%, and possibly much lower, before employers begin a "bidding war" for workers. ...

Essence of the Story

■ The unemployment rate in March 1999 was 4.2 percent, down from 4.4 percent in February, and at its lowest level since 1970.

■ But only 46,000 nonfarm jobs were created in March, down from 297,000 in February. The index of aggregate hours, which rose 0.5 percent in February, fell 0.5 percent in March. And employment in manufacturing fell.

■ Despite the tight labor market, wage increases were moderate.

■ Rosanne Cahn, an economist at Credit Suisse First Boston, said that the unemployment rate would have to drop to at least 4 percent, possibly lower, before wages begin to increase more quickly.

■ Figure 1 shows the inflation rate and the earnings growth rate from January 1997 to December 1998. Inflation was on a downward path through 1997 but was constant during 1998.

■ Figure 2 uses the Phillips curve to interpret the changes in inflation and unemployment.

■ In January 1997, the long-run Phillips curve was $LRPC_0$ at the (assumed) natural unemployment rate of 5.3 percent. The short-run Phillips curve was $SRPC_0$, and unemployment was at the natural rate.

■ Even if the natural rate of unemployment had remained constant, the short-run Phillips curve would have shifted downward to $SRPC_1$ because of a fall in the expected inflation rate.

■ But during 1997, the natural rate of unemployment decreased to (an assumed) 4.5 percent and the long-run Phillips curve shifted leftward to $LRPC_1$. The short-run Phillips curve also shifted leftward, to $SRPC_2$.

■ Through 1998, the unemployment rate was close to the natural rate.

■ It is possible that by the end of 1998 and the beginning of 1999, the unemployment rate was below the natural rate.

■ If the unemployment rate was below the natural rate at the beginning of 1999, the rate of inflation would be predicted to increase during 1999.

■ The view of Rosanne Cahn reported in the news article implies that she believes that the natural rate of unemployment is below 4 percent.

■ But whether inflation is going to continue to increase depends on how rapidly the money supply grows. The Fed is committed to maintaining noninflationary money growth, but Fig. 3 raises some questions about whether it is succeeding.

■ Between February 1997 and November 1998, the M2 growth rate increased. If the M2 growth rate in November 1998, which is close to 9 percent a year, is maintained, inflation will rise and probably to more than 5 percent a year.

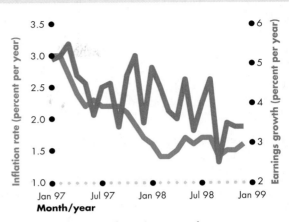

Figure 1 Inflation and earnings growth

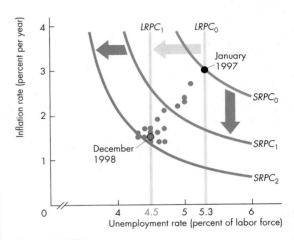

Figure 2 Phillips curves

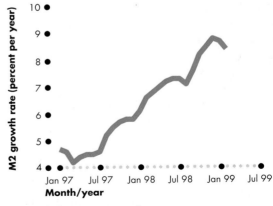

Figure 3 M2 money growth

SUMMARY

KEY POINTS

Inflation and the Price Level (p. 356)

■ Inflation is a process of persistently rising prices and falling value of money.

Demand-Pull Inflation (pp. 357–359)

■ Demand-pull inflation arises from increasing aggregate demand.

■ Its main sources are increases in the money supply or in government purchases.

Cost-Push Inflation (pp. 359–361)

■ Cost-push inflation can result from any factor that decreases aggregate supply.

■ Its main sources are increasing wage rates and increasing prices of key raw materials.

Effects of Inflation (pp. 362–366)

■ Inflation is costly when it is unanticipated because it creates inefficiencies and redistributes income and wealth.

■ People try to anticipate inflation to avoid its costs.

■ Forecasts of inflation based on all the available relevant information are called rational expectations.

■ A moderate anticipated inflation has a small cost. But a rapid anticipated inflation is costly because it decreases potential GDP and slows growth.

Inflation and Unemployment: The Phillips Curve (pp. 366–370)

■ The short-run Phillips curve shows the tradeoff between inflation and unemployment when the expected inflation rate and the natural unemployment rate are constant.

■ The long-run Phillips curve, which is vertical, shows that when the actual inflation rate equals the expected inflation rate, the unemployment rate equals the natural unemployment rate.

■ Unexpected changes in the inflation rate bring movements along the short-run Phillips curve.

■ Changes in expected inflation shift the short-run Phillips curve.

■ Changes in the natural unemployment rate shift both the short-run and long-run Phillips curves.

Interest Rates and Inflation (pp. 370–371)

■ The higher the expected inflation rate, the higher is the nominal interest rate.

■ As the anticipated inflation rate rises, borrowers willingly pay a higher interest rate and lenders successfully demand a higher interest rate.

■ The nominal interest rate adjusts to equal the real interest rate plus the expected inflation rate.

KEY FIGURES

KEY TERMS

PROBLEMS

*1. The figure shows an economy's long-run aggregate supply curve, *LAS*; three aggregate demand curves *AD*$_0$, *AD*$_1$, and *AD*$_2$; and three short-run aggregate supply curves *SAS*$_0$, *SAS*$_1$, and *SAS*$_2$. The economy starts out on the curves *AD*$_0$ and *SAS*$_0$. Some events then occur that generate a demand-pull inflation.

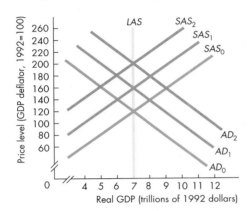

a. List the events that might cause demand-pull inflation.
b. Using the figure, describe the initial effects of demand-pull inflation.
c. Using the figure, describe what happens as a demand-pull inflation spiral unwinds.

2. In the economy described in problem 1, some events then occur that generate a cost-push inflation.
a. List the events that might cause cost-push inflation.
b. Using the figure, describe the initial effects of cost-push inflation.
c. Using the figure, describe what happens as a cost-push inflation spiral unwinds.

*3. In the economy described in problem 1, some events then occur that generate a perfectly anticipated inflation.
a. List the events that might cause a perfectly anticipated inflation.
b. Using the figure, describe the initial effects of anticipated inflation.
c. Using the figure, describe what happens as anticipated inflation proceeds.

4. In the economy described in problem 1, suppose that people anticipate deflation (a falling price level) but aggregate demand turns out not to change.
a. What happens to the short-run and long-run aggregate supply curves? (Draw some new curves if you need to.)
b. Using the figure, describe the initial effects of anticipated deflation.
c. Using the figure, describe what happens as it becomes obvious to everyone that the anticipated deflation is not going to occur.

*5. An economy has an unemployment rate of 4 percent and an inflation rate of 5 percent a year at point *a* in the figure. Some events then occur that move the economy to point *d*.

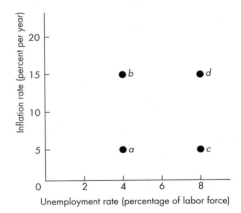

a. Describe the events that could move the economy from point *a* to point *d*.
b. Draw in the diagram the economy's short-run and long-run Phillips curves when the economy is at point *a*.
c. Draw in the diagram the economy's short-run and long-run Phillips curves when the economy is at point *d*.

6. In the economy described in problem 5, some events occur that move the economy from point *b* to point *c*.
a. Describe the events that could move the economy from point *b* to point *c*.
b. Draw in the diagram the economy's short-run and long-run Phillips curves when the economy is at point *b*.
c. Draw in the diagram the economy's short-run and long-run Phillips curves when the economy is at point *c*.

*7. In the economy described in problem 5, some events occur that move the economy in a clockwise loop from *a* to *b* to *d* to *c* and back to *a*.
   a. Describe the events that could create this sequence.
   b. Draw in the diagram the sequence of the economy's short-run and long-run Phillips curves.
   c. Has the economy experienced demand-pull inflation, cost-push inflation, anticipated inflation, or none of these?

8. In the economy described in problem 5, some events occur that move the economy in a counterclockwise loop from *a* to *c* to *d* to *b* and back to *a*.
   a. Describe the events that could create this sequence.
   b. Draw in the diagram the sequence of the economy's short-run and long-run Phillips curves.
   c. Has the economy experienced demand-pull inflation, cost-push inflation, anticipated inflation, or none of these?

*9. An economy with a natural unemployment rate of 4 percent and an expected inflation rate of 6 percent a year has the following inflation and unemployment history:

Year	Inflation rate (percent per year)	Unemployment rate (percent)
1999	10	2
2000	8	3
2001	6	4
2002	4	5
2003	2	6

   a. Draw a diagram of the economy's short-run and long-run Phillips curves.
   b. If the actual inflation rate rises from 6 percent a year to 8 percent a year, what is the change in the unemployment rate? Explain why it occurs.

10. For the economy described in problem 9, the natural unemployment rate rises to 5 percent and the expected inflation rate falls to 5 percent a year. Draw the new short-run and long-run Phillips curves in a diagram.

CRITICAL THINKING

1. Study *Reading Between the Lines* on pp. 372–373 and use the link on the Parkin Web site to obtain the latest data on inflation, unemployment, and money growth. Then answer the following questions:
   a. What happened to the unemployment rate, the inflation rate, and the M2 money growth rate during the months following April 1999 when the news article was written?
   b. Do the events of 1999 support the view of Rosanne Cahn reported in the news article?
   c. Did the Fed keep the M2 money growth rate high, did it speed up the growth rate yet further, or did it slow the growth rate?
   d. Explain the likely effects of the Fed's monetary actions on the inflation rate and the unemployment rate through 1999.
   e. What do you think the Fed should be doing to interest rates and M2 money growth right now? Why?

2. If an inflation rate of 10 percent a year (like that we had during the 1970s) returned in the United States, who would benefit and who would lose?

3. "The Phillips curve is a menu from which the government must choose how much inflation and how much unemployment to buy." Evaluate this statement. Under what conditions is it true? Under what conditions is it false?

4. If the Fed aimed to use monetary policy to lower the unemployment rate to 2 percent, what do you predict would happen to:
   a. Unemployment in the short run?
   b. Unemployment in the long run?
   c. Inflation in the short run?
   d. Inflation in the long run?
   e. The short-run Phillips curve?
   f. The long-run Phillips curve?
   g. Potential GDP?
   h. The growth rate of potential GDP?

5. Use the link on the Parkin Web site to obtain the latest data on inflation, unemployment, and money growth in Japan, Germany, and Canada. Then:
   a. Interpret the data for each country in terms of shifting Phillips curves.
   b. Which country do you think has the lowest expected inflation rate? Why?

Understanding Aggregate Demand and Inflation

Money Chasing Goods

Aggregate demand fluctuations bring recessions and expansions. If aggregate demand expands more rapidly than long-run aggregate supply, we get inflation. So understanding the forces that determine aggregate demand helps us to understand both the business cycle and inflation. ◆ It took economists a long time to achieve this knowledge, and we still don't know enough about aggregate demand to be able to forecast it more than a few months ahead. But we do know the basic factors that influence aggregate demand. And we know a lot about how those factors interact to send shock waves rippling through the economy. ◆ Fundamentally, aggregate demand is a monetary phenomenon. The quantity of money is the single most significant influence on aggregate demand. This insight was first outlined more than 200 years ago by David Hume, a Scottish philosopher and close friend of Adam Smith. Said Hume, "In every Kingdom into which money begins to flow in greater abundance than formerly, every thing takes a new face: labor and industry gain life; the merchant becomes more enterprising, the manufacturer more diligent and skilful, and even the farmer follows his plow with greater alacrity and attention." Milton Friedman and other economists known as *monetarists* also emphasize the central role of money. Money lies at the center of Keynes' theory of aggregate demand as well. But Keynes also called attention to the power of independent changes in government purchases, taxes, and business investment to influence aggregate demand. In the modern world, we also recognize the effect of changes in exports on aggregate demand. ◆ The chapters in this part explain the factors that influence aggregate demand and help you to understand how they interact to bring multiplier effects on aggregate expenditure. Chapter 11 explained the effects of changes in business investment and the multiplier effect they have on consumption expenditure and aggregate expenditure. This chapter also explained how changes in business inventories trigger changes in production and incomes. Chapter 12 looked at fiscal policy and applied the model of Chapter 11 to study the effects of changes in government purchases and taxes. Chapter 13 brought money into the picture and explained exactly what money is and how banks create it. Chapter 14 showed how the Fed controls the quantity of money and thereby influences interest rates and expenditure. Chapter 15 returned to the aggregate supply–aggregate demand framework and explained inflation. It showed how the trends in inflation are determined by the trend in the money supply and how fluctuations in aggregate demand bring fluctuations in inflation, employment, and unemployment. ◆ Many economists have developed the insights you've learned in these chapters. One of the truly outstanding ones is Milton Friedman, whom you can meet on the next page. Another, and one of today's leading macroeconomists, is Bennett McCallum of Carnegie Mellon University, whom you can also meet on the following pages.

The Economist

Milton Friedman *was born into a poor immigrant family in New York City in 1912. He was an undergraduate at Rutgers and graduate student at Columbia University during the Great Depression. Today, Professor Friedman is a Senior Fellow at the Hoover Institution at Stanford University. But his reputation was built between 1946 and 1983, when he was a leading member of the "Chicago School," an approach to economics developed at the University of Chicago and based on the views that free markets allocate resources efficiently and that stable and low money supply growth delivers macroeconomic stability.*

Friedman has advanced our understanding of the forces that determine aggregate demand and clarified the effects of the quantity of money and for this work, he was awarded the (much overdue, in the opinion of his many admirers) 1977 Nobel Prize for Economic Science.

By reasoning from basic economic principles, Friedman predicted that persistent demand stimulation would not increase output but would cause inflation. When output growth slowed and inflation broke out in the 1970s, Friedman seemed like a prophet, and for a time, his policy prescription, known as monetarism, was embraced around the world.

> "Inflation is always and everywhere a monetary phenomenon."
>
> MILTON FRIEDMAN
> *The Counter-Revolution in Monetary Theory*

The Issues

The combination of history and economics has taught us a lot about the causes of inflation. Severe inflation—hyperinflation—arises from a breakdown of the normal fiscal policy processes at times of war or political upheaval. Tax revenues fall short of government spending, and newly printed money fills the gap between them. As inflation increases, the quantity of money that is needed to make payments increases, and a shortage of money can even result. So the rate of money growth increases yet further, and prices rise yet faster. Eventually, the monetary system collapses. Such was the experience of Germany during the 1920s and Brazil during the 1990s.

In earlier times, when commodities were used as money, inflation resulted from the discovery of new sources of money. The most recent occurrence of this type of inflation was at the end of the nineteenth century when gold, then used as money, was discovered in Australia, the Klondike, and South Africa.

In modern times, inflation has resulted from increases in the money supply that has accommodated increases in costs. The most dramatic such inflations occurred during the 1970s when the Fed and other central banks around the world accommodated oil price increases.

To avoid inflation, money supply growth must be held in check. But at times of severe cost pressure, central banks feel a strong tug in the direction of avoiding recession and accommodating the cost pressure.

Yet some countries have avoided inflation more effectively than others have. One source of success is central bank independence. In low-inflation countries, such as Germany and Japan, the central bank decides how much money to create and at what level to set interest rates, and does not take instructions from the government. In high-inflation countries, such as the United Kingdom and Italy, the central bank takes direct orders from the government about interest rates and money supply growth. The architects of a new monetary system for the European Community have noticed this connection between central bank independence and inflation, and they are modeling the European Central Bank on Germany's Bundesbank.

Then

When inflation is especially rapid, as it was in Germany in 1923, money becomes almost worthless. In Germany at that time, bank notes were more valuable as fire kindling than as money, and the sight of people burning Reichmarks was a common one. To avoid having to hold money for too long, wages were paid and spent twice a day. Banks took deposits and made loans, but at interest rates that compensated both depositors and the bank for the falling value of money—interest rates that could exceed 100 percent a month. The price of a dinner would increase during the course of an evening, making lingering over coffee a very expensive pastime.

Now

In 1994, Brazil had a computer-age hyperinflation, an inflation rate that was close to 50 percent a month. Banks installed ATMs on almost every street corner and refilled them several times an hour. Brazilians tried to avoid holding currency. As soon as they were paid, they went shopping and bought enough food to get them through to the next payday. Some shoppers filled as many as six carts on a single monthly trip to the supermarket. Also, instead of using currency, Brazilians used credit cards whenever possible. But they paid their card balances off quickly because the interest rate on unpaid balances was 50 percent a month. Only at such a high interest rate did it pay banks to lend to cardholders, because banks themselves were paying interest rates of 40 percent a month to induce depositors to keep their money in the bank.

Many economists today are working on aggregate demand and inflation. One distinguished contributor, whom you can meet on the following pages, is Bennett McCallum of Carnegie Mellon University.

Bennett T. McCallum

is Professor of Economics at Carnegie Mellon University. He was born in Poteet, Texas, in 1935. As an undergraduate, he attended Rice University, where he earned a degree in chemical engineering in 1958. He earned an MBA from Harvard Business School in 1963 and a Ph.D. in economics from Rice University in 1969.

Professor McCallum's research interests include monetary theory and policy, macroeconomic dynamics, and applied econometrics. Much of his research is aimed toward improving monetary policy, and Professor McCallum's advice is sought by central banks around the world.

Bennett T. McCallum

He has recently spent time at the Reserve Bank of New Zealand as well as the central bank of the Philippines.

Michael Parkin talked with Professor McCallum about his work, how it connects with the work of other great economists, and his insights on monetary policy.

Professor McCallum, how did you become interested in Economics?
I majored in chemical engineering in college and later worked for three years as a process design engineer for a petrochemical firm in Houston, Texas. Then, at my wife's urging, I earned an MBA at Harvard University. While attending

Harvard, I took as many economics, statistics, and operations research courses as possible. I enjoyed these courses and, as a result, decided to enroll in a Ph.D. program in economics.

What I found attractive about economics is its fascinating—even beautiful—theoretical structure combined with its emphasis on thinking analytically about public policy issues. The usual noneconomist approach to policy issues that one gets from the media and other sources seems to consist mostly of moralizing on the basis of the effects that a policy might have on some particular social group, which is very different from thinking analytically.

Many economists of your generation were heavily influenced by John Maynard Keynes. Looking back now on the work of Keynes, what do you think his legacy amounts to?
Keynes was by all accounts an exceptionally brilliant person and very good at his chosen subject of economics. But he was principally interested in the practical side of economics and government policy. During World War II, for instance, he contributed greatly to Britain's wartime finance policy and to the design of the Bretton Woods system that governed international monetary relations from 1945 to 1971. Thus for Keynes, economic theory was something that he did to persuade others of insights that he had. As a consequence, his theoretical work was, in my opinion, badly flawed. His famous *General Theory* contains numerous theoretical mistakes. It nevertheless did make a big contribution to the way that economic analysis is done, primarily by helping to persuade economists to be interested in short-run rather

than just long-run analysis. That was actually a major reorientation in thinking. It was like saying, "Hey, guys, let's pay attention to short-run effects. They're important."

Immediately following Keynes, economists began to emphasize that we can and should use fiscal policy to manipulate aggregate demand. What do we actually know about the ability of governments to manipulate aggregate expenditure using fiscal policy?

If there is a major sustained increase in government spending, starting from a deep recession such as in the 1930s, there will be major effects, as in 1940 to 1944. But if resources are fully employed, then the main real effect will be to shift consumption to the government from households and businesses. If, instead, the government imposes a tax change that's financed by bonds, by borrowing more or less, then the effects will be smaller. From a business cycle point of view, the most important fiscal policy considerations involve the automatic stabilizers, since, at least in the United States, the legislature typically isn't able to take actions promptly enough to be very helpful for any particular economic boom or slump.

What do we know about the Fed's ability to manipulate aggregate expenditure by using monetary policy?

The Fed can act much more quickly, and changes in its policy stance almost certainly affect nominal expenditures, or GDP in dollar terms. In other words, when the central bank pursues a more expansionary policy, the rate of aggregate expenditures will increase. But that is in money terms. What the real effects are depends on how wage and price adjustments occur, and our understanding in that respect is very far from complete. Indeed, my opinion is that the most serious weakness in our understanding of macro and monetary issues is the mechanism by which changes in monetary policy affect real variables such as employment or price-level-adjusted GDP. Although there is a lot of good work going on right now, we don't have agreement on the nature of the wage and price adjustment process.

Can we continue to use monetary policy to prevent inflation? If we can, how? And is Greenspan's current monetary policy on the right track?

Certainly monetary policy can be used to prevent inflation. You just cannot have a serious long-lasting inflation unless the central bank is creating money rapidly. As for gauging whether monetary policy is right or not, I think the best single measure is the rate of growth of the monetary base, by which we mean currency plus bank reserves.

As for recent federal reserve policy, I think it's been quite good over the period since Greenspan

became chairman, but nevertheless, I think that the United States would benefit from legislation stating that the prevention of inflation is the Fed's main objective. Currently, the law fails to state the main responsibility of the Fed. Although Greenspan has been quite consistent on this dimension himself, it's not a good idea to have a system that relies so much on the judgments of a single person. The next Fed chairman might not be so reasonable. Legislation clearly mandating prevention of inflation as the Fed's main responsibility would make it more difficult for Congress to pressure the Fed toward other objectives, which are less suitable.

What should the Fed be doing to minimize the risk of inflation and recession?

There's no question that Fed policies have substantial effects on output and employment, but these effects are temporary. From my perspective, the extent to which the Fed can usefully contribute to reducing cyclical fluctuation is rather limited. So I think the Fed should try to keep total spending, one measure of which would be nominal GDP, growing smoothly at a rate that is basically noninflationary. For example, if the objective is to keep inflation at about 2 percent per year, then the Fed ought to keep nominal GDP growing rather smoothly at about 4 1/2 percent (since real GDP will in any case grow at about 2 1/2 percent, on the average).

In conducting this policy, in which the Fed tightens or loosens depending on whether nominal GDP is growing faster or slower than 4 1/2 percent, you have to use some measure to determine whether you are in fact tightening or loosening, and I would favor looking at the growth rate of the monetary base. Now the Fed does not do that; instead, it looks at the federal funds interest rate. The problem with that approach is that from the perspective of short-run analysis, a high interest rate means tight money, but from the perspective of long-run analysis, a high interest rate reflects loose money (fast money growth). So gauging monetary conditions on the basis of an interest rate is a rather tricky and difficult thing to do. That's why I would prefer to look at a very narrow, controllable monetary measure, such as the monetary base.

What is your assessment of the U.S. deficit? Are deficits inflationary?
Government deficits per se are not all that important at the macroeconomic level. More important is the extent of goods and services that are consumed by the government, rather than the private sector. Deficits are going to be inflationary if the central bank responds to them by creating money in an attempt to keep interest rates from rising. This often happens, especially in countries with poorly developed tax systems. But in the United States, the Fed has not been printing money to finance the deficit. Instead, the Fed has forced the Treasury to finance the deficit by borrowing from the public. So we've not had an accommodating policy from the Fed, and as a result, we've not had much inflation. Much the same has been true in Europe and in many of the developed economies over the last 10 to 15 years.

Who historically are the big contributors to our understanding of aggregate fluctuations? Who are today's big contributors?
There were several macroeconomists who took John Maynard Keynes' general body of reasoning and his idea of focusing on short-run phenomena and made something fairly coherent out them. Economists such as Patinkin, Modigliani, and Hicks developed Keynesian economics as opposed to thoughts that Keynes had himself begun with. What about before Keynes? His teacher, Alfred Marshall, viewed the generation of business cycles in a manner rather consistent with Keynes' views, but he did not give so much attention to that topic. Irving Fisher believed that if you stabilized price levels, it would tend to prevent the problems that create recessions. Marshall believed fairly much the same thing.

Robert Lucas has been easily the most productive economist of the last 25 years, certainly in the area of macroeconomics. Although his information-based theory of fluctuations has not prevailed, he nevertheless set the tone and direction for today's research.

There are two important lessons from Lucas's work. First, is the basic idea of rational expectations—that although people can't forecast the future perfectly, they can and do strive to avoid systematic expectational errors. This implies that in designing macroeconomic policy, governments should not rely on the presumption that people are going to make the same mistakes over and over again. The second main lesson

from Lucas's work is that we should focus on long-run and long-lasting effects of policy actions rather than the temporary, short-term effects emphasized by the Keynesian approach of the 1950s and 1960s. We should try to design good institutions and good rules for policy making rather than being distracted by the alleged crisis of the day. In these teachings, as in many other ways, Lucas was further developing the general approach of Milton Friedman.

Is an economics major a good thing to pursue at the start of the new millenium?
Although only a small fraction of students studying economics will go on to become professional economists, it's an excellent subject to take for preparing for other careers—including business and the law—because of the disciplined, analytical thinking that it teaches.

I'm of the belief that an undergraduate should take subjects that are interesting to him or her. Find something that's enjoyable to you, that you're interested in, and then work hard on that. It doesn't have to be economics. What's unfortunate is for students to just go through the paces while they're undergraduates and miss the opportunity to gain a foundation in some field that will allow them to start off on an intellectually satisfying life.

The Business Cycle

The 1920s were years of unprecedented prosperity for Americans. After the horrors of World War I (1914–1918), the economic machine was back at work, producing such technological marvels as cars and airplanes, telephones and vacuum cleaners. Houses and apartments were being built at a frantic pace. Then, almost without warning, in October 1929, came a devastating stock market crash. Overnight, the values of stocks and shares traded on Wall Street fell by 30 percent. During the four succeeding years, there followed the most severe economic contraction in recorded history. By 1933, real GDP had fallen by 30 percent, unemployment had increased to 25 percent of the labor force, and employment was down 20 percent. What caused the Great Depression? ◆ By the standard of the Great Depression, recent recessions have been mild. But recessions have not gone away. Our economy has experienced 15 recessions since 1920 and 10 since the end of World War II in 1945. For 16 months, from November 1973 through March 1975, real GDP fell by 5 percent. It fell again in back-to-back recessions in 1980 and in 1981–1982. Most recently, real GDP decreased for 8 months in 1990–1991. Between these recessions, expansions took real GDP and income per person to new heights. Since the 1990–1991 recession, real GDP has grown steadily. By the end of 1998, it was some 25 percent higher than it had been in the 1990–1991 recession. What causes a repeating sequence of recessions and expansions in our economy? Must what goes up always come down? Will we have another recession? When?

Must What Goes Up Always Come Down?

◇ We are going to explore the business cycle in this chapter. You will see how all the strands of macroeconomics that you've been following come together and weave a complete picture of the forces and mechanisms that generate economic growth and fluctuations in production, employment and unemployment, and inflation.

After studying this chapter, you will be able to:

■ Distinguish among the different theories of the business cycle

■ Explain the Keynesian and monetarist theories of the business cycle

■ Explain the new classical and new Keynesian theories of the business cycle

■ Explain real business cycle theory

■ Describe the origins of and the mechanisms at work during two recent recessions and during the Great Depression

Cycle Patterns, Impulses, and Mechanisms

YOU'VE LOOKED AT THE BUSINESS CYCLE AT several points in your study of macroeconomics. You met it first in Chapter 5, which defines the phases of the cycle and describes its history. In Chapter 7, you saw how unemployment fluctuates over the business cycle. You learned about a framework for studying the business cycle—the aggregate supply–aggregate demand model—in Chapter 8. In Chapter 12, you focused on business cycle turning points and the inventory changes and expenditure multiplier effects that operate as the economy swings from expansion to recession and from recession to expansion. In Chapter 13, you studied the ways in which fiscal policy influences and is influenced by the business cycle. Finally, you saw in Chapters 14 through 16 how money influences economic fluctuations and how inflation and the business cycle intertwine.

You've also looked at another type of economic fluctuation: the productivity growth slowdown of the 1970s. This slowdown is not classified as a business cycle event, but it has some similarities. It is part of an overall process of economic growth, the pace of which fluctuates. The processes of growth and of the business cycle are intimately connected. In fact, according to one view, they are all manifestations of the same phenomenon.

This chapter brings all these strands in your previous study of macroeconomics together and gives you an opportunity both to review what you have learned and to put it to work in a focused way in interpreting and making sense of particular episodes in our economic history.

We'll get moving by first returning to the facts about the business cycle and looking at the complex patterns it makes.

Business Cycle Patterns

The business cycle is an irregular and nonrepeating up-and-down movement of business activity that takes place around a generally rising trend and that shows great diversity. Each recession, expansion, and turning point has been dated by the National Bureau of Economic Research (NBER). The NBER has identified 15 recessions and expansions since 1920. On the average, recessions have lasted for just over a

year and real GDP has fallen from peak to trough by more than 6 percent. Expansions have lasted for almost 4 years on the average, and real GDP has increased from trough to peak by an average of 22 percent. But these averages hide huge variations from one cycle to another.

Figure 17.1 shows the range of variation across the different recessions and expansions. It shows the total percentage change in real GDP during successive recessions and expansion. You can see that the Great Depression was much more severe than anything that followed it. Over a 43-month period, real GDP shrank by 33 percent. The second most severe recession was also in the 1930s. Another relatively severe recession occurred at the end of World War II in 1945. The only other recession that comes close to these is the OPEC recession of 1974–1975. A four-fold rise in the price of oil brought a 16-month and 5 percent fall in real GDP. The other recessions since 1950, including the most recent 1990–1991 recession, have been much milder than those of the 1930s. The biggest expansion occurred during World War II. But the other two big expansions were in the 1960s and 1980s. There is no correlation between the length of an expansion and the length of the preceding recession.

With this enormous diversity of experience, there is no simple explanation for the business cycle. Also, there is no (currently available) way of forecasting when the next turning point will come. But there is a body of theory about the business cycle that helps us to understand its causes. A good place to begin studying this theory is to distinguish the possible ways in which cycles can be created.

Cycle Impulses and Mechanisms

Cycles are a widespread physical phenomenon. In a tennis match, the ball cycles from one side of the court to the other and back again. Every day, the earth cycles from day to night and back to day. A child on a rocking horse creates a cycle as the horse swings back and forth.

The tennis ball cycle is the simplest. It is caused by the actions of the players. Each time the ball changes direction (at each turning point), the racket (an outside force) is applied. The day-night-day cycle is the most subtle. This cycle is caused by the rotation of the earth. No new force is applied each day to make the sun rise and set. It happens because of

FIGURE 17.1
Some Business Cycle Patterns

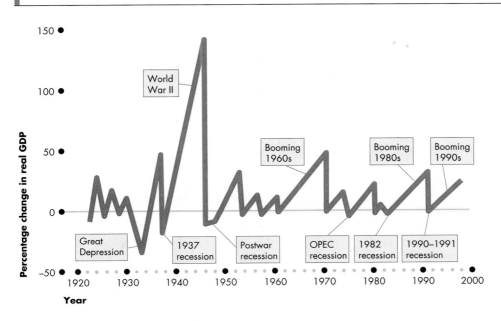

Recessions have lasted from 43 months during the Great Depression, when real GDP fell by 33 percent, to 6 months in 1980, when real GDP fell by 2.5 percent. The mildest recession lasted through most of 1970, when real GDP fell by 1 percent. Recessions have been less severe in the post–World War II period. Expansions have lasted from 6 months in 1980 to more than 100 months during the 1960s. Expansions have become longer and stronger during the post–World War II period.

Source: National Bureau of Economic Research and the author's calculations.

the design of the objects that interact to create the cycle. Nothing happens at a turning point (sunrise and sunset) that is any different from what is happening at other points except that the sun comes into or goes out of view. The child's rocking horse cycle is a combination of these two cases. To start the horse rocking, some outside force must be exerted (as in the tennis ball cycle). But once the horse is rocking, the to-and-fro cycle continues for some time with no further force being applied (as in the day-night-day cycle). The rocking horse cycle eventually dies out unless the horse is pushed again, and each time the horse is pushed, the cycle temporarily becomes more severe.

The economy is a bit like all three of these examples. It can be hit by shocks (like a tennis ball) that send it in one direction or another, it can cycle indefinitely (like the turning of day into night), and it can cycle in swings that get milder until another shock sets off a new burst of bigger swings (like a rocking horse). While none of these analogies is perfect, they all contain some insights into the business cycle.

Different theories of the cycle emphasize different outside forces (different tennis rackets) and different cycle mechanisms (different solar system and rocking horse designs).

Although there are several different theories of the business cycle, they all agree about one aspect of the cycle: the central role played by investment and the accumulation of capital.

The Central Role of Investment and Capital

Whatever the shocks are that hit the economy, they hit one crucial variable: investment. Recessions begin when investment in new capital slows down, and they turn into expansions when investment speeds up. Investment and capital interact like the spinning earth and the sun to create an ongoing cycle.

In an expansion, investment proceeds at a rapid rate and the capital stock grows quickly. But rapid capital growth means that the amount of capital per hour of labor is growing. Equipped with more capital, labor becomes more productive. But the *law of diminishing returns* begins to operate. The law of diminishing returns states that as the quantity of capital increases, with the quantity of labor remaining the same, the gain in productivity from the additional units of capital eventually diminishes. Diminishing returns to capital bring a fall in the profit rate, and with a lower profit rate, the incentive to invest weakens. As a result, investment eventually falls. When it falls by a large amount, recession begins.

In a recession, investment is low and the capital stock grows slowly. In a deep recession, the capital stock might actually fall. Slow capital growth (or even a falling capital stock) means that the amount of capital per hour of labor is falling. With a low amount of capital per hour of labor, businesses begin to see opportunities for profitable investment and the pace of investment eventually picks up. As it does so, recession turns into expansion.

The *AS-AD* Model

Investment and capital are a crucial part of the business cycle mechanism, but they are just one part. To study the broader business cycle mechanism, we need a broader framework. That framework is the *AS-AD* model of Chapter 8. All the theories of the business cycle can be described in terms of the *AS-AD* model. Theories differ both in what they identify as the impulse and in the cycle mechanism. But all theories can be thought of as making assumptions about the factors that make either aggregate supply or aggregate demand fluctuate and assumptions about how they interact with each other to create a business cycle. Business cycle impulses can affect either the supply side or the demand side of the economy or both. But there are no pure supply-side theories. We will classify all theories of the business cycle as either:

1. Aggregate demand theories
2. Real business cycle theory

We'll study the aggregate demand theories first. Then we'll study real business cycle theory, which is a more recent approach that isolates a shock that has both aggregate supply and aggregate demand effects.

Aggregate Demand Theories of the Business Cycle

THREE TYPES OF AGGREGATE DEMAND THEORY OF the business cycle have been proposed. They are:

- Keynesian theory
- Monetarist theory
- Rational expectations theories

Keynesian Theory

The **Keynesian theory of the business cycle** regards volatile expectations as the main source of economic fluctuations. This theory is distilled from Keynes' *General Theory of Employment, Interest, and Money.* We'll explore the Keynesian theory by looking at its main impulse and the mechanism that converts that impulse into a real GDP cycle.

Keynesian Impulse The *impulse* in the Keynesian theory of the business cycle is *expected future sales and profits.* A change in expected future sales and profits changes the demand for new capital and changes the level of investment.

Keynes had a sophisticated theory about *how* expected sales and profits are determined. He reasoned that these expectations would be volatile because most of the events that shape the future are unknown and impossible to forecast. So, he reasoned, news or even rumors about future tax rate changes, interest rate changes, advances in technology, global economic and political events, or any other of the thousands of relevant factors that influence sales and profits change expectations in ways that can't be quantified but that have large effects.

To emphasize the volatility and diversity of sources of changes in expected sales and profits, Keynes described these expectations as *animal spirits.* In using this term, Keynes was not saying that expectations are irrational. Rather, he meant that because future sales and profits are impossible to forecast, it might be rational to take a view about them based on rumors, guesses, intuition, and instinct. Further, it might be rational to *change* one's view of the future, perhaps radically, in the light of scraps of new information.

Keynesian Cycle Mechanism In the Keynesian theory, once a change in animal spirits has changed investment, a cycle mechanism begins to operate that has two key elements. First, the initial change in investment has a multiplier effect. The change in investment changes *aggregate* expenditure, real GDP, and disposable income. The change in disposable income changes consumption expenditure and aggregate demand changes by a multiple of the initial change in investment. (This mechanism is described in detail in Chapter 12, p. 266 and pp. 272–273.) The aggregate demand curve shifts rightward in an expansion and leftward in a recession.

The second element of the Keynesian cycle mechanism is the response of real GDP to a change in aggregate demand. The short-run aggregate supply curve is horizontal (or nearly so). With a horizontal *SAS* curve, swings in aggregate demand translate into swings in real GDP with no changes in the price level. But the short-run aggregate supply curve depends on the money wage rate. If the money wage rate is fixed (sticky), the *SAS* curve does not move. And if the money wage rate changes, the *SAS* curve shifts. In the Keynesian theory, the response of the money wage rate to changes in aggregate demand are *asymmetric*.

On the downside, when aggregate demand decreases and unemployment rises, the money wage rate does not change. It is completely rigid in the downward direction. With a decrease in aggregate demand and no change in the money wage rate, the economy gets stuck in a below full-employment equilibrium. No natural forces operate to restore full employment. The economy remains in that situation until animal spirits are lifted and investment increases.

On the upside, when aggregate demand increases and unemployment falls below the natural rate, the money wage rate rises quickly. It is flexible in the upward direction. At above full employment, the horizontal *SAS* curve plays no role and only the vertical *LAS* curve is relevant. With an increase in aggregate demand and an accompanying rise in the money wage rate, the price level rises quickly to eliminate the shortages and bring the economy back to full employment. The economy remains in that situation until animal spirits fall and investment and aggregate demand decrease.

Figures 17.2 and 17.3 illustrate the Keynesian theory of the business cycle by using the aggregate supply–aggregate demand model. In Fig. 17.2, the economy is initially at full employment (point *a*) on the long-run aggregate supply curve (*LAS*), the aggregate demand curve (*AD*$_0$), and the short-run

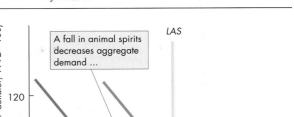

FIGURE 17.2

A Keynesian Recession

The economy is operating at point *a* at the intersection of the long-run aggregate supply curve (*LAS*), the short-run aggregate supply curve (*SAS*), and the aggregate demand curve (*AD*$_0$). A Keynesian recession begins when a fall in animal spirits causes investment demand to decrease. Aggregate demand decreases, and the *AD* curve shifts leftward to *AD*$_1$. With sticky money wages, real GDP decreases to $6 trillion and the price level does not change. The economy moves to point *b*.

aggregate supply curve (*SAS*). A fall in animal spirits decreases investment, and a multiplier process decreases aggregate demand. The aggregate demand curve shifts leftward to *AD*$_1$. With a fixed money wage rate, real GDP falls to $6 trillion and the economy moves to point *b*. Unemployment has increased and there is a surplus of labor. But the money wage rate does not fall, and the economy remains at point *b* until some force moves it away.

That force is shown in Fig. 17.3. Here, starting out at point *b*, a rise in animal spirits increases investment. The multiplier process kicks in, and aggregate demand increases. The *AD* curve shifts to *AD*$_2$, and real GDP begins to increase. An expansion is under way. As long as real GDP remains below potential GDP ($7 trillion in this example), the money wage rate and the price level remain constant. But real

FIGURE 17.3

A Keynesian Expansion

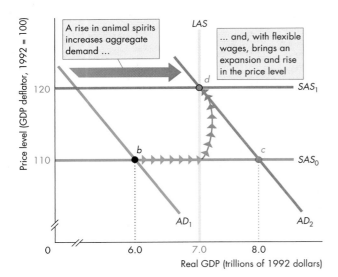

Starting at point *b*, a Keynesian expansion begins when a rise in animal spirits causes investment demand to increase. Aggregate demand increases, and the AD curve shifts rightward to AD_2. With sticky money wages, real GDP increases to $7 trillion. But the economy does not go all the way to point *c*. When full employment is reached, the money wage rate rises and the SAS curve shifts upward toward SAS_1. The price level rises as the economy heads toward point *d*.

GDP never increases to point *c*, the point of intersection of SAS_0 and AD_2. The reason is that once real GDP exceeds potential GDP and unemployment falls below the natural rate, the money wage rate begins to rise and the SAS curve starts to shift upward toward SAS_1. As the money wage rate rises, the price level also rises and real GDP growth slows. The economy follows a path like the one shown by the arrows connecting point *b*, the initial equilibrium, with point *d*, the final equilibrium.

The Keynesian business cycle is mainly like a tennis match. It is caused by outside forces—animal spirits—that change direction and set off a process that ends at an equilibrium that must be hit again by the outside forces to disturb it.

Monetarist Theory

The **monetarist theory of the business cycle** regards fluctuations in the money stock as the main source of economic fluctuations. This theory is distilled from the writings of Milton Friedman and several other economists. We'll explore the monetarist theory as we did the Keynesian theory, by looking first at its main impulse and second at the mechanism that creates a cycle in real GDP.

Monetarist Impulse The *impulse* in the monetarist theory of the business cycle is the *growth rate of the quantity of money*. A speedup in money growth brings expansion, and a slowdown in money growth brings recession. The source of the change in the growth rate of the quantity of money is the monetary policy actions of the Fed.

Monetarist Cycle Mechanism In the monetarist theory, once the Fed has changed the money growth rate, a cycle mechanism begins to operate that, like the Keynesian mechanism, first affects aggregate demand. When the money growth rate increases, the quantity of real money in the economy increases. Interest rates fall, and real money balances increase. The foreign exchange rate also falls—the dollar loses value on the foreign exchange market. These initial financial market effects begin to spill over into other markets. Investment demand and exports increase, and consumers spend more on durable goods. These initial changes in expenditure have a multiplier effect, just as investment has in the Keynesian theory. Through these mechanisms, a speedup in money growth shifts the aggregate demand curve rightward and brings an expansion. Similarly, a slowdown in money growth shifts the aggregate demand curve leftward and brings a recession.

The second element of the monetarist cycle mechanism is the response of aggregate supply to a change in aggregate demand. The short-run aggregate supply curve is upward-sloping. With an upward-sloping SAS curve, swings in aggregate demand translate into swings in both real GDP and the price level. But monetarists believe that real GDP deviations from full employment are temporary in both directions.

In monetarist theory, the money wage rate is only *temporarily sticky*. When aggregate demand decreases and unemployment rises, the money wage rate eventually begins to fall. As the money wage rate falls, so does the price level and after a period of adjustment, full employment is restored. When aggregate demand increases and unemployment falls below the natural rate, the money wage rate begins to rise. As the money wage rate rises, so does the price level. And through a period of adjustment, real GDP returns to potential GDP and the unemployment rate returns to the natural rate.

Figure 17.4 illustrates the monetarist theory. In part (a), the economy is initially at full employment (point *a*) on the long-run aggregate supply curve (*LAS*), the aggregate demand curve (*AD*₀), and the short-run aggregate supply curve (*SAS*₀). A slow-down in the money growth rate decreases aggregate

demand and the aggregate demand curve shifts left-ward to *AD*₁. Real GDP decreases to $6.5 trillion, and the economy goes into recession (point *b*). Unemployment increases and there is a surplus of labor. The money wage rate begins to fall. As the money wage falls, the short-run aggregate supply curve starts to shift rightward toward *SAS*₁. The price level falls, and real GDP begins to expand as the economy moves to point *c*, its new full-employment equilibrium.

Figure 17.4(b) shows the effects of the opposite initial money shock—a speedup in money growth. Here, starting out at point *c*, a speedup in the money growth rate increases aggregate demand and shifts the

---

FIGURE **17.4**

A Monetarist Business Cycle

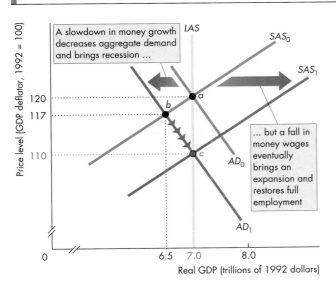

(a) Recession

A monetarist recession begins when a slowdown in money growth decreases aggregate demand. The *AD* curve shifts left-ward from *AD*₀ to *AD*₁ (in part a). With sticky money wages, real GDP decreases to $6.5 trillion and the price level falls to 117 as the economy moves from point *a* to point *b*. With a surplus of labor, the money wage rate falls and the *SAS* curve shifts rightward to *SAS*₁. The price level falls further, and real GDP returns to potential GDP at point *c*.

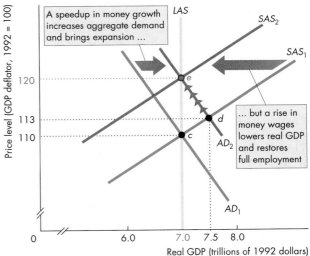

(b) Expansion

Starting at point *c* (part b), a monetarist expansion begins when an increase in money growth increases aggregate demand and shifts the *AD* curve rightward to *AD*₂. With sticky money wages, real GDP rises to $7.5 trillion, the price level rises to 113, and the economy moves to point *d*. With a shortage of labor, the money wage rate rises and the *SAS* curve shifts toward *SAS*₂. The price level rises, and real GDP decreases to potential GDP as the economy heads toward point *e*.

AD curve to *AD₂*. Both real GDP and the price level increase as the economy moves to point *d*, the point of intersection of *SAS₁* and *AD₂*. With real GDP above potential GDP and unemployment below the natural rate, the money wage rate begins to rise and the *SAS* curve starts to shift leftward toward *SAS₂*. As the money wage rate rises, the price level also rises and real GDP decreases. The economy moves from point *d* to point *e*, its new full-employment equilibrium.

The monetarist business cycle is like a rocking horse. It needs an outside force to get it going, but once going, it rocks back and forth (but just once). It doesn't matter in which direction the force initially hits. If it is a money growth slowdown, the economy cycles with a recession followed by expansion. If it is a money growth speedup, the economy cycles with an expansion followed by recession.

Rational Expectations Theories

A **rational expectation** is a forecast that is based on all the available relevant information (see Chapter 16, p. 363). Rational expectations theories of the business cycle are theories based on the view that money wages are determined by a rational expectation of the price level. Two distinctly different rational expectations theories of the cycle have been proposed. A **new classical theory of the business cycle** regards *unanticipated* fluctuations in aggregate demand as the main source of economic fluctuations. This theory is based on the work of Robert E. Lucas, Jr., (see pp. 175–180) and several other economists, including Thomas J. Sargent and Robert J. Barro. A different **new Keynesian theory of the business cycle** also regards *unanticipated* fluctuations in aggregate demand as the main source of economic fluctuations but it leaves room for *anticipated* demand fluctuations to play a role. We'll explore these theories as we did the Keynesian and monetarist theories, by looking first at the main impulse and second at the cycle mechanism.

Rational Expectations Impulse The *impulse* that distinguishes the rational expectations theories from the other aggregate demand theories of the business cycle is the *unanticipated change in aggregate demand*. A larger than anticipated increase in aggregate demand brings an expansion, and a smaller than anticipated increase in aggregate demand brings a recession. Any factor that influences aggregate demand—for example,

fiscal policy, monetary policy, or developments in the world economy that influence exports—whose change is not anticipated can bring a change in real GDP.

Rational Expectations Cycle Mechanisms To describe the rational expectations cycle mechanisms, we'll deal first with the new classical version. When aggregate demand decreases, if the money wage rate doesn't change, real GDP and the price level both decrease. The fall in the price level increases the *real* wage rate, and employment decreases and unemployment increases. In the new classical theory, these events occur only if the decrease in aggregate demand is not anticipated. If the decrease in aggregate demand *is* anticipated, the price level is expected to fall and both firms and workers will agree to a lower money wage rate. By doing so, they can prevent the real wage from rising and avoid a rise in the unemployment rate.

Similarly, if firms and workers anticipate an increase in aggregate demand, they expect the price level to rise and will agree to a higher money wage rate. By doing so, they can prevent the real wage rate from falling and avoid a fall in the unemployment rate below the natural rate.

Only fluctuations in aggregate demand that are unanticipated and not taken into account in wage agreements bring changes in real GDP. *Anticipated* changes in aggregate demand change the price level, but they leave real GDP and unemployment unchanged and do not create a business cycle.

New Keynesian economists, like new classical economists, believe that money wages are influenced by rational expectations of the price level. But new Keynesians emphasize the long-term nature of most wage contracts. They say that *today's* money wages are influenced by *yesterday's* rational expectations. These expectations, which were formed in the past, are based on old information that might now be known to be incorrect. After they have made a long-term wage agreement, both firms and workers might anticipate a change in aggregate demand, which they expect will change the price level. But because they are locked into their agreement, they are unable to change money wages. So money wages are sticky in the new Keynesian theory, and with sticky money wages, even an *anticipated* change in aggregate demand changes real GDP.

New classical economists believe that long-term contracts are renegotiated when conditions change to make them outdated. So they do not regard long-term contracts as an obstacle to money wage flexibility, provided that both parties to an agreement recognize the changed conditions. If both firms and workers expect the price level to change, they will change the agreed money wage rate to reflect that shared expectation. In this situation, anticipated changes in aggregate demand change the money wage rate and the price level and leave real GDP unchanged.

The distinctive feature of both versions of the rational expectations theory of the business cycle is the role of unanticipated changes in aggregate demand. Figure 17.5 illustrates the effect of unanticipated changes on real GDP and the price level.

Potential GDP is $7 trillion, and the long-run aggregate supply curve is *LAS*. Aggregate demand is expected to be *EAD*. Given potential GDP and *EAD*, the money wage rate is set at the level that is expected to bring full employment. At this money wage rate, the short-run aggregate supply curve is *SAS*. Imagine that initially aggregate demand equals expected aggregate demand, so there is full employment. Real GDP is $7 trillion, and the price level is 110. Then, unexpectedly, aggregate demand turns out to be less than expected and the aggregate demand curve shifts leftward to AD_0 (in Fig. 17.5a). Many different aggregate demand shocks, such as a slowdown in the money growth rate or a collapse of exports, could have caused this shift. A recession

FIGURE 17.5

A Rational Expectations Business Cycle

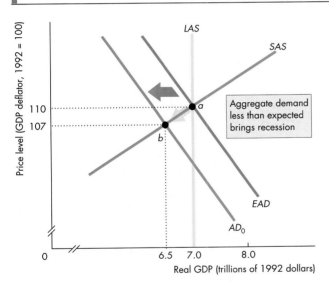

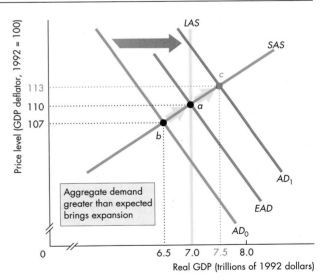

(a) Recession

(b) Expansion

The economy is expected to be at point *a* at the intersection of the long-run aggregate supply curve, *LAS*; the short-run aggregate supply curve, *SAS*; and the *expected* aggregate demand curve, *EAD*. A rational expectations recession begins when an unanticipated fall in aggregate demand shifts the *AD* curve leftward to AD_0. With money wage rates based on the expectation that aggregate demand will be *EAD*, real GDP falls to $6.5 trillion and the price level falls to 107 as the economy moves to point *b*. As long as aggregate demand is *expected* to

be *EAD*, there is no change in the money wage rate.

A rational expectations expansion begins when an unanticipated rise in aggregate demand shifts the *AD* curve rightward from AD_0 to AD_1. With money wage rates based on the expectation that aggregate demand will be *EAD*, real GDP increases to $7.5 trillion and the price level rises to 113 as the economy moves to point *c*. Again, as long as aggregate demand is *expected* to be *EAD*, there is no change in the money wage rate.

begins. Real GDP falls to $6.5 trillion, and the price level falls to 107. The economy moves to point *b*. Unemployment increases, and there is a surplus of labor. But aggregate demand is expected to be at *EAD*, so the money wage rate doesn't change and the short-run aggregate supply curve remains at *SAS*.

The recession ends when aggregate demand increases to its expected level. And a larger increase that takes aggregate demand to a level that exceeds *EAD* brings an expansion. In Fig. 17.5(b), the aggregate demand curve shifts rightward to AD_1. Such an increase in aggregate demand might be caused by a speedup in the money growth rate or an export boom. Real GDP now increases to $7.5 trillion, and the price level rises to 113. The economy moves to point *c*. Unemployment is now below the natural rate. But aggregate demand is expected to be at *EAD*, so the money wage rate doesn't change and the short-run aggregate supply curve remains at *SAS*.

Fluctuations in aggregate demand between AD_0 and AD_1 around expected aggregate demand *EAD* bring fluctuations in real GDP and the price level between points *b* and *c*.

The two versions of the rational expectations theory differ in their predictions about the effects of a change in expected aggregate demand. The new classical theory predicts that as soon as expected aggregate demand changes, the money wage rate also changes, so the *SAS* curve shifts. The new Keynesian theory predicts that the money wage rate changes only gradually when new contracts are made, so the *SAS* curve moves only slowly. This difference between the two theories is crucial for policy. According to the new classical theory, anticipated policy actions change the price level only and have no effect on real GDP and unemployment. The reason is that when policy is expected to change, the money wage rate changes, so the *SAS* curve shifts and offsets the effects of the policy action on real GDP. In contrast, in the new Keynesian theory, because the money wage rate changes only when new contracts are made, even anticipated policy actions change real GDP and can be used in an attempt to stabilize the cycle.

Like the monetarist business cycle, these rational expectations cycles are similar to rocking horses. They need an outside force to get them going, but once going, the economy rocks around its full employment point. The new classical horse rocks faster and comes to rest more quickly than the new Keynesian horse.

AS-AD General Theory

All the theories of the business cycle that we've considered can be viewed as particular cases of the more general *AS-AD* theory. In this more general theory, the impulses of both the Keynesian and monetarist theories can change aggregate demand. A multiplier effect makes aggregate demand change by more than any initial change in one of its components. The money wage rate can be viewed as responding to changes in the expected price level. Even if the money wage is flexible, it will change only to the extent that price level expectations change. As a result, the money wage rate will adjust gradually.

Although in all three types of business cycle theory that we've considered, the cycle is caused by fluctuations in aggregate demand, the possibility that an occasional aggregate supply shock might occur is not ruled out. A recession could occur because aggregate supply falls. For example, a widespread drought that cuts agricultural production could cause a recession in an economy that has a large agricultural sector. But these aggregate demand theories of the cycle regard aggregate supply shocks as rare rather than normal events. Aggregate demand fluctuations are the normal ongoing sources of fluctuations.

REVIEW QUIZ

- What, according to Keynesian theory, causes the business cycle? What are the roles of *animal spirits*, the multiplier, and sticky money wages in this theory?
- What, according to monetarist theory, causes the business cycle? What are the roles of the Fed and the money supply in this theory?
- What, according to new classical theory and new Keynesian theory, causes the business cycle? What are the roles of rational expectations and unanticipated fluctuations in aggregate demand in these theories?
- What are the differences between the new classical theory and the new Keynesian theory concerning the money wage rate over the business cycle?

A new theory of the business cycle challenges the mainstream and traditional aggregate demand theories that you've just studied. It is called the real business cycle theory. Let's look at this new cycle theory.

Real Business Cycle Theory

THE NEWEST THEORY OF THE BUSINESS CYCLE, known as **real business cycle theory** (or RBC theory), regards random fluctuations in productivity as the main source of economic fluctuations. These productivity fluctuations are assumed to result mainly from fluctuations in the pace of technological change, but they might also have other sources such as international disturbances, climate fluctuations, or natural disasters. The origins of real business cycle theory can be traced to the rational expectations revolution set off by Robert E. Lucas, Jr., but the first demonstration of the power of this theory was given by Edward Prescott and Finn Kydland and by John Long and Charles Plosser. Today, real business cycle theory is part of a broad research agenda called *dynamic general equilibrium analysis*, and hundreds of young macroeconomists do research on this topic.

Like our study of the aggregate demand theories, we'll explore RBC theory by looking first at its impulse and second at the mechanism that converts that impulse into a cycle in real GDP.

The RBC Impulse

The *impulse* in RBC theory is the *growth rate of productivity* that results from *technological change*. RBC theorists believe this impulse to be generated mainly by the process of research and development that leads to the creation and use of new technologies. Most of the time, technological change is steady and productivity grows at a moderate pace. But sometimes productivity growth speeds up and occasionally productivity *decreases*—labor becomes less productive, on the average.

A period of rapid productivity growth brings a strong business cycle expansion and a *decrease* in productivity triggers a recession.

It is easy to understand why technological change brings productivity growth. But how does it *decrease* productivity? All technological change eventually increases productivity. But if initially, technological change makes a sufficient amount of existing capital, especially human capital, obsolete, productivity temporarily decreases. At such a time, more jobs are destroyed than created and more businesses fail than start up.

FIGURE 17.6
The Real Business Cycle Impulse

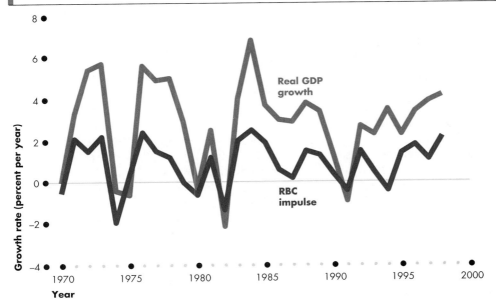

The real business cycle is caused by changes in technology that bring fluctuations in the growth rate of productivity. The fluctuations in productivity growth shown here are calculated by using growth accounting (the one third rule) to remove the contribution of capital accumulation to productivity growth. Productivity fluctuations are correlated with real GDP fluctuations. Economists are not sure what the productivity variable actually measures or what causes it to fluctuate.

Source: *Economic Report of the President, 1999,* and the author's calculations.

To isolate the RBC theory impulse, economists use growth accounting, which is explained in Chapter 11, pp. 233–236. Figure 17.6 shows the RBC impulse for the United States from 1970 to 1998. You can see that fluctuations in productivity growth are correlated with real GDP fluctuations. But this RBC impulse variable is a catch-all and no one knows what it actually measures or what causes it to fluctuate.

The RBC Mechanism

According to RBC theory, two immediate effects follow from a change in productivity that get an expansion or a contraction going:

1. Investment demand changes.
2. The demand for labor changes.

We'll study these effects and their consequences during a recession. In an expansion, they work in the direction opposite to what is described here.

Technological change makes some existing capital obsolete and temporarily decreases productivity. Firms expect the future profits to fall and see their labor productivity falling. With lower profit expectations, they cut back their purchases of new capital, and with lower labor productivity, they plan to lay off some workers. So the initial effect of a temporary fall in productivity is a decrease in investment demand and a decrease in the demand for labor.

Figure 17.7 illustrates these two initial effects of a decrease in productivity. Part (a) shows investment demand, ID, and saving supply, SS (both of which are explained in Chapter 10, pp. 209–210 and 213–214). Initially, investment demand is ID_0 and the equilibrium investment and saving are $1 trillion at a real interest rate of 6 percent a year. A decrease in productivity decreases investment demand and the ID curve shifts leftward to ID_1. The real interest rate falls to 4 percent, and investment and saving decrease to $0.7 trillion.

Part (b) shows the demand for labor, LD, and the supply of labor, LS (which are explained in Chapter 9, pp. 185–190). Initially, the demand for labor is LD_0, and equilibrium employment is 200 billion hours a year at a real wage rate of $15 an hour. The decrease in productivity decreases the demand for labor, and the LD curve shifts leftward to LD_1.

Before we can determine the new level of employment and real wage rate, we need to take a ripple effect into account—the key ripple effect in RBC theory.

The Key Decision: When to Work? According to RBC theory, people decide *when* to work by doing a cost-benefit calculation. They compare the return from working in the current period with the *expected* return from working in a later period. You make such a comparison every day in school. Suppose your goal in this course is to get an A. To achieve this goal, you work pretty hard most of the time. But during the few days before the midterm and final exams, you work especially hard. Why? Because you believe that the return from studying close to the exam is greater than the return from studying when the exam is a long time away. So during the term, you take time off for the movies and other leisure pursuits, but at exam time, you work every evening and weekend.

Real business cycle theory says that workers behave like you. They work fewer hours, sometimes zero hours, when the real wage rate is temporarily low, and they work more hours when the real wage rate is temporarily high. But to properly compare the current wage rate with the expected future wage rate, workers must use the real interest rate. If the real interest rate is 6 percent a year, a real wage of $1 an hour earned this week will become $1.06 a year from now. If the real wage rate is expected to be $1.05 an hour next year, today's real wage of $1 looks good. By working longer hours now and shorter hours a year from now, a person can get a 1 percent higher real wage rate. But suppose the real interest rate is 4 percent a year. In this case, $1 earned now is worth $1.04 next year. Working fewer hours now and more next year is the way to get a 1 percent higher real wage rate.

So the when-to-work decision depends on the real interest rate. The lower the real interest rate, other things remaining the same, the smaller is the supply of labor. Many economists believe this *intertemporal substitution* effect to be of negligible size. RBC theorists believe that the effect is large, and it is the key element in the RBC mechanism.

You saw in Fig. 17.7(a) that the decrease in investment demand lowers the real interest rate. This fall in the real interest rate lowers the return to current work and decreases the supply of labor. In Fig. 17.7(b), the labor supply curve shifts leftward to LS_1. The effect of a productivity shock on the demand for labor is larger than the effect of the fall in the real interest rate on the supply of labor. That is, the LD curve shifts farther leftward than does the LS curve. As a result, the real wage rate falls to $14.50 an hour and the level of employment falls to 195 billion hours. A recession has begun and is intensifying.

FIGURE 17.7

Capital and Labor Markets in a Real Business Cycle

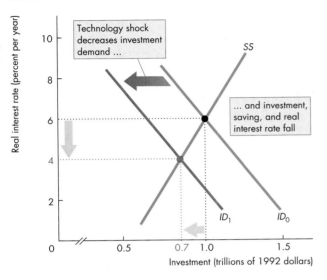

(a) Investment, saving, and interest rate

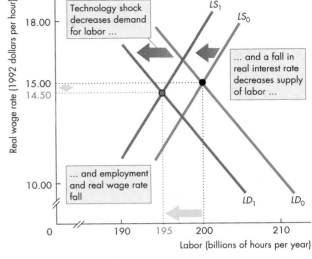

(b) Labor and wage rate

Saving supply is *SS* (part a), and initially, investment demand is ID_0. The real interest rate is 6 percent, and saving and investment are $1 trillion. In the labor market (part b), the demand for labor is LD_0 and the supply of labor is LS_0. The real wage rate is $15 an hour, and employment is 200 billion hours. A technological change temporarily decreases productivity, and both investment demand and the demand for labor decrease.

The two demand curves shift leftward to ID_1 and LD_1. In part (a), the real interest rate falls to 4 percent a year and investment and saving decrease. In part (b), the fall in the real interest rate decreases the supply of labor (the when-to-work decision) and the supply curve shifts leftward to LS_1. Employment falls to 195 billion hours, and the real wage rate falls to $14.50 an hour. A recession is under way.

Real GDP and the Price Level The next part of the RBC story traces the consequences of the changes you've just seen for real GDP and the price level. With a decrease in employment, aggregate supply decreases, and with a decrease in investment demand, aggregate demand decreases. Figure 17.8 illustrates these effects, using the *AS-AD* framework. Initially, the long-run aggregate supply curve is LAS_0, and the aggregate demand curve is AD_0. The price level is 110, and real GDP is $7 trillion. There is no short-run aggregate supply curve in this figure because in RBC theory, the *SAS* curve has no meaning. The labor market moves relentlessly toward its equilibrium, and the money wage rate adjusts freely (either upward or downward) to ensure that the real wage rate keeps the quantity of labor demanded equal to the quantity supplied. In RBC theory, unemployment is always

at the natural rate, and the natural rate fluctuates over the business cycle because the amount of job search fluctuates.

The decrease in employment decreases total production and aggregate supply decreases. The *LAS* curve shifts leftward to LAS_1. The decrease in investment demand decreases aggregate demand, and the *AD* curve shifts leftward to AD_1. The price level falls to 107, and real GDP decreases to $6.8 trillion. The economy has gone through a recession.

What Happened to Money? The name *real* business cycle theory is no accident. It reflects the central prediction of the theory. Real things, not nominal or monetary things, cause the business cycle. If the quantity of money changes, aggregate demand changes. But if there is no real change—with no

FIGURE 17.8

AS-AD in a Real
Business Cycle

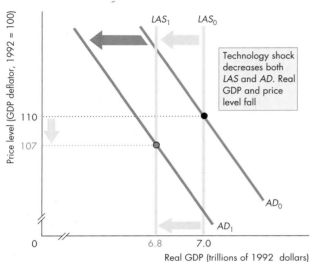

Initially, the long-run aggregate supply curve is LAS_0 and the aggregate demand curve is AD_0. Real GDP is $7 trillion (which equals potential GDP), and the price level is 110. There is no *SAS* curve in the real business cycle theory because the money wage rate is flexible. The technological change described in Fig. 17.7 temporarily decreases potential GDP, and the *LAS* curve shifts leftward to LAS_1. The fall in investment demand decreases aggregate demand, and the AD curve shifts leftward to AD_1. Real GDP decreases to $6.8 trillion, and the price level falls to 107. The economy has gone into recession.

change in the use of resources and no change in potential GDP—the change in money changes only the price level. In real business cycle theory, this outcome occurs because the aggregate supply curve is the *LAS* curve, which pins real GDP down at potential GD. So when *AD* changes, only the price level changes.

Cycles and Growth The shock that drives the business cycle of RBC theory is the same as the force that generates economic growth: technological change. On the average, as technology advances, productivity grows. But it grows at an uneven pace. You saw this fact when you studied growth accounting in Chapter

11. There, we focused on slow-changing trends in productivity growth. Real business cycle theory uses the same idea but says that there are frequent shocks to productivity that are mostly positive but that are occasionally negative.

Criticisms of Real Business Cycle Theory

RBC theory is controversial, and when economists discuss it, they often generate more heat than light. Its detractors claim that its basic assumptions are just too incredible. Money wages *are* sticky, they claim, so to assume otherwise is at odds with a clear fact. Intertemporal substitution is too weak, they say, to account for large fluctuations in labor supply and employment with small real wage changes.

But what really kills the RBC story, say most economists, is an implausible impulse. Technology shocks are not capable of creating the swings in productivity that growth accounting reveals. These swings in productivity are caused by something, they concede, but they are as likely to be caused by *changes in aggregate demand* as by technology. If the fluctuations in productivity are caused by aggregate demand fluctuations, then the traditional demand theories are needed to explain them. Fluctuations in productivity do not cause the cycle but are caused by it!

Building on this theme, the critics point out that the so-called productivity fluctuations that growth accounting measures are correlated with changes in the growth rate of money and other indicators of changes in aggregate demand.

Defense of Real Business Cycle Theory

The defenders of RBC theory claim that the theory works. It explains the macroeconomic facts about the business cycle and is consistent with the facts about economic growth. In effect, a single theory explains *both growth and cycles*. The growth accounting exercise that explains slowly changing trends also explains the more frequent business cycle swings. Its defenders also claim that RBC theory is consistent with a wide range of *micro*economic evidence about labor supply decisions, labor demand and investment demand decisions, and information on the distribution of income between labor and capital.

RBC theorists acknowledge that money and the business cycle are correlated. That is, rapid money growth and expansion go together, and slow money growth and recession go together. But, they argue, causation does not run from money to real GDP as the traditional aggregate demand theories state. Instead, they view causation as running from real GDP to money—so-called reverse causation. In a recession, the initial fall in investment demand that lowers the interest rate decreases the demand for bank loans and lowers the profitability of banking. So banks increase their reserves and decrease their loans. The quantity of bank deposits and hence the quantity of money decrease. This reverse causation is responsible for the correlation between money growth and real GDP according to real business cycle theory.

Its defenders also argue that the RBC view is significant because it at least raises the possibility that the business cycle is efficient. The business cycle does not signal an economy that is misbehaving; it is business as usual. If this view is correct, it means that policy designed to smooth the cycle is misguided. Only by taking out the peaks can the troughs be smoothed out. But peaks are bursts of investment to take advantage of new technologies in a timely way. So smoothing the cycle means delaying the benefits of new technologies.

R E V I E W   Q U I Z

- What, according to real business cycle theory, causes the business cycle? What is the role of fluctuations in the rate of technological change?
- How, according to real business cycle theory, does a fall in productivity growth influence investment demand, the real interest rate, the demand for labor, the supply of labor, employment, and the real wage rate?
- How, according to real business cycle theory, does a fall in productivity growth influence long-run aggregate supply, aggregate demand, real GDP, and the price level?

You've now reviewed the main theories of the business cycle. Your next task is to examine some actual business cycles. In pursuing this task, we will focus on the recession phase of the cycle. We'll do this mainly because it is the recessions that cause the most trouble. We begin by looking at two recent recessions.

Recessions and Expansions During the 1990s

THE 1990s HAVE BROUGHT SOME INTERESTING business cycle experience. In the United States, we had a brief recession during 1990–1991 followed by a period of sustained and at times rapid expansion. In contrast, Japan experienced a decade of slow growth and ended the decade in serious recession. In 1999, while the three fifths of the global economy that includes the United States, Canada, and Western Europe continued to expand vigorously, the other two fifths that includes Japan, some other East Asian countries, and Central Europe was in recession.

In the theories of the business cycle that you've studied, recessions and expansions can be triggered by a variety of forces, some on the aggregate demand side and some on the aggregate supply side. We'll study the shocks that triggered and the processes at work during some of these 1990s episodes. We'll focus on three situations:

- The U.S. recession of 1990–1991
- The U.S. expansion of the 1990s
- The Japanese recession

The U.S. Recession of 1990–1991

At the beginning of 1990, the U.S. economy was at full employment. The unemployment rate was just above 5 percent, and inflation was steady at 4 percent a year. But the events of 1990 disturbed this situation and ended what was then the longest peacetime expansion in U.S. history.

External Shock: The Gulf Crisis   The dominant event of 1990 was a political and military crisis in the Persian Gulf. Iraq's president Saddam Hussein invaded Kuwait, and the United States responded with massive air strikes against Iraq. The Gulf Crisis, as it was known, brought shocks to both aggregate demand and aggregate supply.

The main aggregate demand shock was a decrease in investment. The Gulf Crisis increased uncertainty and lowered expected sales and profits. Investment decreased between 1990 and 1991 by $80 billion. The decrease in investment brought an even greater decrease in aggregate demand because of the multiplier effect on consumption expenditure.

On the supply side, the Gulf Crisis threw the world energy markets into turmoil. Between April 1990 and October 1990, the price of crude oil more than doubled. This oil price increase also led to increases in the prices of other fuels and raw materials, and it decreased short-run aggregate supply.

Fiscal Policy and Monetary Policy   There were no major fiscal policy or monetary policy shocks to trigger the recession. Government purchases increased slightly to cope with the military consequences of the crisis. But this effect was small. Tax revenues decreased and the deficit increased as the normal automatic stabilizers began to operate (see Chapter 13, p. 292).

Monetary policy was unremarkable. The Fed slowed the M2 money growth rate from 4 percent in 1990 to 3 percent in 1991, but real interest rates were lowered. So if monetary policy played a role in this recession, it was in the direction of moderating it.

Aggregate Demand and Aggregate Supply   Figure 17.9 shows the events that started the 1990–1991 recession. In mid-1990, the economy was on aggregate demand curve AD_{90} and short-run aggregate supply curve SAS_{90} with real GDP at $6.14 trillion and the GDP deflator at 94. By mid-1991, the short-run aggregate supply curve had shifted to SAS_{91} and investment uncertainty had shifted the aggregate demand curve to AD_{91}. Real GDP had decreased to $6.08 trillion. The GDP deflator increased to 97, but the inflation rate slowed slightly from 4.3 percent a year in 1990 to 4 percent a year in 1991 and to 2.8 percent a year during 1992.

Labor Market and Productivity   As real GDP decreased, so did employment and aggregate hours. Unemployment increased, but the real wage rate did not change much. Labor productivity growth slowed to about half a percent and overall productivity decreased by more than half a percent during 1991.

After just eight months of contraction, the 1990s recession was over and the economy was expanding again.

The U.S. Expansion of the 1990s

By the end of 1998, the U.S. economy had completed 94 months of uninterrupted expansion and looked set to break the all-time record of 106 months recorded during the 1960s. Real GDP had grown by

FIGURE 17.9

The 1990–1991 Recession

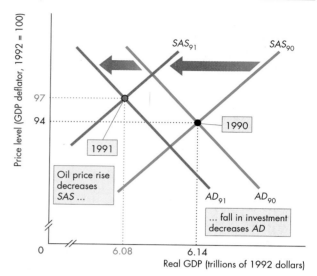

In 1990, the economy was on its aggregate demand curve, AD_{90}, and its short-run aggregate supply curve, SAS_{90}, with real GDP at $6.14 trillion and a GDP deflator of 94. A large increase in oil prices decreased aggregate supply and shifted the short-run aggregate supply curve to SAS_{91}. Uncertainty surrounding the world economy lowered profit expectations, leading to a fall in investment and a decrease in aggregate demand. The aggregate demand curve shifted to AD_{91}. The combination of a decrease in both aggregate supply and aggregate demand puts the economy into recession.

23 percent during this period. What caused this long and strong expansion?

Productivity Growth in the Information Age   The most significant feature of the 1990s was an explosion in the use of the computer. The growth of the Internet is the single most visible consequence of this explosion. But it is just one of many transformations of economic life that has occurred during the 1990s.

The personal computer has changed the way we write, keep financial and other records, and communicate with each other. The microprocessor has revolutionized the way we listen to music, drive a car, use a camera, make a microwave dinner, and check out at the supermarket. It has revolutionized even more the way firms produce goods and services.

But the computer and related technologies are not the whole technological story of the 1990s. Biotechnology changed from being primarily a research activity to a commercial activity in this decade. It was also a decade in which personal services expanded enormously.

All this technological change created profit opportunities but required a large amount of investment to realize those profits. Also, most of the world shared in this technological revolution. And its global nature brought a large increase in U.S. exports.

Between 1991 and 1998, investment increased from $740 billion to $1,332 billion and exports increased from $600 billion to $985 billion (all 1992 dollars). An expansion of aggregate expenditure of this magnitude—almost a trillion dollars—with its multiplier effect on consumption expenditure brought a large increase in aggregate demand.

It also brought a correspondingly large increase in aggregate supply. The capital stock increased by almost $3 trillion (or almost 20 percent), and employment increased by more than 20 billion hours a year (or about 10 percent).

Fiscal Policy and Monetary Policy   The expansion of the 1990s was to some degree made possible by the fiscal policy and monetary policy that accompanied it. The expansion was not caused by these policies, but they encouraged sustained real GDP growth.

Fiscal policy was restrained throughout the expansion. Government purchases of goods and services remained almost constant. Tax revenues increased early in the expansion because of a 1993 tax bill that increased some tax rates. But most of the rising tax revenues and falling transfer payments resulted from the growing economy. The result was that a deficit of $280 billion in 1992 was transformed into a surplus of $75 billion in 1998.

Monetary policy encouraged the expansion. The Fed kept the quantity of money (M2) growing at a low but steady rate that lowered inflation and interest rates throughout the expansion.

Aggregate Demand and Aggregate Supply During the Expansion   Figure 17.10 shows the 1990s expansion using the *AS-AD* model. In 1991, the economy was on aggregate demand curve AD_{91} and short-run aggregate supply curve SAS_{91} with real GDP at $6.08 trillion and the GDP deflator at 97. The long-run

aggregate supply curve was LAS_{91}, and potential GDP exceeded real GDP. There was a recessionary gap. By 1998, capital accumulation, increased labor hours, and technological change had increased potential GDP to $7.6 trillion and the long-run aggregate supply curve had shifted to LAS_{98}. The large increase in investment demand and exports with their multiplier effects increased aggregate demand and the aggregate demand curve shifted to AD_{98}.

The increase in potential GDP increased short-run aggregate supply, but higher money wages decreased short-run aggregate supply. The net effect of these effects was a small decrease in short-run aggregate supply to SAS_{98}. Real GDP increased to $7.6 trillion—equal to potential GDP—and the price level increased to 113.

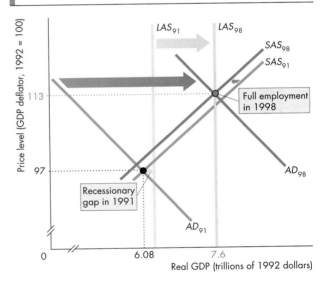

FIGURE 17.10

The 1990s Expansion

In 1991, the economy was on its aggregate demand curve, AD_{91}, and its short-run aggregate supply curve, SAS_{91}, with real GDP at $6.08 trillion and a GDP deflator of 97. Potential GDP (the *LAS* curve) exceeded real GDP by a recessionary gap. Technological advances increased both aggregate demand and aggregate supply. The aggregate demand curve shifted to AD_{98}, the long-run aggregate supply curve shifted to LAS_{98}, and the short-run aggregate supply curve shifted to SAS_{98}, The result of these shifts was an increase in real GDP to $7.6 trillion (equal to potential GDP) and an increase in the price level to 113.

A Real Business Cycle Expansion Phase   The description of the expansion of the 1990s that we've just reviewed looks exactly like the events that real business cycle theory predicts. A strong and sustained burst of technological change brought rising productivity. The result was an increase in investment demand, an increase in the demand for labor, and an increase in the supply of labor. The real interest rate increased, and the real wage rate increased but only slightly.

The expansion in the demand for labor and supply of labor brought a falling unemployment rate. The lower unemployment rate is a lower *natural* rate, not a sign that the economy is overheating.

The Stock Market During the Expansion   The U.S. stock market enjoyed extraordinary growth during the 1990s expansion. The real stock price (the Dow Jones Industrial Average corrected for inflation) increased moderately through 1994. It then exploded. Between 1995 and 1998, real stock prices increased by 130 percent.

The explanation for this huge increase in stock prices is not known with certainty. Some people believe it shows what Fed Chairman Alan Greenspan called "irrational exuberance." But it is possible to rationalize such a large stock price increase as the consequence of people believing that the trend growth rate of the economy has increased. If in 1994, people had been expecting a growth trend of 2 percent a year and if by the late 1990s they had revised this expectation upward to 4 percent a year, a more than doubling of stock prices would be feasible. But whether such a growth rate expectation is realistic is another matter.

While the U.S. economy continued to enjoy its longest peacetime expansion, some economies across the Pacific Ocean were in trouble. One that was in special trouble is Asia's largest economy, Japan. Let's look at the Japanese business cycle during the 1990s.

The Japanese Recession

Between 1992 and 1998, when real GDP in the United States expanded by more than 20 percent, Japan's real GDP expanded by a mere 6 percent—a growth rate of only 0.7 percent per year. By 1998, real GDP in Japan was shrinking at a near 5 percent annual rate.

Why did Japan experience such a low rate of economic growth during the 1990s and a recession in 1998? Several factors seem to have combined to produce Japan's problems. And these factors together with the fiscal policies and monetary policies that Japan has pursued provide valuable information about the validity of the alternative theories of the business cycle that you studied earlier in this chapter.

The main factors that contributed to Japan's weak economy and ultimate recession were:

- Collapse of asset prices
- Fiscal policy
- Monetary policy
- Structural rigidities

Collapse of Asset Prices   During the second half of the 1980s, land prices and stock prices in Japan increased *threefold*. This increase was much larger than that in the United States and Europe. Asset prices increased for three main reasons.

First, investors believed that Japan's medium-term and long-term prospects were bright. Second, financial deregulation brought an increase of foreign investment into Japan. Japan's banks expanded loans to finance the purchase of assets whose prices were rising. Third, the Bank of Japan (the nation's central bank) lowered interest rates between 1985 and 1987 and permitted a rapid growth rate of money. The motivation for rapid monetary expansion was to prevent the yen from rising against the U.S. dollar in the foreign exchange market. (See Chapter 20, pp. 476–477 for an explanation of how monetary policy influences the foreign exchange rate.)

Asset prices collapsed in 1990. And the collapse created a wealth effect. Saving and consumption were not much affected by the decrease in wealth. But investment expenditure decreased sharply, and so did aggregate demand. With a lower investment rate, the capital stock and potential GDP grew more slowly.

Fiscal Policy   From 1991 through 1996, Japan pursued ambitious and substantial fiscal policies to stimulate the economy. In 1991, the government of Japan had a budget surplus equal to 3 percent of GDP. By 1996, this surplus had been transformed into a deficit equal to more than 7 percent of GDP. Six major *discretionary* actions occurred, which are detailed in Table 17.1, that added 12.9 percent to aggregate expenditure. With its associated multiplier effects, this represents an enormous increase in aggregate demand relative to what it would have been in the absence of stimulation. But the stimulation was not persistent during the 1990s.

The removal of temporary tax cuts and cuts in government investment expenditures *lowered* aggregate expenditure by 3 percent of real GDP in 1996–1997. This fiscal policy tightening decreased aggregate demand and contributed to the recession of 1998.

TABLE 17.1
Fiscal Stimulation in Japan

Date proposed	Total stimulation (percent of GDP)
August 1992	2.3
April 1993	2.8
September 1993	1.3
February 1994	3.2
September 1995	3.0
Mid-1996–mid-1997	−3.0
April 1998	3.3
Total	**12.9**

FIGURE 17.11
Japan's Sliding Growth Rate

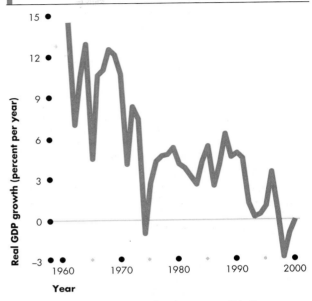

Japan's economic growth rate has been on a slide for many years. Growth of 10 percent a year during the 1960s was followed by growth of 4 percent a year during the 1970s and 1980s and by less than 1 percent a year during the 1990s.

Source: The Penn World Table: An Expanded Set of International Comparisons, 1950–1988, *Quarterly Journal of Economics,* May 1991, 327–368. 1993-1998, International Monetary Fund, *World Economic Outlook* (Washington D.C., October 1998).

Monetary Policy The Bank of Japan lowered its official interest rate (called the official discount rate, or ODR) from 6 percent in 1991 to 1.75 percent by the end of 1993 and to 0.5 percent by 1995. The ODR has remained at this level since 1995. Despite these large cuts in interest rates, a lower inflation rate meant that the real interest rate did not fall as much and so did not act as a stimulus to investment. Also, a strong yen limited the growth of export demand.

Since 1996, a weaker yen and lower real short-term interest rates have had a small but positive effect on aggregate demand in Japan.

Structural Problems Market distortions in agriculture, transportation, retail and wholesale trades, and construction that protect inefficient farms and firms create a lack of competition and low productivity growth. Rich countries such as the United States, Canada, and those in Western Europe have experienced a process of de-industrialization as manufacturing processes have migrated to poorer countries and have been replaced by rapid expansion in the service sector. Japan has not shared this experience.

This aspect of Japan's economy goes to the core of the real business cycle explanation for fluctuations: fluctuations in the productivity growth rate. When viewed on the longer-term context, this factor might have been slowing Japan's growth rate for many years. Figure 17.11 shows Japan's steadily declining growth rate. Slower productivity growth works through the real business cycle mechanism described earlier in this chapter.

REVIEW QUIZ

- What events triggered the 1990–1991 recession in the United States? What role was played by external shocks and by policy? What mechanisms translated the shocks into a recession?
- What factors brought the long and strong expansion in the United States during the 1990s?
- What factors contributed to the slow growth and eventual recession in Japan during the 1990s?

You've now seen how business cycle theory can be used to interpret recessions and expansions during the 1990s. But can we use business cycle theory to explain the greatest of recessions—the Great Depression? Let's find out.

The Great Depression

THE LATE 1920s WERE YEARS OF ECONOMIC boom. New houses and apartments were built on an unprecedented scale, new firms were created, and the capital stock of the nation expanded. At the beginning of 1929, U.S. real GDP exceeded potential GDP and the unemployment rate was a low 3.2 percent. But as that eventful year unfolded, increasing signs of economic weakness began to appear. The most dramatic events occurred in October when the stock market collapsed, losing more than one third of its value in two weeks. The four years that followed were years of monstrous economic depression.

Figure 17.12 shows the dimensions of the Great Depression. On the eve of the Great Depression in 1929, the economy was on aggregate demand curve AD_{29} and short-run aggregate supply curve SAS_{29}. Real GDP was $1,028 billion (1992 dollars), and the GDP deflator was 15.

In 1930, there was a widespread expectation that the price level would fall, and the money wage rate fell. With a lower money wage rate, the short-run aggregate supply curve shifted from SAS_{29} to SAS_{30}. But increased pessimism and uncertainty decreased investment and the demand for consumer durables, and aggregate demand decreased to AD_{30}. In 1930, real GDP decreased to $936 billion (a 9 percent decrease) and the price level fell to 14.6 (a 3 percent fall).

In a normal recession, the economy might have remained below full employment for a year or so and then started to expand. But the recession of 1930 was not a normal one. In 1930 and the next two years, the economy was further bombarded with huge negative demand shocks (the sources of which we'll look at in a moment). The aggregate demand curve shifted leftward all the way to AD_{33}. With a depressed economy, the price level was expected to fall and wages fell in line with those expectations. The money wage fell from 55¢ an hour in 1930 to 44¢ an hour by 1933. As a result of lower wages, the aggregate supply curve shifted from SAS_{30} to SAS_{33}. But the size of the shift of the short-run aggregate supply curve was much less than the decrease in aggregate demand. As a result, the aggregate demand curve and the short-run aggregate supply curve intersected in 1933 at a real GDP of $734 billion (a decrease of 29 percent from 1929) and a GDP deflator of 11.4 (a decrease of 24 percent from 1929).

FIGURE 17.12

The Great Depression

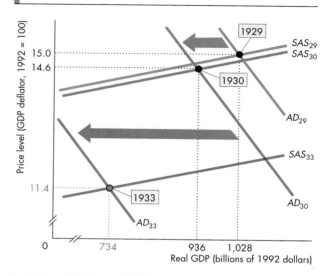

In 1929, real GDP was $1,028 billion and the GDP deflator was 15—at the intersection of AD_{29} and SAS_{29}. Increased pessimism and uncertainty resulted in a decrease in investment and aggregate demand decreased to AD_{30}. The money wage rate decreased, so the short-run aggregate supply curve shifted to SAS_{30}. Real GDP and the price level fell. In the next three years, decreases in the money supply and investment decreased aggregate demand, shifting the aggregate demand curve to AD_{33}. Again, to some degree, the decrease in aggregate demand was anticipated, so wages fell and the short-run aggregate supply curve shifted to SAS_{33}. By 1933, real GDP had fallen to $734 billion (71 percent of its 1929 level) and the GDP deflator had fallen to 11.4 (76 percent of its 1929 level).

Although the Great Depression brought enormous hardship, the distribution of that hardship was uneven. Twenty-five percent of the work force had no jobs at all. Also at that time, there were virtually no organized social security and unemployment programs in place. So for many families there was virtually no income. But the pocketbooks of those who kept their jobs barely noticed the Great Depression. It is true that wages fell from 57¢ an hour in 1929 to 44¢ an hour in 1933. But at the same time, the price level fell by a larger percentage, so real wages actually increased. Thus people who had jobs became better off during the Great Depression.

You can begin to appreciate the magnitude of the Great Depression if you compare it with the two recessions that we studied earlier in this chapter. Between 1973 and 1975, real GDP fell by 1.8 percent. From mid-1990 to mid-1991, it fell by 1.6 percent. A hypothetical 1999 Great Depression would lower real GDP by 30 percent, to less than its 1979 level.

Why the Great Depression Happened

The late 1920s were years of economic boom, but they were also years of increasing uncertainty. The main source of increased uncertainty was international. The world economy was going through tumultuous times. The patterns of world trade were changing as Britain, the traditional economic powerhouse of the world, began its period of relative economic decline and new economic powers such as Japan began to emerge. International currency fluctuations and the introduction of restrictive trade policies by many countries (see Chapter 19) further increased the uncertainty faced by firms. There was also domestic uncertainty arising from the fact that there had been such a strong boom in recent years, especially in the capital goods sector and housing. No one believed that this boom would last forever, but many people thought it had a lot farther to run and there was great uncertainty about how demand would change.

This environment of uncertainty led to a slowdown in consumer spending, especially on new homes and household appliances. By the fall of 1929, the uncertainty had reached a critical level and contributed to the stock market crash. The stock market crash, in turn, heightened people's fears about economic prospects in the foreseeable future. Fear fed fear. Investment collapsed. The building industry almost disappeared. An industry that had been operating flat out just two years earlier was now building virtually no new houses and apartments. It was this drop in investment and a drop in consumer spending on durables that led to the initial leftward shift of the aggregate demand curve from AD_{29} to AD_{30} in Fig. 17.12.

At this stage, what became the Great Depression was no worse than many previous recessions had been. What distinguishes the Great Depression from previous recessions are the events that followed between 1930 and 1933. But economists, even to

this day, have not come to agreement on how to interpret those events. One view, argued by Peter Temin,[1] is that spending continued to fall for a wide variety of reasons—including a continuation of increasing pessimism and uncertainty. According to Temin's view, the continued contraction resulted from a collapse of expenditure that was independent of the decrease in the quantity of money. The investment demand curve shifted leftward. Milton Friedman and Anna J. Schwartz have argued that the continuation of the contraction was almost exclusively the result of the subsequent worsening of financial and monetary conditions.[2] According to Friedman and Schwartz, it was a severe cut in the money supply that lowered aggregate demand, prolonging the contraction and deepening the depression.

Although there is disagreement about the causes of the contraction phase of the Great Depression, the disagreement is not about the elements at work but about the degree of importance attached to each. Everyone agrees that increased pessimism and uncertainty lowered investment demand, and everyone agrees that there was a massive contraction of the real money supply. Temin and his supporters assign primary importance to the fall in autonomous expenditure and secondary importance to the fall in the money supply. Friedman and Schwartz and their supporters assign primary responsibility to the money supply and regard the other factors as being of limited importance.

Let's look at the contraction of aggregate demand a bit more closely. Between 1930 and 1933, the nominal money supply decreased by 20 percent. This decrease in the money supply was not directly induced by the Fed's actions. The *monetary base* (currency in circulation and bank reserves) hardly fell at all. But the bank deposits component of the money supply suffered an enormous collapse. It did so primarily because a large number of banks failed. Before the Great Depression, fueled by increasing stock prices and booming business conditions, bank loans expanded. But after the stock market crash and the downturn, many borrowers found themselves in hard economic times. They could not pay the interest on

---

[1]Peter Temin, *Did Monetary Forces Cause the Great Depression?* (New York: W. W. Norton, 1976).

[2]Milton Friedman and Anna J. Schwartz developed this explanation in *A Monetary History of the United States: 1867–1960* (Princeton, N.J.: Princeton University Press, 1963), Chapter 7.

their loans, and they could not meet the agreed repayment schedules. Banks had deposits that exceeded the realistic value of the loans that they had made. When depositors withdrew funds from the banks, the banks lost reserves. Many of them simply couldn't meet their depositors' demands to be repaid.

Bank failures feed on themselves and create additional failures. Seeing banks fail, people become anxious to protect themselves and so take their money out of the banks. Such were the events of 1930. The quantity of notes and coins in circulation increased, and the volume of bank deposits declined. But the very action of taking money out of the bank to protect one's wealth accentuated the process of banking failure. Banks were increasingly short of cash and unable to meet their obligations.

What role did the stock market crash of 1929 play in producing the Great Depression? It certainly created an atmosphere of fear and panic and probably also contributed to the overall air of uncertainty that dampened investment spending. It also reduced the wealth of stockholders, encouraging them to cut back on their consumption spending. But the direct effect of the stock market crash on consumption, although a contributory factor to the Great Depression, was not the major source of the drop in aggregate demand. It was the collapse in investment arising from increased uncertainty that brought the 1930 decline in aggregate demand.

The stock market crash was a predictor of severe recession. It reflected the expectations of stockholders concerning future profit prospects. As those expectations became pessimistic, people sold their stocks. There were more sellers than buyers and the prices of stocks were bid lower and lower. That is, the behavior of the stock market was a consequence of expectations about future profitability, and those expectations were lowered as a result of increased uncertainty.

Can It Happen Again?

Because we have an incomplete understanding of the causes of the Great Depression, we cannot be sure whether such an event will happen again. The economic turmoil of the 1920s that preceded the Depression certainly can happen again. But there are some significant differences between the economy of the 1990s and that of the 1930s that make a severe depression much less likely today than it was 60 years ago. The most significant features of the economy

that make severe depression less likely today are:

- Bank deposit insurance
- The Fed's role as lender of last resort
- Taxes and government spending
- Multi-income families

Let's examine these in turn.

Bank Deposit Insurance   As a result of the Great Depression, the federal government established, in the 1930s, the Federal Deposit Insurance Corporation (FDIC). The FDIC insures bank deposits for up to $100,000 per deposit, so most depositors need no longer fear bank failure. If a bank fails, the FDIC pays the deposit holders. With federally insured bank deposits, the key event that turned a fairly ordinary recession into the Great Depression is most unlikely to occur. It was the fear of bank failure that caused people to withdraw their deposits from banks. The aggregate consequence of these individually rational acts was to cause the very bank failures that were feared. With deposit insurance, most depositors have nothing to lose if a bank fails and so have no incentive to take actions that are likely to give rise to that failure.

Some recent events reinforce this conclusion. With massive failures of S&Ls in the 1980s and with bank failures in New England in 1990 and 1991, there was no tendency for depositors to panic and withdraw their funds in a self-reinforcing run on similar institutions.

Lender of Last Resort   The Fed is the lender of last resort in the U.S. economy. If a single bank is short of reserves, it can borrow reserves from other banks. If the entire banking system is short of reserves, banks can borrow from the Fed. By making reserves available (at a suitable interest rate), the Fed is able to make the quantity of reserves in the banking system respond flexibly to the demand for those reserves. Bank failure can be prevented, or at least contained to cases in which bad management practices are the source of the problem. Widespread failures of the type that occurred in the Great Depression can be prevented.

It is now generally agreed that the Fed made a serious mistake in its handling of monetary policy during the Great Depression. With one eye on the international situation, the Fed *increased* the discount rate sharply from 1.5 percent to 3.5 percent just when the banks needed to borrow more. It was only long after the event, when Friedman and Schwartz examined the contraction years of the Great Depression, that economists came to realize that the Fed would have had to *decrease* the discount rate and *increase* the monetary base to have prevented the intensification of the contraction. Now that this lesson has been learned and there is such widespread agreement about the matter, there is at least some chance that the mistake will not be repeated.

The last time the Fed was confronted by a similar problem, though on a much smaller scale, was in October 1987. At that time, a severe stock market crash triggered fears of a new Great Depression. The Fed Chairman, Alan Greenspan, told the U.S. banking and financial community that the Fed had both the ability and the intent to maintain calm financial conditions and to supply sufficient reserves to ensure that the banking system did not begin to contract.

Taxes and Government Spending   The government sector was a much smaller part of the economy in 1929 than it has become today. On the eve of that earlier recession, government purchases of goods and services were less than 9 percent of GDP. Today, government purchases exceed 20 percent of GDP. Government transfer payments were less than 6 percent of GDP in 1929. Today, they exceed 15 percent of GDP.

A larger level of government purchases of goods and services means that when recession hits, a large component of aggregate demand does not decline. But government transfer payments are the most sensitive economic stabilizer. When the economy goes into recession and depression, more people qualify for unemployment benefits and social security. As a consequence, although disposable income decreases, the extent of the decrease is moderated by the existence of such programs. Consumption expenditure, in turn, does not decline by as much as it would in the absence of such government programs. The limited decline in consumption spending further limits the overall decrease in aggregate expenditure, thereby limiting the magnitude of an economic downturn.

Multi-Income Families   At the time of the Great Depression, families with more than one wage earner were much less common than they are today. The labor force participation rate in 1929 was around 55 percent. Today, it is 67 percent. Thus even if the unemployment rate increased to around 25 percent today, close to 50 percent of the adult population would actually have jobs. During the Great Depression, less than 40 percent of the adult population had work. Multi-income families have greater security than single-income families do. The chance of both (or all) income earners in a family losing their jobs simultaneously is much lower than the chance of a single earner losing work. With greater family income security, family consumption is likely to be less sensitive to fluctuations in family income that are seen as temporary. Thus when aggregate income falls, it might not induce a cut in consumption. For example, during the OPEC recession, as real GDP fell, personal consumption expenditure actually increased. In 1990–1991, when real GDP fell by $60 billion, consumption expenditure fell by only $26 billion.

For the four reasons we have just reviewed, it appears that the economy has better shock-absorbing characteristics today than it had in the 1920s and 1930s. Even if there is a collapse of confidence, leading to a fall in investment, today's shock absorbers will not translate that initial shock into the large and prolonged fall in real GDP and rise in unemployment that occurred more than 60 years ago.

Because the economy is now more immune to severe recession than it was in the 1930s, even a stock market crash of the magnitude that occurred in 1987 had barely noticeable effects on spending. A crash of a similar magnitude in 1929 resulted in the near collapse of housing investment and consumer durable purchases. In the period following the 1987 stock market crash, investment and spending on durable goods hardly changed.

None of this is to say that there might not be a deep recession or even a Great Depression in the future. But it would take a very severe shock to trigger one.

◆ We have now completed our study of the business cycle. Analysts use the theories you have studied to try to forecast the next business cycle turning point. You can see an example of this activity in *Reading Between the Lines* on pp. 406–407.

We have also completed our study of the science of macroeconomics and learned about the influences on long-term economic growth and inflation as well as the business cycle. We have discovered that these issues pose huge policy challenges. How can we speed up the rate of economic growth while at the same time keeping inflation low and avoiding big swings of the business cycle? Our task in the next chapter is to study these macroeconomic policy challenges.

Is Japan Recovering?

DOW JONES NEWSWIRES, WSJ INTERACTIVE, APRIL 9, 1999

Japan Sticks to Economic Growth Forecast for 1999

TOKYO (AP)—Japan's top economic official on Friday stood by the government's forecast of 0.5% growth for the coming year, despite signs that the country is not close to pulling out of recession.

Japan's economy shrank 0.8% in the last three months of 1998, and is expected to have shrunk for the second year in a row when statistics for the fiscal year ended March 31 emerge.

Independent analysts expect the economy to shrink yet again in the fiscal year that just began.

But Taichi Sakaiya, the director general of Japan's Economic Planning Agency, said the government's record spending and tax-cut program would spur the economy.

"Although I can't say it absolutely, I have considerable confidence" that the official growth target of 0.5% will be reached this fiscal year, Sakaiya told reporters.

The administration of Prime Minister Keizo Obuchi has pledged to avoid three fiscal years in a row of contraction.

The economy shrank 0.4% in the 1997-98 fiscal year and is expected to shrink more than 2% in the just-ended fiscal year.

Also Friday, Takafusa Shioya, the deputy director-general of the Economic Planning Agency, said there would probably not be any major changes in the agency's assessment of the economy in its next monthly report.

In its March report, the EPA described conditions as "extremely severe," but said the economy's "downward movement continues to slow to a halt."

A string of Japanese government officials have voiced optimism about the economy recently, declaring that it had hit its lowest point and would now begin to recover from its worst recession since World War II.

Foreign Minister Masahiko Komura was quoted as telling a group of four U.S. congressmen Friday that the Japanese economy "is poised to bottom out and to move upward." ...

Essence of the Story

- Japan's real GDP shrank 0.4 percent* in the 1997–1998 fiscal year. (Japan's fiscal year runs from April 1 to March 31.) It is expected to shrink more than 2 percent in the 1998–1999 fiscal year.

- In April 1999, independent economic forecasters were predicting that Japan's real GDP would shrink yet again during the 1999–2000 fiscal year.

- But the Japanese government was committed to bringing an expansion in 1999–2000.

- Several Japanese government officials declared that real GDP had hit its lowest point and that Japan would begin to recover from its worst recession since World War II.

*The news article seems to misreport this number. According to the official data, the economy shrank by 3.6 percent (or almost 4 percent) during fiscal year 1997-1998. The economic analysis on the next page uses this corrected number.

■ Figure 1 shows how the Japanese economy got into its worst recession since World War II.

■ We'll assume that before the recession began, in the first quarter of 1997 (1997, Q1), the Japanese economy was at full employment. We'll use index numbers to measure both real GDP and the price level with bases of 100 in 1997, Q1.

■ In 1997, Q1, aggregate demand was AD_{97}, long-run aggregate supply was LAS_{97}, and short-run aggregate supply was SAS_{97}. The aggregate demand curve intersected the short-run aggregate supply curve at potential GDP on the long-run aggregate supply curve (by assumption).

■ During the next two years, asset prices crashed, decreasing wealth. The decrease in wealth brought a large decrease in investment. So the aggregate demand curve shifted leftward to AD_{99}.

■ At the same time, structural problems and widespread business failure decreased short-run aggregate supply. The short-run aggregate supply curve shifted leftward to SAS_{99}.

■ Real GDP decreased over the two-year period by 6 percent to 94. The price level remained constant.

■ Forecasts of where Japan is heading in 1999–2000 differ—but not by much.

■ Figure 2 shows the range of disagreement.

■ The Japanese government believes that it has done enough with tax cuts and spending increases (combined with the Bank of Japan's loose monetary policy) to make aggregate demand increase to AD_{00} (gov).

■ The government probably also believes that short-run aggregate supply will increase to SAS_{00} (gov).

■ If the government is correct, real GDP will increase during 1999 by about 0.5 percent.

■ Independent economic forecasters believe that aggregate demand in Japan will decrease further in 1999 but by a small amount. Their forecast is that aggregate demand will decrease to AD_{00} (ind).

■ These forecasters probably also believe that short-run aggregate supply will decrease to SAS_{00} (ind).

■ If the independent forecasters are correct, real GDP will decrease during 1999 by about 1 percent.

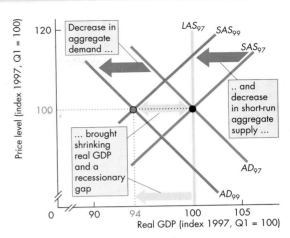

Figure 1   Japan goes into recession

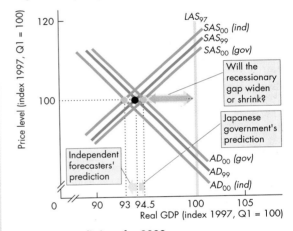

Figure 2   Predictions for 2000

■ Although the independent forecasters and the Japanese government disagree on the *direction* of change of real GDP during 1999, the disagreement about the year-end *level* is within 2 percentage points. This range of disagreement is small relative to the range of uncertainty in macroeconomic forecasts.

SUMMARY

KEY POINTS

Cycle Patterns, Impulses, and Mechanisms (pp. 384–386)

- Since 1920, there have been 15 recessions and expansions.
- The Great Depression was the most severe contraction of real GDP, and the postwar recessions have been milder than the prewar recessions.

Aggregate Demand Theories of the Business Cycle (pp. 386–392)

- Keynesian business cycle theory identifies volatile expectations about future sales and profits as the main source of economic fluctuations.
- Monetarist business cycle theory identifies fluctuations in the money stock as the main source of economic fluctuations.
- Rational expectations theory identifies unanticipated fluctuations in aggregate demand as the main source of economic fluctuations.

Real Business Cycle Theory (pp. 393–397)

- In real business cycle (RBC) theory, economic fluctuations are caused by fluctuations in the influence of technological change on productivity growth.
- A temporary slowdown in the pace of technological change decreases investment demand and both the demand for labor and supply of labor.

Recessions and Expansions During the 1990s (pp. 397–401)

- The 1990–1991 recession resulted from the Gulf Crisis, which increased the price of oil—a decrease in aggregate supply—and a decrease in investment—a decrease in aggregate demand.
- The 1990s expansion resulted from a large increase in the rate of productivity growth that increased investment demand and the demand for and supply of labor and that increased both aggregate demand and aggregate supply.

- The Japanese slowdown and recession of the 1990s were triggered by an asset price collapse combined with structural problems. Policy stimulation occurred, but it was not sufficient to prevent recession, and a tightening of fiscal policy in 1996 and 1997 contributed to the 1998 recession.

The Great Depression (pp. 402–405)

- The Great Depression started with increased uncertainty, which brought a fall in investment (especially in housing) and spending on consumer durables.
- There then followed a near total collapse of the financial system. Banks failed and the money supply fell, resulting in a continued fall in aggregate demand.
- The Great Depression itself produced a series of reforms that make a repeat of such a depression much less likely.

KEY FIGURES

KEY TERMS

PROBLEMS

Use the figure for all the problems.

*1. The figure shows the economy of Virtual Reality. When the economy is in a long-run equilibrium, it is at points *b*, *f*, and *j*. When a recession occurs in Virtual Reality, the economy moves away from these points to one of the two other points identified in each of the three parts of the figure.

   a. If the Keynesian theory is the correct explanation for the recession, to which points does the economy move?

   b. If the monetarist theory is the correct explanation for the recession, to which points does the economy move?

   c. If the new classical theory of the business cycle is the correct explanation for the recession, to which points does the economy move?

   d. If the new Keynesian theory of the business cycle is the correct explanation for the recession, to which points does the economy move?

   e. If real business cycle theory is the correct explanation for the recession, to which points does the economy move?

2. The figure shows the economy of Vital Signs. When the economy is in a long-run equilibrium, it is at points *a*, *e*, and *i*. When an expansion occurs in Vital Signs, the economy moves away from these points to one of the two other points identified in each of the three parts of the figure.

   a. If the Keynesian theory is the correct explanation for the recession, to which points does the economy move?

   b. If the monetarist theory is the correct explanation for the recession, to which points does the economy move?

   c. If the new classical theory of the business cycle is the correct explanation for the recession, to which points does the economy move?

   d. If the new Keynesian theory of the business cycle is the correct explanation for the recession, to which points does the economy move?

   e. If real business cycle theory is the correct explanation for the recession, to which points does the economy move?

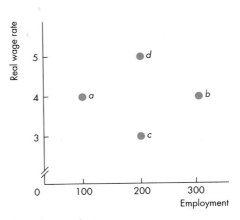

(a) Labor market

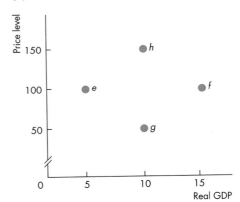

(b) AS-AD

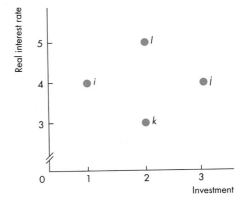

(c) Investment

*3. Suppose that when the recession occurs in Virtual Reality, the economy moves to *d*, *g*, and *k*. Which theory of the business cycle, if any, explains this outcome?

4. Suppose that when the expansion occurs in Vital Signs, the economy moves to *d*, *h*, and *l*. Which theory of the business cycle, if any, explains this outcome?

*5. Suppose that when the recession occurs in Virtual Reality, the economy moves to *c*, *g*, and *k*. Which theory of the business cycle, if any, explains this outcome?

6. Suppose that when the expansion occurs in Vital Signs, the economy moves to *c*, *h*, and *l*. Which theory of the business cycle, if any, explains this outcome?

*7. Suppose that when the recession occurs in Virtual Reality, the economy moves to *d*, *h*, and *k*. Which theory of the business cycle, if any, explains this outcome?

8. Suppose that when the expansion occurs in Vital Signs, the economy moves to *d*, *g*, and *l*. Which theory of the business cycle, if any, explains this outcome?

*9. Suppose that when the recession occurs in Virtual Reality, the economy moves to *c*, *h*, and *k*. Which theory of the business cycle, if any, explains this outcome?

10. Suppose that when the expansion occurs in Vital Signs, the economy moves to *c*, *g*, and *l*. Which theory of the business cycle, if any, explains this outcome?

*11. Suppose that when the recession occurs in Virtual Reality, the economy moves to *d*, *g*, and *l*. Which theory of the business cycle, if any, explains this outcome?

12. Suppose that when the expansion occurs in Vital Signs, the economy moves to *c*, *h*, and *k*. Which theory of the business cycle, if any, explains this outcome?

*13. Suppose that when the recession occurs in Virtual Reality, the economy moves to *c*, *g*, and *l*. Which theory of the business cycle, if any, explains this outcome?

14. Suppose that when the expansion occurs in Vital Signs, the economy moves to *d*, *h*, and *k*. Which theory of the business cycle, if any, explains this outcome?

CRITICAL THINKING

1. Study *Reading Between the Lines* on pp. 406–407 and use the links on the Parkin Web site to obtain the data on Japan's real GDP since the end of 1998. Then answer the following questions:
   a. Given the most recent data on Japan's real GDP, does it appear that the government of Japan or the independent forecasters had the correct view of where Japan was heading during 1999?
   b. Why did the official forecasters believe that Japan was on the road to recovery?
   c. What, according to the different theories of the business cycle, must happen if Japan is to enjoy a strong and sustained recovery?
   d. Can you detect any clues in the news article that tell you whether the Japanese government takes a Keynesian, monetarist, new classical, new Keynesian, or real business cycle view of Japan's recession?
   e. What policy actions, if any, do you think the government of Japan and the Bank of Japan need to take in 2000 to keep the Japanese economy growing and to prevent a new recession?

2. Describe the changes in real GDP, employment and unemployment, and the price level that occurred in the United States during the Great Depression years of 1929–1933.

3. Use the links on the Parkin Web site to obtain information about the current state of the U.S. economy. Then:
   a. List all of the features of the U.S. economy during the current year that you think are consistent with a pessimistic outlook for the next two years.
   b. List all of the features of the U.S. economy during the current year that you think are consistent with an optimistic outlook for the next two years.
   c. Describe how you think the U.S. economy is going to evolve over the next year or two. Explain your predictions, drawing on the pessimistic and optimistic factors that you listed in parts (a) and (b) and on your knowledge of macroeconomic theory.

Chapter 18

Macroeconomic Policy Challenges

From 1991 through 1998, the U.S. economy performed well. Real GDP expanded by 3.2 percent a year, unemployment fell to 4.3 percent, the inflation rate fell to less than 2 percent a year, and a $280 billion federal government budget deficit in 1992 was turned into a $75 billion surplus in 1998. The United States was not alone in achieving a strong economic expansion. Real GDP in Canada grew by 3 percent a year, and despite a recession in 1998, the developing Asian countries expanded by 7.5 percent a year during the 1990s. ◆ But not all countries shared in this solid growth. Japan's real GDP expanded by less than 2 percent a year and shrank in 1998. In Russia, real GDP shrank for five successive years to less than two thirds its 1990 level. ◆ These problems in Japan and Russia raised doubts about the future of the U.S. expansion. There were other questions about the U.S. economy: Had the potential GDP growth rate increased? Had the natural rate of unemployment decreased? Was real GDP above potential GDP? Was inflation about to increase? And when is the next recession coming? ◆ The variety of macroeconomic performance raises questions about macroeconomic policy. Can policy improve performance? Specifically, can the federal government use its fiscal policy to speed up long-term growth, keep inflation in check, and maintain a low unemployment rate? Can the Fed use its monetary policy to achieve any of these ends? Are some policy goals better achieved by fiscal policy and some by monetary policy? What specific policy actions do the best job? Are some ways of conducting policy better than others?

◆ In this chapter, we're going to study the challenges of achieving the highest sustainable long-term growth rate and low unemployment while avoiding inflation. At the end of the chapter, you will have a deeper understanding of the macroeconomic policy problems that face the United States today and of the debates that surround us concerning those problems.

What Can Policy Do?

After studying this chapter, you will be able to:

- **Describe the goals of macroeconomic policy and the main features of fiscal policy and monetary policy since 1960**
- **Explain how fiscal policy and monetary policy influence long-term economic growth**
- **Evaluate fixed-rule and feedback-rule policies to stabilize the business cycle**
- **Explain how fiscal policy influences the natural rate of unemployment**
- **Explain why lowering inflation usually brings recession**

Policy Goals

MACROECONOMIC POLICY GOALS FALL INTO TWO big categories: domestic and international. We study international macroeconomic policy issues in Chapters 19 and 20. Here, we focus on domestic policy. The four main domestic macroeconomic policy goals are to:

- Achieve the highest sustainable rate of potential GDP growth
- Smooth out avoidable business cycle fluctuations
- Maintain low unemployment
- Maintain low inflation

Potential GDP Growth

Rapid sustained real GDP growth can make a profound contribution to economic well being. With a growth rate of 2 percent a year, it takes more than 30 years for production to double. With a growth rate of 5 percent a year, production more than doubles in just 15 years. And with a growth rate of 10 percent a year, as some Asian countries have achieved, production doubles in just 7 years. The limits to *sustainable* growth are determined by the availability of natural resources, by environmental considerations, and by the willingness of people to save and invest in new capital and new technologies rather than consume everything they produce.

How fast can the economy grow over the long term? Between 1988 and 1995, through one complete business cycle, potential GDP grew at a rate of 2 percent a year.[1] But the U.S. population grows at about 1 percent a year, so the growth rate of real GDP per person was 1 percent a year, which means that output per person doubles every 70 years. Most economists believe that the U.S. economy can maintain a long-term growth rate of potential GDP of 2.5 percent a year. This growth rate would double output per person every 48 years. A few economists believe that with the right policies, sustainable growth of 5 percent a year is possible. This growth rate would double output per person every 18 years, increase it more than sixfold over 48 years, and increase it more than twelvefold in 70 years. So increasing the long-term growth rate is of critical importance.

---

[1]This number and the other numbers in this paragraph are based on the official measure of real GDP. If we take inflation bias into account, the growth rates might be as much as 1 percent per year more than these.

The Business Cycle

Potential GDP probably does not grow at a constant rate. Fluctuations in the pace of technological advance and in the pace of investment in new capital bring fluctuations in potential GDP. So some fluctuations in real GDP represent fluctuations in potential GDP. But when real GDP grows less quickly than potential GDP, output is lost, and when real GDP grows more quickly than potential GDP, bottlenecks arise. Keeping real GDP growth steady and equal to potential GDP growth avoids these problems.

It is not known how smooth real GDP growth can be made. Real business cycle theory regards all the fluctuations in real GDP as fluctuations in potential GDP. The aggregate demand theories regard most of the fluctuations in real GDP as being avoidable deviations from potential GDP.

Unemployment

When real GDP growth slows, unemployment rises above the natural rate of unemployment. The higher the unemployment rate, the longer is the time taken by unemployed people to find jobs. Productive labor is wasted, and there is a slowdown in the accumulation of human capital. If high unemployment persists, serious psychological and social problems arise for the unemployed workers and their families.

When real GDP growth speeds up, unemployment decreases and falls below the natural rate of unemployment. The lower the unemployment rate, the harder it becomes for expanding industries to get the labor they need to keep growing. If extremely low unemployment persists, serious bottlenecks and production dislocations occur.

Keeping unemployment at the natural rate avoids both of these problems. But just what is the natural rate of unemployment? Assessments vary. The actual average unemployment rate over the most recent business cycle—1988 to 1998—was 5.7 percent. Most economists think the natural rate has fallen in recent years and would put it at somewhere between 4.5 percent and 5.5 percent today. Real business cycle theorists believe the natural rate fluctuates and always equals the actual unemployment rate.

If the natural rate of unemployment becomes high, then a goal of policy becomes lowering the natural rate itself. This goal is independent of smoothing the business cycle.

Inflation

When inflation fluctuates unpredictably, money becomes less useful as a measuring rod for conducting transactions. In extreme cases, it becomes useless and is abandoned as the means of payment. Borrowers and lenders and employers and workers must take on extra risks. Keeping the inflation rate steady and predictable avoids these problems.

What is the most desirable inflation rate? Some economists say that the *rate* of inflation doesn't matter much as long as the rate is *predictable*. But most economists believe that price stability, which they translate as an inflation rate between 0 and 3 percent a year, is desirable. The reason why zero is not the target is that some price increases are due to quality improvements—a measurement bias in the price index—so a *measured* inflation rate between 0 and 3 percent a year is equivalent to price stability.

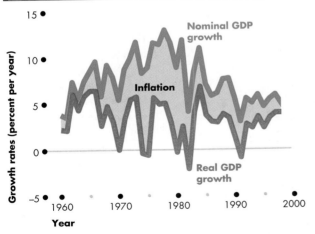

FIGURE 18.1

Macroeconomic Performance: Real GDP and Inflation

Real GDP growth and inflation fluctuate a great deal, and during the 1970s, inflation mushroomed (the height of the green shaded area) and real GDP growth slowed. This macroeconomic performance falls far short of the goals of a high and stable real GDP growth rate and low and predictable inflation.

Source: The Economic Report of the President, 1999.

The Two Core Policy Indicators: Real GDP Growth and Inflation

Although macroeconomic policy pursues the four goals we've just considered, the goals are not independent ones. Three of these goals—increasing the real GDP growth rate, smoothing the business cycle, and maintaining low unemployment—are linked together. Real GDP growth tells us directly about the long-term goal of high sustainable growth and the business cycle. It also has a strong link to unemployment. If growth becomes too rapid, unemployment falls below the natural rate, and if growth becomes too slow, unemployment rises above the natural rate. So keeping real GDP growing steadily at its maximum sustainable rate is equivalent to avoiding business fluctuations and keeping unemployment at the natural rate.

There are some connections between real GDP growth and inflation, but over the long run, these two variables are largely independent. So two variables, real GDP growth and inflation, are the core policy targets.

Policy performance, judged by the two core policy targets—real GDP growth and inflation—is shown in Fig. 18.1. Here the red line shows real GDP growth. Real GDP growth averaged 4 percent a year during the 1960s, but after 1970, the growth rate fell to less than 2.5 percent a year. Real GDP growth has fluctuated between a high of 6.8 percent in 1984 and a low of −2.1 percent in 1982. The height of the green shaded area shows inflation. The inflation rate was low during the 1960s, exploded during the 1970s, and then fell through the 1980s. During the 1990s, inflation returned to its 1960s level.

R E V I E W   Q U I Z

- Why does macroeconomic stabilization policy try to achieve the highest sustainable rate of potential GDP growth, small business cycle fluctuations, low unemployment, and low inflation?
- Can stabilization policy keep the unemployment rate below the natural rate?
- Why are real GDP growth and inflation the two core policy indicators?

We've examined the policy goals. Let's now look at the policy tools and the way they have been used.

Policy Tools and Performance

THE TOOLS THAT ARE USED TO TRY TO ACHIEVE macroeconomic performance objectives are fiscal policy and monetary policy. **Fiscal policy**, which is described in Chapter 13, is the use of the federal budget to achieve macroeconomic objectives. The detailed fiscal policy tools are tax rates, benefit rates, and government purchases of goods and services. These tools work by influencing aggregate supply and aggregate demand in the ways explained in Chapter 8. **Monetary policy**, which is described in Chapter 15, is the adjustment of the quantity of money in circulation and interest rates by the Federal Reserve (the Fed) to achieve macroeconomic objectives. These tools work by changing aggregate demand. How have the tools actually been used in the United States? Let's answer this question by summarizing the main directions of fiscal and monetary policy over the years since 1960.

Fiscal Policy Since 1960

Figure 18.2 gives a broad summary of fiscal policy since 1960. It shows the levels of government revenues and expenditures and the budget balance (each as a percentage of GDP). So that you can see the political context of fiscal policy, the figure also shows the terms of administrations and the names of the incumbent presidents.

Fiscal policy was mildly expansionary during the Kennedy years and strongly expansionary during the later Johnson years when the Vietnam War buildup occurred. During Nixon's presidency, spending growth was kept moderate. But under the pressure of the first OPEC oil shock, spending soared during Ford's presidency. The Carter years began with spending cuts, but then spending climbed to a new high. During the first Reagan term, spending continued to increase at first but it was later held in check, and then during the second Reagan term, spending was cut. During the Bush years, government purchases took an increased percentage of GDP but taxes took a smaller percentage. As the 1991 recession

---

FIGURE 18.2

The Fiscal Policy Record: A Summary

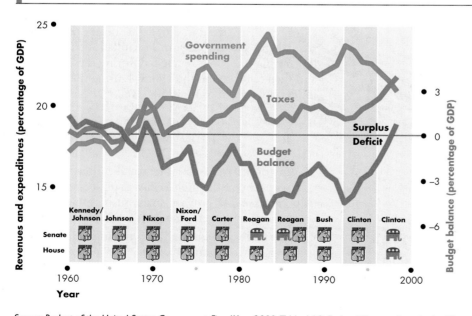

Fiscal policy is summarized here by the performance of government spending, taxes, and the budget balance. Spending has been on an upward trend, and because spending has increased more than taxes, a deficit has emerged. Cycles in spending and taxes have resulted in cycles in the deficit that often have been expansionary in the year before an election and contractionary in the year following an election.

Source: *Budget of the United States Government, Fiscal Year 2000*, Table 14.2, Federal Transactions in the National Income and Product Accounts, and *The Congressional Record*.

intensified and the 1992 election drew closer, tax cuts became the rage, especially in Congress, and revenues decreased. But a tax bill in 1993 increased taxes, so revenues increased during the Clinton presidency. At the same time, spending was held in check and decreased as a percentage of GDP.

The budget balance tells an interesting story. During the terms of Johnson, Nixon, and Ford and the first Reagan term, the budget deficit decreased in the immediate post-election year and increased as the next election approached. Through the Clinton years, the deficit decreased and a surplus emerged.

Monetary Policy Since 1960

Figure 18.3 shows three broad measures of monetary policy. They are the growth rate of M2, the federal funds rate, and the real federal funds rate. The M2 growth rate tells us how monetary policy was influencing an important determinant of aggregate demand. The federal funds rate tells us how the Fed was acting to change money growth. And the real federal funds rate tells us how the Fed was acting

on the opportunity cost of short-term funds that influences spending plans.

Figure 18.3 also identifies the election years, the presidents, and the Fed chairs. The Fed has had five chairs during this period. Notice that the term of a Fed chair does not coincide with the term of a president. William McChesney Martin was a long-serving chair whose term began in 1951. He retired in 1969 and was replaced by Arthur Burns, who served until 1977. William Miller had the shortest term and was replaced by Paul Volcker in 1979. The next chair, Alan Greenspan, was appointed by President Reagan in 1987 and has served under three presidents.

First, let's look at some of the monetary policy trends. During the 1960s, the M2 growth rate averaged 7 percent a year and ranged between a low of 4 percent in 1969 and a high of 9 percent in 1967. It then increased to average 10 percent a year between 1970 and 1983 and hit a peak of 14 percent in 1976. M2 growth fell steadily from 12 percent in 1983 to less than 1 percent in 1994 but then increased in 1995. The federal funds rate trended upward from 1960 through 1981 and then trended downward. The real federal funds rate fell through 1975 and

FIGURE 18.3

The Monetary Policy Record: A Summary

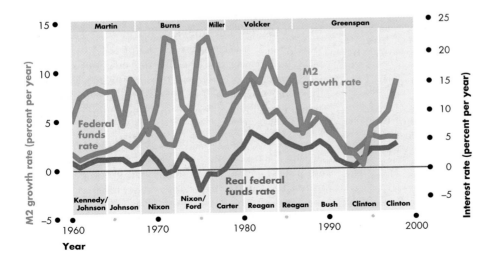

Here the growth rate of M2 and the federal funds rate summarizes the monetary policy record. Fluctuations in M2 growth have coincided with elections, the growth rate usually increasing in the year before an election. Important exceptions are 1979–1980 and 1991–1992, when monetary policy did not become expansionary and the incumbent President lost the election.

Source: The Economic Report of the President, 1999.

then increased and remained high through most of the 1980s. It fell during the early 1990s but then began to rise again through 1998.

The general upward trend in M2 growth brought the 1970s inflation, which brought rising *nominal* interest rates but, at first, falling real interest rates. The subsequent sharp downward trend in M2 growth brought falling inflation and falling nominal interest rates but was accompanied by high real interest rates.

Next, look at the cycles. The peaks and troughs in M2 growth more or less coincide with the opposite turning points in the federal funds rate. When the Fed cuts the federal funds rate, M2 growth speeds up; when the Fed increases the federal funds rate, M2 growth slows down. But notice also a remarkable fact about the monetary policy cycles. There is a tendency for the federal funds rate to rise and the M2 growth rate to decrease immediately following an election and for the federal funds rate to fall and the M2 growth rate to increase as the next election approaches. Usually, the incumbent president or his party's successor has won the election. There are two exceptions. In 1980, M2 growth increased, but not as quickly as the demand for money. Interest rates increased, the economy slowed, and Jimmy Carter lost his reelection bid. In 1992, M2 growth slowed, interest rates rose, and George Bush lost his reelection bids. A coincidence? Perhaps, but presidents take a keen interest in what the Fed is up to.

REVIEW QUIZ

- What were the main features and effects of fiscal policy during the terms of the various presidents from Kennedy in the 1960s to Clinton in the 1990s? What problems did fiscal policy respond to during the late 1960s and the 1970s?
- What were the main features and effects of monetary policy during each decade from the 1960s through the 1990s? In which periods was monetary policy inflationary? In which periods was it used to fight inflation?

You've now studied the goals of policy and seen the broad trends and cycles in fiscal and monetary policy. Let's now study the ways in which policy might be used better to achieve its goals. We'll begin by looking at long-term growth policy.

Long-Term Growth Policy

THE SOURCES OF THE LONG-TERM GROWTH OF potential GDP, which are explained in Chapter 11 (pp. 231–232), are the accumulation of physical and human capital and the advance of technology. Chapter 11 briefly examines the range of policies that might achieve faster growth. Here, we probe more deeply into the problem of boosting the long-term growth rate.

Monetary policy can contribute to long-term growth by keeping the inflation rate low. (Chapter 16, p. 364–365 explains some connections between inflation and growth.) Fiscal policy and other policies can also contribute to growth by influencing the private decisions on which long-term growth depends in three areas. All growth policies increase:

- National saving
- Investment in human capital
- Investment in new technologies

National Saving

National saving equals private saving plus government saving (see Chapter 6, p. 118). Figure 18.4 shows national saving and its private and government components since 1960. From 1960 through 1982, national saving (green line) fluctuated around an average of 20 percent of GDP. There then began a steady slide that saw national saving sink to 14 percent of GDP in 1993 before beginning to rise again. Private saving (blue line) actually increased as a percentage of GDP between 1960 and 1984, when it peaked at 22 percent of GDP. Government saving (the vertical gap between the blue line and the green line) was positive before 1975, became negative (government dissaving) during the 1980s, and returned to positive in 1997.

The data you have just examined are for *gross* saving. Each year, national wealth grows by the amount of *net* saving, which equals gross saving minus the value of capital that is scrapped during the year. Figure 18.4 shows U.S. net saving as a percentage of GDP. You can see that net saving (red line) followed a falling trend through 1993. The reason is that capital depreciated at an increasing rate. During the 1960s, depreciation ranged between 10 percent and 14 percent of GDP. This percentage edged upward and was around 12 percent by the mid-1990s. In the 1982 recession, it reached 14 percent of GDP. As a result of the fall in gross saving and the increase in the depreciation rate, net saving in the United States sank to an all-time low of 2.4 percent of GDP in 1993. But since 1993, the net saving rate has been rising.

U.S. investment, one of the engines of growth, is not limited by U.S. saving. The reason is that foreign saving can be harnessed to finance U.S. investment. But boosting the U.S. saving rate can help to bring faster real GDP growth for two reasons. First, the U.S. economy is a significant proportion of the world economy, so an increase in U.S. saving would increase world saving and bring lower real interest rates around the world. With lower real interest rates, investment would be boosted everywhere. The U.S. economy and the world economy could grow faster. Second, with more domestic saving, there might be an increase in domestic investment in high-risk–high-return new technologies that could boost U.S. growth.

How can national saving be increased? The two points of attack are:

- Increasing government saving
- Increasing private saving

Increasing Government Saving   Government saving was negative between 1975 and 1996, and its average during the 1990s was –1.3 percent of GDP. But government saving increased after 1992 as the federal budget deficit was gradually eliminated and replaced by a surplus. Maintaining a federal budget surplus will be hard work and will be achieved only by resisting tax cuts and increases in expenditures on Social Security, Medicaid, and Medicare.

Increasing Private Saving   Private saving has fallen from its peak of the mid-1980s, but even in the low years of 1992 and 1993, private saving was the same percentage of GDP it had been in 1960. The main way in which government actions can boost private saving is by increasing the after-tax rate of return on saving. This is what government policy has sought to do, but on only one type of asset: individual retirement accounts (IRAs). By putting their savings into IRAs, people can avoid income tax on their interest income. But they cannot use their IRAs (without tax penalties) until they reach the age of 59 1/2. Also, there are limits (that were relaxed somewhat in 1997) to the amount that can be accumulated tax-free in an IRA.

Private saving probably could be stimulated more effectively by cutting taxes on interest income and capital gains (increases in asset values) and replacing the lost government revenue from such a tax cut with a national consumption tax or a national sales tax. Whether such restructuring of taxes is politically feasible or desirable is a question that goes beyond the scope of macroeconomics.

Private Saving and Inflation   Inflation erodes the value of money and other financial assets such as bonds, and uncertainty about future inflation discourages saving. One further policy, therefore, that increases the saving rate is a monetary policy that preserves stable prices and minimizes uncertainty about the future value of money. Chapter 16 (p. 364–365) spells out the broader connection between inflation and real GDP and explains why low inflation brings greater output and faster growth.

FIGURE 18.4

Saving Rates in the United States: 1960–1998

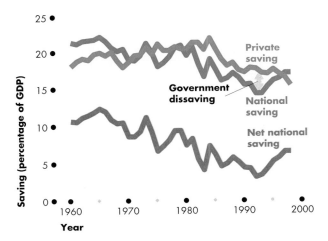

U.S. national saving (green line) peaked in 1979 and has fallen since that year. Both government saving and private saving have contributed to the fall. U.S. net saving (red line) has fallen even faster than national saving and has been on a downward trend since the mid-1960s. It hit an all-time low of 2.4 percent of GDP in 1993. It has increased since then.

Source: The Economic Report of the President, 1999.

Investment in Human Capital

The accumulation of human capital plays a crucial role in economic growth, and two areas are relevant: schooling and on-the-job experience. Economic research shows that both schooling and on-the-job training pay. That is, on the average, the greater the number of years a person remains in school and the greater the number of years of work experience, the higher are that person's earnings. Furthermore, schooling and on-the-job experience yield one of the highest rates of return available.

If education and on-the-job training yield higher earnings, why does the government need a policy toward investment in human capital? Why can't people simply be left to get on with making their own decisions about how much human capital to acquire? The answer is that the *social* returns to human capital probably exceed the *private* returns. The extra productivity that comes from the *interactions* of well-educated and experienced people exceeds what each individual could achieve alone. So, left to ourselves, we would probably accumulate too little human capital. Let's look at some aspects of education and training policies.

Education and Training Policies   Governments attempt to increase human capital by subsidizing schooling. They also help to set the standards of achievement for the school system.

The United States has achieved a high standard on some dimensions of schooling but not on all dimensions. For example, in 1998, 63 percent of high school graduates enrolled in postsecondary education (one of the highest percentages in the world) but 13 percent of high school students dropped out and did not graduate.

The Goals 2000: Educate America Act of 1994 and President Clinton's second term education initiative are examples of attempts to improve the quality of schooling. The 1994 Act pays special attention to improving each child's state of preparation for school and performance in school, especially in mathematics and science, two areas in which U.S. schoolchildren are not leading the world. A further feature of Goals 2000 is to improve college access, especially for adults who can benefit from retraining.

The scope for government training programs is limited, but the government can set an example as an employer and it can encourage best-practice training programs for workers.

Investment in New Technologies

Investment in new technologies is the third area in which policy can influence economic growth. As Chapter 11 explains, investment in new technologies is special for two reasons. First, it appears not to run into the problem of diminishing returns that plague the other types of capital and the other factors of production. Second, the benefits of new technologies spill over to influence all parts of the economy, not just the firms undertaking the investment. For these reasons, increasing the rate of investment in new technologies is a promising way of boosting long-term growth. But how can government policy influence the pace of technological change?

Government can fund and provide tax incentives for research and development activities. Through the National Science Foundation, the public universities, and various research establishments, governments fund a large amount of basic research. Also, the federal government encourages business research with a Research and Experiment Tax Credit (R&E credit). This credit is available to firms that spend more on research and development than some threshold amount. The idea is to stimulate more expenditure on these activities than would occur otherwise. The effectiveness of the R&E credit is not certain, but there is some evidence that it is a cost-effective way of boosting research.

R E V I E W   Q U I Z

- Why do long-term growth policies focus on increasing saving and increasing investment in human capital and new technologies?
- What have been the trends in the U.S. net saving rate since the mid-1970s?
- What actions can the government take that might increase the saving rate?
- What actions can the government take that might increase the rate of investment in human capital?
- What actions can the government take that might increase investment in new technologies?

We've seen how government might use its fiscal and monetary policies to influence long-term growth. How can it influence the business cycle and unemployment? Let's now address this question.

Business Cycle and Unemployment Policy

MANY DIFFERENT FISCAL AND MONETARY POLICIES can be pursued to stabilize the business cycle and cyclical unemployment. But all these polices fall into three broad categories:

- Fixed-rule policies
- Feedback-rule policies
- Discretionary policies

Fixed-Rule Policies

A **fixed-rule policy** specifies an action to be pursued independently of the state of the economy. An everyday life example of a fixed rule is a stop sign. It says, "Stop regardless of the state of the road ahead—even if no other vehicle is trying to use the road." One fixed-rule policy, proposed by Milton Friedman, is to keep the quantity of money growing at a constant rate year in and year out, regardless of the state of the economy, to make the *average* inflation rate zero. Another fixed-rule policy is to balance the federal budget. Fixed rules are rarely followed in practice, but they have some merits in principle, and later in this chapter, we will study how they would work if they were pursued.

Feedback-Rule Policies

A **feedback-rule policy** specifies how policy actions respond to changes in the state of the economy. A yield sign is an everyday feedback rule. It says, "Stop if another vehicle is attempting to use the road ahead, but otherwise, proceed." A macroeconomic feedback-rule policy is one that changes the money supply, interest rates, or even tax rates in response to the state of the economy. Some feedback rules guide the actions of policy makers. For example, the Fed's Federal Open Market Committee used a feedback rule when it kept pushing interest rates ever higher through 1994 in response to persistently falling unemployment and strong real GDP growth. Other feedback-rule policies are automatic. Examples are the automatic increase in tax revenues and decrease in transfer payments during an expansion and the automatic decrease in tax revenues and increase in transfer payments during a recession.

Discretionary Policies

A **discretionary policy** responds to the state of the economy in a possibly unique way that uses all the information available, including perceived lessons from past "mistakes." An everyday discretionary policy occurs at an unmarked intersection. Each driver uses discretion in deciding whether to stop and how slowly to approach the intersection. Most macroeconomic policy actions have an element of discretion because every situation is to some degree unique. For example, through 1998, the Fed cut interest rates several times to maintain economic growth in the face of a sagging Asian economy. The Fed might have delayed cutting rates until it was sure that lower rates were needed and then cut them in larger increments. The Fed used discretion based on lessons it had learned from earlier expansions. But despite the fact that all policy actions have an element of discretion, they can be regarded as modifications of a basic feedback-rule policy.

We'll study the effects of business cycle policy by comparing the performance of real GDP and the price level under a fixed rule and a feedback rule. Because the business cycle can result from demand shocks or supply shocks, we need to consider these two cases. We'll begin by studying demand shocks.

Stabilizing Aggregate Demand Shocks

We'll study an economy that starts out at full employment and has no inflation. Figure 18.5 illustrates this situation. The economy is on aggregate demand curve AD_0 and short-run aggregate supply curve SAS. These curves intersect at a point on the long-run aggregate supply curve, LAS. The GDP deflator is 110, and real GDP is $7 trillion. Now suppose that there is an unexpected and temporary decrease in aggregate demand. Let's see what happens.

Perhaps investment decreases because of a wave of pessimism about the future, or perhaps exports decrease because of a recession in the rest of the world. Regardless of the origin of the decrease in aggregate demand, the aggregate demand curve shifts leftward, to AD_1 in Fig. 18.5. Aggregate demand curve AD_1 intersects the short-run aggregate supply curve, SAS, at a GDP deflator of 105 and a real GDP of $6.5 trillion. The economy is in a recession. Real GDP is less than potential GDP, and unemployment is above its natural rate.

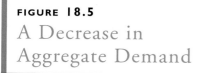

FIGURE 18.5

A Decrease in
Aggregate Demand

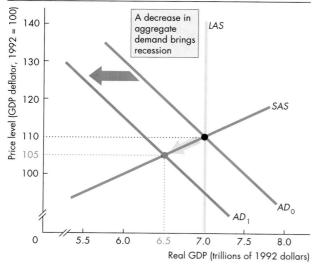

The economy starts out at full employment on aggregate demand curve AD_0 and short-run aggregate supply curve SAS, the two curves intersecting on the long-run aggregate supply curve, LAS. Real GDP is $7 trillion, and the GDP deflator is 110. A fall in aggregate demand (due to pessimism about future profits, for example) unexpectedly shifts the aggregate demand curve to AD_1. Real GDP falls to $6.5 trillion, and the GDP deflator falls to 105. The economy is in a recession.

Suppose that the decrease in aggregate demand from AD_0 to AD_1 is temporary. As confidence in the future improves, firms' investment picks up, or as economic expansion proceeds in the rest of the world, exports gradually increase. As a result, the aggregate demand curve gradually returns to AD_0, but it takes some time to do so.

We are going to work out how the economy responds under two alternative policies during the period in which aggregate demand gradually increases to its original level: a fixed rule and a feedback rule.

Fixed Rule: Monetarism   The fixed rule that we'll study here is one in which government purchases of goods and services, taxes, and the money supply remain constant. Neither fiscal policy nor monetary policy responds to the depressed economy. This is

the rule advocated by monetarists. A **monetarist** is an economist who believes that fluctuations in the money stock are the main source of economic fluctuations—the monetarist theory of the business cycle (see Chapter 17, p. 388).

Figure 18.6(a) illustrates the response of the economy under a fixed rule when the decrease in aggregate demand to AD_1 is *temporary*. Gradually, aggregate demand returns to its original level and the aggregate demand curve shifts rightward to AD_0. As it does so, real GDP and the GDP deflator gradually increase. The GDP deflator gradually returns to 110 and real GDP to $7 trillion, as shown in Fig. 18.6(a). Throughout this process, the economy experiences more rapid growth than usual but beginning from a state in which real GDP is less than potential GDP. Also throughout the adjustment, unemployment remains above the natural rate.

Figure 18.6(b) illustrates the response of the economy under a fixed rule when the decrease in aggregate demand to AD_1 is *permanent*. Gradually, with unemployment above the natural rate, the money wage rate falls and the short-run aggregate supply curve shifts rightward to SAS_1. As it does so, real GDP gradually increases and the GDP deflator falls. Real GDP gradually returns to potential GDP of $7 trillion, and the GDP deflator gradually falls to 95, as shown in Fig. 18.6(b). Again, throughout the adjustment, real GDP is less than potential GDP and unemployment exceeds the natural rate.

Let's contrast the adjustment under a fixed-rule policy with that under a feedback-rule policy.

Feedback Rule: Keynesian Activism   The feedback rule that we'll study is one in which government purchases of goods and services increase, tax rates decrease, and the money supply increases when real GDP falls below potential GDP. In other words, both fiscal policy and monetary policy become expansionary when real GDP is less than potential GDP. When real GDP exceeds potential GDP, both policies operate in reverse, becoming contractionary. This rule is advocated by Keynesian activists. A **Keynesian activist** is an economist who believes that fluctuations in aggregate demand combined with sticky wages (and/or sticky prices) are the main source of economic fluctuations—the Keynesian and new Keynesian theories of the business cycle (see Chapter 17, pp. 386–390).

Figure 18.6(c) illustrates the response of the economy under this feedback-rule policy. When aggregate demand decreases to AD_1, the expansionary fiscal and

FIGURE 18.6

Two Stabilization Policies: Aggregate Demand Shock

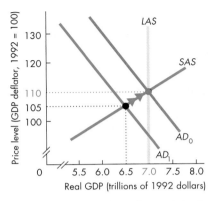
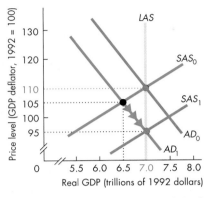
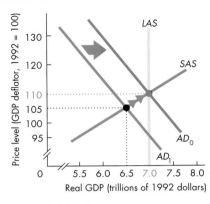

(a) Fixed rule: temporary demand shock   **(b) Fixed rule: permanent demand shock**   **(c) Feedback rule**

Aggregate demand has fallen from AD_0 to AD_1, and the economy is in a recession. Real GDP has fallen to $6.5 trillion, and the GDP deflator has fallen to 105. A fixed-rule stabilization policy (parts a and b) leaves aggregate demand at AD_1, so real GDP remains at $6.5 trillion and the GDP deflator remains at 105. If the aggregate demand shock is temporary (part a), aggregate demand subsequently returns to its original level and the aggregate demand curve shifts back to AD_0. As it does, real GDP increases back to $7 trillion and the GDP deflator increases to 110. If the demand shock is permanent (part b),

aggregate demand remains at AD_1. Eventually, because unemployment is above the natural rate, the money wage rate falls and the SAS curve shifts to SAS_1. The price level falls further (to a GDP deflator of 95), and real GDP returns to $7 trillion. Part (c) shows a feedback rule. With the economy in recession, expansionary fiscal and monetary policies increase aggregate demand and shift the aggregate demand curve from AD_1 to AD_0. Real GDP returns to $7 trillion and the GDP deflator returns to 110.

monetary policies increase aggregate demand, shifting the aggregate demand curve immediately to AD_0. As other influences begin to increase aggregate demand, fiscal and monetary policies become contractionary and hold the aggregate demand curve steady at AD_0. Real GDP is held steady at $7 trillion, and the GDP deflator remains at 110.

The Two Rules Compared   Under a fixed-rule policy, the economy goes into a recession and stays there for as long as it takes for aggregate demand to increase again under its own steam. Only gradually does the aggregate demand curve return to its original position and the recession come to an end.

Under a feedback-rule policy, the economy is pulled out of its recession by the policy action. Once back at potential GDP, real GDP is held there by a gradual, policy-induced decrease in aggregate demand that exactly offsets the increase in aggregate demand coming from private spending decisions.

The price level and real GDP decrease and increase by exactly the same amounts under the two policies, but real GDP stays below potential GDP for longer with a fixed rule than it does with a feedback rule.

The Fed's Feedback Rule: 1992–1998   The Fed operates a feedback rule but also tries to anticipate events. At the end of 1992, real GDP was less than potential GDP and unemployment exceeded the natural rate. Through 1992 the Fed cut interest rates and speeded up money growth. By 1994, real GDP was close to and growing faster than potential GDP. To prevent inflation, the Fed increased interest rates and slowed money growth. As the economy slowed, during 1995, the Fed cut interest rates and speeded up money growth. Real GDP growth again speeded up in 1996. Again, in early 1997, the Fed applied the monetary brake. The economy did not slow in 1998, but because much of Asia was in recession, the Fed cut rates again to try to avoid a U.S. and global recession.

Are Feedback Rules Better?

Is a feedback rule better than a fixed rule? Can the government and the Fed use feedback rules to keep the economy close to full employment with a stable price level? Of course, unforecasted events—such as a collapse in business confidence—will hit the economy from time to time. But by responding with a change in tax rates, spending, interest rates, and money supply, can't the government and the Fed minimize the damage from such a shock? It appears to be so from our analysis, and the Fed did a pretty good job during 1992–1998.

Despite the apparent superiority of a feedback rule, many economists remain convinced that a fixed rule stabilizes aggregate demand more effectively than a feedback rule does. These economists assert that fixed rules are better than feedback rules because:

- Potential GDP is not known.
- Policy lags are longer than the forecast horizon.
- Feedback-rule policies are less predictable than fixed-rule policies.

Knowledge of Potential GDP   To decide whether a feedback policy needs to stimulate or retard aggregate demand, it is necessary to determine whether real GDP is currently above or below potential GDP. But potential GDP is not known with certainty. It depends on a large number of factors, one of which is the level of employment when unemployment is at its natural rate. But uncertainty and disagreement exist about how the labor market works, so we can only estimate the natural rate of unemployment. As a result, there is uncertainty about the *direction* in which a feedback policy should be pushing the level of aggregate demand.

Policy Lags and the Forecast Horizon   The effects of policy actions taken today are spread out over the following two years or even more. But no one is able to forecast accurately that far ahead. The forecast horizon of the policy makers is less than 1 year. Further, it is not possible to predict the precise timing and magnitude of the effects of policy actions. Thus feedback policies that react to today's economy may be inappropriate for the state of the economy at that uncertain future date when the policy's effects are felt.

For example, suppose that today the economy is in recession. The Fed reacts with an increase in the money supply growth rate. When the Fed puts on the monetary accelerator, the first reaction is a fall in interest rates. Some time later, lower interest rates produce an increase in investment and the purchases of consumer durable goods. Some time still later, this increase in expenditure increases income; higher income in turn induces higher consumption expenditure. Later yet, the higher expenditure increases the demand for labor, and eventually, wages and prices rise. The industries and regions in which spending increases occur vary, and so does the impact on employment. It can take from 9 months to 2 years for an initial action by the Fed to cause a change in real GDP, employment, and the inflation rate.

By the time the Fed's actions are having their maximum effect, the economy has moved on to a new situation. Perhaps a world economic slowdown has added a new negative effect on aggregate demand that is offsetting the Fed's expansionary actions. Or perhaps a boost in business confidence has increased aggregate demand yet further, adding to the Fed's own expansionary policy. Whatever the situation, the Fed can take the appropriate actions today only if it can forecast those future shocks to aggregate demand.

Thus to smooth the fluctuations in aggregate demand, the Fed needs to take actions today, based on a forecast of what will be happening over a period stretching 2 or more years into the future. It is no use taking actions a year from today to influence the situation that then prevails. By then it will be too late.

If the Fed is good at economic forecasting and bases its policy actions on its forecasts, then the Fed can deliver the type of aggregate-demand-smoothing performance that we assumed in the model economy that we studied earlier in this chapter. But if the Fed takes policy actions that are based on today's economy rather than on the forecasted economy a year into the future, then those actions will often be inappropriate ones.

When unemployment is high and the Fed puts its foot on the accelerator, it speeds the economy back to full employment. But the Fed might not be able to see far enough ahead to know when to ease off the accelerator and gently tap the brake, holding the economy at its full-employment point. Usually, the Fed keeps its foot on the accelerator for too long, and after the Fed has taken its foot off the accelerator pedal, the economy races through the full-employment point and starts to experience shortages and inflationary pressures. Eventually, when inflation increases and unemployment falls below its natural rate, the Fed steps on the brake, pushing the economy back below full employment.

According to advocates of fixed rules, the Fed's own reactions to the current state of the economy is one of the major sources of fluctuations in aggregate demand and the major factor that people have to forecast to make their own economic choices.

During recent years, the Fed has tried to avoid the problems just described. In 1994, it increased interest rates early in the expansion and by small increments. In 1995, after real GDP growth slowed but before any signs of recession were on the horizon, the Fed began to cut interest rates. In 1997, before inflation turned seriously upward, the Fed squeezed the monetary brake. And in 1998, while the economy expanded strongly, the Fed cut rates to avoid the effects of the Asian recession. So the Fed's actions during 1992–1998 were gentler and better timed than in previous business cycles.

The problems for fiscal policy feedback rules are more severe than those for monetary policy because of the lags in the implementation of fiscal policy. The Fed can take actions relatively quickly. But before a fiscal policy action can be taken, the entire legislative process must be completed. Thus even before a fiscal policy action is implemented, the economy may have moved on to a new situation that calls for a different feedback policy from the one that is in the legislative pipeline.

Predictability of Policies   To make decisions about long-term contracts for employment (wage contracts) and for borrowing and lending, people have to anticipate the future course of prices—the future inflation rate. To forecast the inflation rate, it is necessary to forecast aggregate demand. And to forecast aggregate demand, it is necessary to forecast the policy actions of the government and the Fed.

If the government and the Fed stick to rock-steady, fixed rules for tax rates, spending programs, and money supply growth, then policy itself cannot be a contributor to unexpected fluctuations in aggregate demand.

In contrast, when a feedback rule is being pursued, there is more scope for the policy actions to be unpredictable. The main reason is that feedback rules are not written down for all to see. Rather, they have to be inferred from the behavior of the government and the Fed.

Thus with a feedback policy, it is necessary to predict the variables to which the government and Fed react and the extent to which they react. Consequently, a feedback rule for fiscal and monetary

policies can create more unpredictable fluctuations in aggregate demand than a fixed rule can.

Economists disagree about whether those bigger fluctuations offset the potential stabilizing influence of the predictable changes the Fed makes. No agreed measurements have been made to settle this dispute. Nevertheless, the unpredictability of the Fed in its pursuit of feedback policies is an important fact of economic life. And the Fed does not always go out of its way to make its reactions clear. Even in Congressional testimony, Federal Reserve Board chairmen are reluctant to make the Fed's actions and intentions entirely plain. (It has been suggested that two former chairmen of the Federal Reserve Board, the pipe-puffing Arthur Burns and the cigar-puffing Paul Volcker, carried their own smokescreens around with them, as if to exemplify the Fed's mysteriousness and unpredictability. The nonsmoking Alan Greenspan seems to be running a more open and predictable Fed.)

It is not surprising that the Fed seeks to keep *some* of its actions behind a smokescreen. First, the Fed wants to maintain as much freedom of action as possible and so does not want to state with too great a precision the feedback rules that it will follow in any given circumstances. Second, the Fed is part of a political process and, although legally independent of the federal government, is not immune to subtle influence. For at least these two reasons, the Fed does not specify feedback rules as precisely as the one we've analyzed in this chapter. As a result, the Fed cannot deliver an economic performance that has the stability that we generated in the model economy.

To the extent that the Fed's actions are discretionary and unpredictable, they lead to unpredictable fluctuations in aggregate demand. These fluctuations, in turn, produce fluctuations in real GDP, employment, and unemployment.

If it is difficult for the Fed to pursue a predictable feedback stabilization policy, it is probably impossible for Congress to do so. The stabilization policy of Congress is formulated in terms of spending programs and tax laws. Because these programs and laws are the outcome of a political process that is constrained only by the Constitution, there can be no effective way in which a predictable feedback fiscal policy can be adhered to.

We reviewed three reasons why feedback-rule policies might not be more effective than fixed-rule policies in controlling aggregate demand. But there is a fourth reason why some economists prefer fixed rules: Not all shocks to the economy are on the demand side. Most advocates of feedback rules believe that most fluctuations do come from aggregate demand. Some advocates of fixed rules believe that aggregate supply fluctuations are the dominant ones. Let's now see how aggregate supply fluctuations affect the economy under a fixed rule and a feedback rule. We will also see why the economists who believe that aggregate supply fluctuations are the dominant ones also favor a fixed rule rather than a feedback rule.

Stabilizing Aggregate Supply Shocks

Real business cycle theorists believe that fluctuations in real GDP (and in employment and unemployment) are caused not by fluctuations in aggregate demand but by fluctuations in productivity growth. According to real business cycle theory, there is no useful distinction between long-run aggregate supply and short-run aggregate supply. Because wages are flexible, the labor market is always in equilibrium and unemployment is always at its natural rate. The vertical long-run aggregate supply curve is also the short-run aggregate supply curve. Fluctuations occur because of shifts in the long-run aggregate supply curve. Normally, the long-run aggregate supply curve shifts to the right—the economy expands. But the pace at which the long-run aggregate supply curve shifts to the right varies. Also, on occasion, the long-run aggregate supply curve shifts leftward, bringing a decrease in aggregate supply and a fall in real GDP.

If the real business cycle theory is correct, economic policy that influences the aggregate demand curve has no effect on real GDP. But it does affect the price level. If a feedback-rule policy is used to increase aggregate demand every time real GDP decreases, and if the real business cycle theory is correct, the feedback-rule policy will make price level fluctuations more severe than they otherwise would be. To see why, consider Fig. 18.7.

Imagine that the economy starts out on aggregate demand curve AD_0 and long-run aggregate supply curve LAS_0 at a GDP deflator of 110 and with real GDP equal to $7 trillion. Now suppose that the long-run aggregate supply curve shifts to LAS_1. An actual decrease in long-run aggregate supply can occur as a result of a severe drought or other natural catastrophe or perhaps as the result of a disruption of international trade such as the OPEC embargo of the 1970s.

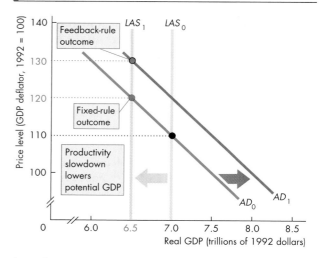

FIGURE 18.7

Responding to a Productivity Growth Slowdown

A productivity growth slowdown shifts the long-run aggregate supply curve from LAS_0 to LAS_1. Real GDP decreases to $6.5 trillion, and the GDP deflator rises to 120. With a fixed rule, there is no change in the money supply, taxes, or government spending; aggregate demand stays at AD_0; and that is the end of the matter. With a feedback rule, the Fed increases the money supply and the Congress cuts taxes or increases spending, intending to increase real GDP. Aggregate demand shifts to AD_1, but the result is an increase in the price level—the GDP deflator rises to 130—with no change in real GDP.

Fixed Rule   With a fixed rule, the fall in the long-run aggregate supply has no effect on the policies of the Fed or the government and no effect on aggregate demand. The aggregate demand curve remains AD_0. Real GDP decreases to $6.5 trillion, and the GDP deflator increases to 120.

Feedback Rule   Now suppose that the Fed and the government use feedback rules. In particular, suppose that when real GDP decreases, the Fed increases the money supply and Congress enacts a tax cut to increase aggregate demand. In this example, the money supply and tax cut shift the aggregate demand curve to AD_1. The policy goal is to bring real GDP back to $7 trillion. But the long-run aggregate supply curve has shifted, and so potential GDP has decreased to $6.5 trillion. The increase in aggregate demand cannot bring forth an increase in output if the economy does not have the capacity to produce that output. So real GDP stays at $6.5 trillion, but the price level rises still further—the GDP deflator goes to 130. You can see that in this case, the attempt to stabilize real GDP using a feedback-rule policy has no effect on real GDP but generates a substantial price level increase.

We've now seen some of the shortcomings of using feedback rules for stabilization policy. Some economists believe that these shortcomings are serious and want to constrain Congress and the Fed so that they use fixed rules. Others, regarding the potential advantages of feedback rules as greater than their costs, advocate the continued use of such policies but with an important modification that we'll now look at.

Nominal GDP Targeting

Nominal GDP targeting is an attempt to keep the growth rate of nominal GDP steady. This policy target was first proposed by a leading Keynesian activist, James Tobin of Yale University. It is a policy that recognizes the strengths of a fixed rule but that regards the monetarist fixed rule as inappropriate. Instead, nominal GDP targeting uses feedback rules for fiscal and monetary policy to hit a fixed nominal GDP growth target.

Because nominal GDP growth equals the real GDP growth rate plus the inflation rate, keeping nominal GDP growth steady does not directly target either real GDP growth or inflation. But nominal GDP usually grows quickly because the inflation rate is high. And nominal GDP usually grows slowly because real GDP growth is negative—the economy is in recession. So the idea is that, by keeping nominal GDP growth steady, both excessive inflation and severe recession might be avoided.

Nominal GDP targeting uses feedback rules. Expansionary fiscal and/or monetary actions increase aggregate demand when nominal GDP is below target and contractionary fiscal and/or monetary actions decrease aggregate demand when nominal GDP is above target. The main problem with nominal GDP targeting is that there are long and variable time lags between the identification of a need to change aggregate demand and the effects of the policy actions that are taken.

Natural Rate Policies

The business cycle and unemployment policies we've considered have been directed at smoothing the business cycle and minimizing *cyclical unemployment*. It is also possible to pursue policies aimed at lowering the natural rate of unemployment. But there are no cost-less ways of lowering the natural rate of unemployment. Let's look at two possible ways.

One policy tool is unemployment insurance. To lower the natural rate of unemployment, the government might reduce the unemployment benefit, or shorten the period for which benefits are paid, or restrict benefits to people who undertake training programs that increase the likelihood of their finding jobs. With reduced benefits, an unemployed person would spend less time looking for a job and would accept a job even if it were not a good match for the person's skills. But such a policy might create hardship and have a cost that exceeds the cost of a high natural rate of unemployment.

The government might lower the minimum real wage rate. It could achieve a cut in the minimum wage either by holding the minimum money wage rate constant and letting inflation cut the minimum real wage rate or by cutting the minimum money wage rate. A lower minimum wage increases the quantity of labor demanded and lowers unemployment. The government faces a tradeoff between real wages and unemployment.

R E V I E W   Q U I Z

- What is a fixed-rule fiscal policy and what is a fixed-rule monetary policy? Can you provide two examples of fixed rules in everyday life (other than those in the text)?
- What is a feedback-rule fiscal policy and what is a feedback-rule monetary policy? When might a feedback-rule policy be used? Can you provide two examples of feedback rules in everyday life (other than those in the text)?
- Why do some economists say that feedback rules do not necessarily deliver a better macroeconomic performance than fixed rules? Do you agree or disagree with them? Why?

We've studied growth policy and business cycle and unemployment policy. Let's now study inflation policy.

Inflation Policy

THERE ARE TWO INFLATION POLICY PROBLEMS. In times of price level stability, the problem is to prevent inflation from breaking out. In times of inflation, the problem is to reduce its rate and restore price stability. Preventing inflation from breaking out means avoiding both demand-pull and cost-push forces. Avoiding demand-pull inflation is the flip side of avoiding demand-driven recession and is achieved by stabilizing aggregate demand. So the business cycle and unemployment policy we've just studied is also an anti-inflation policy. But avoiding cost-push inflation raises some special issues that we need to consider. So we will look at two issues for inflation policy:

- Avoiding cost-push inflation
- Slowing inflation

Avoiding Cost-Push Inflation

Cost-push inflation is inflation that has its origins in cost increases. In 1973–1974 and again in 1979, the world oil price exploded. Cost shocks such as these become inflationary if they are accommodated by an increase in the quantity of money. Such an increase in the quantity of money can occur if a monetary policy feedback rule is used. A fixed-rule policy for the money stock makes cost-push inflation impossible. Let's see why.

Figure 18.8 shows the economy at full employment. Aggregate demand is AD_0, short-run aggregate supply is SAS_0, and long-run aggregate supply is LAS. Real GDP is $7 trillion, and the GDP deflator is 110. Now suppose that OPEC tries to gain a temporary advantage by increasing the price of oil. The short-run aggregate supply curve shifts leftward from SAS_0 to SAS_1.

FIGURE 18.8

Responding to an OPEC Oil Price Increase

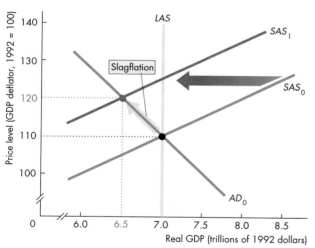

(a) Fixed rule

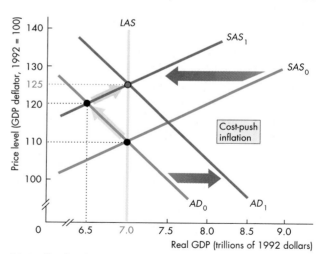

(b) Feedback rule

The economy starts out on AD_0 and SAS_0, with a GDP deflator of 110 and real GDP of $7 trillion. OPEC forces up the price of oil, and the short-run aggregate supply curve shifts to SAS_1. Real GDP decreases to $6.5 trillion, and the GDP deflator increases to 120. With a fixed-rule policy (part a), the Fed makes no change to aggregate demand. The economy stays in

a recession until resource prices fall and the economy returns to its original position. With a feedback-rule policy (part b), the Fed injects additional money and the aggregate demand curve shifts to AD_1. Real GDP returns to $7 trillion (potential GDP), but the GDP deflator increases to 125. The economy is set for another round of cost-push inflation.

Monetarist Fixed Rule Figure 18.8(a) shows what happens if the Fed follows a fixed rule for monetary policy and the government follows a fixed rule for fiscal policy. Suppose that the fixed rule is for zero money growth and no change in taxes or government purchases of goods and services. With these fixed rules, the Fed and the government pay no attention to the fact that there has been an increase in the price of oil. No policy actions are taken. The short-run aggregate supply curve has shifted to SAS_1, but the aggregate demand curve remains at AD_0. The GDP deflator rises to 120, and real GDP falls to $6.5 trillion. The economy has experienced *stagflation*. With unemployment above the natural rate, the money wage rate will eventually fall. The low level of real GDP and low sales will probably also bring a fall in the price of oil. These events will shift the short-run aggregate supply curve back to SAS_0. The GDP deflator will fall to 110, and real GDP will increase to $7 trillion. But this adjustment might take a long time.

Keynesian Feedback Rule Figure 18.8(b) shows what happens if the Fed and government operate a feedback rule. The starting point is the same as before—the economy is on SAS_0 and AD_0 with a GDP deflator of 110 and real GDP of $7 trillion. OPEC raises the price of oil, and the short-run aggregate supply curve shifts to SAS_1. Real GDP decreases to $6.5 trillion, and the price level rises to 120.

A feedback rule is followed. With potential GDP perceived to be $7 trillion and with actual real GDP at $6.5 trillion, the Fed pumps money into the economy and the government increases its spending and lowers taxes. Aggregate demand increases, and the aggregate demand curve shifts rightward to AD_1. The price level rises to 125, and real GDP returns to $7 trillion. The economy moves back to full employment but at a higher price level. The economy has experienced *cost-push inflation.*

The Fed responded in the way we've just described to the first wave of OPEC price increases in the mid-1970s. OPEC sees the same advantage in forcing up the price of oil again. A new rise in the price of oil decreases aggregate supply, and the short-run aggregate supply curve shifts leftward once more. The Fed chases it with an increase in aggregate demand, and the economy is in a freewheeling inflation. Realizing this danger, the Fed did *not* respond in the early 1980s to the second wave of OPEC price increases as it had done before. Instead, the Fed held firm and even slowed down the growth of aggregate demand

to further dampen the inflation consequences of OPEC's actions.

Incentives to Push Up Costs You can see that there are no checks on the incentives to push up *nominal* costs if the Fed accommodates price hikes. If some group sees a temporary gain from pushing up the price at which they are selling their resources and if the Fed always accommodates the increase to prevent unemployment and slack business conditions from emerging, then cost-push elements will have a free rein. But when the Fed pursues a fixed-rule policy, the incentive to attempt to steal a temporary advantage from a price increase is severely weakened. The cost of higher unemployment and lower output is a consequence that each group will have to face and recognize.

Thus a fixed rule can deliver steady inflation, while a feedback rule, in the face of cost-push pressures, leaves inflation free to rise and fall at the whim of whichever group believes a temporary advantage to be available from pushing up its price.

Slowing Inflation

So far, we've concentrated on *avoiding* inflation. But often the problem is not to avoid inflation but to tame it. The United States was in such a situation during the late 1970s and early 1980s. How can inflation, once it has set in, be cured? We'll look at two cases:

- A surprise inflation reduction
- A credible announced inflation reduction

A Surprise Inflation Reduction We'll use two equivalent approaches to study the problem of lowering inflation: the aggregate supply–aggregate demand model and the Phillips curve. The *AS-AD* model tells us about real GDP and the price level, while the Phillips curve, which is explained in Chapter 16 (pp. 366–368), lets us keep track of inflation and unemployment.

Figure 18.9 illustrates the economy at full employment with inflation raging at 10 percent a year. In part (a), the economy is on aggregate demand curve AD_0 and short-run aggregate supply curve SAS_0. Real GDP is $7 trillion, and the GDP deflator is 110. With real GDP equal to potential GDP on the *LAS* curve, the economy is at full employment. Equivalently, in part (b), the economy is on its long-run Phillips curve, *LRPC*, and short-run Phillips curve, $SRPC_0$. The

FIGURE 18.9
Lowering Inflation

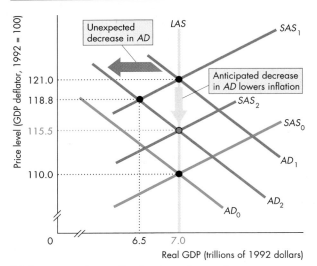

(a) Aggregate demand and aggregate supply

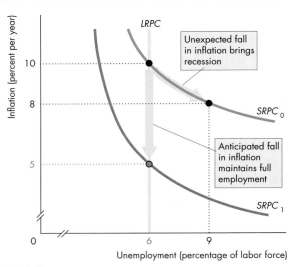

(b) Phillips curves

In part (a), aggregate demand is AD_0, short-run aggregate supply is SAS_0, and real GDP and potential GDP are $7 trillion on the long-run aggregate supply curve LAS. The aggregate demand curve is expected to shift and actually shifts to AD_1. The short-run aggregate supply curve shifts to SAS_1. The GDP deflator rises to 121, but real GDP remains at $7 trillion. Inflation is proceeding at 10 percent a year, and this inflation rate is anticipated. In part (b), which shows this same situation, the economy on the short-run Phillips curve $SRPC_0$ and on the long-run Phillips curve $LRPC$. Unemployment is at the natural rate of 6 percent, and inflation is 10 percent a year. An unex-

pected slowdown in aggregate demand growth means that the aggregate demand curve shifts from AD_0 to AD_2, real GDP falls to $6.5 trillion, and inflation slows to 8 percent (GDP deflator is 118.8). Unemployment rises to 9 percent as the economy slides down $SRPC_0$. An anticipated, credible, announced slowdown in aggregate demand growth means that when the aggregate demand curve shifts from AD_0 to AD_2, the short-run aggregate supply curve shifts from SAS_0 to SAS_2. The short-run Phillips curve shifts to $SRPC_1$. Inflation slows to 5 percent, real GDP remains at $7 trillion, and unemployment remains at its natural rate of 6 percent.

inflation rate of 10 percent a year is anticipated, so unemployment is at its natural rate, 6 percent of the labor force.

Next year, aggregate demand is *expected* to increase and the aggregate demand curve in Fig. 18.9(a) is expected to shift rightward from AD_0 to AD_1. In expectation of this increase in aggregate demand, wages increase to shift the short-run aggregate supply curve from SAS_0 to SAS_1. If expectations are fulfilled, the GDP deflator rises to 121—a 10 percent inflation—and real GDP remains at potential GDP. In part (b), the economy remains at its original position—unemployment is at the natural rate, and the inflation rate is 10 percent a year.

Now suppose that no one is expecting the Fed to change its policy, but the Fed actually tries to slow

inflation. It raises interest rates and slows money growth. Aggregate demand growth slows, and the aggregate demand curve (in part a) shifts rightward from AD_0 not to AD_1, as people expect, but only to AD_2.

With no change in the expected inflation rate, wage rates rise by the same amount as before and the short-run aggregate supply curve shifts leftward from SAS_0 to SAS_1. Real GDP decreases to $6.5 trillion, and the GDP deflator rises to 118.8—an inflation rate of 8 percent a year. In Fig. 18.9(b), the economy moves along the short-run Phillips curve $SRPC_0$ as unemployment rises to 9 percent and inflation falls to 8 percent a year. The Fed's policy has succeeded in slowing inflation but at the cost of recession. Real GDP is below potential GDP, and unemployment is above its natural rate.

A Credible Announced Inflation Reduction Suppose that instead of simply slowing down the growth of aggregate demand, the Fed announces its intention ahead of its action and in a credible and convincing way so that its announcement is believed. That is, the Fed's policy is anticipated. Because the lower level of aggregate demand is expected, wages increase at a pace consistent with the lower level of aggregate demand. The short-run aggregate supply curve (in Fig. 18.9a) shifts leftward from SAS_0 but only to SAS_2. Aggregate demand increases by the amount expected, and the aggregate demand curve shifts from AD_0 to AD_2. The GDP deflator rises to 115.5—an inflation rate of 5 percent a year—and real GDP remains at potential GDP.

In Fig. 18.9(b), the lower expected inflation rate shifts the short-run Phillips curve downward to $SRPC_1$, and inflation falls to 5 percent a year, while unemployment remains at its natural rate of 6 percent.

A credible announced inflation reduction lowers inflation but with no accompanying loss of output or increase in unemployment.

Inflation Reduction in Practice

When the Fed in fact slowed inflation in 1981, we paid a high price. The Fed's policy action was unpredicted. It occurred in the face of wages that had been set at too high a level to be consistent with the growth of aggregate demand that the Fed subsequently allowed. The consequence was recession—a decrease in real GDP and a rise in unemployment. Could the Fed have lowered inflation without causing recession by telling people far enough ahead of time that it did indeed plan to lower inflation?

The answer appears to be no. The main reason is that people expect the Fed to behave in line with its record, not with its stated intentions. How many times have you told yourself that it is your firm intention to take off 10 unwanted pounds or to keep within your budget and put a few dollars away for a rainy day, only to discover that, despite your very best intentions, your old habits win out in the end?

To form expectations of the Fed's actions, people look at the Fed's past *actions*, not its stated intentions. On the basis of such observations—called Fed-watching—they try to work out what the Fed's policy is, to forecast its future actions, and to forecast the effects of those actions on aggregate demand and inflation. The Greenspan Fed, like the Volcker Fed that preceded it, has built a reputation for being anti-inflationary. That reputation is valuable because it helps the Fed to contain inflation and lowers the cost of eliminating inflation if it temporarily returns. The reason is that with a low expected inflation rate, the short-run Phillips curve is in a favorable position (like $SRPC_1$ in Fig. 18.9b). The Fed's actions during the 1990s have been designed to keep inflation expectations low and prevent the gains made during the 1980s recession from being eroded.

A Truly Independent Fed

A radical suggestion for strengthening the Fed's reputation as the guardian of price stability is to make the Fed more independent of government and to charge it with the single responsibility of achieving and maintaining price level stability. Some central banks are more independent than the Fed. The German and Swiss central banks are the best examples. Another example is the New Zealand central bank. All these central banks have the responsibility of stabilizing prices but not real GDP and of pursuing their objective without interference from the government. Recent research on central bank performance has strengthened the view that a more independent central bank can deliver a lower average inflation rate without creating either a higher unemployment rate or a lower real GDP growth rate.

R E V I E W   Q U I Z

- Why does a fixed rule provide more effective protection against a cost-push inflation than a feedback rule?
- Why does a recession usually result as inflation is being tamed?
- How does establishing a reputation of being an inflation fighter improve the Fed's ability to maintain low inflation and to lower the cost of fighting inflation?

◆ *Reading Between the Lines* on pp. 430–431 looks at the challenges the Fed faced in 1999 as it sought to keep the economy expanding but avoid renewed inflation.

You've now completed your study of macroeconomics. In the remaining chapters, we shift our focus to the international economy.

A Feedback Rule?

BARRON'S ONLINE, APRIL 12, 1999

The Fed Catches On

BY JOHN LISCIO

At this stage of the economic expansion, a few things should be abundantly clear. First and foremost, inflation is simply not a threat. Look at any measure of it that tickles your fancy and the message is the same: Cost-push inflation sleeps with the fishes. ...

Productive investment in technology has eased capacity constraints and alleviated upward pressure on wage growth. It's a brave new world out there; and now even the Fed is warming up to it.

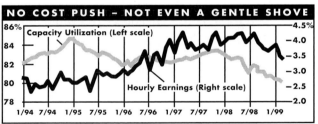

NO COST PUSH – NOT EVEN A GENTLE SHOVE

Capacity Utilization (Left scale)

Hourly Earnings (Right scale)

86% 84 82 80 78 — 4.5% 4.0 3.5 3.0 2.5 2.0

1/94 7/94 1/95 7/95 1/96 7/96 1/97 7/97 1/98 7/98 1/99

BARRON'S/Briefing.com

...

Here is just a small taste of the Fed of the Future (from the minutes of the FOMC's February confab):

"With regard to the outlook for inflation, the members saw no evidence of accelerating price inflation despite high levels of business activity and very tight labor markets across most of the nation. Indeed, the conjuncture over an extended period of strong economic growth, very low rates of unemployment, and the absence of any buildup of inflation could not be explained in terms of normal historical relationships. While temporary factors, such as declining oil prices, had played a role in depressing inflation, the persistence of very low inflation under these conditions most likely also resulted from more lasting changes in economic relationships."...

By accepting these new economic relationships, Fed officials are making it clear that they will not raise rates until and unless inflation actually picks up. We have long been arguing that there will be no preemptive tightening, as the Fed no longer has any confidence that there is anything to preempt.

Essence of the Story

■ Inflation is not a threat in the United States.

■ The Fed says that there is "no evidence of accelerating price inflation despite high levels of business activity and very tight labor markets."

■ The Fed believes that there is a new relationship between inflation and unemployment.

■ The Fed will not raise interest rates until and unless inflation actually increases.

■ The Fed will not tighten monetary policy in anticipation of increased inflation because the Fed does not foresee inflation increasing.

Economic Analysis

■ This article argues that inflation is dead, that the economy is governed by new relationships, and that the Fed should not and likely will not act to raise interest rates in anticipation of renewed inflation but instead will wait until the inflation rate actually increases.

■ Waiting until the inflation rate increases and then reacting to it is an example of a feedback-rule policy.

■ The belief that the economy is governed by new relationships is a belief that the growth rate of potential GDP has increased and that the natural rate of unemployment has decreased.

■ Both the growth rate of potential GDP and the natural unemployment rate change from time to time. The growth rate decreased and the natural rate increased during the 1970s. The growth rate increased and the natural rate decreased during the 1990s.

■ To pursue a feedback-rule policy, the Fed must estimate the growth rate of potential GDP so that it can estimate the position of the long-run aggregate supply curve.

■ Figure 1 shows how the economy will behave in 1999 if the Fed gets things right.

■ The Fed expects potential GDP to be $7.7 trillion. The long-run aggregate supply curve is expected to be LAS_{99}, and the short-run aggregate supply curve is expected to be SAS_{99}. The Fed holds interest rates steady and expects the aggregate demand curve to be AD_{99}.

■ If all these expectations are correct, real GDP increases and equals potential GDP and the price level rises, but at roughly the same rate as in 1998.

■ Figure 2 shows what happens in 1999 if the Fed gets potential GDP wrong. Here, potential GDP remains at $7.6 trillion.

■ The aggregate demand curve is AD_0, and the short-run aggregate supply curve is SAS_0. Initially, real GDP increases to $7.7 trillion and there is an inflationary gap.

■ Wage rates now begin to rise, and the SAS curve starts to shift leftward. Inflation increases as the price level rises, and real GDP decreases.

■ Now that inflation has taken off, the Fed tightens its monetary policy by raising interest rates. Aggregate demand decreases, and the AD curve shifts leftward to AD_1. The Fed's action

limits inflation. The price level rises to 116 rather than 117. But the economy goes into recession.

■ Some economists believe that the scene just described will occur because the Fed has permitted the quantity of money to grow too quickly during 1998 and early 1999.

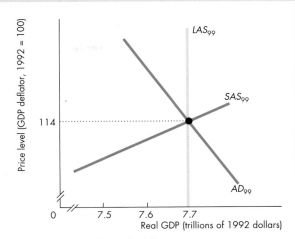

Figure 1   The Fed gets it right

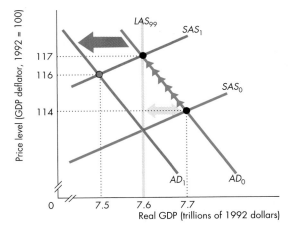

Figure 2   The Fed waits for inflation to return

You're The Voter

■ Why does the Fed need to estimate potential GDP?

■ What are the main pros and cons if the Fed ignores potential GDP and fixes the growth rate of M2?

SUMMARY

KEY POINTS

Policy Goals (pp. 412–413)

■ The goals of macroeconomic policy are to achieve the highest sustainable rate of long-term real GDP growth, smooth unavoidable business cycle fluctuations, maintain low unemployment, and avoid inflation.

Policy Tools and Performance (pp. 414–416)

■ Fiscal policy was expansionary during the Kennedy years, the late 1960s and early 1970s, and the early Reagan 1980s. It was contractionary during the Carter, later Reagan, and Clinton years.

■ The M2 growth rate increased during the 1970s, peaked in 1976, and then fell.

Long-Term Growth Policy (pp. 416–418)

■ Policies to increase the long-term growth rate focus on increasing saving and investment in human capital and new technologies.

■ To increase the saving rate, government saving must increase or incentives for private saving must be strengthened by increasing after-tax returns.

■ Human capital investment might be increased with improved education and by improving on-the-job training programs.

■ Investment in new technologies can be encouraged by tax incentives.

Business Cycle and Unemployment Policy (pp. 419–425)

■ In the face of an aggregate demand shock, a fixed-rule policy takes no action. Real GDP and the price level fluctuate.

■ In the face of an aggregate demand shock, a feedback-rule policy takes offsetting fiscal and monetary action. An ideal feedback rule keeps the economy at full employment, with stable prices.

■ Some economists say that a feedback rule creates fluctuations because it requires greater knowledge of the economy than we have, operates with time

lags that extend beyond the forecast horizon, and introduces unpredictability about policy reactions.

■ In the face of a productivity growth slowdown, both rules have the same effect on output. A feedback rule brings a higher inflation rate than a fixed rule does.

■ Nominal GDP targeting might avoid the extremes of inflation and recession.

Inflation Policy (pp. 426–429)

■ A fixed rule minimizes the threat of cost-push inflation. A feedback rule validates cost-push inflation and leaves the price level and inflation rate free to move to wherever they are pushed.

■ Inflation can be tamed, at little or no cost in terms of lost output or excessive unemployment, by slowing the growth of aggregate demand in a credible and predictable way. But usually, when inflation is slowed down, a recession occurs.

KEY FIGURES

KEY TERMS

PROBLEMS

*1. A productivity growth slowdown has occurred. Explain its possible origins and describe a policy package that is designed to speed up growth again.

2. A nation is experiencing a falling saving rate. Explain its possible origins and describe a policy package that is designed to increase the saving rate.

*3. The economy shown in the figure is initially on aggregate demand curve AD_0 and short-run aggregate supply curve SAS_0. Then aggregate demand decreases and the aggregate demand curve shifts leftward to AD_1.

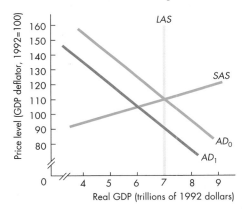

a. What are the initial equilibrium real GDP and price level?

b. If the decrease in aggregate demand is temporary and the government follows a fixed-rule fiscal policy, what happens to real GDP and the price level? Trace the immediate effects and the adjustment as aggregate demand returns to its original level.

c. If the decrease in aggregate demand is temporary and the government follows a feedback-rule fiscal policy, what happens to real GDP and the price level? Trace the immediate effects and the adjustment as aggregate demand returns to its original level.

d. If the decrease in aggregate demand is permanent and the government follows a fixed-rule fiscal policy, what happens to real GDP and the price level?

e. If the decrease in aggregate demand is permanent and the government follows a feedback-rule fiscal policy, what happens to real GDP and the price level?

4. The economy shown in the figure is initially on aggregate demand curve AD_0 and short-run aggregate supply curve SAS_0. Then short-run aggregate supply decreases and the short-run aggregate supply curve shifts leftward to SAS_1.

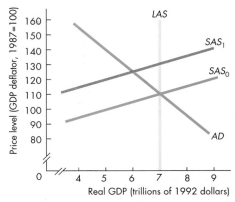

a. What are the initial equilibrium real GDP and price level?

b. What type of event could have caused the decrease in short-run aggregate supply?

c. If the government follows a fixed-rule monetary policy, what happens to real GDP and the price level? Trace the immediate effects and the adjustment as aggregate demand and short-run aggregate supply return to its original level.

d. If the government follows a feedback-rule monetary policy, what happens to real GDP and the price level? Trace the immediate effects and the adjustment as aggregate demand and short-run aggregate supply respond to the policy action.

*5. The economy is experiencing 10 percent inflation and 7 percent unemployment. Real GDP growth has sagged to 1 percent a year. The stock market has crashed.

a. Explain how the economy might have gotten into its current state.

b. Set out policies for the Fed and Congress to pursue that will lower inflation, lower unemployment, and speed real GDP growth.

c. Explain how and why your proposed policies will work.

6. The inflation rate has fallen to less than 1 percent a year, and the unemployment rate has fallen to less then 4 percent. Real GDP is growing at almost 5 percent a year. The stock market is at a record high.

a. Explain how the economy might have gotten into its current state.

b. Set out policies for the Fed and Congress to pursue that will lower inflation, lower unemployment, and speed real GDP growth.

c. Explain how and why your proposed policies will work.

*7. When the economies of Indonesia, Korea, Thailand, Malaya, and the Philippines entered into recession in 1997, the International Monetary Fund (IMF) made loans but only on condition that the recipients of the loans increased interest rates, raised taxes, and cut government expenditures.

a. Would you describe the IMF prescription as a feedback-rule policy or a fixed-rule policy?

b. What do you predict the effects of the IMF policies would be?

c. Do you have any criticisms of the IMF polices? What would you have required these countries to do? Why?

8. As the U.S. economy continued to expand and its stock market soared to new record levels during 1998, the Fed cut interest rates.

a. Would you describe the Fed's actions as a feedback-rule policy or a fixed-rule policy?

b. What do you predict the effects of the Fed's policies would be?

c. Do you have any criticisms of the Fed's polices? What monetary policy would you have pursued? Why?

CRITICAL THINKING

1. Study *Reading Between the Lines* on pp. 430–431 and then:

a. Describe the challenge faced by the Fed and explain why the challenge was particularly interesting during 1999.

b. In what state is the economy when the inflation rate increases?

c. What signs would you look for to determine whether inflation was about to take off?

d. What in your opinion does the Fed's challenge of 1999 tell us about the relative merits of a fixed-rule monetary policy and a feedback-rule monetary policy?

2. The economy is booming and inflation is beginning to rise, but it is widely agreed that a massive recession is just around the corner. Provide Congress with testimony that summarizes your opinion on whether a fixed-rule policy or a feedback-rule policy is better able to deal with the situation.

3. The economy is in a recession, and inflation is falling. It is widely agreed that a strong recovery is just around the corner. Provide the Fed with a memorandum that summarizes your opinion on whether a fixed-rule policy or a feedback-rule policy is better able to deal with the situation.

4. You have been hired to draw up an economic plan that will maximize the chance that the President will be re-elected.

a. What are the macroeconomic stabilization policy elements in that plan?

b. What do you have to make the economy do in an election year?

c. What policy actions would help the President achieve re-election?

(In dealing with this problem, be careful to take into account the effects of your proposed policy on expectations and the effects of those expectations on actual economic performance.)

 5. Use the link on the Parkin Web site to obtain the latest *Economic Report of the President.* Review Chapter 2 on Macroeconomic Policy and Performance. Write a summary and critique of this chapter.

Understanding Stabilization Problems and Policies

Boom and Bust

To cure a disease, doctors must first understand how the disease responds to different treatments. It helps to understand the mechanisms that operate to cause the disease, but sometimes, a workable cure can be found even before the full story of the causes has been told. ◆ Curing economic ills is similar to curing our medical ills. We need to understand how the economy responds to the treatments we might prescribe for it. And sometimes, we want to try a cure even though we don't fully understand the reasons for the problem we're trying to control. ◆ You've seen how the pace of capital accumulation and technological change determine the long-term growth trend. You've learned how fluctuations around the long-term trend can be generated by changes in aggregate demand and aggregate supply. And you've learned about the key sources of fluctuations in aggregate demand and aggregate supply. ◆ The two chapters in this part have built on everything you've studied in macroeconomics. The central tool they use is the *AS-AD* model. But they use it to explain the big picture or grand vision that different schools of thought hold concerning the way the economy operates and what is important. ◆ In Chapter 17, we learned about alternative visions of the business cycle. All of these visions can be translated into the *AS-AD* model. And doing so helps us to compare and contrast the competing visions. But one theory of the cycle, the new *real business cycle (RBC)* theory, is more at home with the demand and supply model of microeconomics (Chapter 4) than the *AS-AD* model. Most economists have not embraced the real business cycle approach. It is an extreme view. But the method that real business cycle theory uses is here to stay. This method is to build a (mathematical) model of the entire economy and then see, in a computer simulation, what kind of cycle the model creates. The economy on the computer is then calibrated to the real economy, and the cycles are compared. The computer model can be treated with a variety of "medications" and their effects observed. This new style of business cycle research cannot be explained in detail without using advanced mathematical ideas. But Chapter 16 explained the economics that underlies it and showed you the type of model that real business cycle theorists use. ◆ Chapter 17 described the policy debate and explained the alternative approaches that have been proposed to speed growth, smooth the business cycle, and contain inflation. Again, the *AS-AD* model was the workhorse that was used to compare the effects of alternative policy strategies. ◆ The economist you're going to meet on the following page, Irving Fisher, developed ideas about business cycles that have never been in the mainstream but that are becoming fashionable today. Frederic S. Mishkin has helped to refine modern business cycle theory and has worked as the senior research economist at the New York Fed.

435

The Economist

Irving Fisher *(1867-1947)*
ranks among the greatest American-born economists. The son of a Congregational minister who died as Irving was finishing high school, he paid his way through Yale and earned enough to keep his mother and younger brother by tutoring his fellow students.

Irving Fisher came to economics by way of mathematics. He was Yale's first Ph.D. student in pure economics, but in the math department!

The contributions that Fisher made to economics cover the entire subject. He is best known for his work on the quantity theory of money (Chapter 14, pp. 321–324) and the relation between interest rates and inflation (Chapter 16, pp. 370–371). But he also wrote on the business cycle. He believed that the Great Depression was caused because the fall in the price level increased the real burden of debts. He wrote from experience. He had borrowed heavily to buy stocks in the rising market of the late 1920s and lost a fortune of perhaps 10 million dollars in the crash of 1929.

> "...in the great booms and depressions, ... the two big bad actors are debt disturbances and price level disturbances."
>
> Irving Fisher
> *"The Debt Deflation Theory of Depressions"*
> ECONOMETRICA, 1933

The Issues

Economic activity has fluctuated between boom and bust for as long as we've had records. And understanding the sources of economic fluctuations has turned out to be difficult. One reason is that there are no simple patterns. Every new episode of the business cycle is different from its predecessor in some way. Some cycles are long and some short, some are mild and some severe, some begin in the United States and some abroad. We never know with any certainty when the next turning point (down or up) is coming or what will cause it. A second reason is that the apparent waste of resources during a recession or a depression seems to contradict the very foundation of economics: Resources are limited and people have unlimited wants—there is scarcity. A satisfactory theory of the business cycle must explain why scarce resources don't *always* get fully employed.

One theory is that recessions result from insufficient aggregate demand. The solution is to increase government spending, cut taxes, and cut interest rates. But demand stimulation must not be overdone. Countries that stimulate aggregate demand too much, such as the Brazil, find their economic growth rates sagging, unemployment rising, and inflation accelerating.

Today's new theory, real business cycle theory, predicts that fluctuations in aggregate demand have *no* effect on output and employment and change only the price level and inflation rate. But this theory ignores the *real* effects of financial collapse of the type that occurred in the 1930s. If banks fail on a large scale and people lose their wealth, other firms also begin to fail and jobs are destroyed. Unemployed people cut their spending, and output falls yet further. Demand stimulation might not be called for, but action to ensure that sound banks survive certainly is.

While economists are trying to understand the sources of the business cycle, the government and the Fed are doing the best they can to moderate the cycle. In the years since World War II, there appears to have been some success. Although the business cycle has not disappeared, it has become much less severe.

Then

What happens to the economy when people lose confidence in banks? They withdraw their funds. These withdrawals feed on themselves, creating a snowball of withdrawals and, eventually, panic. Short of funds with which to repay depositors, banks call in loans and previously sound businesses are faced with financial distress. They close down and lay off workers. And recession deepens and turns into depression. Bank failures and the resulting decline in the nation's supply of money and credit were a significant factor in deepening and prolonging the Great Depression. But they taught us the importance of stable financial institutions and gave rise to the establishment of federal deposit insurance to prevent future financial collapse.

Now

How can a building designed as a shop have no better use than to be boarded up and left empty? Not enough aggregate demand, say the Keynesians. Not so, say the real business cycle theorists. Technological change has reduced the building's current productivity as a shop to zero. But its expected future productivity is sufficiently high that it is not efficient to refit the building for some other purpose.

All unemployment, whether of buildings or people, can be explained in a similar way. For example, how can it be that during a recession, a person trained as a shop clerk is without work? Not enough aggregate demand is one answer. Another is that the current productivity of shop clerks is low but their expected future productivity is sufficiently high that it does not pay an unemployed clerk to retrain for a job that is currently available.

It is now almost 70 years since the Great Depression. Although we've had many recessions since then, none of them compare with the severity of that event. Some credit for avoiding another major depression must go to the Federal Reserve Board and the monetary policy it has pursued. Next you can meet Professor Frederic Mishkin of Columbia University and former vice-president and director of research at the Federal Reserve Bank of New York.

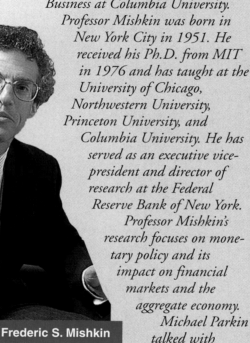

Frederic S. Mishkin

Frederic S. Mishkin

is the A. Barton Hepburn Professor of Economics in the Graduate School of Business at Columbia University. Professor Mishkin was born in New York City in 1951. He received his Ph.D. from MIT in 1976 and has taught at the University of Chicago, Northwestern University, Princeton University, and Columbia University. He has served as an executive vice-president and director of research at the Federal Reserve Bank of New York. Professor Mishkin's research focuses on monetary policy and its impact on financial markets and the aggregate economy.
Michael Parkin talked with Professor Mishkin about his work, the role the Fed plays in monetary policy, and the legacy of Irving Fisher.

Why are you an economist?
The Great Depression was the most important event in my father's life, and we talked about it continually at the dinner table. We also talked about the stock market. These discussions piqued my interest in economics. When I went to college, I thought of becoming a physicist, but I realized that economics has many of same attributes. Both disciplines demand thinking logically and are consistently based on models. The real-world problems that were implicit

in the study of economics proved much more interesting to me then. I realized that economics was my calling, and in fact, it was one of the best choices I've ever made.

What are the most basic principles that you find yourself repeatedly returning to in your professional life, and especially in your life as the director of research at the New York Fed.
A key principle is that incentives are everything. Particularly in today's world, where you need creativity, you cannot motivate people to do good research by just commanding them. You instead need to motivate them by saying, "Do your own work, figure it out yourself, but, on the other hand, I'm going to give you the right incentives." A second principle is the concept of backward induction. If you think about where you want to be and work backwards, you are frequently way ahead of the game. Not only are these two concepts extremely useful in thinking about real-world economic problems, they've been absolutely invaluable to me in managing the Fed's research group of 150 people. We have an annual evaluation process followed by a salary review, and promotions are determined by how well people are doing and how well they respond to incentives.

Does the work of Federal Reserve banks directly contribute to the quality of the monetary policy that is developed?
In economics we never really have answers, but we are able to understand things better through research that initiates debate and makes good policy outcomes more likely. Many of the new

ideas that are published in the academic journals have helped to guide policy makers. I have stressed the value of basic research here at the Federal Reserve Bank of New York and have emphasized our need to be at the very frontier of ideas. We also have to make decisions from day to day that involves much more nitty-gritty research. For example, we have to forecast the economy and try to understand what's going on in the inflation process.

We are enjoying one of longest uninterrupted recoveries in U.S. economic history, and there's little sign of either serious inflation or a serious recession. To what do you attribute this successful run? What part do you think the Fed can take credit for, and where else would you allocate credit, if anywhere?
There's a fair amount of credit due to the Fed, but I'm going to use an adage that my mother always said to me, "It's better to be lucky than good, but it's even better to be good and lucky." The Fed has been both good and lucky. The "good" part is that the Fed has acted in accordance with the results of economic research that indicates that good monetary policy is forward looking. There are lags from monetary policy to inflation on the order of two to three years. This indicates that monetary policy actions today have little effect on today's inflation but are highly relevant to what will happen to

future inflation. We must look to the future if we are to promote a stable economic environment in which we have very low inflation. In February 1994, when the Fed started to raise interest rates, unemployment was close to the 7 percent range and inflation pressures were nonexistent. Yet, looking several years down the road, we realized that if we did not start to raise interest rates and tighten monetary policy, then we would eventually have an overheated

economy with inflation out of control. The preemptive policy of raising interest rates was extremely successful because it helped the inflation rate to stay very low, and the economy continued to grow at a sustainable pace. Another benefit of pursuing a preemptive policy is that markets and businesses understand that the central bank will be serious about controlling inflation. That produces a much more stable environment because businesses know they can't solve their problems by just raising prices. Instead, they have to be efficient and keep costs low. The Fed has also been "lucky." Even if the Fed is doing the right thing during a business cycle expansion, there may be a tendency for the economy to overheat a little bit and a little bit of inflation to occur. This has not hap-

pened. The economy is about as good as it can get, and that requires not only good policy but also some luck.

The traditional categories for discussing policy involve terms such as *rules*, *discretion*, and *fixed rules* versus *feedback rules*. Is that language of use in thinking about Fed policy?
I think that there's a problem with the dichotomy between rules and discretion. One part of the literature views rules as being critical to solving problems such as time inconsistency. Trying to do what looks good right now but not worrying about the future may result in a sequence of policies that lead to poor outcomes in the long run. You have to avoid the temptation to do what looks like the right thing today and ignore the long run. That's one of the reasons why people feel that rules are important. On the other hand, the criticism of rules is that they are too rigid, particularly for dealing with unexpected events. Rules can, in that situation, lead to a very bad outcome. An alternative is to pursue a policy that is basically constrained discretion. It's rulelike, but without a rigid rule. For example, inflation-targeting regimes that have been pursued in many countries throughout the world in recent years are neither a rule nor discretion. They are, instead, constrained discretion. My view is that a good monetary policy should always be rulelike; but, on the other hand, the idea of putting in fixed rules is probably not a good idea.

For the past 15 years the real business cycle research agenda has downplayed the role of money. How do you evaluate the recent real business cycle research program?

The real business cycle literature takes the view that monetary policy is not important to the actual short-term business cycle. I think that monetary policy is more important to the business cycle than real business cycle models give credit for. There is evidence that monetary policy has been important. For example, during the early 1980s, the Federal Reserve took very active steps to get inflation under control and the result was a quite severe recession, but eventually the tight monetary policy produced the right outcome, which was low inflation. I would also characterize the Great Depression as a period where monetary policy performed very poorly and contributed to the most severe economic contraction in the U.S. history. I think monetary policy actions were extremely important during that episode and extremely important during the period 1980 to 1982. On the other hand, real business cycle literature points out that the degree of control that monetary policy authorities can exert on the business cycle is indeed limited, and I am quite sympathetic to this view. The idea that the monetary authorities are able to tweak the business cycle at every turn is just not correct because the actual degree of certainty as to what will happen as a result of certain monetary policy actions is by no

means clear. The real business cycle literature has made people aware that monetary policy cannot be fully in control of what happens in the business cycle. On the other hand, I think that it's overstretching to say that monetary policy actions don't have real effects.

How can students help themselves to be more able to address interesting, real problems?

It is critical to get students to apply what they learn in class to their everyday lives. I tell my students that they must be reading newspapers such as *The Wall Street Journal, The Financial Times,* or *The New York Times* for business and financial news. I also tell students that they actually can use economic principles such as adverse selection and moral hazard to solve real-world problems every day. For example, if somebody's a rich person and is thinking about getting married, he or she faces an adverse selection problem: Does the other person love me because I'm wealthy rather than because I'm a lovable person?

In addition to managing the research group, I participate in the management committee of the bank. I've been able to actively contribute to the management of this bank because I can use economic principles to discuss what I think would be sensible solutions to problems. Economics is wonderful training for being able to solve many problems that hit you every day.

What, for you, is the legacy of Irving Fisher?

Irving Fisher is one of the extraordinary American economists. He's famous for the quantity theory of money, which is extremely useful in thinking about the importance of money to the economy. He was a pioneer whose work on interest rates is still valuable today in thinking about how to conduct monetary policy. He also did pathbreaking work for which he was not famous. For example, his paper "The Debt Deflation Theory of the Great Depression" has led to a much better understanding of financial crises in today's world.

What can an undergraduate gain from taking an economics course?

Economics is an important part of a liberal arts education and is essential for law and MBA students. For the first time in my life, I've actually been a manager, and one of the things that is really striking is how useful economic concepts have been to helping me to be effective. I now can go back to my MBA students and show them that many of these concepts are ones that I actually used in practice to make me a better manager.

Economics is not only useful in helping people become professionals, but also extremely useful in terms of making them better educated citizens. Yes, I do want to train people to help them be successful directly in their careers, but I also want to make them more successful, generally, as people. I think economics is a very powerful tool in achieving that.

Chapter 19

Trading with the World

Silk Routes and Sucking Sounds

Since ancient times, people have expanded their trading as far as technology allowed. Marco Polo opened up the silk route between Europe and China in the thirteenth century. Today, container ships laden with cars and machines and Boeing 747s stuffed with farm-fresh foods ply sea and air routes, carrying billions of dollars worth of goods. Why do people go to such great lengths to trade with those in other nations? ◆ Low-wage Mexico has entered into a free trade agreement with high-wage Canada and the United States—the North American Free Trade Agreement, or NAFTA. According to Texas billionaire Ross Perot, this agreement has caused a "giant sucking sound" and transferred jobs from Michigan to Mexico. Is Ross Perot right? How can we compete with a country that pays its workers a fraction of U.S. wages? Are there any industries, besides perhaps the Hollywood movie industry, in which we have an advantage? ◆ In 1930, Congress passed the Smoot-Hawley Act, which imposed a 45 percent tariff (rising to 60 percent by 1933) on one third of U.S. imports. This move provoked widespread retaliation and a tariff war among the world's major trading countries. After World War II, a process of trade liberalization brought about a gradual reduction of tariffs. What are the effects of tariffs on international trade? Why don't we have completely unrestricted international trade?

◆ In this chapter, we're going to learn about international trade. We'll discover how all nations can gain by specializing in producing the goods and services in which they have a comparative advantage and trading with other countries. We'll discover that *all* countries can compete, no matter how high their wages. We'll also explain why countries restrict trade.

After studying this chapter, you will be able to:

- Describe the patterns in international trade

- Explain comparative advantage and explain why all countries can gain from international trade

- Explain how economies of scale and diversity of taste lead to gains from trade

- Explain why trade restrictions reduce our imports, exports, and consumption possibilities

- Explain the arguments used to justify trade restrictions and show how they are flawed

- Explain why we have trade restrictions

Patterns and Trends in International Trade

THE GOODS AND SERVICES THAT WE BUY FROM people in other countries are called **imports**. The goods and services that we sell to people in other countries are called **exports**. What are the most important things that we import and export? Most people would probably guess that a rich nation such as the United States imports raw materials and exports manufactured goods. Although that is one feature of U.S. international trade, it is not its most important feature. The vast bulk of our exports *and* imports is manufactured goods. We sell foreigners earth-moving equipment, airplanes, supercomputers, and scientific equipment, and we buy televisions, VCRs, blue jeans, and T-shirts from them. Also, we are a major exporter of agricultural products and raw materials. We also import and export a huge volume of services.

Trade in Goods

Manufactured goods account for 50 percent of our exports and for 60 percent of our imports. Industrial materials (raw materials and semimanufactured items) account for 17 percent of our exports and for 20 percent of our imports, and agricultural products account for only 7 percent of our exports and 3 percent of our imports. Our largest individual export and import items are capital goods and autos.

But goods account for only 74 percent of our exports and 83 percent of our imports. The rest of our international trade is in services.

Trade in Services

You may be wondering how a country can "export" and "import" services. Here are some examples.

If you take a vacation in France and travel there on an Air France flight from New York, you import transportation services from France. The money you spend in France on hotel bills and restaurant meals is also a U.S. import of services. Similarly, the vacation taken by a French student in the United States counts as an U.S. export of services to France.

When we import TV sets from South Korea, the owner of the ship that transports them might be Greek and the company that insures them might be British. The payments that we make for the transportation

and insurance are U.S. imports of services. Similarly, when an American shipping company transports California wine to Tokyo, the transportation cost is an American export of a service to Japan. Our international trade in these types of services is large and growing.

Geographical Patterns

The United States has trading links with every part of the world, but Canada is our biggest single trading partner for both exports and imports. We buy 45 percent of our imports from Japan and other Asian countries such as China, Hong Kong, South Korea, and Taiwan, and we sell a similar percentage of our exports to Asia, Europe, Latin America, and Canada.

Trends in the Volume of Trade

In 1960, we exported less than 5 percent of total output and imported 4 1/2 percent of the goods and services that we bought. In 1998, we exported 11 percent of total output and imported 13 percent of the goods and services that we bought.

On the export side, capital goods, automobiles, food, and raw materials have remained large items and held a roughly constant share of total exports, but the composition of imports has changed. Food and raw material imports have fallen steadily. Imports of fuel increased dramatically during the 1970s but fell during the 1980s. Imports of machinery have grown, and today they approach 50 percent of total imports.

Balance of Trade and International Borrowing

The value of exports minus the value of imports is called the **balance of trade.** In 1998, the U.S. balance of trade was a negative $170 billion. Our imports were $170 billion more than our exports. When we import more than we export, as we did in 1998, we borrow from foreigners or sell some of our assets. When we export more than we import, we make loans to foreigners or buy some of their assets.

We study the *balance* of trade in Chapter 20. In this chapter, our goal is to understand the factors that influence the *volume* and *directions* of international trade rather than its balance. And the keys to this understanding are the concepts of opportunity cost and comparative advantage.

Opportunity Cost and Comparative Advantage

THE FUNDAMENTAL FORCE THAT GENERATES international trade is *comparative advantage*. And the basis of comparative advantage is divergent *opportunity costs*. You met these ideas in Chapter 3, when we learned about the gains from specialization and exchange between Tom and Nancy.

Tom and Nancy each specialize in producing just one good and then trade with each other. Most nations do not go to the extreme of specializing in a single good and importing everything else. Nonetheless, nations can increase the consumption of all goods if they redirect their scarce resources toward the production of those goods and services in which they have a comparative advantage.

To see how this outcome occurs, we'll apply the same basic ideas we learned in the case of Tom and Nancy to trade among nations. We'll begin by recalling how we can use the production possibility frontier to measure opportunity cost. Then we'll see how divergent opportunity costs bring comparative advantage and gains from trade for countries as well as for individuals even though no country completely specializes in the production of just one good.

Opportunity Cost in Farmland

Farmland (a fictitious country) can produce grain and cars at any point inside or along its production possibility frontier, *PPF*, shown in Fig. 19.1. (We're holding constant the output of all the other goods that Farmland produces.) The Farmers (the people of Farmland) are consuming all the grain and cars that they produce, and they are operating at point *a* in the figure. That is, Farmland is producing and consuming 15 billion bushels of grain and 8 million cars each year. What is the opportunity cost of a car in Farmland?

We can answer that question by calculating the slope of the production possibility frontier at point *a*. The magnitude of the slope of the frontier measures the opportunity cost of one good in terms of the other. To measure the slope of the frontier at point *a*, place a straight line tangential to the frontier at point *a* and calculate the slope of that straight line. Recall that the formula for the slope of a line is the change in the value of the variable measured on the *y*-axis divided by the change in the value of the variable measured on the *x*-axis as we move along the line.

Here, the variable measured on the *y*-axis is billions of bushels of grain, and the variable measured on the *x*-axis is millions of cars. So the slope is the change in the number of bushels of grain divided by the change in the number of cars.

As you can see from the red triangle at point *a* in the figure, if the number of cars produced increases by 2 million, grain production decreases by 18 billion bushels. Therefore the magnitude of the slope is 18 billion divided by 2 million, which equals 9,000. To get one more car, the people of Farmland must give up 9,000 bushels of grain. Thus the opportunity cost of 1 car is 9,000 bushels of grain. Equivalently, 9,000 bushels of grain cost 1 car. For the people of Farmland, these opportunity costs are the prices they face. The price of a car is 9,000 bushels of grain, and the price of 9,000 bushels of grain is 1 car.

FIGURE 19.1

Opportunity Cost in Farmland

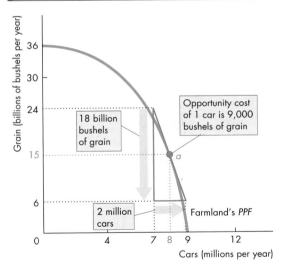

Farmland produces and consumes 15 billion bushels of grain and 8 million cars a year. That is, it produces and consumes at point *a* on its production possibility frontier. Opportunity cost is equal to the magnitude of the slope of the production possibility frontier. The red triangle tells us that at point *a*, 18 billion bushels of grain must be forgone to get 2 million cars. That is, at point *a*, 2 million cars cost 18 billion bushels of grain. Equivalently, 1 car costs 9,000 bushels of grain or 9,000 bushels cost 1 car.

Opportunity Cost in Mobilia

Figure 19.2 shows the production possibility frontier of Mobilia (another fictitious country). Like the Farmers, the Mobilians consume all the grain and cars that they produce. Mobilia consumes 18 billion bushels of grain a year and 4 million cars, at point a'.

Let's calculate the opportunity costs in Mobilia. At point a', the opportunity cost of a car is equal to the magnitude of the slope of the red line tangential to the production possibility frontier, *PPF*. You can see from the red triangle that the magnitude of the slope of Mobilia's production possibility frontier is 6 billion bushels of grain divided by 6 million cars, which equals 1,000 bushels of grain per car. To get one more car, the Mobilians must give up 1,000 bushels of grain. Thus the opportunity cost of 1 car is 1,000 bushels of grain, or, equivalently, the opportunity cost of 1,000 bushels of grain is 1 car. These are the prices faced in Mobilia.

FIGURE 19.2

Opportunity Cost in Mobilia

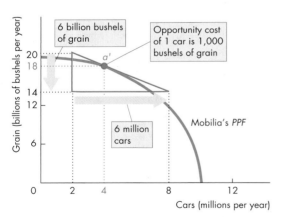

Mobilia produces and consumes 18 billion bushels of grain and 4 million cars a year. That is, it produces and consumes at point a' on its production possibility frontier. Opportunity cost is equal to the magnitude of the slope of the production possibility frontier. The red triangle tells us that at point a', 6 billion bushels of grain must be forgone to get 6 million cars. That is, at point a', the opportunity cost of 6 million cars is 6 billion bushels of grain. Equivalently, 1 car costs 1,000 bushels of grain or 1,000 bushels of grain cost 1 car.

Comparative Advantage

Cars are cheaper in Mobilia than in Farmland. One car costs 9,000 bushels of grain in Farmland but only 1,000 bushels of grain in Mobilia. But grain is cheaper in Farmland than in Mobilia—9,000 bushels of grain costs only 1 car in Farmland, while that same amount of grain costs 9 cars in Mobilia.

Mobilia has a comparative advantage in car production. Farmland has a comparative advantage in grain production. A country has a **comparative advantage** in producing a good if it can produce that good at a lower opportunity cost than any other country.

Let's see how opportunity cost differences and comparative advantage generate gains from international trade.

Gains from Trade

IF MOBILIA BOUGHT GRAIN FOR WHAT IT COSTS Farmland to produce it, then Mobilia could buy 9,000 bushels of grain for 1 car. That is much lower than the cost of growing grain in Mobilia, for there it costs 9 cars to produce 9,000 bushels of grain. If the Mobilians can buy grain at the low Farmland price, they will reap some gains.

If the Farmers can buy cars for what it costs Mobilia to produce them, they will be able to obtain a car for 1,000 bushels of grain. Because it costs 9,000 bushels of grain to produce a car in Farmland, the Farmers would gain from such an opportunity.

In this situation, it makes sense for Mobilians to buy their grain from Farmers and for Farmers to buy their cars from Mobilians. But at what price will Farmland and Mobilia engage in mutually beneficial international trade?

The Terms of Trade

The quantity of grain that Farmland must pay Mobilia for a car is Farmland's **terms of trade** with Mobilia. Because the United States exports and imports many different goods and services, we measure the terms of trade in the real world as an index number that averages the terms of trade over all the items we trade.

The forces of international supply and demand determine the terms of trade. Figure 19.3 illustrates these forces in the Farmland-Mobilia international car market. The quantity of cars *traded internationally* is measured on the *x*-axis. On the *y*-axis, we measure the

FIGURE 19.3

International Trade
in Cars

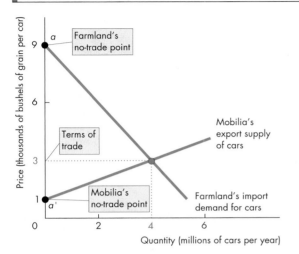

As the price of a car falls, the quantity of imports demanded by Farmland increases—Farmland's import demand curve for cars is downward sloping. As the price of a car rises, the quantity of cars supplied by Mobilia for export increases—Mobilia's export supply curve of cars is upward sloping. Without international trade, the price of a car is 9,000 bushels of grain in Farmland (point *a*) and 1,000 bushels of grain in Mobilia (point *a'*).

With free international trade, the price (terms of trade) is determined where the export supply curve intersects the import demand curve—3,000 bushels of grain per car. At that price, 4 million cars a year are imported by Farmland and exported by Mobilia. The value of grain exported by Farmland and imported by Mobilia is 12 billion bushels a year, the quantity required to pay for the cars imported.

price of a car. This price is expressed as the *terms of trade*—bushels of grain per car. If no international trade takes place, the price of a car in Farmland is 9,000 bushels of grain, its opportunity cost, as indicated by point *a* in the figure. Again, if no trade takes place, the price of a car in Mobilia is 1,000 bushels of grain, its opportunity cost, as indicated by point *a'* in the figure. The no-trade points *a* and *a'* in Fig. 19.3 correspond to the points identified by those same letters in Figs. 19.1 and 19.2. The lower the price of a car (terms of trade), the greater is the quantity of cars that the Farmers are willing to import from the Mobilians. This fact is illustrated by the downward-sloping curve, which shows Farmland's import demand for cars.

The Mobilians respond in the opposite direction. The higher the price of a car (terms of trade), the greater is the quantity of cars that Mobilians are willing to export to Farmers. This fact is reflected in Mobilia's export supply of cars—the upward-sloping line in Fig. 19.3.

The international market in cars determines the equilibrium price (terms of trade) and quantity traded. This equilibrium occurs where the import demand curve intersects the export supply curve. In this case, the equilibrium price is 3,000 bushels of grain per car. Mobilia exports and Farmland imports four million cars a year. Notice that the terms of trade are lower than the initial price in Farmland but higher than the initial price in Mobilia.

Balanced Trade

The number of cars exported by Mobilia—4 million a year—is exactly equal to the number of cars imported by Farmland. How does Farmland pay for its cars? By exporting grain. How much grain does Farmland export? You can find the answer by noticing that for 1 car, Farmland has to pay 3,000 bushels of grain. Hence, for 4 million cars, they have to pay 12 billion bushels of grain. Thus Farmland's exports of grain are 12 billion bushels a year. Mobilia imports this same quantity of grain.

Mobilia is exchanging 4 million cars for 12 billion bushels of grain each year, and Farmland is doing the opposite, exchanging 12 billion bushels of grain for 4 million cars. Trade is balanced between these two countries. The value received from exports equals the value paid out for imports.

Changes in Production and Consumption

We've seen that international trade makes it possible for Farmers to buy cars at a lower price than that at which they can produce them for themselves. Equivalently, Farmers can sell their grain for a higher price. International trade also enables Mobilians to sell their cars for a higher price. Equivalently, Mobilians can buy grain for a lower price. Thus everybody gains. How is it possible for *everyone* to gain? What are the changes in production and consumption that accompany these gains?

An economy that does not trade with other economies has identical production and consumption possibilities. Without trade, the economy can consume only what it produces. But with international trade, an economy can consume different quantities of goods from those that it produces. The production possibility frontier describes the limit of what a country can produce, but it does not describe the limits to what it can consume. Figure 19.4 will help you to see the distinction between production possibilities and consumption possibilities when a country trades with other countries.

First of all, notice that the figure has two parts, part (a) for Farmland and part (b) for Mobilia. The production possibility frontiers that you saw in Figs. 19.1 and 19.2 are reproduced here. The slopes of the two black lines in the figure represent the opportunity costs in the two countries when there is no international trade. Farmland produces and consumes at point a, and Mobilia produces and consumes at a'. Cars cost 9,000 bushels of grain in Farmland, and 1,000 bushels of grain in Mobilia.

Consumption Possibilities   The red line in each part of Fig. 19.4 shows the country's consumption possibilities with international trade. These two red lines have the same slope, and the magnitude of that slope is the opportunity cost of a car in terms of grain on the world market—3,000 bushels per car. The *slope* of the consumption possibilities line is common to both countries because its magnitude equals the *world* price. But the position of a country's consumption possibilities line depends on the country's production possibilities. A country cannot produce outside its production possibility curve, so its consumption possibility curve touches its production possibility curve. Thus Farmland could choose to consume at point b with no international trade or at any point on its red consumption possibilities line with international trade.

Free Trade Equilibrium   With international trade, the producers of cars in Mobilia can get a higher price for their output. As a result, they increase the quantity of car production. At the same time, grain producers in Mobilia get a lower price for their grain, and so they reduce production. Producers in Mobilia adjust their output by moving along their production possibility frontier until the opportunity cost in Mobilia equals the world price (the opportunity cost in the world market). This situation arises when Mobilia is producing at point b' in Fig. 19.4(b).

But the Mobilians do not consume at point b'. That is, they do not increase their consumption of

cars and decrease their consumption of grain. Instead, they sell some of their car production to Farmland in exchange for some of Farmland's grain. They trade internationally. But to see how that works out, we first need to check in with Farmland to see what's happening there.

In Farmland, producers of cars now get a lower price and producers of grain get a higher price. As a consequence, producers in Farmland decrease car production and increase grain production. They adjust their outputs by moving along the production possibility frontier until the opportunity cost of a car in terms of grain equals the world price (the opportunity cost on the world market). They move to point b in part (a). But the Farmers do not consume at point b. Instead, they trade some of their additional grain production for the now cheaper cars from Mobilia.

The figure shows us the quantities consumed in the two countries. We saw in Fig. 19.3 that Mobilia exports 4 million cars a year and Farmland imports those cars. We also saw that Farmland exports 12 billion bushels of grain a year and Mobilia imports that grain. Thus Farmland's consumption of grain is 12 billion bushels a year less than it produces, and its consumption of cars is 4 million a year more than it produces. Farmland consumes at point c in Fig. 19.4(a).

Similarly, we know that Mobilia consumes 12 billion bushels of grain more than it produces and 4 million cars fewer than it produces. Thus Mobilia consumes at point c' in Fig. 19.4(b).

Calculating the Gains from Trade

You can now literally see the gains from trade in Fig. 19.4. Without trade, Farmers produce and consume at point a (part a)—a point on Farmland's production possibility frontier. With international trade, Farmers consume at point c in part (a)—a point *outside* the production possibility frontier. At point c, Farmers are consuming 3 billion bushels of grain a year and 1 million cars a year more than before. These increases in consumption of both cars and grain, beyond the limits of the production possibility frontier, are the gains from international trade. Mobilians also gain. Without trade, they consume at point a' in part (b)—a point on Mobilia's production possibility frontier. With international trade, they consume at point c'—a point outside the

FIGURE 19.4
Expanding Consumption Possibilities

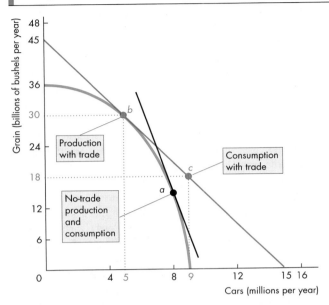

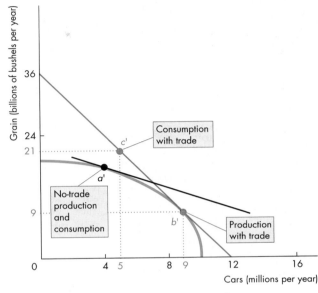

(a) Farmland

With no international trade, the Farmers produce and consume at point *a* and the opportunity cost of a car is 9,000 bushels of grain (the slope of the black line in part a). Also, with no international trade, the Mobilians produce and consume at point *a'* and the opportunity cost of 1,000 bushels of grain is 1 car (the slope of the black line in part b). Goods can be exchanged internationally at a price of 3,000 bushels of grain for 1 car along the red line in each part of the figure. In part (a), Farmland decreases its production of cars and

(b) Mobilia

increases its production of grain, moving from *a* to *b*. It exports grain and imports cars, and it consumes at point *c*. The Farmers have more of both cars and grain than they would if they produced all their own goods—at point *a*. In part (b), Mobilia increases car production and decreases grain production, moving from *a'* to *b'*. Mobilia exports cars and imports grain, and it consumes at point *c'*. The Mobilians have more of both cars and grain than they would if they produced all their own goods—at point *a'*.

production possibility frontier. With international trade, Mobilia consumes 3 billion bushels of grain a year and 1 million cars a year more than without trade. These are the gains from international trade for Mobilia.

Gains for All

Trade between the Farmers and the Mobilians does not create winners and losers. Everyone wins. Sellers add the net demand of foreigners to their domestic demand, and so their market expands. Buyers are faced with domestic supply plus net foreign supply and so have a larger supply available to them.

REVIEW QUIZ

In what circumstances can countries gain from international trade?

■ What determines the goods and services that a country will export? What determines the goods and services that a country will import?

■ What is a comparative advantage and what role does it play in determining the amount and type of international trade that occurs?.

■ How can it be that all countries gain from international trade and that there are no losers?

Gains from Trade in Reality

THE GAINS FROM TRADE THAT WE HAVE JUST studied between Farmland and Mobilia in grain and cars occur in a model economy—in a world economy that we have imagined. But these same phenomena occur every day in the real global economy.

Comparative Advantage in the Global Economy

We buy TVs and VCRs from Korea, machinery from Europe, and fashion goods from Hong Kong. In exchange, we sell machinery, grain and lumber, airplanes, computers and financial services. All this international trade is generated by comparative advantage, just like the international trade between Farmland and Mobilia in our model economy. All international trade arises from comparative advantage, even when trade is in similar goods such as tools and machines. At first thought, it seems puzzling that countries exchange manufactured goods. Why doesn't each developed country produce all the manufactured goods its citizens want to buy?

Trade in Similar Goods

Why does the United States produce automobiles for export and at the same time import large quantities of them from Canada, Japan, Korea, and Western Europe? Wouldn't it make more sense to produce all the cars that we buy here in the United States? After all, we have access to the best technology available for producing cars. Autoworkers in the United States are surely as productive as their fellow workers in Canada, Western Europe, and Asian countries. So why does the United States have a comparative advantage in some types of cars and Japan and Europe in others?

Diversity of Taste and Economies of Scale

The first part of the answer is that people have a tremendous diversity of taste. Let's stick with the example of cars. Some people prefer a sports car, some prefer a limousine, some prefer a regular, full-size car, and some prefer a minivan. In addition to size and type of car, there are many other dimensions in which cars vary. Some have low fuel consumption, some

have high performance, some are spacious and comfortable, some have a large trunk, some have four-wheel drive, some have front-wheel drive, some have a radiator grill that looks like a Greek temple, and others look like a wedge. People's preferences across these many dimensions vary. The tremendous diversity in tastes for cars means that people value variety and are willing to pay for it in the marketplace.

The second part of the answer to the puzzle is *economies of scale*—the tendency for the average cost to be lower, the larger the scale of production. In such situations, larger and larger production runs lead to ever lower average costs. Many goods, including cars, experience economies of scale. For example, if a car producer makes only a few hundred (or perhaps a few thousand) cars of a particular type and design, the producer must use production techniques that are much more labor-intensive and much less automated than those employed to make hundreds of thousands of cars in a particular model. With short production runs and labor-intensive production techniques, costs are high. With very large production runs and automated assembly lines, production costs are much lower. But to obtain lower costs, the automated assembly lines have to produce a large number of cars.

It is the combination of diversity of taste and economies of scale that determines opportunity cost, produces comparative advantages, and generates such a large amount of international trade in similar commodities. With international trade, each car manufacturer has the whole world market to serve. Each producer can specialize in a limited range of products and then sell its output to the entire world market. This arrangement enables large production runs on the most popular cars and feasible production runs even on the most customized cars demanded by only a handful of people in each country.

The situation in the market for cars is also present in many other industries, especially those producing specialized equipment and parts. For example, the United States exports computer central processor chips but imports memory chips, exports mainframe computers but imports PCs, exports specialized video equipment but imports VCRs. Thus international exchange of similar but slightly differentiated manufactured products is a highly profitable activity.

Let's next see what happens when governments restrict international trade. We'll see that free trade brings the greatest possible benefits. We'll also see why, in spite of the benefits of free trade, governments sometimes restrict trade.

Trade Restrictions

GOVERNMENTS RESTRICT INTERNATIONAL TRADE to protect domestic industries from foreign competition by using two main tools:

1. Tariffs
2. Nontariff barriers

A **tariff** is a tax that is imposed by the importing country when an imported good crosses its international boundary. A **nontariff barrier** is any action other than a tariff that restricts international trade. Examples of nontariff barriers are quantitative restrictions and licensing regulations that limit imports. First, let's look at tariffs.

The History of Tariffs

U.S. tariffs today are modest compared with their historical levels. Figure 19.5 shows the average tariff rate—total tariffs as a percentage of total imports.

You can see in this figure that this average reached a peak of 20 percent in 1933. In that year, three years after the passage of the Smoot-Hawley Act, one third of imports was subject to a tariff, and on those imports, the tariff rate was 60 percent. (The average tariff in Fig. 19.5 for 1933 is 60 percent multiplied by 0.33, which equals 20 percent.) Today, the average tariff rate is only 4 percent.

The reduction in tariffs since World War II followed the signing in 1947 of the **General Agreement on Tariffs and Trade** (GATT). Since its formation, the GATT has organized several rounds of negotiations that have resulted in tariff reductions. One of these, the Kennedy Round, which began in the early 1960s, resulted in large tariff cuts starting in 1967. Another, the Tokyo Round, resulted in further tariff cuts in 1979. The most recent, the Uruguay Round, which started in 1986 and was completed in 1994, was the most ambitious and comprehensive of the rounds. The Uruguay Round also led to the creation of a new **World Trade Organization** (WTO). Membership of the WTO brings greater obligations on countries to observe the GATT rules.

FIGURE 19.5

U.S. Tariffs: 1930–1998

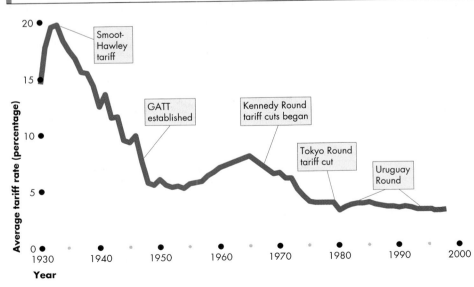

The Smoot-Hawley Act, which was passed in 1930, took U.S. tariffs to a peak average rate of 20 percent in 1933. (One third of imports was subject to a tariff rate of 60 percent.) Since the establishment of GATT in 1947, tariffs have steadily declined in a series of negotiating rounds, the most significant of which are identified in the figure. Tariffs are now as low as they have ever been.

Sources: U.S. Bureau of the Census, *Historical Statistics of the United States, Colonial Times to 1970*, Bicentennial Edition, Part 1 (Washington, D.C., 1975), Series U-212; *Statistical Abstract of the United States: 1986*, 106th edition (Washington, D.C., 1985); and *Statistical Abstract of the United States: 1998*, 118th edition (Washington, D.C., 1998).

In addition to the agreements under the GATT and the WTO, the United States is a party to the **North American Free Trade Agreement** (NAFTA), which became effective on January 1, 1994, and under which barriers to international trade between the United States, Canada, and Mexico will be virtually eliminated after a 15-year phasing-in period.

In other parts of the world, trade barriers have virtually been eliminated among the member countries of the European Union, which has created the largest unified tariff-free market in the world. In 1994, discussions among the Asia-Pacific Economic group (APEC) led to an agreement in principle to work toward a free-trade area that embraces China, all the economies of East Asia and the South Pacific, and the United States and Canada. These countries include the fastest-growing economies and hold the promise of heralding a global free-trade area.

The effort to achieve freer trade underlines the fact that trade in some goods is still subject to extremely high tariffs. The highest tariffs faced by U.S. buyers are those on textiles and footwear. A tariff of more than 10 percent (on the average) is imposed on almost all our imports of textiles and footwear. For example, when you buy a pair of blue jeans for $20, you pay about $5 more than you would if there were no tariffs on textiles. Other goods protected by tariffs are agricultural products, energy and chemicals, minerals, and metals. The meat, cheese, and sugar that you consume cost significantly more because of protection than they would with free international trade.

The temptation on governments to impose tariffs is a strong one. First, tariffs provide revenue to the government. Second, they enable the government to satisfy special interest groups in import-competing industries. But, as we'll see, free international trade brings enormous benefits that are reduced when tariffs are imposed. Let's see how.

How Tariffs Work

To analyze how tariffs work, let's return to the example of trade between Farmland and Mobilia. Figure 19.6 shows the international market for cars in which these two countries are the only traders. The volume of trade and the price of a car are determined at the point of intersection of Mobilia's export supply curve of cars and Farmland's import demand curve for cars.

FIGURE 19.6
The Effects of a Tariff

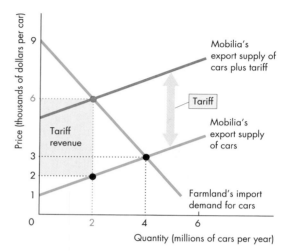

Farmland imposes a tariff on car imports from Mobilia. The tariff increases the price that Farmers have to pay for cars. It shifts the supply curve of cars in Farmland leftward. The vertical distance between the original supply curve and the new one is the amount of the tariff, $4,000 per car. The price of cars in Farmland increases, and the quantity of cars imported decreases. The government of Farmland collects a tariff revenue of $4,000 per car—a total of $8 billion on the 2 million cars imported. Farmland's exports of grain decrease because Mobilia now has a lower income from its exports of cars.

In Fig. 19.6, these two countries trade cars and grain in exactly the same way that we saw in Fig. 19.3. Mobilia exports cars, and Farmland exports grain. The volume of car imports into Farmland is 4 million a year, and the world market price of a car is 3,000 bushels of grain. Fig. 19.6 expresses prices in dollars rather than in units of grain and is based on a money price of grain of $1 a bushel. With grain costing $1 a bushel, the money price of a car is $3,000.

Now suppose that the government of Farmland, perhaps under pressure from car producers, decides to impose a tariff on imported cars. In particular, suppose that a tariff of $4,000 per car is imposed. (This is a huge tariff, but the car producers of Farmland are pretty fed up with competition from Mobilia.) What happens?

- The supply of cars in Farmland decreases.
- The price of a car in Farmland rises.
- The quantity of cars imported by Farmland decreases.
- The government of Farmland collects the tariff revenue.
- Resource use is inefficient.
- The *value* of exports changes by the same amount as the *value* of imports and trade remains balanced.

Change in the Supply of Cars   Farmland cannot buy cars at Mobilia's export supply price. It must pay that price plus the $4,000 tariff. So the supply curve in Farmland shifts leftward. The new supply curve is that labeled "Mobilia's export supply of cars plus tariff." The vertical distance between Mobilia's export supply curve and the new supply curve is the tariff of $4,000 a car.

Rise in Price of Cars   A new equilibrium occurs where the new supply curve intersects Farmland's import demand curve for cars. That equilibrium is at a price of $6,000 a car, up from $3,000 with free trade.

Fall in Imports   Car imports fall from 4 million to 2 million cars a year. At the higher price of $6,000 a car, Farmland's car producers increase their production. Grain production in Farmland decreases as resources are moved into the expanding car industry.

Tariff Revenue   Total expenditure on imported cars by the Farmers is $6,000 a car multiplied by the 2 million cars imported ($12 billion). But not all of that money goes to the Mobilians. They receive $2,000 a car, or $4 billion for the 2 million cars. The difference—$4,000 a car, or a total of $8 billion for the 2 million cars—is collected by the government of Farmland as tariff revenue.

Inefficiency   The people of Farmland are willing to pay $6,000 for the marginal car imported. But the opportunity cost of that car is $2,000. So there is a gain from trading an extra car. In fact, there are gains—willingness to pay exceeds opportunity cost—all the way up to 4 million cars a year. Only when 4 million cars are being traded is the maximum price that a Farmer is willing to pay equal to the minimum price that is acceptable to a Mobilian. Thus restricting trade reduces the gains from trade.

Trade Remains Balanced   With free trade, Farmland was paying $3,000 a car and buying 4 million cars a year from Mobilia. Thus the total amount paid to Mobilia for imports was $12 billion a year. With a tariff, Farmland's imports have been cut to 2 million cars a year and the price paid to Mobilia has also been cut to only $2,000 a car. Thus the total amount paid to Mobilia for imports has been cut to $4 billion a year. Doesn't this fact mean that Farmland now has a balance of trade surplus?

It does not. The price of cars in Mobilia has fallen. But the price of grain remains at $1 a bushel. So the relative price of cars has fallen, and the relative price of grain has increased. With free trade, the Mobilians could buy 3,000 bushels of grain for one car. Now they can buy only 2,000 bushels for a car. With a higher relative price of grain, the quantity demanded by the Mobilians decreases and Mobilia imports less grain. But because Mobilia imports less grain, Farmland exports less grain. In fact, Farmland's grain industry suffers from two sources. First, there is a decrease in the quantity of grain sold to Mobilia. Second, there is increased competition for inputs from the now expanded car industry. Thus the tariff leads to a contraction in the scale of the grain industry in Farmland.

It seems paradoxical at first that a country imposing a tariff on cars hurts its own export industry, decreasing its exports of grain. It may help to think of it this way: Mobilians buy grain with the money they make from exporting cars to Farmland. If they export fewer cars, they cannot afford to buy as much grain. In fact, in the absence of any international borrowing and lending, Mobilia must cut its imports of grain by exactly the same amount as the loss in revenue from its export of cars. Grain imports into Mobilia are cut back to a value of $4 billion, the amount that can be paid for by the new lower revenue from Mobilia's car exports. Thus trade is still balanced. The tariff cuts imports and exports by the same amount. The tariff has no effect on the *balance* of trade, but it reduces the *volume* of trade.

The result that we have just derived is perhaps one of the most misunderstood aspects of international economics. On countless occasions, politicians and others call for tariffs to remove a balance of trade deficit or argue that lowering tariffs would produce a balance of trade deficit. They reach this conclusion by failing to work out all the implications of a tariff.

Let's now turn our attention to the other tool for restricting trade: nontariff barriers.

Nontariff Barriers

The two main forms of nontariff barriers are:

1. Quotas
2. Voluntary export restraints

A **quota** is a quantitative restriction on the import of a particular good, which specifies the maximum amount of the good that can be imported in a given period of time. A **voluntary export restraint** (VER) is an agreement between two governments in which the government of the exporting country agrees to restrain the volume of its own exports.

Quotas are especially prominent in textiles and agriculture. Voluntary export restraints are used to regulate trade between Japan and the United States.

How Quotas and VERs Work

To see how a quota works, suppose that Farmland imposes a quota that restricts its car imports to 2 million cars a year. Figure 19.7 shows the effects of this action. The quota is shown by the vertical red line at 2 million cars a year. Because it is illegal to exceed the quota, car importers buy only that quantity from Mobilia, for which they pay $2,000 a car. But because the import supply of cars is restricted to 2 million cars a year, people in Farmland are willing to pay $6,000 per car. This is the price of a car in Farmland.

The value of imports falls to $4 billion, exactly the same as in the case of the tariff. So with lower incomes from car exports and with a higher relative price of grain, Mobilians cut back on their imports of grain in exactly the same way that they did under a tariff.

The key difference between a quota and a tariff lies in who collects the gap between the import supply price and the domestic price. In the case of a tariff, it is the government of the importing country. In the case of a quota, it goes to the person who has the right to import under the import quota regulations.

A voluntary export restraint is like a quota arrangement in which quotas are allocated to each exporting country. The effects of voluntary export restraints are similar to those of quotas but differ from them in that the gap between the price in the importing country and the export price is captured not by domestic importers but by the foreign exporter. The government of the exporting country has to establish procedures for allocating the restricted volume of exports among its producers.

FIGURE 19.7
The Effects of a Quota

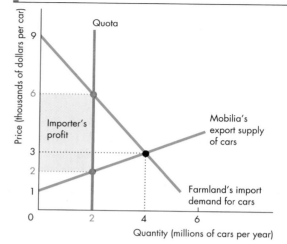

Farmland imposes a quota of 2 million cars a year on car imports from Mobilia. That quantity appears as the vertical line labeled "Quota." Because the quantity of cars supplied by Mobilia is restricted to 2 million, the price at which those cars will be traded increases to $6,000. Importing cars is profitable because Mobilia is willing to supply cars at $2,000 each. There is competition for import quotas.

REVIEW QUIZ

- What happens to a country's consumption possibilities when it opens itself up to international trade and trades freely at world market prices?
- What do trade restrictions do to the gains from international trade?
- What is best for a country: restricted trade, no trade, or free trade?
- What does a tariff on imports do to the volume of imports and the volume of exports?
- In the absence of international borrowing and lending, how do tariffs and other trade restrictions influence the total value of imports and exports and the balance of trade—the value of exports minus the value of imports?

Let's now look at some commonly heard arguments for restricting international trade.

The Case Against Protection

FOR AS LONG AS NATIONS AND INTERNATIONAL trade have existed, people have debated whether a country is better off with free international trade or with protection from foreign competition. The debate continues, but for most economists, a verdict has been delivered and is the one you have just seen. Free trade promotes prosperity for all; protection is inefficient. We've seen the most powerful case for free trade in the example of how Farmland and Mobilia both benefit from their comparative advantage. But there is a broader range of issues in the free trade versus protection debate. Let's review these issues.

Three arguments for restricting international trade are:

■ The national security argument
■ The infant-industry argument
■ The dumping argument

Let's look at each in turn.

The National Security Argument

The national security argument for protection is that a country must protect industries that produce defense equipment and armaments and those on which the defense industries rely for their raw materials and other intermediate inputs. This argument for protection does not withstand close scrutiny.

First, it is an argument for international isolation, for in a time of war, there is no industry that does not contribute to national defense. Second, if the case is made for boosting the output of a strategic industry, it is more efficient to achieve this outcome with a subsidy to the firms in the industry financed out of taxes. Such a subsidy would keep the industry operating at the scale judged appropriate, and free international trade would keep the prices faced by consumers at their world market levels.

The Infant-Industry Argument

The so-called **infant-industry argument** for protection is that it is necessary to protect a new industry to enable it to grow into a mature industry that can compete in world markets. The argument is based on the idea of *dynamic comparative advantage*, which can arise from *learning-by-doing* (see Chapter 3).

Learning-by-doing is a powerful engine of productivity growth, and comparative advantage evolves and changes because of on-the-job experience. But these facts do not justify protection.

First, the infant-industry argument is valid only if the benefits of learning-by-doing *not only* accrue to the owners and workers of the firms in the infant industry but also *spill over* to other industries and parts of the economy. For example, there are huge productivity gains from learning-by-doing in the manufacture of aircraft. But almost all of these gains benefit the stockholders and workers of Boeing and other aircraft producers. Because the people making the decisions, bearing the risk, and doing the work are the ones who benefit, they take the dynamic gains into account when they decide on the scale of their activities. In this case, almost no benefits spill over to other parts of the economy, so there is no need for government assistance to achieve an efficient outcome.

Second, even if the case is made for protecting an infant industry, it is more efficient to do so by a subsidy to the firms in the industry, with the subsidy financed out of taxes.

The Dumping Argument

Dumping occurs when a foreign firm sells its exports at a lower price than its cost of production. Dumping might be used by a firm that wants to gain a global monopoly. In this case, the foreign firm sells its output at a price below its cost to drive domestic firms out of business. When the domestic firms have gone, the foreign firm takes advantage of its monopoly position and charges a higher price for its product. Dumping is usually regarded as a justification for temporary countervailing tariffs.

But there are powerful reasons to resist the dumping argument for protection. First, it is virtually impossible to detect dumping because it is hard to determine a firm's costs. As a result, the test for dumping is whether a firm's export price is below its domestic price. But this test is a weak one because it can be rational for a firm to charge a low price in markets in which the quantity demanded is highly sensitive to price and a higher price in a market in which demand is less price-sensitive.

Second, it is hard to think of a good that is produced by a natural *global* monopoly. So even if all the domestic firms were driven out of business in some industry, it would always be possible to find several and usually many alternative foreign sources of supply and to buy at prices determined in competitive markets.

Third, if a good or service were a truly global natural monopoly, the best way of dealing with it would be by regulation—just as in the case of domestic monopolies. Such regulation would require international cooperation.

The three arguments for protection that we've just examined have an element of credibility. The counterarguments are in general stronger, so these arguments do not make the case for protection. But they are not the only arguments that you might encounter. The many other arguments that are commonly heard are quite simply wrong. They are fatally flawed. The most common of them are that protection:

- Saves jobs
- Allows us to compete with cheap foreign labor
- Brings diversity and stability
- Penalizes lax environmental standards
- Protects national culture
- Prevents rich countries from exploiting developing countries

Saves Jobs

The argument is: When we buy shoes from Brazil or shirts from Taiwan, U.S. workers lose their jobs. With no earnings and poor prospects, these workers become a drain on welfare and spend less, causing a ripple effect of further job losses. The proposed solution to this problem is to ban imports of cheap foreign goods and protect U.S. jobs. The proposal is flawed for the following reasons.

First, free trade does cost some jobs, but it also creates other jobs. It brings about a global rationalization of labor and allocates labor resources to their highest-value activities. Because of international trade in textiles, tens of thousands of workers in the United States have lost jobs because textile mills and other factories have closed. But tens of thousands of workers in other countries have gotten jobs because textile mills have opened there. And tens of thousands of U.S. workers have gotten better-paying jobs than textile workers because other export industries have expanded and created more jobs than have been destroyed.

Second, imports create jobs. They create jobs for retailers that sell imported goods and firms that service those goods. They also create jobs by creating incomes in the rest of the world, some of which are spent on imports of U.S.-made goods and services.

Although protection does save particular jobs, it does so at inordinate cost. For example, textile jobs are protected in the United States by quotas imposed under an international agreement called the Multifiber Arrangement. It has been estimated by the U.S. International Trade Commission (ITC) that because of quotas, 72,000 jobs exist in textiles that would otherwise disappear and annual clothing expenditure in the United States is $15.9 billion, or $160 per family higher than it would be with free trade. Equivalently, the ITC estimates that each textile job saved costs $221,000 a year.

Allows Us to Compete with Cheap Foreign Labor

With the removal of protective tariffs in U.S. trade with Mexico, Ross Perot said we would hear a "giant sucking sound" of jobs rushing to Mexico (one of which is shown in the cartoon). Let's see what's wrong with this view.

The labor cost of a unit of output equals the wage rate divided by labor productivity. For example, if a U.S. auto worker earns $30 an hour and produces 15

"I don't know what the hell happened—one minute I'm at work in Flint, Michigan, then there's a giant sucking sound and suddenly here I am in Mexico."

Drawing by M. Stevens; © 1993
The New Yorker Magazine, Inc.

units of output an hour, the average labor cost of a unit of output is $2. If a Mexican auto assembly worker earns $3 an hour and produces 1 unit of output an hour, the average labor cost of a unit of output is $3. Other things remaining the same, the higher a worker's productivity, the higher is the worker's wage rate. High-wage workers have high productivity. Low-wage workers have low productivity.

Although high-wage U.S. workers are more productive, on the average, than low-wage Mexican workers, there are differences across industries. U.S. labor is relatively more productive in some activities than in others. For example, the productivity of U.S. workers in producing movies, financial services, and customized computer chips is relatively higher than in the production of metals and some standardized machine parts. The activities in which U.S. workers are relatively more productive than their Mexican counterparts are those in which the United States has a *comparative advantage*. By engaging in free trade, increasing our production and exports of the goods and services in which we have a comparative advantage and decreasing our production and increasing our imports of the goods and services in which our trading partners have a comparative advantage, we can make ourselves and the citizens of other countries better off.

Brings Diversity and Stability

A diversified investment portfolio is less risky than one that has all the eggs in one basket. The same is true for an economy's production. A diversified economy fluctuates less than an economy that produces only one or two goods.

But big, rich, diversified economies like those of the United States, Japan, and Europe do not have this type of stability problem. Even a country like Saudi Arabia that produces almost only one good (oil) can benefit from specializing in the activity at which it has a comparative advantage and then investing in a wide range of other countries to bring greater stability to its income and consumption.

Penalizes Lax Environmental Standards

A new argument for protection is that many poorer countries, such as Mexico, do not have the same environment policies that we have and, because they

are willing to pollute and we are not, we cannot compete with them without tariffs. So if they want free trade with the richer and "greener" countries, they must clean up their environments to our standards.

This argument for trade restrictions is weak. First, not all poorer countries have significantly lower environmental standards than the United States has. Many poor countries and the former Communist countries of Eastern Europe do have bad environment records. But some countries enforce strict laws. Second, a poor country cannot afford to be as concerned about its environment as a rich country can. The best hope for a better environment in Mexico and in other developing countries is rapid income growth through free trade. As their incomes grow, developing countries will have the *means* to match their desires to improve their environment. Third, poor countries have a comparative advantage at doing "dirty" work, which helps rich countries achieve higher environment standards than they otherwise could.

Protects National Culture

The national culture argument for protection is not heard much in the United States, but it is a commonly heard argument in Canada and Europe.

The expressed fear is that free trade in books, magazines, movies, and television programs means U.S. domination and the end of local culture. So, the reasoning continues, it is necessary to protect domestic culture industries from free international trade to ensure the survival of a national cultural identity.

Protection of these industries is common and takes the form of nontariff barriers. For example, local content regulations on radio and television broadcasting and in magazines is often required.

The cultural identity argument for protection has no merit, and it is one more example of rent seeking. Writers, publishers, and broadcasters want to limit foreign competition so that they can earn larger economic profits. There is no actual danger to national culture. In fact, many of the creators of so-called American cultural products are not Americans, but the talented citizens of other countries, ensuring the survival of their national cultural identities in Hollywood! Also, if national culture is in danger, there is no surer way of helping it on its way out than by impoverishing the nation whose culture it is. And protection is an effective way of doing just that.

Prevents Rich Countries from Exploiting Developing Countries

Another new argument for protection is that international trade must be restricted to prevent the people of the rich industrial world from exploiting the poorer people of the developing countries, forcing them to work for slave wages.

Wage rates in some developing countries are indeed very low. But by trading with developing countries, we increase the demand for the goods that these countries produce, and, more significantly, we increase the demand for their labor. When the demand for labor in developing countries increases, the wage rate also increases. So, far from exploiting people in developing countries, trade improves their opportunities and increases their incomes.

We have reviewed the arguments that are commonly heard in favor of protection and the counter-arguments against them. There is one counter-argument to protection that is general and quite overwhelming. Protection invites retaliation and can trigger a trade war. The best example of a trade war occurred during the Great Depression of the 1930s when the Smoot-Hawley Tariff was introduced. Country after country retaliated with its own tariff, and in a short period, world trade had almost disappeared. The costs to all countries were large and led to a renewed international resolve to avoid such self-defeating moves in the future. They also led to the creation of GATT and are the impetus behind NAFTA, APEC, and the European Union.

R E V I E W   Q U I Z

- Is there any merit to the view that we should restrict international trade to achieve national security goals, to stimulate the growth of new industries, or to restrain foreign monopoly?

- Is there any merit to the view that we should restrict international trade to save jobs, compensate for low foreign wages, make the economy more diversified, compensate for costly environmental policies, protect national culture, or protect developing countries from being exploited?

- Is there any merit to the view that we should restrict international trade for any reason? What is the main argument against trade restrictions?

Why Is International Trade Restricted?

WHY, DESPITE ALL THE ARGUMENTS AGAINST protection, is trade restricted? There are two key reasons:

- Tariff revenue
- Rent seeking

Tariff Revenue

Government revenue is costly to collect. In the developed countries such as the United States, a well-organized tax-collection system is in place that can generate billions of dollars of income tax and sales tax revenues. This tax-collecting system is made possible by the fact that most economic transactions are done by firms that must keep properly audited financial records. Without such records, the revenue collection agencies (the Internal Revenue Service in the United States) would be severely hampered in the work. Even with audited financial accounts, some proportion of potential tax revenue is lost. Nonetheless, for the industrialized countries, the income tax and sales taxes are the major sources of revenue and the tariff plays a very small role.

But governments in developing countries have a difficult time collecting taxes from their citizens. Much economic activity takes place in an informal economy with few financial records. So only a small amount of revenue is collected from income taxes and sales taxes in these countries. The one area in which economic transactions are well recorded and audited is in international trade. So this activity is an attractive base for tax collection in these countries and is used much more extensively than in the developed countries.

Rent Seeking

The major reason why international trade is restricted is because of rent seeking. Free trade increases consumption possibilities *on the average,* but not everyone shares in the gain and some people even lose. Free trade brings benefits to some and imposes costs on others, with total benefits exceeding total costs. It is the uneven distribution of costs and benefits that is the principal source of impediment to achieving more liberal international trade.

Returning to our example of trade in cars and grain between Farmland and Mobilia, the benefits to Farmland from free trade accrue to all the producers of grain and those producers of cars who would not have to bear the costs of adjusting to a smaller car industry. These costs are transition costs, not permanent costs. The costs of moving to free trade are borne by those car producers and their employees who have to become grain producers. The number of people who gain will, in general, be enormous compared with the number who lose. The gain per person will therefore be rather small. The loss per person to those who bear the loss will be large. Because the loss that falls on those who bear it is large, it will pay those people to incur considerable expense to lobby against free trade. On the other hand, it will not pay those who gain to organize to achieve free trade. The gain from trade for any one individual is too small for that individual to spend much time or money on a political organization to achieve free trade. The loss from free trade will be seen as being so great by those bearing that loss that they *will* find it profitable to join a political organization to prevent free trade. Each group is optimizing—weighing benefits against costs and choosing the best action for themselves. The anti-free-trade group will, however, undertake a larger quantity of political lobbying than the pro-free-trade group.

Compensating Losers

If, in total, the gains from free international trade exceed the losses, why don't those who gain compensate those who lose so that everyone is in favor of free trade? To some degree, such compensation does take place. When Congress approved the NAFTA deal with Canada and Mexico, it set up a $56 million fund to support and retrain workers who lost their jobs because of the new trade agreement. During the first six months of the operation of NAFTA, only 5,000 workers applied for benefits under this scheme.

The losers from freer international trade are also compensated indirectly through the normal unemployment compensation arrangements. But only limited attempts are made to compensate those who lose from free international trade. The main reason why full compensation is not attempted is that the costs of identifying all the losers and estimating the value of

their losses would be enormous. Also, it would never be clear whether a person who has fallen on hard times is suffering because of free trade or for other reasons, perhaps reasons that are largely under the control of the individual. Furthermore, some people who look like losers at one point in time may, in fact, wind up gaining. The young auto worker who loses his job in Michigan and becomes a computer assembly worker in Minneapolis resents the loss of work and the need to move. But a year or two later, looking back on events, he counts himself fortunate. He has made a move that has increased his income and given him greater job security.

It is because we do not, in general, compensate the losers from free international trade that protectionism is such a popular and permanent feature of our national economic and political life.

R E V I E W   Q U I Z

- What are the two main reasons for imposing a tariff on imports?
- What type of country benefits most from the revenue that tariffs generate? Does the United States need to use tariffs to raise revenue for the government?
- If trade restrictions are costly, why do we use them? Why don't the people who gain from trade organize a political force that is strong enough to ensure that their interests are protected?

◇ You've now seen how free international trade enables all nations to gain from specialization and trade. By producing goods in which we have a comparative advantage and trading some of our production for that of others, we expand our consumption possibilities. Placing impediments on that trade restricts the extent to which we can gain from specialization and trade. Opening our country up to free international trade expands the market for the things that we sell and raises their relative price. The market for the things that we buy also expands, and the relative price falls. *Reading Between the Lines* on pp. 458–459 looks at a recent example of an international trade dispute between the United States and Europe.

In the final chapter, we're going to examine the balance of international trade and the forces that influence the exchange rate.

Tariffs in Action

T H E   N E W   Y O R K   T I M E S , MARCH 4, 1999

Miffed at Europe, U.S. Raises Tariffs for Luxury Goods

BY DAVID E. SANGER

The United States heated up two politically contentious trade disputes with Europe today, slapping 100 percent tariffs on $520 million in European products and threatening to ban Europe's supersonic pride, the Concorde, from landing in the United States.

The tariffs imposed by the Clinton Administration on goods such as Louis Vuitton handbags, Parma ham, pecorino cheese and Scottish cashmere sweaters, which essentially double their price and make it much harder for European exporters to sell them in this country, are part of a six-year battle over trade in bananas.

The threat to ban the Concorde is in a bill passed overwhelmingly in the House of Representatives today, in retaliation for a European ruling that would ban many older American airplanes from landing in Europe. American officials say Europe's restriction is designed to promote the sale of new engines and aircraft made by European manufacturers.

But both battles are really about the enormous tensions that have erupted between the United States and a Europe newly unified by a common currency. On both continents, politicians are feeling the heat from slowing exports, and fear a slowdown in economic growth later this year. And Washington and the European Union find themselves unable to resolve seemingly ordinary economic disputes, with each accusing the other of defying the World Trade Organization, the four-year-old court of international trade.

The court has stepped in to arbitrate the banana dispute, which involves European limits on imports, and has become the battleground over other politically sensitive issues, including Europe's ban on imported beef from cattle raised with hormones. ...

The trade fight with Europe has become a major issue at the White House, with President Clinton becoming directly involved in some of the negotiations, most recently with French President Jacques Chirac. But the economic impact is relatively modest: The United States imported $176.3 billion in goods from nations in the European Union last year, meaning that today's sanctions apply to one-quarter of 1 percent of goods imported from Europe. ...

Essence of the Story

■ The United States imposed a 100 percent tariff on $520 million of European products such as Louis Vuitton handbags, Parma ham, pecorino cheese, and Scottish cashmere sweaters in a six-year battle over trade in bananas.

■ The United States also threatened to ban the Concorde (the supersonic airplane) from landing in the United States in retaliation for a European ruling that would ban many older American airplanes from landing in Europe.

■ The economic impact of the tariff is relatively modest because it applies to one quarter of 1 percent of the goods imported from Europe.

Economic Analysis

■ Figure 1 shows the U.S. market for a luxury good such as a high-quality handbag or a cashmere sweater.

■ The demand curve of U.S. buyers of this luxury good is D.

■ There are two supply curves: the supply curve of the European producers, S_E, and the supply curve of U.S. producers, S_{US}.

■ With no tariff, the quantity of this luxury good bought in the United States is QC_0. Of these, QP_0 are produced in the United States and the rest are imported, as shown by the arrow in Fig. 1.

■ Now the United States puts a 100 percent tariff on the imports of these items. The foreign good is now supplied to the U.S. market at the original supply price, $100, plus the tariff, $100, so the supply curve of this luxury good from Europe shifts to become S_E + *tariff*.

■ With the tariff, the quantity of the good bought in the United States is QC_1. Of these, QP_1 are produced in the United States and the rest are imported from Europe, as shown by the arrow in Fig. 1.

■ The tariff decreases U.S. consumption and imports and increases U.S. production.

■ Figure 2 shows the winners and the losers in the United States.

■ The winners include U.S producers who gain additional economic profit, which is shown by the blue area in Fig. 2.

■ Another winner is the U.S. government, which collects additional revenue shown by the purple area in Fig. 2.

■ The losers are the U.S. consumers. The consumers' loss equals the producers' gain plus the government's gain plus two other losses. One is an increase in the opportunity cost of producing the good in the United States, which is shown by the red area. Another is deadweight loss, which is shown by the gray area.

■ The sum of the blue, red, purple, and gray areas is the loss of consumer surplus that results from the tariff.

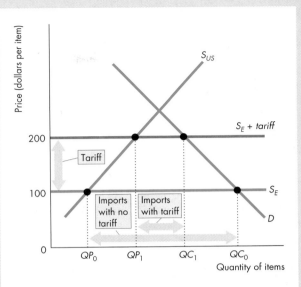

Figure 1 Tariffs and imports

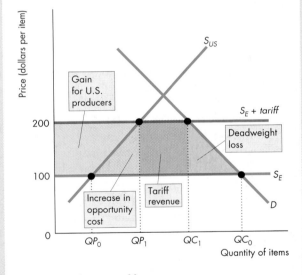

Figure 2 Winners and losers

You're The Voter

■ Are you for or against the tariff on luxury goods from Europe?

■ Write a report to your member of Congress explaining why you favor or oppose the luxury good tariff.

SUMMARY

KEY POINTS

Patterns and Trends in International Trade (p. 442)

■ Large flows of trade take place between countries, most of which is in manufactured goods exchanged among rich industrialized countries.

■ Since 1960, the volume of U.S. trade, as a percentage of total output, has more than doubled.

Opportunity Cost and Comparative Advantage (pp. 443–444)

■ When opportunity costs between countries diverge, comparative advantage enables countries to gain from international trade.

Gains from Trade (pp. 444–447)

■ By increasing its production of goods in which it has a comparative advantage and then trading some of the increased output, a country can consume at a point outside its production possibility frontier.

■ In the absence of international borrowing and lending, trade is balanced as prices adjust to reflect the international supply of and demand for goods.

■ The world price balances the production and consumption plans of the trading parties. At the equilibrium price, trade is balanced.

Gains from Trade in Reality (p. 448)

■ Comparative advantage explains the international trade that takes place in the world.

■ But trade in similar goods arises from economies of scale in the face of diversified tastes.

Trade Restrictions (pp. 449–452)

■ Countries restrict international trade by imposing tariffs and quotas.

■ Trade restrictions raise the domestic price of imported goods, lower the volume of imports, and reduce the total value of imports.

■ Trade restrictions also reduce the total value of exports by the same amount as the reduction in the value of imports.

The Case Against Protection (pp. 453–456)

■ Arguments that protection is necessary for national security, to allow infant industries the chance to grow, and to prevent dumping are weak.

■ Arguments that protection saves jobs, allows us to compete with cheap foreign labor, makes the economy diversified and stable, protects national culture, and is needed to offset the costs of environmental policies are fatally flawed.

Why Is International Trade Restricted? (pp. 456–457)

■ Trade is restricted because tariffs raise government revenue and because protection brings a small loss to a large number of people and a large gain per person to a small number of people.

KEY FIGURES

KEY TERMS

PROBLEMS

*1. The table provides information about Virtual Reality's production possibilities.

TV sets (per day)		Computers (per day)
0	and	36
10	and	35
20	and	33
30	and	30
40	and	26
50	and	21
60	and	15
70	and	8
80	and	0

  a. Calculate Virtual Reality's opportunity cost of a TV set when it produces 10 sets a day.
  b. Calculate Virtual Reality's opportunity cost of a TV set when it produces 40 sets a day.
  c. Calculate Virtual Reality's opportunity cost of a TV set when it produces 70 sets a day.
  d. Using the answers to parts (a), (b), and (c), sketch the relationship between the opportunity cost of a TV set and the quantity of TV sets produced in Virtual Reality.

2. The table provides information about Vital Sign's production possibilities.

TV sets (per day)		Computers (per day)
0	and	18.0
10	and	17.5
20	and	16.5
30	and	15.0
40	and	13.0
50	and	10.5
60	and	7.5
70	and	4.0
80	and	0

  a. Calculate Vital Sign's opportunity cost of a TV set when it produces 10 sets a day.
  b. Calculate Vital Sign's opportunity cost of a TV set when it produces 40 sets a day.
  c. Calculate Vital Sign's opportunity cost of a TV set when it produces 70 sets a day.
  d. Using the answers to parts (a), (b), and (c), sketch the relationship between the opportunity cost of a TV set and the quantity of TV sets produced in Vital Signs.

*3. Suppose that with no international trade, Virtual Reality in problem 1 produces and consumes 10 TV sets a day and Vital Signs produces and consumes 60 TV sets a day. Now suppose that the two countries begin to trade with each other.
  a. Which country exports TV sets?
  b. What adjustments are made to the amount of each good produced by each country?
  c. What adjustments are made to the amount of each good consumed by each country?
  d. What can you say about the terms of trade (the price of a TV set expressed as computers per TV set) under free trade?

4. Suppose that with no international trade, Virtual Reality in problem 1 produces and consumes 50 TV sets a day and Vital Signs produces and consumes 20 TV sets a day. Now suppose that the two countries begin to trade with each other.
  a. Which country exports TV sets?
  b. What adjustments are made to the amount of each good produced by each country?
  c. What adjustments are made to the amount of each good consumed by each country?
  d. What can you say about the terms of trade (the price of a TV set expressed as computers per TV set) under free trade?

*5. Compare the total quantities of each good produced in problems 1 and 2 with the total quantities of each good produced in problems 3 and 4.
  a. Does free trade increase or decrease the total quantities of TV sets and computers produced in both cases? Why?
  b. What happens to the price of a TV set in Virtual Reality in the two cases? Why does it rise in one case and fall in the other?
  c. What happens to the price of a computer in Vital Signs in the two cases? Why does it rise in one case and fall in the other?

6. Compare the international trade in problem 3 with that in problem 4.
  a. Why does Virtual Reality export TV sets in one of the cases and import them in the other case?
  b. Do the TV producers or the computer producers gain in each case?
  c. Do consumers gain in each case?

*7. The figure depicts the international market for soybeans.

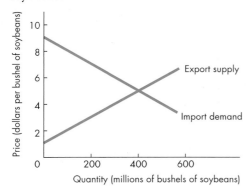

a. If the two countries did not engage in international trade, what would be the prices of soybeans in the two countries?
b. What is the world price of soybeans if there is free trade between these countries?
c. What quantities of soybeans are exported and imported?
d. What is the balance of trade?

8. If the country in problem 7(b) that imports soybeans imposes a tariff of $2 per bushel, what is the world price of soybeans and what quantity of soybeans gets traded internationally? What is the price of soybeans in the importing country? Calculate the tariff revenue.

*9. The importing country in problem 7(b) imposes a quota of 300 million bushels on imports of soybeans.
a. What is the price of soybeans in the importing country?
b. What is the revenue from the quota?
c. Who gets this revenue?

10. The exporting country in problem 7(b) imposes a VER of 300 million bushels on its exports of soybeans.
a. What is the world price of soybeans now?
b. What is the revenue of soybean growers in the exporting country?
c. Which country gains from the VER?

CRITICAL THINKING

1. Study *Reading Between the Lines* on pp. 458–459 and then answer the following questions:
a. Why did the United States impose a tariff on luxury goods from Europe?
b. What are the effects of the tariff on these goods? Explain your answer.
c. Who are the winners and who are the losers from the tariff?
d. Why do you think that the government cares about banana growers? (Hint: Think about where bananas grow and think about who owns the firms that produce bananas.)
e. The news article talks about a U.S. ban on Concorde landings in retaliation for the European ban on some older U.S aircraft types. How would you go about analyzing the effects of this action? Who gains and who loses?

2. Visit the Parkin Web site and study the *Web Reading Between the Lines* on steel dumping. Then answer the following questions:
a. What is the argument in the news article for limiting steel imports?
b. Evaluate the argument. Is it correct or incorrect in your opinion? Why?
c. Would you vote to limit steel imports? Why or why not?
d. Would you vote differently if you lived in another steel-producing country? Why or why not?

3. Use the links on the Parkin Web site to visit the Public Citizen Global Trade Watch and the State of Arizona Department of Commerce Web sites. Review the general message provided by the two sites about NAFTA and then answer the following questions:
a. What is the message that the Public Citizen Global Trade Watch wants to give?
b. What is the basic message of the Arizona Commerce Department?
c. Which message do you think is the correct one and why?
d. Would you vote to maintain NAFTA? Why or why not?

20

International Finance

Yes! The yen (¥), the euro (€), and the dollar ($) are the world's three big currencies. The yen (the currency of Japan) and the dollar (the currency of the United States) have been around for a long time. The euro is new. It was launched on January 1, 1999, as the fledgling currency of 11 members of the European Union, and it will not be used for ordinary transactions until 2002. But it is already an international currency. Most of the world's international trade and finance is conducted using these three currencies. ◆ Currencies fluctuate in value. In 1971, one U.S. dollar bought 360 Japanese yen. In 1999, it bought 121 yen and four years earlier, it had bought only 84 yen. In 1997 and 1998, during the Asian financial crisis, the currency of Indonesian fell against our dollar to less that one third of its pre-crisis value. The Russian ruble also crashed during 1998 to a quarter of its initial value. ◆ Why does our dollar fluctuate against other currencies? Is there anything we can do or should do to stabilize the value of the dollar? ◆ Although the U.S. dollar is the world's most important currency, the position of the United States in the global economy is changing. In 1988, Americans owned foreign assets equal in value to the assets that foreigners owned in the United States. Before 1988, American ownership of foreign assets exceeded foreign ownership of U.S. assets. After 1988, the balance tipped increasingly the other way. Foreign entrepreneurs like Australian-born Rupert Murdoch and Sony's Akio Mori have roamed the United States with giant shopping carts and loaded them up with such items as the L. A. Dodgers, Twentieth Century Fox, the Rockefeller Center, and MGM. Why have foreigners been buying more U.S. real estate and businesses than Americans have been buying abroad?

◆ We're going to discover why the U.S. economy has become attractive for foreign investors, what determines the amount of international borrowing and lending, and why the dollar fluctuates against other currencies.

¥€$!

After studying this chapter, you will be able to:

■ Explain how international trade is financed

■ Describe a country's balance of payments accounts

■ Explain what determines the amount of international borrowing and lending

■ Explain why the United States changed from being a lender to being a borrower in the mid-1980s

■ Explain how the foreign exchange value of the dollar is determined

■ Explain why the foreign exchange value of the dollar fluctuates

Financing International Trade

WHEN A SONY STORE IN THE UNITED STATES imports CD players from Japan, it does not pay for them with U.S. dollars—it uses Japanese yen. And when a French construction company buys an earth mover from Caterpillar, Inc., it uses U.S. dollars. Whenever we buy things from another country, we use the currency of that country to make the transaction. It doesn't make any difference what the item being traded is; it might be a consumption good or a capital good, a building, or even a firm.

We're going to study the markets in which money—different types of currency—is bought and sold. But first we're going to look at the scale of international trading and borrowing and lending and at the way in which we keep our records of these transactions. Such records are called the balance of payments accounts.

Balance of Payments Accounts

A country's **balance of payments accounts** records its international trading, borrowing, and lending. There are in fact three balance of payments accounts:

1. Current account
2. Capital account
3. Official settlements account

The **current account** records payments for imports of goods and services from abroad, receipts from exports of goods and services sold abroad, net interest paid abroad, and net transfers (such as foreign aid payments). The *current account balance* equals exports minus imports, net interest, and net transfers. The **capital account** records foreign investment in the United States minus U.S. investment abroad. The **official settlements account** records the change in official U.S. reserves. **Official U.S. reserves** are the government's holdings of foreign currency. If U.S. official reserves increase, the *official settlements account balance* is negative. The reason is that holding foreign money is like investing abroad. U.S. investment abroad is a minus item in the capital account. By the same reasoning, if official reserves decrease, the *official settlements account balance* is positive.

The sum of the balances on the three accounts always equals zero. That is, to pay for our current account deficit, we must either borrow more from abroad than we lend abroad or use our official reserves to cover the shortfall.

Table 20.1 shows the U.S. balance of payments accounts in 1998. Items in the current account and capital account that provide foreign currency to the United States have a plus sign; items that cost the United States foreign currency have a minus sign. The table shows that in 1998, U.S. imports exceeded U.S. exports and the current account had a deficit of $230 billion. How do we pay for imports that exceed the value of our exports? That is, how do we pay for our current account deficit? We pay by borrowing from the rest of the world. The capital account tells us by how much. We borrowed $540 billion (foreign investment in the United States) but made loans of $310 billion (U.S. investment abroad). Thus our net foreign borrowing was $230 billion. In some years, the accounts show a statistical discrepancy between our capital account and current account transactions. But in 1998, the statistical discrepancy was small. The statistical discrepancy arises because of illegal and hidden transactions.

TABLE 20.1

U.S. Balance of Payments Accounts in 1998

Current account	Billions of dollars
Imports of goods and services	−1,120
Exports of goods and services	+910
Net interest income	+20
Net transfers	−40
Current account balance	−230
Capital account	
Foreign investment in the United States	+540
U.S. investment abroad	−310
Capital account balance	+230
Official settlements account	
Increase in official U.S. reserves	—

Source: Selected Estimates from the International Transactions news release, March 11, 1999, Bureau of Economic Analysis, U.S. Department of Commerce, Washington, D.C. All the items are rounded to the nearest $10 billion.

Our net borrowing from abroad minus our current account deficit is the change in official U.S. reserves. In 1998, reserves barely changed because our net foreign borrowing of $230 billion equaled our current account deficit of $230 billion. When our reserves do change, we record an *increase* in reserves as a negative number in our international accounts. Why? Because an increase in our reserves is like making a loan to the rest of the world.

The numbers in Table 20.1 give a snapshot of the balance of payments accounts in 1998. Figure 20.1 puts that snapshot into perspective by showing the balance of payments between 1980 and 1998. Because the economy grows and the price level rises, changes in the dollar value of the balance of payments do not convey much information. To remove the influences of growth and inflation, Fig. 20.1 shows the balance of payments as a percentage of nominal GDP.

As you can see, the capital account balance is almost a mirror image of the current account balance. The official settlements balance is very small in comparison with the balances on these other two accounts. A large current account deficit (and capital account surplus) emerged during the 1980s but declined from 1987 to 1991. Since then, it has increased again.

You will perhaps obtain a better understanding of the balance of payments accounts and the way in which they are linked together if you consider the income and expenditure, borrowing and lending, and bank account of an individual.

Individual Analogy An individual's current account records the income from supplying the services of factors of production and the expenditure on goods and services. Consider, for example, Joanne. She worked in 1995 and earned an income of $25,000. Joanne has $10,000 worth of investments that earned her an interest income of $1,000. Joanne's current account shows an income of $26,000. Joanne spent $18,000 buying goods and services for consumption. She also bought a new house, which cost her $60,000. So Joanne's total expenditure was $78,000. The difference between her expenditure and income is $52,000 ($78,000 minus $26,000). This amount is Joanne's current account deficit.

FIGURE 20.1

The Balance of Payments: 1975–1998

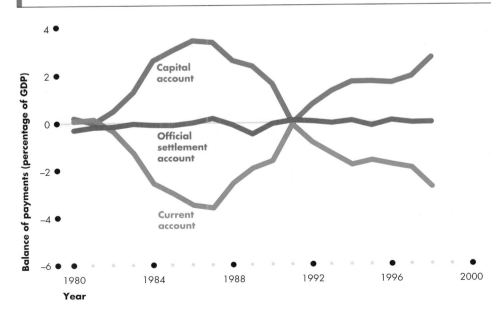

During the 1980s, a large current account deficit arose. That deficit decreased in the late 1980s but increased again after 1991. The capital account balance mirrors the current account balance. When the current account balance is negative, the capital account balance is positive— we borrow from the rest of the world. Fluctuations in the official settlements balance are small in comparison with fluctuations in the current account balance and the capital account balance.

Source: Economic Report of the President, 1999, and Table 20.1.

To pay for an expenditure of $52,000 in excess of her income, Joanne has to use the money that she has in the bank or has to take out a loan. In fact, Joanne took a mortgage of $50,000 to help buy her house. This mortgage was the only borrowing that Joanne did, so her capital account surplus was $50,000. With a current account deficit of $52,000 and a capital account surplus of $50,000, Joanne is still $2,000 short. She got that $2,000 from her own bank account. Her cash holdings decreased by $2,000.

Joanne's income from her work is analogous to a country's income from its exports. Her income from her investments is analogous to a country's interest income from foreigners. Her purchases of goods and services, including her purchase of a house, are analogous to a country's imports. Joanne's mortgage—borrowing from someone else—is analogous to a country's borrowing from the rest of the world. The change in her own bank account is analogous to the change in the country's official reserves.

Borrowers and Lenders, Debtors and Creditors

A country that is borrowing more from the rest of the world than it is lending to it is called a **net borrower**. Similarly, a **net lender** is a country that is lending more to the rest of the world than it is borrowing from it.

The United States is a net borrower but it is a relative newcomer to the ranks of net borrower nations. Throughout the 1960s and most of the 1970s, the United States was a net lender to the rest of the world. It had a surplus on its current account and a deficit on its capital account. It was not until 1983 that the United States became a significant net borrower from the rest of the world. Between 1983 and 1987, its borrowing increased each year. It then decreased and was briefly zero in 1991, after which it started to increase again. The average net foreign borrowing by the United States between 1983 and 1998 was $102 billion a year.

Most countries are net borrowers like the United States. But a small number of countries, including Japan and oil-rich Saudi Arabia, are net lenders.

A net borrower might be reducing its net assets held in the rest of the world or it might be going deeper into debt. A nation's total stock of foreign investment determines whether it is a debtor or creditor. A **debtor nation** is a country that during its entire history has borrowed more from the rest of the world than it has lent to it. It has a stock of outstanding debt to the rest of the world that exceeds the stock of its own claims on the rest of the world. A **creditor nation** is a country that has invested more in the rest of the world than other countries have invested in it.

At the heart of the distinction between a net borrower/net lender and a debtor/creditor nation is the distinction between flows and stocks, which you have encountered many times in your study of macroeconomics. Borrowing and lending are flows—amounts borrowed or lent per unit of time. Debts are stocks—amounts owed at a point in time. The flow of borrowing and lending changes the stock of debt.

The United States was a debtor nation through the 19th century as we borrowed from Europe to finance our westward expansion, railroads, and industrialization. We paid off our debt and became a creditor nation for most of the current century. But following a string of current account deficits, we became a debtor nation again in 1989.

Since 1989, total stock of U.S. borrowing from the rest of the world has exceeded U.S. lending to the rest of the world. The largest debtor nations are the capital-hungry developing countries (like the United States was during the 19th century). The international debt of these countries grew from less than a third to more than a half of their gross domestic product during the 1980s and created what was called the "Third World debt crisis."

Should we be concerned that the United States is a net borrower? The answer to this question depends mainly on what the net borrower is doing with the borrowed money. If borrowing is financing investment that in turn is generating economic growth and higher income, borrowing is not a problem. If the borrowed money is being used to finance consumption, then higher interest payments are being incurred, and consequently, consumption will eventually have to be reduced. In this case the more the borrowing and the longer it goes on, the greater is the reduction in consumption that will eventually be necessary. We'll see below whether the United States is borrowing for investment or for consumption.

Current Account Balance

What determines a country's current account balance and net foreign borrowing? You've seen that net exports (*NX*) is the main item in the current account.

We can define the current account balance (*CAB*) as

$$CAB = NX + \text{Net interest income} + \text{Net transfers.}$$

Fluctuations in net exports are the main source of fluctuations in the current account balance. The other two items are small and have trends but do not fluctuate much. So we can study the current account balance by looking at what determines net exports.

Net Exports

Net exports are determined by the government budget and private saving and investment. To see how net exports are determined, we need to recall some of the things that we learned about the national income accounts in Chapter 6. Table 20.2 will refresh your memory and summarize some calculations.

Part (a) lists the national income variables that are needed, with their symbols. Part (b) defines three surpluses and deficits. **Net exports** is exports of goods and services minus imports of goods and services.

The **government sector surplus or deficit** is equal to net taxes minus government purchases of goods and services. If that number is positive, a government sector surplus is lent to other sectors; if that number is negative, a government deficit must be financed by borrowing from other sectors. The government sector deficit is the sum of the deficits of the federal, state, and local governments.

The **private sector surplus or deficit** is saving minus investment. If saving exceeds investment, a private sector surplus is lent to other sectors. If investment exceeds saving, a private sector deficit is financed by borrowing from other sectors.

Part (b) also shows the values of these deficits and surpluses for the United States in 1998. As you can see, net exports were –$151 billion, a deficit of $151 billion. The government sector's revenue from net taxes was $1,563 billion and it purchased $1,487 billion worth of goods and services. The government sector surplus was $76 billion. The private sector saved $1,140 billion and invested $1,367 billion, so it had a deficit of $227 billion.

Part (c) shows the relationship among the three deficits. From the national income accounts, we know that real GDP, *Y*, is the sum of consumption expenditure, *C*, investment, government purchases, and net exports. It also equals the sum of consumption expenditure, saving, and taxes. Rearranging these equations tells us that net exports is the sum of the government sector deficit and the private sector deficit. In the United

TABLE 20.2

Net Exports, the Government Budget, Saving, and Investment

	Symbols and equations	United States in 1998 (billions of dollars)
(a) Variables		
Exports	X	959
Imports	M	1,110
Government purchases	G	1,487
Net taxes	T	1,563
Investment	I	1,367
Saving	S	1,140
(b) Surpluses and deficits		
Net exports	$X - M$	$959 - 1,110 = -151$
Government sector	$T - G$	$1,563 - 1,487 = 76$
Private sector	$S - I$	$1,140 - 1,367 = -227$
(c) Relationship among surpluses and deficits		
National accounts	$Y = C + I + G + X - M$	
	$= C + S + T$	
Rearranging:	$X - M = S - I + T - G$	
Net exports	$X - M$	-151
equals:		
Government sector	$T - G$	76
plus		
Private sector	$S - I$	-227

Source: National Income and Product Accounts and *Survey of Current Business*, (March, 1999).

The National Income and Product Accounts measures of exports and imports are different from the Balance of Payments Accounts measures in Table 20.1 on p. 464.

States in 1998, the government sector had a surplus of $76 billion and the private sector had a deficit of $227 billion. The government sector deficit plus the private sector deficit equals net exports of –$151 billion.

The Twin Deficits

You've seen that net exports equal the sum of the government sector deficit and the private sector deficit. But how do these deficits fluctuate over time? Figure 20.2 answers this question. It shows the government sector deficit (the red line) and net exports *two years later* (the blue line).

You can see that there is a strong tendency for net exports to decrease (to become increasingly negative) when the government budget has gone into a deeper deficit (has become increasingly negative). Because of the tendency for the government sector deficit and the

net exports deficit to move in the same direction, they are sometimes called the **twin deficits**.

Why are the two deficits linked? It is because capital is highly mobile in today's world. If the U.S. government increases expenditure or lowers taxes, total spending in the United States rises. But with the economy at or near full employment, the extra goods and services demanded are sucked in from the rest of the world. Imports rise. Capital flows in to pay for those imports. Saving and investment don't change. In reality, these adjustments take time, which is why net exports lag behind the government sector deficit by about two years.

Is U.S. Borrowing for Consumption or Investment?

In 1998, net exports were a negative $151 billion and we borrowed this amount from abroad. Did we borrow for consumption or investment? In 1998, private investment in buildings, plant, and equipment was $1,376 billion. Government investment in defense equipment and public structures such as highways, and dams was $240 billion a year. All this investment added to the nation's capital and much of it increased productivity. Government also spends on education and health-care services, which increase *human capital*. Our international borrowing is financing private and public investment, not consumption.

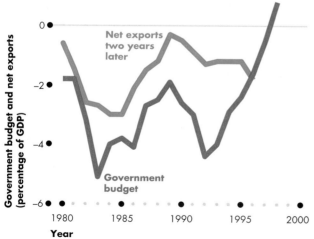

FIGURE 20.2

The Twin Deficits

Net exports and the government budget deficit move in similar ways but with a time lag of two years. If the government budget deficit increases, as it did in 1980–1983 and again in 1990–1992, net exports decrease two years later, as they did in 1982–1985 and again in 1992–1994.

Source: Survey of Current Business, March 1999.

R E V I E W   Q U I Z

- When an American art dealer buys a painting from a French gallery, which currency gets used to make the transaction?
- When a German car maker buys parts from a Detroit car maker, which currency gets used to make the transaction?
- What types of transactions do we record in the balance of payments accounts?
- What transactions does the current account record? What transactions does the capital account record? What transactions does the official settlements account record?
- How are the current account deficit, the government sector deficit, and the private sector surplus related?

The Exchange Rate

W̲HEN WE BUY FOREIGN GOODS OR INVEST IN another country, we have to obtain some of that country's currency to make the transaction. When foreigners buy U.S.-produced goods or invest in the United States, they have to obtain some U.S. dollars. We get foreign currency, and foreigners get U.S. dollars in the foreign exchange market. The **foreign exchange market** is the market in which the currency of one country is exchanged for the currency of another. The foreign exchange market is not a place like a downtown flea market or produce market. The market is made up of thousands of people—importers and exporters, banks, and specialists in the buying and selling of foreign exchange, called foreign exchange brokers. The foreign exchange market opens on Monday morning in Hong Kong, which is still Sunday evening in New York. As the day advances, markets open in Singapore, Tokyo, Bahrain, Frankfurt, London, New York, Chicago, and San Francisco. As the West Coast markets close, Hong Kong is only an hour away from opening for the next day of business. The sun barely sets on the foreign exchange market. Dealers around the world are in continual contact by telephone, and on a typical day in 1996, $1.3 trillion changed hands.

The price at which one currency exchanges for another is called a **foreign exchange rate**. For example, in March 1999, one U.S. dollar bought 121 Japanese yen. The exchange rate was 121 yen per dollar.

Figure 20.3 shows the exchange rate of the U.S. dollar in terms of the Japanese yen between 1980 and 1999. From 1982 to 1995, and again in early 1999, the value of the dollar fell against the yen—the dollar depreciated.

Currency depreciation is the fall in the value of one currency in terms of another currency. For example if the dollar falls from 100 yen to 80 yen, the dollar depreciates by 20 percent. From 1980 to 1982 and again during 1996 and 1998, the dollar rose in value against the yen—the dollar appreciated. **Currency appreciation** is the rise in the value of one currency in terms of another currency. For example if the dollar rises from 100 yen to 120 yen, the dollar appreciates against the yen by 20 percent.

We've just expressed the value of the U.S. dollar in terms of the yen. But we can express the value of the dollar in terms of any currency. Also, we can

FIGURE 20.3

The Exchange Rate

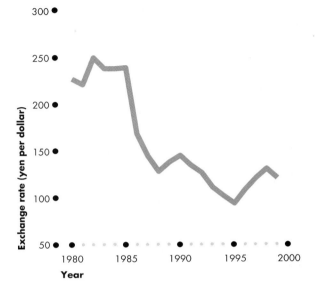

The exchange rate is the price at which two currencies can be traded. The yen-dollar exchange rate, expressed as yen per dollar, shows that the dollar has generally fallen in value—depreciated—against the yen. But since 1995, the dollar has risen against the yen.

Source: Economic Report of the President, 1999.

express the exchange rate of the yen in terms of the dollar as a number of dollars per yen.

When the U.S. dollar appreciates against the yen, the yen depreciates against the dollar.

Why does the U.S. dollar fluctuate in value? Why does it sometimes depreciate and sometimes appreciate? What happened during 1997 to make the dollar appreciate and in early 1999 to make it depreciate against the yen? To answer these questions, we need to understand the forces that determine the exchange rate.

The exchange rate is a price—the price of one country's money in terms of another country's money. And like all prices, demand and supply determine the exchange rate. So to understand the forces that determine the exchange rate, we need to study demand and supply in the foreign exchange market. We'll begin by looking at the demand side of the market.

Demand in the Foreign Exchange Market

The quantity of dollars demanded in the foreign exchange market is the amount that traders plan to buy during a given time period at a given exchange rate. This quantity depends on many factors. The main ones are:

■ The exchange rate
■ Interest rates in the United States and other countries
■ The expected future exchange rate

Let's look first at the relationship between the quantity of dollars demanded in the foreign exchange market and the exchange rate.

The Law of Demand for Foreign Exchange

People do not buy dollars because they enjoy them. The demand for dollars is a *derived demand*. People demand dollars so that they can buy U.S.-made goods and services (U.S. exports). They also demand dollars so that they can buy U.S. assets such as bank accounts, bonds, stocks, businesses, and real estate. Nevertheless, the law of demand applies to dollars just as it does to anything else that people value.

Other things remaining the same, the higher the exchange rate, the smaller is the quantity of dollars demanded in the foreign exchange market. For example, if the price of the U.S. dollar rises from 100 yen to 120 yen but nothing else changes, the quantity of U.S. dollars that people plan to buy in the foreign exchange market decreases. Why does the exchange rate influence the quantity of dollars demanded?

There are two separate reasons, and they are related to the two sources of the derived demand for dollars:

■ Exports effect
■ Expected profit effect

Exports Effect   The larger the value of U.S. exports, the larger is the quantity of dollars demanded in the foreign exchange market. But the value of U.S. exports depends on the exchange rate. The lower the exchange rate, with everything else the same, the cheaper are U.S.-produced goods and services and the greater is the value of U.S. exports and the greater is the quantity of U.S. dollars demanded on the foreign exchange market to pay for these exports.

Expected Profit Effect   The larger the expected profit from holding dollars, the greater is the quantity of dollars demanded in the foreign exchange market. But expected profit depends on the exchange rate. The lower the exchange rate, other things remaining the same, the larger is the expected profit from buying dollars and the greater is the quantity of dollars demanded on the foreign exchange market.

To understand this effect, suppose you think the dollar will be worth 120 yen by the end of the month. If today, a dollar costs 115 yen, you buy dollars. But a person who thinks that the dollar will be worth 115 yen at the end of the month does not buy dollars. Now suppose the exchange rate falls to 110 yen per dollar. More people think they can profit from buying dollars, so the quantity of dollars demanded increases.

For the two reasons we've just reviewed, other things remaining the same, when the foreign exchange rate rises, the quantity of dollars demanded decreases, and when the foreign exchange rate falls, the quantity of dollars demanded increases. Figure 20.4 shows the demand curve for U.S. dollars in the foreign exchange market. In this figure, when the foreign exchange rate rises, other things remaining the same, there is a decrease in the quantity of dollars demanded and a movement upward along the demand curve as shown by the arrow. When the exchange rate falls, other things remaining the same, there is an increase in the quantity of dollars demanded and a movement downward along the demand curve as shown by the arrow.

Changes in the Demand for Dollars

A change in any other influence on the dollars that people plan to buy in the foreign exchange market brings a change in the demand for dollars and a shift in the demand curve for dollars. Demand either increases or decreases. These other influences are:

■ Interest rates in the United States and other countries
■ The expected future exchange rate

Interest Rates in the United States and Other Countries   People and businesses buy financial assets to make a return. The higher the interest rate that people can make on U.S. assets compared with foreign assets, the more U.S. assets they buy. What matters is not the level of U.S. interest rates, but the U.S. interest rate minus the foreign interest rate, a

FIGURE 20.4

The Demand for Dollars

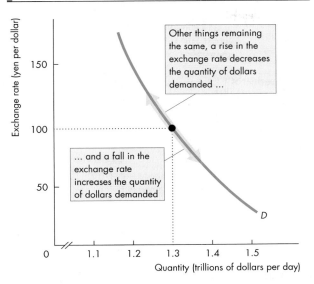

Other things remaining the same, a rise in the exchange rate decreases the quantity of dollars demanded ...

... and a fall in the exchange rate increases the quantity of dollars demanded

The quantity of dollars that people plan to buy depends on the exchange rate. Other things remaining the same, if the exchange rate rises, the quantity of dollars demanded decreases and there is a movement upward along the demand curve for dollars. If the exchange rate falls, the quantity of dollars demanded increases and there is a movement downward along the demand curve for dollars.

gap that is called the **U.S. interest rate differential**. If the U.S. interest rate rises and the foreign interest rate remains constant, the U.S. interest rate differential increases. The larger the U.S. interest rate differential, the greater is the demand for U.S. assets and the greater is the demand for dollars on the foreign exchange market.

The Expected Future Exchange Rate   Other things remaining the same, the higher the expected future exchange rate, the greater is the demand for dollars. To see why, suppose you are Toyota's finance manager. The exchange rate is 100 yen per dollar and you think that by the end of the month, it will be 120 yen per dollar. You spend 100,000 yen today and buy $1,000. At the end of the month, the dollar is 120 yen, as you predicted it would be, and you sell the $1,000. You get 120,000 yen. You've made a profit of 20,000 yen, or almost $167. The higher the expected

future exchange rate, other things remaining the same, the greater is the expected profit and the greater is the demand for dollars today.

Figure 20.5 summarizes the above discussion of the influences on the demand for dollars. A rise in the U.S. interest differential or a rise in the expected future exchange rate increases the demand for dollars and shifts the demand curve rightward from D_0 to D_1. A fall in the U.S. interest differential or a fall in the expected future exchange rate decreases the demand for dollars and shifts the demand curve leftward from D_0 to D_2.

FIGURE 20.5

Changes in the Demand for Dollars

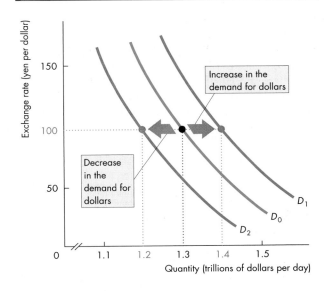

Increase in the demand for dollars

Decrease in the demand for dollars

A change in any influence on the quantity of dollars that people plan to buy, other than the exchange rate, brings a change in the demand for dollars.

The demand for dollars:

Increases if:	Decreases if:
▪ The U.S. interest rate differential increases	▪ The U.S. interest rate differential decreases
▪ The expected future exchange rate rises	▪ The expected future exchange rate falls

Supply in the Foreign Exchange Market

The quantity of U.S. dollars supplied in the foreign exchange market is the amount that traders plan to sell during a given time period at a given exchange rate. This quantity depends on many factors. The main ones are:

- The exchange rate
- Interest rates in the United States and other countries
- The expected future exchange rate

Let's look first at the relationship between the quantity of dollars supplied in the foreign exchange market and the exchange rate.

The Law of Supply of Foreign Exchange

People supply dollars in the foreign exchange market when they buy other currencies. And they buy other currencies so that they can buy foreign-made goods and services (U.S. imports). They also supply dollars and buy foreign currencies so that they can buy foreign assets such as bank accounts, bonds, stocks, businesses, and real estate. The law of supply applies to dollars just as it does to anything else that people plan to sell.

Other things remaining the same, the higher the exchange rate, the greater is the quantity of dollars supplied in the foreign exchange market. For example, if the price of the U.S. dollar rises from 100 yen to 120 yen but nothing else changes, the quantity of yen that people plan to buy in the foreign exchange market increases and so the quantity of U.S. dollars supplied increases. Why does the exchange rate influence the quantity of dollars supplied?

There are two reasons and they parallel the two reasons on the demand side of the market:

- Imports effect
- Expected profit effect

Imports Effect   The larger the value of U.S. imports, the larger is the quantity of foreign currency demanded to pay for these imports. And when people buy foreign currency, they supply dollars. So the larger the value of U.S. imports, the greater is the quantity of

dollars supplied in the foreign exchange market. But the value of U.S. imports depends on the exchange rate. The higher the exchange rate, with everything else the same, the cheaper are foreign-produced good and services to Americans, the more the United States imports, and the greater is the quantity of U.S. dollars supplied on the foreign exchange market to pay for these imports.

Expected Profit Effect   The larger the expected profit from holding a foreign currency, the greater is the quantity of that currency demanded and the greater is the quantity of dollars supplied in the foreign exchange market. But the expected profit from holding a foreign currency depends on the exchange rate. The higher the exchange rate, other things remaining the same, the larger is the expected profit from selling dollars and the greater is the quantity of dollars supplied on the foreign exchange market.

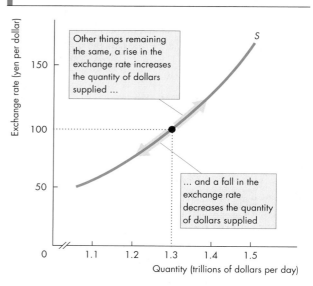

FIGURE 20.6

The Supply of Dollars

The quantity of dollars that people plan to sell depends on the exchange rate. Other things remaining the same, if the exchange rate rises, the quantity of dollars supplied increases and there is a movement upward along the supply curve for dollars. If the exchange rate falls, the quantity of dollars supplied decreases and there is a movement downward along the supply curve for dollars.

For the two reasons we've just reviewed, other things remaining the same, when the foreign exchange rate rises, the quantity of dollars supplied increases, and when the foreign exchange rate falls, the quantity of dollars supplied decreases. Figure 20.6 shows the supply curve for U.S. dollars in the foreign exchange market. In this figure, when the foreign exchange rate rises, other things remaining the same, there is an increase in the quantity of dollars supplied and a movement upward along the supply curve as shown by the arrow. When the exchange rate falls, other things remaining the same, there is a decrease in the quantity of dollars supplied and a movement downward along the supply curve as shown by the arrow.

Changes in the Supply of Dollars

A change in any other influence on the dollars that people plan to sell in the foreign exchange market brings a change in the supply of dollars and a shift in the supply curve for dollars. Supply either increases or decreases. These other influences parallel the other influences on demand but have exactly the opposite effects. These influences are:

- Interest rates in the United States and other countries
- The expected future exchange rate

Interest Rates in the United States and Other Countries The larger the U.S. interest rate differential, the smaller is the demand for foreign assets and so the smaller is the supply of dollars in the foreign exchange market.

The Expected Future Exchange Rate Other things remaining the same, the higher the expected future exchange rate, the smaller is the supply of dollars. To see why, suppose the dollar is trading at 100 yen per dollar today and you think that by the end of the month, the dollar will be 120 yen per dollar. You were planning on selling dollars today, but you decide to hold off and wait until the end of the month. If you supply dollars today, you get only 100 yen per dollar. But at the end of the month, if the dollar is 120 yen per dollar as you predict, you'll get 120 yen for each dollar you supply. You'll make a profit of 20 percent. So, the higher the expected future exchange

rate, other things remaining the same, the smaller is the expected profit from selling U.S. dollars today and the smaller is the supply of dollars today.

Figure 20.7 summarizes the above discussion of the influences on the supply of dollars. A rise in the U.S. interest differential or a rise in the expected future exchange rate decreases the supply of dollars and shifts the demand curve leftward from S_0 to S_1. A fall in the U.S. interest differential or a fall in the expected future exchange rate increases the supply of dollars and shifts the supply curve rightward from S_0 to S_2.

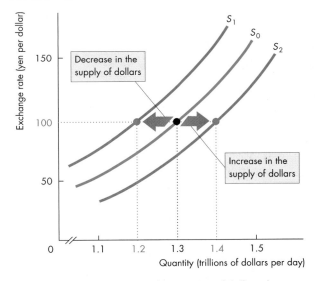

FIGURE 20.7

Changes in the Supply of Dollars

A change in any influence on the quantity of dollars that people plan to sell, other than the exchange rate, brings a change in the supply of dollars.

The supply of dollars:

Increases if:

- The U.S. interest rate differential decreases
- The expected future exchange rate falls

Decreases if:

- The U.S. interest rate differential increases
- The expected future exchange rate rises

Market Equilibrium

Figure 20.8 shows how demand and supply in the foreign exchange market determine the exchange rate. The demand curve is *D*, and the supply curve is *S*. Just like all the other markets you've studied, the price (the exchange rate) acts as a regulator.

If the exchange rate is too high, there is a surplus of dollars—the quantity supplied exceeds the quantity demanded. In Fig. 20.8, if the exchange rate is 150 yen per dollar, there is a surplus of dollars. If the exchange rate is too low, there is a shortage of dollars—the quantity supplied is less than the quantity demanded. In Fig. 20.8, if the exchange rate is 50 yen per dollar, there is a shortage of dollars.

At the equilibrium exchange rate, there is neither a shortage nor a surplus. The quantity supplied equals the quantity demanded. In Fig. 20.8, the equilibrium exchange rate is 100 yen per dollar. At this

exchange rate, the quantity demanded equals the quantity supplied and $1.3 trillion a day is bought and sold.

The foreign exchange market is constantly pulled to its equilibrium by the forces of supply and demand. Foreign exchange dealers are constantly looking for the best price they can get. If they are selling, they want the highest price available. If they are buying, they want the lowest price available. Information flows from dealer to dealer through the worldwide computer network, and the price adjusts second by second to keep buying plans and selling plans in balance. That is, price adjusts second by second to keep the market at its equilibrium.

Changes in the Exchange Rate

If the demand for dollars increases and the supply of dollars does not change, the exchange rate rises. If the demand for dollars decreases and the supply of dollars does not change, the exchange rate falls. Similarly, if the supply of dollars decreases and the demand for dollars does not change, the exchange rate rises. If the supply of dollars increases and the demand for dollars does not change, the exchange rate falls.

These predictions about the effects of changes in demand and supply are the same as for other markets.

Why the Exchange Rate Is Volatile   Sometimes the dollar depreciates and at other times it appreciates, but the quantity of dollars traded each day barely changes. Why? The main reason is that supply and demand are not independent of each other in the foreign exchange market.

When we studied the demand for dollars and the supply of dollars, we saw that unlike other markets, the demand side and the supply side of the market have some common influences. A change in the expected future exchange rate or a change in the U.S. interest rate differential changes both demand and supply—and in opposite directions. These common influences on both demand and supply explain why the exchange rate can be volatile at times, even though the quantity of dollars traded does not change.

Everyone in the foreign exchange market is potentially a demander and a supplier. Each has a price above which he or she will sell and below which he or she will buy. Let's see how these common supply and demand effects work by looking at two episodes: one in which the dollar appreciated and one in which it depreciated.

FIGURE 20.8
Equilibrium Exchange Rate

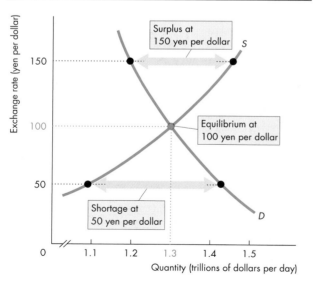

The demand curve for dollars is *D*, and the supply curve is *S*. If the exchange rate is 150 yen per dollar, there is a surplus of dollars and the exchange rate falls. If the exchange rate is 50 yen per dollar, there is a shortage of dollars and the exchange rate rises. If the exchange rate is 100 yen per dollar, there is neither a shortage nor a surplus of dollars and the exchange rate remains constant. The market is in equilibrium.

A Depreciating Dollar: 1994–1995   Between 1994 and the summer of 1995, the dollar fell from 100 yen to a low of 84 yen per dollar. Figure 20.9(a) explains this fall. In 1994, the demand and supply curves were those labeled D_{94} and S_{94}. The exchange rate was 100 yen per dollar. During 1994, traders expected the U.S. dollar to depreciate. They expected a lower exchange rate. As a result, the demand for dollars decreased and the supply of dollars increased. The demand curve shifted leftward to D_{95}, and the supply curve shifted rightward to S_{95}. The exchange rate fell to 84 yen per dollar.

An Appreciating Dollar: 1995–1998   Between 1995 and 1998, the dollar appreciated against the yen. It rose from 84 yen to 130 yen per dollar. Figure 20.9(b) explains why this happened. In 1995, the demand and supply curves were those labeled D_{95} and S_{95}. The exchange rate was 84 yen per dollar—where the supply and demand curves intersect. During the next two years, Japan was in recession

and the U.S. economy was expanding. Interest rates in Japan fell, and the yen was expected to depreciate. The demand for yen decreased. As a result, the demand for dollars increased, and the supply of dollars decreased. The demand curve shifted from D_{95} to D_{98}, and the supply curve shifted from S_{95} to S_{98}. These two shifts reinforced each other, and the exchange rate increased to 130 yen per dollar.

Exchange Rate Expectations

The changes in the exchange rate that we've just examined occurred in part because the exchange rate was *expected to change*. This explanation sounds a bit like a self-fulfilling forecast. But what makes expectations change? The answer is new information about the deeper forces that influence the value of money. Two such forces are:

■ Purchasing power parity
■ Interest rate parity

FIGURE 20.9
Exchange Rate Fluctuations

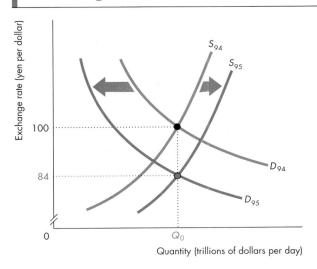

(a) 1994 to 1995

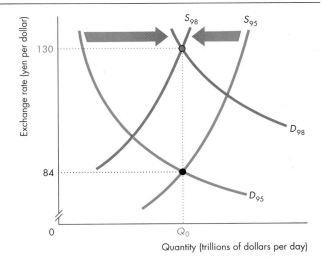

(b) 1995 to 1998

The exchange rate fluctuates because changes in demand and supply are not independent of each other. Everyone in the foreign exchange market is a potential buyer and seller. Between 1994 and 1995 (in part a), the dollar depreciated from 100 to 84 yen per dollar. The exchange rate was expected to depreciate, which decreased the demand for dollars and increased the

supply. Between 1995 and 1998 (part b), the dollar appreciated from 84 to 130 yen per dollar. This appreciation occurred because a weak Japanese economy and low interest rates in Japan generated an expectation of a weak yen and a strong dollar. The supply of dollars decreased, the demand for dollars increased, and the dollar rose in value.

Purchasing Power Parity   Money is worth what it will buy. But two kinds of money, U.S. dollars and Canadian dollars for example, might buy different amounts of goods and services. Suppose a Big Mac costs $4 (Canadian) in Toronto and $3 (U.S.) in New York. If the Canadian dollar exchange rate is $1.33 Canadian per U.S. dollar, the two monies have the same value. You can buy a Big Mac in both Toronto and New York for either $4 Canadian or $3 U.S.

The situation we've just described is called **purchasing power parity**, which means *equal value of money*. If purchasing power parity does not prevail, some powerful forces go to work. To understand these forces, let's suppose that the price of a Big Mac in New York rises to $4 U.S., but in Toronto it remains at $4 Canadian. Suppose the exchange rate remains at $1.33 Canadian per U.S. dollar. In this case, a Big Mac in Toronto still costs $4 Canadian or $3 U.S. But in New York, it costs $4 U.S. or $5.33 Canadian. Money buys more in Canada than in the United States. Money is not of equal value in both countries.

If all (or most) prices have increased in the United States and not increased in Canada, then people will generally expect that the value of the U.S. dollar on the foreign exchange market must fall. In this situation, the exchange rate is expected to fall. The demand for U.S. dollars decreases, and the supply of U.S. dollars increases. The exchange rate falls, as expected. If the exchange rate falls to $1.00 Canadian and there are no further price changes, purchasing power parity is restored. A Big Mac now costs $4 in either U.S. or Canadian dollars in both New York and Toronto.

If prices increase in Canada and other countries but remain constant in the United States, then people will generally expect that the value of the U.S. dollar on the foreign exchange market is too low and that it is going to rise. In this situation, the exchange rate is expected to rise. The demand for U.S. dollars increases, and the supply of U.S. dollars decreases. The exchange rate rises, as expected.

Ultimately, the value of money is determined by the price level, which in turn is determined by aggregate supply and aggregate demand (see Chapter 8, pp. 162–163 and Chapter 16, pp. 357–361.) So the deeper forces that influence the exchange rate have tentacles that spread throughout the economy. If prices in the United States rise faster than those in other countries, the exchange rate falls. And if prices rise more slowly in the United States than in other countries, the exchange rate rises.

Interest Rate Parity   Money is worth what it can earn. Again, two kinds of money, Canadian dollars and U.S. dollars, for example, might earn different amounts. Suppose a Canadian dollar bank deposit in Toronto earns 5 percent a year and a U.S. dollar bank deposit in New York earns 3 percent a year. In this situation, why does anyone deposit money in New York? Why doesn't all the money flow to Toronto? The answer is: Because of exchange rate expectations. Suppose people expect the Canadian dollar to depreciate by 2 percent a year. This 2 percent depreciation must be subtracted from the 5 percent interest to obtain the net return of 3 percent a year that an American expects to earn by depositing funds in a Toronto bank. The two returns are equal. This situation is one of **interest rate parity**, which means *equal interest rates.*

Adjusted for risk, interest rate parity always prevails. Funds move to get the highest return available. If for a few seconds a higher return is available in New York than in Toronto, the demand for U.S. dollars rises and the exchange rate rises until expected interest rates are equal.

The Fed in the Foreign Exchange Market

Interest rates in the United States are determined by the demand for and supply of money (see Chapter 15, pp. 343–344). But the supply of money is influenced by the Fed, so ultimately, the exchange rate is influenced by monetary policy. When interest rates in the United States rise, relative to those in other countries, the demand for U.S. dollars increases, the supply decreases, and the exchange rate rises. (Similarly, when interest rates in the United States fall, relative to those in other countries, the demand for U.S. dollars decreases, the supply increases, and the exchange rate falls.)

But the Fed can intervene directly in the foreign exchange market. It can buy or sell dollars and try to smooth out fluctuations in the exchange rate. Let's look at the foreign exchange interventions that the Fed can make.

Suppose the Fed wants the exchange rate to be steady at 120 yen per dollar. If the exchange rate rises above 120 yen per dollar, the Fed sells dollars. If the exchange rate falls below 120 yen per dollar, the Fed buys dollars. By these actions, it changes supply or demand and keeps the exchange rate close to its target rate of 120 yen per dollar.

Figure 20.10 shows this Fed intervention in the foreign exchange market. The supply of dollars is S, and initially the demand for dollars is D_0. The equilibrium exchange rate is 120 yen per dollar. This exchange rate is the Fed's target rate, shown by the horizontal red line in the figure.

When the demand for dollars increases and the demand curve shifts rightward to D_1, the Fed sells $0.1 trillion. This action increases the supply of dollars by $0.1 trillion and prevents the exchange rate from rising. When the demand for dollars decreases and the demand curve shifts leftward to D_2, the Fed buys $0.1 trillion. This action decreases the supply of dollars by $0.1 trillion and prevents the exchange rate from falling.

If the demand for dollars fluctuates between D_1 and D_2 and on the average is D_0, the Fed can repeatedly intervene in the way we've just seen. Sometimes the Fed buys and sometimes it sells, but on the average, it neither buys nor sells.

But suppose the demand for dollars increases permanently from D_0 to D_1. The Fed cannot now maintain the exchange rate at 120 yen per dollar indefinitely. To do so, the Fed would have to sell dollars every day. When the Fed sells dollars in the foreign exchange market, it buys foreign currency. So the Fed would be piling up foreign currency.

Now suppose the demand for dollars decreases permanently from D_0 to D_2. Again the Fed cannot maintain the exchange rate at 120 yen per dollar indefinitely. In this situation, to hold the exchange rate at 120 yen per dollars, the Fed would have to buy dollars every day. When the Fed buys dollars in the foreign exchange market, it uses its holdings of foreign currency. So the Fed would be losing foreign currency. Eventually, it would run out of foreign currency and would then have to abandon its attempt to fix the exchange rate.

FIGURE 20.10

Foreign Exchange Market Intervention

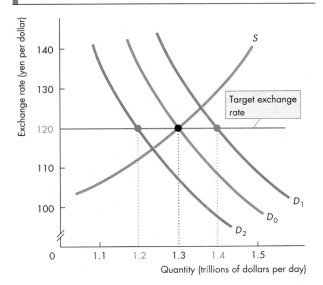

Initially, the demand for dollars is D_0, the supply of dollars is S, and the exchange rate is 120 yen per dollar. The Fed can intervene in the foreign exchange market to keep the exchange rate close to its target rate (120 yen in this example). If demand increases from D_0 to D_1, the Fed sells dollars to increase supply. If demand decreases from D_0 to D_2, the Fed buys dollars to decrease supply. Persistent intervention on one side of the market cannot be sustained.

REVIEW QUIZ

- What is the exchange rate and how is it determined?
- What are the influences of interest rates and the expected future exchange rate on the demand for and supply of dollars in the foreign exchange market?
- How do changes in the expected future exchange rate influence the actual exchange rate?
- How do purchasing power parity and interest rate parity affect exchange rate expectations?
- How can the Fed influence the foreign exchange market?

Reading Between the Lines on pages 478–479 looks at exchange rates in 1999 and the relative purchasing power of different currencies in terms of a Big Mac.

You have now reached the end of your economics course. Go back to the big ideas that define the way of economic thinking (on pp. 6–11) and see how much more they mean to you now than they did when you first read them. I hope that your instructor and I have helped to open your eyes and shown you a new way of seeing the world. If we have, you can now do your own "reading between the lines" every day. Keep your economics text handy. Use it to refresh you memory of the economic principles that help you make sense of your world.

Purchasing Power Parity

T H E   E C O N O M I S T , APRIL 3, 1999

Big MacCurrencies

... The Big Mac Index was devised 13 years ago as a light-hearted guide to whether currencies are at their "correct" level. It is based upon one of the oldest concepts in international economics: purchasing power parity (PPP)—the notion that a dollar, say, should buy the same amount in all countries. In the long run, argue PPP fans, currencies should move towards the rate which equalizes the prices of an identical basket of goods and services in each country.

Out "basket" is a McDonald's Big Mac, which is produced in more than 100 countries. The Big Mac PPP is the exchange rate that would leave hamburgers costing the same in America as abroad. Comparing actual exchange rates with PPPs signals whether a currency is under- or over-valued. ...

The American price (the average of four cities, including tax) has dropped by 5% over the past year, to $2.43. Elsewhere the cheapest Big Mac is in Malaysia ($1.19), whereas in Switzerland it costs a beefy $3.97. Hence the Swiss franc is the most overvalued currency (by 64%) the ringgit the most undervalued (by 51%). ...

The hamburger standard

	Big Mac prices		Under(-)/over(+) valuation against the dollar, %
	In local currency	In dollars	
United States‡	$2.43	2.43	—
Argentina	Peso2.50	2.50	+3
Australia	A$2.65	1.66	−32
Brazil	Real2.95	1.73	−30
Britain	£ 1.90	3.07	+26
Canada	C$2.99	1.98	−19
Chile	Peso1,25	2.60	+7
China	Yuan9.90	1.20	−51
Denmark	DKr24.75	3.58	+47
Euro area	Euro2.52	2.71	+11
France	FFr8.50	2.87	+18
Germany	DM4.95	2.72	+12
Italy	Lire4,500	2.50	+3
Netherlands	Fl5.45	2.66	+10
Spain	Pta375	2.43	0
Hong Kong	HK$10.2	1.32	−46
Hungary	Forint299	1.26	−48
Indonesia	Rupiah14,500	1.66	−32
Israel	Shekel13.9	3.44	+42
Japan	¥294	2.44	0
Malaysia	M$4.52	1.15	−51
Mexico	Peso19.9	2.05	−14
New Zealand	NZ$3.40	1.82	−25
Poland	Zloty5.50	1.38	−43
Russia	Rouble33.5	1.35	−44
Singapore	S$3.20	1.85	−24
South Africa	Rand8.60	1.38	−43
South Korea	Won3,000	2.46	+1
Sweden	SKr24.0	2.86	+19
Switzerland	SFr5.90	3.97	+64
Taiwan	NT$70.0	2.11	−13
Thailand	Baht52.0	1.38	−43

Essence of the Story

- *The Economist* publishes a Big Mac index of currencies.

- The index is based on the price of a McDonald's Big Mac, which is now produced in over 100 countries.

- The Big Mac purchasing power parity (PPP) is the exchange rate that makes a Big Mac cost the same in all countries.

- *The Economist* uses this index to judge whether currencies are at their "correct" PPP level.

- In April 1999, the Big Mac cost an average of $2.43 in the United States. It cost least in Malaysia, $1.19, and most in Switzerland, $3.97.

- *The Economist* concludes that the Malaysian ringgit is the most undervalued currency (by 51%) and the Swiss franc is the most overvalued (by 64%).

■ Although *The Economist* is having a bit of fun with its Big Mac index, it is also doing some misleading and potentially wrong economics.

■ The basic assumption is that a Big Mac is the same good the world over. Because it is the same good, it should have the same price. Any price differences are due to currencies being undervalued or overvalued.

■ The assumption is wrong. When McDonald's sells a Big Mac, it sells a *service*—a fast food service—as well as a good.

■ The price of the service component of a Big Mac varies from place to place and depends on local demand and supply conditions.

■ Figure 1 shows the range of prices *inside the United States*. The highest price is in New York City, where a Big Mac costs $3.13 with tax. The lowest price is in Jonesboro, Arkansas, where the price is $1.80.

■ More than half the countries in *The Economist's* table have prices that fall inside the range of those in the United States.

■ Only three of *The Economist's* countries—Switzerland, Denmark, and Israel—have prices that exceed the price in New York City.

■ Only eleven of *The Economist's* countries have prices below the price in Jonesboro, Arkansas.

■ There are many reasons why the local prices of a Big Mac vary—some on the demand side and some on the supply side.

■ A major supply side influence is the cost of labor. An hour of labor in Switzerland costs 75 times that of an hour of labor in Malaysia.

■ To make PPP comparisons, we must use goods that are easily transported among countries and that have a small or no service component. The price of a floppy disk, a PC, or a computer chip would do a much better job of revealing PPP than the price of a Big Mac.

■ *The Economist* should replace its Big Mac standard with the Intel chip standard.

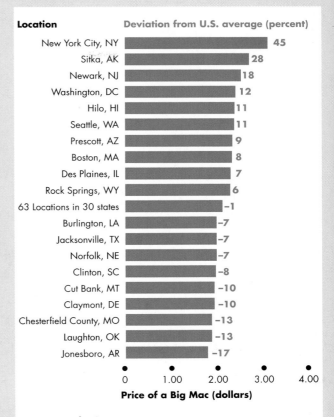

PPP Across the States

■ Why does it matter whether the dollar is undervalued or overvalued?

■ What can the Fed do if it believes that the dollar is undervalued or overvalued?

■ Thinking only about your own economic well-being, what is better for you: an undervalued dollar or an overvalued dollar?

479

SUMMARY

KEY POINTS

Financing International Trade (pp. 464–468)

- International trade, borrowing, and lending are financed by using foreign currency.
- A country's international transactions are recorded in its balance of payments accounts.
- Historically, the United States has been a net lender to the rest of the world, but in 1983, that situation changed and the United States became a net borrower. In 1989, the United States became a net debtor.
- The net exports deficit is equal to the government sector deficit plus the private sector deficit.

The Exchange Rate (pp. 469–477)

- Foreign currency is obtained in exchange for domestic currency in the foreign exchange market.
- The exchange rate is determined by demand and supply in the foreign exchange market.
- The lower the exchange rate, the greater is the quantity of dollars demanded. A change in the exchange rate brings a movement along the demand curve for dollars.
- Changes in the U.S. interest rate differential and the expected future exchange rate change the demand for dollars and shift the demand curve.
- The lower the exchange rate, the smaller is the quantity of dollars supplied. A change in the exchange rate brings a movement along the supply curve for dollars.
- Changes in the U.S. interest rate differential and the expected future exchange rate change the supply of dollars and shift the supply curve.
- Fluctuations in the exchange rate occur because fluctuations in the demand for and supply of dollars are not independent.
- The Fed can intervene in the foreign exchange market to smooth fluctuations in the dollar.

KEY FIGURES AND TABLE

KEY TERMS

PROBLEMS

*1. The citizens of Silecon, whose currency is the grain, conduct the following transactions in 1999:

Item	Billions of grains
Imports of goods and services	350
Exports of goods and services	500
Borrowing from the rest of the world	60
Lending to the rest of the world	200
Increase in official holdings of foreign currency	10

   a. Set out the three balance of payments accounts for Silecon.
   b. Does Silecon have a flexible exchange rate?

2. The citizens of Spin, whose currency is the wheel, conduct the following transactions in 1999:

Item	Wheels
Imports of goods and services	50
Exports of goods and services	60
Borrowing from the rest of the world	2
Lending to the rest of the world	12
Increase in official holdings of foreign currency	0

   a. Set out the three balance of payments accounts for Spin.
   b. Does Spin have a flexible exchange rate?

*3. The figure below shows the flows of income and expenditure in Dream Land in 2000. The amounts are in millions of dollars. GDP in Dream Land is $60 million.
   a. Calculate Dream Land's net exports.
   b. Calculate saving in Dream Land.
   c. How is Dream Land's investment financed?

4. The figure below shows the flows of income and expenditure in Dream Land in 2001. The amounts are in millions of dollars. Dream Land's GDP has increased to $65 million, but all the other items whose values are provided in the figure remain the same as they were in 2000.
   a. Calculate Dream Land's net exports in 2001.
   b. Calculate saving in Dream Land in 2001.
   c. How is Dream Land's investment financed?

*5. The following table tells you about Ecflex, a country with a flexible exchange rate whose currency is the band.

   Calculate the following for Ecflex:
   a. Imports of goods and services
   b. Current account balance
   c. Capital account balance
   d. Net taxes
   e. Private sector surplus

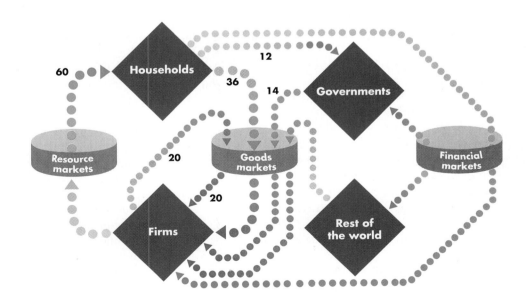

Item	Billion bands
GDP	100
Consumption expenditure	60
Government purchases of goods and services	24

Item	Billion bands
Investment	22
Exports of goods and services	20
Government budget deficit	4

6. You are told the following about Ecfix, a country with a fixed exchange rate whose currency is the rock:

Item	Billion rocks
GDP	200
Consumption expenditure	120
Government purchases of goods and services	50
Investment	50
Exports of goods and services	40
Saving	45

Calculate the following for Ecfix:
  a. Imports of goods and services
  b. Current account balance
  c. Capital account balance
  d. Net taxes
  e. Private sector surplus
  f. Government deficit or surplus

💻 *7. A country's currency appreciates, and its official holdings of foreign currency increase. What can you say about:
  a. The exchange rate system being pursued by the country?
  b. The possible central bank sources of the currency appreciation?
  c. The possible private actions behind the appreciation?

💻 8. A country's currency depreciates, and its official holdings of foreign currency decrease. What can you say about:
  a. The exchange rate system being pursued by the country?
  b. The possible sources of the currency depreciation?
  c. The possible private actions behind the depreciation?

CRITICAL THINKING

1. Study *Reading Between the Lines* on pp. 478–479 and then answer the following questions.
  a. Which currencies does *The Economist* claim are undervalued and which does it claim are overvalued?
  b. What is PPP?
  c. What is the key assumption used by *The Economist* to make its PPP calculations?
  d. What is wrong with *The Economist*'s assumptions?
  e. Use the Bulletin Board on the Parkin Web site to share information on the prices of floppy disks around the world and do a PPP comparison based on the floppy disk standard.

🌐 2. Use the link on the Parkin Web site to visit FRED, the database of the Federal Reserve Bank of St. Louis, and find data on the exchange rate and international trade.
  a. When did the United States last have a current account surplus?
  b. Does the United States have a surplus or a deficit in its trade in goods?
  c. Does the United States have a surplus or a deficit in its trade in services?
  d. What has happened to foreign investment in the United States during the past ten years?
  e. Do you think that the U.S. balance of payments record is a matter for concern? Why or why not?

🌐 3. Use the link on the Parkin Web site to get recent data on the exchange rate of the U.S. dollar against two other currencies that interest you over the past month. Then:
  a. Use the demand and supply model of the foreign exchange market to explain the changes (or absence of changes) in the exchange rates.
  b. What specific events might have changed exchange rate expectations?
  c. What forces might have prevented the exchange rates from changing?
  d. What information would you need to be able to determine whether central bank intervention has prevented either exchange rate from changing by as much as it otherwise would have?

Understanding the Global Economy

It's a Small World

The scale of international trade, borrowing, and lending, both in absolute dollar terms and as a percentage of total world production, expands every year. One country, Singapore, imports and exports goods and services in a volume that exceeds its gross domestic product. The world's largest nation, China, returned to the international economic stage during the 1980s and is now a major producer of manufactured goods. ◆ International economic activity is large because today's economic world is small and because communication is so incredibly fast. But today's world is not a new world. From the beginning of recorded history, people have traded over large and steadily increasing distances. The great Western civilizations of Greece and Rome traded not only around the Mediterranean but also into the Gulf of Arabia. The great Eastern civilizations traded around the Indian Ocean. By the Middle Ages, the East and the West were trading routinely overland on routes pioneered by Venetian traders and explorers such as Marco Polo. When, in 1497, Vasco da Gama opened a sea route between the Atlantic and Indian Oceans around Africa, a new trade between East and West began, which brought tumbling prices of Eastern goods in Western markets. ◆ The European discovery of America and the subsequent opening up of Atlantic trade continued the process of steady globalization. So the developments of the 1990s, amazing though many of them were, represent a continuation of an ongoing expansion of human horizons.
◆ These two chapters study the interaction of nations in today's global economy.
◆ Chapter 19 described and explained international trade in goods and services. In this chapter, you came face to face with one of the biggest policy issues of all ages: free trade versus protection. The chapter explained how all nations can benefit from free international trade. And it showed how protection from competition brings big benefits to a few and small losses to many. The total gains from protection are dwarfed by the losses, but because the losses are spread thinly and the gains thickly, protectionism always has supporters and political backers. ◆ Chapter 20 explained some of the fundamentals of international borrowing and lending and the exchange rate. It explained the poorly understood fact that the size of a nation's international deficit depends not on how efficient it is, but on how much its citizens save relative to how much they invest. Nations with low saving rates, everything else remaining the same, have international deficits. ◆ This chapter also explains why foreign exchange rates fluctuate so much. ◆ The global economy is big news these days. And it has always attracted attention. On the next page, you can meet the economist who first understood comparative advantage: David Ricardo. And you can meet one of today's leading international economists, Stanley Fischer, formally a professor at MIT and now Deputy Managing Director of the International Monetary Fund.

The Economist

David Ricardo *(1772–1832) was a highly successful 27-year-old stockbroker when he stumbled on a copy of Adam Smith's* Wealth of Nations *(see p. 56) on a weekend visit to the country. He was immediately hooked and went on to become the most celebrated economist of his age and one of the all-time great economists. One of his many contributions was to develop the principle of comparative advantage, the foundation on which the modern theory of international trade is built. The example he used to illustrate this principle was the trade between England and Portugal in cloth and wine.*

The General Agreement on Tariffs and Trade was established as a reaction against the devastation wrought by beggar-my-neighbor tariffs imposed during the 1930s. But it is also a triumph for the logic first worked out by Smith and Ricardo.

The Issues

Until the mid-eighteenth century, it was generally believed that the purpose of international trade was to keep exports greater than imports and pile up gold. If gold was accumulated, it was believed, the nation would prosper; if gold was lost through an international deficit, the nation would be drained of money and impoverished. These beliefs are called *mercantilism*, and the *mercantilists* were pamphleteers who advocated with missionary

fervor the pursuit of an international surplus. If exports did not exceed imports, the mercantilists wanted imports restricted.

In the 1740s, David Hume explained that as the quantity of money (gold) changes, so also does the price level, and the nation's *real* wealth is unaffected. In the 1770s, Adam Smith argued that import restrictions would lower the gains from specialization and make a nation poorer. Thirty years later, David Ricardo proved the law of comparative advantage and demonstrated the superiority of free trade. Mercantilism was intellectually bankrupt but remained politically powerful.

Gradually, through the nineteenth century, the mercantilist influence waned and North America and Western Europe prospered in an environment of increasingly free international trade. But despite remarkable advances in economic understanding, mercantilism never quite died. It had a brief and devastating revival in the 1920s and 1930s when tariff hikes brought about the collapse of international trade and accentuated the Great Depression. It subsided again after World War II with the establishment of the General Agreement on Tariffs and Trade (GATT).

But mercantilism lingers on. The often expressed view that the United States should restrict Japanese imports and reduce its deficit with Japan and fears that NAFTA will bring economic ruin to the United States are modern manifestations of mercantilism. It would be interesting to have David

Hume, Adam Smith, and David Ricardo commenting on these views. But we know what they would say—the same things that they said to the eighteenth-century mercantilists. And they would still be right today.

Then

In the eighteenth century, when mercantilists and economists were debating the pros and cons of free international exchange, the transportation technology that was available limited the gains from international trade. Sailing ships with tiny cargo holds took close to a month to cross the Atlantic Ocean. But the potential gains were large, and so was the incentive to cut shipping costs. By the 1850s, the clipper ship had been developed, cutting the journey from Boston to Liverpool to only 12¼ days. Half a century later, 10,000-ton steamships were sailing between America and England in just 4 days. As sailing times and costs declined, the gains from international trade increased and the volume of trade expanded.

Now

The container ship has revolutionized international trade and contributed to its continued expansion. Today, most goods cross the oceans in containers—metal boxes—packed into and piled on top of ships like this one. Container technology has cut the cost of ocean shipping by economizing on handling and by making cargoes harder to steal, lowering insurance costs. It is unlikely that there would be much international trade in goods such as television sets and VCRs without this technology. High-value and perishable cargoes such as flowers and fresh foods, as well as urgent courier packages, travel by air. Every day, dozens of cargo-laden 747s fly between every major U.S. city and to destinations across the Atlantic and Pacific oceans.

As the world economy has become more integrated, new international institutions have evolved. One of these institutions is the International Monetary Fund, or IMF. Let's talk with one of today's outstanding economists who now plays a leading role at the IMF and has become a household name during the Asia crisis, Stanley Fischer.

Stanley Fischer *has served as the First Deputy Managing Director of the International Monetary Fund (The IMF) since 1994. Born in Zambia in 1943, he received a B.S. and an M.S. from the London School of Economics in 1965 and 1966, respectively, and a Ph.D. from MIT in 1969. Professor Fischer has taught at the University of Chicago and MIT. He served as Vice President of Development Economics and Chief Economist at the World Bank from 1988 to 1992. Michael Parkin talked with Stanley Fischer about his work at the IMF, the goals of that institution, and the lessons that we've learned from the Asian financial crisis.*

Stanley Fischer

How did you get into economics?
I was at high school in Zimbabwe (then Rhodesia) and in the sixth form I began to specialize in physics, chemistry, and math. Then I heard about economics. I switched one of my science courses to economics and I loved it.

This was the perfect field, one that provided an analytic way of understanding an important part of how societies work and also one in which I could use my quantitative skills. I went to the London School of Economics for my bachelor's and master's degrees and then to MIT for my Ph.D. My first appointment was at the University of Chicago

at a time when Milton Friedman was still the dominant influence there.

Can we talk first about the amazing liberalization and growth of world trade during the post–World War II years? Has this growth of world trade brought economic growth for all countries? Or have some gained more than others?
If you were to look at what has happened in the postwar period to the industrialized countries—which, despite some slowing since the 1960s, have grown faster, more consistently, and with less disruption than in any period of similar length in history—you would have to say that the architecture of the postwar economy has been very successful. And then if you look at the developing countries, you will find that, on the average, they have grown faster yet. In the most populous part of the globe, namely, East Asia, China, and, to some extent, India, we have had absolutely unprecedented growth. Every one of the successful East Asian countries has succeeded by integrating with the world economy, by promoting exports and increasing imports, especially of capital and intermediate goods. This process of opening up and using world markets for exports and imports has been absolutely critical. This outcome is what most economists from Adam Smith and David Ricardo on would have predicted.

The one part of the world where progress has, on the average, been most disappointing, is Africa. But there are countries in Africa that have done well. The countries that have been serious about trying to trade in the global economy and about implementing market-friendly policies have done better on the whole. We have seen significant growth in per capita income in Africa in the last few years. The prospects for South Africa look good, and that could be very important for a large part of the continent. In addition, countries such as Mozambique and Uganda have begun growing very fast after terrible civil wars, and Botswana has been one of the fastest-growing economies in the world for the past two decades.

What is the role of the IMF and what are the main problems that it seeks to address?

The IMF has several main functions. The first is *surveillance:* It is an institution in which countries discuss problems of the international economy, as well as each other's economies. Twice a year, the Fund staff presents its survey of the world economy, the *World Economic Outlook.*

In addition, Fund staff presents an annual report—the Article IV report—on the economy of each member country. The Article IV reports are based on the staff's analysis and discussions with the economic policy makers in each country.

Another function of the Fund is to *make loans to countries* in economic trouble. These loans typically provide balance of payments support to countries in crisis and countries to which the private capital markets are reluctant to lend.

One such crisis began in 1997—the financial crisis of Asia, Russia, Brazil, and other countries. What was its central feature?

Financial system weakness was a feature of almost all the crisis countries except Brazil. All the crises were driven and worsened by rapid international movements of capital. Investors pushed money into the crisis countries and then pulled it out, very rapidly, as the crisis approached its peak. The crisis featured *contagion*, spreading fast from one country to another.

What are the lessons of this episode of financial crisis?

The main lesson is that individual countries and the international financial system must adapt to the new circumstances of globally integrated financial markets. We must reduce the volatility of international capital flows and improve the capacity of financial systems and economies to cope with shifts in market confidence and investor sentiment that will inevitably occur in future.

Work is now under way in the emerging market economies, industrialized countries, and international institutions, to identify the polices and reforms that are needed.

For the *emerging market countries*, the list of items that need attention is a long one. Efforts

must focus on sound macroeconomic policies, which include avoiding operating fixed exchange rate systems, which have been crisis-prone. Banking systems must be restructured, and the supervision and regulation of banks must be improved. Better economic and financial information on private and public sector activities must be provided. Business financial practices and bankruptcy laws must be improved. And these countries need to find ways of dealing with rapid and large reversals in international capital flows.

Countries need to think carefully about how fast and in what order to free capital account transactions and to make sure their borrowing is not too short term. They also need adequate reserves and, possibly, lines of credit that will give them access to liquidity when they need it.

The *advanced industrialized countries* need to pursue macroeconomic policies that bring sustainable growth. When these countries are not expanding, developing countries, too, find it difficult to grow. The advanced countries also need to maintain healthy financial systems and to regulate their own financial institutions to minimize potential disruptive capital flows to emerging market countries.

The *international financial institutions*, the IMF among them, must act as well. One example of an important initiative is the design and adoption of international standards for bank operation and supervision and for reporting fiscal and monetary data. Another is the effort to encourage the provision of better economic and financial data to the public by emerging market economies. A third is the effort to strengthen *surveillance* by the IMF. The IMF reports regularly on each country's economy, assessing its policies and practices, thereby encouraging the country to do better. Fourth, IMF member countries are gradually coming to the view that IMF reports, the Article IV reports, should be published so that the general public and investors can share information that so far has been available only to governments. Fifth, we are finding ways of making sure that private investors do their share in solving crises. One important criticism of IMF programs has been that the official sector bails out the private sector, providing loans so that the private sector can take its money out of a country in trouble. This is a very complicated issue, but we are definitely making progress on what is known as "bailing in" the private sector, finding ways of discouraging the private sector from taking its money out when a crisis hits.

What big conclusions should we draw from the special features of Russia's economic and financial condition?

A key question that has been asked since the onset of Russia's crisis in 1999 is: Was the reform strategy of the previous Russian government wrong? My conclusion is, fundamentally, no. The problem was not that the basic strategy was wrong, but that it was not pursued vigorously or deeply enough. What has been necessary in Russia

for some time has been a comprehensive strategy for moving boldly to tackle a large fiscal imbalance and to deal with important structural problems related to the way its economy operates—in particular, the nonpayment problem. Such a strategy was at the heart of the July 1998 program agreed on with the IMF. But by then, the financial situation and market confidence were too precarious and vulnerable to any missteps in implementation, which indeed happened and quickly led to the August collapse.

Put differently, the conclusion is that stabilization is not enough. Russia stabilized its economy extremely successfully from about the middle of 1995, with an appropriate degree of monetary discipline accompanied by a fixed exchange rate regime, which stabilizes inflationary expectations following a prolonged period of high inflation. However, the fiscal adjustment needed was not forthcoming, so there was a massive and rapid buildup in public debt. Ultimately, the government was not able to service its debt out of its own resources and could not convince investors to continue financing its ongoing deficit. This led to both the devaluation of the ruble and the government default on its treasury bills in August 1998.

Moreover, a critical reason why the fiscal adjustment could not be implemented was the lack of progress in industrial restructuring and other structural reforms; thus the stabilization was not sustainable. A very large part of the Russian economy remains

> So the failure of structural reforms underlies the fiscal problem in Russia.

unreformed, has not been part of the monetary economy, and is conducting its operations largely through barter—not only literally barter of goods against goods, but in many cases barter through very sophisticated financial mechanisms that do not involve the use of money. This situation has arisen because of a vast number of factors, including poor enforcement of tax obligations, an unfair tax system, weak bankruptcy laws, poor lending practices by banks, and corrupt business practices. Thus, much of the productive sector was either losing money in real terms or not paying a fair share of taxes. So the failure of structural reforms underlies the fiscal problem in Russia. Without these reforms, the budget will not balance, growth will not materialize, and eventually financial stability will be compromised.

Why do you believe that the IMF can play a role as the lender of last resort?

The IMF already is increasingly playing that role, both as crisis lender and as crisis manager. As crisis lender, the IMF, whose financial structure is similar to that of a credit union, has access to a pool of resources. As crisis manager, it has been taking the lead in negotiating with its member countries that are experiencing a financial crisis. It also has played an important coordinating and

> **Should the IMF function as an international lender of last resort? I believe that there is a need for an agency that will act as such a lender to countries facing a crisis.**

advisory role in arranging financing packages to help countries work out their debt problems with their foreign creditors.

Some have asked whether the IMF has enough resources to act as crisis lender. While the resources available have grown less than the size of the world economy since the IMF's inception in 1945, the IMF can still assemble a sizable financial package in response to a crisis, including, in special circumstances, by borrowing from members' central banks and by creating additional reserves for its members through the issuance of Special Drawing Rights (SDRs).

Should the IMF function as an international lender of last resort? I believe that there is a need for an agency that will act as such a lender to countries facing a crisis. The need arises because international capital flows are both extremely volatile and contagious, exhibiting the classic signs of financial panics, and an international lender of last resort can help to mitigate the effects of this instability and perhaps even help prevent the instability itself. Again, the IMF has already been acting in many ways as such a lender, and there is ongoing work to help make the IMF more effective in that capacity.

Of the main criticisms leveled at the IMF during the Asian crisis, which are the easiest to dismiss, and which, if any, should we take more seriously?

This is a complex question that cannot be easily answered in a few words. While I will try, I should say that the IMF has taken all the criticisms seriously and indeed has produced a comprehensive study of the experience in Indonesia, Korea, and Thailand, which I would encourage those interested to read.

The programs in the Asian crisis countries supported by the IMF sought to restore macroeconomic stability and the conditions for growth while addressing deep-rooted structural weaknesses that lay at the heart of the crisis in each country. These programs have been attacked from a number of angles, but here again I believe that, particularly in the highly fluid and uncertain circumstances, the approach taken and choices made were basically correct.

A frequent criticism is that the policy of high interest rates worsened financial problems being experienced by corporations and therefore made the recessions worse in these countries. However, their currencies were collapsing, and it was critical to avoid a depreciation-inflation spiral. Indeed, the critics fail to recognize that, in addition to the well-known negative effects on growth of high inflation, in a situation where companies and banks had borrowed heavily abroad, the further depreciations implied by lower interest rates would have exacerbated financial problems by

increasing the burden of servicing dollar-denominated debts.

Another criticism is that the programs entailed unduly contractionary fiscal policies. The original programs in these countries, formulated in the initial stages of the crisis, included some degree of fiscal adjustment to lessen the burden that might be placed on the private sector in the face of the large adjustment in the current account of the balance of payments that was needed. The truth is that, even then, the fiscal adjustment that was planned was rather small in both Korea and Indonesia and was substantial only in Thailand, where the initial fiscal imbalance was larger. Moreover, as economic activity deteriorated over the course of the programs, fiscal policy was progressively allowed to become more expansionary. In fact, our study concluded that fiscal policy was not a major factor accounting for the output decline in these countries.

The inclusion of structural measures in our programs also has drawn criticism. Financial and corporate sector inefficiencies were at the heart of these crises, and it was clear from the start that the restoration of durable growth required financial and corporate restructuring. Still, some argued that these reforms, while sensible over the medium term, impose large costs in the short term, and therefore it was a mistake to put them in place when economic activity was already so weak. While this is a valid concern, I think that attempting to stabilize the situation without attempting to address the underlying causes of the crisis would have been akin to treating the symptom without addressing the real cause of the disease. And delay does not make the structural problem any easier to deal with; indeed, as the problem of the Japanese banking sector in the 1990s clearly demonstrates, it makes it worse.

All this said, why did the programs work less well than we all hoped? Why was the economic downturn worse than initially foreseen? Clearly, the projections embodied in the original programs were somewhat more optimistic than the consensus view. However, very few observers foresaw the severity of the downturn—neither the governments, private forecasters, nor academic observers. A number of factors conspired to make matters worse than foreseen. First, the external environment for the crisis countries worsened markedly. In particular, the Japanese recession has been deeper and more prolonged than anticipated, hurting the exports of the crisis countries. Second, several factors—an initial reluctance by governments to implement the programs, political uncertainties, and lack of public support for the programs—made it much more difficult for market confidence to be restored than had been assumed. This led to greater

> The Japanese recession has been deeper and more prolonged than anticipated, hurting the exports of the crisis countries.

capital outflows and put additional upward pressure on interest rates and downward pressure on exchange rates, and forced a larger downward adjustment of domestic demand.

While I believe the basic approach of the programs was right, that doesn't mean that we shouldn't try to do better. As I already discussed, the recent financial crises have revealed weaknesses in the international financial system that we must try to deal with. As briefly described above, the IMF and other international institutions are doing their part to help in that endeavor.

What kinds of jobs do economics graduates get in organizations such as the IMF and the World Bank? What should students be doing as undergraduates to prepare themselves for such positions?

People who want to work in the Fund and the Bank should take courses in macroeconomics, international trade and finance,

development, monetary economics, and public finance. From the viewpoint of the Bank, it would also be useful to study micro-oriented policy issues. The Fund and the Bank have entry programs for people who may be destined for their professional ranks. The World Bank's is called Young Professionals, and the IMF's is called the Economist Program.

The IMF and the World Bank are terrific places to work. You use your analytic skills all the time, in the real world. You have to decide what really matters, you have to be sure that what you're recommending will improve the lives of people. Then if you work in the operational parts of the Fund or Bank, you have to persuade the countries with which you're working that you're right. If you are right and you succeed, you have the satisfaction of having done something useful.

In the process, you'll have had the benefit of learning some diplomacy. You are also likely to learn some humility—for you will realize that the really hard work of implementing policies is done by the politicians and officials of the countries that undertake them. Your job is to help them do their own jobs better, always bearing in mind that the benefits or costs are borne by their people.

Solutions to Odd-Numbered Problems

CHAPTER 1

1. The opportunity cost of going to school is $9,600 of goods and services.

   The opportunity cost of going to school this summer is the highest-valued activity that you will give up so that you can go to summer school. In going to summer school, you will forgo all the goods and services that you could have bought with the income from your summer job ($6,000) plus the expenditure on tuition ($2,000), textbooks ($200), and living expenses ($1,400).

3. No, parking at this mall is not free. Yes, you did impose a cost on Harry.

   Finding a parking space takes about 30 minutes, so you incur an opportunity cost when you park your car. The opportunity cost is the highest-valued activity that you forgo by spending 30 minutes parking your car. If you would have spent those 30 minutes studying, then the opportunity cost of parking at this mall is 30 minutes of studying.

   The cost that you imposed on Harry is the additional 30 minutes that Harry will have to spend searching for a parking space.

CHAPTER 2

1a. To make a time-series graph, plot the year on the x-axis and the inflation rate on the y-axis. The graph will be a line joining all the points.

1b. (i) 1980 (ii) 1986 (iii) 1984, 1987–1990, 1995–1996 (iv) 1981–1983, 1985–1986, 1991–1992, 1994, 1997–1998 (v) 1987 (vi) 1982

1c. Inflation has had a downward trend. The line tends to slope down to the right.

3. To make a scatter diagram, plot the inflation rate on the x-axis and the interest rate on the y-axis. The graph will be a set of dots. The pattern made by the dots tells us that as the inflation rate increases, the interest rate usually increases.

5a. To make a graph that shows the relationship between x and y, plot x on the x-axis and y on the y-axis. The relationship is positive because x and y move together: As x increases, y increases.

5b. The slope increases as x increases. Slope is equal to the change in y divided by the change in x as we move along the curve. When x increases from 1 to 2 (a change of 1), y increases from 1 to 4 (a change of 3), so the slope is 3. But when x increases from 7 to 8 (a change of 1), y increases from 49 to 64 (a change of 15), so the slope is 15.

5c. The taller the building, the bigger is the cost of building it. The higher the unemployment rate, the higher is the crime rate. The longer the flight, the larger is the amount of fuel used.

The slope equals 8.

The slope of the curve at the point where x is 4 is equal to the slope of the tangent to the curve at that point. Plot the relationship and then draw the tangent line at the point where x is 4 and y is 16. Now calculate the slope of this tangent line. To do this, you must find another point on the tangent. The tangent line will cut the x-axis at 2, so another point is x equals 2 and y equals 0. Slope equals rise/run. The rise is 16 and the run is 2, so the slope is 8.

The slope is 7.

The slope of the relationship across the arc when x increases from 3 to 4 is equal to the slope of the straight line joining the points on the curve at x equals 3 and x equals 4. In the graph, draw this straight line. When x increases from 3 to 4, y increases from 9 to 16. Slope equals rise/run. The rise is 7 (16 minus 9) and the run is 1 (4 minus 3), so the slope across the arc is 7.

The slope is −5/4.

The curve is a straight line, so its slope is the same at all points on the curve. Slope equals the change in the variable on the y-axis divided by the change in the variable on the x-axis. To calculate the slope, you must select two points on the line. One point is at 10 on the y-axis and 0 on the x-axis, and another is at 8 on the x-axis and 0 on the y-axis. The change in y from 10 to 0 is associated with the change in x from 0 to 8. Therefore the slope of the curve equals −10/8, which equals −5/4.

13a. The slope at point a is −2, and the slope at point b is −0.75.

To calculate the slope at a point on a curved line, draw the tangent to the line at the point. Then find a second point on the tangent and calculate the slope of the tangent.

The tangent at point a cuts the y-axis at 10. The slope of the tangent equals the change in y divided by the change in x. The change in y equals 4 (10 minus 6) and the change in x equals −2 (0 minus 2). The slope at point a is 4/−2, which equals −2.

Similarly, the slope at point b is −0.75. The tangent at point b cuts the x-axis at 8. The change in y equals 1.5, and the change in x equals −2. The slope at point b is −0.75.

13b. The slope across the arc ab is −1.125.

The slope across an arc ab equals the change in y, which is 4.5 (6.0 minus 1.5) divided by the change in x, which equals −4 (2 minus 6). The slope across the arc ab equals 4.5/−4, which is −1.125.

15a. A set of curves, one for each different temperature.

To draw a graph of the relationship between the price and the number of rides, keep the temperature at 50°F and plot the data in that column against the price. The curve that you draw is the relationship between price and number of rides when the temperature is 50°F. Now repeat the exercise but keep the temperature at 70°F. Then repeat the exercise but keep the temperature at 90°F.

15b. A set of curves, one for each different price.

To draw a graph of the relationship between the temperature and the number of rides, keep the price at $5.00 a ride and plot the data in that row against the temperature. The curve shows the relationship between temperature and the number of rides when the price is $5.00 a ride. Now repeat the exercise but keep the price at $10.00 a ride. Repeat the exercise again and keep the price at $15.00 a ride and then at $20.00 a ride.

15c. A set of curves, one for each different number of rides.

To draw a graph of the relationship between the temperature and price, keep the number of rides at 32 and plot the data along the diagonal in the table. The curve is the relationship between temperature and price at which 32 rides are taken. Now repeat the exercise and keep the number of rides at 27. Repeat the exercise again and keep the number of rides at 18 and then at 40.

CHAPTER 3

1a. Wendell's opportunity cost is 5 percentage points.

When Wendell increases the time he plays tennis from 4 hours to 6 hours, his grade in economics falls from 75 percent to 70 percent. His opportunity cost is 5 percentage points.

1b. Wendell's opportunity cost is 10 percentage points.

When Wendell increases the time he plays tennis from 6 hours to 8 hours, his grade in economics falls from 70 percent to 60 percent. His opportunity cost is 10 percentage points.

3. Wendell's opportunity cost of playing tennis increases as he spends more time on tennis.

When Wendell increases the time he plays tennis from 4 hours to 6 hours, his opportunity cost is 5 percentage points. But when he increases the time he plays tennis from 6 hours to 8 hours, his opportunity cost is 10 percentage points. Wendell's opportunity cost of playing tennis increases as he spends more time on tennis.

5a. Wendell's grade in economics is 66 percent.

When Wendell increases the time he plays tennis from 4 hours to 6 hours, his opportunity cost of the additional 2 hours of tennis is 5 percentage points. So his opportunity cost of an additional 1 hour is 2.5 percentage points. But when he increases the time he plays tennis from 6 hours to 8 hours, his opportunity cost of the additional 2 hours of tennis is 10 percentage points. So his opportunity cost of the additional 1 hour of tennis is 5 percentage points. Wendell's opportunity cost of playing tennis increases as he spends more time on tennis. Opportunity cost is plotted at the midpoint of the range. This curve is Wendell's marginal cost of a additional hour of tennis.

Wendell uses his time efficiently if he plays tennis for 7 hours a week—marginal benefit from tennis equals its marginal cost. Wendell's marginal benefit is 5 percentage points and his marginal cost is 5 percentage points. When Wendell plays 7 hours of tennis, his grade in economics (from his *PPF*) is 66 percent.

5b. If Wendell studied for enough hours to get a higher grade, he would have fewer hours to play tennis. Wendell's marginal benefit from tennis would be greater than his marginal cost, so he would be more efficient if he played more hours of tennis and took a lower grade.

7a. Leisureland's *PPF* is a straight line.

To make a graph of Leisureland's *PPF* measure the quantity of one good on the *x*-axis and the quantity of the other good on the *y*-axis. Then plot the quantities in each row of the table and join up the points.

7b. The opportunity cost of 1 pound of food is 1/2 gallon of sunscreen.

The opportunity cost of the first 100 pounds of food is 50 gallons of sunscreen. To find the opportunity cost of the first 100 pounds of food, increase the quantity of food from 0 pounds to 100 pounds. In doing so, Leisureland's production of sunscreen decreases from 150 gallons to 100 gallons. The opportunity cost of the first 100 pounds of food is 50 gallons of sunscreen. Similarly, the opportunity costs of producing the second 100 pounds and the third 100 pounds of food are 50 gallons of sunscreen.

The opportunity cost of 1 gallon of sunscreen is 2 pounds of food. The opportunity cost of producing the first 50 gallons of sunscreen is 100 pounds of food. To calculate this opportunity cost, increase the quantity of sunscreen from 0 gallons to 50 gallons. Leisureland's production of food decreases from 300 pounds to 200 pounds. Similarly, the opportunity cost of producing the second 50 gallons and the third 50 gallons of sunscreen are 100 pounds of food.

9a. The marginal benefit curve slopes downward.

To draw the marginal benefit from sunscreen, plot the quantity of sunscreen on the *x*-axis and the willingness to pay for sunscreen (that is, the number of pounds of food that they are willing to give up to get a gallon of sunscreen) on the *y*-axis.

9b. The efficient quantity is 75 gallons a month.

The efficient quantity to produce is such that the marginal benefit from the last gallon equals the opportunity cost of producing it. The opportunity cost of a gallon of sunscreen is 2 pounds of sunscreen. The marginal benefit of the 75th gallon of sunscreen is 2 pounds of food. And the marginal cost of the 75th gallon of sunscreen is 2 pounds of food.

Busyland's opportunity cost of a pound of food is 2 gallons of sunscreen, and its opportunity cost of a gallon of sunscreen is 1/2 pound of food.

When Busyland increases the food it produces by 50 pounds a month, it produces 100 gallons of sunscreen less. The opportunity cost of 1 pound of food is 2 gallons of sunscreen. Similarly, when Busyland increases the sunscreen it produces by 100 gallons a month, it produces 50 pounds of food less. The opportunity cost of 1 gallon of sunscreen is 1/2 pound of food.

13a. Leisureland sells food and buys sunscreen.

Leisureland sells the good in which it has a comparative advantage and buys the other good from Busyland. Leisureland's opportunity cost of 1 pound of food is 1/2 gallon of sunscreen, while Busyland's opportunity cost of 1 pound of food is 2 gallons of sunscreen. Leisureland's opportunity cost of food is less than Busyland's, so Leisureland has a comparative advantage in producing food.

Leisureland's opportunity cost of 1 gallon of sunscreen is 2 pounds of food, while Busyland's opportunity cost of 1 gallon of sunscreen is 1/2 pound of food. Busyland's opportunity cost of sunscreen is less than Leisureland's, so Busyland has a comparative advantage in producing sunscreen.

13b. The gains from trade for each country are 50 pounds of food and 50 gallons of sunscreen.

With specialization and trade, together they can produce 300 pounds of food and 300 gallons of sunscreen. So each will get 150 pounds of food and 150 gallons of sunscreen—an additional 50 pounds of food and 50 gallons of sunscreen.

CHAPTER 4

1a. The price of a tape will rise, and the quantity of tapes sold will increase.

CDs and tapes are substitutes. If the price of a CD rises, people will buy more tapes and fewer CDs. The demand for tapes will increase. The price of a tape will rise, and more tapes will be sold.

1b. The price of a tape will fall, and fewer tapes will be sold.

Walkmans and tapes are complements. If the price of a Walkman rises, fewer Walkmans will be bought. The demand for tapes will decrease. The price of a tape will fall, and people will buy fewer tapes.

1c. The price of a tape will fall and fewer tapes will be sold.

The increase in the supply of CD players will lower the price of a CD player. With CD players cheaper than they were, some people will buy CD players. The demand for CDs will increase, and the demand for tapes will decrease. The price of a tape will fall, and people will buy fewer tapes.

1d. The price of a tape will rise, and the quantity sold will increase.

An increase in consumers' income will increase the demand for tapes. As a result, the price of a tape will rise and the quantity bought will increase.

1e. The price of a tape will rise, and the quantity sold will decrease.

If the workers who make tapes get a pay raise, the cost of making a tape increases and the supply of tapes decreases. The price will rise, and people will buy fewer tapes.

1f. The quantity sold will decrease, but the price might rise, fall, or stay the same.

Walkmans and tapes are complements. If the price of a Walkman rises, fewer Walkmans will be bought and so the demand for tapes will decrease. The price of a tape will fall, and people will buy fewer tapes. If the wages paid to workers who make tapes rise, the supply of tapes

decreases. The quantity of tapes sold will decrease, and the price of a tape will rise. Taking the two events together, the quantity sold will decrease, but the price might rise, fall, or stay the same.

3a. (ii) and (iii)

If the price of crude oil (the resource used to make gasoline) rises, the supply of gasoline decreases. The demand for gasoline does not change, so the price of gasoline rises and there is a movement along the demand curve. The quantity demanded of gasoline decreases.

3b. (i) and (iv)

If the price of a car rises, the quantity of cars bought decreases. So the demand for gasoline decreases. The supply of gasoline does not change, so the price of gasoline falls and there is a movement down the supply curve of gasoline. The quantity supplied of gasoline decreases.

3c. (i) and (iv)

If all speed limits on highways are abolished, people will drive faster and use more gasoline. The demand for gasoline increases. The supply of gasoline does not change, so the price of gasoline rises and there is a movement up along the supply curve. The quantity supplied of gasoline increases.

3d. (i) and (iv)

If robot production plants lower the cost of producing a car, the supply of cars will increase. With no change in the demand for cars, the price of a car will fall and more cars will be bought. The demand for gasoline increases. The supply of gasoline does not change, so the price of gasoline rises and the quantity of gasoline supplied increases.

5a. The demand curve is the curve that slopes down toward the right. The supply curve is the curve that slopes up toward the right.

5b. The equilibrium price is $14 a pizza, and the equilibrium quantity is 200 pizzas a day.

Market equilibrium is determined at the intersection of the demand curve and supply curve.

7a. The equilibrium price is 50 cents a pack, and the equilibrium quantity is 120 million packs a week.

The price of a pack adjusts until the quantity demanded equals the quantity supplied. At 50 cents a pack, the quantity demanded is 120 million packs a week and the quantity supplied is 120 million packs a week.

7b. At 70 cents a pack, there will be a surplus of gum and the price will fall.

At 70 cents a pack, the quantity demanded is 80 million packs a week and the quantity supplied is 160 million packs a week. There is a surplus of 80 million packs a week. The price will fall until market equilibrium is restored—50 cents a pack.

9a. The supply curve has shifted leftward.

As the number of gum-producing factories decreases, the supply of gum decreases. There is a new supply schedule, and the supply curve shifts leftward.

9b. There has been a movement along the demand curve.

The supply of gum decreases, and the supply curve shifts leftward. Demand does not change, so the price rises along the demand curve.

9c. The equilibrium price is 60 cents, and the equilibrium quantity is 100 million packs a week.

Supply decreases by 40 millions packs a week. That is, the quantity supplied at each price decreases by 40 million packs. The quantity supplied at 50 cents is now 80 million packs, and there is a shortage of gum. The price rises to 60 cents a pack, at which the quantity supplied equals the quantity demanded (100 million packs a week).

The new price is 70 cents a pack, and the quantity is 120 million packs a week.

The demand for gum increases, and the demand curve shifts rightward. The quantity demanded at each price increases by 40 million packs. The result of the fire is a price of 60 cents a pack. At this price, there is now a shortage of gum. The price of gum will rise until the shortage is eliminated.

CHAPTER 5

1. Go to *Economics in Action*, Chapter 22, Problem 1, and use the graph provided to find the solution to this problem.

3a. The growth rate in India was positive in every year from 1989 to 1996. The growth rate was fastest in 1989.

3b. The growth rate was not negative in Pakistan in this period. The growth rate was slowest in 1993.

3c. From 1989 to 1993, when India's growth rate increased, Pakistan's decreased. But from 1993 to 1995, both growth rates increased. In 1996, they were the same.

5a. Germany had one recession in the third and fourth quarters of 1992.

A recession is a period during which real GDP decreases for at least two successive quarters. Real GDP decreased in the third and fourth quarters of 1992.

5b. Germany experienced a business cycle peak in the fourth quarter of 1991.

A business cycle peak is the upper turning point. A peak occurs when real GDP stops growing and starts to decrease.

5c. Germany experienced a business cycle trough in the fourth quarter of 1992.

A business cycle trough is the lower turning point of a business cycle where a recession ends and an expansion begins.

5d. Germany experienced an expansion during the third and fourth quarters of 1991 and from the first quarter of 1993 through the second quarter of 1994.

An expansion is a period during which real GDP increases.

7. Go to *Economics in Action*, Chapter 22, Problem 7, and use the graph provided to find the solution to this problem.

9. Go to *Economics in Action*, Chapter 22, Problem 9, and use the graph provided to find the solution to this problem.

CHAPTER 6

1. Martha's initial capital stock is 5 copiers, depreciation is 1 copier per year, gross investment is 3 copiers, net investment is 2 copiers, and the final capital stock is 7 copiers.

Final capital stock equals initial capital stock plus net investment. Net investment equals gross investment minus depreciation.

3a. Aggregate expenditure is $60 million.

Aggregate expenditure is the sum of consumption expenditure, investment, government purchases, and net exports. In the figure, B is consumption expenditure, D is investment, C is government purchases, and E is net exports. Therefore aggregate expenditure equals $30 million plus $15 million plus $12 million plus $3 million, which is $60 million.

3b. Aggregate income is $60 million.

Aggregate income equals aggregate expenditure, which from 3(a) is $60 million.

3c. GDP is $60 million.

GDP equals aggregate expenditure, which from 3(a) is $60 million.

3d. Government budget deficit is $2 million.

Government budget deficit equals government purchases minus taxes. C is government purchases, and A is taxes. So the government budget deficit equals $12 million minus $10 million, which is $2 million.

3e. Household saving is $20 million.

Household saving equals aggregate income minus consumption expenditure minus taxes. In the figure, B is consumption expenditure and A is taxes. Therefore household saving equals $60 million minus $30 million minus $10 million, which is $20 million.

3f. Government saving is minus $2 million.

Government saving equals taxes minus government purchases. In the figure, A is taxes and C is government expenditure. Therefore government saving equals $10 million minus $12 million, which is minus $2 million.

3g. Foreign borrowing is $3 million.

Foreign borrowing equals net exports. E is net exports, and net exports equals $3 million. We are in surplus, so foreigners are in deficit and they must borrow from us to pay for their deficit. Foreign borrowing equals $3 million.

3h. National saving is $18 million.

National saving equals the sum of household saving and government saving. Household saving is $20 million (see answer 3e). Government saving is minus $2 million (see answer 3f). Therefore national saving equals $20 million minus $2 million, which is $18 million.

5a. Ecoland's GDP is $1,100,000.

GDP equals the sum of consumption expenditure plus investment plus government purchases plus net exports. That is, GDP equals $600,000 plus $250,000 plus $200,000 plus $300,000 minus $250,000. GDP equals $1,100,000.

5b. Expenditure approach. Income approach cannot be used because there are no data on interest, rent, depreciation, and indirect taxes and subsidies.

5c. Investment is financed by private saving (saving), government saving (taxes minus transfer payments minus purchases of goods and services) plus net foreign borrowing (imports minus exports).

These items are $300,000 + $250,000 − $50,000 − $200,000 + $250,000 − $300,000 = $250,000.

7a. The basket used in the CPI is 10 bottles of juice and 5 lengths of cloth.

The basket used in the CPI is the typical basket consumed in the base year. In the base year, the typical family spends $40 on juice and juice costs $4 a bottle, so the family buys 10 bottles of juice. In the base year, the typical family spends $25 on cloth and cloth costs $5 a length, so the family buys 5 lengths of cloth.

7b. The CPI in the current year is 107.69.

Expenditure on the CPI basket in the current year is 10 bottles of juice @ $4 a bottle plus 5 lengths of cloth @ $6 a length, which is $70. The expenditure on the CPI basket in the base year is $40 plus $25, which is $65. The CPI in the current year equals the expenditure on the basket in the current year divided by the expenditure on the basket in the base year, multiplied by 100. The CPI is 107.69.

7c. The inflation rate in the current year is 7.69 percent.

The CPI in the base year is 100 and the CPI in the current year is 107.69, so the inflation rate is the rate of change of the CPI. The inflation rate equals (107.69 − 100)/100, which is 7.69 percent.

9a. In 1997, GDP is $7,000 and real GDP is $7,000. In 1998, GDP is $7,500 and real GDP is $7,475.

GDP is equal to total expenditure on the goods and services produced by Bananaland in 1997. Expenditure on bananas is 1,000 bunches @ $2 a bunch, which is $2,000. Expenditure on sunscreen is 500 bottles @ $10 a bottle, which is $5,000. So total expenditure is $7,000.

Because 1997 is the base year, real GDP in 1997 equals GDP in 1997.

GDP in 1998 is equal to total expenditure in 1998 on bananas and sunscreen. That is, 1,100 bunches @ $3 a bunch, which is $3,300. Expenditure on sunscreen is 525 bottles @ $8 a bottle, which is $4,200. So total expenditure is $7,500.

Real GDP in 1998 is equal to real GDP in 1997 ($7,000) multiplied by the chain-weighted output index (divided by 100) which is 1.0679.

To obtain the chain weighted quantity index, calculate: (1) the value of the 1997 quantities at the 1998 prices—$7,000; (2) the 1998 quantities at the 1997 prices—$7,450; (3) an output index in 1997 prices—$7,450/$7,000 = 1.0643; (4) an output index in 1998 prices—$7,500/$7,000 = 1.0714; (5) the geometric mean of the two output indexes, calculated by multiplying 1.0643 by 1.0714 and taking the square root of the product. The answer equals 1.0679.

9b. The growth rate of real GDP in 1998 is 6.79 percent.

The growth rate equals the increase in real GDP from 1997 to 1998 expressed as a percentage of real GDP in 1997. That is, the growth rate equals ($7,475 − $7,000)/$7,000, which is 6.79 percent.

9c. The GDP deflator in 1998 is 100.33.

GDP deflator equals GDP in 1998 divided by real GDP in 1998, multiplied by 100. GDP deflator equals ($7,500/$7,475) × 100 = 100.33.

CHAPTER 7

1a. Unemployment rate is 4.7 percent.

The unemployment rate is the percentage of the labor force that is unemployed. The labor force is the sum of the people unemployed and the people employed. So the number of people who are unemployed is 137,169,000 minus 130,777,000, which is 6,392,000.

The unemployment rate equals (the number of people unemployed divided by the labor force) multiplied by 100. That is, (6,392,000/137,169,000) × 100, which is 4.7 percent.

1b. The labor force participation rate is 67.2 percent.

The labor force participation rate is the percentage of the working-age population that is in the labor force. The working-age population is 204,020,000 and the labor force is 137,169,000, so the labor force participation rate equals (137,169,000/204,020,000) × 100, which equals 67.2 percent.

1c. The employment-to-population ratio is 64.1 percent.

The employment-to-population ratio is the percentage of the people of working age who have jobs. The employment-to-population ratio is equal to the number of people employed divided by the working-age population all multiplied by 100. The employment-to-population ratio is (130,777,000/204,020,000) × 100, which is 64.1 percent.

3. Unemployment decreased by 769,000. The number of discouraged workers has decreased.

During 1997, employment in the United States increased by 2,878,000 and the labor force increased by 2,109,000. The number of unemployed is calculated as the labor force minus the number employed. When the labor force increased by 2,109,000 and employment increased by 2,878,000, unemployment decreased by 769,000.

Discouraged workers are people who leave the labor force temporarily during a recession and re-enter the labor force and become job seekers during an expansion. To measure the number of discouraged workers, we need to know about new entrants and retirements. But if new entrants exceed retirements, which they most likely do, because employment increased by more than the increase in the working-age population, most likely the number of discouraged workers decreased.

5a. The number of job losers probably decreased. The number of job leavers probably did not change much.

The decrease in the unemployment rate is an indication that the economy was in an expansion, and normally, in an expansion, the number of job losers decreases but the number of job leavers does not change much.

5b. Labor force entrants and re-entrants probably increased.

In an expansion, discouraged workers re-enter the labor force. So it is likely that entrants and re-entrants increased.

7a. The labor force in July is 15,344,000. It is the number employed plus the number unemployed.

7b. The unemployment rate in July is 10.1 percent. It is the number unemployed as a percentage of the labor force.

7c. The working-age population is 22,729,000. It is the sum of the labor force and the number of people who are not in the labor force.

7d. The employment-to-population ratio is 60.7. It is the number employed as a percentage of the working-age population.

7e. The number of people who are unemployed at the end of August is 1,546,995. It equals the number unemployed in July plus job losers, job leavers, entrants, and reentrants minus hires, recalls, and withdrawals.

7f. The number of people who are employed at the end of August is 13,796,971. It equals the number employed in July minus job losers and job leavers plus hires and recalls.

7g. The labor force at the end of August is 15,343,966. It equals the number employed plus the number unemployed.

7h. The unemployment rate at the end of August is 10.1 percent. It equals the number unemployed as a percentage of the labor force.

7i. The employment-to-population ratio at the end of August is 58.9. It equals the number employed as a percentage of the working-age population. The working-age population is the labor force multiplied by 100 and divided by the labor force participation rate.

9. At the peak of a business cycle, the labor force participation rate is high, employment is high, the unemployment rate is low, the duration of unemployment is low, and fewer workers are discouraged.

CHAPTER 8

1a. A deep recession in the world economy will decrease real GDP, and the price level will fall. A sharp rise in oil prices will decrease real GDP, and the price level will rise. When businesses expect huge losses in the near future, real GDP will decrease and the price level will fall.

A deep recession in the world economy will decrease world income, which in turn will reduce Toughtimes's exports of goods and services. Toughtimes's aggregate demand curve will shift leftward. In Toughtimes, real GDP will decrease and the price level will fall.

A sharp rise in oil prices will decrease short-run aggregate supply and shift the short-run aggregate supply curve leftward. In Toughtimes, the real GDP will decrease and the price level will rise.

When businesses expect huge losses in the near future, they will reduce investment now. Aggregate demand will decrease, and the aggregate demand curve will shift leftward. In Toughtimes, real GDP will decrease and the price level will fall.

1b. Real GDP will decrease and the price level might rise, fall, or stay the same.

In 1(a), each of the events decreases real GDP, so together they will decrease real GDP. But the recession and the expected business losses will lead to a fall in the price level, while the sharp rise in the oil price will lead to a rise in the price level. So together, the price level might rise, fall, or stay the same.

1c. To increase aggregate demand, the government might increase its expenditures or cut taxes and the Fed might increase the quantity of money and decrease interest rates. These policies will increase real GDP.

3a. To plot the aggregate demand curve, plot the price and the quantity of real GDP demanded. To plot the short-run aggregate supply curve, plot the price and the quantity of real GDP supplied in the short-run.

3b. Real GDP is $400 billion, and the price level is 100.
Short-run macroeconomic equilibrium occurs at the intersection of the aggregate demand curve and the short-run aggregate supply curve.

3c. The long-run aggregate supply curve is a vertical line at real GDP of $500 billion.

5. Real GDP increases to $450 billion, and the price level rises to 110.
Aggregate demand increases by $100 billion at each value of the price level, and the aggregate demand curve shifts rightward by $100 billion. The new aggregate demand curve intersects the short-run aggregate supply curve at a real GDP of $450 billion and a price level of 110.

7. Real GDP decreases to $350 billion, and the price level rises to 110.
Short-run aggregate supply decreases by $100 billion at each value of the price level and the short-run aggregate supply curve shifts leftward by $100 billion. The new short-run aggregate supply curve intersects the aggregate demand curve at a real GDP of $350 billion and a price level of 110.

9a. Point c.
The aggregate demand curve is the red curve AD_1. The short-run aggregate supply curve is the blue curve SAS_0. These curves intersect at point c.

9b. Point d.
The short-run aggregate supply curve is the red curve SAS_1. The aggregate demand curve is now the red curve AD_1 These curves intersect at point d.

9c. Aggregate demand increases if (1) expected future incomes, inflation, or profits increase; (2) the government increases its purchases or reduces taxes; (3) the Fed increases the quantity of money and decrease interest rates; or (4) the exchange rate decreases or foreign income increases.

9d. Short-run aggregate supply decreases if resource prices increase.

CHAPTER 9

1a. The graph plots leisure on the x-axis and real GDP on the y-axis. As leisure increases from zero to 12 hours a day, real GDP decreases from $30 to $0 a day.

1b. The table replaces leisure with labor and labor equals 12 hours a day minus leisure hours. The graph plots labor on the x-axis and real GDP on the y-axis. As labor increases from zero to 12 hours a day, real GDP increases from $0 to $30 a day.

1c. When labor increases from 0 to 2 hours a day, the marginal product of labor is $5. When labor increases from 2 to 4 hours a day, the marginal product of labor is $4. When labor increases from 4 to 6 hours a day, the marginal product of labor is $3. When labor increases from 6 to 8 hours a day, the marginal product of labor is $2.

When labor increases from 8 to 10 hours a day, the marginal product of labor is $1. When labor increases from 10 to 12 hours a day, the marginal product of labor is $0. Marginal product is the change in real GDP divided by the change in labor hours.

3a. The demand for labor schedule is the same as the marginal product of labor schedule The marginal product of labor schedule is described in solution 1c. The marginal product must be aligned with the midpoint of the change in labor. So, for example, the marginal product of $5 an hour is aligned with 1 hour of work—the midpoint between 0 and 2 hours.

The graph plots a marginal product of $5 at 1 hour and a marginal product of $1 at 9 hours of labor and is a straight line between these points. At 2 hours of labor, the marginal product is $4.50.

3b. The table lists hours of labor from zero to 12 a day. Against each hour, the wage rate at which Crusoe is willing to supply labor is $4.50 an hour.

Crusoe's supply curve is horizontal at $4.50 an hour.

3c. The full-employment equilibrium real wage rate is $4.50 an hour, and the quantity of labor employed is 2 hours a day.

The full-employment equilibrium real wage rate is $4.50 an hour because Crusoe is willing to work any number of hours at this wage rate. The equilibrium level of employment is 2 hours a day because this is the number of hours at which Crusoe's marginal product of labor is $4.50 an hour.

3d. Potential GDP is $10 a day.

Potential GDP is $10 a day because this quantity of real GDP is produced when labor is 2 hours a day.

5a. The new production function table lists real GDP against labor hours. Real GDP is $15 at 2 hours of labor, $27 at 4 hours, $36 at 6 hours, $42 at 8 hours, $45 at 10 hours, and $45 at 12 hours.

The new demand for labor schedule has labor of 2 hours at $6.75 and 9 hours at $1.50.

To calculate the new demand for labor schedule, calculate the new marginal product (old marginal product multiplied by 1.5) at each level of employment.

5b. The full-employment equilibrium real wage rate is $4.50 an hour and the quantity of labor employed is 5 hours a day.

The equilibrium level of employment is 5 hours a day because this is the number of hours at which Crusoe's marginal product of labor is $4.50 an hour.

5c. Potential GDP is $21 a day.

Potential GDP is $21 a day because this quantity of real GDP is produced when labor is 5 hours a day.

5d. The increase in productivity shifts the production function upward by 50 percent. The marginal product of labor increases by 50 percent. Employment increases and so does potential GDP.

7a. Real wage rate is $3 an hour and employment is 3,000 hours a day.

This wage rate and quantity of labor are at the intersection of the demand curve and the supply curve in the figure.

7b. Potential GDP is $13,500 a day.

To calculate potential GDP, use the fact that the real wage rate on the demand for labor curve is the marginal product of labor. Remember that it is plotted midway between the initial and final level of real GDP from which it is calculated. Do the marginal product calculation in reverse and obtain the level of real GDP at 3,000 hours, which is $13,500 a day.

7c. The natural rate of unemployment is 25 percent.

The natural rate of unemployment occurs at full employment when job search is 1,000 hours. Employment is 3,000 hours, and job search, which is unemployment, is 1,000 hours. The labor force (employment plus unemployment) is 4,000 hours. The natural rate of unemployment is 25 percent (1,000/4,000 multiplied by 100).

CHAPTER 10

1a. Yes.

1b. Yes.

1c. No.

The firm receives a total revenue of $17 million. It spends $16 million ($10 million on the plant, $3 million on labor and $3 million on fuel). Before paying interest, the firm has a surplus of $1 million. If the interest rate is 5 percent a year, the interest cost is $0.5 million. If the interest rate is 10 percent a year, the interest cost is $1 million. If the interest rate is 15 percent a year, the interest cost is $1.5 million. So the firm earns a profit at 5 percent, breaks even at 10 percent, and incurs a loss at 15 percent. The firm will not invest to incur a loss.

3a. A graph that has saving on the x-axis and the interest rate on the y-axis. Three points are plotted at $10,000 and 4 percent; $12,500 and 6 percent; and $15,000 and 8 percent. The saving supply (SS) curve passes through these points.

3b. Saving decreases, and the saving supply curve shifts leftward.

3c. Saving increases, and the saving supply curve shifts rightward.

An increase in expected future income increases consumption expenditure and decreases saving. An increase in disposable income increases both consumption expenditure and saving.

5a. 5 percent a year.

5b. $6 trillion (3050 dollars).

5c. $6 trillion (3050 dollars).

Given the saving supply schedule and the investment demand schedule, the real interest rate at which saving equals investment is 5 percent a year. At this real interest rate, saving and investment equal $6 trillion.

7a. 5 percent a year.

7b. $6 trillion (3050 dollars).

Private saving increases by an amount equal to the decrease in government saving. Total saving remains constant. So the equilibrium real interest rate and saving and investment do not change.

9a. 6 percent a year.

9b. $15 trillion (3050 dollars).

9c. $15 trillion (3050 dollars).

9d. Saving decreases, and investment increases.

To find the galactic equilibrium, find the sum of saving on Earth and Alpha Centura at each real interest rate and find the sum of investment on the two planets at each real interest rate. At a real interest rate of 6 percent a year, galactic saving equals galactic investment at $15 trillion.

In isolation, the real interest rate on Alpha Centura is 7 percent a year. So the real interest rate on Alpha Centura falls. Saving decreases, and investment increases.

CHAPTER 11

1. No. The economy conforms to a one-half rule.

In this economy, an x percent increase in the capital stock per hour of work leads to a $0.5x$ percent increase in real GDP per hour of work. You can confirm this fact by calculating the percentage change in capital and real GDP at each of the levels provided in the table and then dividing the percentage change in real GDP by the percentage change in capital. For example, when capital increases by 100 percent from $10 to $20, real GDP increases by 50 percent from $3.80 to $5.70.

3a. Yes.

Diminishing returns are present if the marginal product of capital diminishes as capital increases, holding technology constant. You can calculate the marginal product of capital from the schedule provided and see that it does diminish. The increase in real GDP per hour of work that occurred in the question resulted from an increase in capital *and an advance in technology*. We know this because to produce $10.29 in 1999 would have required a capital stock of $60 per hour of work, and in 2001, this output can be produced by a capital stock of $50. The change in real GDP divided by the change in capital is not the marginal product of labor because technology is not constant.

3b. $1.04.

This number is calculated as the percentage increase in real GDP that is equal to one half the percentage increase in capital.

3c. $0.94.

This number is calculated as the change in real GDP minus $1.04.

5a. 6 billion hours per year.

This quantity is the quantity demanded and the quantity supplied when the real wage rate is $7 an hour.

5b. The real wage rate rises.

When the demand for labor increases, there is a shortage of labor at the current wage rate. So the real wage rate rises.

5c. The population begins to grow.

The reason for the population growth is that the real wage rate exceeds the subsistence level.

5d. 7 billion hours a year.

This is the quantity of labor demanded at the subsistence real wage rate of $7 an hour. Only when the population has grown by a sufficient amount to make the quantity of labor supplied equal 7 billion hours a year does the population stop growing.

7. When the demand for capital raises the real interest rate above the target rate, the capital stock and real GDP begin to grow and keep on growing. In contrast, in the neoclassical Martha's Island, as the capital stock grows, the real interest rate falls (because of diminishing returns) and growth eventually ends.

CHAPTER 12

1a. The marginal propensity to consume is 0.5.

The marginal propensity to consume is the fraction of a change in disposable income that is consumed. On Heron Island, when disposable income increases by $10 million per year, consumption expenditure increases by $5 million per year. The marginal propensity to consume is 0.5.

1b. The table that shows Heron Island's saving lists disposable income from zero to 40 in increments of 10. Against each level of disposable income are the amounts of saving, which equal disposable income minus consumption expenditure. These amounts run from −5 at zero disposable income to 15 at a disposable income of 40. For each increase in disposable income of $1, saving increases by 50 cents.

1c. Marginal propensity to save is 0.5.

The marginal propensity to consume plus the marginal propensity to save equals 1. Because consumption expenditure and saving exhaust disposable income, 0.5 of each dollar increase in disposable income is consumed and the remaining part (0.5) is saved.

3a. Autonomous expenditure is $2.0 billion.

Autonomous expenditure is expenditure that does not depend on real GDP. Autonomous expenditure equals the value of aggregate planned expenditure when real GDP is zero.

3b. Marginal propensity to consume is 0.6.

When the country has no imports or exports and no income taxes, the slope of the *AE* curve equals the marginal propensity to consume. When income increases from 0 to $6 billion, aggregate planned expenditure increases from $2 billion to $5.6 billion. That is, when real GDP increases by $6 billion, aggregate planned expenditure increases by $3.6 billion. The marginal propensity to consume is $3.6 billion/$6 billion, which is 0.6.

3c. Equilibrium expenditure is $4 billion.

Equilibrium expenditure is the level of aggregate expenditure at which aggregate expenditure equals real GDP. In terms of the graph, equilibrium expenditure occurs at the intersection of the *AE* curve and the 45° line. Draw in the 45° line, and you'll see that the intersection occurs at $4 billion.

3d. There is no change in inventories.

When the economy is at equilibrium expenditure, inventories equal the planned level and there is no unplanned change in inventories.

3e. Firms are accumulating inventories. That is, unplanned inventory investment is positive.

When real GDP is $6 billion, aggregate planned expenditure is less than real GDP, so firms cannot sell all that they produce. Inventories pile up.

3f. The multiplier is 2.5.

The multiplier equals $1/(1 - MPC)$. The marginal propensity to consume is 0.6, so the multiplier equals $1/(1 - 0.6)$, which equals 2.5.

5a. The consumption function is $C = 100 + 0.9(Y - T)$.

The consumption function is the relationship between consumption expenditure and disposable income, other things remaining the same.

5b. The equation to the AE curve is:

$AE = 600 + 0.9Y$,

where Y is real GDP.

Aggregate planned expenditure is the sum of consumption expenditure, investment, government purchases, and net exports. Using the symbol AE for aggregate planned expenditure, aggregate planned expenditure is:

$AE = 100 + 0.9(Y - 400) + 460 + 400$

$AE = 100 + 0.9Y - 360 + 460 + 400$

$AE = 600 + 0.9Y$

5c. Equilibrium expenditure is $6,000 billion.

Equilibrium expenditure is the level of aggregate expenditure that occurs when aggregate planned expenditure equals real GDP. That is,

$AE = 600 + 0.9Y$

and

$AE = Y$

Solving these two equations for Y gives equilibrium expenditure of $6,000 billion.

5d. Equilibrium real expenditure decreases by $1,000 billion, and the multiplier is 10.

The multiplier equals $1/(1 - $ the slope of the AE curve). The equation to the AE curve tells us that the slope of the AE curve is 0.9. So the multiplier is $1/(1 - 0.9)$, which is 10.

The change in equilibrium expenditure equals the change in investment multiplied by 10.

7a. The quantity demanded increases by $1,000 billion.

The increase in investment shifts the aggregate demand curve rightward by the change in investment times the multiplier. The multiplier is 10 and the change in investment is $100 billion, so the aggregate demand curve shifts rightward by $1,000 billion.

7b. In the short-run, real GDP increases by less than $1,000 billion.

Real GDP is determined by the intersection of the AD curve and the SAS curve. In the short run, the price level will rise and real GDP will increase but by an amount less than the shift of the AD curve.

7c. In the long-run, real GDP will equal potential GDP, so real GDP does not increase.

Real GDP is determined by the intersection of the AD curve and the SAS curve. After the initial increase in investment, money wages increase, the SAS curve shifts leftward, and in the long run, real GDP moves back to potential GDP.

7d. In the short run, the price level rises. In the long run, the price level rises.

CHAPTER 13

1a. Equilibrium expenditure decreases by $100 billion.

The government purchases multiplier is the amount by which a change in government purchases on goods and services is multiplied to determine the change in equilibrium expenditure that results. Zapland has no induced taxes or imports, so the government purchases multiplier is $1/(1 - MPC)$, which equals 10. The multiplier tells us that when government purchases decrease by $10 billion, equilibrium expenditure decreases by 10 times as much or $100 billion.

1b. The government purchases multiplier is 10.

1c. Equilibrium expenditure increases by $90 billion.

The lump-sum tax multiplier equals $-MPC/(1 - MPC)$, which is -9. That is, when lump-sum taxes are changed by $10 billion, equilibrium expenditure changes by -9 times the change in lump-sum taxes. A cut in lump-sum taxes of $10 billion will increase equilibrium expenditure by $90 billion.

1d. The lump-sum tax multiplier is -9.

1e. Equilibrium expenditure decreases by $10 billion.

The decrease in government purchases decreases equilibrium expenditure by $100 billion and the cut in taxes increases equilibrium expenditure by $90 billion. So together, equilibrium expenditure decreases by $10 billion.

3a. The quantity of real GDP demanded increases by $100 billion.

The government purchases multiplier tells us that when government purchases increase by $10 billion, equilibrium expenditure increases by 10 times as much, or $100 billion. At the price level 100, the quantity of real GDP demanded increases by an amount equal to the change in equilibrium expenditure. That is, the quantity of real GDP demanded increases by $100 billion.

3b. The aggregate demand curve shifts rightward by $100 billion at each price level.

The AE curve shifts upward by $10 billion, equilibrium expenditure increases by $100 billion, and the AD curve shifts rightward by $100 billion.

3c. In the short run, real GDP increases by less than the $100 billion increase in the quantity of real GDP demanded.

In the short run, real GDP is determined by the short-run aggregate supply and aggregate demand. Because the short-run aggregate supply curve slopes upward, the price level rises and real GDP increases but by less than $100 billion.

3d. In the long run, the increase in real GDP will be zero. Real GDP will return to potential GDP.

In the short run, real GDP exceeds potential GDP and wage rates will start to rise. The short-run aggregate supply will begin to decrease and the price level will rise. The short-run aggregate supply will continue to decrease and the price level will continue to rise until real GDP equals potential GDP.

3e. The price level rises.

In the short run, aggregate demand and short-run aggregate supply determine the price level. Because the short-run aggregate supply curve slopes upward and because aggregate demand increases, the price level rises.

3f. The price level rises.

In the long run, aggregate demand and long-run aggregate supply determine the price level. The short-run aggregate supply curve shifts leftward because the money wage rate rises. Because the long-run aggregate supply curve is vertical and because aggregate demand increases, the price level rises. And it rises by more in the long run than it does in the short run.

5a. The government budget balance is zero.

The government's tax revenues equal its expenditures, so its budget is balanced.

5b. Dreamland does not have a structural or a cyclical deficit.

Because at potential GDP, the budget is balanced, Dreamland does not have a structural surplus or deficit. Because real GDP equals potential GDP, Dreamland does not have a cyclical surplus or deficit.

5c. The budget balance is a deficit of $40 million.

At a real GDP of $30 million, tax revenues equal $80 million and expenditures equal $120 million, so the budget is in deficit. The size of the deficit is $40 million.

5d. Dreamland does not have a structural deficit, but it does have a cyclical deficit of $40 million.

Because at potential GDP, the budget is balanced, Dreamland does not have a structural surplus or deficit. Because real GDP is less than potential GDP and it has a deficit, Dreamland's deficit is a cyclical deficit. The cyclical deficit is $40 million.

5e. Dreamland does not have a structural deficit but it does have a cyclical surplus of $40 million.

Because at potential GDP, the budget is balanced, Dreamland does not have a structural surplus or deficit. Because real GDP exceeds potential GDP and it has a surplus, Dreamland's surplus is a cyclical surplus. The cyclical surplus is $40 million.

CHAPTER 14

1. Money in the United States includes the quarters inside public telephones and the U.S. dollar bills in your wallet.

Money is composed of currency outside the banks and deposits at financial institutions. Currency inside the cash machines, Visa cards, checks, and loans are not money.

3. M1 increases by $1,000; M2 does not change.

M1 is the sum of currency outside the banks, traveler's checks, and checking deposits. M2 is the sum of M1 plus savings deposits, time deposits, and money market mutual funds and other deposits.. The withdrawal of $1,000 from a savings account leaves M2 unchanged because the

$1,000 goes into M1 types of money, which is part of M2. The $50 held as cash and the $950 held in a checking account increase M1 by $1,000.

5a. The balance sheet has the following assets: Reserves, $250 million; Loans, $1,000 million; Other assets, $1,250 billion. It has the following liabilities: Deposits, $2,000 billion; Other liabilities, $500 billion.

5b. The reserve ratio is 12.5 percent.

The reserve ratio is the percentage of deposits that are held as reserves. Reserves are $250 million and deposits are $2,000, so the reserve ratio is 12.5 percent.

5c. The deposit multiplier is 8.

The deposit multiplier equals 1/(required reserve ratio). The required reserve ratio is 12.5, so the deposit multiplier is 8.

7a. The initial increase in the quantity of money is $1,200.

Money is equal to bank deposits and currency outside the banks. Deposits increase by $1,200, so the initial increase in the quantity of money is $1,200.

7b. The initial increase in the quantity of bank deposits is $1,200.

Deposits increase by $1,200 because the immigrant places all the new money on deposit.

7c. The bank initially lends out $1,080.

The bank has a new deposit of $1,200, and it keeps 10 percent of it ($120) as reserves and lends the rest ($1,200 minus $120), which equals $1,080.

7d. The immigrant's bank has loaned $1,080. This amount returns to the banks as new deposits. The banks keep $108 in reserves and lend a further $972.

The banks have now created deposits of $1,200 plus $1,080, which equals $2,280.

7e. The quantity of money has increased by $3,252.

The first loan is $1,080, and the quantity of money increases by $1,080. When this money is spent and returned to the bank as a deposit, the banks keep 10 percent of it ($108) as reserves and lend out the rest ($972). The banks create $972 of new money. So the quantity of money has increased by $1,200 + $1,080 + $972, which equals $3,252.

7f. The quantity of money increases by $12,000. Deposits increase by $12,000. Loans increase by $10,800.

The deposit multiplier is 1/0.1, which equals 10. The deposit multiplier tells us that when reserves increase by $1,200 and the required reserve ratio is 10 percent, deposits will increase by 10 times $1,200, which is $12,000.

The quantity of money increases by the amount of the increase in deposits.

Deposits increase by $12,000 and the reserve ratio is 10 percent, so reserves increase $1,200. Therefore bank loans increase by $12,000 minus $1,200, which is $10,800.

9a. Aggregate demand increases.

9b. The price level rises and real GDP increases in the short run.

9c. In the long run, real GDP returns to potential GDP and the price level is higher than it otherwise would have been by the same percentage as the percentage increase in the quantity of money.

11a. $40 million.

Because $MV = PY$, we know that $M = PY/V$. With $P = 200$, $Y = \$400$ million, and $V = 20$, $M = \$40$ million.

11b. $48 million.

Money grows by 20 percent, which is $8 million.

11c. 240.

Because the quantity theory holds and because the factors that influence real GDP have not changed, the price level rises by the same percentage as the increase in money, which is 20 percent.

11d. $400 billion.

Because the factors that influence real GDP have not changed, real GDP is unchanged.

11e. 20.

Because the factors that influence velocity have not changed, velocity is unchanged.

CHAPTER 15

1a. The monetary base is $45 billion.

The monetary base is the sum of the central bank's notes outside the bank, banks' deposits at the central bank, and coins held by households, firms, and banks. There are $30 billion in notes held by households and firms, banks' deposits at the central bank are $10 billion (2/3 of $15 billion), the banks hold other reserves of $5 billion (which are notes), and there are no coins. The monetary base is $45 billion.

1b. The money supply is $330 billion.

In Nocoin, deposits are $300 billion and currency is $30 billion, so the quantity of money is $330 billion.

1c. The banks' reserve ratio is 5 percent.

The banks' reserve ratio is the percent of deposits that is held as reserves. In Nocoin, deposits are $300 billion and reserves are $15 billion, so the reserve ratio equals ($15 billion/$300 billion) × 100, which is 5 percent.

1d. The currency drain is 9.09 percent.

The currency drain is the percent of the quantity of money that is held as currency by households and firms. In Nocoin, deposits are $300 billion and currency is $30 billion, so the quantity of money is $330 billion. The currency drain equals ($30 billion/$330 billion) × 100, which is 9.09 percent.

3a. The money supply is $337.33 billion.

The money supply increases by the change in the monetary base multiplied by the money multiplier. The money multiplier is the ratio of the money supply to the monetary base, which equals $330 billion divided by $45 billion, which equals 7.33.

So when the monetary base increases by $1 billion, the money supply increases by $7.33 billion. Initially, the money supply was $330 billion, so the new money supply is $337.33 billion.

3b. Currency in circulation is $30.67 billion.

The currency drain in Nocoin equals ($30 billion/$330 billion) × 100, which is 9.09 percent. And 9.09 percent of $337.33 is $30.67.

3c. Bank deposits are $306.67 billion.

Deposits equal the quantity of money minus currency in circulation, which equals $337.33 billion minus $30.67 billion.

3d. Bank reserves are $15.33 billion.

The banks' reserve ratio is 5 percent and 5 percent of deposits of $306.67 billion equals $15.33 billion.

5a. People buy securities, and the interest rate falls.

5b. People sell securities, and the interest rate rises.

5c. People neither buy nor sell securities, and the interest rate remains constant at 4 percent a year.

With real GDP of $20 billion ($Y_1$ in the spreadsheet), column C shows the demand for money schedule. The quantity of money supplied is $3 billion, so the equilibrium interest rate is 4 percent a year.

If the interest rate exceeds 4 percent a year, people are holding more money than they demand. So they try to decrease the amount of money held by buying securities. The prices of securities rise, and the interest rate falls.

If the interest rate is less than 4 percent a year, people are holding less money than they demand. So they try to increase the amount of money held by selling securities. The prices of securities fall, and the interest rate rises.

If the interest rate equals 4 percent a year, people are holding exactly the quantity of money that they demand. So they take no actions to try to change the amount of money held. The interest rate remains constant.

7a. The interest rate rises to 5 percent a year.

7b. The interest rate falls to 3 percent a year.

When real GDP increases in an expansion to $30 billion ($Y_2$ in the spreadsheet), column D shows the demand for money schedule. The quantity of money supplied is $3 billion, so the equilibrium interest rate is 5 percent a year.

When real GDP decreases in a recession to $10 billion ($Y_0$ in the spreadsheet), column B shows the demand for money schedule. The quantity of money supplied is $3 billion, so the equilibrium interest rate is 3 percent a year.

9a. The money supply curve is vertical at 1 trillion 1990 yaks.

When the real money supply is 1 trillion 1990 yaks, the equilibrium interest rate is 3 percent a year at the intersection of the demand for money and supply of money curves.

9b. Must increase the real money supply by 0.5 trillion 1990 yaks.

When the real money supply increases to 1.5 trillion 1990 yaks, the equilibrium interest rate falls to 2 percent a year.

9c. Must make an open market purchase.

When the central bank makes an open market purchase, it increases the amount of money in circulation and decreases the amount of securities.

11. An open market purchase increases the quantity of money and increases aggregate demand. The AD curve shifts rightward. In the short run, real GDP increases and the price level rises.

Starting from above-full employment, this action increases the size of the inflationary gap and increases the inflation rate.

In the long run, real GDP equals potential GDP. The central bank's action has no effect on potential GDP and so does not lower real GDP in the long run.

CHAPTER 16

1a. An increase in the quantity of money, an increase in government purchases, a tax cut, an increase in exports.

Anything that increases aggregate demand can set off a demand-pull inflation. But to sustain such an inflation, the quantity of money must keep increasing.

1b. Starting out on AD_0 and SAS_0, the price level is 120 and real GDP is at potential GDP of $7 trillion. Aggregate demand increases and the AD curve shifts rightward to AD_1. The price level rises and real GDP increases to the intersection of AD_1 and SAS_0. There is now an inflationary gap.

1c. Starting out on AD_1 and SAS_0 with an inflationary gap, the money wage rate rises and short-run aggregate supply decreases. The SAS curve starts to shift leftward toward SAS_1. The price level keeps rising, but real GDP now decreases. The process now repeats. AD shifts to AD_2, an inflationary gap opens again, the money wage rate rises again, and the SAS curve shifts toward SAS_2.

3a. An *anticipated* increase in the quantity of money, an increase in government purchases, a tax cut, an increase in exports.

Anything that increases aggregate demand can set off an anticipated inflation as long as the event is anticipated. But to sustain such an anticipated inflation, the quantity of money must keep increasing along its anticipated path.

3b. Starting out on AD_0 and SAS_0, the price level is 120 and real GDP is at potential GDP of $7 trillion. Aggregate demand increases, and the AD curve shifts rightward to AD_1. The increase in aggregate demand is anticipated so the money wage rate rises and the SAS curve shifts to SAS_1. The price level rises, and real GDP remains at potential GDP.

3c. Starting out on AD_1 and SAS_1, a further anticipated increase in aggregate demand occurs. The AD curve shifts to AD_2, and because the increase in aggregate demand is anticipated, the money wage rate rises again and the SAS curve shifts to SAS_2. Again, the price level rises and real GDP remains at potential GDP.

5a. Both the inflation rate and the unemployment rate have increased. So the expected inflation rate has increased and the natural rate of unemployment might have increased (but has not definitely increased). Any of the events that can increase the expected inflation rate might have occurred. Most likely, the expected growth rate of the money supply has increased. If the natural rate of unemployment has not increased, the economy is in a recession, despite the fact that the inflation rate has increased.

5b. If point a is a long-run equilibrium, the *LRPC* is vertical at an unemployment rate of 4 percent. The *SRPC* slopes downward and passes through point a. If point a is *not* a long-run equilibrium, the *SRPC* still passes through point a but the *LRPC* is vertical at whatever unemployment rate is the natural rate.

5c. If point d is a long-run equilibrium, the *LRPC* is vertical at an unemployment rate of 8 percent. The *SRPC* slopes downward and passes through point d. If point d is *not* a long-run equilibrium, the *SRPC* still passes through point d but the *LRPC* is vertical at whatever unemployment rate is the natural rate.

7a. The most likely events that could create the clockwise sequence described is a mixture of swings in aggregate demand that are initially unanticipated. Aggregate demand increases, unemployment decreases, and the economy is at point a, where there is an inflationary gap. The inflation rate rises, and the expected inflation rate also rises. The *SRPC* shifts upward, and the economy moves from a to b. Aggregate demand now decreases, but at first the decrease is unanticipated and a recession occurs. The economy moves from b to d. There is now a recessionary gap. The inflation rate slows, and the expected inflation rate falls. So the *SRPC* shifts downward and the economy moves from d to c. Aggregate demand now increases again and an expansion moves the economy from c to a.

7b. In your diagram, the *LRPC* is vertical at an unemployment rate of 6 percent. The *SRPC* slopes downward and passes through point a initially. The *SRPC* then shifts upward to pass through point b and keeps shifting upward to pass through point d. The *SRPC* then shifts downward to pass through point c and keeps shifting downward until it again passes through point a.

7c. The economy has experienced a demand-pull inflation. The reason is that a change in aggregate demand triggered the rise and subsequent fall in the inflation rate.

9a. If the natural unemployment rate and the expected inflation rate remain constant between 1999 and 2003, the *SRPC* is linear and passes through the data points listed in the table provided. Note that one of these points is the natural rate of unemployment (4 percent) and the expected inflation rate (6 percent). The *LRPC* is vertical at an unemployment rate of 4 percent.

9b. If the actual inflation rate rises from 6 percent to 8 percent, the unemployment rate falls from 4 percent to 3 percent. This change would occur if there were an unexpected increase in aggregate demand.

CHAPTER 17

1a. Possible combinations are a or d, e or g, and i or k.

A Keynesian recession results from a decrease in investment caused by a decrease in expected profit. In an extreme case, no prices change, so the move is to a, e, and i. But a more general possibility is that the money wage rate doesn't change but the price level falls, real wage rate rises, and the interest rate falls. In this case, the move is to d, g, and k.

1b. d, g, and l.

A monetarist recession results from a decrease in the quantity of money. The interest rate rises, and investment decreases. Aggregate demand decreases, but the money wage rate doesn't change. Real GDP and the price level decrease, the real wage rate rises, and employment decreases. The move is to d, g, and l.

1c. *d, g,* and *i, k,* or *l.*

1d. *d, g,* and *i, k,* or *l.*

Either type of rational expectations recession results from an unanticipated decrease in aggregate demand. Any of several factors could initiate the decrease in aggregate demand, and the interest rate could rise, fall, or remain constant. Aggregate demand decreases, but the money wage rate either doesn't change or doesn't change by enough to maintain full employment. So real GDP and the price level decrease, the real wage rate rises, and employment decreases.

1e. *c, e, g,* or *h,* and *k.*

In a real business cycle recession, a decrease in productivity decreases the demand for labor and capital. The interest rate and the real wage rate fall and investment and employment decrease. Aggregate demand *and* aggregate supply decrease, so real GDP decreases but the price level might fall, rise, or remain unchanged.

3. This recession is consistent with Keynesian or rational expectations theories (see the solutions 1(a), 1(c), and 1(d)).

5. This recession is consistent with real business cycle theory (see the solution 1(e)).

7. This recession is not consistent with any of the theories and is an unlikely combination of events. The price level does not usually rise when the real wage rate rises.

9. This recession is consistent the real business cycle theory (see the solution 1(e)).

11. This recession is consistent with monetarist theory (see the solution 1(b)).

13. This recession is not consistent with any of the theories and is an unlikely combination of events. The real wage rate does not usually fall when the price level falls.

CHAPTER 18

1. Anything that slows investment in physical or human capital or slows the pace of technological change will create a productivity growth slowdown. For the factors at work during the U.S. productivity growth slowdown of the 1970s, review pp. 227-228 of Chapter 11.

Improvements in incentives to invest in physical or human capital or to innovate and speed up the pace of technological change will counteract a productivity growth slowdown. See p. 228 of Chapter 11 and pp. 410-412 of Chapter 18.

3a. Real GDP is $7 trillion and the price level is 110. These values are determined at the intersection of AD_0 and SAS_0.

3b. Real GDP falls to $6 trillion and the price level falls to 105. Then, as aggregate demand returns to AD_0, the price level and real GDP return to their initial levels.

3c. Real GDP falls to $6 trillion and the price level falls to 105. The government increases aggregate demand to AD_0, and the price level and real GDP return to their initial levels. Aggregate demand then increases (because the decrease is temporary), and real GDP rises above potential GDP. An inflationary gap arises. The money wage rate rises and

so does the price level. Real GDP moves back toward potential GDP.

3d. Real GDP falls to $6 trillion, and the price level falls to 105. The economy is stuck at this point until the money wage rate falls, short-run aggregate supply increases, and the economy moves back to potential GDP at an even lower price level. This move will likely take a long time.

3e. Real GDP falls to $6 trillion, and the price level falls to 105. The government increases aggregate demand to AD_0, and the price level and real GDP return to their initial levels. Because the decrease in aggregate demand is permanent, this is the end of the action.

5a. The economy might have gotten into its described state because of a combination of rapid money supply growth (which brings inflation) and large structural changes (which bring high unemployment and slow productivity growth).

5b. A slowdown in money growth will lower the inflation rate. Improvements in incentives to invest in physical or human capital or to innovate and speed up the pace of technological change will speed productivity growth.

5c. Study pp. 410-412 and pp. 420-423 for explanations of how these policy actions work.

7a. These policy actions were part of a feedback rule. The actions were taken *because* of the crises.

7b. The required domestic policies all decrease aggregate demand. They lower real GDP and lower the price level (compared with what would have happened).

7c. A possible criticism, and one that some economists have made, is that the countries should have adopted policies to expand real GDP even at the risk of a rise in inflation, rather than adopt policies that decrease aggregate demand.

CHAPTER 19

1a. 0.10 computer per TV set at 10 TV sets.

1b. 0.40 computer per TV set at 40 TV sets.

1c. 0.70 computer per TV set at 70 TV sets.

1d. The graph shows an upward-sloping line that passes through the three points described in solutions 1a, 1b, and 1c.

The opportunity cost of a TV set is calculated as the decrease in the number of computers produced divided by the increase in the number of TV sets produced as we move along the *PPF*. The opportunity cost of a TV set increases as the quantity of TV sets produced increases.

3a. Virtual Reality exports TV sets to Vital Signs.

At the no-trade production levels, the opportunity cost of a TV set is 0.10 computer in Virtual Reality and 0.30 computer in Vital Signs. Because it costs less to produce a TV set in Virtual Reality, Vital Signs can import TV sets for a lower price than it can produce them. And because a computer costs less in Vital Signs than in Virtual Reality, Virtual Reality can import computers at a lower cost than it can produce them.

3b. Virtual Reality increases the production of TV sets and Vital Signs decreases the production of TV sets. Virtual

Reality decreases the production of computers and Vital Signs increases the production of computers.

Virtual Reality increases production of TV sets to export some to Vital Signs and Vital Signs decreases production of TV sets because it now imports some from Virtual Reality.

3c. Each country consumes more of at least one good and possibly of both goods.

Because each country has a lower opportunity cost than the other at producing one of the goods, total production of both goods can increase.

3d. The price of a TV set is greater than 0.10 computer and less than 0.30 computer.

The price will be higher than the no-trade opportunity cost in Virtual Reality (0.10 computer) and lower than the no-trade opportunity cost in Vital Signs (0.30 computer).

5a. Free trade increases the production of at least one good (but not necessarily both goods) in both cases because each country increases the production of the good at which it has a comparative advantage.

5b. In problem 3, the price of a TV set rises in Virtual Reality. In problem 4, it falls.

The reason is that in problem 3, Virtual Reality produces a small number of TV sets with no trade and has the lower opportunity cost per TV set. But in problem 4, Virtual Reality produces a large number of TV sets with no trade and has the higher opportunity cost per TV set. So in problem 3, Virtual Reality becomes an exporter and increases production. The price of a TV set rises. In problem 4, Virtual Reality becomes an importer and decreases production, and the price of a TV set falls.

5c. In problem 3, the price of a computer rises in Vital Signs. In problem 4, it falls.

The reason is that in problem 3, Vital Signs produces a small number of computers with no trade and has the lower opportunity cost per computer. But in problem 4, Vital Signs produces a large number of computers with no trade and has the higher opportunity cost per computer. So in problem 3, Vital Signs becomes an exporter of computers and increases production. The price of a computer rises. In problem 4, Vital Signs becomes an importer of computers and decreases production, and the price of a computer falls.

7a. $9 per bushel in the importing country and $1 per bushel in the exporting country.

These are the prices at which each country wishes to import and export a zero quantity.

7b. $5 per bushel.

This is the price at which the quantity demanded by the importer equals the quantity supplied by the exporter.

7c. 400 million bushels.

This is the quantity demanded and supplied at the equilibrium price.

7d. Zero.

The balance of trade is zero because the value imported equals the value exported.

9a. $6 per bushel.

The quantity demanded by the importer equals the quantity available under the quota of 300 million bushels at this price.

9b. $600 million.

The price at which the exporters are willing to sell 300 million bushels is $4 a bushel. So there is a profit of $2 a bushel. The total revenue from the quota is 300 million multiplied by $2.

9c. The importing agents to whom the quota is allocated.

CHAPTER 20

1a. A table like Table 37.1 on p. 844 with the numbers provided in the problem.

The current account shows Imports of goods and services: −350 billions of grains, Exports of goods and services: 500 billions of grains, Net interest income: unknown, and Net transfers, unknown. You cannot calculate the current account balance from these numbers because of the two unknown items.

The capital account shows Foreign investment in Silecon: 60 billions of grains, Silecon investment abroad: −200 billions of grains. The capital account balance is −140 billions of grains (a deficit).

The official settlements account shows Increase in official Silecon reserves: −10 billions of grains (minus because it is an increase).

Because the sum of the three balances is zero, you can now calculate the current account balance: 150 billions of grains, a surplus. Exports of goods and services minus imports of goods and services equal 150 billions of grains. So the sum of Net interest income and Net transfers is zero, but we don't know the values of these two items separately.

1b. Silecon does not have a flexible exchange rate. The central bank intervenes in the foreign exchange market.

We know that the central bank intervenes in the foreign exchange market because its official reserves changed.

3a. Net exports are −$10 million.

Use the fact that

$Y = C + I + G + NX$ and solve for NX as

$NX = Y − C − I − G$, which equals

$NX = 60 − 36 − 20 − 14 = −10$.

3b. Saving is $12 million.

Use the fact that

$Y = C + S + T$ and solve for S as

$S = Y − C − T$, which equals

$NX = 60 − 36 − 12 = 12$.

3c. Investment is financed by national saving and foreign borrowing.

$I = S + T - G - NX$, which equals

$I = 12 + 12 - 14 - (-10) = 20$.

5a. Imports of goods and services are 26 billion bands.

Use the fact that

$Y = C + I + G + X - M$ and solve for M as

$M = -Y + C + I + G + X$, which is

$M = -100 + 60 + 22 + 24 + 20 = 26$.

5b. The current account balance is -6 billion bands (assuming that net interest income plus net transfers is zero).

Use the fact that

$CAB = X - M$

$CAB = 20 - 26 = -6$.

5c. The capital account balance is $+6$ billion bands.

The reason is that Ecflex has a flexible exchange rate, so we know that the official settlements account balance is zero.

5d. Net taxes are 20 billion bands.

Use the fact that

Gov. budget deficit $= G - T$, so

$T = G -$ *Gov. budget deficit*, which is

$T = 24 - 4 = 20$.

5e. The private sector balance is -2 billion bands (a deficit).

Use the fact that

Private sector surplus $= S - I$, with

$S = Y - C - NT$, or

Private sector surplus $= Y - C - T - I$, which is

Private sector surplus $= 100 - 60 - 20 - 22 = -2$.

7a. The country intervenes in the foreign exchange market to limit movements in the exchange rate.

If the exchange rate were flexible, there would be no change in the stock of foreign currency holdings. If the exchange rate were fixed, there would be no change in the exchange rate.

7b. The central bank might have conducted an open market operation in the bond market to increase the interest rate.

The central bank's intervention in the foreign exchange market did not bring appreciation. On the contrary, its intervention limited the extent of the appreciation.

7c. Private traders in the foreign exchange market might have increased their demand for the currency perhaps because they expected the exchange rate to appreciate in the future.

Glossary

Above full-employment equilibrium A macroeconomic equilibrium in which real GDP exceeds potential GDP.

Absolute advantage A person has an absolute advantage in the production of two goods if by using the same quantities of inputs, that person can produce more of both goods than another person; a country has an absolute advantage if its output per unit of inputs of all goods is larger than that of another country.

Aggregate demand The relationship between the aggregate quantity of real GDP demanded and the price level.

Aggregate hours The total number of hours worked by all the people employed, both full time and part time, during a year.

Aggregate planned expenditure The expenditure that households, firms, governments, and foreigners plan to undertake in given circumstances. It is the sum of planned consumption expenditure, planned investment, planned government purchases of goods and services, and planned exports minus planned imports.

Aggregate production function The relationship between the quantity of real GDP supplied and the quantities of labor and capital and the state of technology.

Automatic fiscal policy A change in fiscal policy that is triggered by the state of the economy.

Automatic stabilizers Mechanisms that stabilize real GDP without explicit action by the government.

Autonomous expenditure The sum of those components of aggregate planned expenditure that are not influenced by real GDP.

Balanced budget A government budget in which tax revenues and expenditures are equal.

Balance of payments accounts A country's record of international trading, borrowing, and lending.

Balance of trade The value of exports minus the value of imports.

Barter The direct exchange of one good or service for other goods and services.

Below full-employment equilibrium A macroeconomic equilibrium in which potential GDP exceeds real GDP.

Budget deficit A government's budget balance that is negative—expenditures exceed tax revenues.

Budget surplus A government's budget balance that is positive—tax revenues exceed expenditures.

Business cycle The periodic but irregular up-and-down movement in production.

Capital The plant, equipment, buildings, and inventories of raw materials and semifinished goods and services that are used to produce other goods and services.

Capital account A record of foreign investment in a country minus its investment abroad.

Capital stock The total quantity of plant, equipment, buildings, and inventories.

Central bank A bank's bank and a public authority charged with regulating and controlling a country's monetary policy and financial institutions and markets.

Ceteris paribus Other things being equal—all other relevant things remaining the same.

Chain-weighted output index An index that measures the growth rate of real GDP.

Change in demand A change in buyers' plans that occurs when some influence on those plans other than the price of the good changes. It is illustrated by a shift of the demand curve.

Change in supply A change in sellers' plans that occurs when some influence on those plans other than the price of the good changes. It is illustrated by a shift of the supply curve.

Change in the quantity demanded A change in buyers' plans that occurs when the price of a good changes but all other influences on buyers' plans remains unchanged. It is illustrated by a movement along the demand curve.

Change in the quantity supplied A change in sellers' plans that occurs when the price of a good changes but all other influences on sellers' plans remain unchanged. It is illustrated by a movement along the supply curve.

Classical growth theory A theory of economic growth based on the view that real GDP growth is temporary and that when real GDP per person increases above subsistence level, a population explosion brings real GDP back to subsistence level.

Command system A system in which some people give orders and other people obey them.

Commercial bank A firm, licensed either by the Comptroller of the Currency (in the U.S. Treasury) or by a state agency to receive deposits and make loans.

Comparative advantage A person or country has a comparative advantage in an activity if that person or country can perform the activity at a lower opportunity cost than anyone else or any other country.

Complement A good that is used in conjunction with another good.

Consumer Price Index An index that measures the average level of prices of the goods and services that a typical urban family buys.

Consumption expenditure The total amount spent on consumption goods and services.

Consumption function The relationship between consumption expenditure and disposable income, other things remaining the same.

Contractionary fiscal policy A decrease in government expenditures or an increase in tax revenues.

Cost-push inflation An inflation that results from an initial increase in costs.

Council of Economic Advisers The President's council whose main work is to monitor the economy and keep the President and the public well informed about the current state of the economy and the best available forecasts of where it is heading.

Creditor nation A country that during its entire history has invested more in the rest of the world than other countries have invested in it.

Credit union A financial intermediary owned by its depositors, who are a social or economic group, that accepts savings deposits and makes mostly consumer loans.

Cross-section graph A graph that shows the values of an economic variable for different groups in a population at a point in time.

Crowding-out effect The tendency for a government budget deficit to decrease in investment.

Currency The bills and coins that we use today.

Currency appreciation The rise in the value of one currency in terms of another currency.

Currency depreciation The fall in the value of one currency in terms of another currency.

Currency drain An increase in currency held outside the banks.

Current account A record of receipts from the sale of goods and services to foreigners, the payments for goods and services bought from foreigners, the interest payments paid to and received from the rest of the world, and net transfers paid to foreigners.

Cyclical surplus or deficit The actual surplus or deficit minus the structural surplus or deficit.

Cyclical unemployment The fluctuations in unemployment over the business cycle,

Debtor nation A country that during its entire history has borrowed more from the rest of the world than it has lent to it.

Deflation A process in which the price level falls—a negative inflation.

Demand The relationship between the quantity of a good that consumers plan to buy and the price of the good when all other influences on buyers' plans remain the same. It is described by a schedule and illustrated by a demand curve.

Demand curve A curve that shows the relationship between the quantity demanded of a good and its price when all other influences on consumers' planned purchases remain the same.

Demand for labor The relationship between the quantity of labor demanded and the real wage rate when all other influences on firm's hiring plans remain the same.

Demand-pull inflation An inflation that results from an initial increase in aggregate demand.

Deposit multiplier The amount by which an increase in bank reserves is multiplied to calculate the increase in bank deposits.

Depreciation The decrease in the capital stock resulting from wear and tear and obsolescence.

Direct relationship A relationship between two variables that move in the same direction.

Discount rate The interest rate at which the Fed stands ready to lend reserves to commercial banks.

Discouraged workers People who are available and willing to work but who have given up the effort to find work.

Discretionary fiscal policy A policy action that is initiated by an act of Congress.

Discretionary policy A policy that responds to the state of the economy in a possibly unique way that uses all the information available, including perceived lessons from past "mistakes."

Disposable income Aggregate income minus taxes plus transfer payments.

Dumping The sale of a good or service to a foreign country at a price that is less than the cost of producing the good or service.

Dynamic comparative advantage A comparative advantage that a person or country possesses as a result of having specialized in a particular activity and then, as a result of learning-by-doing, having become the producer with the lowest opportunity cost.

Economic growth The expansion of production possibilities that results from capital accumulation and technological change.

Economic growth rate The percentage change in the quantity of goods and services produced from one year to the next.

Economic model A description of some aspect of the economic world that includes only those features of the world that are needed for the purpose at hand.

Economics The science that explains the choices we make and how those choices change as we cope with scarcity.

Economic theory A generalization that summarizes what we think we understand about the economic choices that people make and the performance of industries and entire economies.

Economic welfare A comprehensive measure of the general state of economic well-being.

Efficiency wage A real wage rate that is set above the full-employment equilibrium wage rate and that balances the costs and benefits of this higher wage rate to maximize the firm's profit.

Efficient Resource use is efficient when we produce the goods and services that we value most highly.

Employment Act of 1946 A landmark Congressional act that recognized a role for government actions to reduce unemployment, keep the economy expanding, and keep inflation in check.

Employment-to-population ratio The percentage of people of working age who have jobs.

Entitlement spending Spending on government programs that entitle suitably qualified individuals and businesses to receive benefits and that result in transfer payments that depend on the economic state of individual citizens and businesses.

Entrants People who enter the labor force.

Entrepreneurship The resource that organizes the other three factors of production: labor, land, and capital. Entrepreneurs come up with new ideas about what, how, when, and where to produce, make business decisions, and bear the risk that arises from their decisions.

Equation of exchange An equation that states that the quantity of money multiplied by the velocity of circulation equals GDP.

Equilibrium expenditure The level of aggregate expenditure that occurs when aggregate planned expenditure equals real GDP.

Equilibrium price The price at which the quantity demanded equals the quantity supplied.

Equilibrium quantity The quantity bought and sold at the equilibrium price.

Excess reserves A bank's actual reserves minus its required reserves.

Expansion A business cycle phase in which real GDP increases.

Expansionary fiscal policy An increase in government expenditure or a decrease in tax revenues.

Expenditure The price of a good multiplied by the quantity of the good that is bought is the expenditure on a good.

Exports The goods and services that we sell to people in other countries.

Federal budget A statement of the federal government's financial plan, itemizing programs and their costs, tax revenues, and the proposed deficit or surplus.

Federal Open Market Committee The main policy-making organ of the Federal Reserve System.

Federal Reserve System The central bank of the United States.

Feedback-rule policy A rule that specifies how policy actions respond to changes in the state of the economy.

Financial innovation The development of new financial products—new ways of borrowing and lending.

Financial intermediary A firm that takes deposits from households and firms and makes loans to other households and firms.

Fiscal policy The government's attempt to influence the economy by setting and changing taxes, its pur-

chases of goods and services, and transfer payments to achieve macroeconomic objectives such as full employment, sustained long-term economic growth, and low inflation.

Fixed-rule policy A rule that specifies an action to be pursued independently of the state of the economy.

Flow A quantity per unit of time.

Foreign exchange market The market in which the currency of one country is exchanged for the currency of another.

Foreign exchange rate The price at which one currency exchanges for another.

Frictional unemployment The unemployment that arises from normal labor turnover—people entering and leaving the labor force and from ongoing creation and destruction of jobs.

Full employment A situation in which the quantity of labor demanded equals the quantity supplied. At full employment, the unemployment rate equals the natural rate of unemployment and all unemployment is frictional and structural.

GDP deflator A price index that measures the average level of the prices of all goods and services that are included in GDP.

General Agreement on Tariffs and Trade (GATT) An international agreement designed to reduce tariffs on international trade.

Goods and services All the things that people are willing to pay for.

Government budget deficit The deficit that arises when federal government expenditure exceeds the taxes collected.

Government budget surplus The surplus that arises when the federal government collects more in taxes than its expenditure.

Government debt The total amount of borrowing that the government has undertaken. It equals the sum of past budget deficits minus budget surpluses.

Government purchases Goods and services bought by the government.

Government purchases multiplier The magnification effect of a change in government purchases of goods and services on equilibrium expenditure and real GDP.

Government sector surplus or deficit An amount equal to net taxes minus government purchases of goods and services.

Great Depression A decade (1929–1939) of high unemployment and stagnant production throughout the world economy.

Gross domestic product (GDP) The value of aggregate production of goods and services in a country during a given time period—usually a year.

Gross investment The total amount spent on adding to the capital stock and on replacing depreciated capital.

Growth accounting A method of calculating how much real GDP growth has resulted from growth of labor and capital and how much is attributable to technological change.

Human capital The skill and knowledge of people, arising from their education and on-the-job training.

Imports The goods and services that we buy from people in other countries.

Incentive An inducement to take a particular action.

Income The amount of money that someone earns by working.

Induced expenditure The sum of the components of aggregate expenditure that varies with real GDP.

Induced taxes Taxes that vary as real GDP varies.

Infant-industry argument The proposition that protection is necessary to enable an infant industry to grow into a mature industry that can compete in world markets.

Inferior good A good for which demand decreases as income increases.

Inflation A process in which the price level is rising and money is losing value.

Inflationary gap The amount by which real GDP exceeds potential GDP.

Inflation rate The percentage change in the price level from one year to the next.

Interest rate parity A situation in which the return on assets in different currencies are equal.

Intermediate goods and services Goods and services that firms buy from each other and use as inputs in the goods and services that they eventually sell to final users.

Inverse relationship A relationship between variables that move in opposite directions.

Investment The purchase of new plant, equipment, and buildings and additions to inventories.

Investment demand The relationship between investment and real interest rate, other influences on investment remaining the same.

Job leavers People who voluntarily quit their jobs.

Job losers People who are laid off, either permanently or temporarily, from their jobs.

Job rationing The practice of paying a real wage rate above the equilibrium level and then rationing jobs by some method.

Job search The activity of people looking for acceptable vacant jobs.

Keynesian activist An economist who believes that fluctuations in aggregate demand combined with sticky wages (and/or sticky prices) are the main source of economic fluctuations.

Keynesian theory of the business cycle A theory that regards volatile expectations as the main source of economic fluctuations.

Labor The time and effort that people allocate to producing goods and services.

Labor force The sum of the people who are employed and who are unemployed.

Labor force participation rate The percentage of the working-age population who are members of the labor force.

Labor productivity Real GDP per hour of work.

Labor supply curve A curve that shows the quantity of labor that households plan to supply at each possible real wage rate.

Land All the gifts of nature that we use to produce goods and services.

Law of diminishing returns A law stating that as the quantity of one input increases with the quantities of all other inputs remaining the same, output increases but by ever smaller increments.

Learning-by-doing People become more productive in an activity (learn) just by repeatedly producing a particular good or service (doing).

Linear relationship A relationship between two variables that is illustrated by a straight line.

Liquidity The property of being instantly convertible into a means of payment with little loss in value.

Long-run aggregate supply curve The relationship between the real GDP supplied and the price level in the long run when real GDP equals potential GDP.

Long-run macroeconomic equilibrium A situation that occurs when real GDP equals potential GDP—the economy is on its long-run aggregate supply curve.

Long-run Phillips curve A curve that shows the relationship between inflation and unemployment when the actual inflation rate equals the expected inflation rate.

Lump-sum taxes Taxes that do not vary with real GDP.

Lump-sum tax multiplier The magnification effect of a change in lump-sum taxes on equilibrium expenditure and real GDP.

M1 A measure of money that consists of currency and traveler's checks plus checking deposits owned by individuals and businesses.

M2 A measure of money that consists of M1 plus savings deposits and time deposits.

Macroeconomic long run A time frame that is sufficiently long for real GDP to return to potential GDP.

Macroeconomics The study of the national economy and the global economy, the way in which economic aggregates grow and fluctuate, and the effects of government actions on them.

Macroeconomic short run A period during real GDP has decreased below or increased above potential GDP.

Margin When a choice is changed by a small amount or by a little at a time, the choice is made at the margin.

Marginal benefit The benefit that a person receives from consuming one more unit of a good or service. It is measured as the maximum amount that a person is willing to pay for one more unit of the good or service.

Marginal cost The opportunity cost of producing one more unit of a good or service. It is the best alternative forgone. It is calculated as the increase in total cost divided by the increase in output.

Marginal product of labor The additional real GDP produced by an additional hour of labor when all other influences on production remain the same.

Marginal propensity to consume The fraction of an increase in disposable income that is consumed.

Marginal propensity to import The fraction of an increase in real GDP that is spent on imports.

Marginal propensity to save The fraction of an increase in disposable income that is saved.

Market Any arrangement that enables buyers and sellers to get information and to do business with each other.

Market failure A state in which the market does not use resources efficiently

Means of payment A method of settling a debt.

Microeconomics The study of the decisions of people and businesses, the interactions of those decisions in markets, and the effects of government regulation and taxes on the prices and quantities of goods and services.

Minimum wage The lowest wage rate at which a firm may legally hire labor.

Monetarist An economist who believes that fluctuations in the money stock are the main source of economic fluctuations.

Monetarist theory of the business cycle A theory that regards fluctuations in the money stock as the main source of economic fluctuations.

Monetary base The sum of the Federal Reserve notes, coins, and banks' deposits at the Fed.

Monetary policy The Federal Reserve's attempt to keep inflation in check, maintain full employment, moderate the business cycle, and contribute towards achieving long-term growth by adjusting the quantity of money in circulation and interest rates.

Money Any commodity or token that is generally acceptable as a means of payment.

Money market mutual fund A financial institution that obtains funds by selling shares and that uses these funds to buy highly liquid assets such as U.S. Treasury bills.

Money multiplier The amount by which a change in the monetary base is multiplied to determine the resulting change in the quantity of money.

Money wage rate The number of dollars that an hour of labor earns.

Multiplier The amount by which a change in autonomous expenditure is magnified or multiplied to determine the change in equilibrium expenditure and real GDP.

National saving Saving by households and businesses plus government saving.

Natural rate of unemployment The unemployment rate when the economy is at full employment. There is no cyclical unemployment; all unemployment is frictional and structural.

Negative relationship A relationship between variables that move in opposite directions.

Neoclassical growth theory A theory of economic growth that proposes that real GDP grows because technological change induces saving and investment.

Net borrower A country that is borrowing more from the rest of the world than it is lending to it.

Net exports The exports of goods and services minus imports of goods and services.

Net investment Net increase in the capital stock—gross investment minus depreciation.

Net lender A country that is lending more to the rest of the world than it is borrowing from it.

Net taxes Taxes paid to governments minus transfer payments received from governments.

New classical theory of the business cycle A rational expectations theory of the business cycle that regards unanticipated fluctuations in aggregate demand as the main source of economic fluctuations.

New growth theory A theory of economic growth based on the idea that real GDP grows because of the choices that people make in the pursuit of ever greater profit and that growth can persist indefinitely.

New Keynesian theory of the business cycle A rational expectations theory of the business cycle that regards unanticipated fluctuations in aggregate demand as the main source of economic fluctuations but leaves room for anticipated demand fluctuations to play a role.

Nominal GDP The value of the current period's production in current period prices.

Nominal GDP targeting An attempt to keep the growth rate of nominal GDP steady.

Nontariff barrier An action other than a tariff that restricts international trade.

Normal good A good for which demand increases as income increases.

North American Free Trade Agreement An agreement signed in 1994 between the United States, Canada, and Mexico to virtually eliminate all barriers to international trade between them in 15 years.

Official settlements account A record of the change in a country's official reserves.

Official U.S. reserves The government's holdings of foreign currency.

Open market operation The purchase or sale of government securities by the Federal Reserve System in the open market.

Opportunity cost The opportunity cost of an action is the highest-valued alternative forgone.

Phillips curve A curve that shows a relationship between inflation and unemployment.

Positive relationship A relationship between two variables that move in the same direction.

Potential GDP The value of production (real GDP) when all the economy's resources (labor, land, capital, and entrepreneurship) are fully employed. Unemployment is at its natural rate and the economy is at full employment.

Price level The average level of prices as measured by a price index.

Private sector surplus or deficit An amount equal to saving minus investment.

Production efficiency A situation in which the economy cannot produce more of one good without producing less of some other good.

Production function The relationship between real GDP and the quantity of labor when all other influences on production remain the same.

Production possibility frontier The boundary between those combinations of goods and services that can be produced and those that cannot.

Productivity Production per unit of resource used in the production of goods and services.

Productivity function A relationship that shows how real GDP per hour of labor changes as the amount of capital per hour of labor changes with a given state of technology.

Productivity growth slowdown A slowdown in the growth rate of output per person.

Property rights Social arrangements that govern the ownership, use, and disposal of resources, goods, and services.

Purchasing power parity The equal value of different monies.

Quantity demanded The amount of a good or service that consumers plan to buy during a given time period at a particular price.

Quantity of labor demanded The labor hours hired by the firms in the economy.

Quantity of labor supplied The number of labor hours that all households in the economy plan to work.

Quantity supplied The amount of a good or service that producers plan to sell during a given time period at a particular price.

Quantity theory of money The proposition that in the long run, an increase in the quantity of money brings an equal percentage increase in the price level.

Quota A quantitative restriction on the import of a particular good, which specifies the maximum amount that can be imported in a given time period.

Rational expectation A forecast based on all available relevant information.

Real business cycle theory A theory that regards random fluctuations in productivity as the main source of economic fluctuations.

Real Gross Domestic Product (real GDP) The value of aggregate production of goods and services in a country in a given time period in the prices of a base year.

Real interest rate The nominal interest rate adjusted for inflation; the nominal interest rate minus the inflation rate.

Real wage rate The quantity of goods ands services that an hour's work can buy.

Recession A business cycle phase in which real GDP decreases for at least two successive quarters.

Recessionary gap The amount by which potential GDP exceeds real GDP.

Reentrants People who reenter the labor force.

Relative price The ratio of the price of one good or service to the price of another good or service. A relative price is an opportunity cost.

Required reserve ratio The ratio of reserves to deposits that banks are required, by regulation, to hold.

Reserve ratio The fraction of a bank's total deposits that are held in reserves.

Reserves Cash in a bank's vault plus the bank's deposits at Federal Reserve banks.

Saving The amount of income remaining after meeting consumption expenditures.

Saving function The relationship between saving and disposable income, other things remaining the same.

Savings and loan association (S&L) A financial intermediary that receives checking deposits and savings deposits and that makes personal, commercial, and home-purchase loans.

Savings bank A financial intermediary that is owned by its depositors and accepts deposits and makes loans, mostly home-purchase loans.

Saving supply The relationship between saving and the real interest rate, other things remaining the same.

Scarcity The state in which the resources available are insufficient to satisfy people's wants.

Scatter diagram A diagram that plots the value of one economic variable against the value of another.

Short-run aggregate supply curve A curve that shows the relationship between the quantity of real GDP supplied and the price level in the short run when the money wage rate, other resource prices, and potential GDP remain constant.

Short-run macroeconomic equilibrium A situation that occurs when the quantity of real GDP demanded equals quantity of real GDP supplied—at the point of intersection of the *AD* curve and the *SAS* curve.

Short-run Phillips curve A curve that shows the relationship between inflation and unemployment, when the expected inflation rate and the natural rate of unemployment remain the same.

Slope The change in the value of the variable measured on the y-axis divided by the change in the value of the variable measured on the x-axis.

Stagflation The combination of a rise in the price level and a decrease in real GDP.

Stock A quantity that exists at a point in time.

Structural surplus or deficit The budget balance that would occur if the economy were at full employment and real GDP equalled potential GDP.

Structural unemployment The unemployment that arises when changes in technology or international competition change the skills needed to perform jobs or change the locations of jobs.

Subsistence real wage rate The minimum real wage rate needed to maintain life.

Substitute A good that can be used in place of another good.

Supply The relationship between the quantity of a good that producers plan to sell and the price of the good when all other influences on sellers' plans remaining the same. It is described by a supply schedule and illustrated by a supply curve.

Supply of labor The relationship between the quantity of labor supplied and the real wage rate when all other influences on work plans remain the same.

Supply curve A curve that shows the relationship between the quantity supplied and the price of a good when all other influences on producers' planned sales remaining the same.

Tariff A tax that is imposed by the importing country when an imported good crosses its international boundary.

Technological change The development of new goods and better ways of producing goods and services.

Terms of trade The quantity of goods and services that a country exports to pay for its imports of goods and services.

Thrift institutions Thrift institutions include savings and loan associations, savings banks, and credit unions.

Time-series graph A graph that measures time (for example, months or years) on the *x*-axis and the variable or variables in which we are interested on the *y*-axis.

Tradeoff A constraint that involves giving up one thing to get something else.

Trend The general direction (rising or falling) in which a variable is moving over the long term.

Twin deficits The tendency for the government sector deficit and the net exports deficit to move together.

Unemployment Resources that are available but are not being used.

Unemployment rate The percentage of the people in the labor force who are unemployed.

U.S. interest rate differential The interest rate on a U.S. dollar asset minus the interest rate on a foreign currency asset.

Value added The value of a firm's output minus the value of the intermediate goods that the firm buys from other firms.

Value of production The value of the goods and services produced.

Velocity of circulation The average number of times a dollar of money is used annually to buy the goods and services that make up GDP.

Voluntary exchange A transaction between people, businesses, or countries that is undertaken voluntarily.

Voluntary export restraint A self-imposed restriction by an exporting country on the volume of its exports of a particular good. Voluntary export restraints are often called VERs.

Wealth The value of all the things that people own.

Working-age population The total number of people aged 16 years and over who are not in jail, hospital, or some other form of institutional care.

World Trade Organization An international organization that places obligations on its member countries to observe the GATT rules.

Index

Key concepts and pages on which they are defined appear in **boldface type**.

The Addison-Wesley Series in Economics

Abel/Bernanke
Macroeconomics

Berndt
The Practice of Econometrics

Bierman/Fernandez
Game Theory with Economic Applications

Binger/Hoffman
Microeconomics with Calculus

Boyer
Principles of Transportation Economics

Branson
Macroeconomic Theory and Policy

Bruce
Public Finance and the American Economy

Burgess
The Economics of Regulation and Antitrust

Byrns/Stone
Economics

Carlton/Perloff
Modern Industrial Organization

Caves/Frankel/Jones
World Trade and Payments: An Introduction

Chapman
Environmental Economics: Theory, Application, and Policy

Cooter/Ulen
Law and Economics

Copeland
Exchange Rates and International Finance

Downs
An Economic Theory of Democracy

Eaton/Mishkin
Readings to accompany The Economics of Money, Banking, and Financial Markets

Ehrenberg/Smith
Modern Labor Economics

Ekelund/Tollison
Economics: Private Markets and Public Choice

Fusfeld
The Age of the Economist

Gerber
International Economics

Ghiara
Learning Economics: A Practical Workbook

Gibson
International Finance

Gordon
Macroeconomics

Gregory
Essentials of Economics

Gregory/Stuart
Russian and Soviet Economic Performance and Structure

Griffiths/Wall
Intermediate Microeconomics: Theory and Applications

Gros/Steinherr
Winds of Change: Economic Transition in Central and Eastern Europe

Hartwick/Olewiler
The Economics of Natural Resource Use

Hoy/Livernois/McKenna/Rees/Stengos
Mathematics for Economics

Hubbard
Money, the Financial System, and the Economy

Hughes/Cain
American Economic History

Husted/Melvin
International Economics

Jehle/Reny
Advanced Microeconomic Theory

Klein
Mathematical Methods for Economics

Krugman/Obstfeld
International Economics: Theory and Policy

Laidler
The Demand for Money: Theories, Evidence, and Problems

Lesser/Dodds/Zerbe
Environmental Economics and Policy

Lipsey/Courant/Ragan
Economics

McCarty
Dollars and Sense: An Introduction to Economics

Melvin
International Money and Finance

Miller
Economics Today

Miller/Benjamin/North
The Economics of Public Issues

Miller/VanHoose
Essentials of Money, Banking, and Financial Markets

Mills/Hamilton
Urban Economics

Mishkin
The Economics of Money, Banking, and Financial Markets

Parkin
Economics

Parkin/Bade
Economics in Action Software

Perloff
Microeconomics

Phelps
Health Economics

Riddell/Shackelford/Stamos
Economics: A Tool for Critically Understanding Society

Ritter/Silber/Udell
Principles of Money, Banking, and Financial Markets

Rohlf
Introduction to Economic Reasoning

Ruffin/Gregory
Principles of Economics

Salvatore
Microeconomics

Sargent
Rational Expectations and Inflation

Scherer
Industry Structure, Strategy, and Public Policy

Schotter
Microeconomics

Sherman/Kolk
Business Cycles and Forecasting

Smith
Case Studies in Economic Development

Studenmund
Using Econometrics

Su
Economic Fluctuations and Forecasting

Thomas
Modern Econometrics

Tietenberg
Environmental and Natural Resource Economics

Tietenberg
Environmental Economics and Policy

Todaro
Economic Development

Waldman/Jensen
Industrial Organization: Theory and Practice